Learn iOS 11 Programming with Swift 4
Second Edition

Learn the fundamentals of iOS app development with Swift 4 and Xcode 9

Craig Clayton

BIRMINGHAM - MUMBAI

Learn iOS 11 Programming with Swift 4
Second Edition

Copyright © 2018 Packt Publishing

All rights reserved. No part of this book may be reproduced, stored in a retrieval system, or transmitted in any form or by any means, without the prior written permission of the publisher, except in the case of brief quotations embedded in critical articles or reviews.

Every effort has been made in the preparation of this book to ensure the accuracy of the information presented. However, the information contained in this book is sold without warranty, either express or implied. Neither the author, nor Packt Publishing or its dealers and distributors, will be held liable for any damages caused or alleged to have been caused directly or indirectly by this book.

Packt Publishing has endeavored to provide trademark information about all of the companies and products mentioned in this book by the appropriate use of capitals. However, Packt Publishing cannot guarantee the accuracy of this information.

Acquisition Editor: Reshma Raman
Content Development Editor: Vikas Tiwari
Technical Editor: Madhunikita Sunil Chindarkar
Copy Editor: Muktikant Garimella
Project Coordinator: Ulhas Kambali
Proofreader: Safis Editing
Indexer: Tejal Daruwale Soni
Graphics: Jason Monteiro, Tom Scaria
Production Coordinator: Shantanu N. Zagade

First published: December 2016
Second edition: January 2018

Production reference: 1290118

Published by Packt Publishing Ltd.
Livery Place
35 Livery Street
Birmingham
B3 2PB, UK.

ISBN 978-1-78839-075-0

www.packtpub.com

mapt.io

Mapt is an online digital library that gives you full access to over 5,000 books and videos, as well as industry leading tools to help you plan your personal development and advance your career. For more information, please visit our website.

Why subscribe?

- Spend less time learning and more time coding with practical eBooks and Videos from over 4,000 industry professionals

- Improve your learning with Skill Plans built especially for you

- Get a free eBook or video every month

- Mapt is fully searchable

- Copy and paste, print, and bookmark content

PacktPub.com

Did you know that Packt offers eBook versions of every book published, with PDF and ePub files available? You can upgrade to the eBook version at www.PacktPub.com and as a print book customer, you are entitled to a discount on the eBook copy. Get in touch with us at service@packtpub.com for more details.

At www.PacktPub.com, you can also read a collection of free technical articles, sign up for a range of free newsletters, and receive exclusive discounts and offers on Packt books and eBooks.

Contributors

About the author

Craig Clayton is a self-taught, senior iOS engineer at Adept Mobile specializing in building mobile experiences for NBA and NFL teams. He also volunteers as the organizer of the Suncoast iOS meetup group in the Tampa/St. Petersburg area, and prepares presentations and hands-on talks for this group and other groups in the community. He has also launched Cocoa Academy online, which specializes in bringing a diverse list of iOS courses ranging from building apps to games for all programming levels.

About the reviewer

Cecil Costa, also known as Eduardo Campos in Latin countries, is a Euro-Brazilian freelance developer. He has been giving onsite courses for companies such as Ericsson, Roche, TVE (a Spanish TV channel), and others. He has also worked for different companies, including IBM, Qualcomm, Spanish Lottery, and Dia. He is also the author of *Swift Cookbook*, *Swift 2 Blueprints*, *Reactive Programming with Swift*, and a video course called *Building iOS 10 Applications with Swift*, by Packt Publishing.

Packt is searching for authors like you

If you're interested in becoming an author for Packt, please visit `authors.packtpub.com` and apply today. We have worked with thousands of developers and tech professionals, just like you, to help them share their insight with the global tech community. You can make a general application, apply for a specific hot topic that we are recruiting an author for, or submit your own idea.

Table of Contents

Preface	1
Chapter 1: Getting Familiar with Xcode	7
Getting started	8
The Xcode interface	13
Navigator panel	14
Standard editor	14
Utilities panel	15
Debug panel	15
Toolbar	15
Generic iOS device	18
iOS device	18
Connecting wirelessly	23
Window pane controls	25
Summary	27
Chapter 2: Building a Foundation with Swift	29
Playgrounds – an interactive coding environment	30
Data types – where it all starts	33
String	33
Integer data type	34
Floating-point numbers	35
Booleans	35
Variables and constants – where data is held	36
Creating a variable with a string	36
Creating a variable with an integer (Int)	37
Debug and print() – detecting your bugs	37
Adding floating-point numbers	38
Creating a Boolean	40
Hungarian notation	41
Why constants versus variables?	42
Comments – leaving yourself notes or reminders	42
Type safety and type inference	43
Concatenating strings	43
String interpolation	44
Operations with our integers	45

Increment and decrement	47
Comparison operators	48
Summary	48

Chapter 3: Building on the Swift Foundation — 49

Creating a Playground project	50
The if statements – having fun with logic statements	51
Optionals and optional bindings	58
Why optionals?	63
Functions	64
Summary	73

Chapter 4: Digging Deeper — 75

Creating a Playground project	76
Ranges	77
Closed range	77
Half-closed range	79
Control flow	80
The for...in loop	81
One-sided range	85
The while loop	86
The repeat...while loop	89
Summary	91

Chapter 5: Digging into Collections — 93

Arrays	93
Creating an empty array	94
Creating an array with initial values	95
Creating a mutable array	95
Adding items to an array	96
Checking the number of elements in an array	101
Checking for an empty array	102
Retrieving a value from an array	103
Iterating over an array	107
Removing items from an array	108
Dictionaries	112
Creating a dictionary	112
Adding and updating dictionary elements	114
Accessing an item in a dictionary	118
Iterating over dictionary values	119

[ii]

Iterating over dictionary keys	120
Iterating over dictionary keys and values	120
Checking the number of items in a dictionary	121
Removing items from a dictionary	124
Sets	**126**
Creating an empty set	127
Creating a set with an array literal	127
Creating a mutable set	128
Adding items into a set	128
Checking if a set contains an item	130
Iterating over a set	131
Intersecting two sets	134
Joining two sets	136
Removing items from a set	137
Summary	**140**
Chapter 6: Starting the UI Setup	**141**
Useful terms	**142**
View Controller	142
Table View Controller	142
Collection View Controller	143
Navigation Controller	144
Tab Bar Controller	145
Storyboard	146
Segue	147
Auto Layout	147
Model View Controller (MVC)	147
App tour	**148**
Explore tab	148
Locations	150
Restaurant listings	150
Restaurant detail	152
Map tab	153
Project setup	**154**
Creating a new project	154
Summary	**157**
Chapter 7: Setting Up the Basic Structure	**159**
Starting from scratch	**159**
Storyboard setup	**161**

Table of Contents

Adding our app assets	165
Storyboards	178
Creating our launch screen	179
Adding a Navigation Controller	188
Summary	**192**
Chapter 8: Building Our App Structure in Storyboard	**193**
Adding a Collection View Controller	196
Hooking up our outlets	199
Creating a custom color	205
Setting up our cell	209
Section header	211
Updating the grid	215
Adding a modal	217
Updating Bar Button Items	225
Unwinding our Cancel button	226
Adding our first Table View	227
Summary	**228**
Chapter 9: Finishing Up Our App Structure in Storyboard	**229**
Adding our Restaurant List View	230
Hooking up our outlets	230
Setting up our cell	231
Adding Reviews View	239
Viewing reviews	241
Map Kit View	244
Summary	**249**
Chapter 10: Designing Cells	**251**
Setting up the Explore header	251
Adding Auto Layout to the Explore header	256
Setting up the Explore cell	258
Adding Auto Layout to the Explore cell	260
Setting up the Restaurant cell	261
Adding Auto Layout to the Restaurant cell	265
Location cell	268
Summary	**269**
Chapter 11: Designing Static Tables	**271**
Setting up cells	272
Creating our section headers	273

Creating our address section	277
Adding Auto Layout to the headers	279
Photos section	280
Adding Auto Layout to the photos section	283
Reviews section	285
Adding Auto Layout to the Review cells	294
Updating the reservation times cells	298
Reservation information	299
Reservation header	302
Summary	306

Chapter 12: Designing a Photo Filter and Review Form — 307

Setting up our View Controllers	307
Adding our Photo Filter View	309
Adding Auto Layout for the Photo Filter View	313
Creating the Photo Filter View cell	314
Adding Auto Layout to our Photo Filter cell	315
Creating reviews	316
Setting up the Review storyboard	316
Creating a Review form	318
Updating the Review cells	319
Updating our first cell	319
Positioning UI elements	319
Adding Auto Layout for creating reviews	322
Refactoring the storyboard	324
Creating a new storyboard for the Map tab	325
Creating a new storyboard for the Explore tab	327
Summary	334

Chapter 13: Getting Started with the Grid — 335

Understanding the Model View Controller architecture	335
Getting familiar with the setup	337
Classes and structures	337
Controllers and classes	343
Creating our controller	344
Understanding Collection View controllers and Collection View cells	352
Getting data into Collection View	355
Understanding the data source	356
Summary	358

Chapter 14: Getting Data into Our Grid — 359

[v]

Model — 360
ExploreData.plist — 361
ExploreItem.swift — 362
ExploreDataManager.swift — 364
Getting data — 368
Connecting to our cell — 371
Hooking up our UI with IBOutlets — 372
Restaurant listing — 377
Summary — 381

Chapter 15: Getting Started with the List — 383
Creating our Location View Controller class — 383
Connecting our Table View with our Location View Controller — 384
Digging into our Table View code — 387
Adding the data source and delegate — 387
Adding locations to our Table View — 392
Creating our first property list (plist) — 394
Adding data to our property list — 395
Creating our location data manager — 399
Working with our data manager — 400
Creating folders — 401
Summary — 405

Chapter 16: Where Are We? — 407
Setting up map annotations — 407
What is an MKAnnotation? — 407
Creating a restaurant annotation — 408
Creating our Map Data Manager — 413
Creating a base class — 415
Refactoring code — 417
Refactoring ExploreDataManager — 418
Creating and adding annotations — 419
Creating our Map View Controller — 419
Creating custom annotations — 424
Map to restaurant detail — 428
Creating a storyboard reference — 429
Map to restaurant detail — 432
Passing data to restaurant detail — 433
Organizing your code — 438
Refactoring ExploreViewController — 439

Using the MARK comment	442
Refactoring RestaurantViewController	443
Refactoring MapViewController	447
Summary	452

Chapter 17: Working with an API — 453

Creating an API Manager	454
What is an API?	454
Understanding a JSON file	454
Exploring the API Manager file	456
Location list	458
Selecting a location	458
Adding a Header view	460
Passing a selected location back to Explore View	461
Unwinding our Done button	463
Getting the last selected location	466
Passing location and cuisine to the restaurant list	469
Creating our restaurant cell class	474
Setting up restaurant list cell outlets	475
Creating a restaurant data manager	478
Handling no data	482
Summary	490

Chapter 18: Displaying Data in Restaurant Detail — 491

Adding a navigation button	499
Displaying data in our static Table View	505
Summary	509

Chapter 19: Foodie Reviews — 511

Getting started with reviews	511
Displaying ratings in our custom UIControl	513
Adding our touch events	519
Setting up the unwind segues	522
Setting up our rating control	523
Creating our review form controller	524
Summary	530

Chapter 20: Working with Photo Filters — 531

Understanding filters	531
Creating our filter scroller	535
Creating a filter cell	539
Creating our apply filter view controller	542

[vii]

Getting permission	550
Summary	553
Chapter 21: Understanding Core Data	**555**
What is Core Data?	555
Creating a data model	557
Entity auto-generation	564
Restaurant Photo Entity	565
Review item	566
Core Data manager	568
Summary	574
Chapter 22: Saving Reviews	**575**
Saving reviews	575
Saving photos	578
Setting up the cell UI	584
Adding Auto Layout	585
Adding an overall rating	587
Summary	589
Chapter 23: Universal	**591**
Explore	591
Location listing	600
Restaurant listing	601
Updating restaurant details	608
Summary	609
Chapter 24: iMessages	**611**
Understanding iMessages	612
Creating our extension	613
Updating our assets	617
Implementing our Messages UI	618
Adding Auto Layout to our cell	622
Creating a framework	623
Connecting our message cell	631
Showing restaurants	633
iMessage crashing	637
Sending reservations	640
Summary	643
Chapter 25: Notifications	**645**

Starting with the basics	646
Getting permission	646
Setting up notifications	647
Showing notifications	653
Customizing our notifications	656
Embedding images	656
Adding buttons	662
Custom UI in notifications	665
Summary	671

Chapter 26: Just a Peek — 673

Adding 3D Touch quick actions	673
Adding favorites	686
Creating a new model object	687
Updating our Core Data manager	692
Summary	700

Chapter 27: Drag and Drop — 701

Accepting drag from other apps	701
Dragging and dropping filter items	706
Summary	712

Chapter 28: SiriKit — 713

Understanding SiriKit	714
Supported intents	715
Enable Siri capabilities	716
Creating users	725
Updating our intent handler	726
Testing Siri	728
Summary	735

Chapter 29: Beta and Store Submission — 737

Creating a bundle identifier	739
Creating a certificate signing request	746
Creating production and development certificates	750
Creating a production provisioning profile	756
Creating a Development Provisioning Profile	763
Creating an App Store listing	766
Creating an archive build	769
Internal and external testing	776
Internal testing	776

Table of Contents

External testing	779
Summary	783
Other Books You May Enjoy	785
Index	789

Preface

In this book, we will build a restaurant reservation app called *Let's Eat*. We will start the book off by exploring Xcode, our programming environment, which is also known as Interface Development Environment (IDE). Next, you will start learning the foundations of Swift, the programming language used in iOS apps. Once we are comfortable with the basics of Swift, we will dig deeper to build a more solid foundation.

After we have a solid foundation of using Swift, we will start creating the visual aspects of our *Let's Eat* app. During this process, we will work with storyboards and connect our app's structure together using segues. With our UI complete, we will go over the different ways in which we can display data. To display our data in a grid, we will use Collection Views, and to display our data in a list, we will use Table Views.

We will also look at how to add basic and custom annotations on to a map. Finally, it's time to get real data; we will look at what an Application Programming Interface (API) is and how we can get real restaurant data into our Collection Views, Table Views, and Map.

We now have a complete app, but how about adding some bells and whistles? The first place we can add a feature will be on the restaurant detail page where we can add restaurant reviews. Here, users will be able to take or choose a picture and apply a filter on to their picture. They will also be able to give the restaurant a rating as well as a review. When they are done, we will save this data using Core Data.

Since we built our app to work on both iPhone and iPad, we should add the ability to make our app support iPad Multitasking. Doing this will allow our app to be open alongside another app at the same time.

If we want to be able to send our reservation to a friend, we can create a custom UI for iMessages, which will send them the details for the reservation along with the app it came from. The one thing missing from our app is the ability to notify the user with a custom notification to alert when they have an upcoming reservation.

Finally, let's create a quick access for our app using 3D touch where, by tapping our app icon, the user can quickly jump to their reservations. Now that we have added some bells and whistles, let's get this app to our friends using TestFlight, and finally get it into the App Store.

Preface

Who this book is for

This book is for beginners who want to be able to create iOS applications. If you have some programming experience, this book is a great way to get a full understanding of how to create an iOS application from scratch and submit it to the App Store. You do not need any knowledge of Swift or any prior programming experience.

What this book covers

Chapter 1, *Getting Familiar with Xcode,* takes you through a tour of Xcode and talks about all the different panels that we will use throughout the book.

Chapter 2, *Building a Foundation with Swift,* deals with the basics of Swift.

Chapter 3, *Building on the Swift Foundation,* teaches us to build on our Swift foundation and learn some more basics of Swift.

Chapter 4, *Digging Deeper,* talks about ranges and control flow.

Chapter 5, *Digging into Collections,* talks about the different types of Collections.

Chapter 6, *Starting the UI Setup,* is about building the Let's Eat app. We will focus on getting our structure set up using storyboards.

Chapter 7, *Setting Up the Basic Structure,* deals with working on our Let's Eat app in a storyboard.

Chapter 8, *Building Our App Structure in Storyboard,* is about adding more to our app structure in the storyboard

Chapter 9, *Finishing Up Our App Structure in Storyboard,* finishes up our app structure in the storyboard

Chapter 10, *Designing Cells,* is about designing the table and collection view cells in storyboard.

Chapter 11, *Designing Static Tables,* teaches how to work with a static table view.

Chapter 12, *Designing a Photo Filter and Review Form,* teaches you how to design a basic form.

Chapter 13, *Getting Started with the Grid,* is about working with Collection Views and how we can use them to display a grid of items.

Chapter 14, *Getting Data into Our Grid*, is about getting data into our Collection Views.

Chapter 15, *Getting Started with the List*, teaches us to work with Table View and takes a deep look at dynamic Table Views.

Chapter 16, *Where Are We?*, deals with working with MapKit and learning how to add annotations to a map. We will also create custom annotations for our map.

Chapter 17, *Working with an API*, is about learning how to use a JSON API within our app.

Chapter 18, *Displaying Data in Restaurant Detail*, teaches you how to pass data using segues.

Chapter 19, *Foodie Reviews*, talks about working with the phone's camera and library.

Chapter 20, *Working with Photo Filters*, takes a look at how to apply filters to our photos.

Chapter 21, *Understanding Core Data*, teaches us the basics of using Core Data.

Chapter 22, *Saving Reviews*, wraps up Reviews by saving them using Core Data.

Chapter 23, *Universal*, deals with multitasking on the iPad, and how we can get an update to be supported on all devices.

Chapter 24, *iMessages*, is about building a custom message app UI. We will also create a framework to share data between both apps.

Chapter 25, *Notifications*, provides learning on how to build basic notifications. Then, we will look at embedding images into our notifications as well as building a custom UI.

Chapter 26, *Drag and Drop*, is about learning how to add drag and drop both within the app and accepting drag and drop from other apps.

Chapter 27, *Just a Peek*, looks at 3D touch and how to add quick actions to our app. We will also look at how we can add peek and pop to our restaurant list.

Chapter 28, *SiriKit*, teaches how to use Siri to create money requests.

Chapter 29, *Beta and Store Submission*, is about how to submit apps for testing as well as submitting apps to the App Store.

To get the most out of this book

You need to have Xcode 9 installed in your system. To download Xcode 9 visit `https://developer.apple.com/xcode/`.

Download the example code files

You can download the example code files for this book from your account at `www.packtpub.com`. If you purchased this book elsewhere, you can visit `www.packtpub.com/support` and register to have the files emailed directly to you.

You can download the code files by following these steps:

1. Log in or register at `www.packtpub.com`.
2. Select the **SUPPORT** tab.
3. Click on **Code Downloads & Errata**.
4. Enter the name of the book in the **Search** box and follow the onscreen instructions.

Once the file is downloaded, please make sure that you unzip or extract the folder using the latest version of:

- WinRAR/7-Zip for Windows
- Zipeg/iZip/UnRarX for Mac
- 7-Zip/PeaZip for Linux

The code bundle for the book is also hosted on GitHub at `https://github.com/PacktPublishing/Learn-iOS-11-Programming-with-Swift-4-Second-Edition`. We also have other code bundles from our rich catalog of books and videos available at `https://github.com/PacktPublishing/`. Check them out!

Download the color images

We also provide a PDF file that has color images of the screenshots/diagrams used in this book. You can download it here: `https://www.packtpub.com/sites/default/files/downloads/LearniOS11ProgrammingwithSwift4SecondEdition_ColorImages.pdf`.

Conventions used

There are a number of text conventions used throughout this book.

`CodeInText`: Indicates code words in text, database table names, folder names, filenames, file extensions, pathnames, dummy URLs, user input, and Twitter handles. Here is an example: "As we have done throughout the book, we are going to create a `Manager` class."

A block of code is set as follows:

```
let arrOfInts:[Int] = []
let arrStrings = [String]()
```

Bold: Indicates a new term, an important word, or words that you see onscreen. For example, words in menus or dialog boxes appear in the text like this. Here is an example: "Once installed, launch Xcode, and you should see the following **Welcome to Xcode screen**."

Warnings or important notes appear like this.

Tips and tricks appear like this.

Get in touch

Feedback from our readers is always welcome.

General feedback: Email `feedback@packtpub.com` and mention the book title in the subject of your message. If you have questions about any aspect of this book, please email us at `questions@packtpub.com`.

Errata: Although we have taken every care to ensure the accuracy of our content, mistakes do happen. If you have found a mistake in this book, we would be grateful if you would report this to us. Please visit `www.packtpub.com/submit-errata`, selecting your book, clicking on the Errata Submission Form link, and entering the details.

Piracy: If you come across any illegal copies of our works in any form on the Internet, we would be grateful if you would provide us with the location address or website name. Please contact us at `copyright@packtpub.com` with a link to the material.

If you are interested in becoming an author: If there is a topic that you have expertise in and you are interested in either writing or contributing to a book, please visit `authors.packtpub.com`.

Reviews

Please leave a review. Once you have read and used this book, why not leave a review on the site that you purchased it from? Potential readers can then see and use your unbiased opinion to make purchase decisions, we at Packt can understand what you think about our products, and our authors can see your feedback on their book. Thank you!

For more information about Packt, please visit `packtpub.com`.

1
Getting Familiar with Xcode

So, you want to get into iOS development? I was in your shoes on January 27th, 2010, when Apple first announced the iPad. Literally as soon as the conference was over, I knew that I wanted to learn how to create apps for the iPad. I signed up to the Apple Developer website and paid my $99 annual fee. But then, I realized that I did not know where to begin. A large variety of instructional books or videos did not exist, especially since the iPad had not yet been released. I had previous programming experience; however, I had no idea how to write Objective-C (the original programming language for iOS). Therefore, I had to teach myself the basics. In this book, we will learn what it takes to become an iOS developer together.

If you are new to programming, take your time. You should understand the lessons in one chapter before moving on to the next chapter. These important skills will set you up with a solid foundation in iOS development. If you have previous programming experience, you should still review the earlier chapters, as they will be a refresher for you.

Throughout this book, we will work in Xcode, specifically Xcode 9 (and Swift 4, which we will tackle later in the book). Xcode is known as an **Integrated Development Environment** (**IDE**). Using Xcode gives us everything we will need in order to build apps for iOS, tvOS, macOS (formerly, OS X), and watchOS. In this chapter, we will explore Xcode in order to help you get more comfortable using it. If you are not on Xcode 9, make sure to update Xcode, as the code in this book will not run properly otherwise.

Our focus in this book will be on creating a universal iOS app (an app for both the iPhone and iPad). The best way to do this is to create a project to familiarize yourself with where everything is and how to find what you need. So, let's first download and install Xcode.

Getting started

In order to download Xcode, launch the App Store on your Mac and then type `Xcode` into the search bar in the upper-right corner:

For better quality of images, download the graphics bundle from `https://www.packtpub.com/sites/default/files/downloads/LearniOS11ProgrammingwithSwift4SecondEdition_ColorImages.pdf`.

Next, click on **INSTALL**:

Getting Familiar with Xcode

Once installed, launch Xcode and you should see the following **Welcome to Xcode** screen:

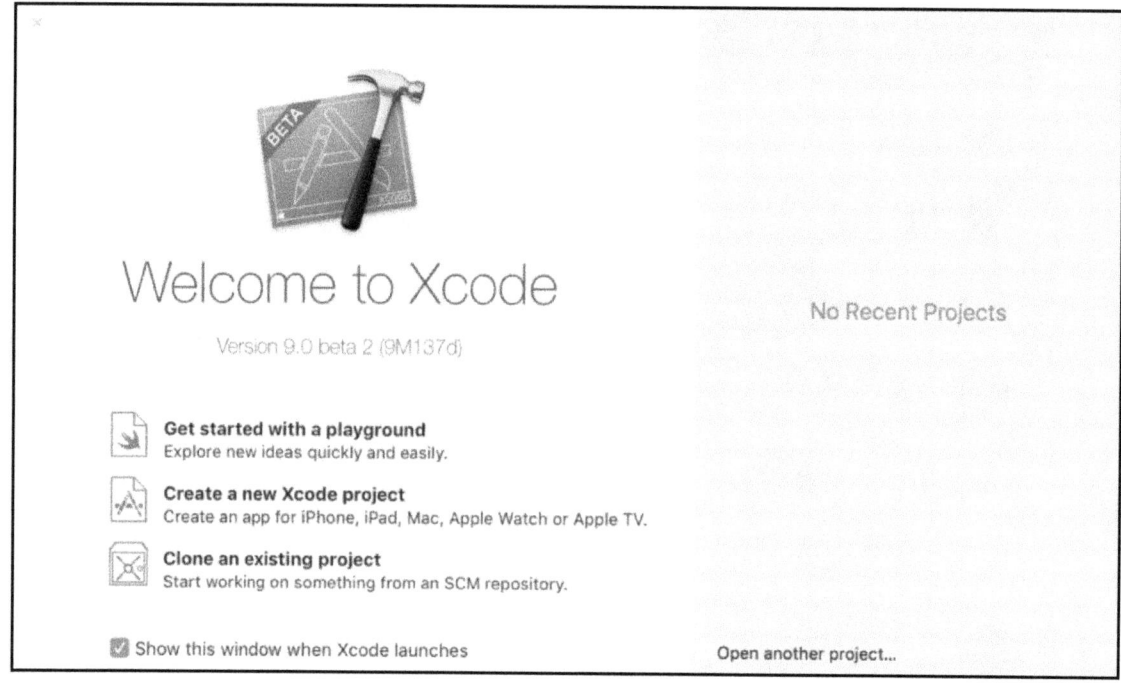

Chapter 1

If this is the first time you have launched Xcode, then you will see **No Recent Projects** in the right panel. If you have previously created projects, then you will see those listed to the right. To get started, we are going to click on **Create a new Xcode project** in the left panel of the welcome screen. This will take us to the new project screen:

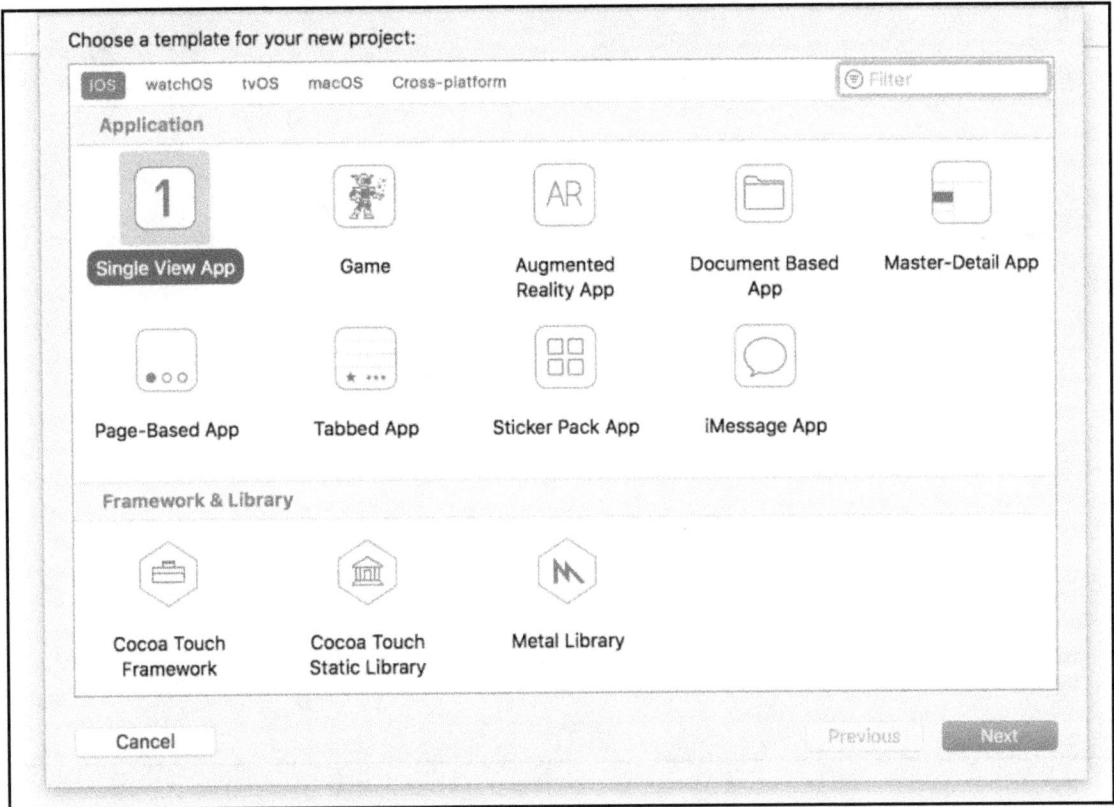

Getting Familiar with Xcode

Across the top of this screen, you can select one of the following items: **iOS**, **watchOS**, **tvOS**, **macOS**, and **Cross-platform**. Since we are creating apps for iOS, make sure that you have iOS selected. Then, select **Single View App** and click on **Next**. Now, you will see an options screen for a new project:

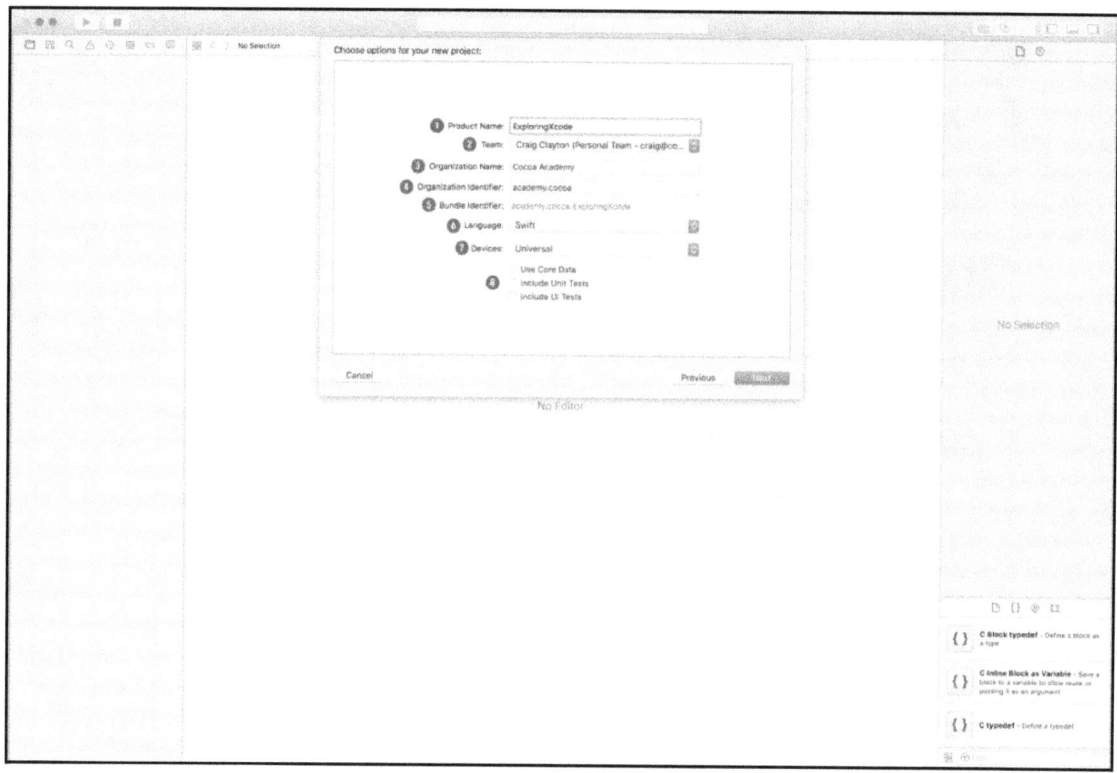

This option screen has the following seven items to complete or choose:

1. **Product Name**: The product name is your app. We are going to set ours as `ExploringXcode`.
2. **Team**: The team is connected to your Apple account. We are going to ignore this for now, because it is not needed for this chapter. If you have a team set up, just leave it as is. We will cover this in greater detail later in the book.
3. **Organization Name**: You can set the organization name to your company name or just your name.

[12]

4. **Organizer Identifier**: You will set the organizer identifier to be your domain name in reverse. For example, my website URL is `cocoa.academy`, and therefore, my identifier is `academy.cocoa`. Since URLs are unique, it will ensure that no one else will have your identifier. If you do not have a domain, then just use your first and last name for now. You will eventually have to purchase a domain if you want to submit your app to the Apple Store.
5. **Bundle Identifier**: When you create a new project, Apple will combine your **Product Name** with your **Organizer Identifier** to create your unique bundle identifier. So, even if 10,000 people create this project, each person will have a different bundle identifier.
6. **Language**: Make sure your language is set to Swift.
7. **Checkboxes**: You can uncheck **Use Core Data**, **Include Unit Tests**, and **Include UI Tests**, as these are things we will not be using in this chapter.

Now, select **Next**, and Xcode will prompt us to save our project. I have a dedicated folder for all my projects, but you can save it on your desktop for easy access.

The Xcode interface

Your project is now open and it is time for us to get familiar with all of the panels. If this is your first time in Xcode, then it will probably be a bit overwhelming for you. Therefore, we will break it down into five parts:

- **NAVIGATOR PANEL**
- **STANDARD EDITOR**
- **UTILITIES PANEL**
- **DEBUG PANEL**

Getting Familiar with Xcode

- TOOLBAR
- WINDOW PANE CONTROLS

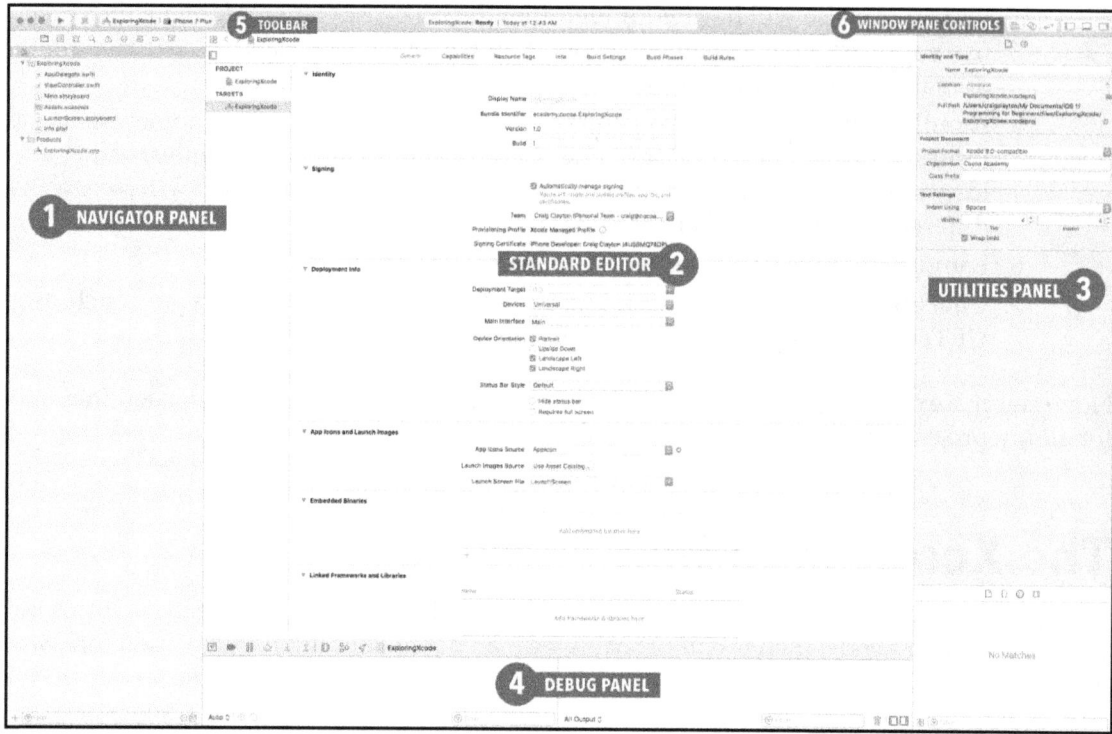

Navigator panel

The primary use for the navigator panel is to add new files and/or select existing files. The other icons are used from time to time; we will cover them as we need them.

Standard editor

The standard editor is a single panel view used to edit files. The standard editor area is the primary area in which you will work. In this area, we can view storyboard files, see our Swift files, or view our project settings.

Utilities panel

The utilities panel can be a bit confusing when you first use Xcode, because this menu changes based on what you have selected in the standard editor. When we start building an app, we will dig deeper into this. For now, just know that the utilities panel is made up of the inspector pane at the top and the library pane at the bottom. The inspector pane allows you to change the attributes or properties of things you put in your storyboard-the library pane allows you to insert objects, image assets, and code snippets into your app.

Debug panel

The debug panel will allow us to see log messages from our app. You will become very familiar with this panel by the time you finish this book. The debug panel is one of the greatest tools for getting feedback on what your app is doing or not doing.

Toolbar

Next, we look at the toolbar:

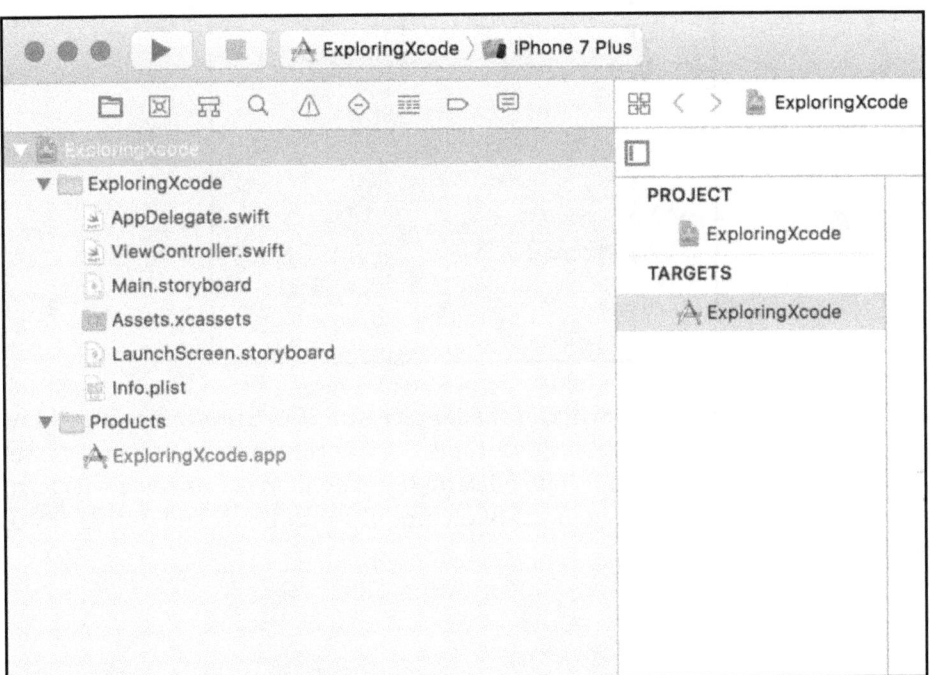

Getting Familiar with Xcode

First, we have a play button, which is how we launch our app (or use *cmd + R*). Next, you will see a stop button, which will not be active until you run your app. This stop button (or *cmd + .*) is used to stop your app from running. To the right of the stop button, you will see your target (your project name) along with the current Simulator selected. If you click on your project name, you will see a screen similar to this:

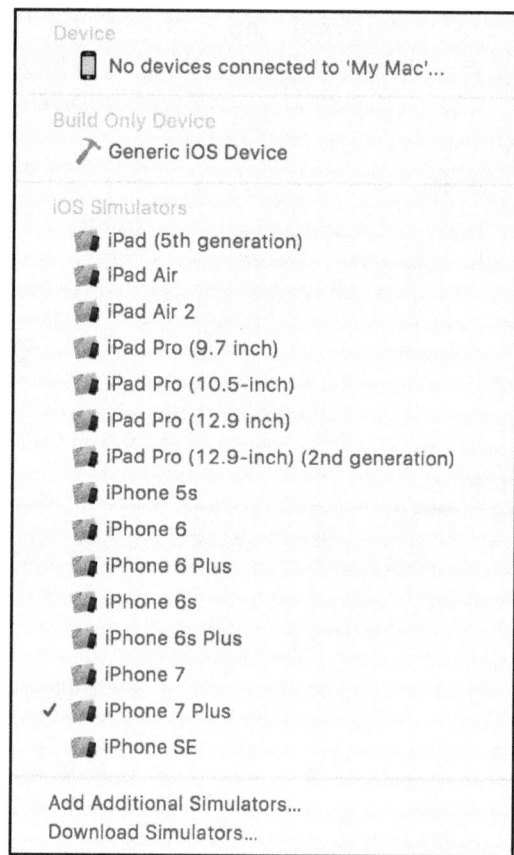

This drop-down menu, which we will call the **Device** and **iOS Simulators** drop-down menu, allows you to change your Simulator type. For the purposes of our project, select **iPhone7 Plus** as your Simulator and then click on the play icon (or use *cmd + R*) to run your app. Your app will be blank and will most likely not fit the entire screen (unless you are on a large screen).

Chapter 1

In order to see the entire screen, you can scroll right and left; however, doing this gets harder once you have elements in your app. So, an alternative to scrolling is to resize your app to fit the screen. We can do this by going to your **Simulator** menu and navigating to **Window** | **Scale**:

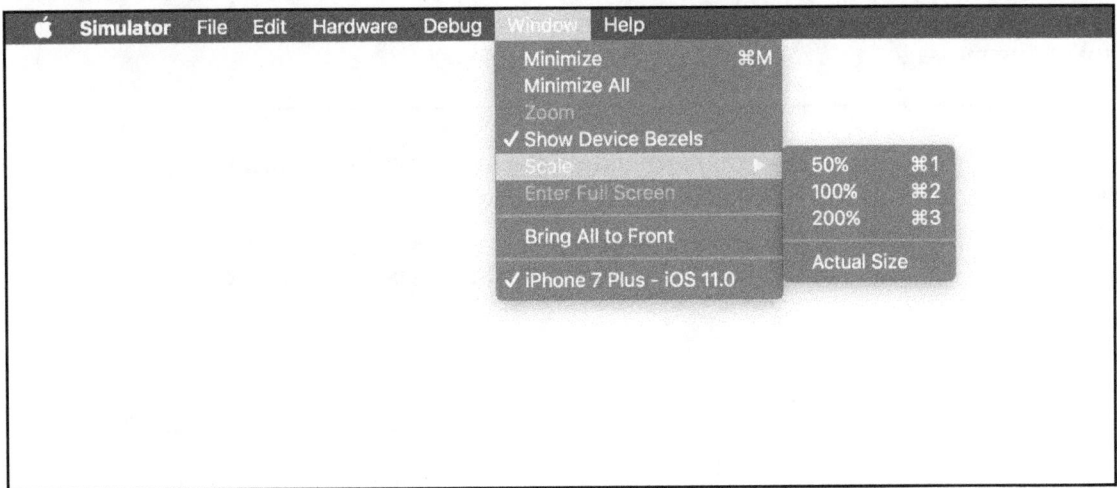

Here, you will be able to scale from **200%** to **100%**, or **50%** (select whichever percentage allows the app to best fit your screen size).

Now, let's return to Xcode and select the stop button (or use *cmd + .*).

If you use the keyboard shortcut, make sure Xcode is in focus; otherwise, this shortcut will not work. I work on a 15-inch MacBook Pro Retina - therefore, when I am working on an app, I will use the iPhone 6 or iPad Air 2 simulator in landscape. They both fit nicely on my screen without having to resize either.

In addition to the **Simulator**, there is a **Build Only Device** as well as a **Device** section, both at the top of the **Device** and **Simulator** drop-down menu that was shown earlier in this chapter. Note that, for our purposes, you will only need a Simulator while we are building the app; however, you can add an iOS device if you would like (see under **iOS Device**).

Generic iOS device

The **Generic iOS Device**, under the **Build Only Device** section of the **Device** and **Simulator** drop-down menu, is used for when you need to archive your app, which means that you are preparing your app for submission to Apple (either to the App Store or to Test Flight). If you try to select **Generic iOS Device** now and run the app, you will get the following message:

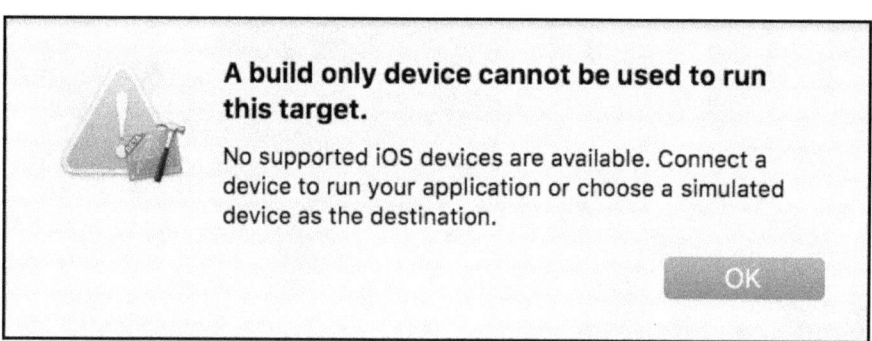

Therefore, change **Generic iOS Device** to an actual Simulator, and then you will be able to continue.

iOS device

If you do not have a device connected to the computer, you will see **No devices connected...** under the **Device** section of the Device and Simulator drop-down menu.

As noted earlier, when we start building the *Let's Eat* app, you will have the option of using the Simulator or connecting a device to Xcode. Using a device is slower; however, the simulator will not perform in the same way as a device will.

In the past, you needed to have a paid account to build your app on a device. Now, you do not need a developer account in order to run the app on your device. Note that, if you decide to connect your device instead of using a Simulator, you will need iOS 11 installed on it. Introduced in Xcode 9 is the ability to connect your phone wirelessly. We will look at the traditional way first and then we will go over how you connect your phone wirelessly.

Chapter 1

The following steps are only for those who do not want to pay for the Apple Developer Program at this time:

1. Connect your iOS device via USB
2. In the drop-down menu, select your device (here, **Xclusive iPhone 6 Plus**):

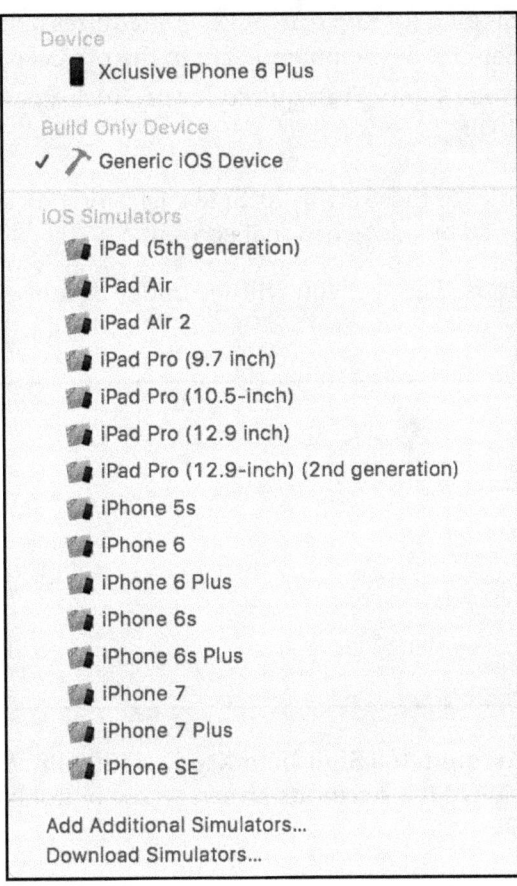

Getting Familiar with Xcode

3. Wait for Xcode 9 to finish indexing and processing. This may take a bit of time. Once complete, the status will say **Ready**.
4. Run the project by hitting the Play button (or use *cmd + R*).

You will get two errors that state the following:

- Signing for `ExploringXcode` requires a development team. Select a development team in the project editor.
- Code signing is required for product type application in SDK iOS 10.0.

Ignore the specifics of these errors as they basically indicate that we need to create an account and add our device to that account:

5. Now, in the standard editor, you will see under **Signing** that you need to add an account:

6. Click on **Add Account**. If a **Sign in to Xcode with your Apple ID** dialog box does not pop up, inside of the **Accounts** screen on the bottom left, click on the + and select **Apple ID**:

[20]

Chapter 1

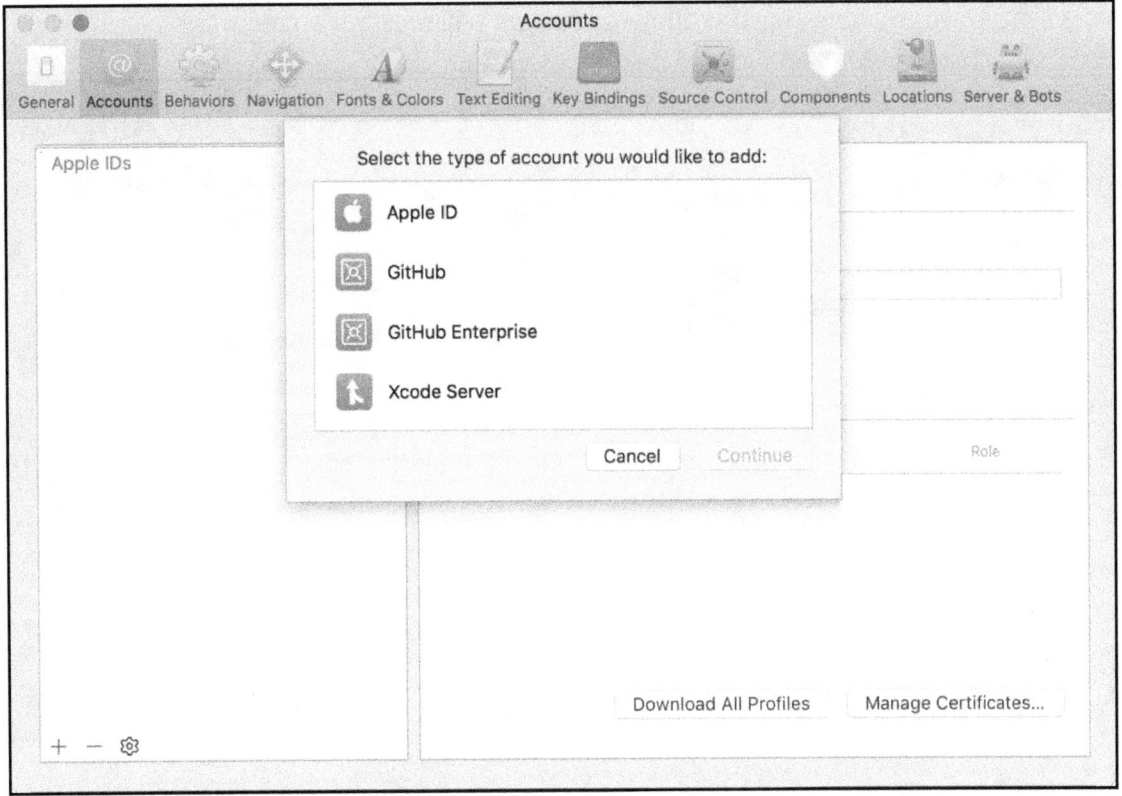

7. Then, you will click on **Create Apple ID**. You will be asked to enter your birth date, name, email, and password, along with security questions. Make sure that you verify your email before you answer the security questions; otherwise, you will have to come back to this screen and add **Apple ID** again.

8. Once you have finished all the steps, you will see your account:

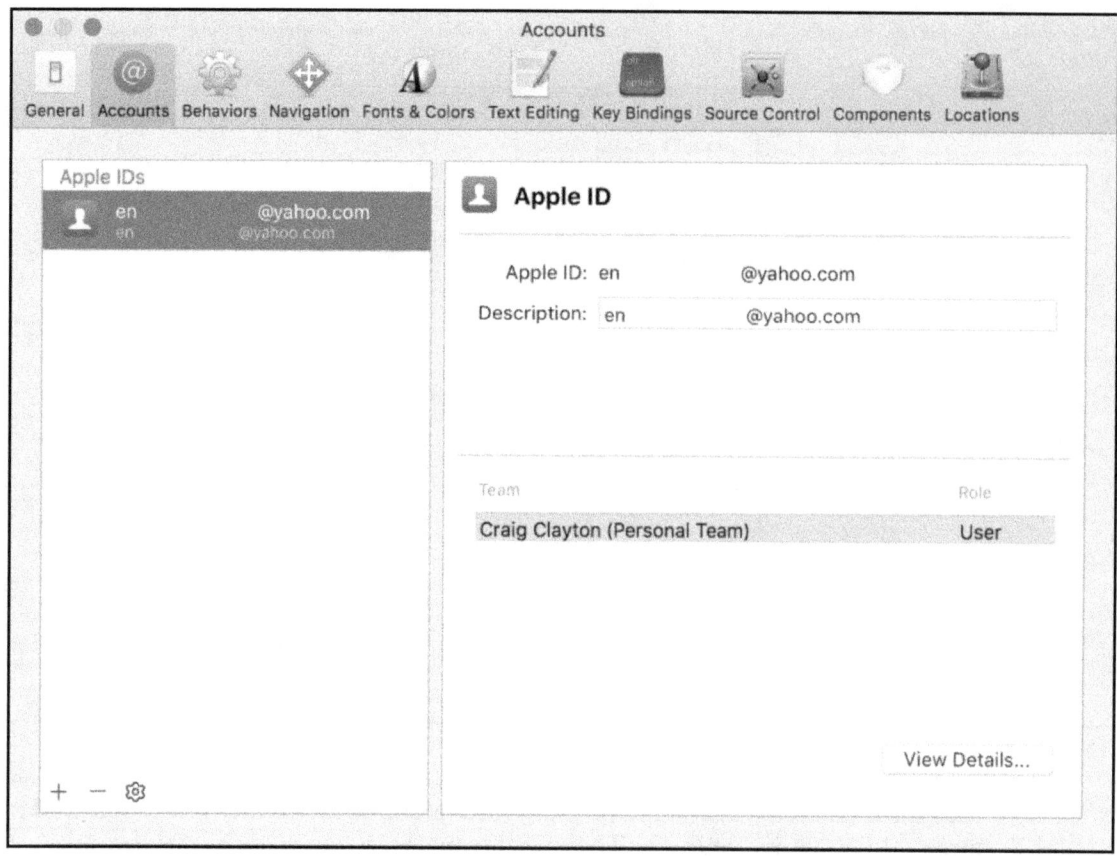

If you already have an account, then, instead of seeing **Add Account**, you will see a drop-down menu with your account listed. If your device is not connected to this account, you might see a message asking if you would like to add your device to your account.

Connecting wirelessly

Now that you have your phone and account connected it is easy to get your phone set up to run it wirelessly. With your device already connected via USB, go to **Window** | **Devices** and **Simulators**. Click on the Checkbox marked **Connect via network**:

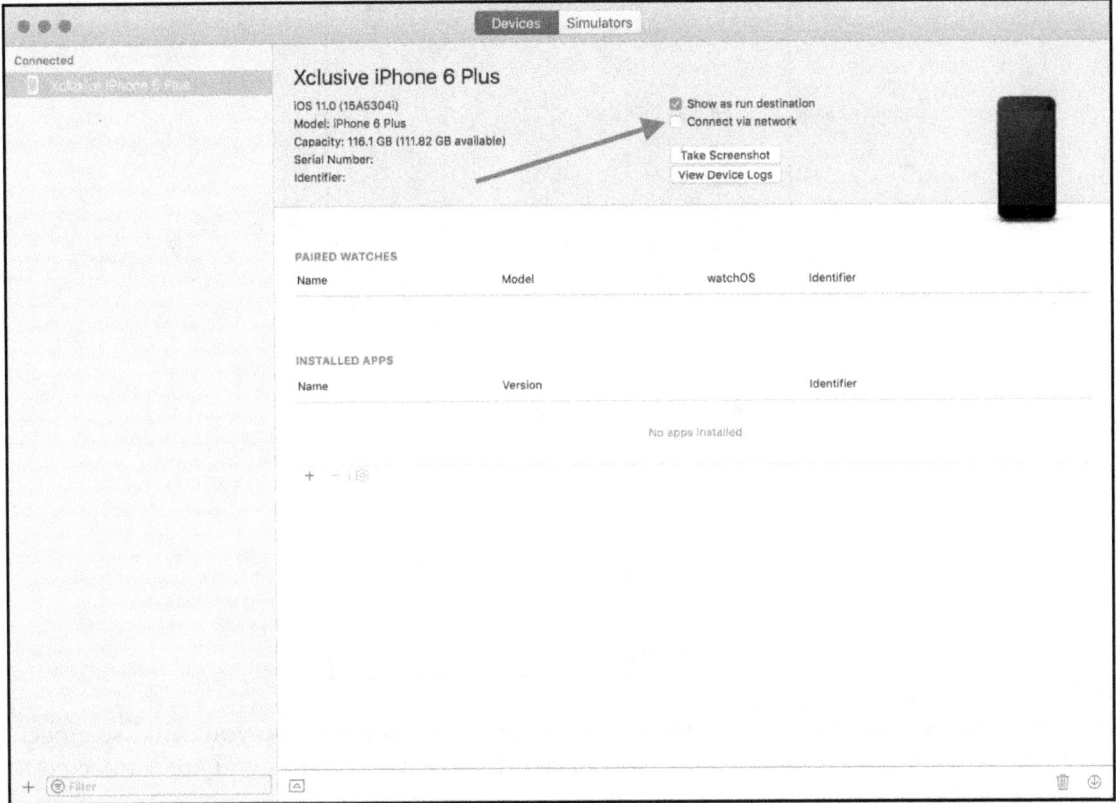

Make sure that your phone and your computer are connected to the same Wi-Fi network.

When I first connected to my device, I saw a globe icon in Xcode that lets you know that you are connected via the network.

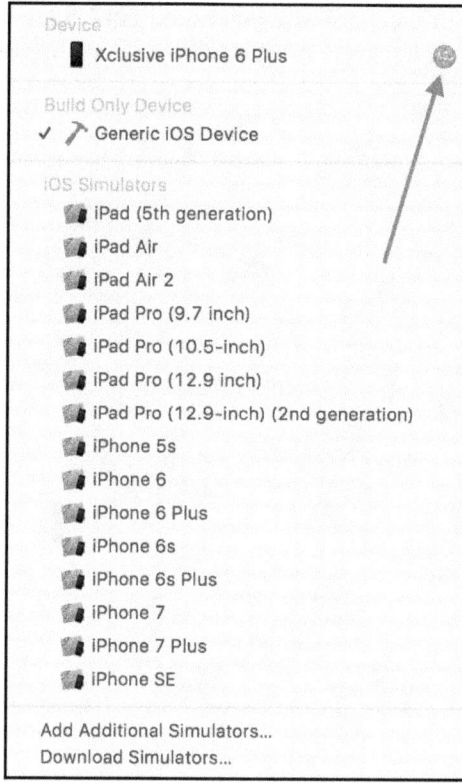

After a short time, the globe went away. Even if you do not see the icon you can disconnect the USB and your device should still be connected to Xcode (as long as you are connected to the same Wi-Fi network).

You will not need to use a device for the majority of this book; however, depending on the type of MacBook you have, you might need to use a device.

Before we get to the right side of the Toolbar, select the `Main.storyboard` file in your navigator panel. This file is used to do all of your visual setup for your entire app. We will cover this in detail later in the book. After you select the file, you should see the following:

Chapter 1

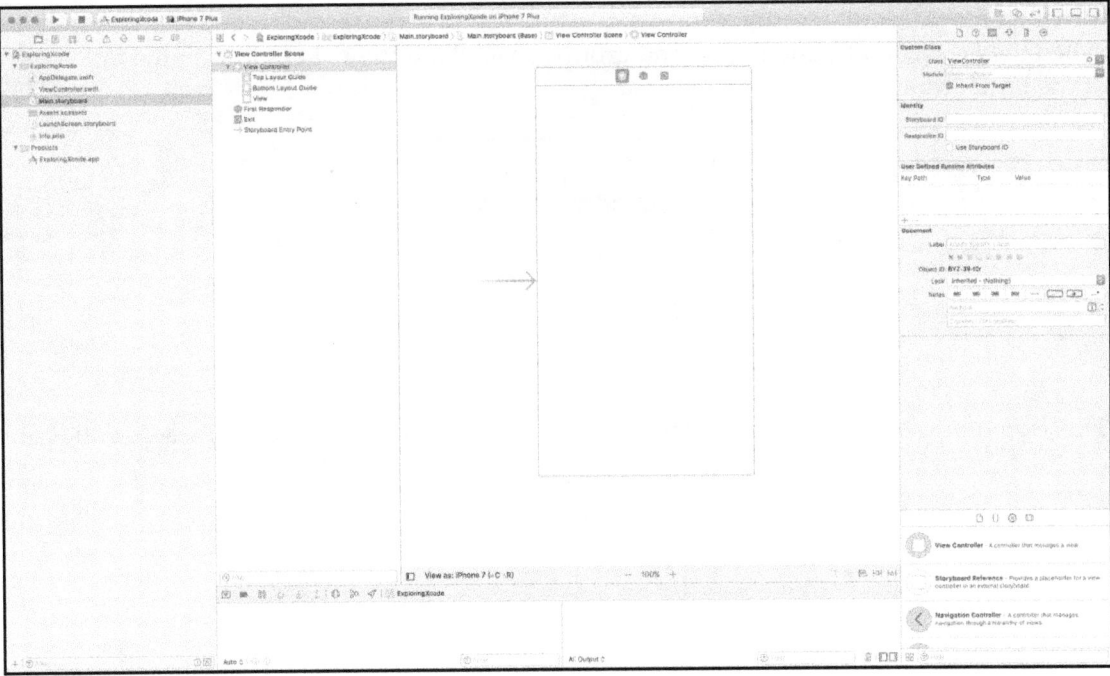

Window pane controls

The following screenshot shows the window pane controls:

Moving onto the window pane controls, you will see two groups of icons. The first group is called the Editor Mode, and the second group is called the View. Let's look at the functions of the Editor Mode icons:

This icon controls the standard editor (which is the center panel in the earlier screenshot of the `Main.storyboard` file in the navigator panel).

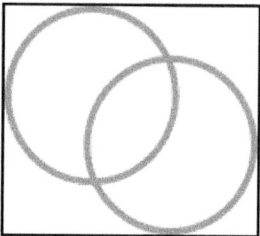

This icon splits the Standard editor into two panels, where you will see the `ViewController.swift` file on the right. We will use this split screen throughout the book.

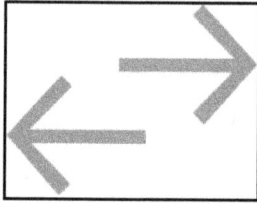

This icon is the Version editor. We will not address the Version editor in this book, since it is a more advanced feature.

At this point, you might be thinking that there are way too many panels open, and I would agree with you. This is where the last group of View icons in the toolbar comes in handy.

Let's look at these icons and their functions in the following table:

This icon will toggle (hide or show) the navigator panel (or use *cmd + 0*).

This icon will toggle (hide or show) the debug panel (or use *cmd + shift + Y*).

This icon will toggle (hide or show) the utilities panel (or use *cmd + alt + 0*).

Summary

Congratulations! You have finished exploring the basics of Xcode. When we start building our app, we will cover the more important parts of Xcode in depth. It is now time to start learning Swift 4.

2
Building a Foundation with Swift

Now that we have had a short tour of Xcode, it is time to start learning about Swift. Remember, if you are new to programming, things will be very different for you, so take your time. The important skills that you will learn here will set you up with a solid foundation in iOS development. If you have previous programming experience, you should still review this chapter, as it can only enhance your programming skills and act as a refresher for you.

On June 2, 2014, Apple changed the game for iOS development, because this was the day Swift was announced to the world. With this announcement, everybody was put on an even playing field, because they had to learn a new programming language. Swift has brought a more modern approach to developing apps and has seen a huge influx of new developers of all ages wanting to build iOS apps. But enough about history! Let's dig in and see what you are going to learn.

The following will be covered in this chapter:

- Playgrounds
- Data types
- Variables and constants
- Debug and print()
- Comments

Playgrounds – an interactive coding environment

Before we jump into building the app that we will be creating in later chapters, called *Let's Eat*, we need to understand the basics of Swift. An easy way to experiment with Swift is to use **Playgrounds**. It is an interactive coding environment that evaluates your code and displays the results. Using Playgrounds gives us the ability to work with Swift without needing to create a project. It is great for prototyping a particular part of your app. So, whether you are learning or experimenting, Playgrounds are an invaluable tool. In order to create a Playground, we need to launch Xcode and click on **Get started with a playground**:

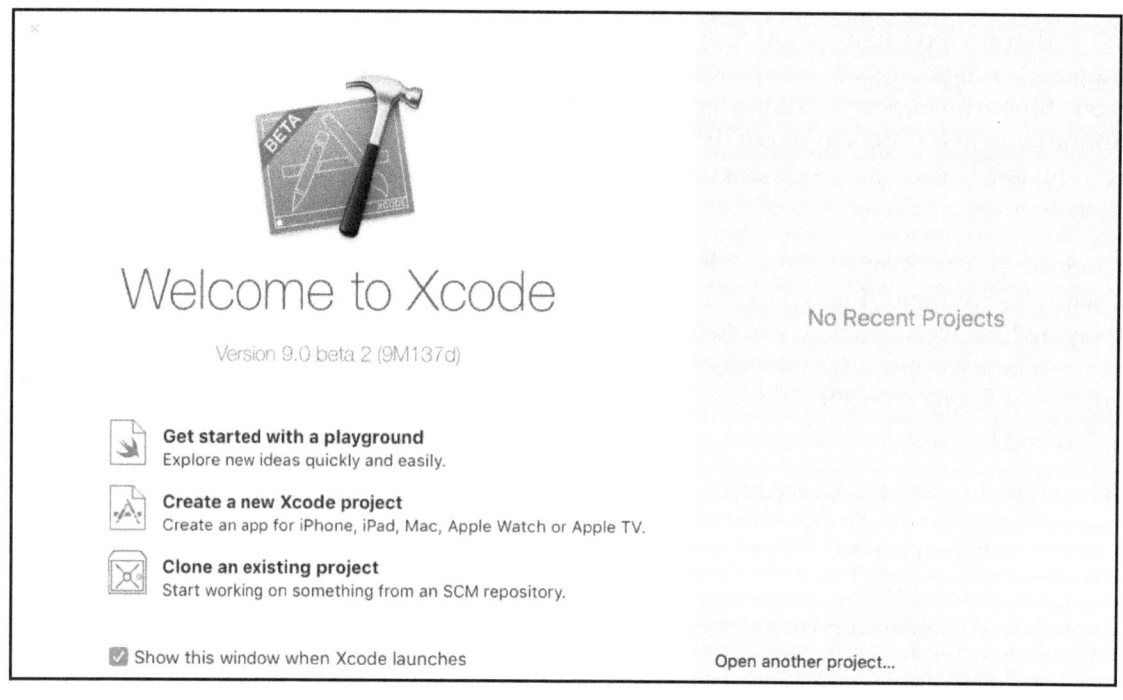

The **Playground** template screen will appear. Make sure that you select **iOS**, then choose **Blank** and hit **Next**:

You will be asked to give your project a name and a location to save the file; name your new `Playground iOS11-Programming-for-Beginners-Ch2`. You can save the file anywhere that you like. Now, with the project saved, we can explore Playgrounds a bit.

When you launch the app, you will see five distinct areas:

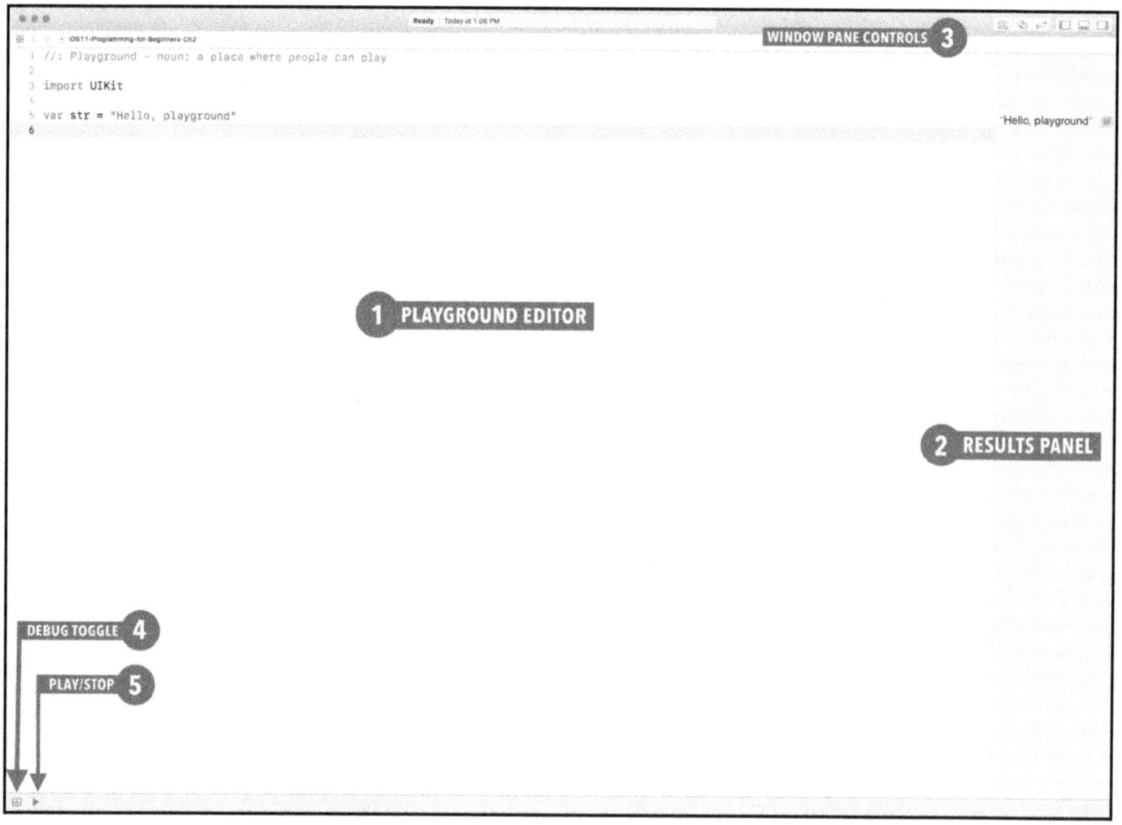

WINDOW PANE CONTROLS 3
//: Playground - noun: a place where people can play
import UIKit
var str = "Hello, playground"
"Hello, playground"
1 PLAYGROUND EDITOR
2 RESULTS PANEL
DEBUG TOGGLE 4
PLAY/STOP 5

Let's break down each area in Playgrounds:

- **Playground editor**: This area is where you will write all of your code.
- **Results panel**: The **Results panel** is a feature only found in Playgrounds and provides immediate feedback.
- **Window Pane Controls**: The **Window Pane Controls** have two groups of icons:

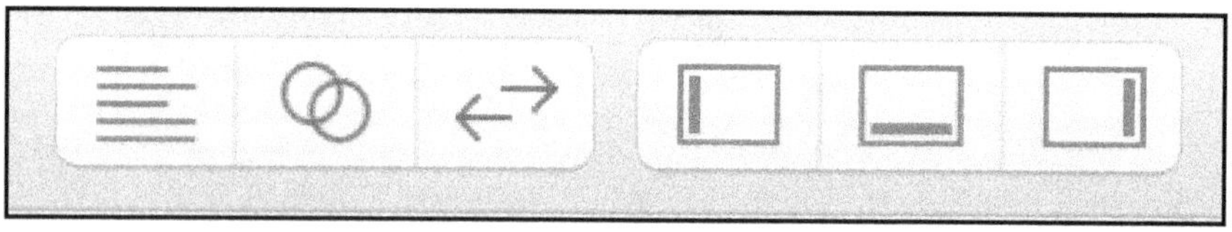

Chapter 2

As we discussed earlier, the first group is called the **Editor Mode** and the second group is called the **View**. Refer to the detailed description of these icons in the previous chapter for information about what each does.

- **Debug toggle**: This button allows you to hide and show the Debug panel and toggle on the Debug panel.
- **Play/Stop**: This button is used in order to make Playgrounds executes code or to stop Playgrounds from running. Typically, Playgrounds runs on its own, but sometimes you need to manually toggle this feature on when Playgrounds does not execute your code for you.

Now that we have our setup finished, delete everything in this file. Your Playground should have three open panels: your Playground editor, the Results panel, and the Debug panel. Let's start digging into some code.

Data types – where it all starts

Swift offers a collection of built-in data types. Its data types are string, integer, floating-point numbers, and Booleans. These data types can be found in most programming languages. Therefore, if you are not new to programming, you can skip this section and start at the variables and constants—where data is held section later.

Let's walk-through each data type for those of you who are new to programming or would like a refresher.

String

The first data type we will discuss is string. A string is represented by a series of characters. Strings are used to display text in an app. When a string is wrapped in quotes, it is known as a string literal. In programming, we cannot just add text into Playgrounds. So, in order to write a string, we must wrap our string inside quotes.

Building a Foundation with Swift

Let's now add our name into Playgrounds wrapped in quotes:

In Playgrounds, your values also will appear inside of your Results panel. So, we now know that, in order to create a String, we need to use quotes.

Integer data type

Integers (**Ints**) are whole numbers, such as 32 and –100. Integers are useful for when you need to do calculations (that is, adding, subtracting, multiplication, and so on). Let's add some numbers into Playgrounds. On the next line, under your name, type 32 and then, on the following line, –100:

Again, you will see both `32` and `-100` in the Results panel under your name.

Floating-point numbers

Floating-point numbers are numbers with a fractional component, such as 4.993, 0.5, and -234.99. Let's add these values into Playgrounds as well:

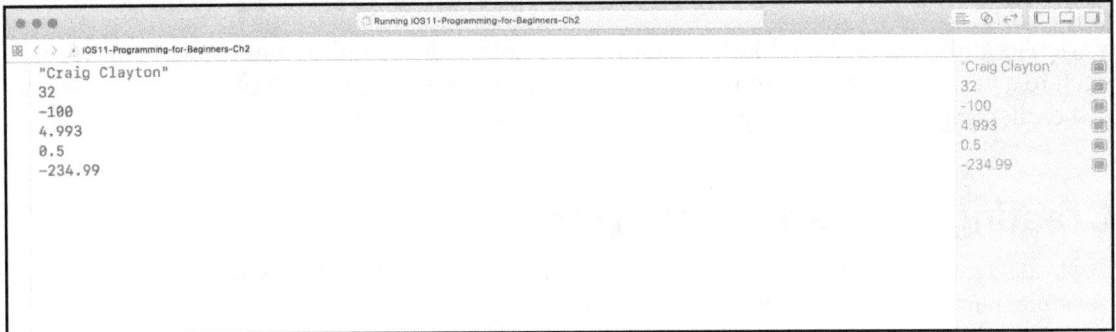

Booleans

Booleans (**bools** for short), are referred to as logical, because they either can be true or false. Booleans are used when you need to determine whether some logic is true or false. For example, did the user log in? This statement would either be true, yes, they did or false, no, they did not. So, in Playgrounds, add `true` and `false`:

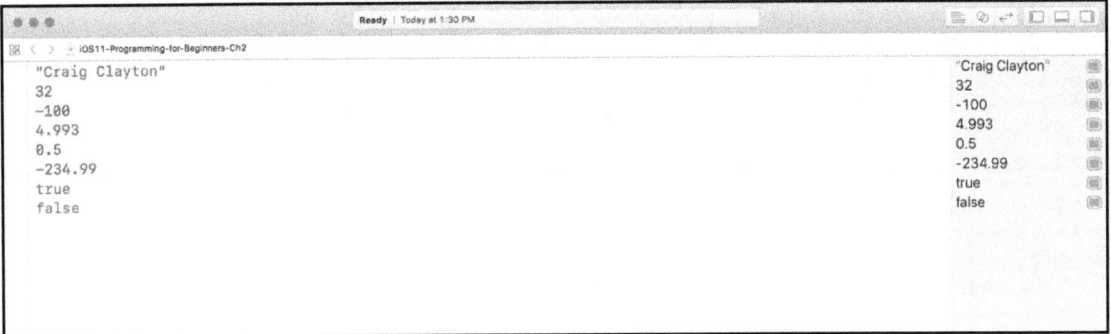

So, now we covered all of the basic data types in Swift. Right now, we have no way to use these data types. This is where variables and constants come into play.

Variables and constants – where data is held

Variables and constants are like a container that holds some kind of data. When you want to declare a variable, you have to use the var keyword. Let's declare each of the data types we did earlier, but, this time, using variables and constants instead.

Creating a variable with a string

First, delete what you have entered into Playgrounds already, and now let's declare our first variable, named `fullName`, and set it to your name:

```
var fullName = "Craig Clayton"
```

The preceding code says that we have a variable named `fullName` and that it is holding a string value of `Craig Clayton`. Your Results panel will have your actual name as its data:

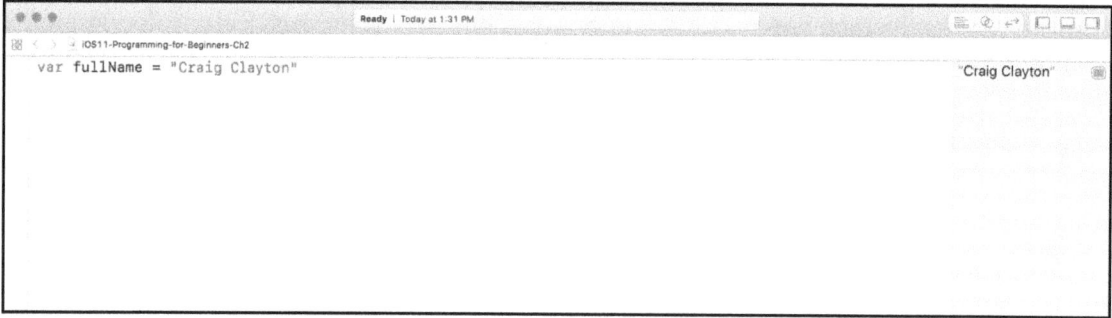

Creating a variable with an integer (Int)

Now, let's create a variable with an Int called `age` and set it to our age (or whatever you want your age to be) by adding the following:

```
var age = 40
```

Our program now knows that age is an Int. You should see both your name and age in the Results panel, just like you did previously:

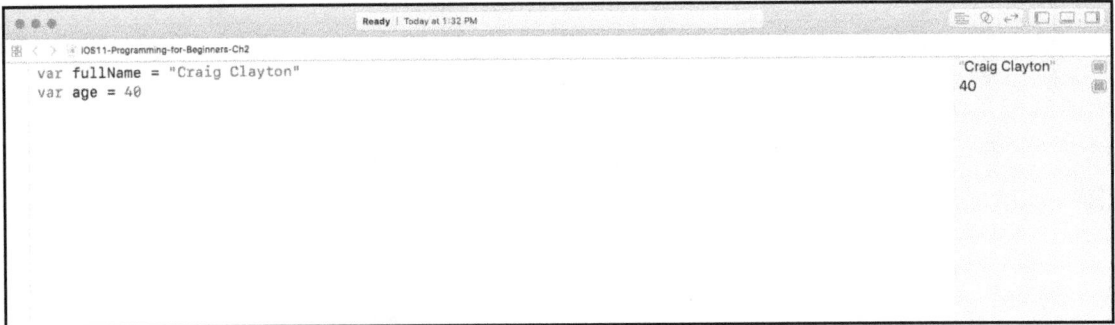

Debug and print() – detecting your bugs

We can use the Debug panel (at the bottom of the following screenshot) using `print()`. So, let's see how `print()` works by printing both our name and age. We can do this by adding the following:

```
print(fullName)
print(age)
```

It should appear on your screen as follows:

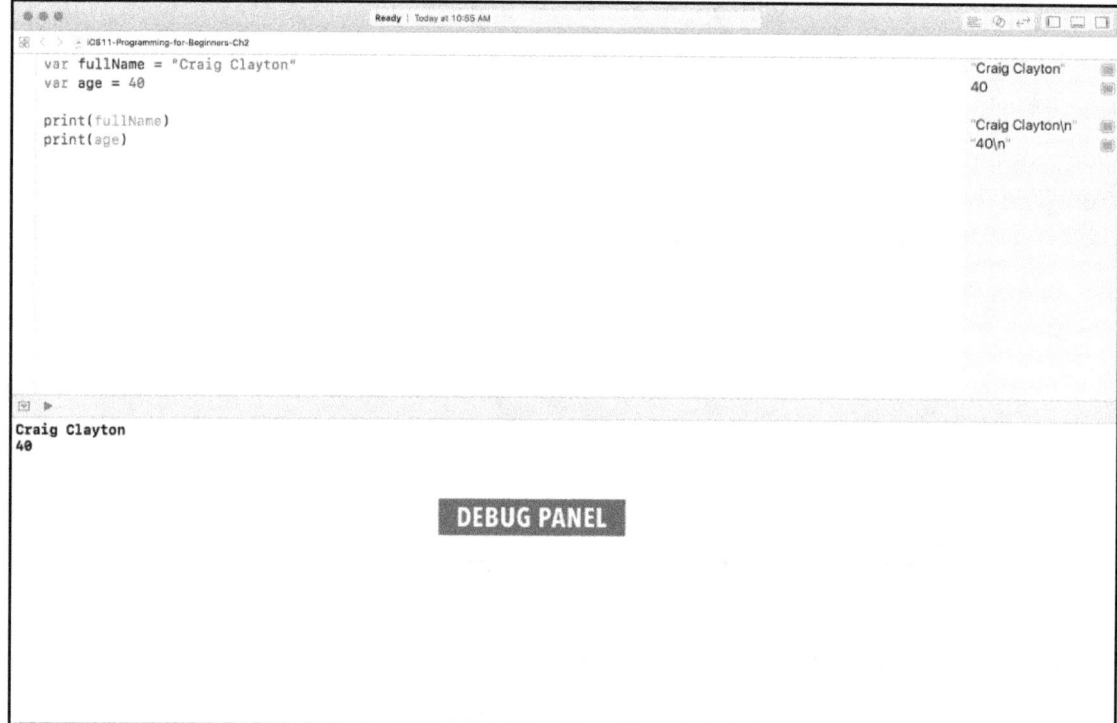

You should now see the output in both the Results and Debug panels. Using print() allows us to see things in our Debug panel and therefore verify expected results. This is a very useful debugging tool.

Adding floating-point numbers

Let's now add floating-point numbers, using the let constant in the Playground:

```
let gradeAvg = 2.9
let version = 1.1
```

Chapter 2

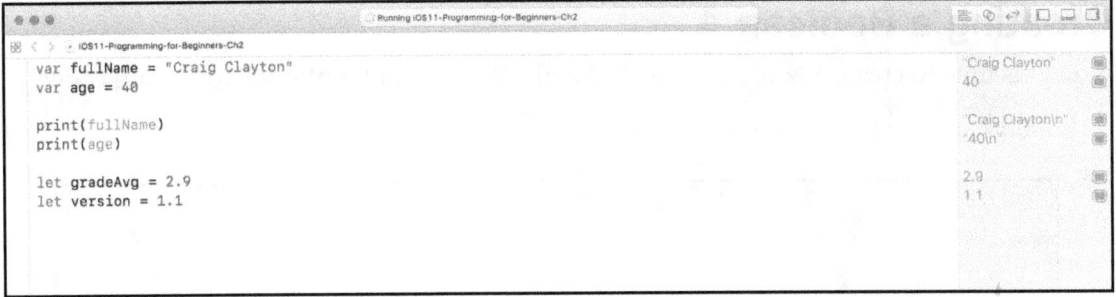

You will notice that a couple of things are different. First, we are using the `let` keyword. Using `let` tells our program that this is a constant. Constants are variables that cannot be changed once they are set (as opposed to a non-constant variable, which can be changed after being set).

The other thing you might have noticed is that we explicitly set our `version` to `Float`. When dealing with a floating-point number, it can be a `Double` or a `Float`. Without getting too technical, a `Double` is much more precise than a `Float`. The best way to explain this is to use pi as an example. Pi is a number in which the digits go on forever. Well, we cannot use a number that goes on forever; however, a `Double` and `Float` will handle how precise that number will be. Let's look at the following diagram to see what I mean by precise:

Double vs Float

let lessPrecisePI = Float("3.14")
let morePrecisePI = Float("3.1415926536")

So, in the preceding example, you can see that `Float` will only display `3.14`, whereas `Double` will give you a much more accurate number. In Swift, a `Double` is preferred. Therefore, if you do not explicitly set the floating-point number to a `Float`, Swift will default it to a `Double`. To set `version` to a `Float`, you must purposely set it that way.

Building a Foundation with Swift

Creating a Boolean

Now it is time to create a `Bool`, and we will make it a constant. Enter the following code:

```
let isConstant:Bool = true
```

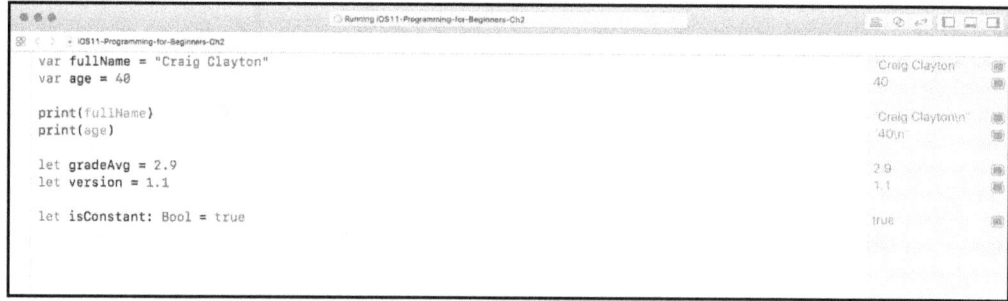

Since `isConstant` is set, let's make it `false` by adding this:

```
isConstant = false
```

On the same line as what you just entered, you now will see a red circle with a white dot. The red circle means that there is an error. The white circle inside of it means that Xcode can fix the error for you (most of the time):

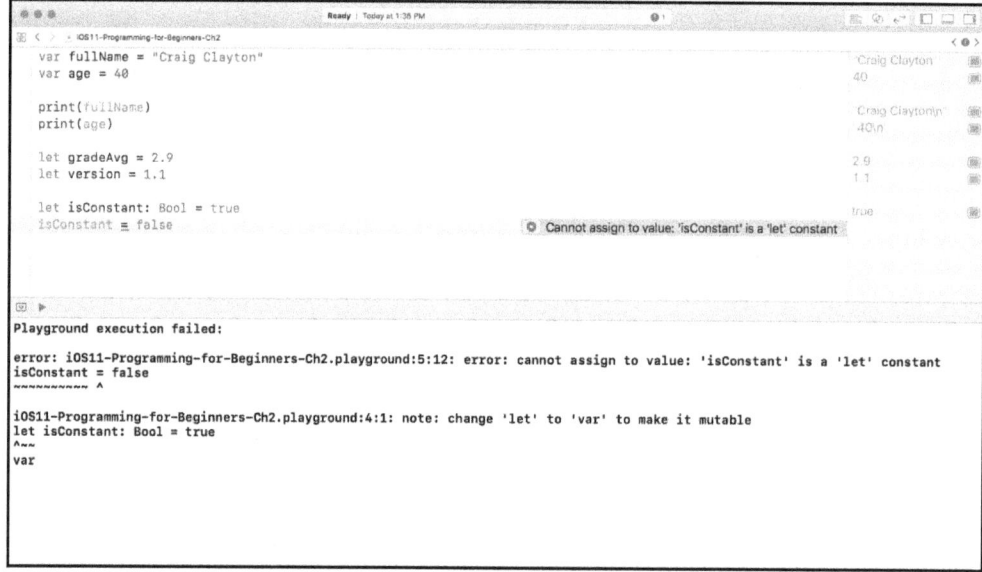

[40]

Chapter 2

You also will notice an error in your Debug panel, which is just a more detailed version of the error. This error is telling us that we are trying to change the value of a constant when we cannot do so.

If you tap on the circle, you will see that Playgrounds suggests that you change the `var` to a `let`, since you cannot assign a value to a constant:

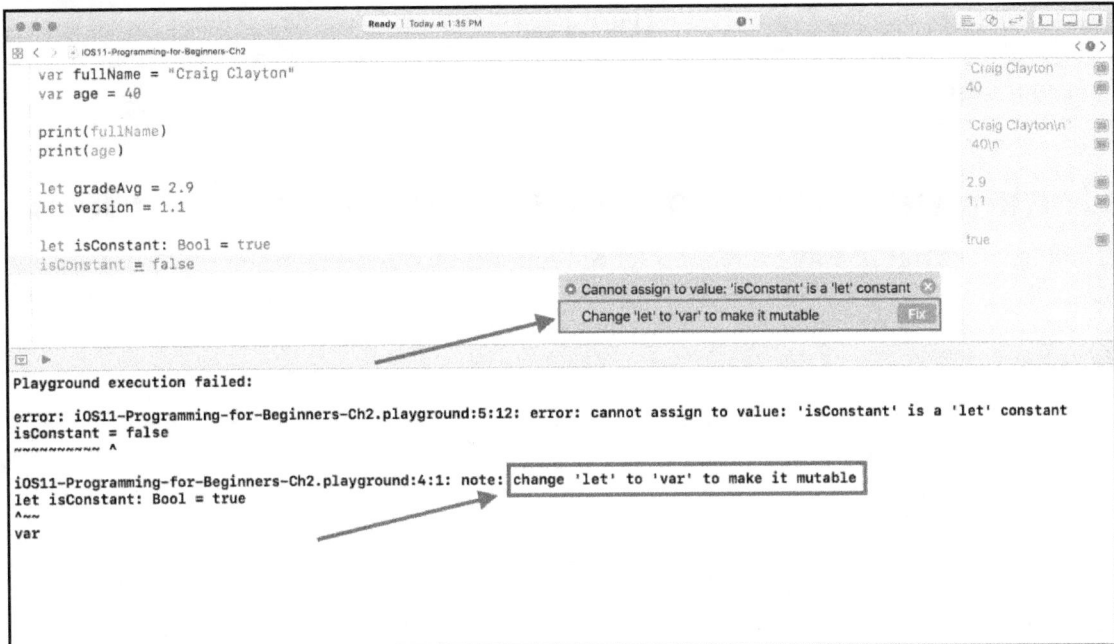

Since we want it to remain a constant, let's delete the line `isConstant = false`. We have covered basic data types, but there are some other programming basics we should discuss as well.

Hungarian notation

Typically, I like to use Hungarian notation when writing variables, because it acts as an identifier for the data type of the variable. For example, earlier we wrote `fullName` and `gradeAvg`. Throughout this book, you will see that I use Hungarian notation.

[41]

Why constants versus variables?

You might be asking yourself *"Why would you ever want to make something constant?"* Since constants cannot change after you run your app, they keep you from accidentally changing a value that should not be changed. Another really good use for constants is for base URLs, as you would not want these to change. When you are getting data, you do not want to accidentally change the value midway through your app. Apple recommends that you use `let` whenever possible. Typically, I will use a `let` until Xcode warns me that a `var` is preferable. If I change the value from `let` to `var`, then I am verifying that this is the behavior I want.

Comments – leaving yourself notes or reminders

Comments are a great way to create notes or reminders to yourself. When you comment code, it means that it will not be executed when your code runs. There are two types of comment used: `//` or `/* */`. `//` is typically used for a one-line comment and `/**/` is used for a block of text.

You can add comments to your code, such as a To-Do item or just a brief explanation of what something is doing.

Let's see what both of these look like:

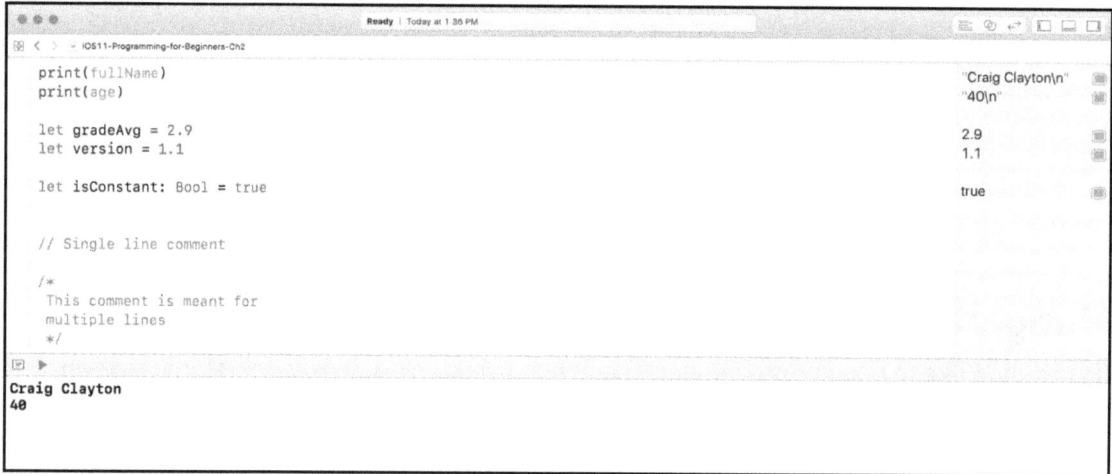

Type safety and type inference

Swift is a type-safe language, which means that you are encouraged to be clear about the value types with which your code will work. Type inference means that, before your code runs, it will be able to quickly check to ensure that you did not set anything to a different type. If you do, Xcode will give you an error. Why is this good? Let's say that you have an app in the store and that you set one of your variables as a String in one part of your code, but then accidentally set the same variable as an Int in another part of your code. This error may cause some bad behavior in your app that could cause it to crash. Finding these kinds of error is like finding a needle in a haystack. Therefore, type checking helps you write safer code by helping you avoid errors when working with different types.

We have now looked at data types and know that strings are for textual data, Int for integer, Bool for boolean, and Double and Float for floating-point numbers. Let's look a bit deeper into data types and see how we can do more than just assign them to variables.

Concatenating strings

String concatenation is the result of combining multiple string literals together to form an expression. So, let's create one by first entering two String literals:

Combining these two gives us a String concatenation. We can combine Strings by using the + operator. Add the following:

```
let full = firstName + lastName
```

Building a Foundation with Swift

When you look in the Results panel, you will notice that there is no space between our first and last names.

In addition, if we just put the variables in quotes, they will revert to simple string literals and will no longer be variables.

String interpolation

In order to correct that, we can put these variables inside of quotes, which is known as string interpolation, using a backslash and parentheses around each of our variables inside of the string interpolation. Let's update our name variable to be the following, and you will see the space in the name in the Results panel:

```
let full = "\(firstName) \(lastName)"
```

After adding the line our code should look something like this:

Now that we know about using variables inside of quotes, we can do the same inside of `print()`. Let's put the `firstName` and `lastName` inside of `print()`, as follows:

```
print("\(firstName) \(lastName)")
```

Chapter 2

The print statements are great for checking to see you are getting the value you want:

```
let firstName = "Craig"                             "Craig"
let lastName = "Clayton"                            "Clayton"

let full = "\(firstName) \(lastName)"               "Craig Clayton"
print("\(firstName) \(lastName)")                   "Craig Clayton\n"
```

Craig Clayton

Bam! Now, we have a way to see multiple variables inside of print() and to create string interpolation by combining multiple strings together. We can do much more with Strings, and we will cover them later in the book.

Operations with our integers

In our Playground, we know that age is an Int, but with Int, we also can write arithmetic expressions using numbers, variables/constants, operators, and parentheses. Let's start with addition, subtraction, multiplication, and division. Add the following into Xcode:

```
// (+) operator
let sum = 23 + 20                                   43
// (-) operator
let result = 32 - sum                               -11
// (*) operator
let total = result * 5                              -55
// (/) operator
let divide = total / 10                             -5
```

[45]

Building a Foundation with Swift

So, sum added two integers (+ operator) together, totaling 43 in our preceding example. Then, we subtracted (- operator) sum from 32 to create result (-11 in our example). After that, we took result and multiplied (* operator) it by 5 (see -55 in the Results panel). All of this is pretty basic math; however, you may have noticed something different with our division equation (/ operator). When you divide two integers, the result will be a third integer. So, instead of -55 divided by 10 equaling -5.5, our result was -5. In order to get the correct floating-point value of -5.5, we need to make our division value a Double. Therefore, let's add the following:

```
let divide2 = Double(total) / 10
```

After adding the preceding line of code, your code should look something like this:

```
// (+) operator
let sum = 23 + 20                          43
// (-) operator
let result = 32 - sum                      -11
// (*) operator
let total = result * 5                     -55
// (/) operator
let divide = total / 10                    -5
let divide2 = Double(total) / 10           -5.5
```

All of these operations will look familiar to you, but there is one with which you might not be familiar and that is the remainder operator. The remainder operator returns the remainder when one number is divided by another.

So, for example, 7 divided by 3 equals 2.33. When we apply the remainder operator, we get back 1. Add the following to Playgrounds:

```
let mod = 7 % 3
```

Now, your code should look something like this:

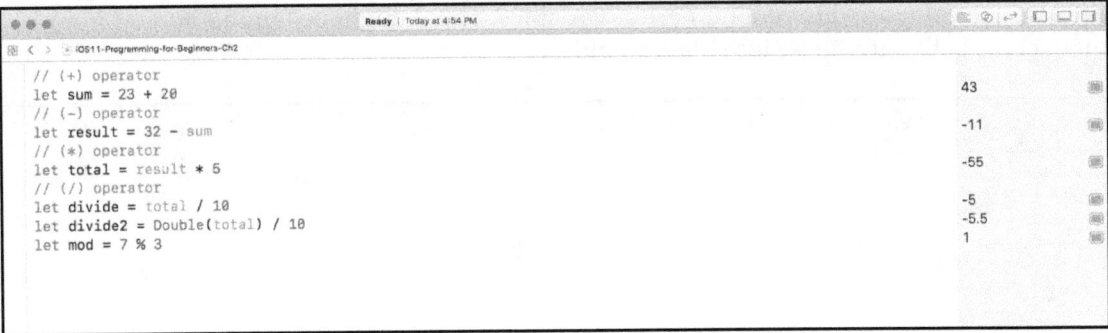

Increment and decrement

There will be times when you need to increment (increase) or decrement (decrease) a value. There are two ways you can accomplish this. Add the following into Playgrounds:

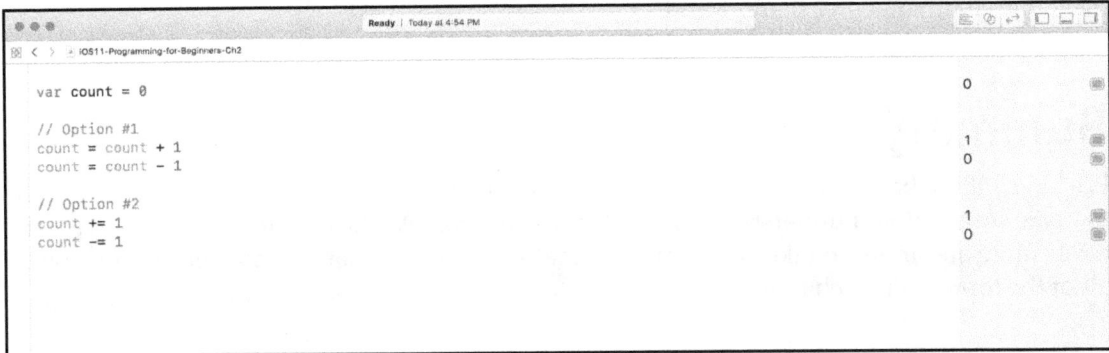

Both of these options do the same thing, but option #2 is just written in shorthand. The preferred way is to use option #2, the += (addition assignment operator) and -= (subtraction assignment operator), but it really is your preference.

Comparison operators

We also can compare different numerical variables. These might be familiar to you from math class. Let's enter these into Playgrounds:

```
let firstValue = 1                              1
let secondValue = 2                             2

// Checking for greater than
firstValue > secondValue                        false
// Checking for less than
firstValue < secondValue                        true
// Checking for greater than or equal
firstValue >= secondValue                       false
// Checking for less than or equal
firstValue <= secondValue                       true
// Checking for equal
firstValue == secondValue                       false
// Checking for not equal
firstValue != secondValue                       true
```

As you can see in the Results panel, these comparison entries result in true or false based on the values that you enter (here, 1 and 2).

Summary

We have hit the basics and, from this point, if you are new to programming it is a good idea to make sure that you understand each topic we covered. As the chapters progress, we will cover more and more so take your time and really make sure that you are comfortable with all of the topics in this chapter.

3
Building on the Swift Foundation

In the last chapter, we went through the basics of understanding data types and how to create variables and constants. Now that we are comfortable with those topics, let's look at adding more building blocks. This chapter will build on what we learned in the last chapter and get a bit closer to better understanding Swift.

The following will be covered in this chapter:

- Type safety and type inference
- Operations with Integers
- `if` statements
- Optionals and optional bindings
- Functions

Data types are good, but we will need to add some logic to our app. For example, we want to be able to control whether someone should see a login screen when they launch the app or if they should go right into the app. You will use logic a lot, so let's look at what an `if` statement is and how to use it.

Creating a Playground project

As you learned earlier, launch Xcode and click on **Get started with a playground**:

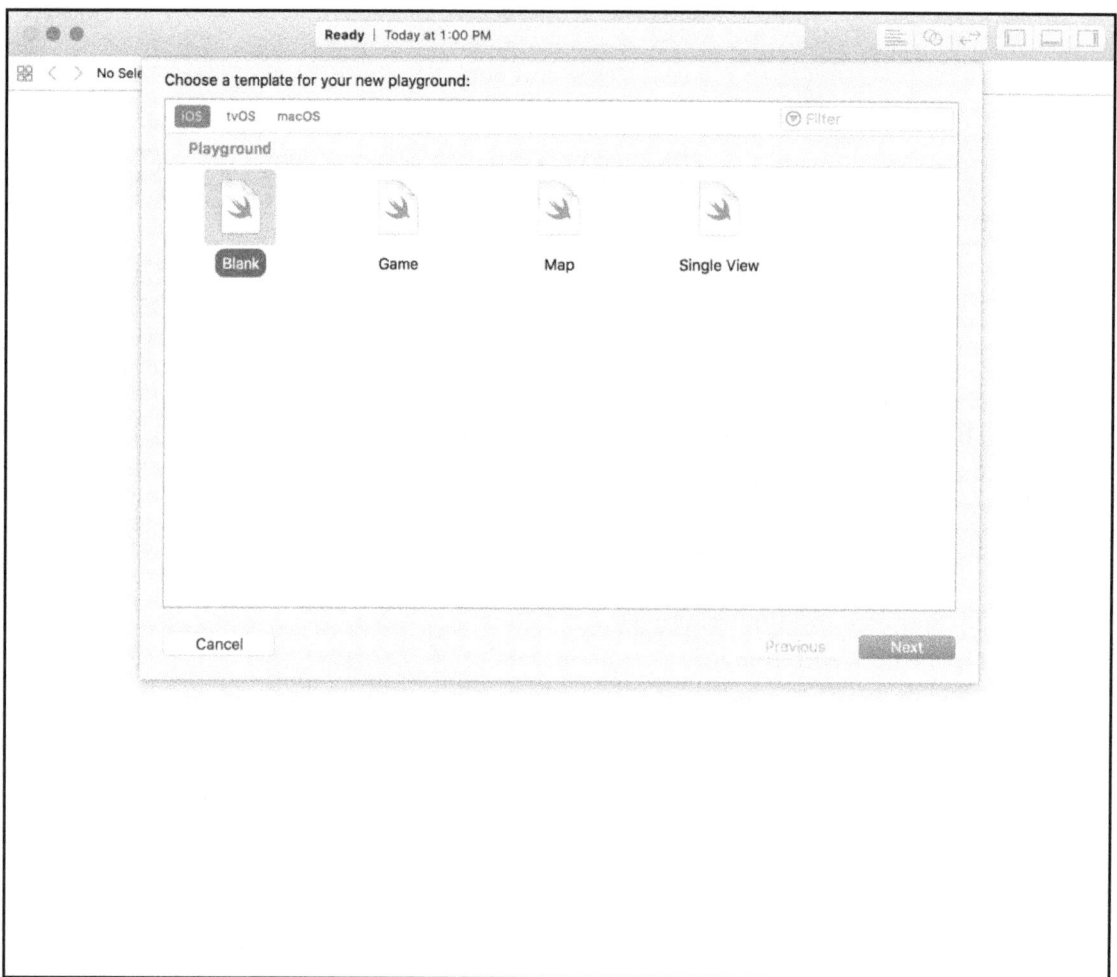

The Playground template screen will appear. Make sure that you select **iOS** and then choose **Blank** and hit **Next**. You will be asked to give your project a name and a location to save the file; name your new Playground iOS11-Programming-for-Beginners-Ch3. You can save the file anywhere that you like. Now, with the project saved, we can explore Playgrounds a bit.

The if statements – having fun with logic statements

Let's add our first piece of logic using an `if` statement. An `if` statement is a simple statement to determine whether or not a statement is true. Input the following into Xcode:

In the first line of the preceding code, we created a constant named, `isPictureVisible`, and we set it to `true`. The next line starts our `if` statement and is read as follows: if `isPictureVisible` is `true`, then print `Picture is visible`. When we write `if` statements, we must use the curly braces to enclose our logic. It is good practice to put the opening curly brace (`{`) on the same line as the `if` and the closing curly brace (`}`) on the line immediately after your logic.

When writing `if` statements using a `bool`, you are always checking for `true`; however, if you wanted to check for `false`, you would do the following:

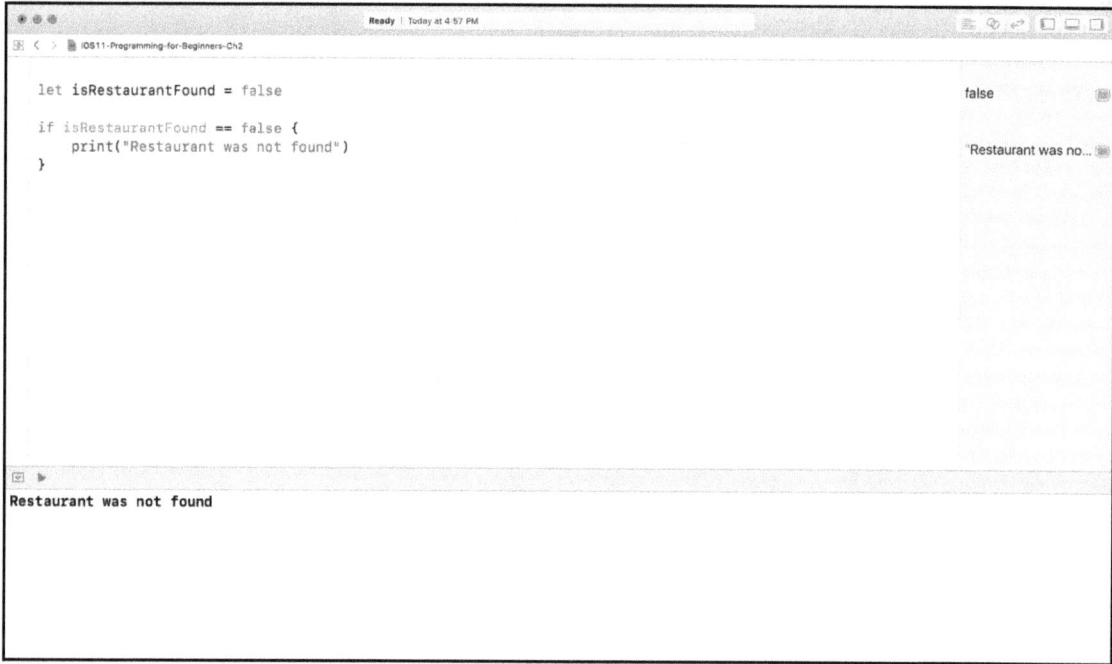

Bools work great with `if` statements, but we also can use them with other data types. Let's try an `if` statement with an `Int` next. Write the following into Playgrounds:

Chapter 3

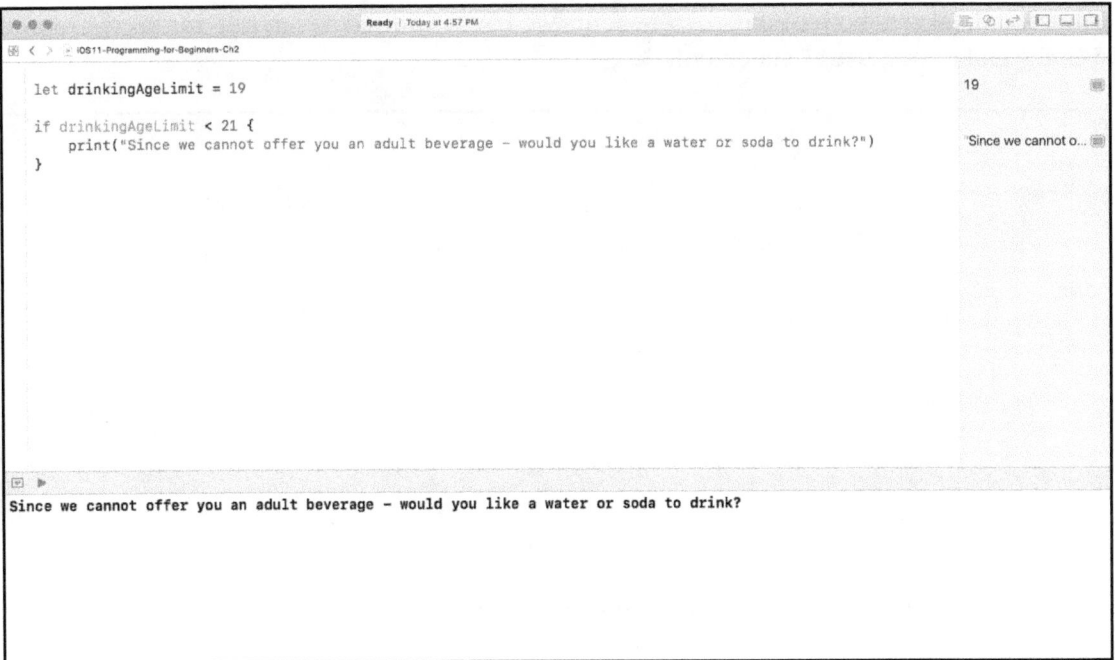

In the preceding example, we first created another constant with our Int set to 19. The next line says—if drinkingAgeLimit is less than 21, then print Since we cannot offer you an adult beverage - would you like a water or soda to drink? When you are using Int within if statements, you will use the comparison operators (<, >, <=, >=, ==, or !=). However, our last if statement feels incomplete, because we are not doing anything for someone over 21. This is where you will utilize an if...else statement. You enter an if...else statement exactly as you did an if statement, but, at the end, you add the word else.

You can add else to both of the `if` statements we have inputted so far, but, for now, just add it to the end of our last `if` statement:

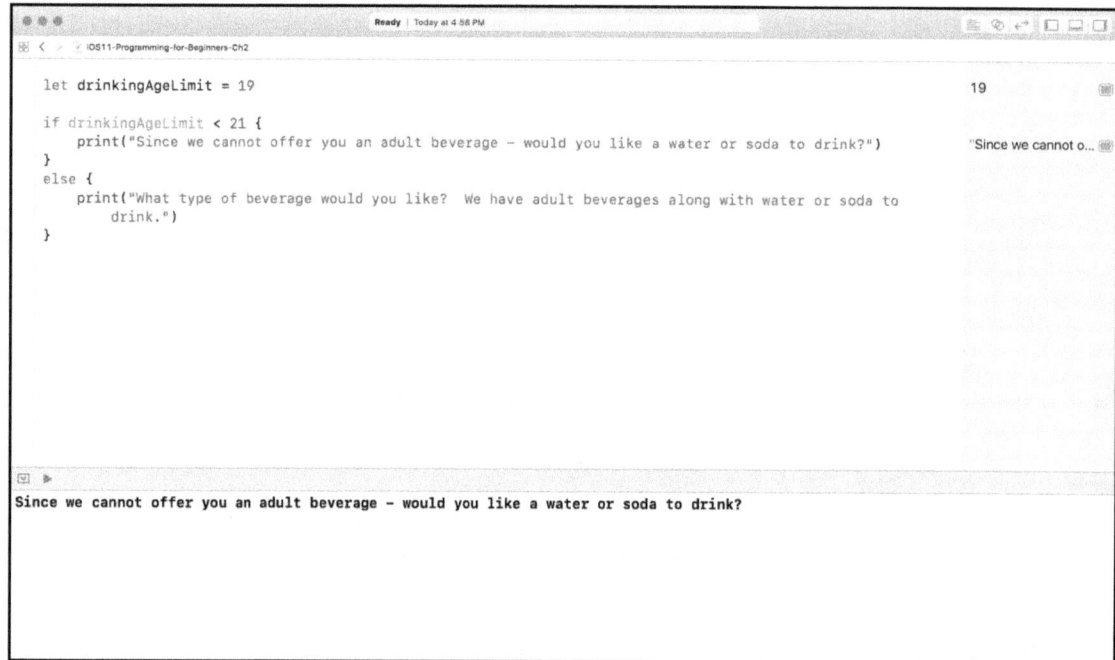

With else added onto the end of our `if` statement, it turns into an `if...else` statement, which now reads—if `drinkingAgeLimit` is less than `21`, then print `Since we cannot offer you an adult beverage - would you like a water or soda to drink?` Otherwise (or `else`), print `What type of beverage would you like? We have adult beverages along with water or soda to drink.`

Now, our `if...else` statement can handle both conditions. Based on the value 19 for our `drinkingAgeLimit`, we can see in the Debug panel: `Since we cannot offer you an adult beverage - would you like a water or soda to drink?` If we change `drinkingAgeLimit` to 30, our Debug panel says, `What type of beverage would you like? We have adult beverages along with water or soda to drink.` Go ahead and change 19 to 30 in Playgrounds:

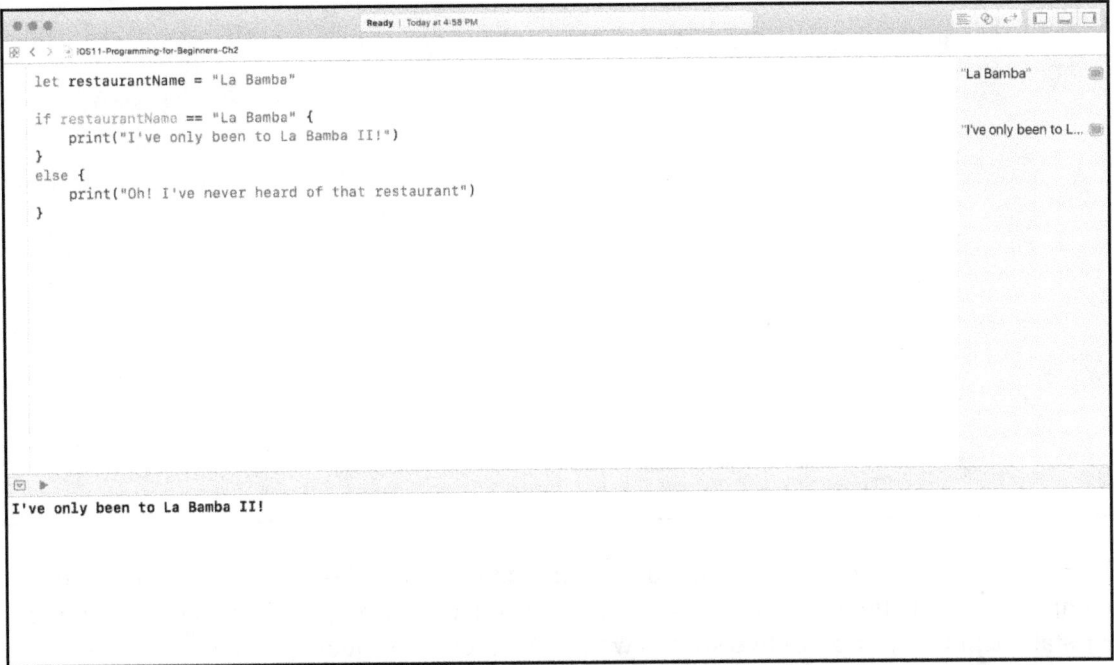

Note that we got the behavior we wanted in the Debug panel.

Building on the Swift Foundation

So far, we have covered using an `if` statement with a `bool` and an `Int`. Let's take a look at one more example using a string. Add this next bit of code into Playgrounds:

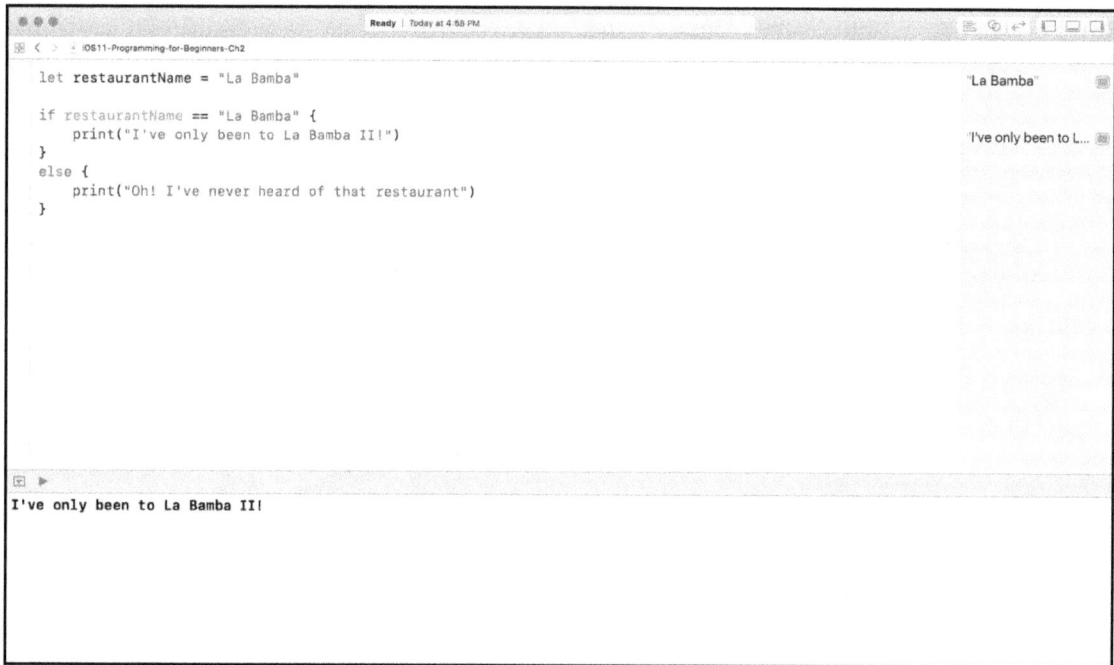

In programming, we use equals (=) when setting data to variables. However, in order to compare two data types, we must use the double equals (==). Therefore, when we write an `if` statement that compares two strings we must use double equals (==) instead of just equals (=) to determine equality.

An `if...else` statement only lets us check two conditions, whether they are `true` or `not`. If we wanted to add more conditions, we would not be able to simply use an `if...else` statement. In order to accomplish this, we would use what is called an `if...else...if...else`. This statement gives us the ability to add any number of `else-if`s inside of our `if...else` statement. We will not go overboard, so let's just add one. Update your last `if...else` statement to the following:

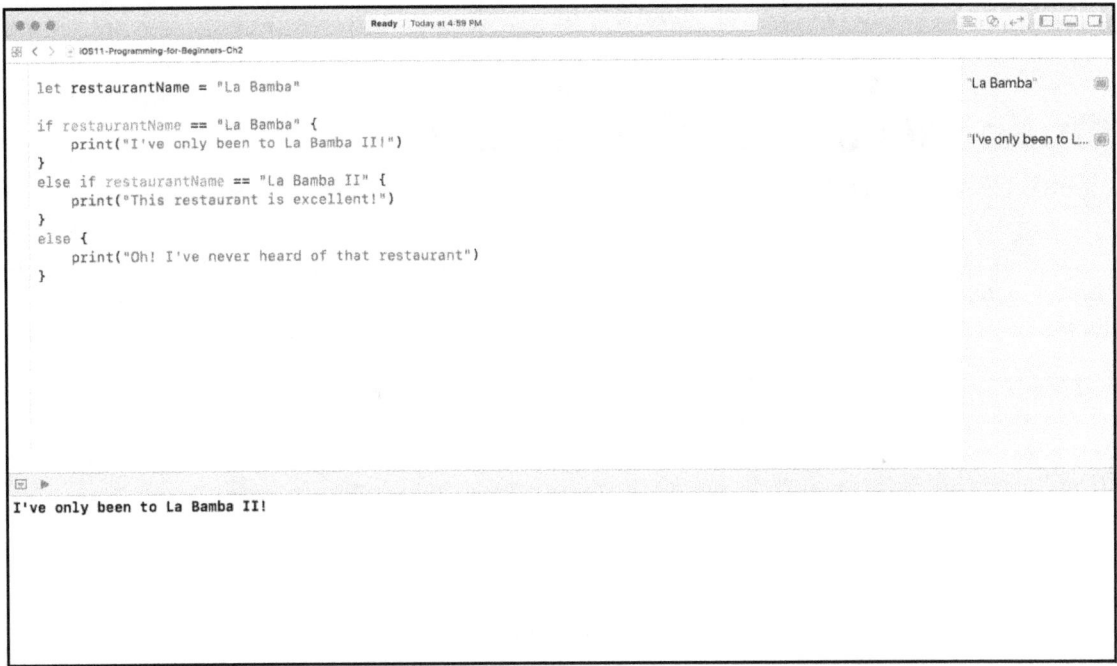

Building on the Swift Foundation

In this example of an `if...else...if...else` statement, we are checking whether `restaurantName` equals `La Bamba`, print `I've only been to La Bamba II!` else, if `restaurantName` equals `This restaurant is excellent!` else print `Oh! I've never heard of that restaurant.`

Using `if`, `if...else` and `if...else if...else` statements really helps you create simple or complex logic for your app. Being able to use them with `Strings`, `bools`, `Ints`, and floating-point numbers gives you more flexibility.

Optionals and optional bindings

Optionals are used when a value cannot be set. Think of optionals as a container that can take either a value or nil. This gives us the ability to check whether the value is nil or not. In order to create an optional value, you will have to give it a data type followed by a question mark (?). Before we do that, let's create a string that is not an optional. Add the following to Playgrounds:

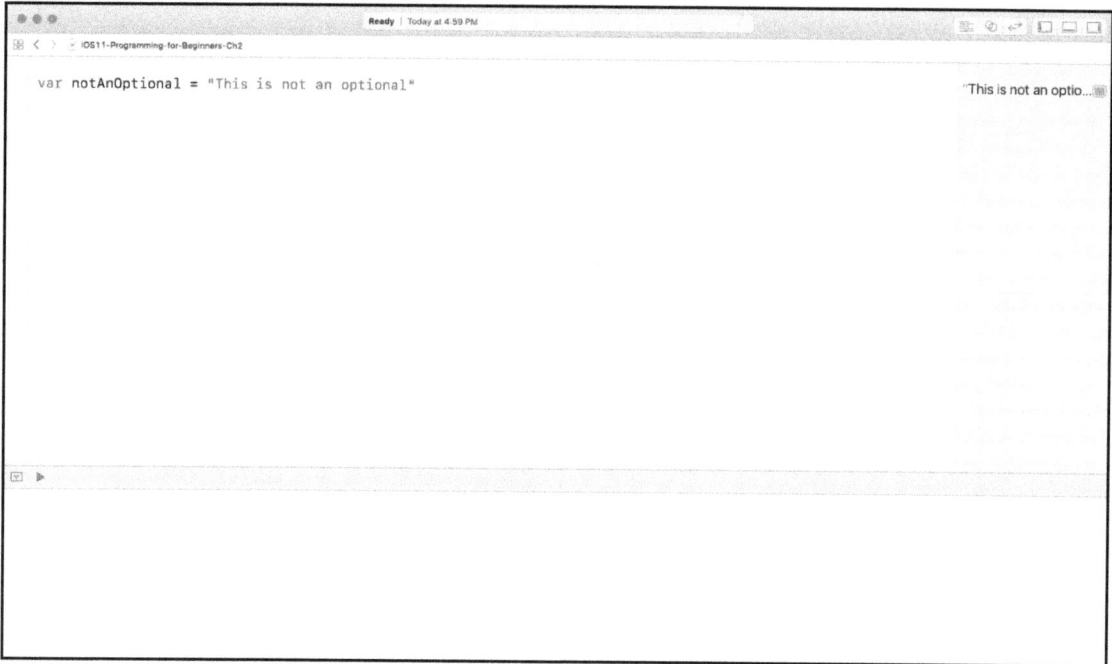

Now, let's add an optional to Playgrounds:

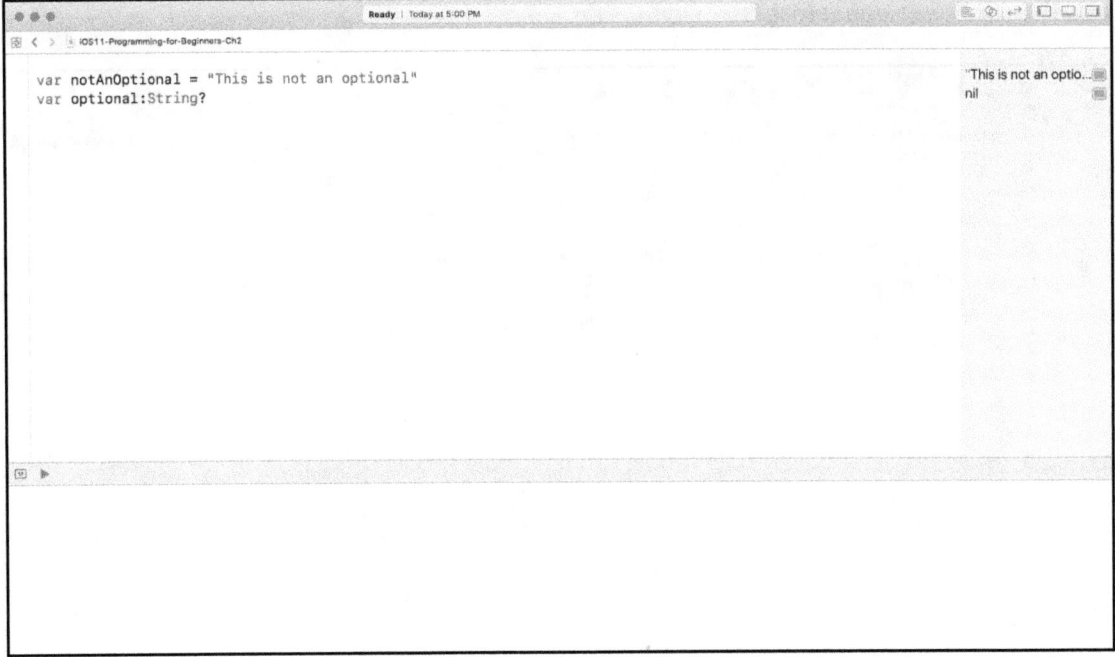

Building on the Swift Foundation

In this example, we created a string optional, and, if you notice in the Results panel, it is nil. But for our `notAnOptional`, we see `This is not an optional`. Now, on the next line, let's set `optional` equal to `This is an optional`:

Chapter 3

In our Results panel, we see `This is an optional`. Let's now print both `strNotAnOptional` and `strOptional`, as you will see a difference between the two:

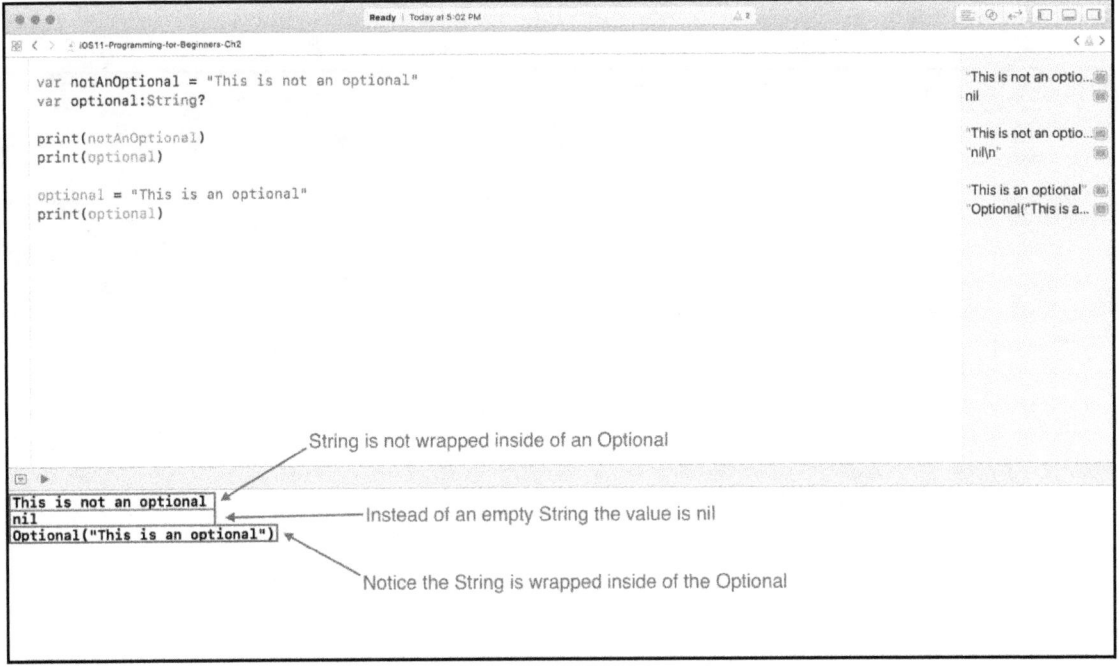

Note that our `notAnOptional` variable looks fine, but `optional` has an optional wrapped (`""`) around the `String`. This means that, in order for us to access the value, we must unwrap the optional. One way we could do this is by force-unwrapping the optional using an (`!`). Let's update our `print` statement and change it to the following:

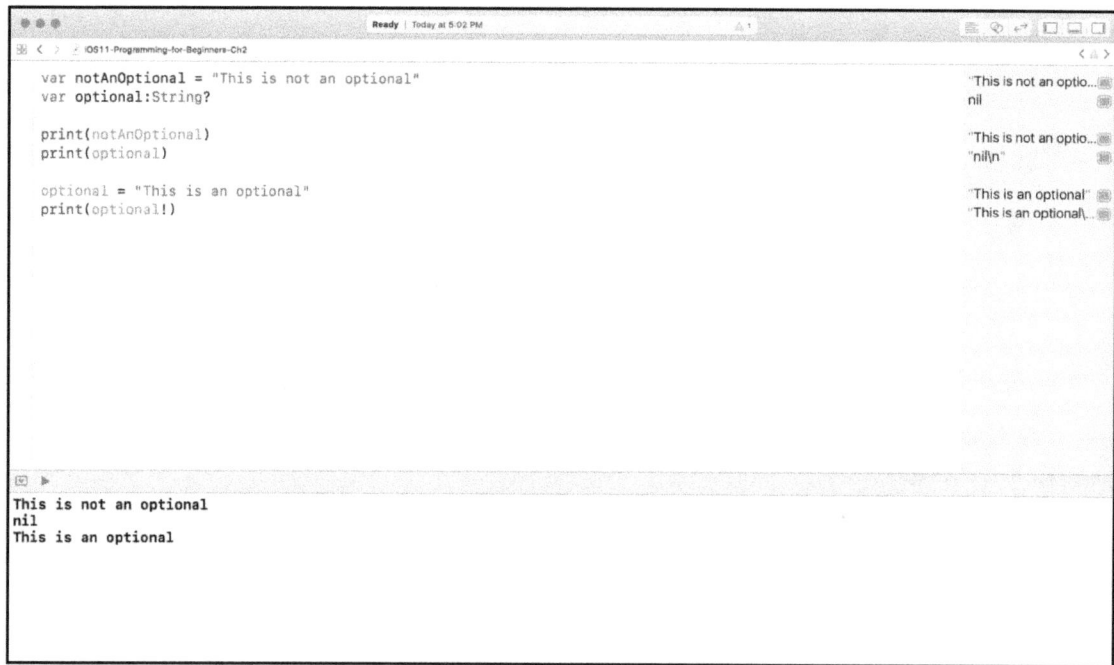

We just force-unwrapped our optional, but this method is not recommended. We should use what is called **optional binding**, which is the safe way to access the value using an `if...let` statement. Remove the (`!`) from the `print` statement and instead write the following optional binding:

Chapter 3

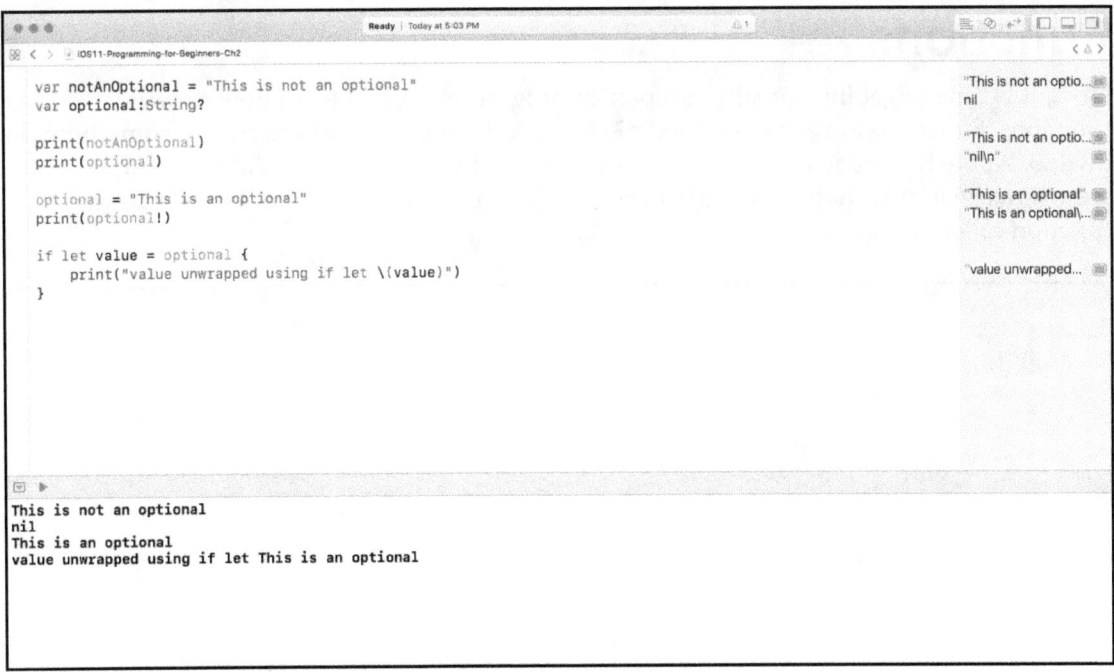

This `if...let` statement is saying that if the optional is not nil, set it to `strValue`—but, if this optional is nil, ignore it and do nothing. We now do not have to worry about anything setting our value and causing our app to crash.

Why optionals?

So, now you are probably asking: Why do you have to do this? Trust me, when I first learned about optionals, I felt the same way. Optionals were actually made for your protection. For now, just understand that, when you see a data type followed by a question mark, this variable is an optional. As we work with optionals more and more throughout the book, it will become clearer to you.

Building on the Swift Foundation

Functions

Now, it is time to get into a really fun part of programming and learn how to write functions. Functions are self-contained pieces of code that you want to run on something. In Swift 3, Apple has made a change to how you should write functions. All of the functions we will write in this chapter will perform an action (think of verbs). Let's create a simple function called `greet()`:

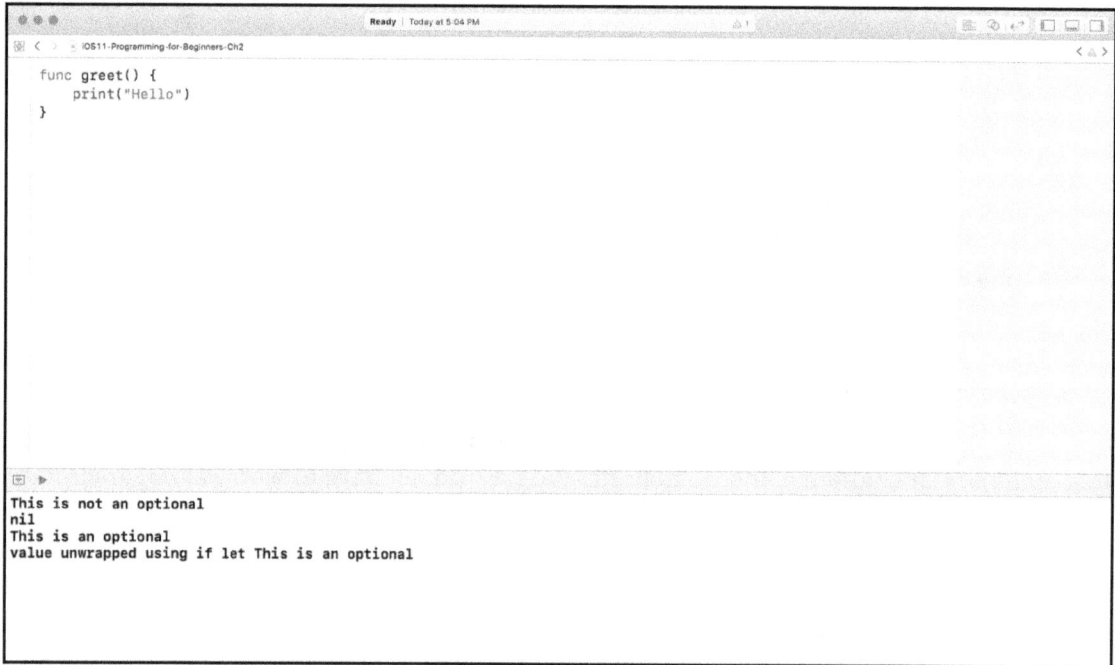

This example is a basic function with a `print` statement in it. In programming, functions do not actually run until you call them. We call a function simply by calling its name. So, let's call greet:

```
greet()
```

Chapter 3

Once we add this to the code, this is what we'll see on the screen:

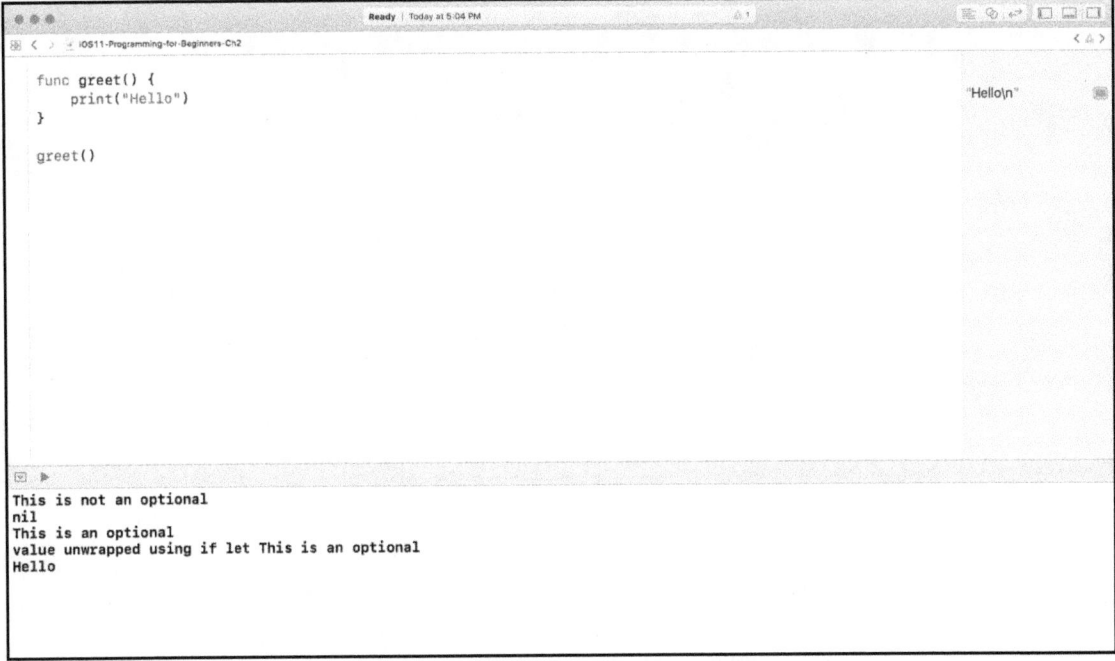

That's it! We just created our first function and called it. However, functions can do so much more. We can add what is called a parameter to a function. A parameter allows us to accept data types inside our parentheses. Doing this allows us to build more reusable chunks of code. So, let's update our `greet()` function to accept a parameter called `name`:

```
func greet(name:String) {
print("Hello")
}
```

Building on the Swift Foundation

After you update the function, you will get an error:

```
func greet(name:String) {
    print("Hello")
}

greet()                                                    ⊘ Missing argument for parameter 'name' in call
```

```
Playground execution failed: error: iOS11-Programming-for-Beginners-Ch3.playground:87:7: error: missing argument for parameter 'name' in call
greet()
      ^
       name: <#String#>

iOS11-Programming-for-Beginners-Ch3.playground:83:6: note: 'greet(name:)' declared here
func greet(name:String) {
     ^

* thread #1, queue = 'com.apple.main-thread', stop reason = breakpoint 1.2
  * frame #0: 0x000000010c4bd3b0 iOS11-Programming-for-Beginners-Ch3`executePlayground
    frame #1: 0x000000010c4bc9b0 iOS11-Programming-for-Beginners-Ch3`__37-[XCPAppDelegate enqueueRunLoopBlock]_block_invoke + 32
    frame #2: 0x000000010cfceb5c CoreFoundation`__CFRUNLOOP_IS_CALLING_OUT_TO_A_BLOCK__ + 12
    frame #3: 0x000000010cfb3e54 CoreFoundation`__CFRunLoopDoBlocks + 356
    frame #4: 0x000000010cfb35ee CoreFoundation`__CFRunLoopRun + 894
    frame #5: 0x000000010cfb3016 CoreFoundation`CFRunLoopRunSpecific + 406
    frame #6: 0x000000011246ca24 GraphicsServices`GSEventRunModal + 62
    frame #7: 0x000000010db350d4 UIKit`UIApplicationMain + 159
    frame #8: 0x000000010c4bc6d9 iOS11-Programming-for-Beginners-Ch3`main + 201
    frame #9: 0x00000001105fe65d libdyld.dylib`start + 1
```

We received this error because we updated our function, but we did not update the line where we called it. Let's update where we call `greet()` to the following:

```
greet(name: "Joshua")
```

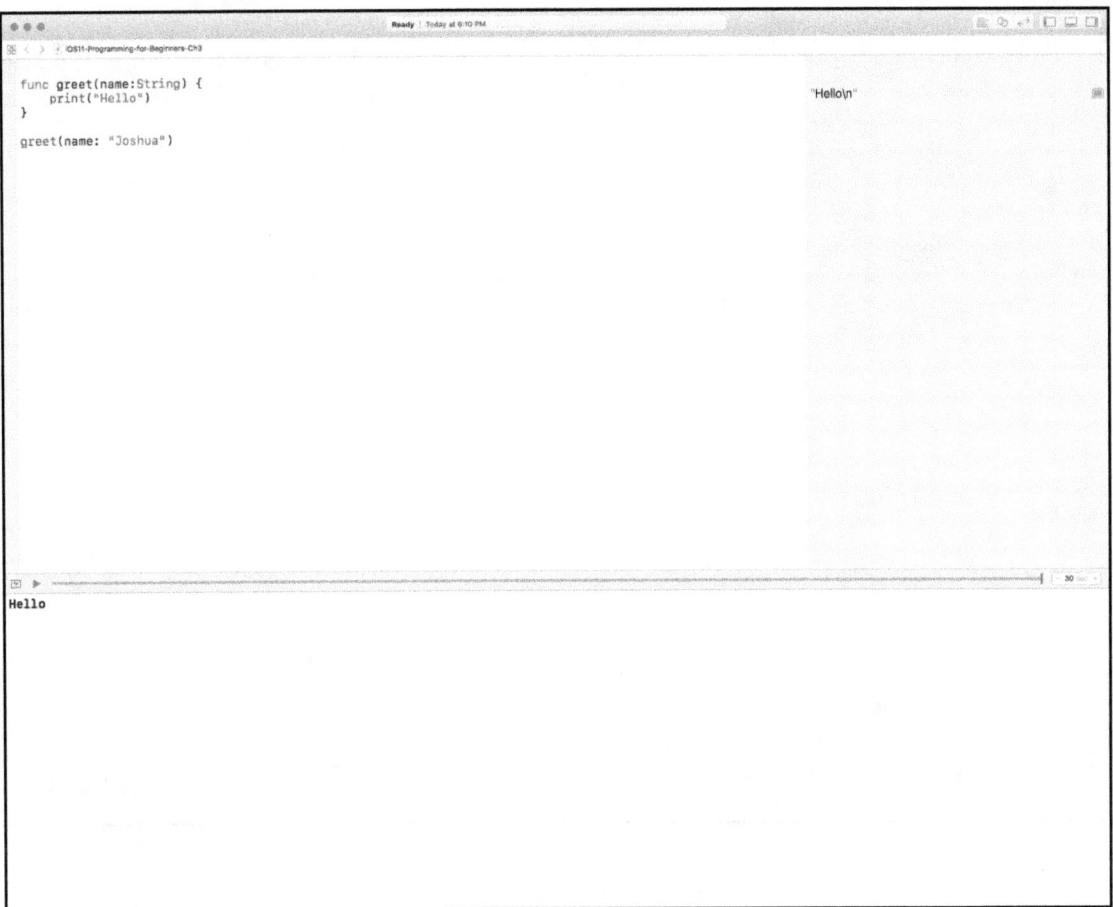

This looks good; however, the Debug panel shows us that we are not using the name in our greeting. Earlier, you learned how to create a string interpolation. So, we just need to append our variable name inside of our `print` statement, as follows:

```
print("Hello \(name)")
```

This is how your code will now look:

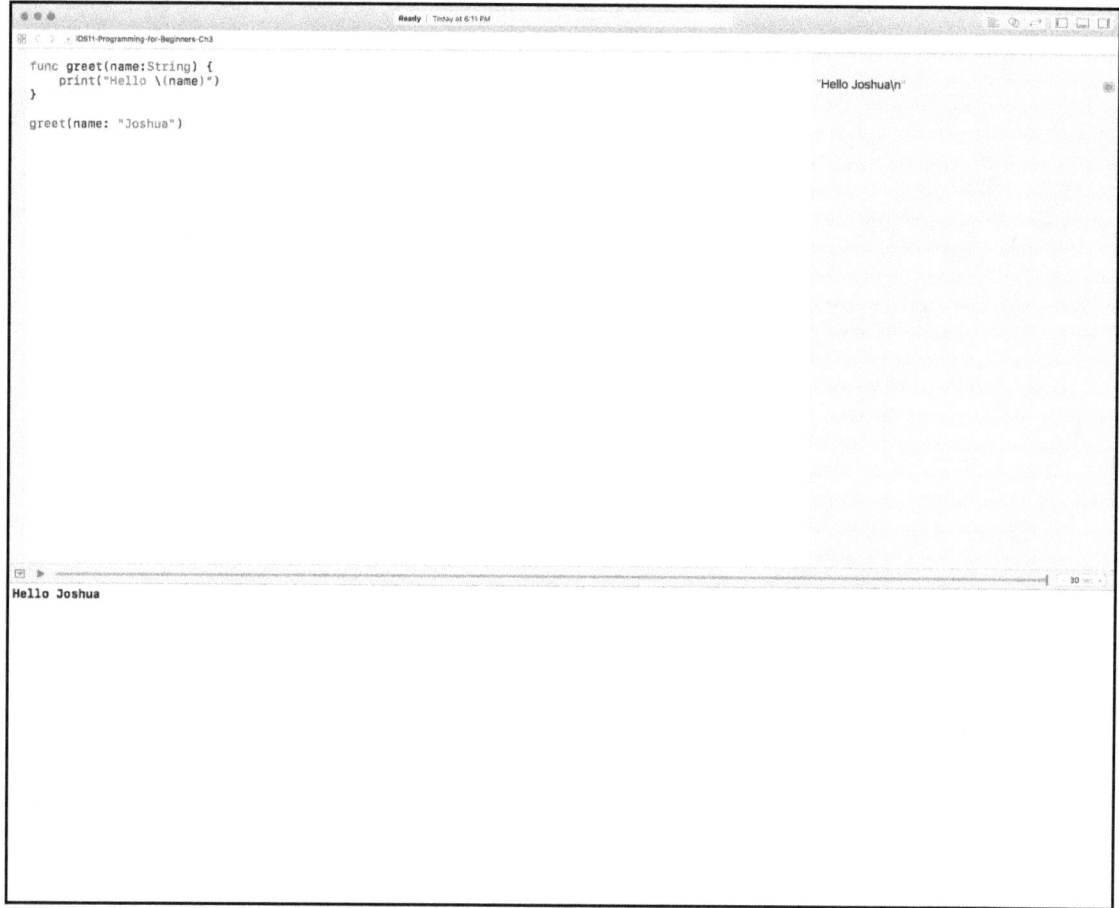

Chapter 3

Functions can take multiple parameters, so let's create another `greet()` function that takes two parameters, a first name and a last name:

```
func greet(first:String, last:String) {
    print("Hello \(first) \(last)")
}
```

Now, your code and its output should look as shown in the following screenshot:

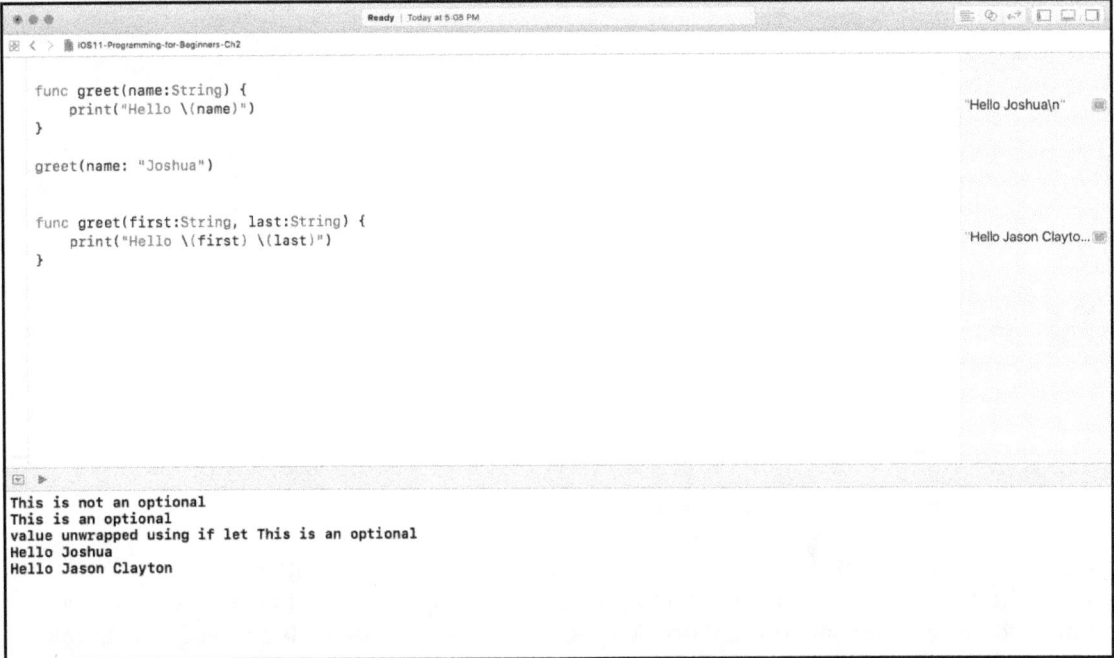

We also need to update where we called `greet()` to accept multiple parameters as well:

```
greet(first: "Craig", last: "Clayton")
```

Building on the Swift Foundation

Now, your code and output screen should look something like this:

```
func greet(name:String) {
    print("Hello \(name)")
}

greet(name: "Joshua")


func greet(first:String, last:String) {
    print("Hello \(first) \(last)")
}

greet(first: "Jason", last: "Clayton")
```

```
This is not an optional
This is an optional
value unwrapped using if let This is an optional
Hello Joshua
Hello Jason Clayton
```

We now have a function that accepts multiple parameters.

What would be great is if we could make a function that return the greeting to us. Well, we can! Whenever we want our function to return something, we need to use a noun as a way to describe what our function will do. We just created a function called `greet()` that takes a first and last name and creates a full name.

Now, let's create another function called `greeting()`, which will return a full name back with a greeting. Let's see what this looks like:

```
func greeting(with first:String, last:String) -> String {
    return "Hello \(first) \(last)"
}
```

This is how your code and output screen should look:

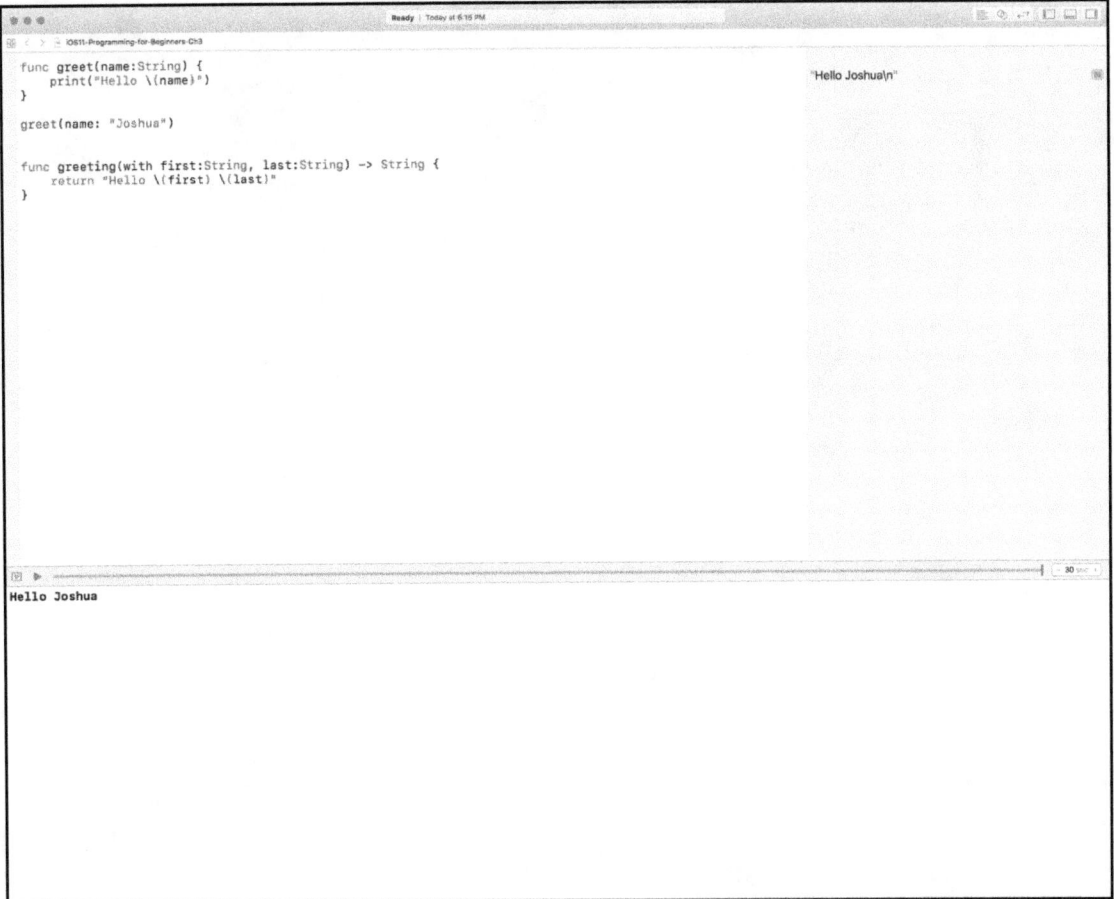

This function is almost the same as the previous one, but with a couple of new things. First -> String tells the function that we want to return a string. Inside of our function, we return "Hello \(first) \(last)". Since we said that we want to return something after our parentheses, then we have to do just that. Now, let's see how we do this. Enter the following:

```
print(greeting(with:"Teena", last:"Harris"))
```

Building on the Swift Foundation

Now, this is how your code and output screen should look:

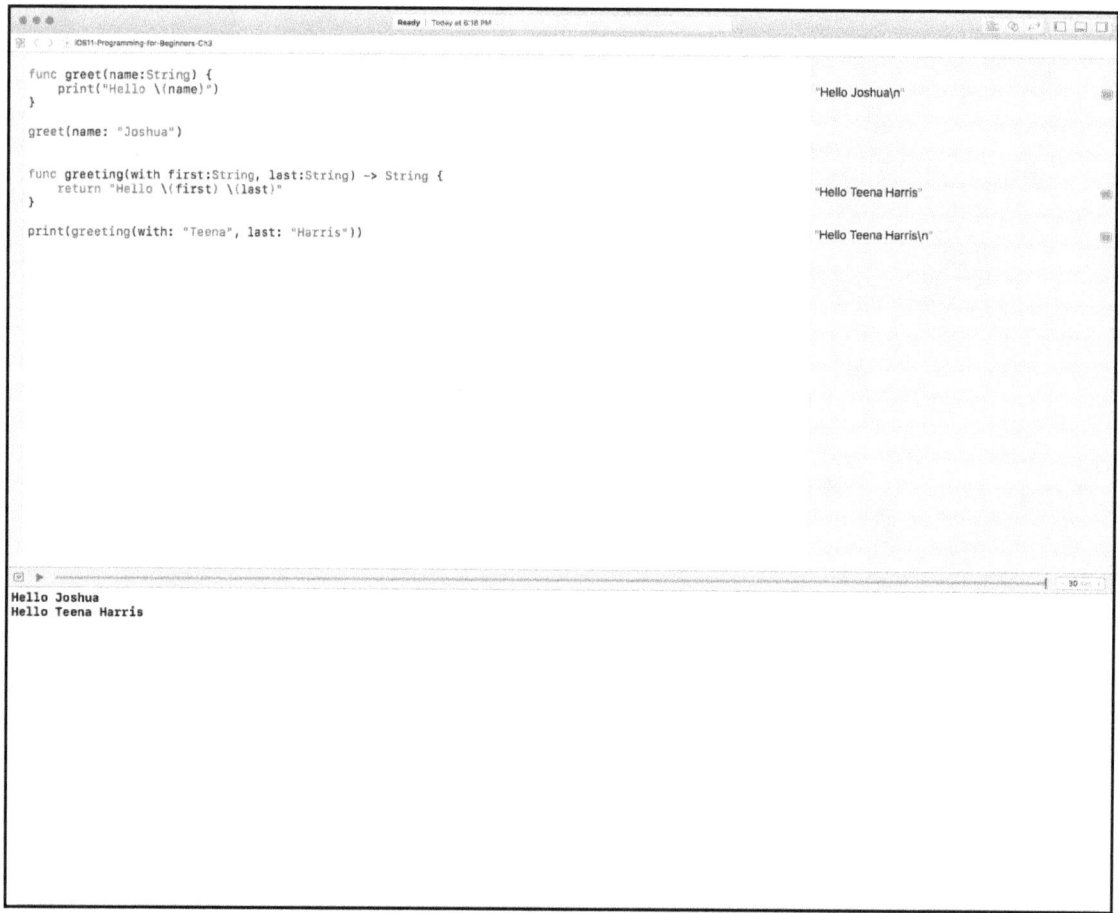

If you notice, in the Debug panel we now have our full name with `Hello` added to the beginning. As you start to build on functions, you really start to see the power.

These are just the basics of functions. We will cover more advanced functions throughout our *Let's Eat* app. The main thing beginning programmers forget is that functions should be small. Your function should do one thing and one thing only. If your function is too long, then you need to break it up into smaller chunks. Sometimes longer functions are unavoidable, but you should always be mindful of keeping them as small as possible. Nice work!

Let's work

We covered a lot in this chapter, and now it is time to put everything we covered into practice. Here are two challenges. If you are comfortable with them, then work on them on your own. Otherwise, go back into this chapter and you can follow along with me and see how to do each one:

- **Challenge 1**: Write a function that accepts and returns a custom greeting (other than `Hello`, which we addressed earlier in this chapter) along with your first and last name
- **Challenge 2**: Write a function that will take two numbers and add, subtract, multiply, or divide those two numbers

Summary

In this chapter, we learned what type safety is, as well as type inference. We also learned about operations with integers as well as working our way through `if` statements. Finally, we discussed the power of optionals and learned about what functions are and how to use them.

In the next chapter, we will move on to some more Swift basics by digging into Swift collections. Learning these well will really help you progress in Swift, because you will use them all the time.

4
Digging Deeper

When I first started programming, I was in my mid-twenties. I started a lot older than most, but I will say that grasping the basics took me a bit longer than most. I remember when I bought my first programming book and I read and reread chapters over and over again until the concepts made sense to me. I found that a lot of books talked to me like I had majored in computer science. As you progress through this book, take your time-and, if you need to go back, it is okay to do so. No one is going to care that it took you an extra day to understand a concept. It is more important that you fully understand that concept.

One tip I would give you is not to copy and paste code. No matter where you find the code and no matter how long it takes, it benefits you to type it out. Doing this really helped me as I eventually started to remember the code and it became second nature to me.

In the last chapter, we went over the basics of Swift to get you warmed up. Now, we will dig deeper and learn some more programming concepts. These concepts will build on what you have already learned. In this chapter, we will cover:

- Ranges
- Control flow

Let's begin by creating a new Playground project.

Digging Deeper

Creating a Playground project

As you learned earlier, launch Xcode and click on **Get started with a playground**:

The Playground template screen will appear. Make sure that you select **iOS** and then choose **Blank** and hit **Next**. You will be asked to give your project a name and a location to save the file; name your new Playground `iOS11-Programming-for-Beginners-Ch4`. You can save the file anywhere you like. Now, with the project saved, we can explore Playgrounds a bit.

Next, delete everything inside of your file and toggle on the Debug panel using the toggle button (*cmd* + *Shift* + *Y*). You should now have a blank screen with the Results panel on the right and the Debug panel on the bottom opened.

We focused on the basics earlier and now we will build upon those skills. Ranges are one such data type that we should learn and are very useful and can come in handy for a variety of reasons. Let's take a look at what Ranges are and then start to understand the difference between a *closed Range*, a *half-closed Range*, and a *one-sided Range*.

Ranges

Ranges are generic data types that represent a sequence of numbers. Let's look at the following image to understand:

| 10 11 12 13 14 15 16 17 18 19 20 |

Closed range

Notice that, in the preceding image, we have numbers ranging from **10** to **20**. Rather than having to write each value, we can use Ranges to represent all of these numbers in shorthand form. In order to do this, let's remove all of the numbers in the image except for **10** and **20**:

| 10   20 |

[77]

Digging Deeper

Now that we have removed those numbers, we need a way to tell Swift that we want to include all of the numbers that we just deleted. This is where the range operator (...) comes into play. Therefore, in Playgrounds, let's create a constant called range and set it equal to `10...20`:

```
let range = 10...20
```

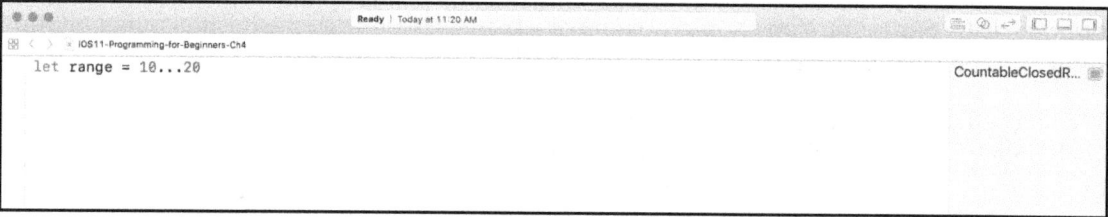

The range that we just entered says that we want the numbers between `10` and `20` as well as both `10` and `20` themselves. This type of Range is known as a closed Range.

Inside of Playground, in the result you will see a Show Result icon:

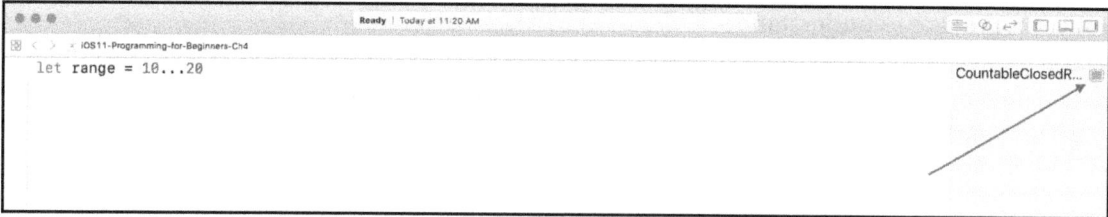

If you hover over the result you will also see Quick Look:

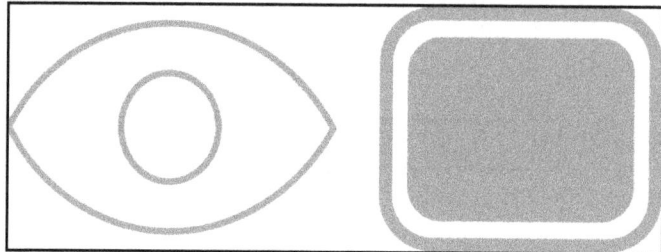

Select the Show Result icon so that you can see the result:

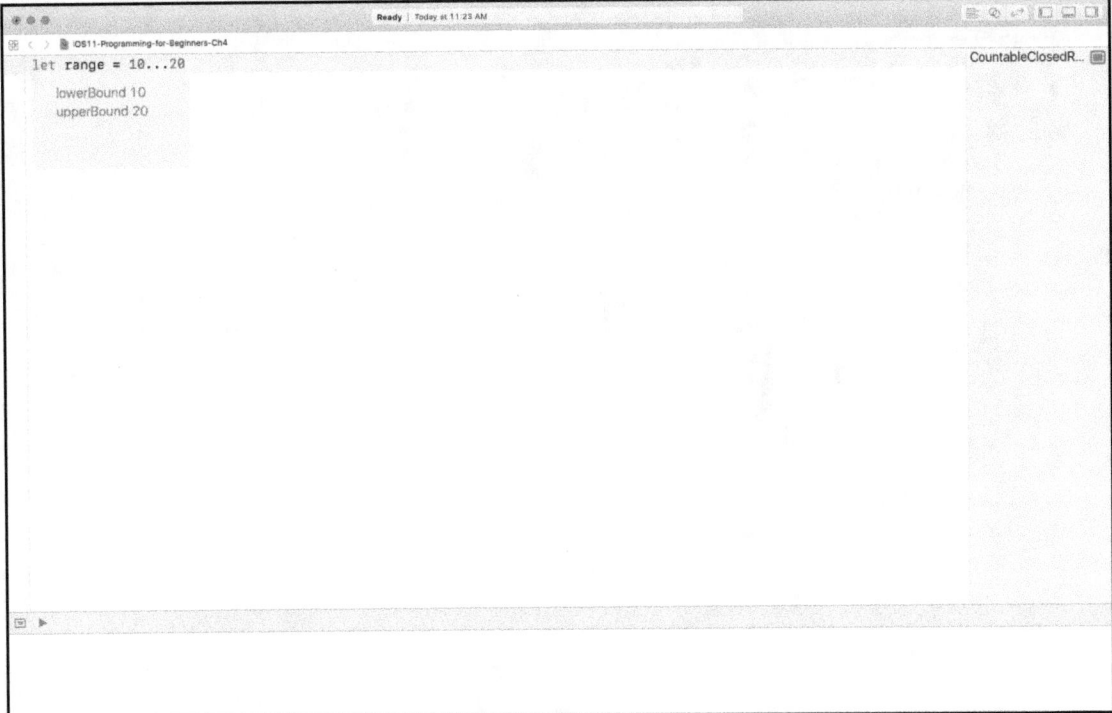

Next, we also have what is called a half-closed Range.

Half-closed range

Let's make another constant that is known as a half-closed Range and set it equal to 10 < 20. Add the following into Playgrounds:

```
let halfClosedRange = 10..<20
```

Digging Deeper

Your code should now look like this:

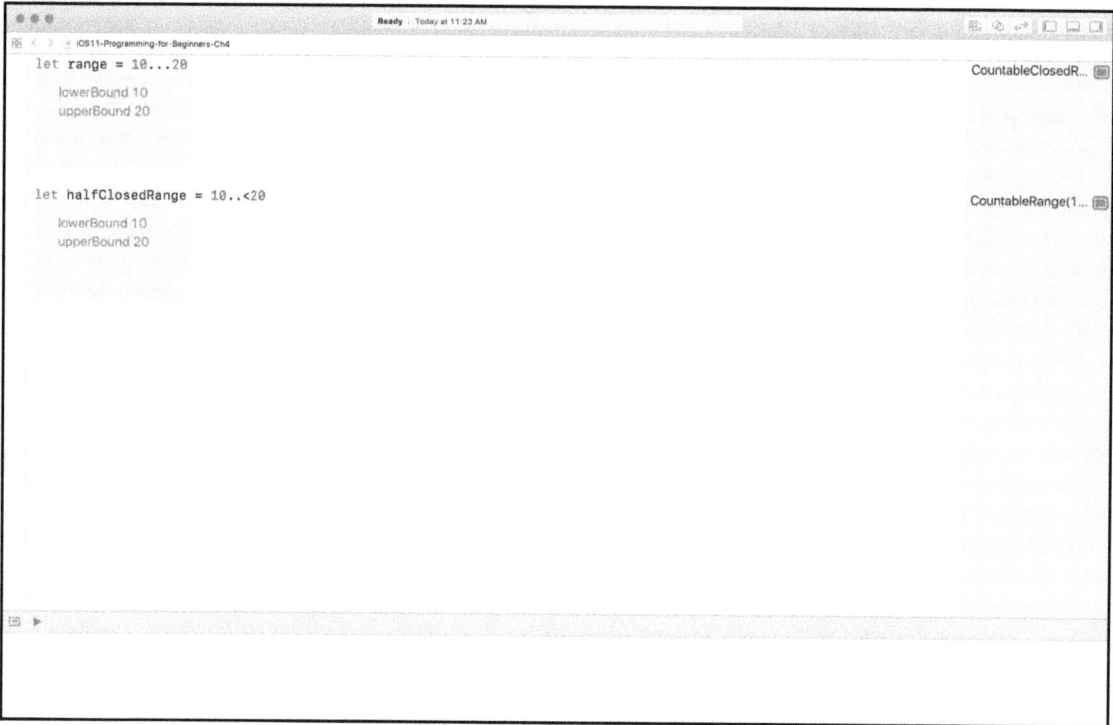

A half-closed Range is the same as a closed Range, except that the end value will not be included. In this example, that means that 10 through 19 will be included and 20 will be excluded.

At this point, you will notice that your Results panel shows you `CountableClosedRange(10...20)` and `CountableRange(10..<20)`. We cannot see all the numbers within the Range. In order to see all the numbers, we need to use a loop.

Control flow

In programming, control flow is the order in which your code is executed. When working with Swift, we can use a variety of control statements. Loops, in particular, are useful for when you want to repeat a task multiple times. Let's take a look at a few different types of loop.

The for...in loop

One of the most common control statements is a `for...in` loop. It allows you to iterate over each element in a sequence. Let's see what a `for...in` loop looks like:

```
for <value> in <sequence> {
  // Code here
}
```

We start the `for...in` loop with for, which is proceeded by `<value>`. This is actually a local constant (only the `for...in` loop can access it) and can be any name you like. Typically, you will want to give this value an expressive name. Next, we have in, which is followed by `<sequence>`. This is where we want to give it our sequence of numbers. Let's write the following into Playgrounds:

```
for value in range {
    print("closed range - \(value)")
}
```

(11 times)

```
closed range - 10
closed range - 11
closed range - 12
closed range - 13
closed range - 14
closed range - 15
closed range - 16
closed range - 17
closed range - 18
closed range - 19
closed range - 20
```

Digging Deeper

Notice that, in our Debug panel, we see all of the numbers we wanted in our range.

Let's do the same for our `halfClosedRange` variable, by adding the following:

```
for index in halfClosedRange {
    print("half closed range - \(index)")
}
```

```
half closed range - 10
half closed range - 11
half closed range - 12
half closed range - 13
half closed range - 14
half closed range - 15
half closed range - 16
half closed range - 17
half closed range - 18
half closed range - 19
```

In our Debug panel, we see that we get the numbers 10 through 19. One thing to note is that these two `for...in` loops have different variables. In the first loop, we used value, and in the second one, we used index. You can make these whatever you choose them to be.

In addition, in the two preceding examples, we used constants, but we could actually just use the Ranges within the loop. Add the following:

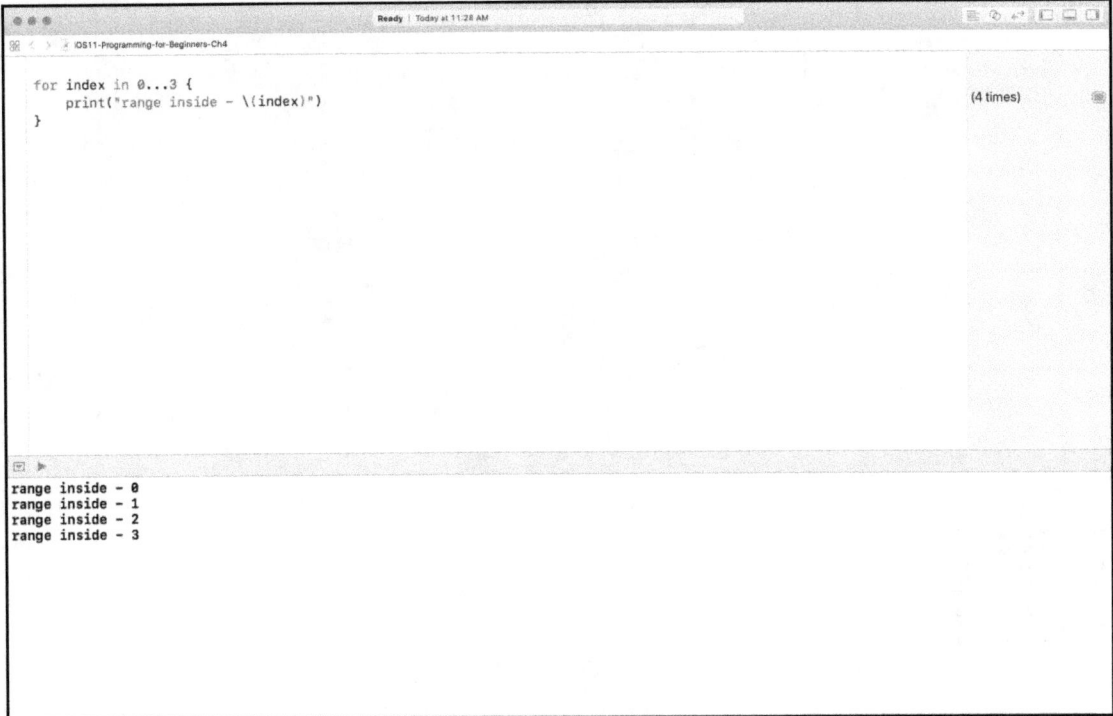

Now, you see 0 to 3 print inside of the Debug panel.

Digging Deeper

What if you wanted the numbers to go in reverse order? Let's input the following `for...in` loop:

```
for index in (10...20).reversed() {
    print("reversed range - \(index)")
}
```

```
reversed range - 20
reversed range - 19
reversed range - 18
reversed range - 17
reversed range - 16
reversed range - 15
reversed range - 14
reversed range - 13
reversed range - 12
reversed range - 11
reversed range - 10
```

We now have the numbers in descending order in our Debug panel. When we add Ranges into a `for...in` loop, we have to wrap our range inside parentheses so that Swift recognizes that our period before `reversed()` is not a decimal. Now that we are familiar with loops, there is one more range we need to look at.

One-sided range

A one-sided Range operator allows you to use ranges that continue as far as possible in one direction. If you wanted to have the range just continue then this is what you would use. Let's look at a one sided range:

```
let names = ["Craig", "Teena", "Jason", "Joshua", "Myah", "Tiffany", "Kim", "Veronica", "Mikki(KK)", "Milan", "Shelby", "Kaysey"]

for name in names[2...] {
    print(name)
}
```

Output:
```
Jason
Joshua
Myah
Tiffany
Kim
Veronica
Mikki(KK)
Milan
Shelby
Kaysey
```

```
for name in names[...6] {
    print("")
}

// Craig
// Teena
```

```
// Jason
// Joshua
// Myah
// Tiffany
// Kim
```

```
for name in names[...6] {
    print(name)
}
```
(7 times)

```
Craig
Teena
Jason
Joshua
Myah
Tiffany
Kim
```

Another useful loop is the `while` loop. Let's take a look at how the `while` loop is used.

The while loop

A `while` loop executes a bool expression at the start of the loop and the set of statements run until a condition becomes false. It is important to note that `while` loops can be executed zero or more times. Here is the basic syntax of a while loop:

```
while <condition> {
    // statement
}
```

Let's write a `while` loop in Playgrounds and see how it works. Add the following:

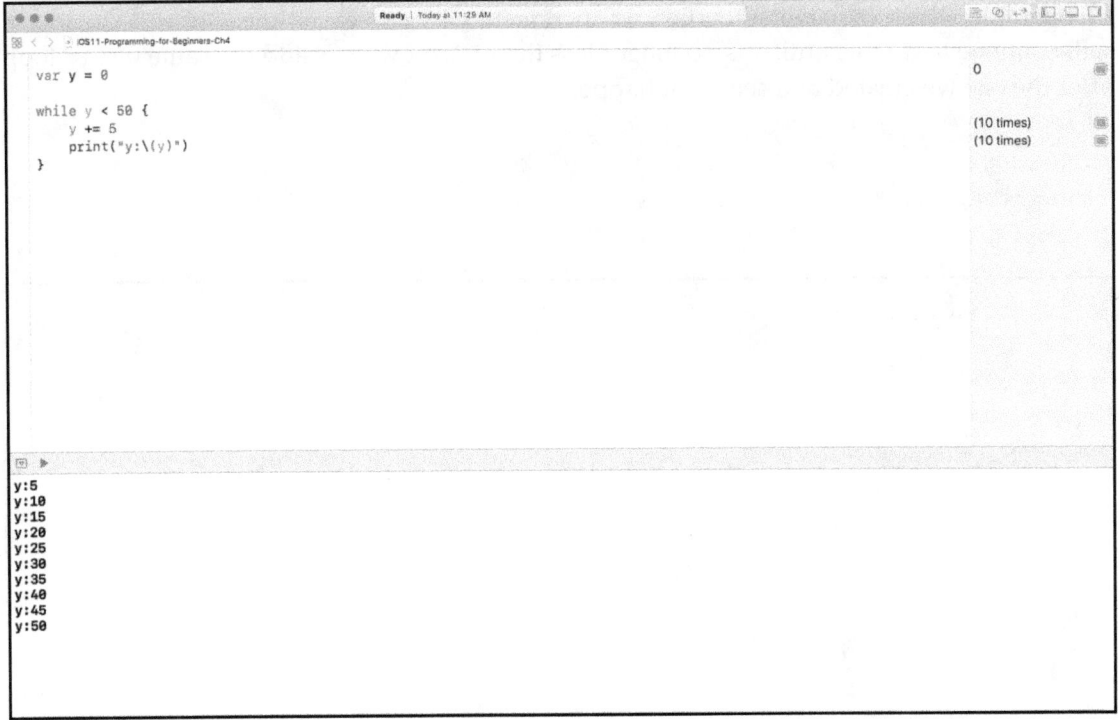

Digging Deeper

So, this `while` loop starts with a variable that begins at zero. Before the `while` loop executes, it checks to see if `y` is less than `50`-and, if so, it continues into the loop. Using the `+=` operator, which we covered earlier, we increment `y` by five each time. Our `while` loop will continue to do this until `y` is no longer less than `50`. Now, let's add the same `while` loop after the one we created and see what happens:

```
while y < 50 {
y += 5
print("y:\(y)")
}
```

```
var y = 0                                                    0

while y < 50 {
    y += 5                                                   (10 times)
    print("y:\(y)")                                          (10 times)
}

while y < 50 {
    y += 5
    print("y:\(y)")
}
```

```
y:5
y:10
y:15
y:20
y:25
y:30
y:35
y:40
y:45
y:50
```

You will notice that the second `while` loop never runs. This may not seem like it is important until we look at our next type of loop.

The repeat...while loop

The `repeat...while` loop is pretty similar to a `while` loop, in that it continues to execute the set of statements until a condition becomes false. The main difference is that the `repeat...while` loop does not evaluate its bool condition until the end of the loop. Here is the basic syntax of a `repeat...while` loop:

```
repeat {
// statement
} <condition>
```

Let's write a `repeat...while` loop in Playgrounds and see how it works. Add the following into Playgrounds:

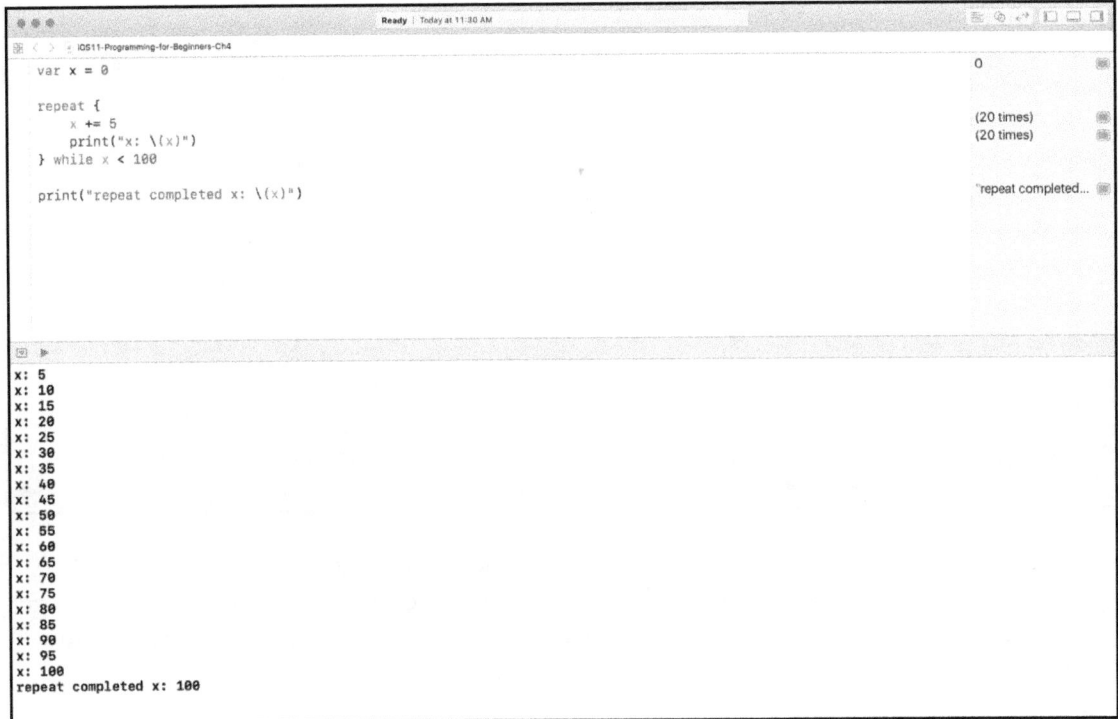

Digging Deeper

You will notice that our `repeat...while` loop executes first and increments x by 5, and after (as opposed to checking the condition before, as with a `while` loop), it checks to see if x is less than 100. This means that our `repeat...while` loop will continue until the condition hits 100. Here is where it gets interesting.

Let's add another `repeat...while` loop after the one we just created:

```
var x = 0                                                          0

repeat {
    x += 5                                                         (20 times)
    print("x: \(x)")                                               (20 times)
} while x < 100

print("repeat completed x: \(x)")                                  "repeat completed...

repeat {
    x += 5                                                         105
    print("x: \(x)")                                               "x: 105\n"
} while x < 100
```

```
x: 5
x: 10
x: 15
x: 20
x: 25
x: 30
x: 35
x: 40
x: 45
x: 50
x: 55
x: 60
x: 65
x: 70
x: 75
x: 80
x: 85
x: 90
x: 95
x: 100
repeat completed x: 100
x: 105
```

Now, you can see that our `repeat...while` loop incremented to 105 instead of 100, like the previous `repeat...while` loop. This happens because the bool expression does not get evaluated until after it is incremented by 5. Knowing this behavior will help you pick the right loop for your situation.

Summary

So far, we have looked at three loops: the `for...in` loop, the `while` loop, and the `repeat-while` loop. We will use the `for...in` loop again, but first we need to talk about collections. In the next chapter, we will focus on what collections are and how to use them when working with data. Make sure you fully understand loops, because we will build on them in the next chapter and throughout the book. Therefore, review as much as you need in order to make sure you feel that you are proficient in the topics contained in this chapter.

5
Digging into Collections

In the last couple of chapters, we reviewed the basics of Swift to get you warmed up. Before we start building our app, we need to look at one more programming concept—collections. In Swift, we have three primary collection types, which we will cover in this chapter:

- Arrays
- Dictionaries
- Sets

We will dig deeper into each one, but we will start with the most common collection type—arrays.

Arrays

Arrays are ordered collections of values and can hold any number of items, for example, a list of Strings, Ints, floating-point values, and so on. Arrays are stored in an ordered list, starting at 0. Let's look at a diagram:

0	Florida		0	45		0	Florida
1	Ohio		1	66		1	California
2	California		2	23		2	32
3	North Carolina		3	10		3	New York
4	Colorado		4	88		4	99
5	Nevada					5	true
6	New York					6	9.0

Starting from left to right in the preceding examples, we first have an array that holds a collection of Strings. In the second example, we have another array that holds a collection of Ints. In our third example, we have an array that holds a collection of floating-point values.

Now, let's review the following diagram, which is a mixed array:

0	Florida
1	California
2	32
3	New York
4	99
5	true
6	9.0

Since this example contains mixed data types, such as Strings, Ints, and bools, we would have to name this an array type of Any. This means that we can have mixed data types inside of our array. Until you are really comfortable with arrays, I would not recommend using them. Try to stick to arrays with the same data type because you know the exact data type of each element.

An array can hold any data type, but making the array strongly typed means every element in it must be of the same type.

Creating an empty array

Let's now create a few arrays in Playgrounds.

Sometimes, you may want to remove your prior entries from your Playground, so that it makes it easier for you to see each new `print` statement. Do that now and input the following:

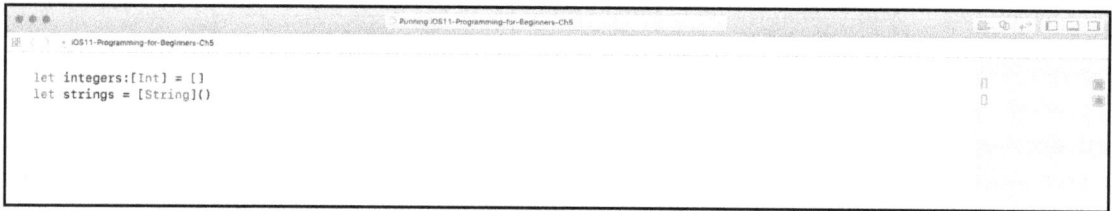

Chapter 5

We just created our first two arrays. The data types within each set of brackets tells Swift what type of an array we want to create. The first array (integers) we created has a data type of Ints, and our second array (strings) has a data type of Strings.

Creating an array with initial values

Arrays can have initial values when they are created. Let's see how this would look by entering the following in Playgrounds:

```
let integers2 = [54, 29]
```

Your code will now look like this:

The array that we just entered uses type inference to declare the data type of the array using its initial values. In this case, Swift understands that it is an array of Ints, because the values we entered are integers. In addition, when we use a constant (`let`) on an array, we are telling Swift that the array is an immutable array, which means that the contents or size cannot change once it is instantiated.

Creating a mutable array

It is best practice to make all arrays (and for that matter, collections) immutable, but there are some cases where you will need to create an array that is mutable. Let's have some fun and create a mutable array:

```
var states:[String] = []
```

As an aside, when creating a mutable array (or any variable), note that each variable must be unique.

One use for a mutable array is so that we can change an array. Let's look at some ways we can do this.

Digging into Collections

Adding items to an array

Let's add some data to our array. There are a few different convenience methods for adding data to an array.

A convenience method is, just as its name implies, a method that makes things convenient. A method is a function that lives inside of a class. We will discuss classes later in this book. If this is starting to get overwhelming, it is understandable. You do not need to worry about every single detail at this time. We will cover this again and things will slowly start to click at some point. Everyone learns differently, so there is no reason to worry if someone else understands something more quickly. Just go at your own pace.

The first convenience method we will look at is the `append()` method:

```
states.append(23)
```

Your code and the output window should now look like this:

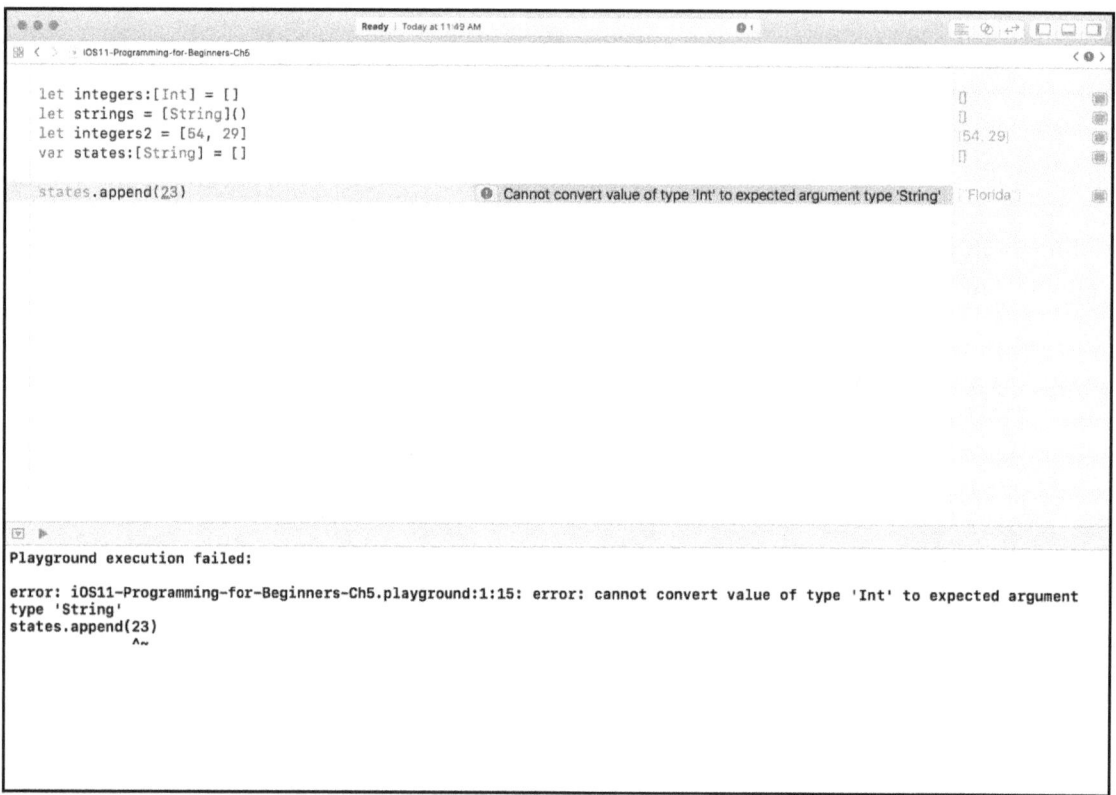

Chapter 5

Houston, we have a problem! You will see that we are getting an error. Actually, I did this for a couple of reasons. Getting errors is normal and common. Most people who start out coding are afraid to make a mistake or get scared about getting or seeing errors. Trust me, I have been coding for years and I make mistakes all the time. The error is telling us that we tried to add an Int into an array that can only hold Strings.

Every developer, from a beginner to an experienced one, will face a time when he or she will encounter an error that he or she cannot figure out. This error might get you frustrated to the point where you want to throw the computer across the room (I have been there a few times). The best advice my boss ever gave me was to take a walk for 10-15 minutes or do something to take your mind off of it. Sometimes this helps and you will come up with an idea after you walk away. Even if you come back and it still takes you hours to figure out what is wrong, this is still part of the process. The best errors are the ones that were the simplest thing you overlooked and you had to spend hours trying to figure out. You might have lost time, but you will have learned a great lesson. Lessons like these will stay with you forever and you will never forget the error the next time you encounter it. So, if your coding results in an error, even in this book, embrace the challenge, because there is no greater feeling than figuring out a challenging error.

So, let's correct what we just did by revising the array to show the following:

```
states.append("Florida")
```

This is how your code should now look:

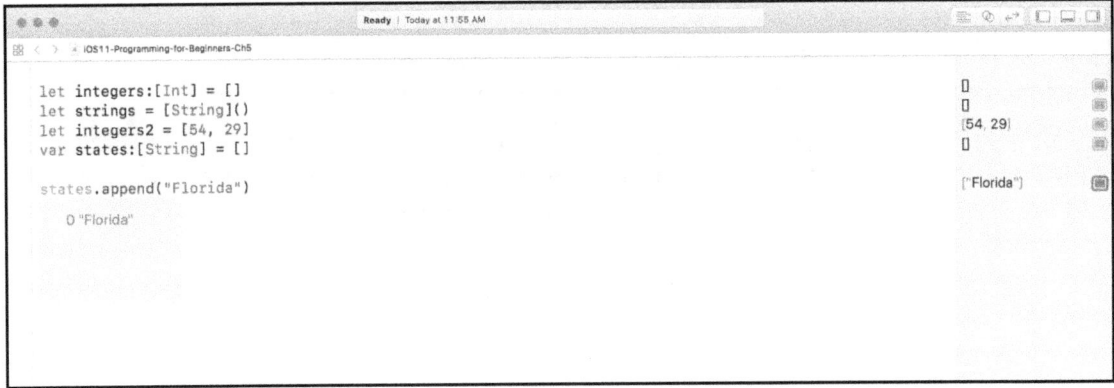

Digging into Collections

In the Results panel, you can actually see the contents of our corrected array.

Since an array can hold any number of items, let's add some more. Earlier, I mentioned that we have a variety of ways to add items to an array. The `append()` method allows us to add only one item at a time. In order to add multiple items, we can use the convenience called `append(contentsOf:)`.

Add the following to Playgrounds:

```
states.append(contentsOf:["California", "New York"])
```

Now, your code should look like this:

```
let integers:[Int] = []
let strings = [String]()
let integers2 = [54, 29]
var states:[String] = []

states.append("Florida")

states.append(contentsOf: ["California", "New York"])
```

We added two more items into our array, but, so far, every example we have utilized has added items at the end of our array. We have two convenience methods that allow us to add items at any index position that is available in the array.

Chapter 5

The first method we can use to do this is called `insert(at:)`, which allows us to add a single item at a certain index position. We also have `insert(contentsOf:at:)`, which allows us to add multiple items into an array at a certain index position. Let's use them both and add `Ohio` after California and then `North Carolina`, `South Carolina`, and `Nevada` after `Ohio`:

```
states.insert("Ohio", at:1)
states.insert(contentsOf:["North Carolina", "South Carolina",
"Nevada"],at:3)
```

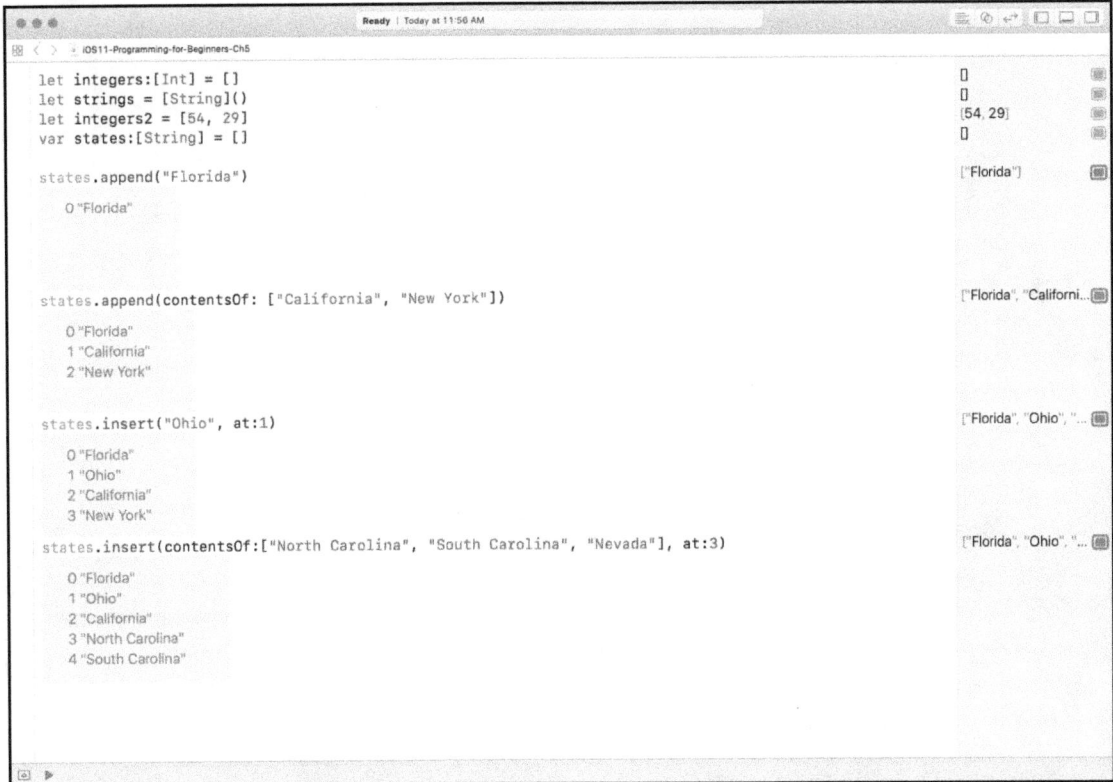

[99]

Digging into Collections

We just added items to our array using `append(contentsOf:)`, but there also is a shorthand version of this using the `+=` operator. Let's add the following:

```
states += ["Texas", "Colorado"]
```

Now, your code should look like this:

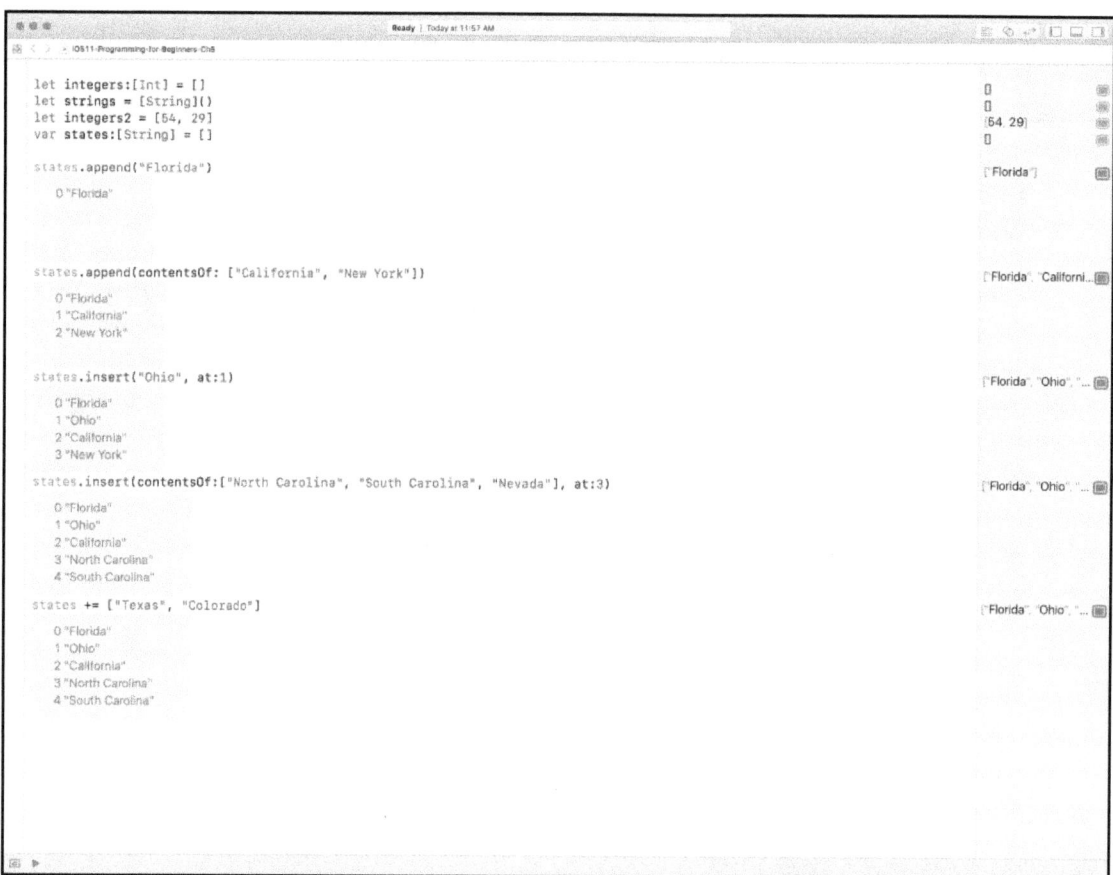

This technique for adding items is much more concise and is my preferred way of inserting items into an array. Writing less code is not always better but, in this case, using the `+=` operator is my go-to method.

Checking the number of elements in an array

If you are keeping track, we now have nine items in our array. Luckily, we do not have to keep track of how many items are in our array, because we have a property called `count`. This property will keep track of the current item count and give us the total count of our array when we want to check. Let's look at the count for states:

```
states.count
```

Your code will now look like this:

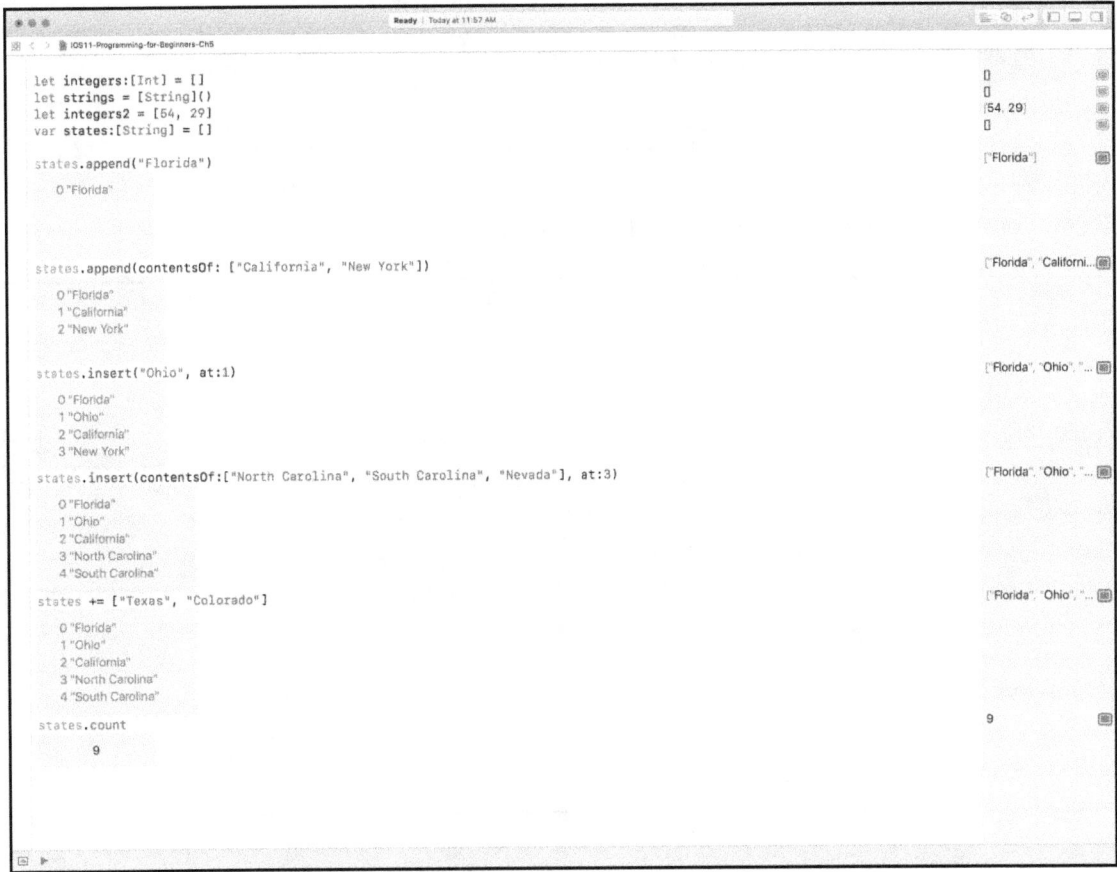

Checking for an empty array

The `count` property is not the only property we can use to calculate how many items are in an array. The most commonly used property for an array is called `isEmpty`. This property uses the `count` property by checking to see if the count is greater than 0. This method will return true or false, depending on whether there are any items within our array. Since you learned that `if...else` statements work well with bools, let's use this `isEmpty` property in an `if...else` statement.

Add the following into Playgrounds:

```
if states.isEmpty {
   print("There are no items in the array")
}
else {
   print("There are currently (states.count) total items in our array")
}
```

Now, your code and the output should look like this:

Now, our Debug panel prints: `There are currently total nine items in our array.`

One thing to remember in programming is that sometimes there are multiple ways of writing a piece of code. It is not shocking to meet someone who will approach the same problem differently than you did. To me, this is why programming is so great. Ultimately, all that matters is that it works as expected, especially when you are new to programming.

All programming languages have what is known as a style guide, which is a preferred way to write code, and it is no different in Swift. Preferred just means a suggested method, but even then, you will notice that most preferred methods vary on certain things. For now, you do not need to worry about different style guides, other than to know that they exist. In this book, we will follow a style that I have adopted into my code.

Once you get comfortable, I recommend that you start to look at style guides and adapt them into your code. Knowing different styles helps you to know your options as well as to understand what others are doing with their code, even if you do not agree with how they write something. If you write your code with a certain structure or style throughout a project, it will make it easier for you to come back to your code if you, for instance, had to take a break for some reason, such as starting another project or just taking some time off.

Retrieving a value from an array

We discussed creating arrays as well as adding items into an array. Now, let's turn to retrieving a value from an array. Since arrays are stored by their index, we can use their index to retrieve values. Let's retrieve California:

```
let state = states[3]
```

Digging into Collections

Now, your code should look like this:

```swift
let integers:[Int] = []                                                         []
let strings = [String]()                                                        []
let integers2 = [54, 29]                                                        [54, 29]
var states:[String] = []                                                        []

states.append("Florida")                                                        ["Florida"]
states.append(contentsOf: ["California", "New York"])                           ["Florida", "Californi...
states.insert("Ohio", at:1)                                                     ["Florida", "Ohio", "...
states.insert(contentsOf:["North Carolina", "South Carolina", "Nevada"], at:3)  ["Florida", "Ohio", "...
states += ["Texas", "Colorado"]                                                 ["Florida", "Ohio", "...
states.count                                                                    9


if states.isEmpty {
    print("There are no items in the array")
}
else {
    print("There are currently \(states.count) total items in our array")       "There are currently...
}

let state = states[3]                                                           "North Carolina"
    North Carolina
```

[104]

The Results panels shows North Carolina and not California. Remember, arrays start at 0, not 1. Therefore, in order for us to get California, we would actually need use the index position of 2. Let's make that update in Playgrounds:

```
let state = states[2]
```

```
let integers:[Int] = []
let strings = [String]()
let integers2 = [54, 29]
var states:[String] = []

states.append("Florida")
states.append(contentsOf: ["California", "New York"])
states.insert("Ohio", at:1)
states.insert(contentsOf:["North Carolina", "South Carolina", "Nevada"], at:3)
states += ["Texas", "Colorado"]
states.count

if states.isEmpty {
    print("There are no items in the array")
}
else {
    print("There are currently \(states.count) total items in our array")
}

let state = states[2]
    California
```

There we go!

Digging into Collections

We now have this great list of states, but someone told you that Arizona also is amazing. Instead of just adding Arizona to our list, you decide that you'd actually prefer to replace South Carolina with Arizona. We could simply look at our array and see in which index South Carolina is. This would not be helpful, however, if it were to change or if the state for which you were searching did not exist. So, the safe way to code this is to check the array for an item, and, if that item is found, then Swift will give us its current index position. The `index(of:)` method is what we will use to get the index position of South Carolina:

```
if let index = states.index(of:"South Carolina") {
  print("Current index position is \(index)")
}
```

This is how our code and output should now look:

```
let integers:[Int] = []
let strings = [String]()
let integers2 = [54, 29]
var states:[String] = []

states.append("Florida")
states.append(contentsOf: ["California", "New York"])
states.insert("Ohio", at:1)
states.insert(contentsOf:["North Carolina", "South Carolina", "Nevada"], at:3)
states += ["Texas", "Colorado"]
states.count

if states.isEmpty {
    print("There are no items in the array")
}
else {
    print("There are currently \(states.count) total items in our array")
}

let state = states[2]
    California

if let index = states.index(of: "South Carolina") {
    print("Current index position of South Carolina is \(index)")
}
```

Output:
```
There are currently 9 total items in our array
Current index position of South Carolina is 4
```

Now that we have the position, we can replace South Carolina with Arizona, like so:

```
if let index = states.index(of:"South Carolina") {
   states[index] = "Arizona"
}
```

This is how our code should now look:

```
let integers:[Int] = []
let strings = [String]()
let integers2 = [54, 29]
var states:[String] = []

states.append("Florida")
states.append(contentsOf: ["California", "New York"])
states.insert("Ohio", at:1)
states.insert(contentsOf:["North Carolina", "South Carolina", "Nevada"], at:3)
states += ["Texas", "Colorado"]
states.count

if states.isEmpty {
    print("There are no items in the array")
}
else {
    print("There are currently \(states.count) total items in our array")
}

let state = states[2]
    California

if let index = states.index(of: "South Carolina") {
    states[index] = "Arizona"
}
```

Iterating over an array

It would be nice if we could see a list of the states in our array. Earlier, you learned that `for...in` loops work with sequences. Since our array is a sequence, we can use `for...in` loops to loop through each element. When working on a project that has arrays, it is helpful to use a `print` statement inside of a `for...in` loop. This lets us print every item in our array to the Debug panel. So, let's use a `for...in` loop to look at the contents of our array:

```
for state in states {
  print(state)
}
```

Digging into Collections

This is how our code and output should now look:

Removing items from an array

Now, it is time to start deleting items from our array. Let's delete the first item from our list. We have a convenience method for removing items from an array, called `removeFirst()`. This method will remove the first item from our array, which in our case is Florida. Let's remove Florida and add this line above our `for...in` loop:

```
states.removeFirst()
```

Chapter 5

This is how our code and output should now look:

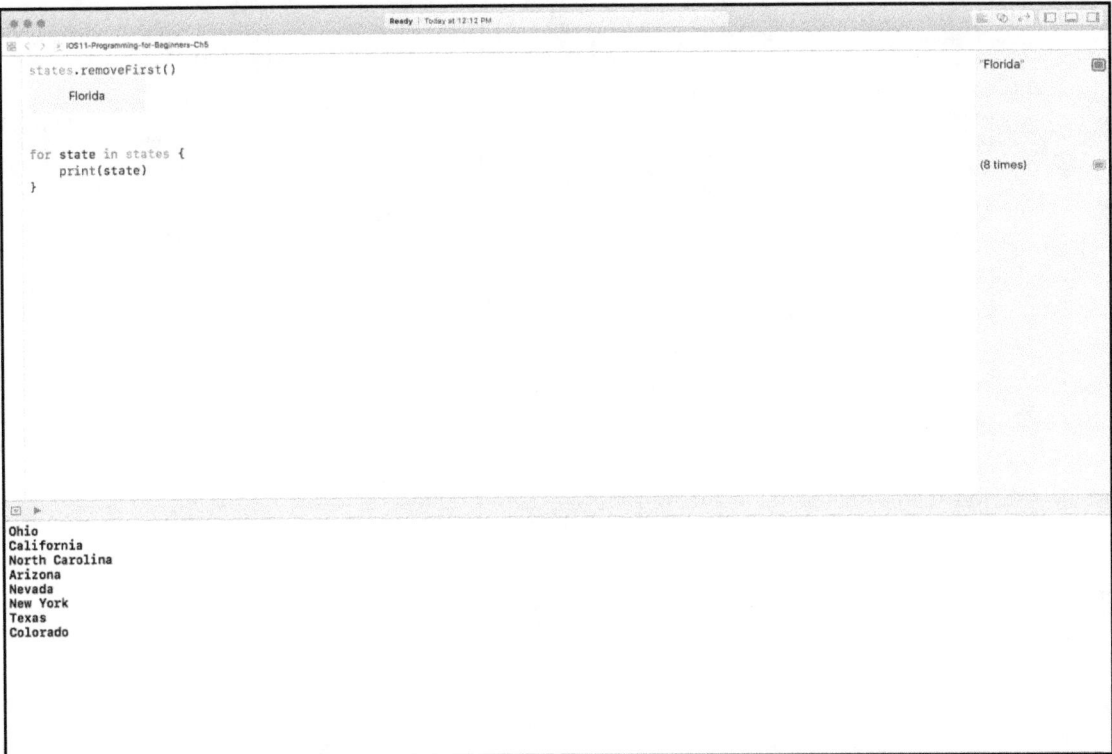

Since we removed Florida, all of our states' index positions will be updated to move one position closer to the top of the array. But what if we wanted to remove an item that was not first? In order to do this, we can use the `remove(at:)` convenience. So, let's remove North Carolina and New York, which are sitting at positions 2 and 4, respectively. We will add the following above our `for...in` loop:

```
states.remove(at:2)
states.remove(at:4)
```

This is how our code and output should now look:

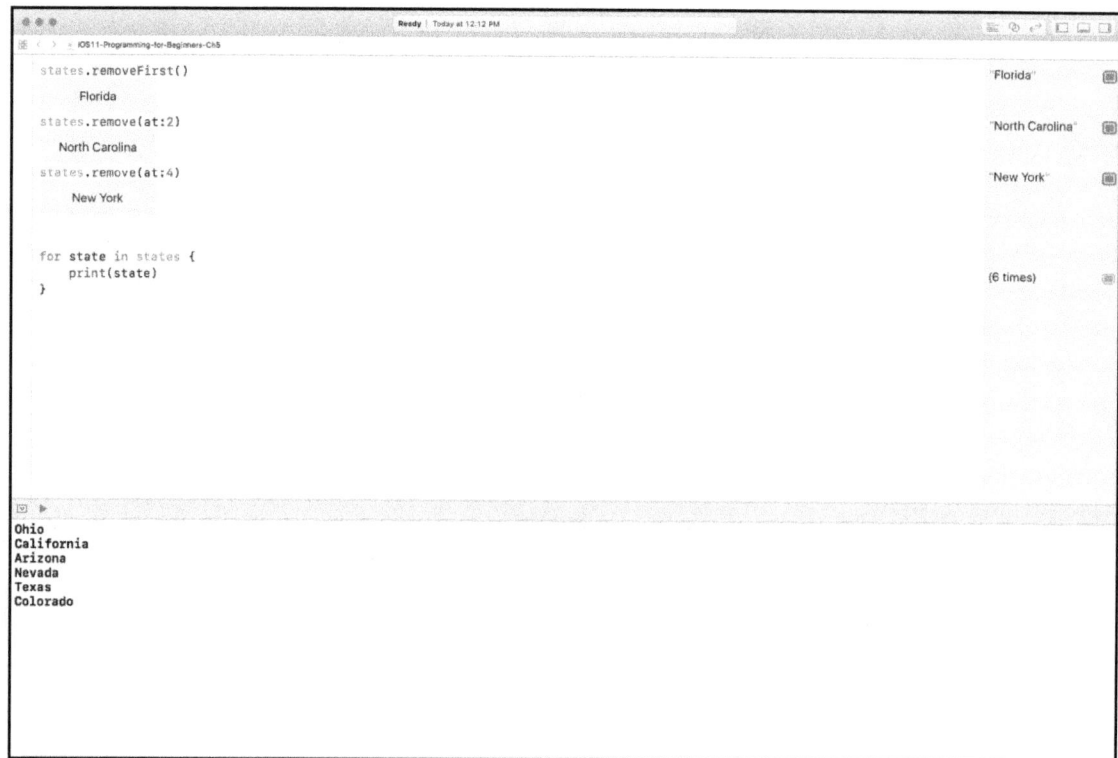

Now, both North Carolina and New York have been removed. You will see that California and Ohio did not move, but Colorado and Nevada moved up closer to the top of the list. To remove the remaining six items, we could use `remove(at:)` for each one, but instead we will use the simpler method of `removeAll()`. So, let's use `removeAll()` in Playgrounds:

```
states.removeAll()
```

Now, your code should look something like this:

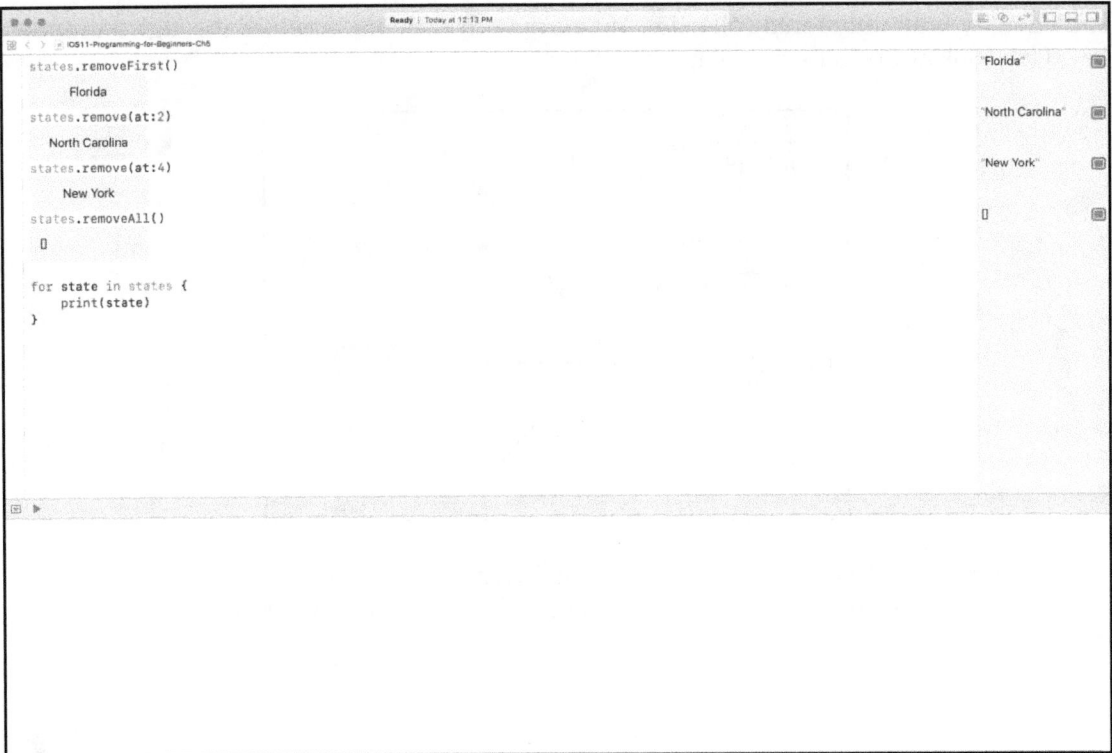

Now, we are back to where we started with an empty array. We have only scratched the surface for arrays. We will do more with arrays later in this book, but we first need to look at the next collection type: dictionaries.

Dictionaries

A dictionary is an unordered collection of values with each one accessed through a unique key. Let's look at the following diagram:

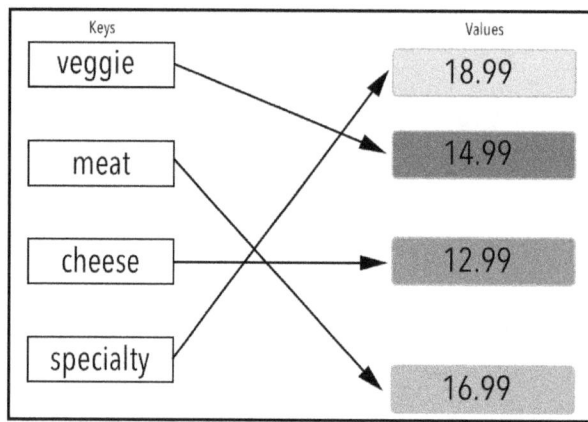

In our diagram, we have a dictionary of pizzas (**keys**) with their prices (**values**). In order to find something inside of a dictionary, we must look it up by its key. Let's look at a dictionary syntax:

```
Dictionary<Key, Value>
```

Creating a dictionary

The traditional way of creating a dictionary is to first declare it as a dictionary and then, inside angle brackets, declare a type for the key and value. Let's create our first dictionary inside Playgrounds:

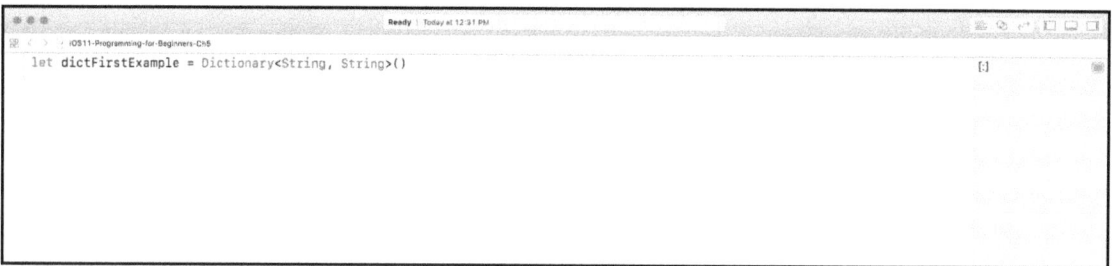

Chapter 5

The immutable dictionary we created earlier has a data type of String for both its key and value. We have multiple ways to create a dictionary. Let's look at another by adding the following into Playgrounds:

```
let dictSecondExample = [String: Int]()
```

Your code should now look like this:

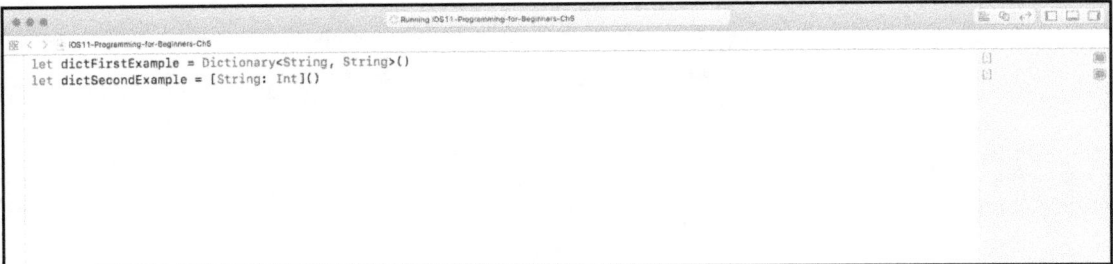

In this latest example, we created another immutable dictionary, with its key having a data type of String and its value having a data type of Int.

If we wanted to use our pizza diagram, the key would have a data type of a String and the value would have a data type of a Double. Let's create this dictionary in Playgrounds, but, this time, we will make it a mutable dictionary and give it an initial value:

```
var dictThirdExample = Dictionary<String, Double>(dictionaryLiteral:
("veggie", 14.99), ("meat", 16.99))
```

Your code should now look like this:

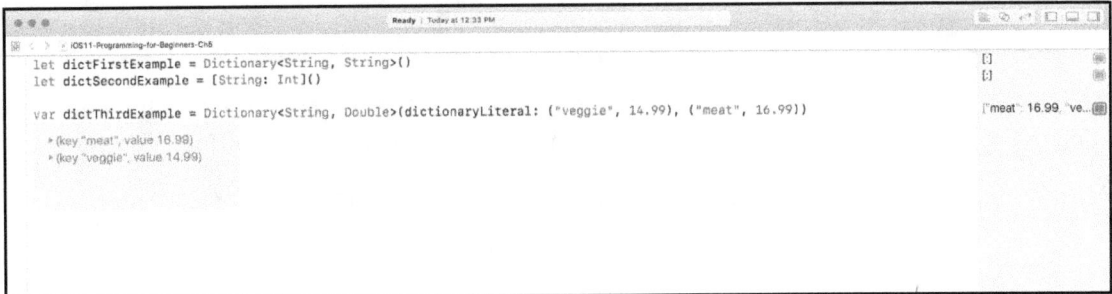

[113]

Digging into Collections

The preceding way is just one way of creating a dictionary for our pizza diagram example. Let's look at a much more common way using type inference:

```
var dictPizzas = ["veggie": 14.99]
```

Once you add this to your code, your code should look something like this:

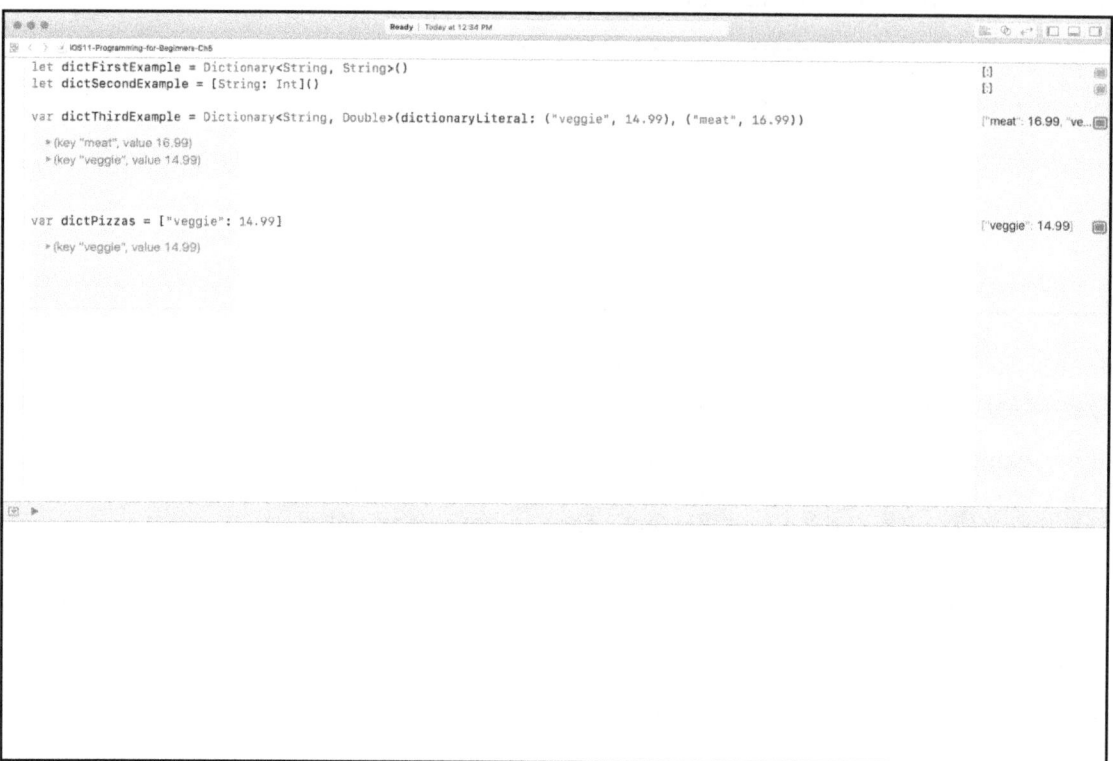

This is a much simpler way to create a dictionary with an initial value. When initializing a dictionary, it can have any number of items. In our case, we are starting off with just one.

Now, let's look at how we can add more pizzas into our dictionary.

Adding and updating dictionary elements

Let's add another item to our `dictPizzas` dictionary:

```
dictPizzas["meat"] = 17.99
```

Once you add this line of code, your code snippet should look like this:

```
let dictFirstExample = Dictionary<String, String>()                                         [:]
let dictSecondExample = [String: Int]()                                                     [:]

var dictThirdExample = Dictionary<String, Double>(dictionaryLiteral: ("veggie", 14.99), ("meat", 16.99))   ["meat": 16.99, "ve...
  ▸ (key "meat", value 16.99)
  ▸ (key "veggie", value 14.99)

var dictPizzas = ["veggie": 14.99]                                                          ["veggie": 14.99]
  ▸ (key "veggie", value 14.99)

dictPizzas["meat"] = 17.99                                                                  17.99
17.9899999999999...
```

This is the shorthand method for adding an item to a dictionary. After the dictionary variable, we add the key inside the brackets. Since the key for this dictionary is Strings, we must put this key in quotes. Next, we assign a Double to our value. Now, our dictionary has two items. This syntax is also used to update a dictionary item. Let's change the price of meat pizza to `16.99`:

```
dictPizzas["meat"] = 16.99
```

Have a look at the code, it should look like this:

```
let dictFirstExample = Dictionary<String, String>()                                         [:]
let dictSecondExample = [String: Int]()                                                     [:]

var dictThirdExample = Dictionary<String, Double>(dictionaryLiteral: ("veggie", 14.99), ("meat", 16.99))   ["meat": 16.99, "ve...
  ▸ (key "meat", value 16.99)
  ▸ (key "veggie", value 14.99)

var dictPizzas = ["veggie": 14.99]                                                          ["veggie": 14.99]
  ▸ (key "veggie", value 14.99)

dictPizzas["meat"] = 17.99                                                                  17.99
17.9899999999999...
dictPizzas["meat"] = 16.99                                                                  16.99
16.9899999999999...
```

Digging into Collections

Instead of using the shorthand syntax, you can use the `updateValue(_:forKey:)` method. This method does almost the same thing as the shorthand syntax. If the value does not exist, it creates the item; if it does exist, it will update the item. The only difference is that, when using the `updateValue(_:forKey:)`, it actually returns the old value after performing the update. Using this method, you will get an optional value, because it is possible that no value exists in the dictionary. Let's change the value now from `16.99` to `15.99`:

```
if let oldValue = dictPizzas.updateValue(15.99, forKey: "meat") {
    print("old value \(oldValue)")
}
```

Your code should now look like this:

```
let dictFirstExample = Dictionary<String, String>()
let dictSecondExample = [String: Int]()

var dictThirdExample = Dictionary<String, Double>(dictionaryLiteral: ("veggie", 14.99), ("meat", 16.99))
   ▸ (key "meat", value 16.99)
   ▸ (key "veggie", value 14.99)

var dictPizzas = ["veggie": 14.99]
   ▸ (key "veggie", value 14.99)

dictPizzas["meat"] = 17.99
   17.9899999999999...
dictPizzas["meat"] = 16.99
   16.9899999999999...

if let oldValue = dictPizzas.updateValue(15.99, forKey: "meat") {
    print("old value \(oldValue)")
}

old value 16.99
```

Chapter 5

Since we do not need the old value, we will just use the shorthand syntax to add a couple more pizzas:

```
dictPizzas["specialty"] = 18.99
dictPizzas["chicken"] = 16.99
```

Your code and output should now look like this:

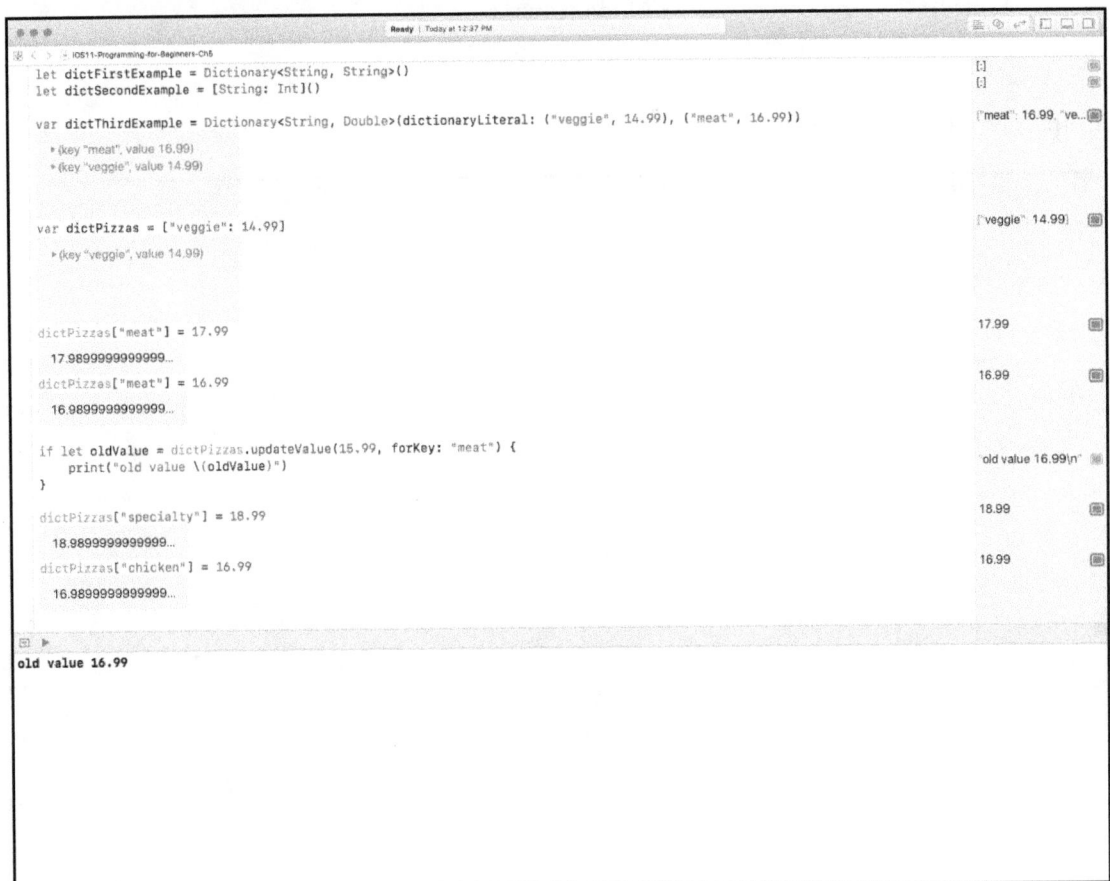

Now that we have some data inside our dictionary, let's see how we can access that data.

Accessing an item in a dictionary

When trying to access an item inside a dictionary, you will always receive an optional value. The reason for this is that you could potentially receive a nil value if the value does not exist. So, you should always use an `if...let` statement in order to safeguard your code:

```
if let numChickenPrice = dictPizzas["chicken"] {
  print(numChickenPrice)
}
```

Your code should now look like this:

Iterating over dictionary values

Just like an array, we can iterate through our dictionary; however, there are a few differences. Since a dictionary is unordered, each time you loop through, the values will never be in the same order. With dictionaries, you can loop through both the values and keys.

Let's iterate over a dictionary's values using a `for...in` loop. Add the following into Playgrounds:

```
for value in dictPizzas.values {
   print(value)
}
```

Your code should now look like this:

[119]

Digging into Collections

Iterating over dictionary keys

To iterate over a dictionary's keys using a `for...in` loop, add the following into Playgrounds:

```
for key in dictPizzas.keys {
    print(key)
}
```

Your code and output should now look like this:

```
let dictFirstExample = Dictionary<String, String>()                                    [:]
let dictSecondExample = [String: Int]()                                                [:]

var dictThirdExample = Dictionary<String, Double>(dictionaryLiteral: ("veggie", 14.99), ("meat", 16.99))   ["meat": 16.99, "ve...
var dictPizzas = ["veggie": 14.99]                                                     ["veggie": 14.99]
dictPizzas["meat"] = 17.99                                                             17.99
dictPizzas["meat"] = 16.99                                                             16.99

if let oldValue = dictPizzas.updateValue(15.99, forKey: "meat") {
    print("old value \(oldValue)")                                                     "old value 16.99\n"
}

dictPizzas["specialty"] = 18.99                                                        18.99
dictPizzas["chicken"] = 16.99                                                          16.99

if let numChickenPrice = dictPizzas["chicken"] {
    print(numChickenPrice)                                                             "16.99\n"
}

for value in dictPizzas.values {
    print(value)                                                                       (4 times)
}

for value in dictPizzas.keys {
    print(value)                                                                       (4 times)
}
```

```
old value 16.99
16.99
16.99
15.99
14.99
18.99
chicken
meat
veggie
specialty
```

Iterating over dictionary keys and values

When you need to iterate over both dictionary keys and values using a `for...in` loop, you use the following:

```
for (key, value) in dictPizzas {
   print("\(key): \(value)")
}
```

Your code and output should now look like this:

```
let dictFirstExample = Dictionary<String, String>()
let dictSecondExample = [String: Int]()
var dictThirdExample = Dictionary<String, Double>(dictionaryLiteral: ("veggie", 14.99), ("meat", 16.99))
var dictPizzas = ["veggie": 14.99]
dictPizzas["meat"] = 17.99
dictPizzas["meat"] = 16.99

if let oldValue = dictPizzas.updateValue(15.99, forKey: "meat") {
    print("old value \(oldValue)")
}

dictPizzas["specialty"] = 18.99
dictPizzas["chicken"] = 16.99

if let numChickenPrice = dictPizzas["chicken"] {
    print(numChickenPrice)
}

for value in dictPizzas.values {
    print(value)
}

for value in dictPizzas.keys {
    print(value)
}

for (key, value) in dictPizzas {
    print("\(key): \(value)")
}
```

```
old value 16.99
16.99
16.99
15.99
14.99
18.99
chicken
meat
veggie
specialty
chicken: 16.99
meat: 15.99
veggie: 14.99
specialty: 18.99
```

So, we have now looked at how to loop through a dictionary.

Checking the number of items in a dictionary

In addition to keys and values, we have other useful properties. We can see the number of items in a dictionary using the `count` property. Let's try that by adding the following:

```
print("There are \(dictPizzas.count) total pizzas.")
```

Now, your code and output should look like this:

```
let dictFirstExample = Dictionary<String, String>()
let dictSecondExample = [String: Int]()

var dictThirdExample = Dictionary<String, Double>(dictionaryLiteral: ("veggie", 14.99), ("meat", 16.99))
var dictPizzas = ["veggie": 14.99]
dictPizzas["meat"] = 17.99
dictPizzas["meat"] = 16.99

if let oldValue = dictPizzas.updateValue(15.99, forKey: "meat") {
    print("old value \(oldValue)")
}

dictPizzas["specialty"] = 18.99
dictPizzas["chicken"] = 16.99

if let numChickenPrice = dictPizzas["chicken"] {
    print(numChickenPrice)
}

for value in dictPizzas.values {
    print(value)
}

for value in dictPizzas.keys {
    print(value)
}

for (key, value) in dictPizzas {
    print("\(key): \(value)")
}

print("There are \(dictPizzas.count) total pizzas.")
```

```
old value 16.99
16.99
16.99
15.99
14.99
18.99
chicken
meat
veggie
specialty
chicken: 16.99
meat: 15.99
veggie: 14.99
specialty: 18.99
There are 4 total pizzas.
```

Along with count, we can check whether a dictionary `isEmpty` or not. Let's use this in an `if...else` statement by adding the following:

```
if dictPizzas.isEmpty {
  print("there are no pizzas")
}
else {
```

```
    print("There are \(dictPizzas.count) total pizzas.")
}
```

Now, your code and output should look like this:

This kind of logic is helpful when you want to display something back to the user or hide a UI.

Digging into Collections

Removing items from a dictionary

Next, let's learn how to remove an item from a dictionary. When deleting items from a dictionary, we have two primary ways of doing this. The first uses `removeValue(forKey:)`. Let's add this right above our `if...else` statement that checks if the dictionary `isEmpty`:

```
dictPizzas.removeValue(forKey: "chicken")
```

Your code should now look like this:

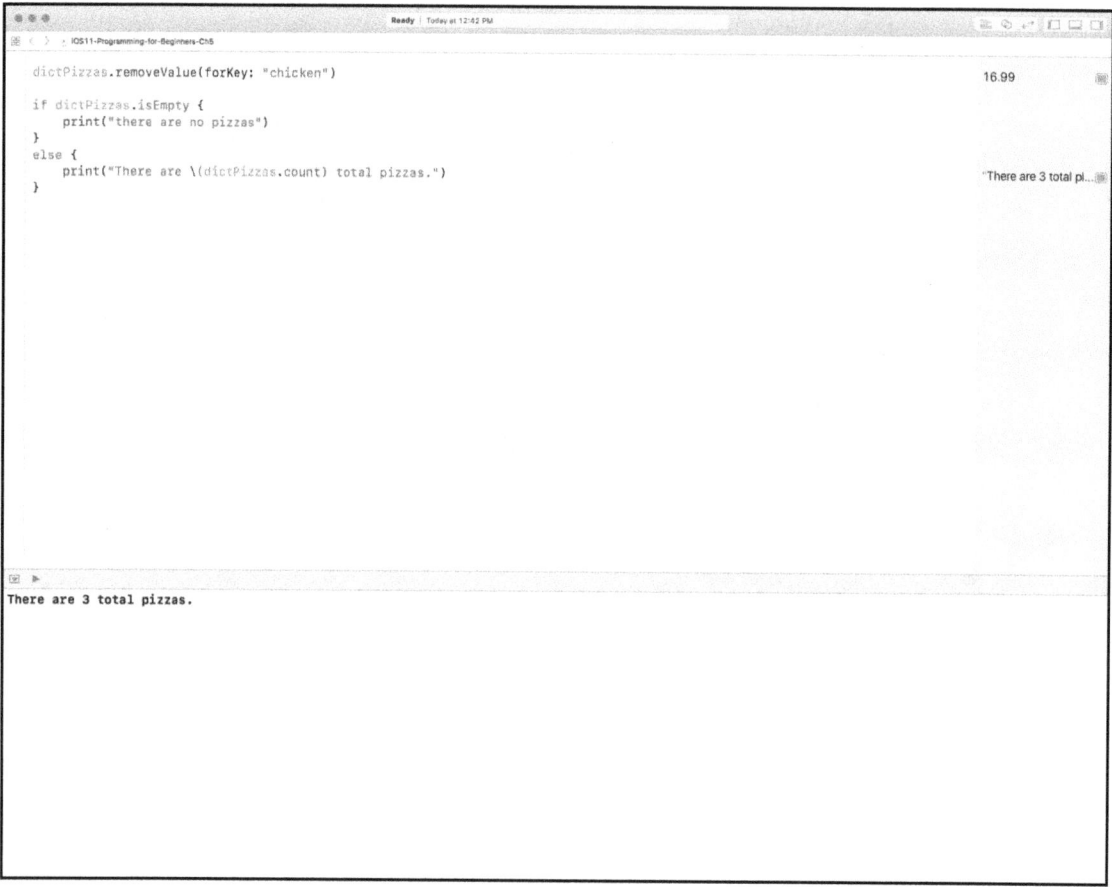

Let's look at the second way of removing dictionary items, the shorthand syntax. Add the following to Playgrounds following the `removeValue(forKey:)`:

```
dictPizzas["meat"] = nil
```

Your code should now look like this:

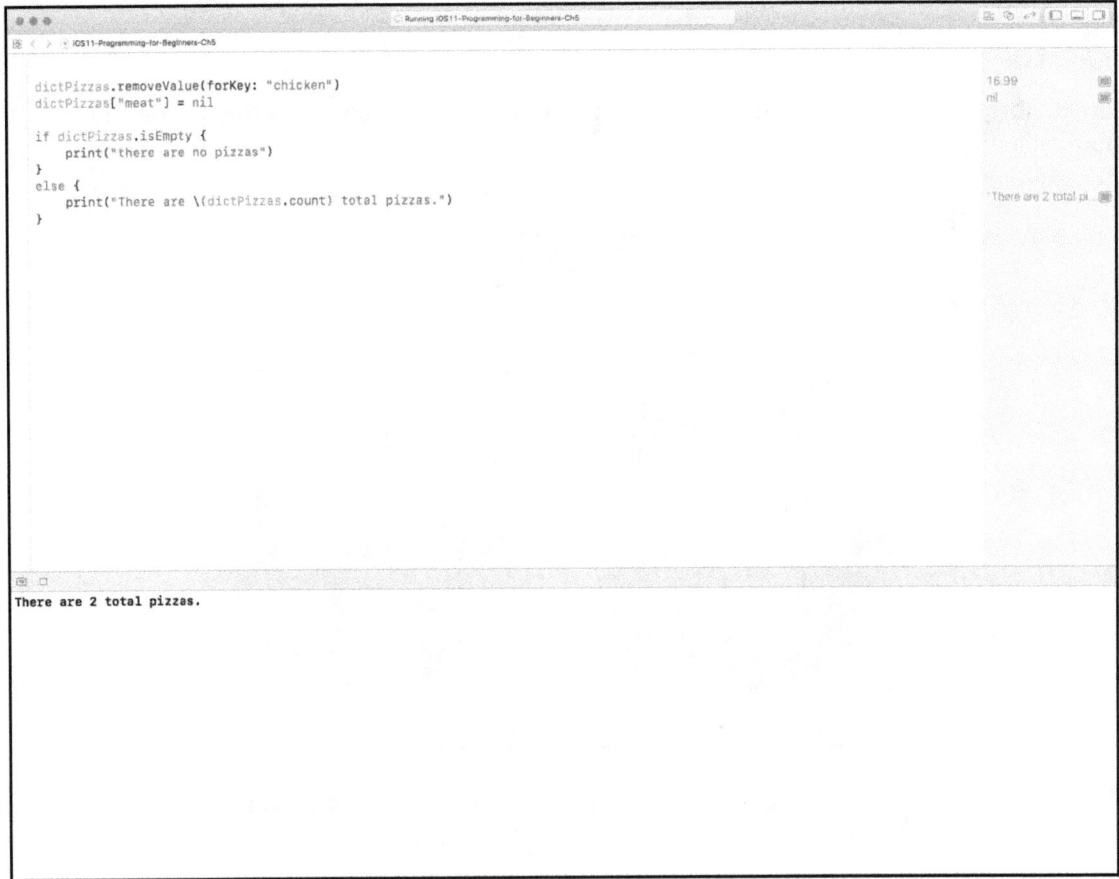

Digging into Collections

Notice that, just like with `updateValue(_:forKey:)`, `removeValue(forKey:)` will return you the value before it is removed. If you do not need the value, the shorthand syntax is the preferred method.

So far, we covered arrays and dictionaries, and now we will review one last collection: sets.

Sets

A set stores unique values of the same type in a collection without a defined order. Let's look at a diagram:

In the preceding diagram, we have two circles, both of which represent a set. On the left, we have Craig's favorite movies and on the right, we have Gabe's favorite movies.

Creating an empty set

Before we create these sets, let's just create an empty set and see what that looks like:

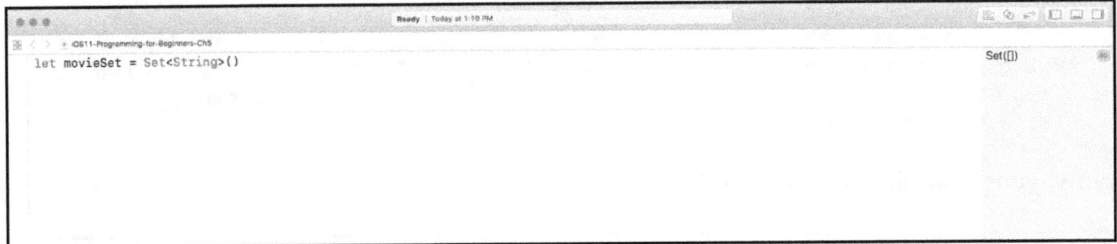

In this first set, after the equals sign, we create the set and give it a data type of String. Then, we use the parentheses to initialize the set.

Creating a set with an array literal

Our first set was an empty String set, but we can create a set using an array literal. Let's add the following into Playgrounds:

```
let numberSet = Set<Int>([])
```

Your code should now look like this:

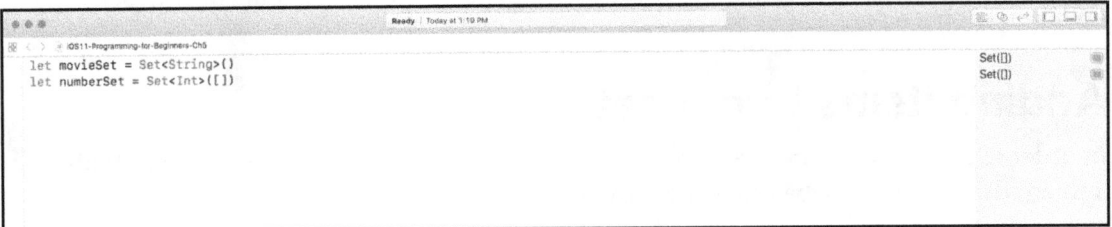

This preceding immutable set has a data type of Int, but in the parentheses we pass an empty array literal when we used the brackets.

Creating a mutable set

Now that we are familiar with the way sets are created, let's create a mutable set for Craig's favorite movies and one for Gabe's favorite movies. Add the following into Playgrounds:

```
var craigsFavMovieSet = Set<String>([])
var gabesFavMovieSet = Set<String>(["Fight Club", "Matrix", "Evil Dead", "Big Trouble in Little China", "Aliens", "Winter Solider", "The Illusionist", "Predator"])
```

Now, your code should look like this:

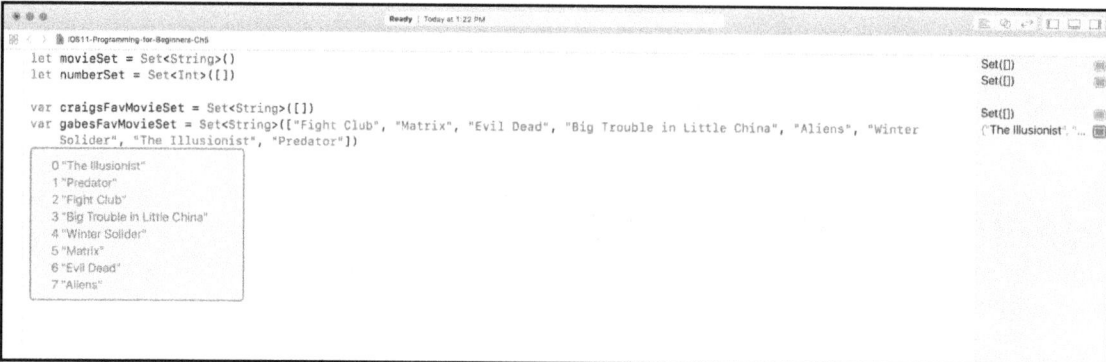

We now have two mutable sets. The first set is created with an empty array literal and the second set is created with some initial values. Let's add some more items to both sets.

Adding items into a set

In order to add an item into a set, we have to use the `insert()` method. Let's use that to add another movie to Gabe's favorite movies:

```
gabesFavMovieSet.insert("Terminator")
gabesFavMovieSet
```

Your code should now look like this:

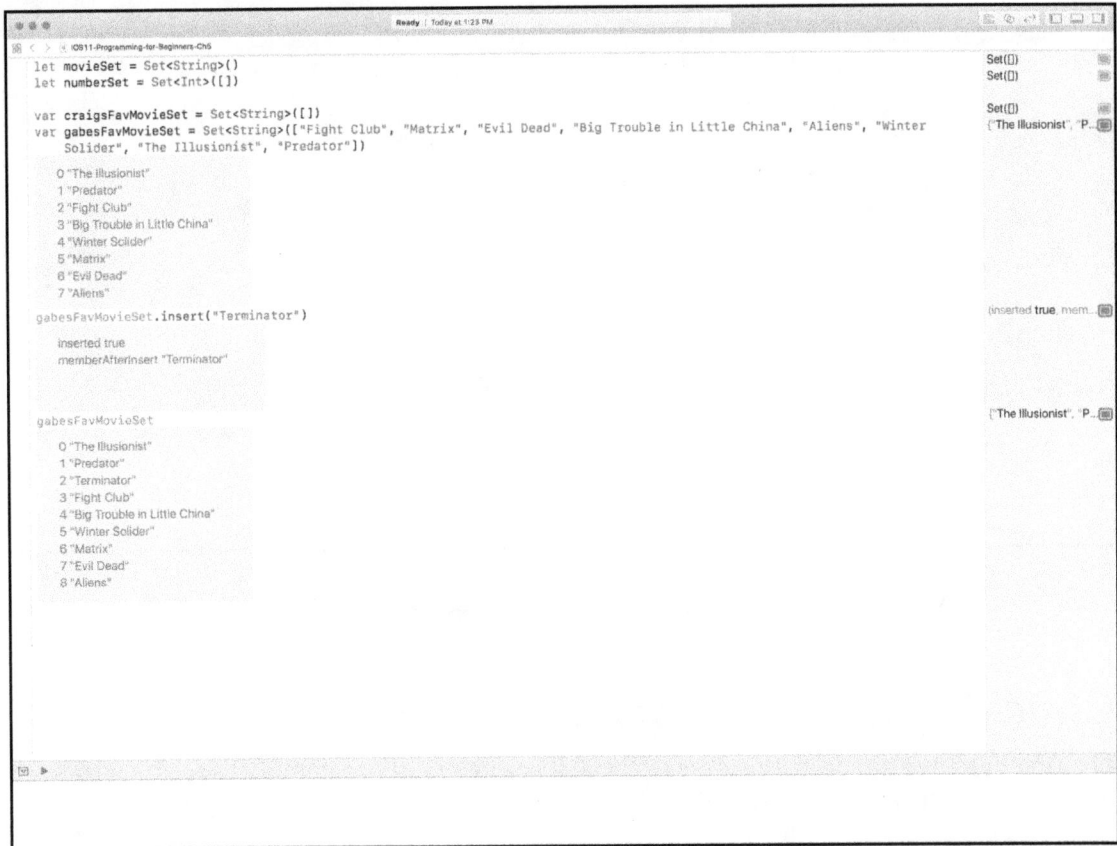

Now, Gabe has nine movies and Craig still has none. We added the `gabeFaveMovieSet` variable again so that we can see the contents update in the Results panel. In order to add multiple items into a set, we can use an array literal.

Let's add 10 movies to Craig's list, as follows:

```
craigsFavMovieSet = ["The Pianist", "The Shawshank Redemption", "Dark
Knight", "Black Swan", "Ip Man", "The Illusionist", "The Silence of the
Lambs", "Winter Solider", "Green Mile", "Se7en"]
```

Your code should now look like this:

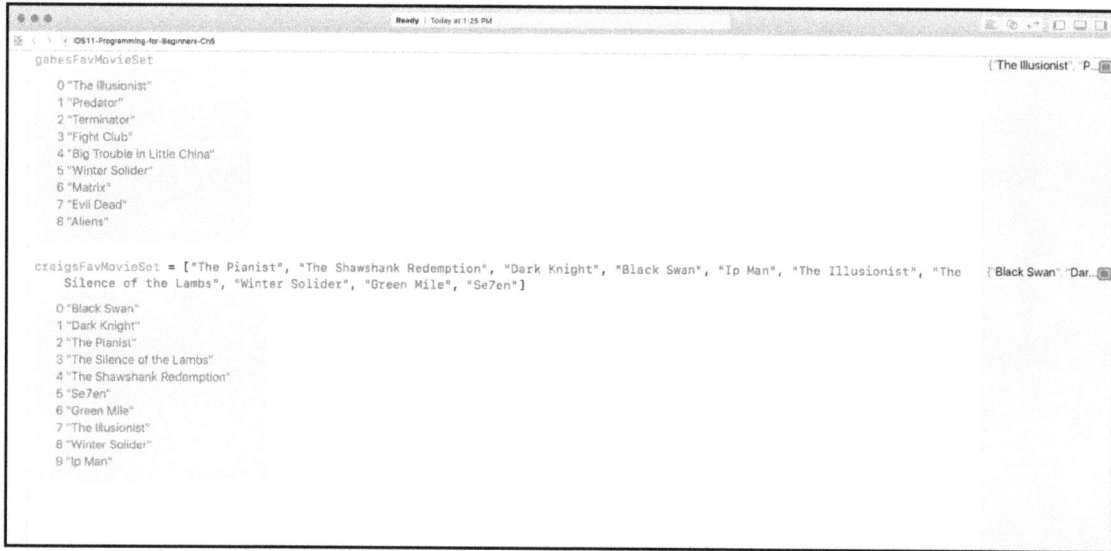

Craig's set now has 10 movies. Next, let's see how we can work with sets.

Checking if a set contains an item

The first thing we can do with sets is to check if a set contains an item. Let's see if Craig's movie list has the movie Green Mile:

```
if craigsFavMovieSet.contains("Green Mile") {
  print("Green Mile found")
}
```

Chapter 5

Your code should now look like this:

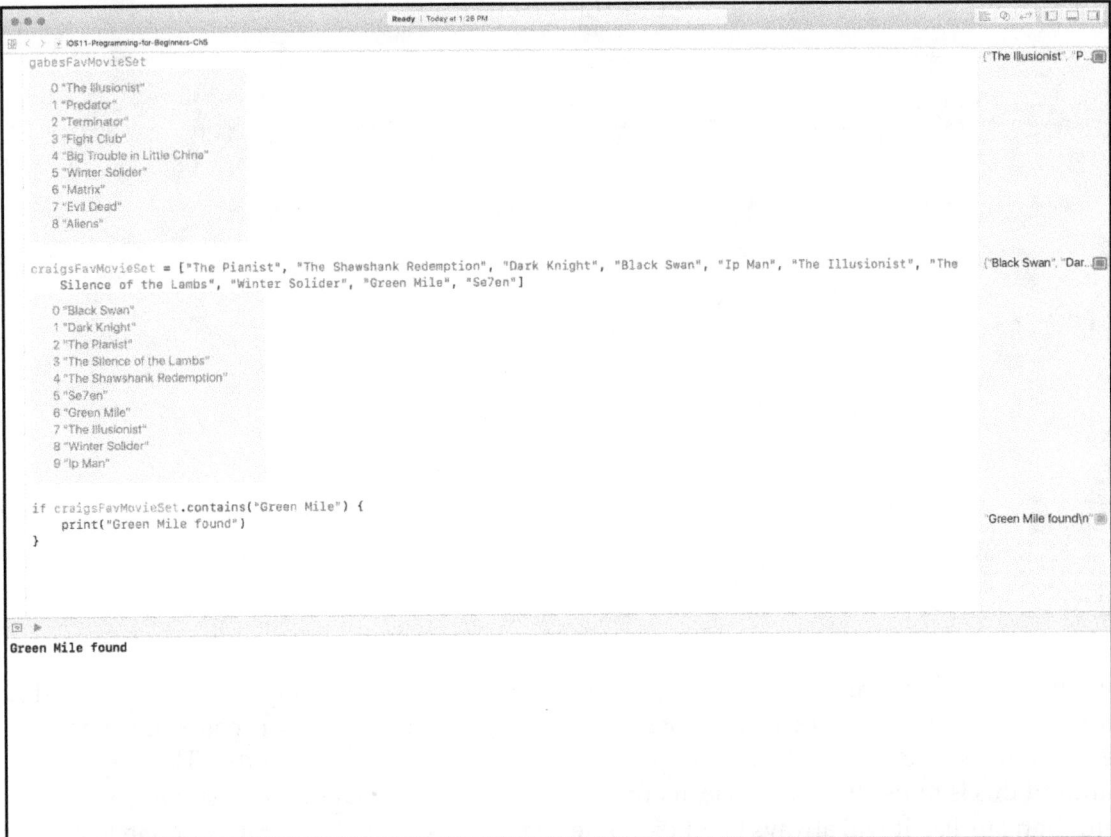

In this preceding example, we used the `contains()` method in order to discover whether an item is in the set.

Iterating over a set

If we want a list of all the movies in Gabe's list, we can use a `for...loop`. Let's see how that works:

```
for movie in gabesFavMovieSet {
  print("Gabe's movie - \(movie)")
}
```

[131]

Digging into Collections

Your code should now look like this:

```
let movieSet = Set<String>()
let numberSet = Set<Int>([])

var craigsFavMovieSet = Set<String>([])
var gabesFavMovieSet = Set<String>(["Fight Club", "Matrix", "Evil Dead", "Big Trouble in Little China", "Aliens", "Winter
    Solider", "The Illusionist", "Predator"])
gabesFavMovieSet.insert("Terminator")
gabesFavMovieSet

craigsFavMovieSet = ["The Pianist", "The Shawshank Redemption", "Dark Knight", "Black Swan", "Ip Man", "The Illusionist", "The
    Silence of the Lambs", "Winter Solider", "Green Mile", "Se7en"]

if craigsFavMovieSet.contains("Green Mile") {
    print("Green Mile found")
}

for movie in gabesFavMovieSet {
    print("Gabe's movie - \(movie)")
}
```

Output:
```
Gabe's movie - The Illusionist
Gabe's movie - Predator
Gabe's movie - Terminator
Gabe's movie - Fight Club
Gabe's movie - Big Trouble in Little China
Gabe's movie - Winter Solider
Gabe's movie - Matrix
Gabe's movie - Evil Dead
Gabe's movie - Aliens
```

Now that we have seen a `for...in` loop for all three collections, arrays, dictionaries, and sets, you can see that there are a lot of similarities. Remember, since sets come unordered, every time we run our `for...in` loop we will get a list in a different order. The way around this is to use the `sorted()` method. This will ensure that every time we loop through our list, it will always be in the same order. Let's do that on Craig's movie list:

```
for movie in craigsFavMovieSet.sorted() {
  print("Craig's movie - \(movie)")
}
```

Your code should now look like this:

```swift
let movieSet = Set<String>()
let numberSet = Set<Int>([])

var craigsFavMovieSet = Set<String>([])
var gabesFavMovieSet = Set<String>(["Fight Club", "Matrix", "Evil Dead", "Big Trouble in Little China", "Aliens", "Winter Solider", "The Illusionist", "Predator"])
gabesFavMovieSet.insert("Terminator")
gabesFavMovieSet

craigsFavMovieSet = ["The Pianist", "The Shawshank Redemption", "Dark Knight", "Black Swan", "Ip Man", "The Illusionist", "The Silence of the Lambs", "Winter Solider", "Green Mile", "Se7en"]

if craigsFavMovieSet.contains("Green Mile") {
    print("Green Mile found")
}

for movie in gabesFavMovieSet {
    print("Gabe's movie - \(movie)")
}

for movie in craigsFavMovieSet.sorted() {
    print("Craig's movie - \(movie)")
}
```

```
Craig's movie - Black Swan
Craig's movie - Dark Knight
Craig's movie - Green Mile
Craig's movie - Ip Man
Craig's movie - Se7en
Craig's movie - The Illusionist
Craig's movie - The Pianist
Craig's movie - The Shawshank Redemption
Craig's movie - The Silence of the Lambs
Craig's movie - Winter Solider
```

Now that we have our set sorted, let's look at the real power of using sets.

Intersecting two sets

In the following diagram, we see that, if we intersect both sets together, we should get a list of any movies they have in common:

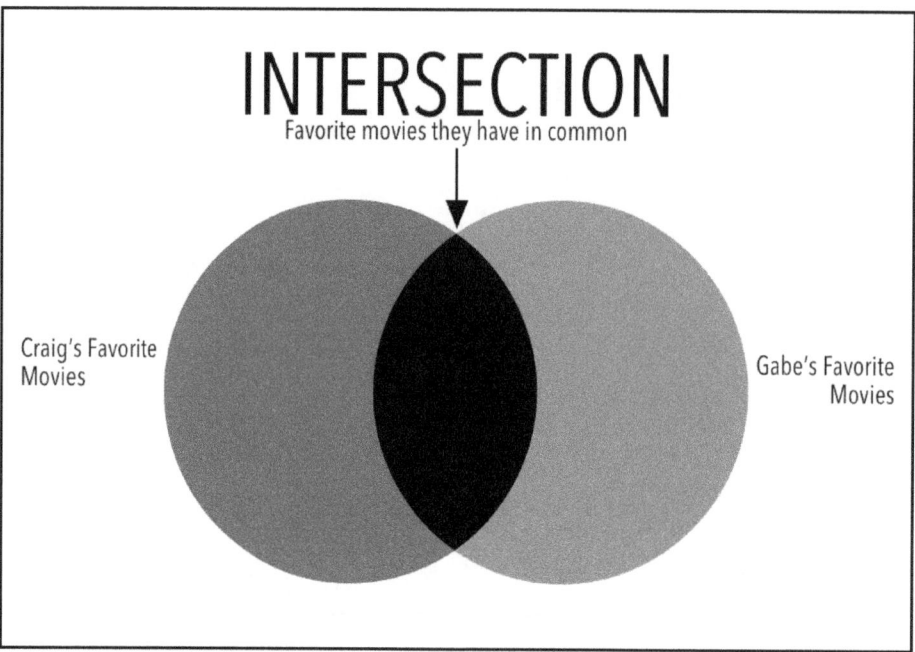

We can do the same using the `intersection()` method in our code. Let's intersect both movie lists and see what happens:

```
craigsFavMovieSet.intersection(gabesFavMovieSet)
```

Your code and output should now look like this:

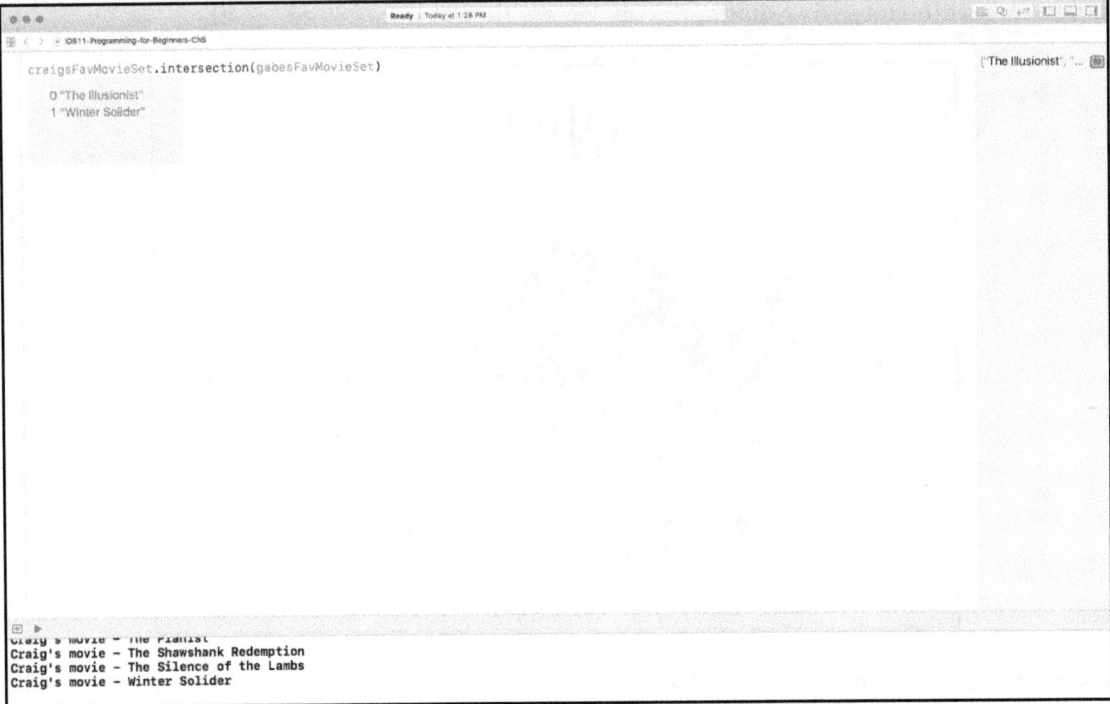

We can see that the only two movies these sets have in common are *Winter Solider* and *The Illusionist*. In addition to seeing which movies the two sets have in common, we also can join the lists to get one consolidated list of the movies from both sets.

Joining two sets

If you look at the following diagram, you can see the two sets joined together:

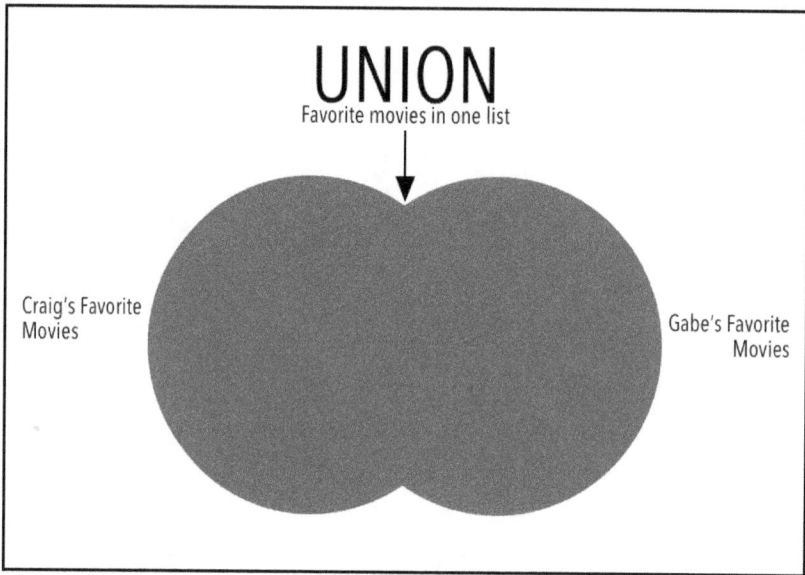

Using the `union()` method, we get a consolidated list of items with no duplicates. Let's try this in Playgrounds:

```
craigsFavMovieSet.union(gabesFavMovieSet)
```

Your code should now look like this:

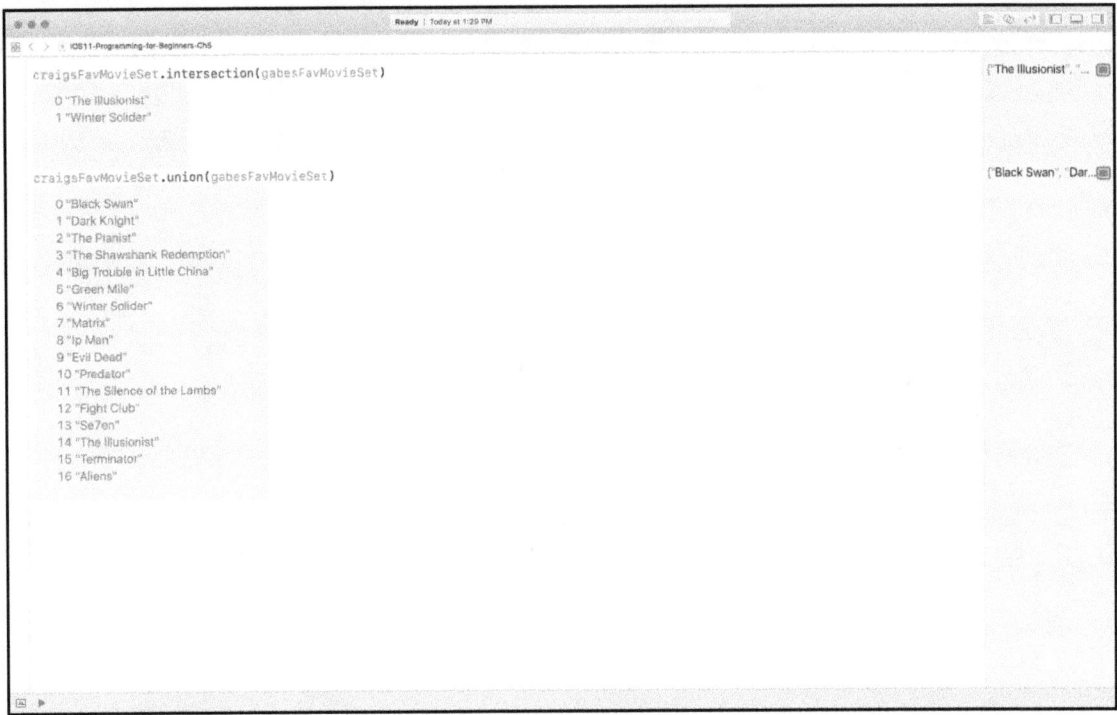

We have a combined list of movies that includes all the movies that the two sets did not have in common and the two movies that were in common, but only listed once. As you can see, sets are really powerful and you can use them to manipulate data. Finally, we need to look at how you can remove items from a set.

Removing items from a set

In order to remove an item from a set, we can use the `remove()` method. When we use this method, we just input the item we want to remove in the parentheses. Let's remove *Winter Solider* from Craig's movie list:

```
craigsFavMovieSet.remove("Winter Solider")
```

Digging into Collections

Your code should now look like this:

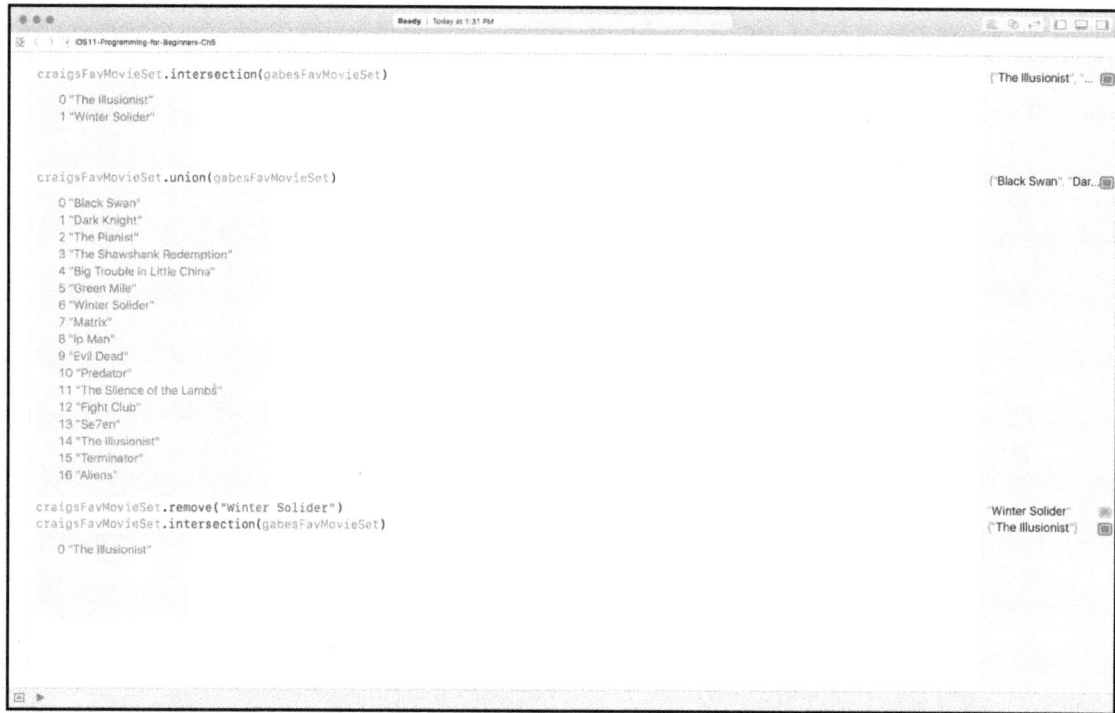

If you wanted to remove more than a single item from a set (for instance, all of the items), then you can use the `removeAll()` method or give it an empty array literal:

```
craigsFavMovieSet.removeAll()
gabesFavMovieSet = []
```

Your code should now look like this:

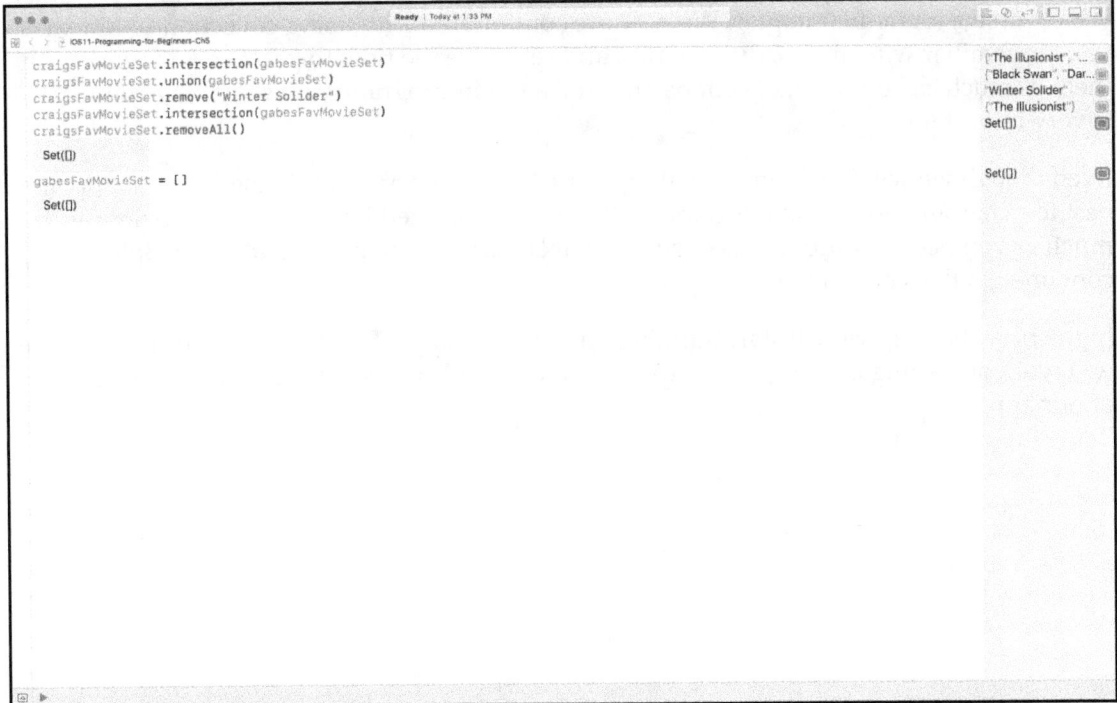

Now, both sets are empty.

Summary

We covered a lot in this chapter. We now are comfortable with using collections. Now that you are familiar with arrays, dictionaries, and sets, take the time to practice and work with them as much as you can. Collections are used a ton in programming so getting comfortable is very important.

Even though we will touch on these things throughout the creation of the *Let's Eat* app, it is best to make sure you are comfortable with what we covered here. So, please review as much as you need in order to make sure you feel that you are proficient in the topics contained in this chapter.

In the next chapter, we will start building our *Let's Eat* app. Over the next two chapters, we will work on getting our project set up and then we will start working on the visual aspects of our app.

6
Starting the UI Setup

Now that you have learned Swift, which will help you to understand a lot of the boilerplate code you will see later, it is time to start building our *Let's Eat* app. Let's begin by getting an overview of what we are going to build. We will review the finished product and then get into how to build this app. Before we start, there will be a lot of new terms and things with which you may or may not be familiar. Learn as much as you can and do not let the finer details stop you from progressing.

We will cover the following topics in this chapter:

- Useful terms
- App tour
- Project setup
- Storyboards
- Creating a custom title view

Useful terms

Before we dig in and start getting our UI set up, we need to take a few minutes to introduce (or re-introduce) you to some terms that you should understand while we build our app:

- View Controller
- Table View Controller
- Collection View Controller
- Navigation Controller
- Tab Bar Controller
- Storyboard
- Segue
- Auto layout
- **Model View Controller (MVC)**

View Controller

View Controllers (`UIViewControllers`) are blank scenes that you can use to hold other UI elements. They give you the ability to create a custom interface.

Table View Controller

A Table View Controller (`UITableViewController`), which inherits from `UIViewController`, is one of the most common UI elements and is used to display a list of items. For example, Apple's Settings screen uses Table View Controller to display the list of settings a user can access and change:

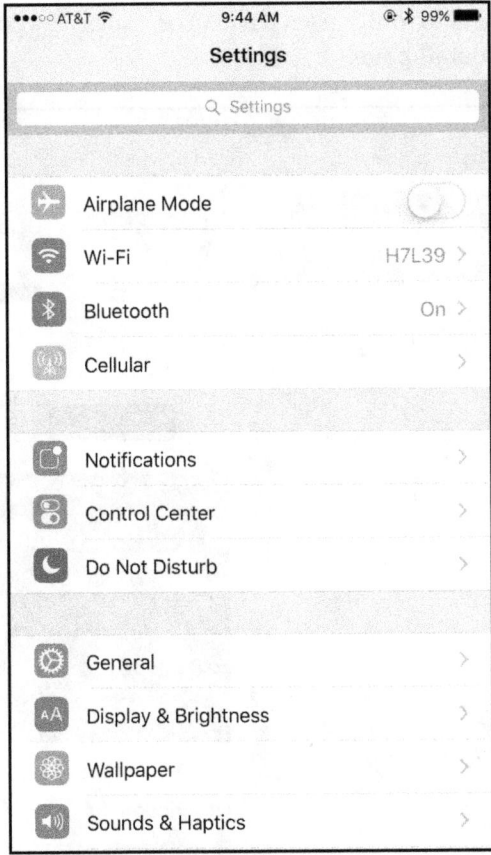

Collection View Controller

Collection View Controllers (`UICollectionViewControllers`) are typically used when you want to display elements within a grid. They are highly customizable and, because of that, are becoming more popular in non-grid based layouts.

Starting the UI Setup

The App Store, for example, currently uses `UICollectionViewControllers` for both its featured page and its app detail page:

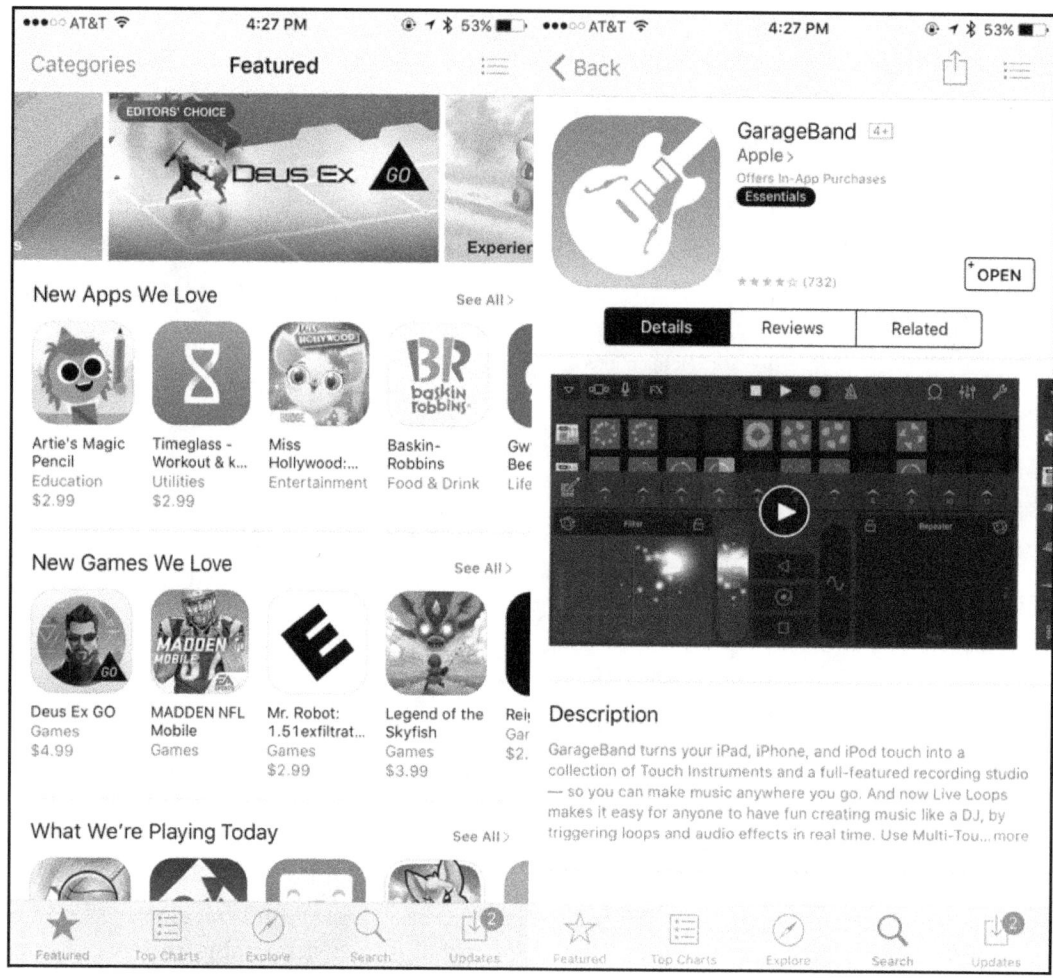

Navigation Controller

A Navigation Controller (`UINavigationController`) is a UI element that allows you to build a drill-down interface for hierarchical content. When you embed a Navigation Controller into a View Controller, Table View Controller, or Collection View Controller, it manages navigation from one controller to another controller.

Chapter 6

Tab Bar Controller

The Tab Bar Controller (`UITabBarController`) manages an array of View Controllers. Our *Let's Eat* app will use a Tab Bar Controller. This controller will give us the ability to have navigation for our app with minimal setup.

Apple has a few apps with which you might be familiar that use the Tab Bar Controller:

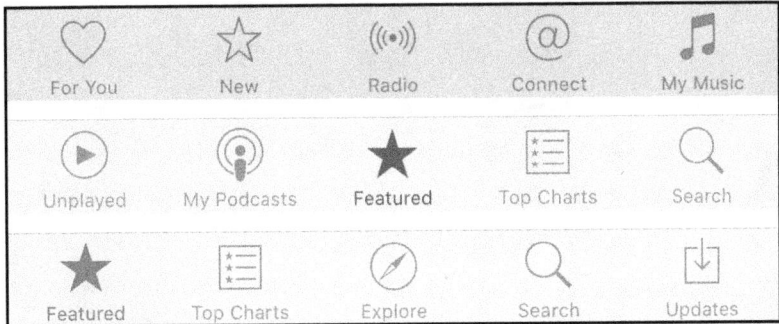

A `UITabBarController` can only have five tabs on the iPhone. If your `UITabBarController` has more than five tabs on the iPhone, the fifth tab and any after that move underneath a **More** button:

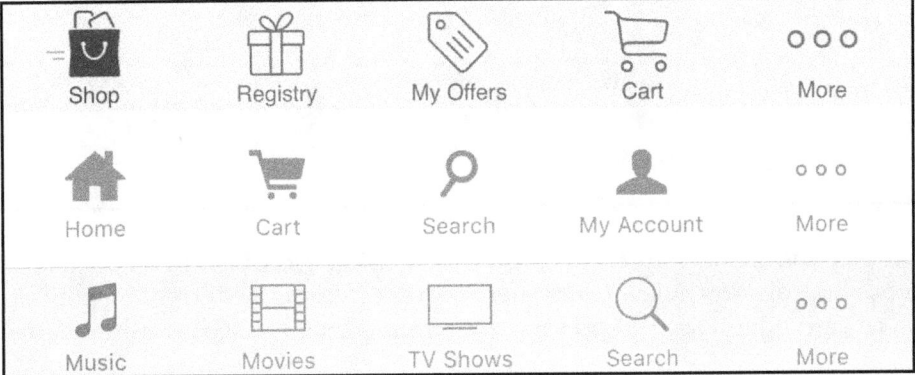

Starting the UI Setup

Storyboard

A storyboard is a file displays a visual representation of your app's UI. This is what a storyboard looks like for an app:

Storyboards let you create your entire app visually using View Controllers, Table View Controllers, and Collection View Controllers as scenes. Along with creating your app visually, you can connect scenes and set up transitions between scenes using segues.

Segue

Segues are used to connect one controller to another controller. In the storyboard, segues are represented by an arrow with an icon:

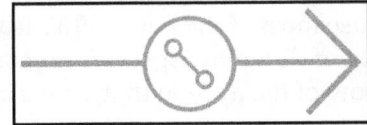

Segues also give you the ability to specify a transition from one scene to another, with very little to no programming.

Auto Layout

Auto layout is an excellent tool that allows you to support different screen sizes and device rotation. With auto layout, you can set different constraints on UI elements for it to adjust to changes in size and rotation. Using auto layout in your app allows you to use one storyboard for all devices.

Model View Controller (MVC)

MVC is a standard software design pattern, which is a solution for commonly occurring problems within software design. Apple has built iOS apps on the MVC design pattern. This pattern divides our app into three camps known as the Model, View, and Controller. We will cover this in detail later in this book.

Starting the UI Setup

App tour

The *Let's Eat* app that we are building is a restaurant reservation app that allows users to find restaurants in a specific area and create reservations from within the app (although our app does not book those reservations). I chose a restaurant reservation app for the purposes of the lessons in this book, because most of the new iOS 11 features work well together in such an app. The app covers a lot of different aspects from maps to iMessage extensions. Let's take a look at the overall flow of the app, so that, as we build, you have a good idea of the direction we are heading in:

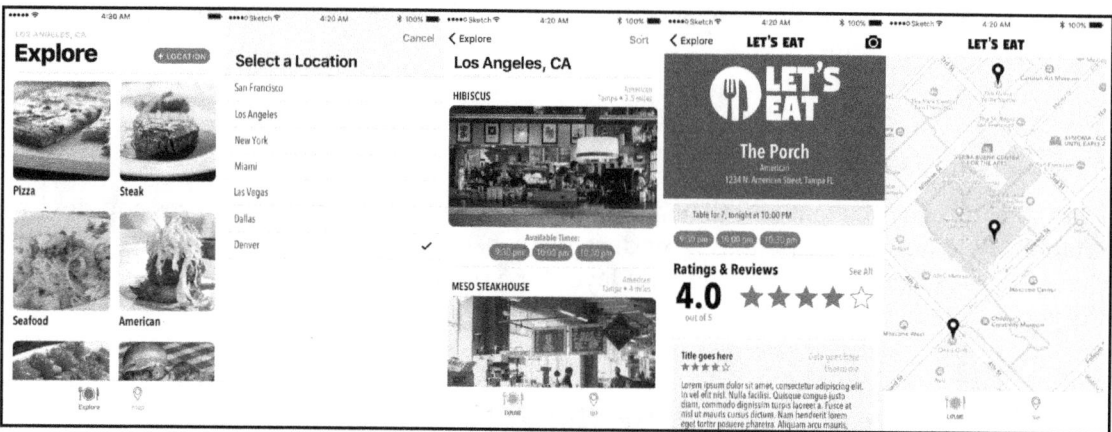

Explore tab

When the app launches, you will see the **Explore** tab. This tab will allow users to pick a particular cuisine that they would like and to select a specific predefined location. Let's break down each component in this view:

Chapter 6

For this screen, we will work with an empty View Controller, which is where all of our UI components live. As you can see, this view in our app is designed to be a grid, so we will be using a Collection View Controller. We will be setting up this Collection View Controller ourselves.

When I build apps, I typically start with a blank Collection View or Table View, because it gives more flexibility in my code as well as with my user interface.

Locations

The Locations view is a list of cities that is accessed from the **Explore** tab. We load this list of cities from a local file-and, if the user selects a city, the app loads all of the restaurants from that area:

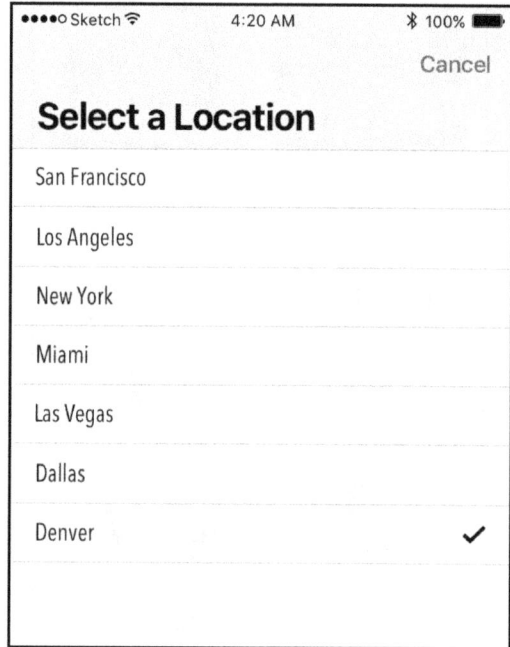

For this Locations view, we will be working with a View Controller that uses a Table View.

Restaurant listings

In Restaurant listings, we see restaurants in the area by the selected cuisine:

We will be covering both `UICollectionViews` and `UITableViews` in this book, but, as an introduction, you should know that `UICollectionViews` are very powerful. The reason they are powerful is that you can customize them to look how you want. For example, the App Store detail is a custom `UICollectionView`.

One great feature when using `UICollectionView` is that, when you are building a universal app like this one, you can make your view look like a list for the iPhone, but appear as a grid on the iPad with minimal effort.

Starting the UI Setup

Restaurant detail

Our Restaurant detail has more information about the restaurant. This view is built using a `UITableView` that uses static cells:

Chapter 6

Map tab

Our **Map** tab is a View Controller with a map that has pins dropped on it from a specific location, denoting all of the restaurants in the area:

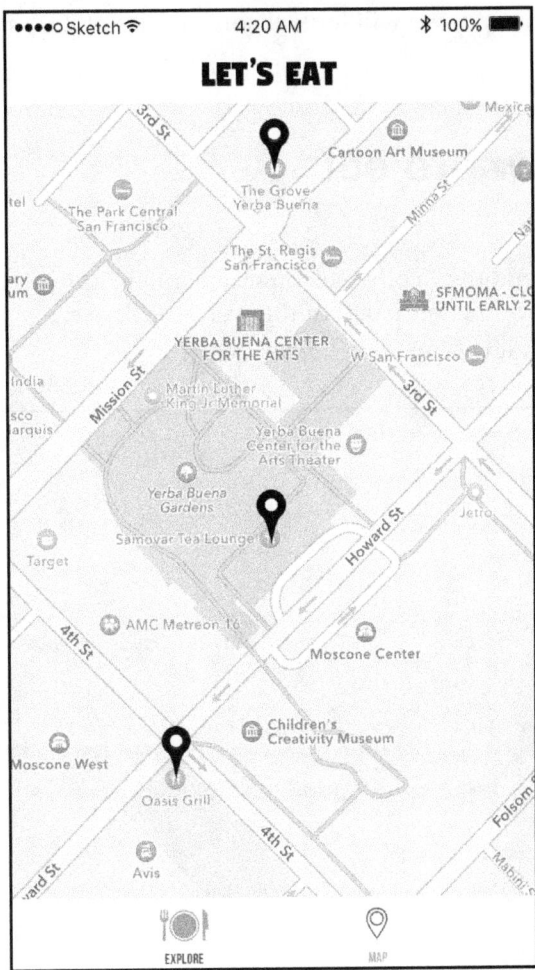

[153]

Starting the UI Setup

Project setup

Now that we have gotten a tour of the app, we are going to build the *Let's Eat* app. First, we need to create the app, then work on the UI and lastly, design our app in a storyboard.

For the initial setup of the app, we will look at some basics of iOS, starting with creating a new project.

Creating a new project

To create a new project:

1. Open Xcode, and the Xcode welcome screen will appear. Click on **Create a new Xcode project** in the left panel of the welcome screen.
2. Select **Single View App** and click on **Next**:

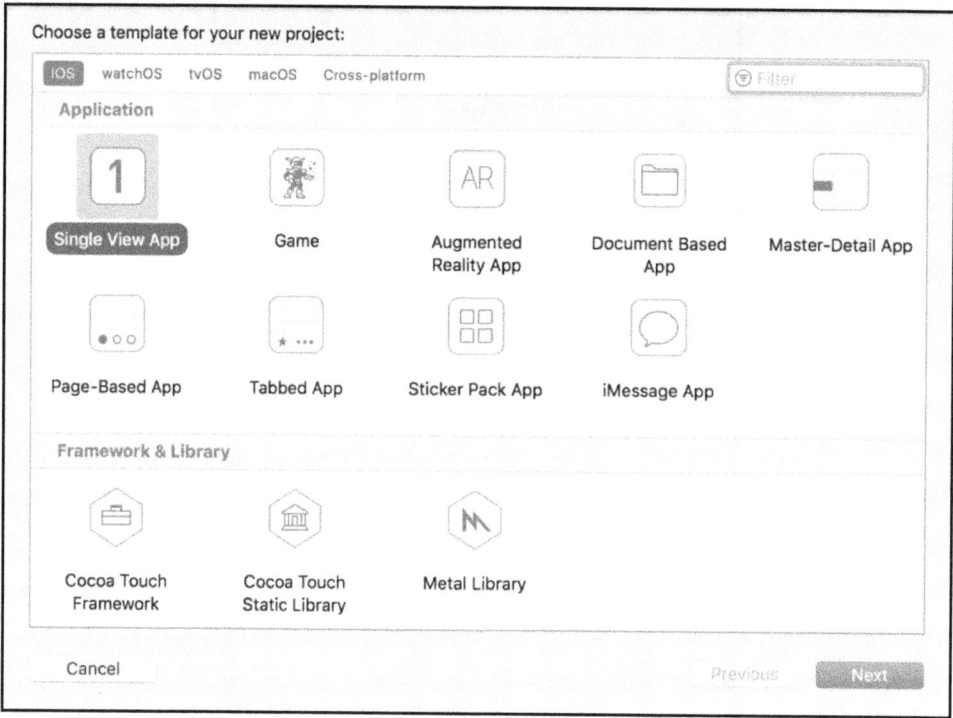

Chapter 6

3. In the options screen that will appear, there will be a number of items to complete or choose. Add the following into that options screen and then hit **Next**:

- **Product Name**: LetsEat
- **Team**: Your account or leave blank
- **Organization Name**: Your name/company name
- **Organization Identifier**: Your domain name in reverse order
- **Language**: Swift
- **Devices**: Universal
- **Use Core Data**: Unchecked
- **Include Unit Tests**: Unchecked
- **Include UI Tests**: Unchecked

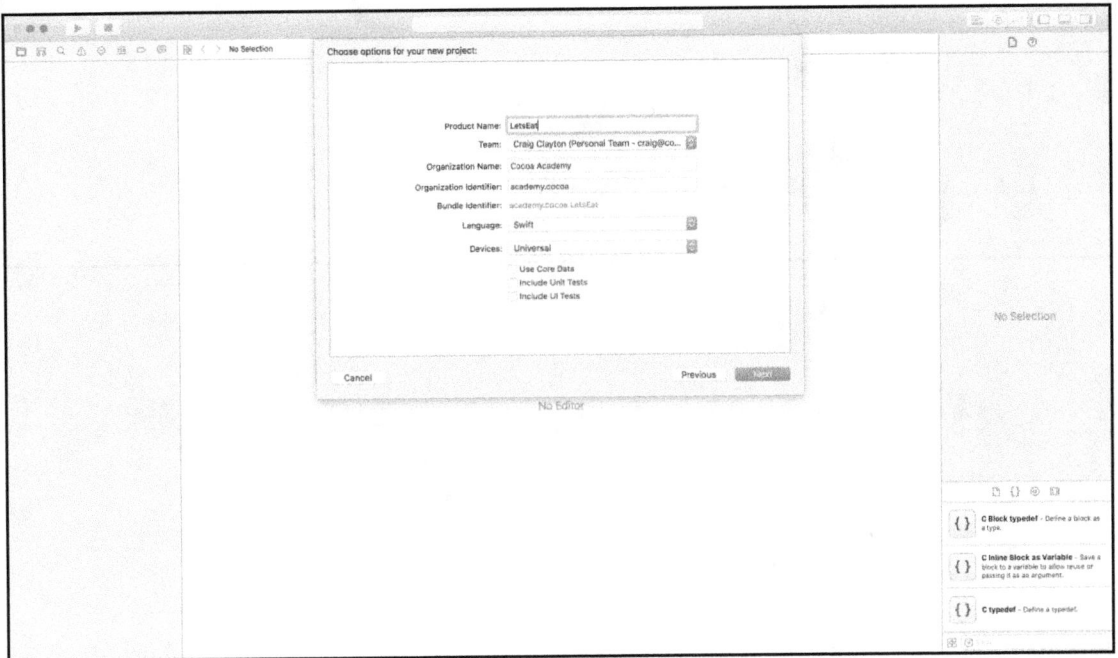

Starting the UI Setup

4. Choose your desktop or a folder in which to save your project and then hit **Create**:

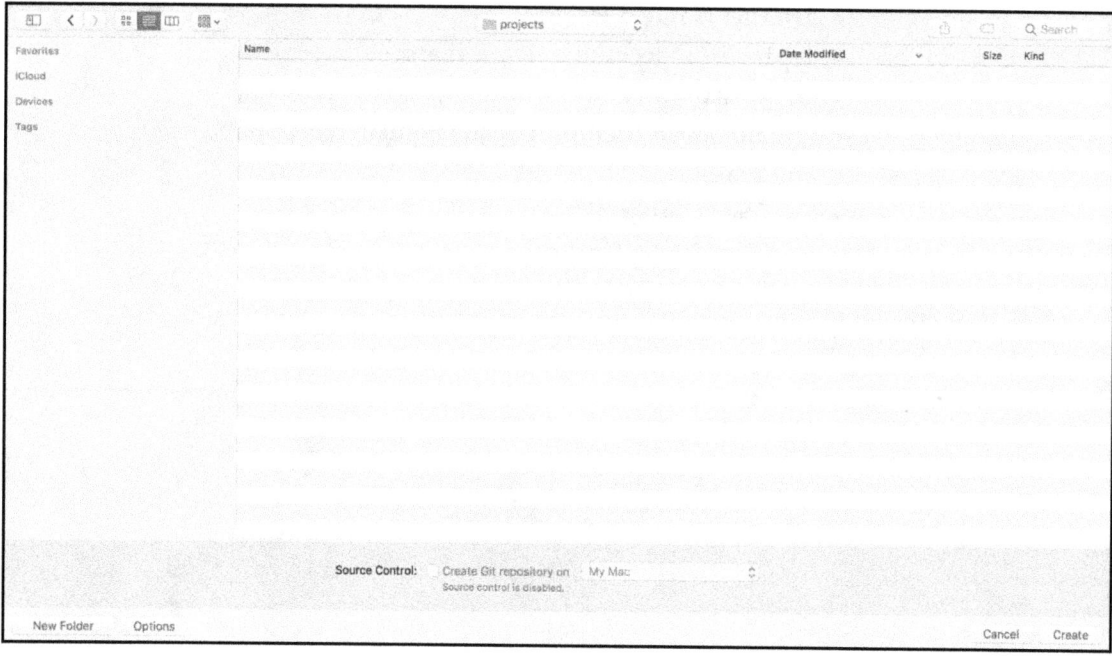

Chapter 6

5. After you save, you will be presented with the following screen:

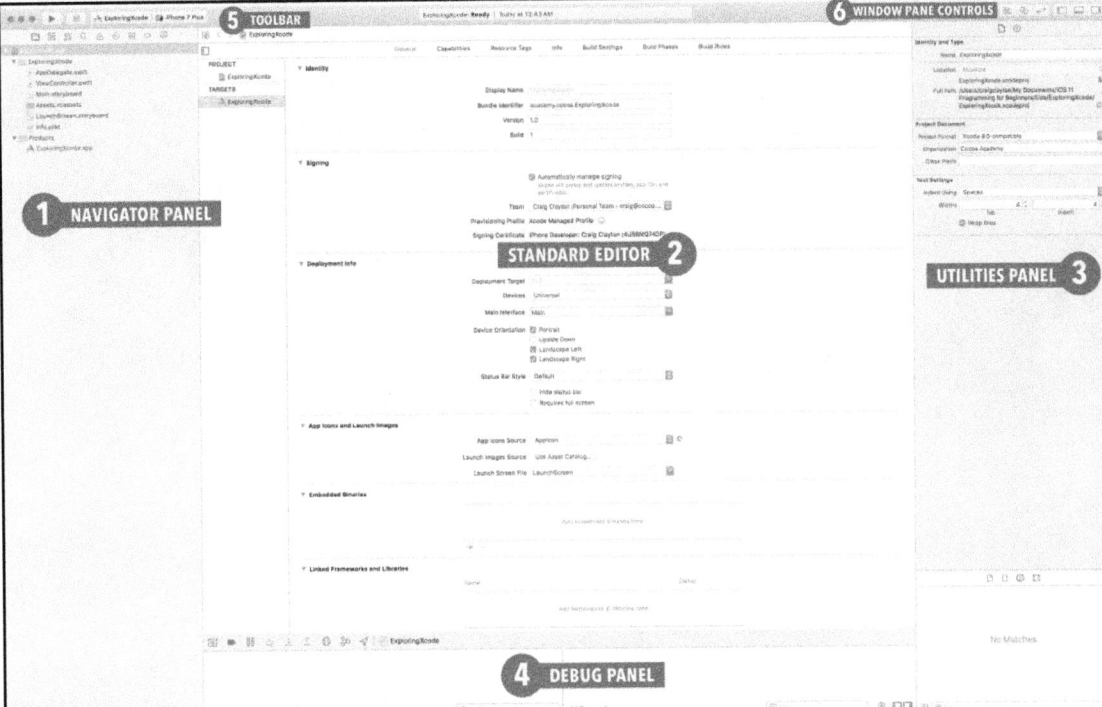

Your project is now created and we can start working on creating our first iOS app.

Summary

In this chapter, we covered useful terms that we will use throughout the book. We also looked at what we are going to build throughout the app and now we have a good idea of what the app will look like.

Next, let's dig in and start working inside of storyboard and getting the UI of the application set up. In the next few chapters, we will work strictly in the storyboard to get our app set up. Once we have everything set up, we will focus on code throughout the rest of the book.

7
Setting Up the Basic Structure

Typically, before I write any code when working on a project, I like to set up my storyboard. This allows me to focus on coding without having to go back and forth from storyboard to code. In this book, we will do some of our layout in code in order to show you how to do that. But first, as I mentioned earlier, my preference is to set up as much as I can inside of storyboard.

The following will be covered in this chapter:

- Creating a Tab Bar Controller
- Tab bar buttons
- Launch screens
- Navigation controllers

In the last chapter, we created our project, and now we are going to continue with that by creating a Tab Bar Controller from scratch. Although there is a Tab Bar Controller template that has everything you need, I find that starting from scratch is an excellent way to learn. Also, I find that it is easier to start to clean, rather than fix or update the template. However, you may want to utilize the template to begin your project in the future. Let's start setting up our app.

Starting from scratch

We will be creating all of our files from scratch, so we will delete the existing files in our project and recreate them in proceeding chapters. The reason for this is so you can become comfortable with a project and understand how it was set up.

Setting Up the Basic Structure

To delete the `ViewController.swift` file, you do the following:

1. Select the `ViewController.swift` file in the Navigator panel:

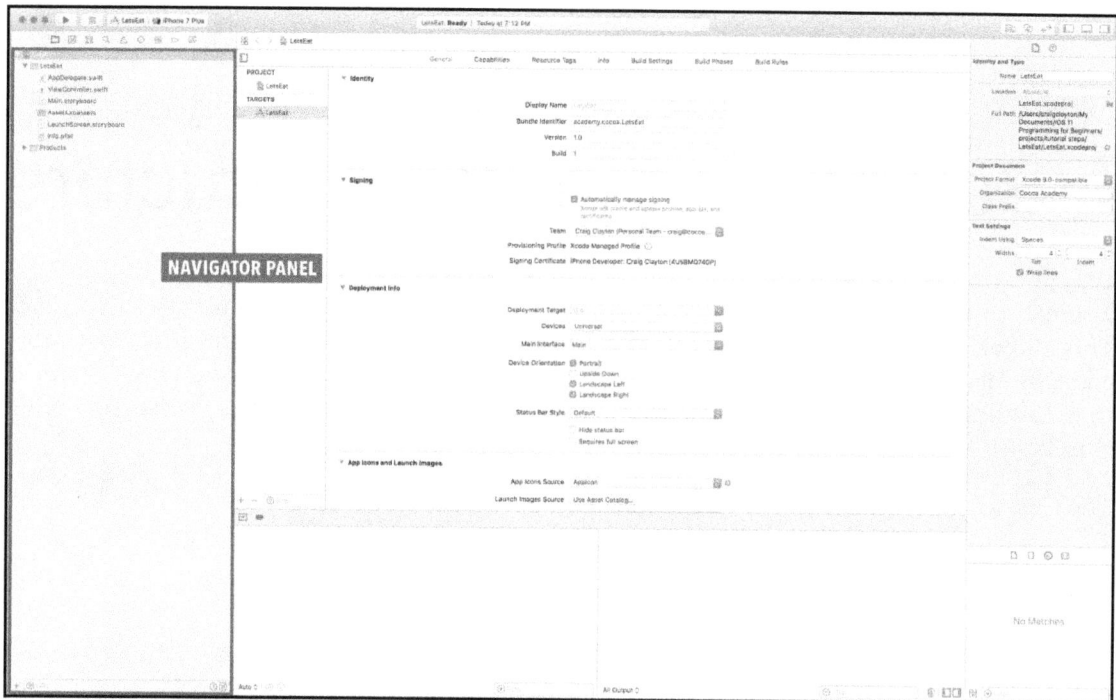

2. With the file selected, hit the *Delete/Backspace* key. You will get the following message:

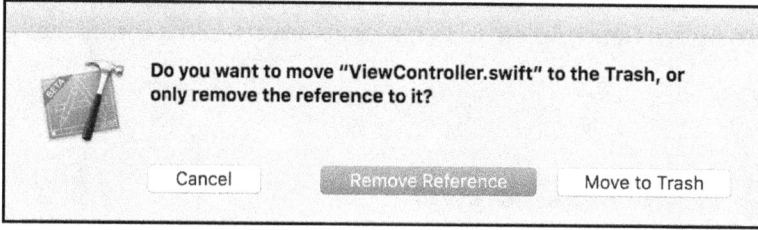

[160]

Chapter 7

3. Select **Move to Trash**.

Now we can continue to the setup of the storyboard.

Storyboard setup

Let's get familiar with the UI setup. In order to update your `Main.storyboard`, do the following:

1. Select the `Main.storyboard` file in the Navigator panel:

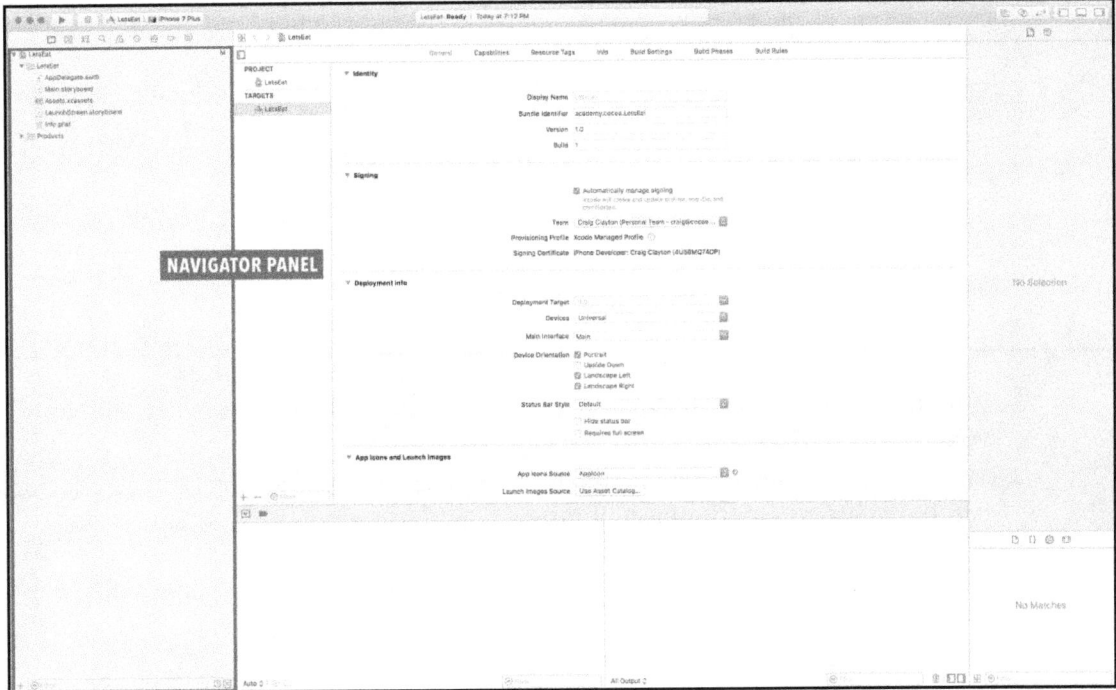

Setting Up the Basic Structure

2. In this storyboard file, select **View Controller scene** in the Outline view:

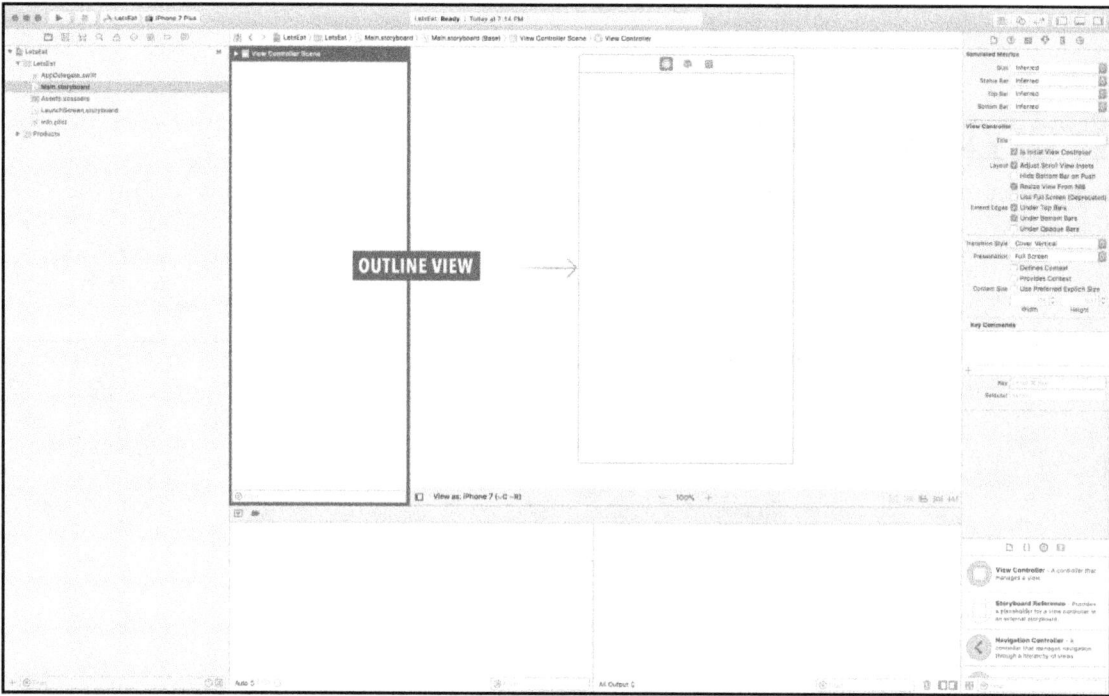

3. With the scene selected, you are going to press the *Delete/Backspace* key, and now your `Main.storyboard` file will be empty.
4. Then, in your Utilities panel, in the bottom pane, you will see the Library selector bar. In the bar, select the object library:

Chapter 7

5. Next, you should pull up on the Library selector bar in order to view more of the object library:

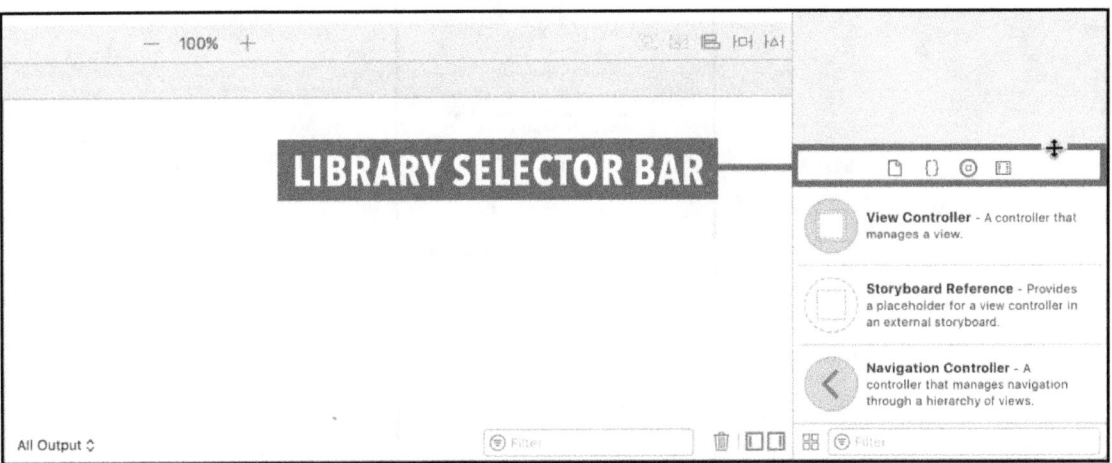

[163]

Setting Up the Basic Structure

6. Find the **Tab Bar Controller**:

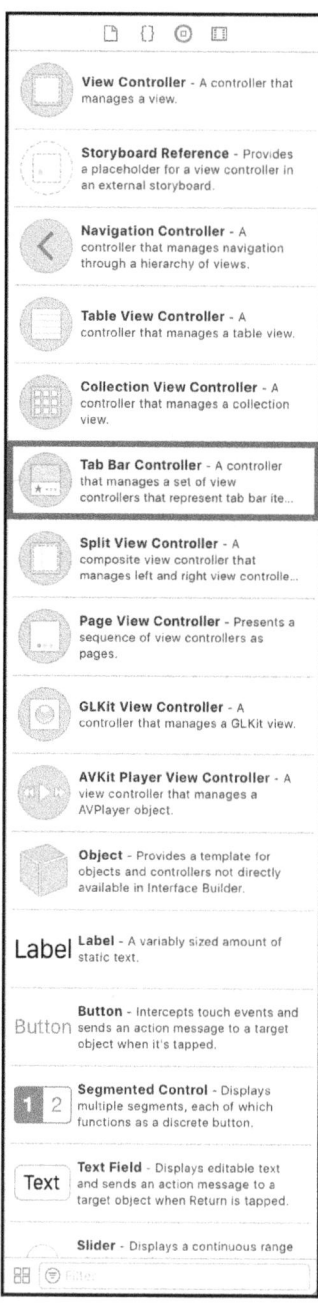

Chapter 7

7. Now, drag the **Tab Bar Controller** out onto the canvas:

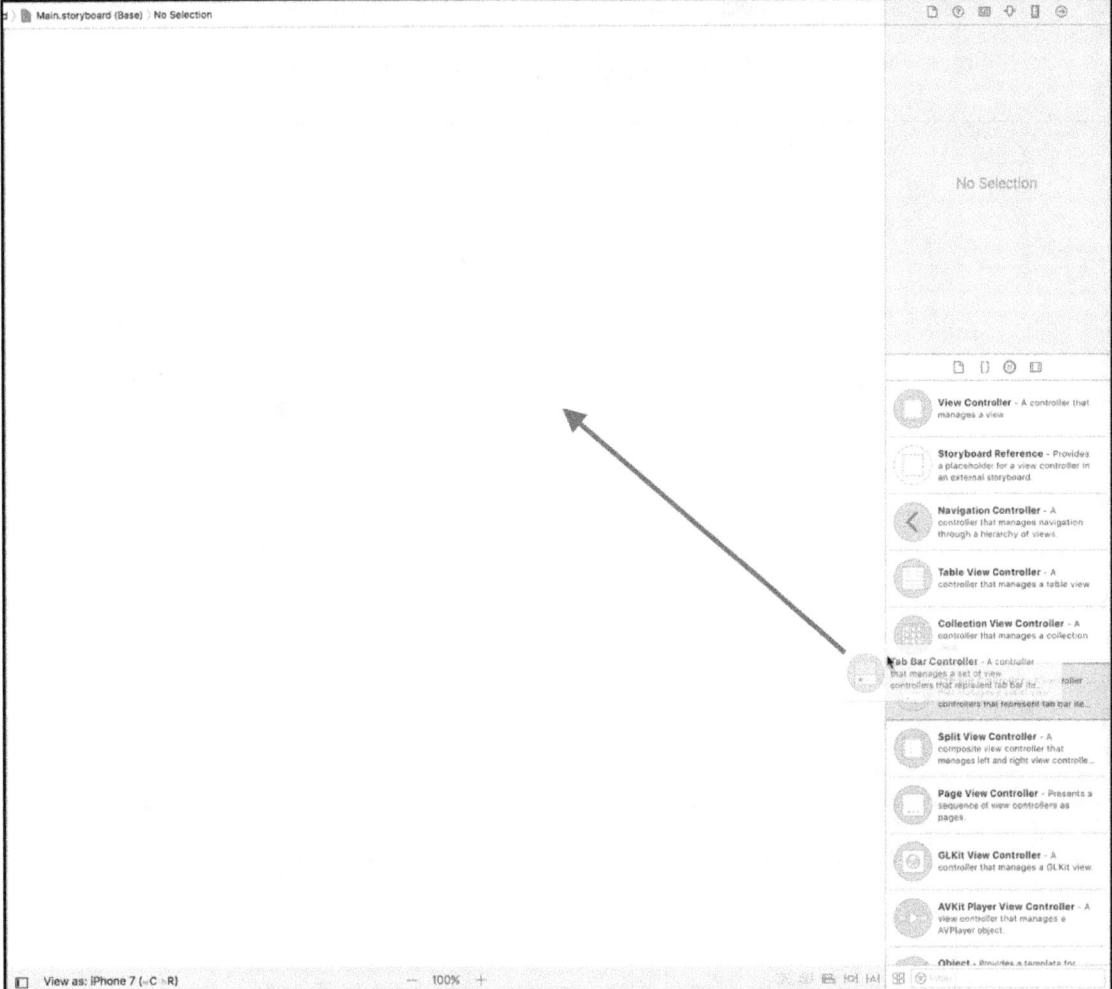

We now have our **Tab Bar Controller**, which will only have two tabs.

Next, we will get our app assets set up so that we can give our tabs image icons.

[165]

Setting Up the Basic Structure

Adding our app assets

Let's add images into our project:

1. Select the `Assets.xcassets` folder in the Navigator panel:

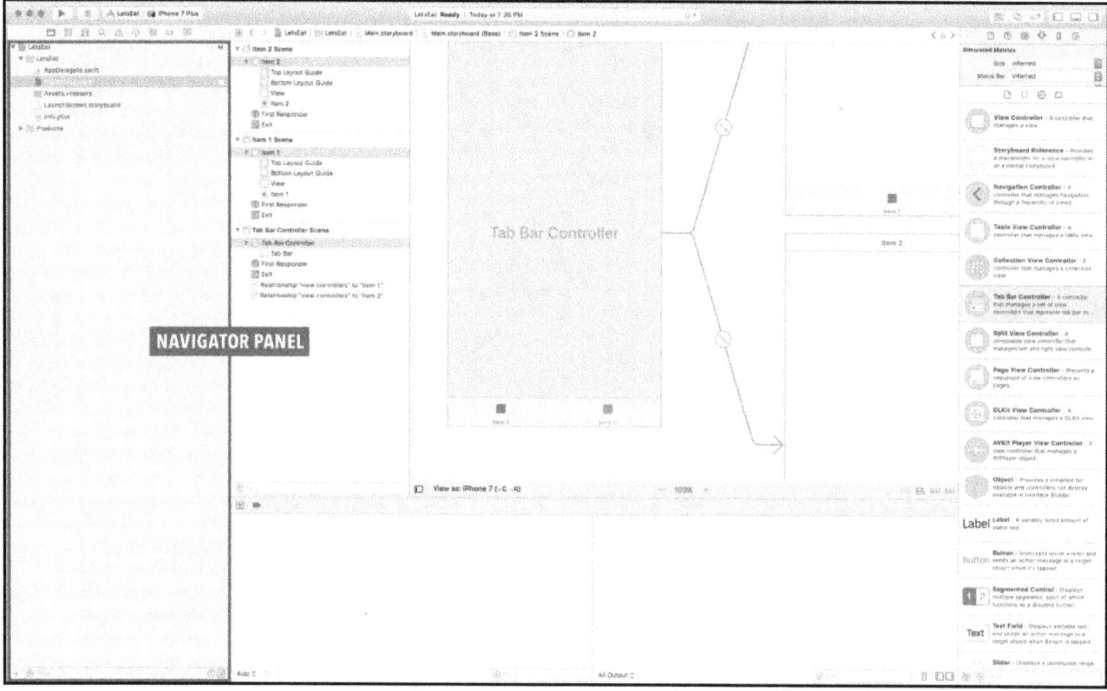

2. Hit the *Delete/Backspace* button, and you will get the following message:

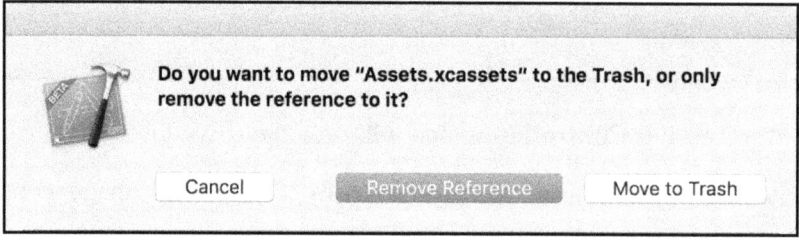

3. Select **Move to Trash**.

Chapter 7

4. Open the project `assets` folder that you downloaded from Packt's website or GitHub. Open `Chapter_07`. Drag the `Assets.xcassets` folder into your project in the Navigator panel:

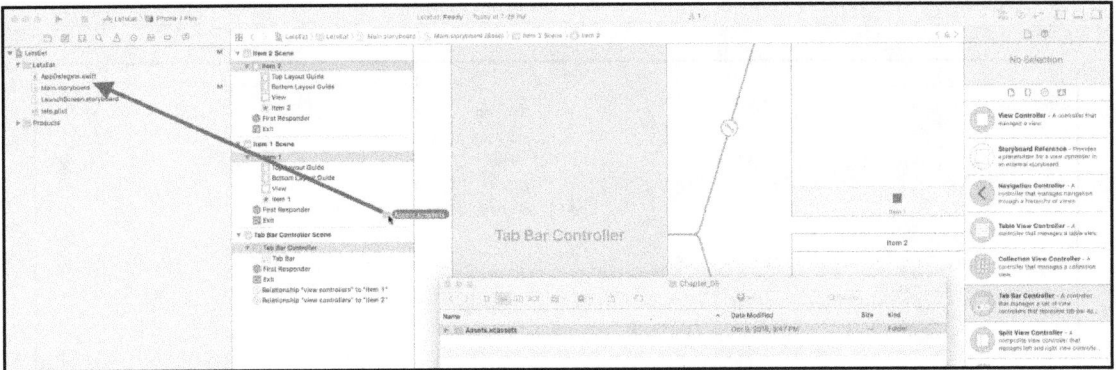

5. When you drop the folder, you will get the following message:

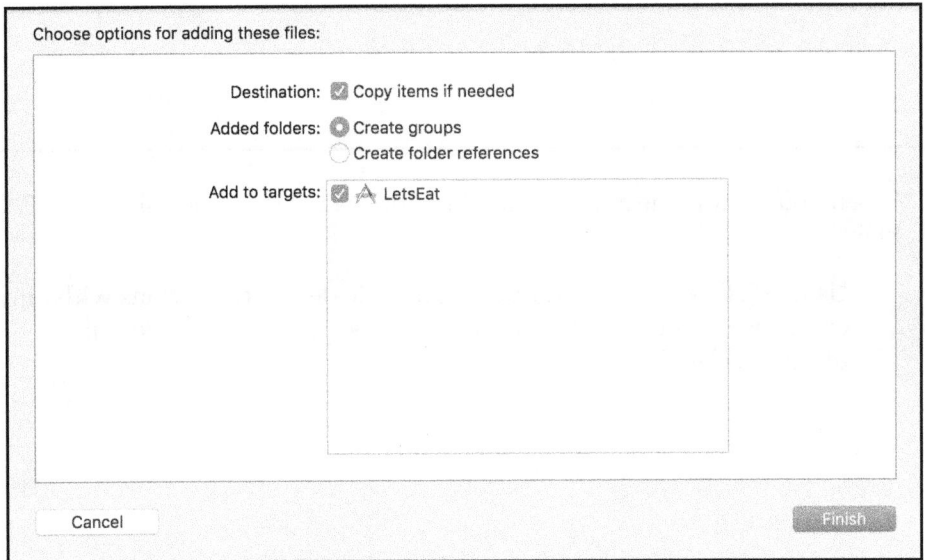

[167]

Setting Up the Basic Structure

6. Make sure that both **Copy items if needed** and **Create groups** are selected. Then, hit **Finish**.

   If you open the `Assets.xcassets` folder, you will now see all the assets for your entire project:

   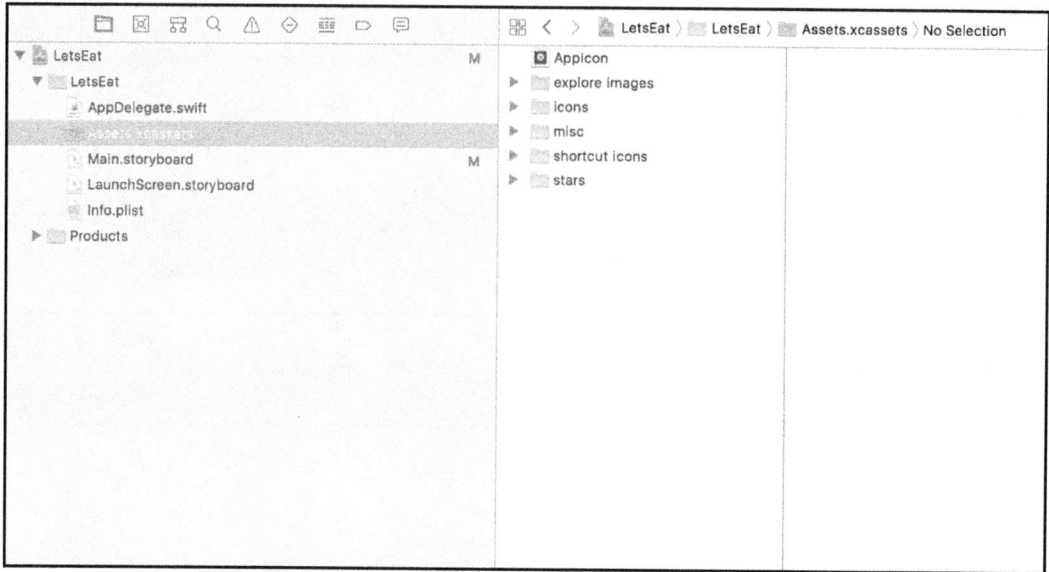

   When you explore the assets, you will notice that we will be using both PNGs and PDFs.

    Using PDFs allows us to support multiple device resolutions with only one image. Therefore, Xcode can handle supplying assets for all resolutions.

Chapter 7

7. Select `Main.storyboard` again, and, in the Outline view, you will select both disclosure arrows for `Item 1 Scene` and `Item 2 Scene`, in order to have them face downwards:

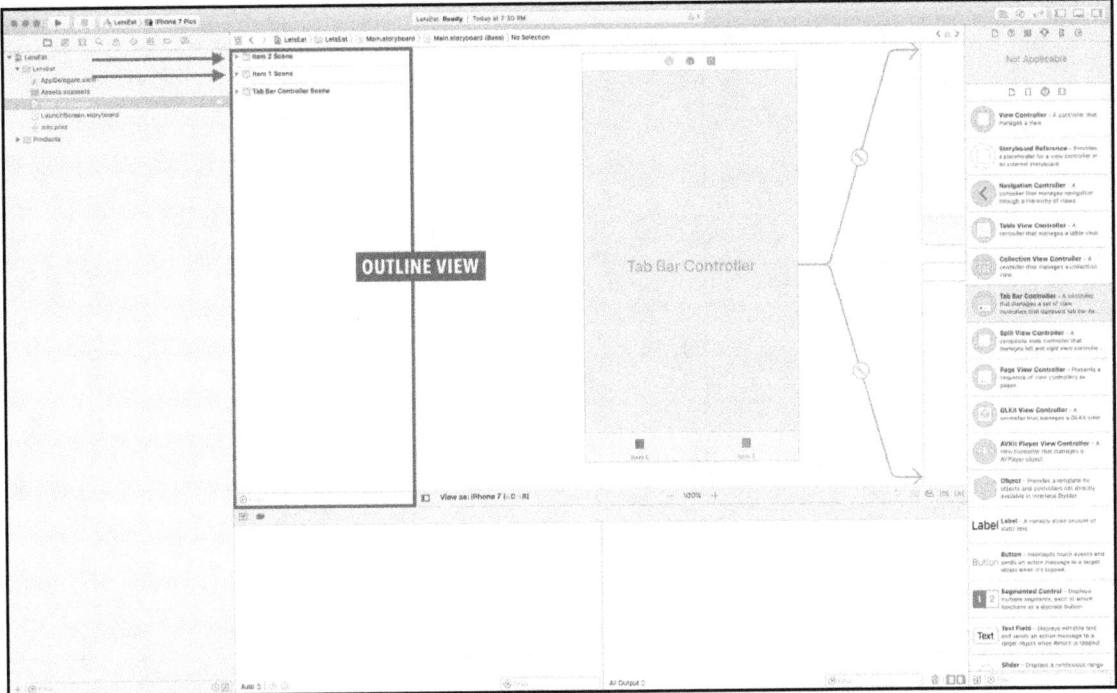

Setting Up the Basic Structure

8. Now, select both disclosure arrows for **Item 1** under `Item 1 Scene` and **Item 2** under `Item 2 Scene`. Both should be downward-facing:

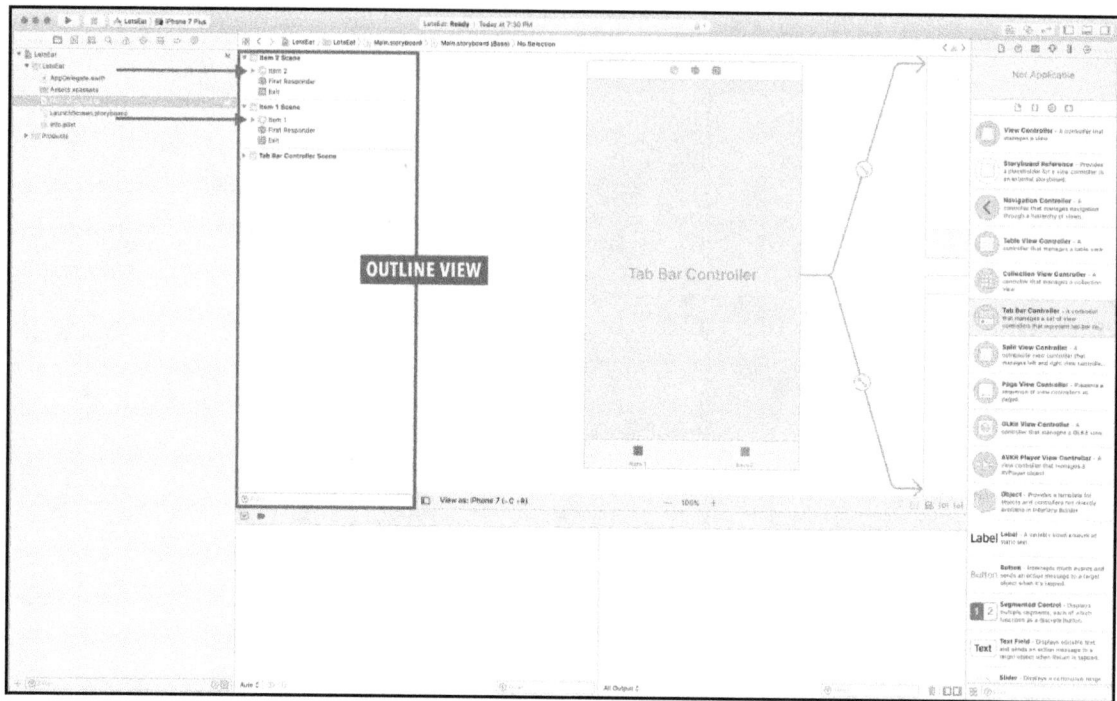

9. Select **Item 1** with the blue star to the left of it, and then select the Attributes inspector in the Utilities panel:

[170]

Chapter 7

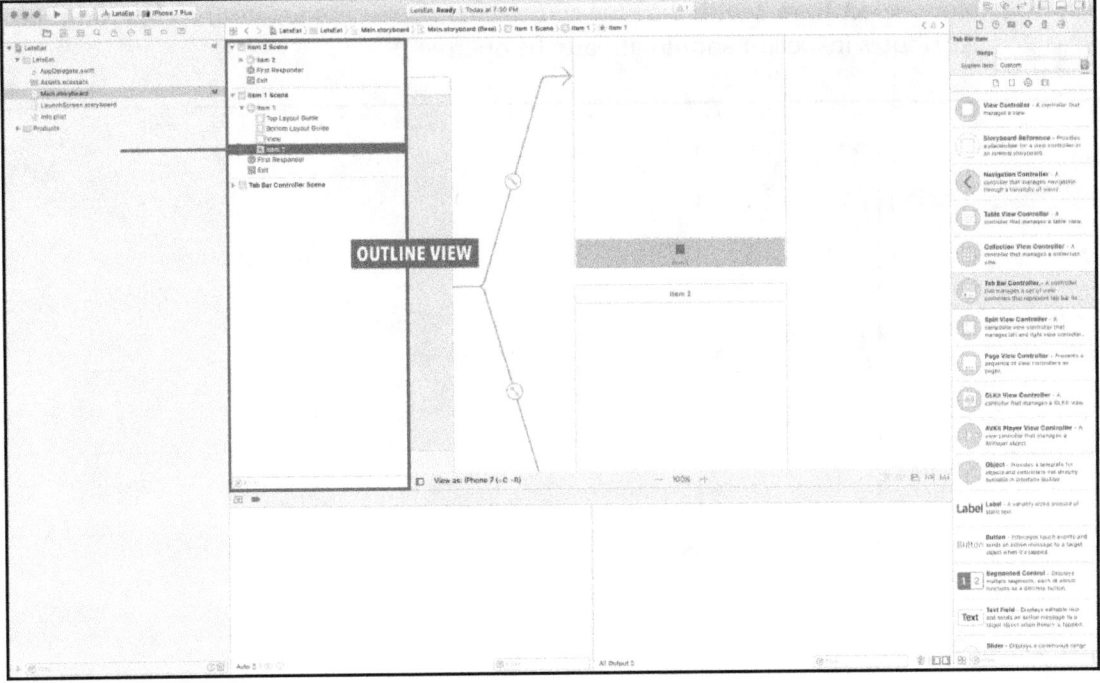

10. In the panel, use the following values to update your first tab icons:

    - In the **Tab Bar Item**, enter the following details:
        - **Badge:** Leave this field blank
        - **System Item:** Select **Custom** from the dropdown list
        - **Selected Image:** icon-explore-on
        - **Title Position:** Select **Default Position** from the dropdown list

    - In the **Bar Item**, enter the following details:
        - **Title:** Type Explore in this field
        - **Image:** icon-explore-off
        - **Tag:** Enter 0 in this field
        - **Enabled:** This checkbox should be checked

Setting Up the Basic Structure

11. Now, select **Item 2** with the blue star to the left of it in the Outline view, and the Attributes inspector should already be open:

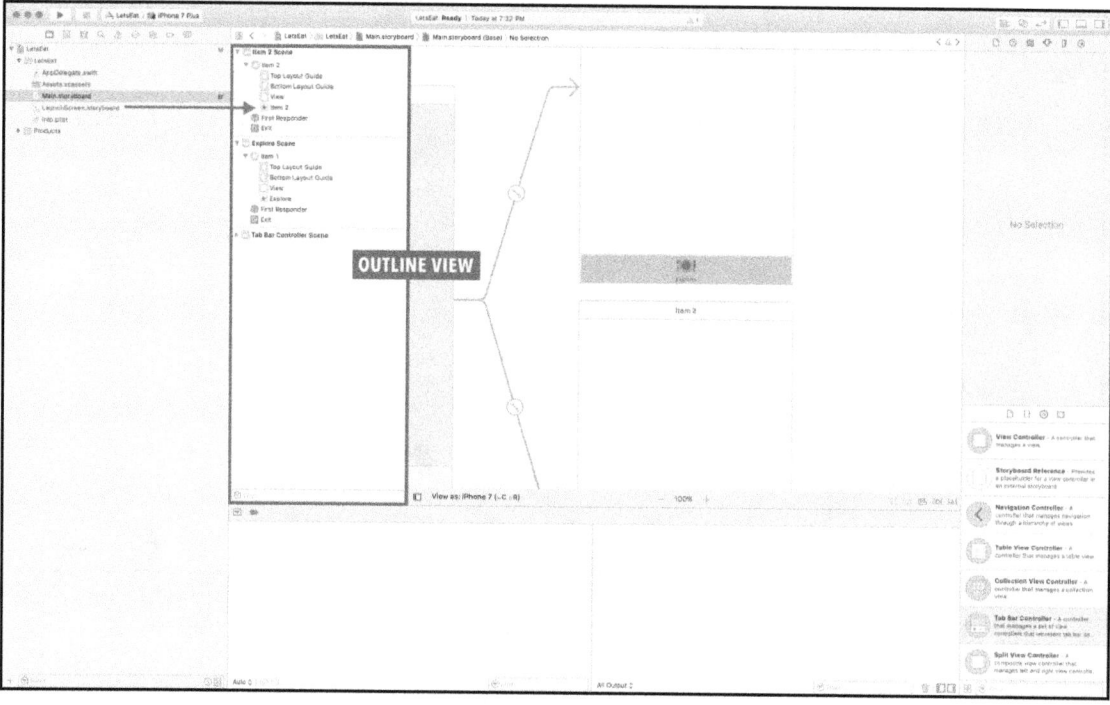

12. Add the following into the panel:

    - In the **Tab Bar Item**, enter the following details:
        - **Badge**: Leave this field blank
        - **System Item**: Select **Custom** from the dropdown list
        - **Selected Image**: icon-map-on
        - **Title Position**: Select **Default Position** from the dropdown list
    - In the **Bar Item**, enter the following details
        - **Title**: Type Map in this field
        - **Image**: icon-map-off
        - **Tag**: Enter 0 in this field
        - **Enabled**: This checkbox should be checked

13. Now, let's run the project by hitting the play button (or use *cmd + R*) in order to see where we are:

Setting Up the Basic Structure

As you may have noticed, this screen does not look like an app. Since we are building a Tab Bar Controller from scratch, we need to add an entry point. Close the simulator, and continue with the following steps:

14. Select `Main.storyboard` again in the Outline view, and make sure that the disclosure arrow is down for the `Tab Bar Controller Scene`:

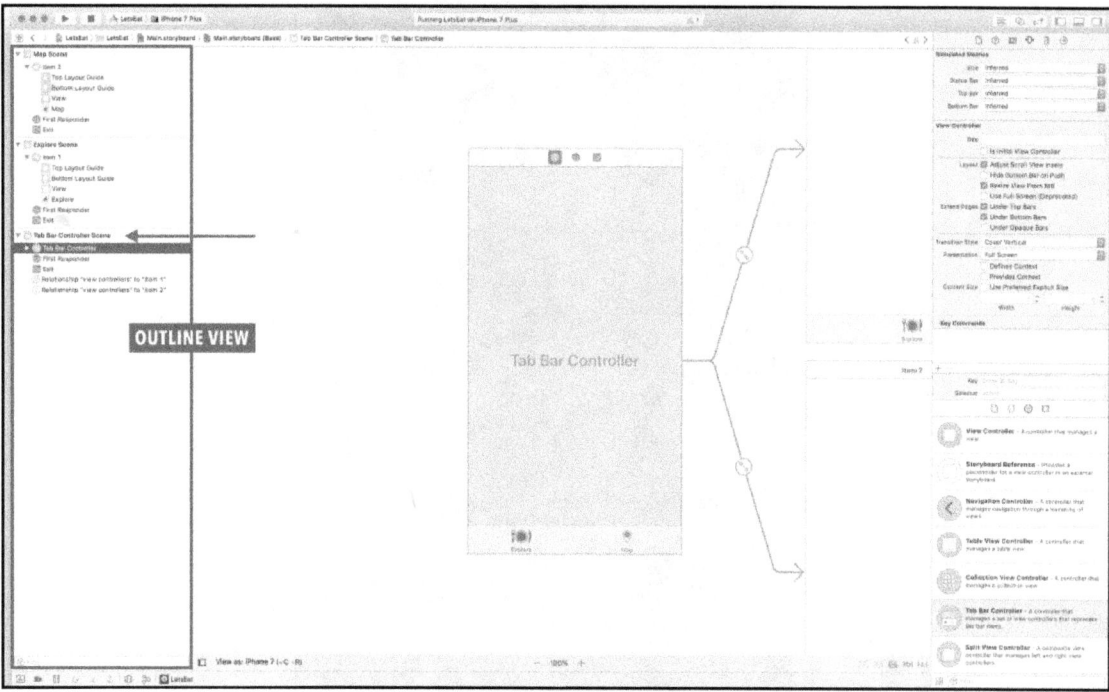

Chapter 7

15. Select the `Tab Bar Controller` under the `Tab Bar Controller Scene`, and, in the Utilities panel, make sure that the Attributes inspector is selected:

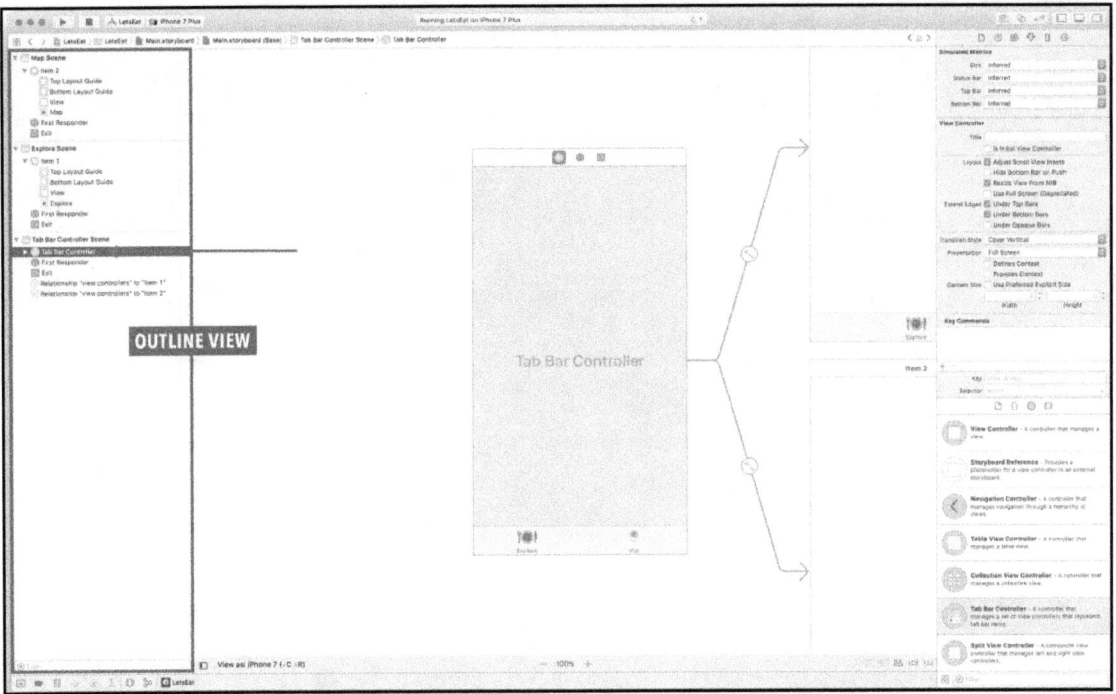

Setting Up the Basic Structure

16. Now, under the **View Controller** section, you will need to check the box for **Is Initial View Controller**:

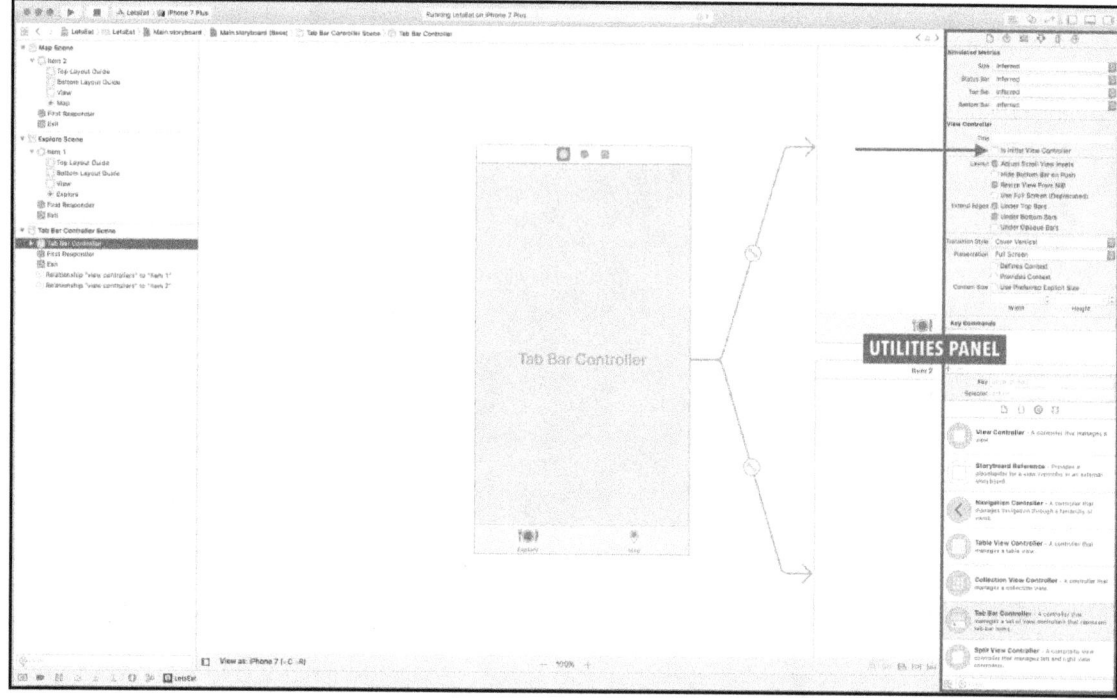

17. After you set the initial **View Controller**, there will be an arrow now pointing to the **Tab Bar Controller**. This arrow signifies the entry point of our app:

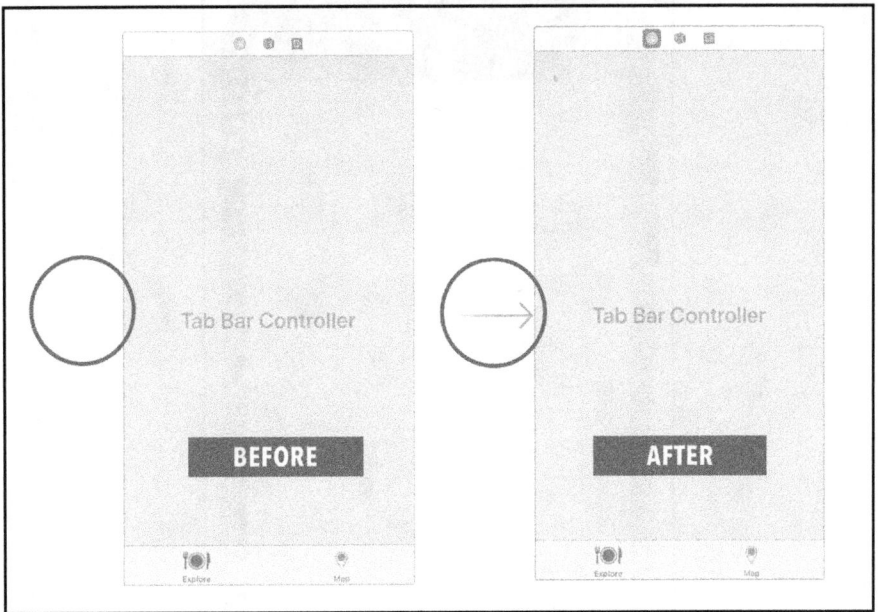

Setting Up the Basic Structure

18. Let's run the project again by hitting the play button (or use *cmd + R*):

Perfect! Now, with our basic structure established, we can start adding more specific elements to our views.

Storyboards

Before we do that, let's update `LaunchScreen.storyboard`. This storyboard is used when our app first launches.

Chapter 7

Creating our launch screen

Launch screens can be created using images, but that would mean that you would have to create images for every device and device orientation. Using the `LaunchScreen.storyboard` gives us the ability to create just one asset for all devices and orientations:

1. Select the `LaunchScreen.storyboard` file, and, in the Outline view, make sure that the disclosure arrows for `View Controller Scene` and then `View Controller` are facing downwards. Then, select `View` under `View Controller`:

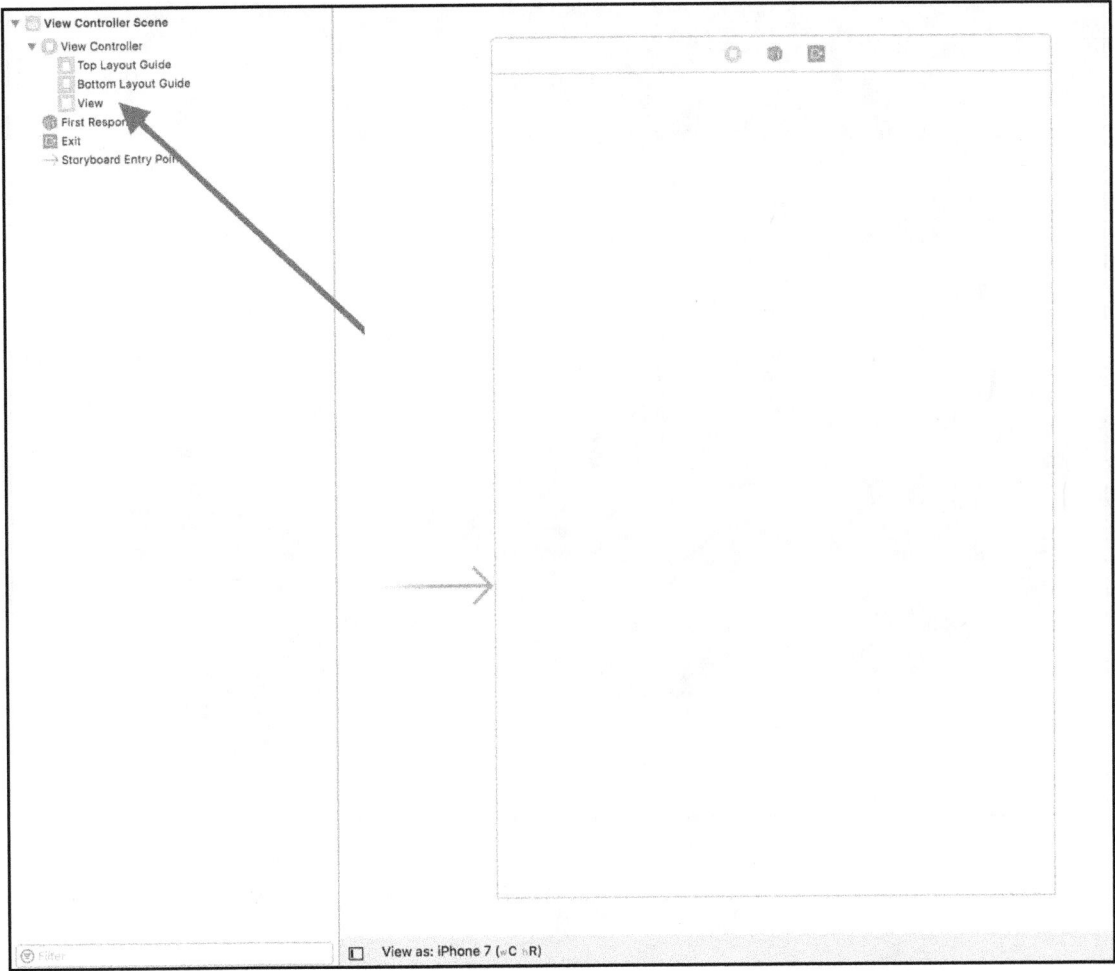

Setting Up the Basic Structure

2. In the Utilities panel, select the Attributes inspector, and click on the white **Background** bar:

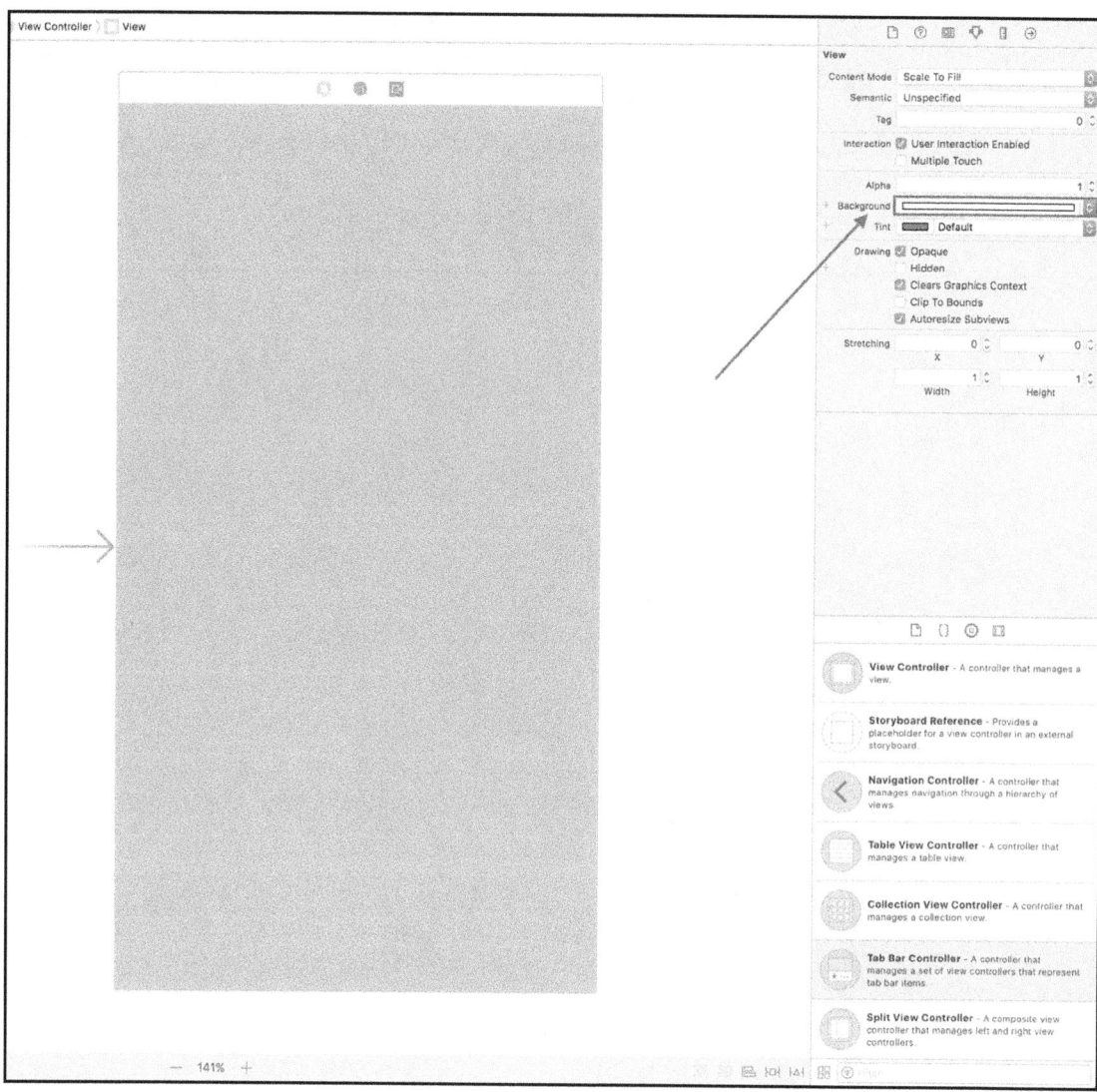

3. Now, you will see a **Colors** panel appear. Select the second tab, which is called the **Color Slider**:

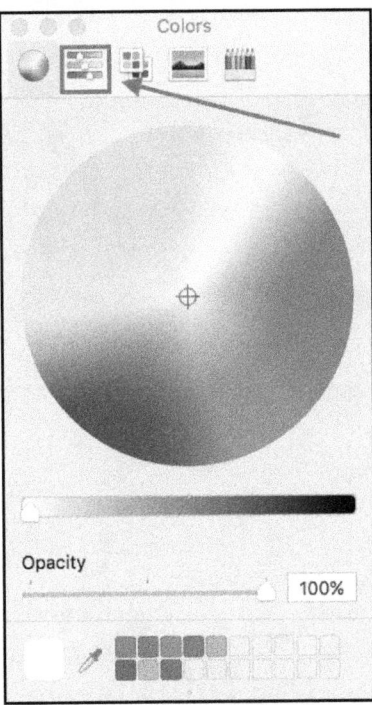

Setting Up the Basic Structure

4. Under **RGB Sliders**, **Hex Color #**, update the value from FFFFFF to 4A4A4A. This should change your background color from white to a dark grey:

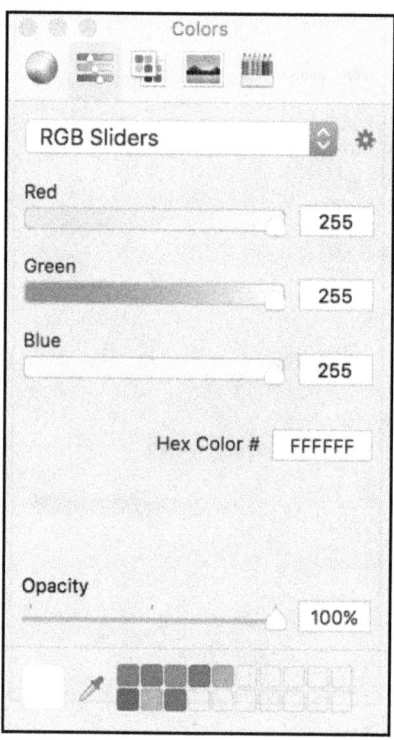

Chapter 7

5. You might have to select the background color a second time. If so, just select the **Background** bar in the Attributes inspector again, which should change the **Hex Color #** back to `FFFFFF`. Then, just change it again to `4A4A4A`. You now can close the **Color** panel, and you should see the background color update in your Standard Editor panel:

Setting Up the Basic Structure

Next, we need to bring the app logo onto the screen:

1. While still in `LaunchScreen.storyboard`, select Media Library under the Library selector bar in the Utilities panel:

Chapter 7

The Media Library allows us to access our image assets, and it will place them inside of a `UIImageView` for us.

2. In the filter, at the bottom of the Library pane, type `detail-logo`. Once that appears, drag and drop the logo onto the `LaunchScreen.storyboard`:

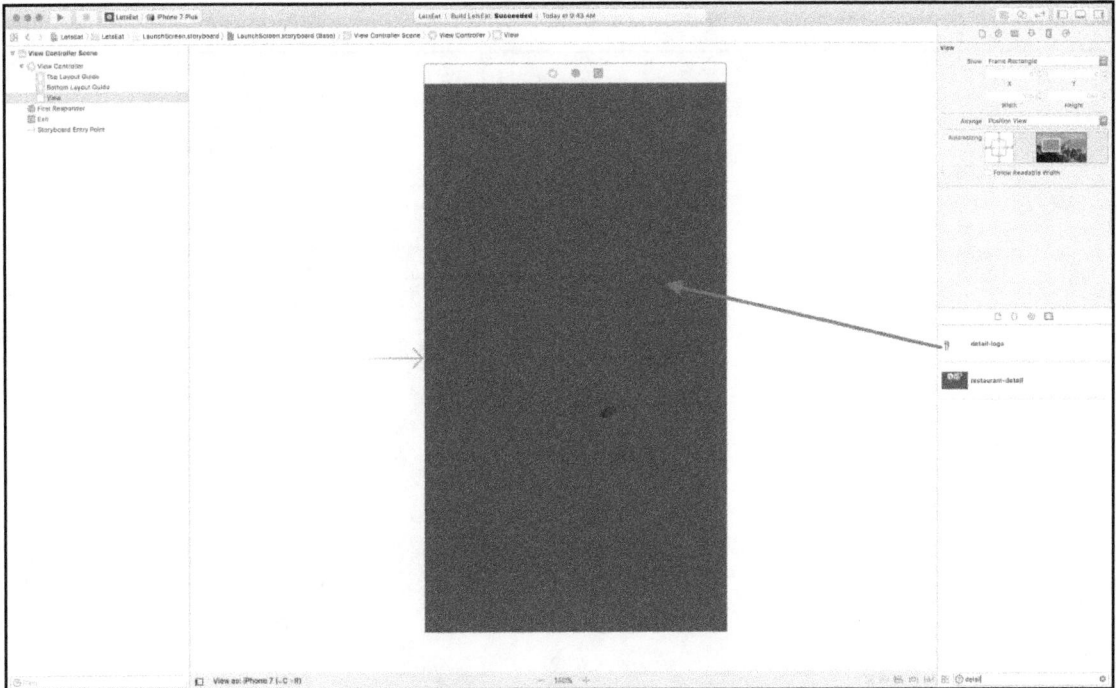

 There might be a bug in Xcode and, therefore, sometimes, when you drag the logo out, the width and height will not be set, and you will need to manually enter the width and height.

[185]

Setting Up the Basic Structure

3. If your logo does not drag out to size, then do this step: with the logo selected, open the Size inspector in the Utilities panel, and set the width and height to the following:

    - **Width**: 220
    - **Height**: 112

4. We want our *Let's Eat* logo to appear in the center of the screen. In order for our logo to appear in the center for all devices, we need to apply auto layout. Select `detail-logo`, and then select the Pin icon near the Filter bar:

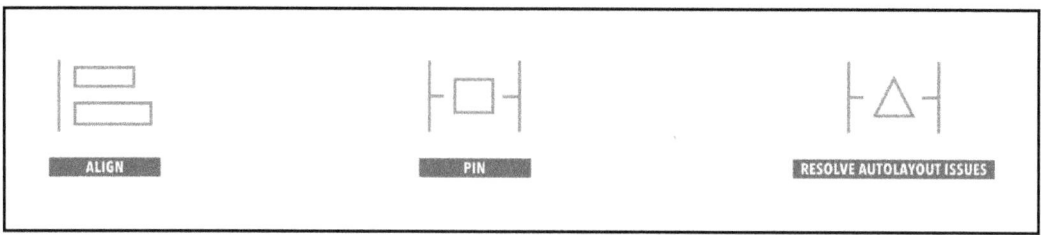

5. Next, select the Align icon (shown in the preceding image), which is to the left of the Pin icon, and check the following boxes that appear:

    - Horizontally in container
    - Vertically in container

6. Then, click on **Add 2 Constraints**.

When you are done, you will see the following:

Our launch screen is now set up for all devices. If you run the project again, you will now see your launch screen with the *Let's Eat* logo and new background color.

Let's move onto adding detail to our **Explore** tab, since this is the first thing a user will see after the app launches.

Setting Up the Basic Structure

Adding a Navigation Controller

We first need to add a Navigation Controller to our **Explore** tab. This will allow us to do a few things, such as adding a button into the title bar of the navigation in order to present our cities list.

1. Select `Main.storyboard`, and, in the Outline view, select `Explore` with the blue star to the left of it, under `Item 1` in the `Explore Scene`:

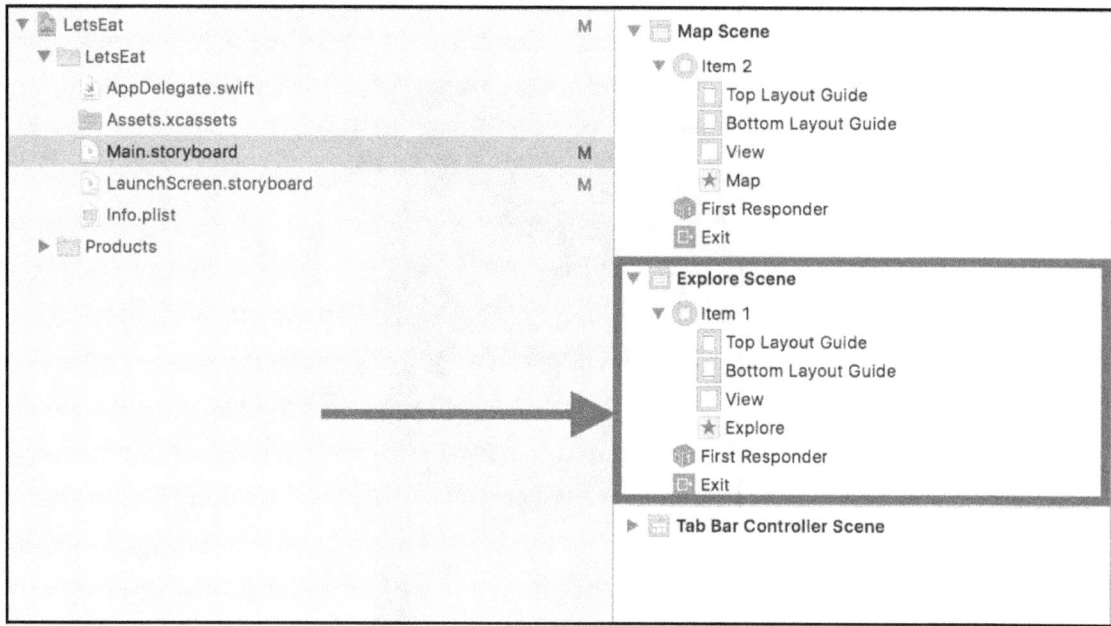

[188]

2. Then, navigate to **Editor** | **Embed In** | **Navigation Controller**:

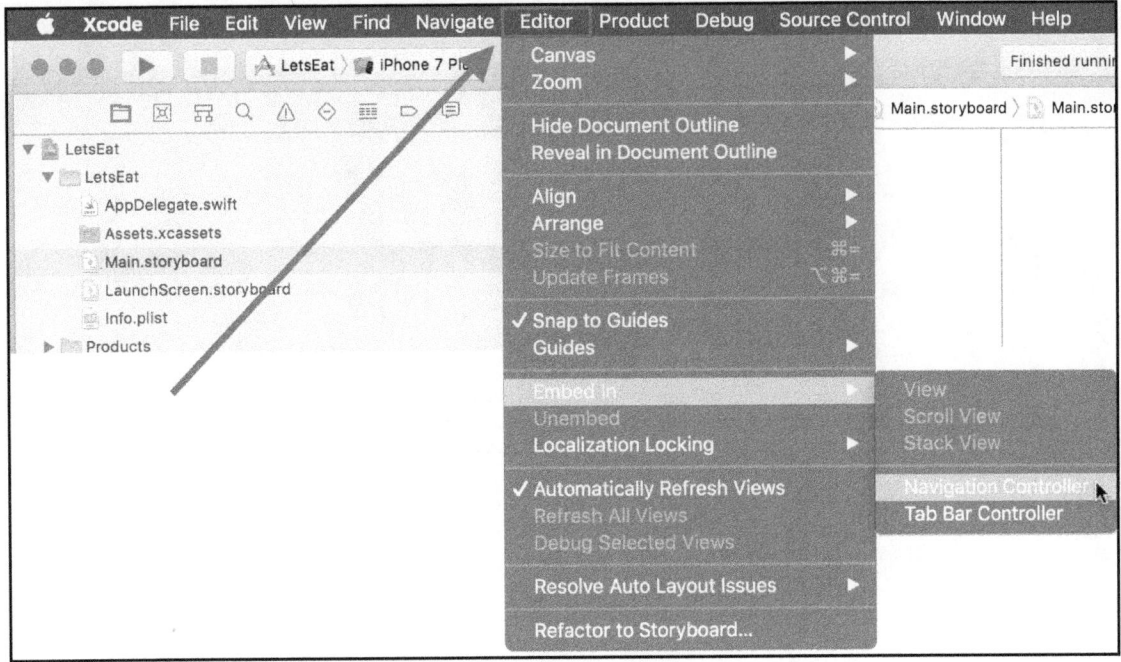

Setting Up the Basic Structure

3. Now, our View Controller has a Navigation Controller:

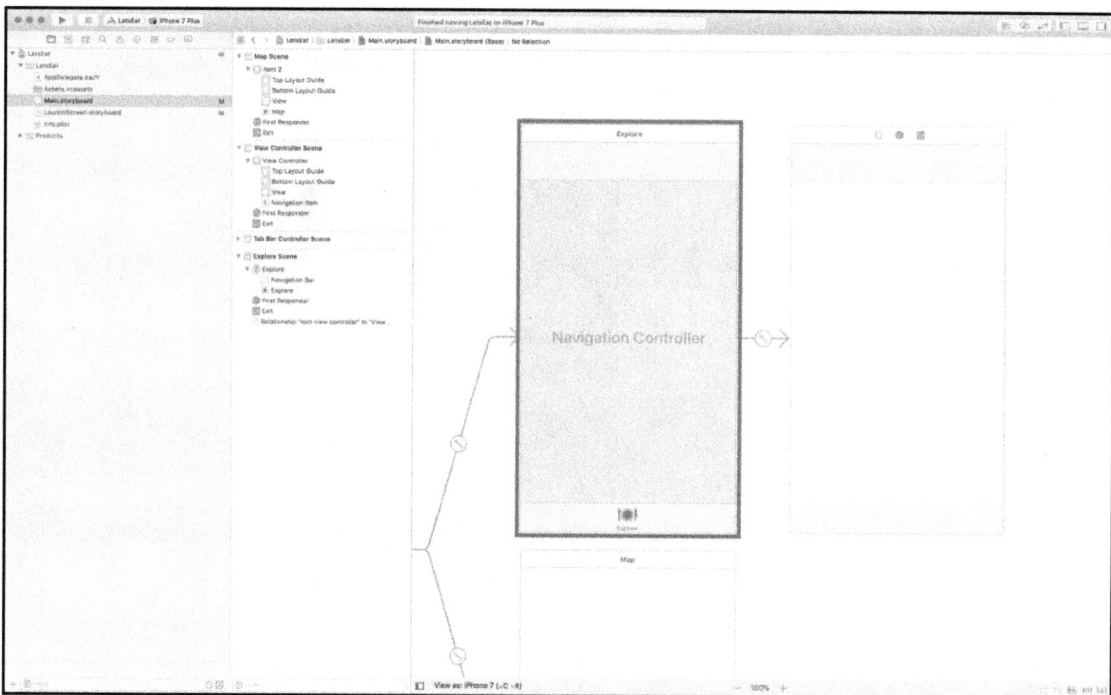

[190]

4. Let's run the project by hitting the Play button (or use *cmd* + *R*):

Repeat steps 1 to 4 under **Adding a Navigation Controller** above for the **Map** tab. Now that we have added both Navigation Controllers, in the next chapter, we will continue to create other View Controllers.

Summary

Storyboarding is one of the things I enjoy doing. It is quick and easy to set up your UI with storyboards. Being able to drag and drop what you need onto the canvas is such an efficient method of developing app storyboards. There are times when you will need to code, but being able to work on things without having to write any code is a wonderful capability. My preference is to use storyboards as much as possible, but there are many developers who prefer to do it in code. If you come from another programming language, try to keep an open mind and really learn storyboarding.

When you work on a project that uses storyboards, you can get a high-level overview of the project. When everything is written in code, it takes more time to get a basic idea of how the app is structured, and its overall flow. Again, there are people who love to code their UI, and we will do some of that in this book. My main point is that you have to find what works for you. This book leans more toward the storyboard side versus the coding side of setting up your UI.

In the next chapter, we will continue setting up our UI, and get familiar with more of the UI elements that you have seen in many iOS apps.

8
Building Our App Structure in Storyboard

In the last chapter, we created our Tab Bar Controller. In this chapter, we will be creating other View Controllers that we need in our app. Our goal for the end of this chapter is to be able to navigate through the app with the least amount of code needed.

The following will be covered in this chapter:

- Collection View
- Outlets
- Modals

Before we begin setting up our Collection View Controller, you will need to add two files, `ExploreViewController` and `RestaurantViewController`, which you'd have downloaded from Packt's website or GitHub. By adding these files and then a bit of code, we will be able to focus on the design of our app.

Building Our App Structure in Storyboard

Later in the book, we will delete these files, and create them ourselves. But, for the purposes of this chapter, let's add these two files into our project:

1. Open the project `assets` folder that you downloaded from Packt's website or GitHub. Open `Chapter_08` and drag the two files in the folder into your project in the Navigator panel:

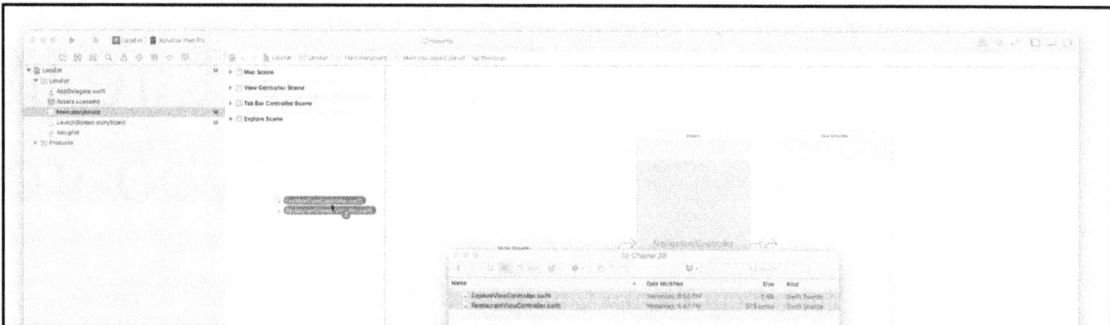

2. When you drop the folder, you will get the following message:

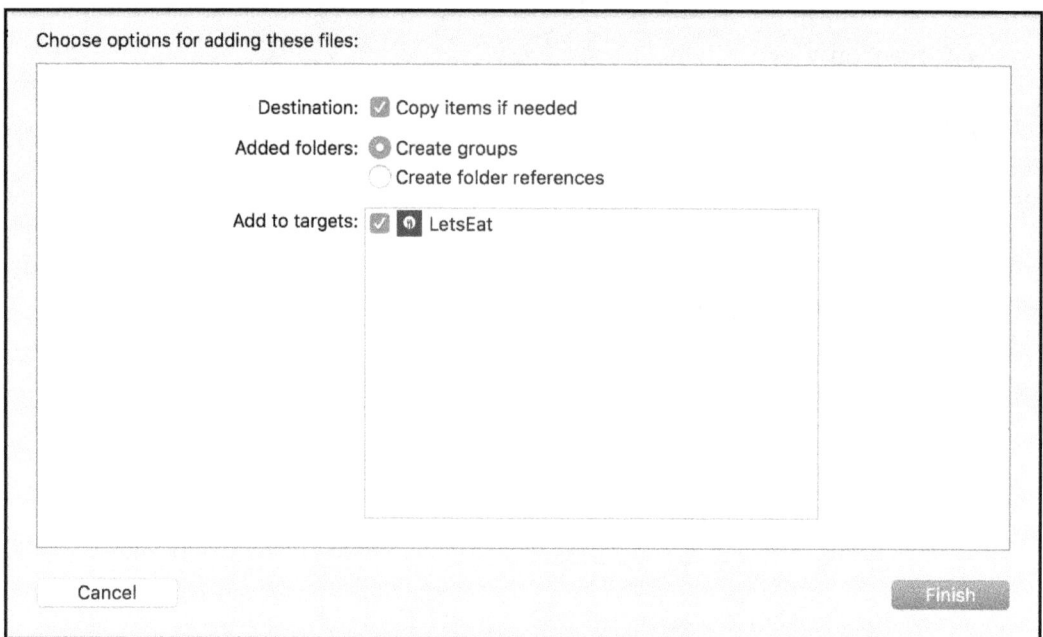

Chapter 8

3. Make sure you have both **Copy items if needed** and **Create groups** selected. Then, hit **Finish**.
4. Now we can add code to these new files, which will allow us to dismiss modals that we will create later in this chapter. A modal is a container that opens on top of the current content showing in an app, and allows you to take more action without opening up all of the information on the screen being viewed. Let's add the code to enable us to dismiss modals:
5. Open the `ExploreViewController.swift` file and, under where it says `// Add Unwind here` at the bottom of the file, add the following code:

```swift
@IBAction func unwindLocationCancel(segue:UIStoryboardSegue) {}
```

```swift
//
// ViewController.swift
// CollectionViewTest
//
// Created by Craig Clayton on 6/30/17.
// Copyright © 2017 Cocoa Academy. All rights reserved.
//

import UIKit

class ExploreViewController: UIViewController {
    
    @IBOutlet weak var collectionView: UICollectionView!
    
    override func viewDidLoad() {
        super.viewDidLoad()
        
        let layout = UICollectionViewFlowLayout()
        layout.headerReferenceSize = CGSize(width: 0, height: 100)
        layout.sectionHeadersPinToVisibleBounds = true
        collectionView.collectionViewLayout = layout
    }
    
    override func didReceiveMemoryWarning() {
        super.didReceiveMemoryWarning()
        // Dispose of any resources that can be recreated.
    }
    
    func collectionView(_ collectionView: UICollectionView, viewForSupplementaryElementOfKind kind: String, at indexPath: IndexPath) -> UICollectionReusableView {
        let headerView = collectionView.dequeueReusableSupplementaryView(ofKind: kind, withReuseIdentifier: "header", for: indexPath)
        return headerView
    }
    
    func collectionView(_ collectionView: UICollectionView, cellForItemAt indexPath: IndexPath) -> UICollectionViewCell {
        return collectionView.dequeueReusableCell(withReuseIdentifier: "exploreCell", for: indexPath)
    }
    
    func numberOfSections(in collectionView: UICollectionView) -> Int {
        return 1
    }
    
    func collectionView(_ collectionView: UICollectionView, numberOfItemsInSection section: Int) -> Int {
        return 20
    }
    
    // Add Unwind here
}
```

If we look at our app design, which we reviewed earlier in this book, in our first tab, the **Explore** tab, we show a grid of food cuisines as well as a list of locations. First, we will set up our grid.

Adding a Collection View Controller

As we discussed earlier in the book, Collection View Controllers allow us to display elements within a grid. Let's set up our **Collection View**:

1. Select the `Main.storyboard` file, making sure that you are zoomed out and can see all of your scenes. In the Utilities panel, ensure that you have the object library tab selected.
2. Next, in the filter field, type: `collectionview`:

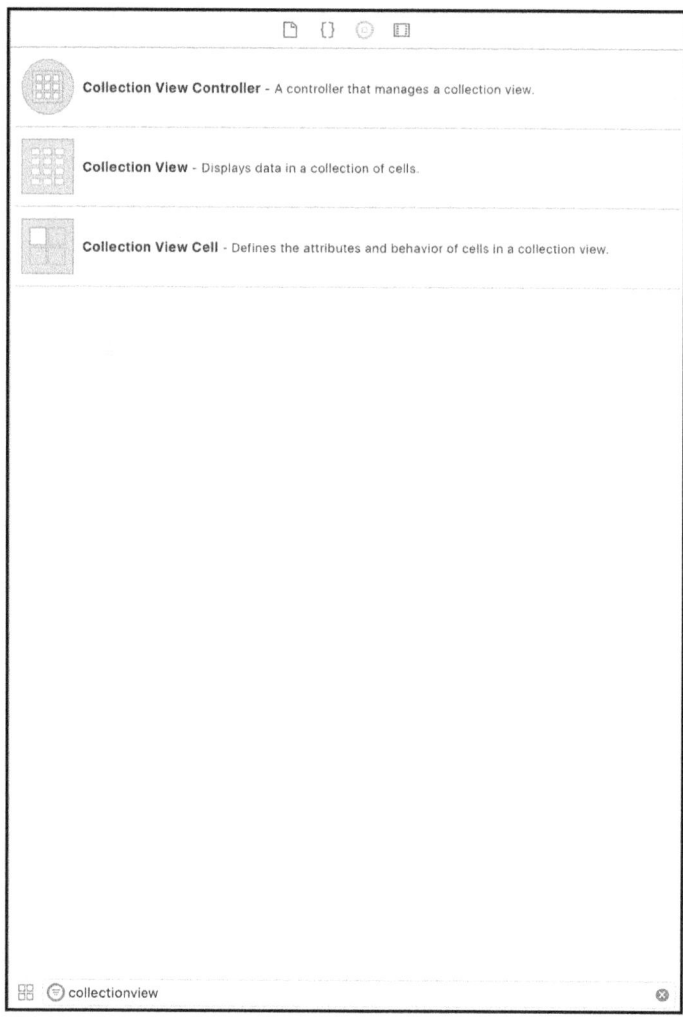

Chapter 8

3. Click on and drag **Collection View**, and drop it onto the **Explore View Controller**:

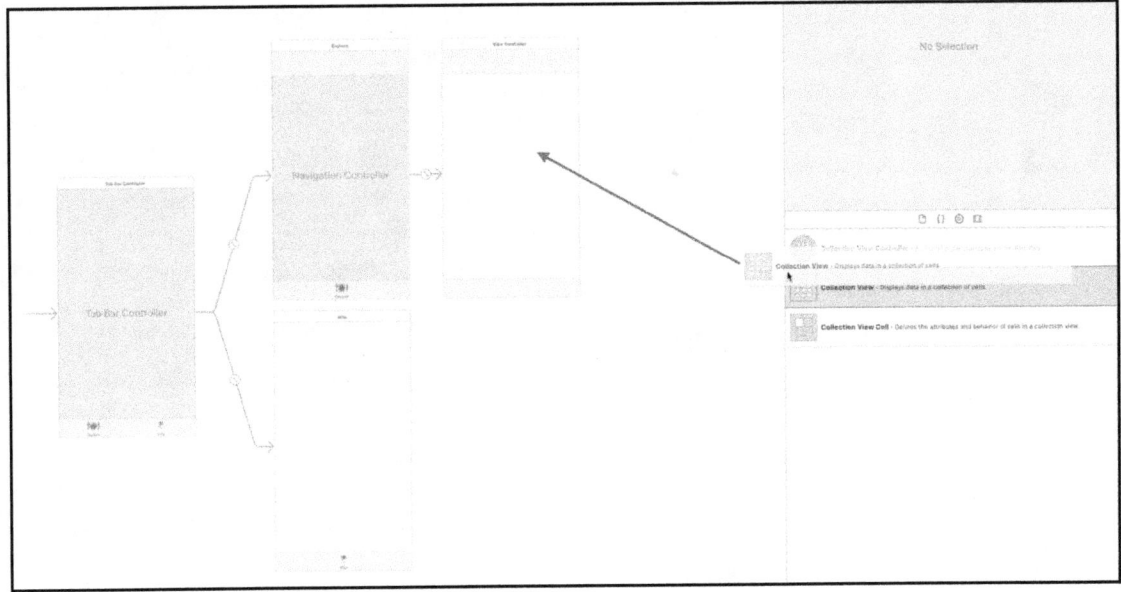

Building Our App Structure in Storyboard

4. After you drop it onto the scene, you will see small boxes around the entire **Collection View** component. Select the Pin icon, and enter the following values:

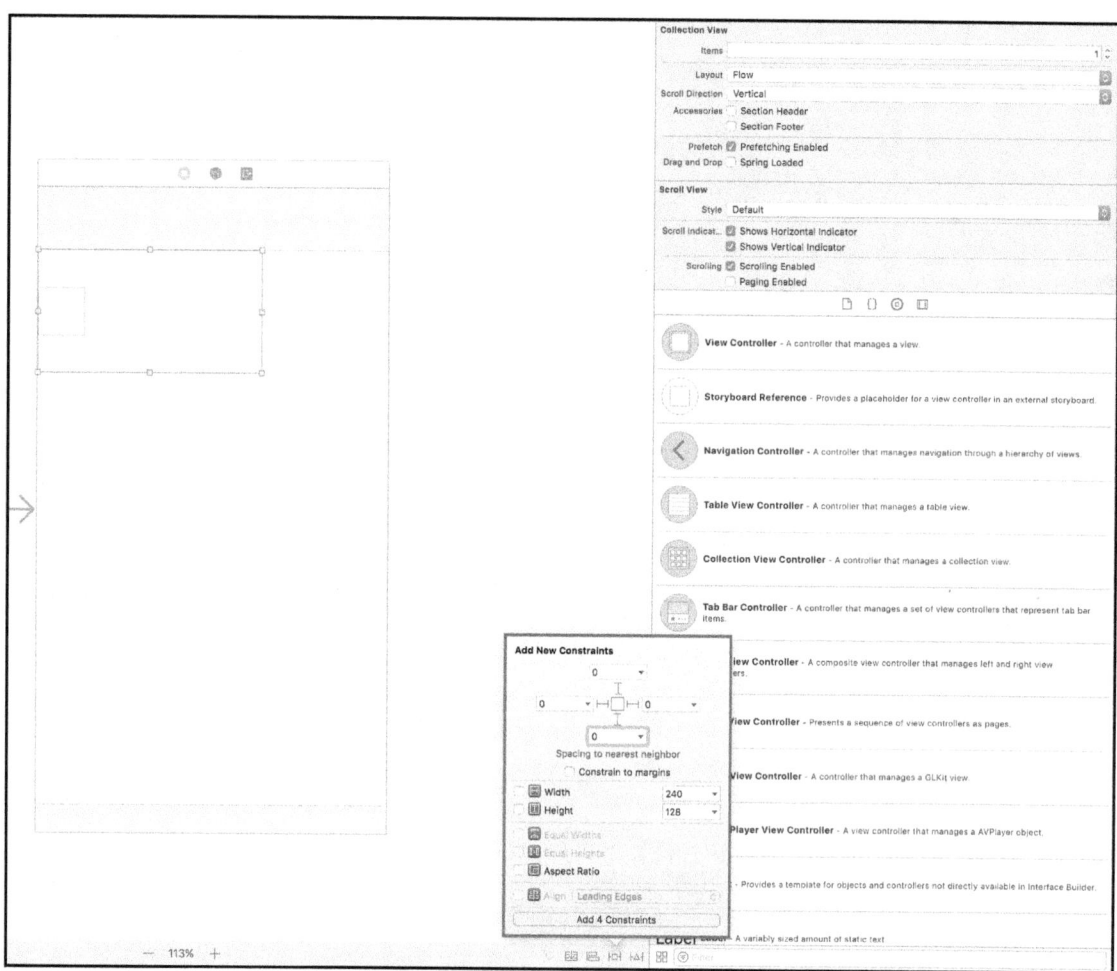

Chapter 8

 All values under **Add New Constraints** are set to 0.

5. Click on **Add 4 Constraints**.

We now have our **Collection View** component set up for our **Explore** tab.

Hooking up our outlets

Let's now link our file, `ExploreViewController`, to our `UIViewController` in storyboard:

1. While still in the `Main.storyboard` file, select the `UIViewController` with the **Collection View** that we just created, by clicking on the left-most icon at the top of that controller:

Building Our App Structure in Storyboard

2. Now, in the Utilities panel, select the Identity Inspector, which is the third icon from the left:

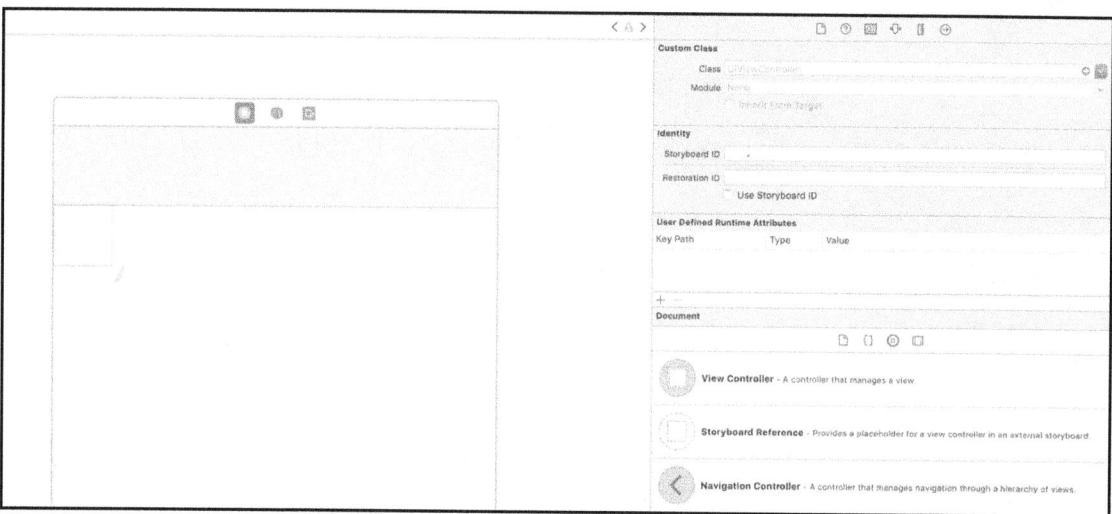

3. Under **Custom Class**, in the **Class** dropdown menu, select `ExploreViewController` and hit *Enter*.
4. After you hit *Enter*, select the **Connections Inspector**, the last icon on the right, in the Utilities panel:

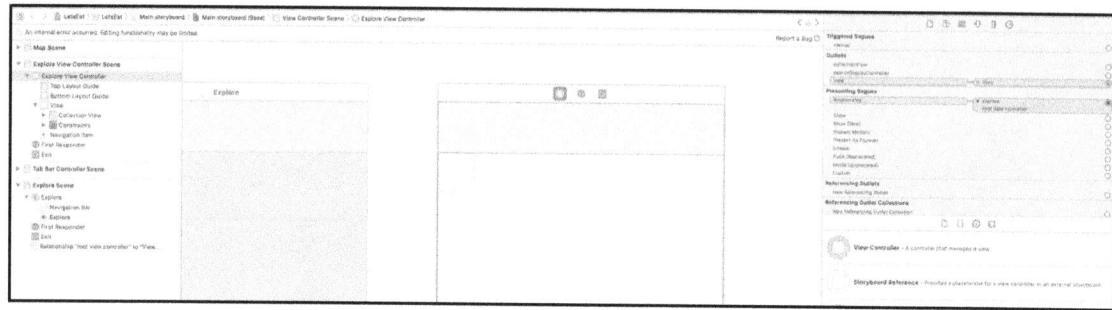

Chapter 8

5. Under **Outlets**, you will see **collectionView** and an empty circle:

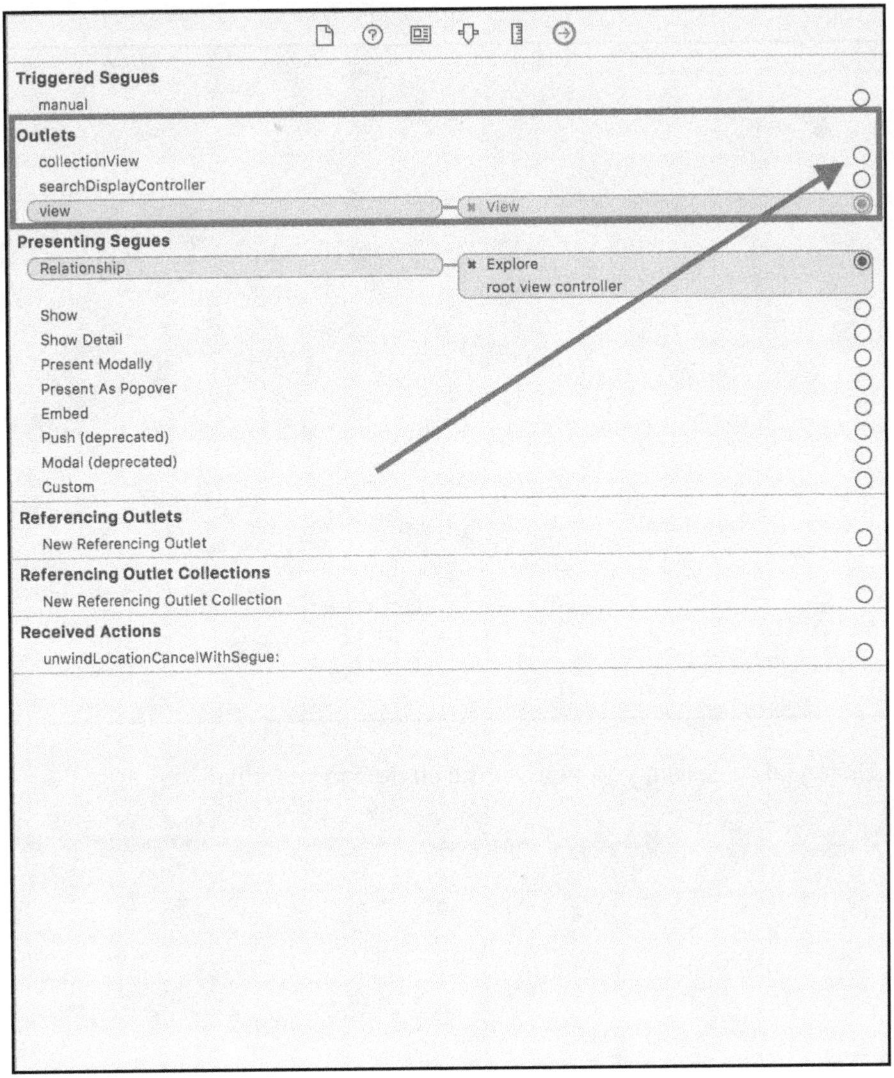

 `IBOutlet` is a way to a connect to a UI element. We have a **Collection View** on our `UIViewController`; now, we are hooking into that variable. Later in the book, you will learn how to create these variables.

[201]

Building Our App Structure in Storyboard

6. Click on the **collectionView** circle, and drag from the circle to the **Collection View** that we just added inside of the `UIViewController`:

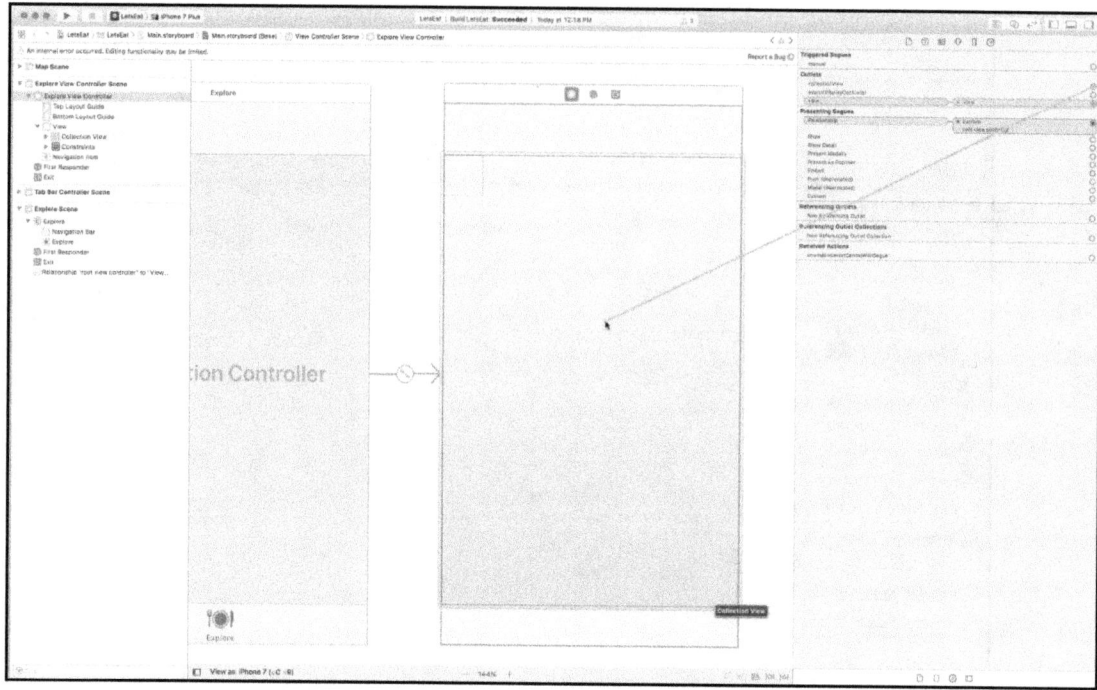

7. Once you release it, you will see the circle become filled:

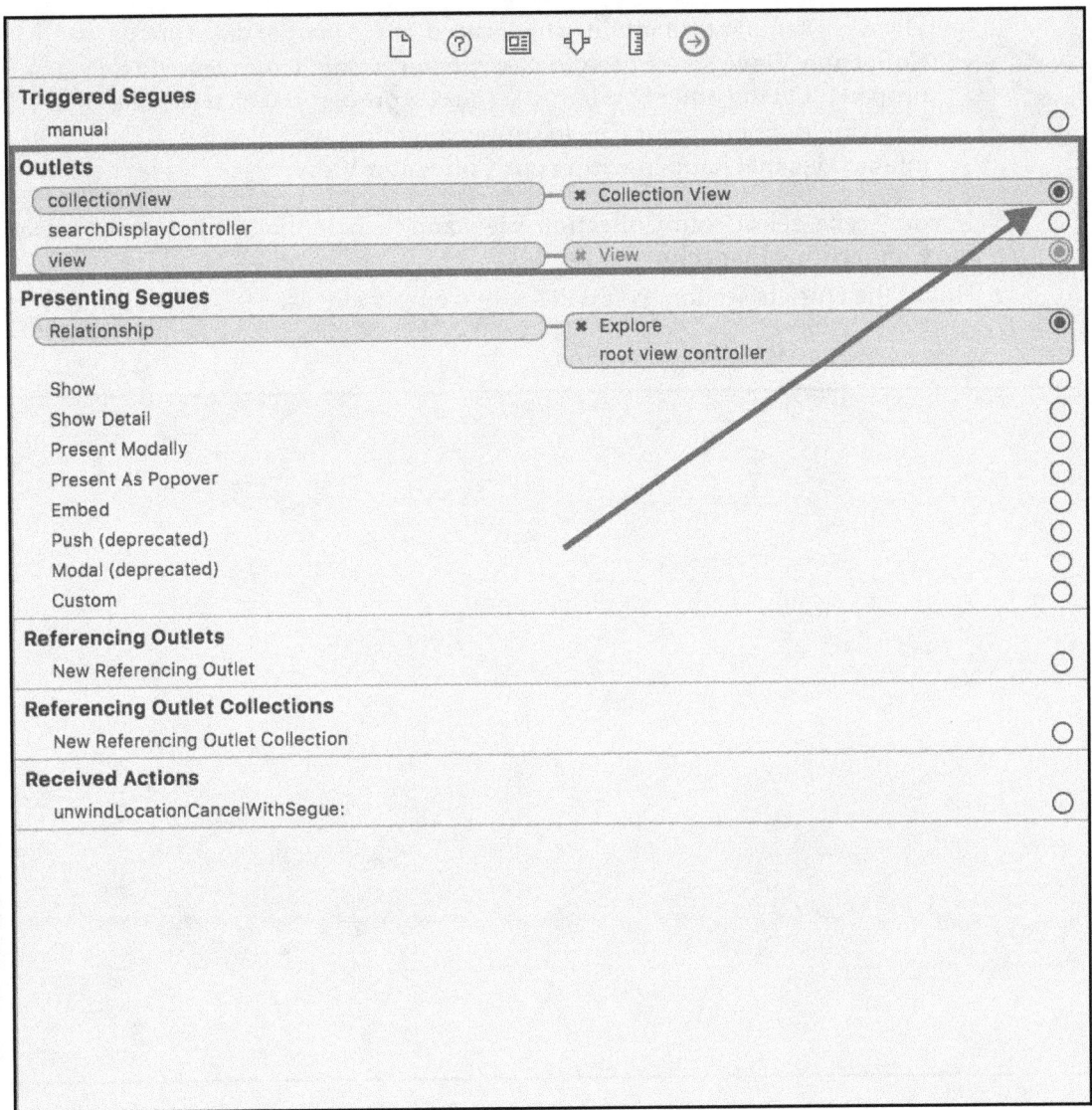

Next, we need to hook up the data source and delegate. This allows us to pass data to our **Collection View**, as well as know when our **Collection View** has some kind of interaction.

Building Our App Structure in Storyboard

 The `dataSource` property is what is used to supply the data for our **Collection View**, so we need to pass whatever data we have to this property. On the other hand, the `delegate` property, which supplies the behavior, does not require us to supply anything, as it receives interactions that happen within our **Collection View**.

8. In your scene, select your **Collection View** and then, in the Utilities panel, select the **Connections Inspector**.
9. Under the **Outlets** section, you will see two empty circles, `dataSource` and `delegate`:

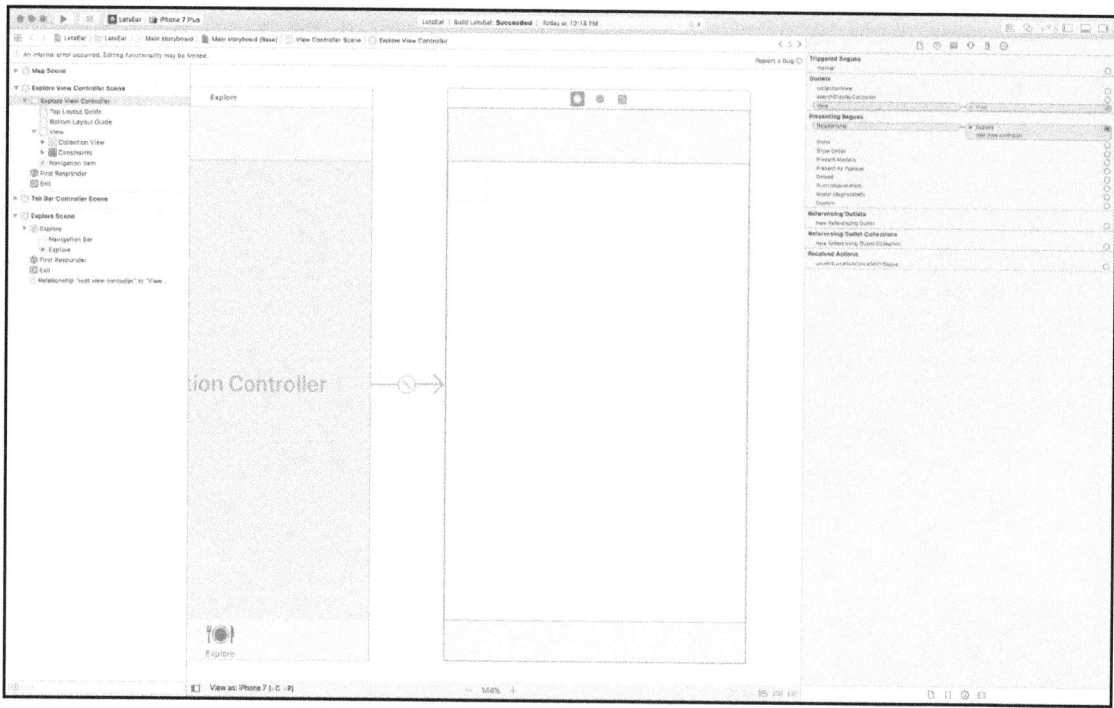

Chapter 8

10. Click on and drag from the empty circle of the `dataSource` property to the **Explore View Controller** in your Outline view, and then release:

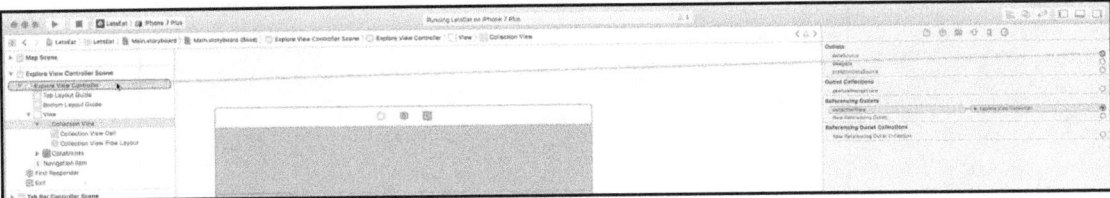

11. Repeat for the `delegate` property:

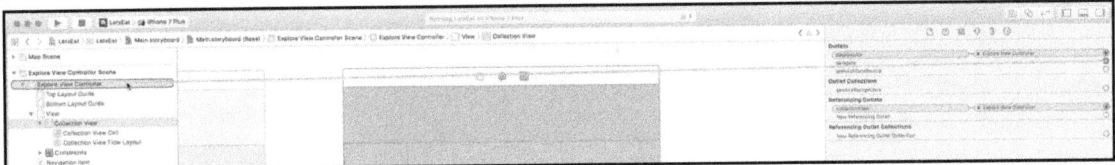

Next, let's set up our **Collection View** prototype cell to have a color.

Creating a custom color

In Xcode 9, we are now able to add colors to your `Assets.xcassets` folder. This is great when you want to have all your colors in one location. Before we update our explore cell, let's create a new color:

1. Open the `Assets.xcassets` file.

[205]

Building Our App Structure in Storyboard

2. Right-click inside of the `Assets.xcassets`, where you will see folders, and create a new folder called colors:

3. Next, right-click the `Color` folder, and this time, select **New Color Set**. You will see a new color added to your folder. Select the Attributes inspector in the Utilities panel:

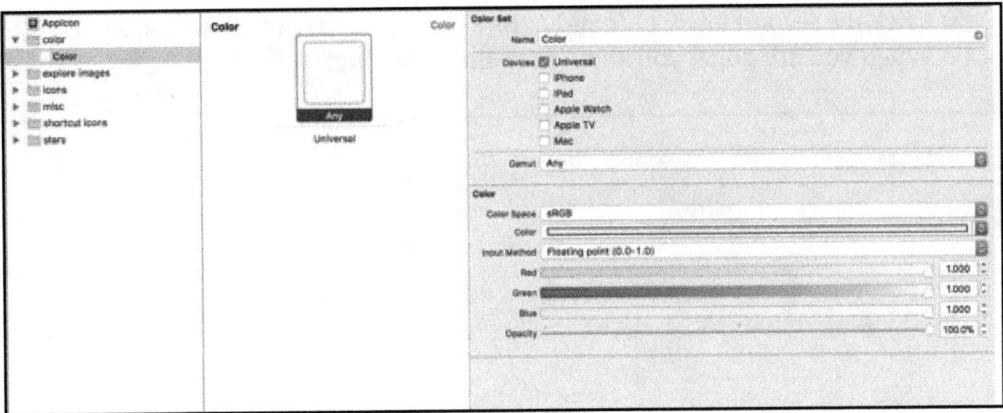

4. Under **Color** set, update name: `Demo Grey`.
5. Under **Color**, click on the color, and you will see a color panel:

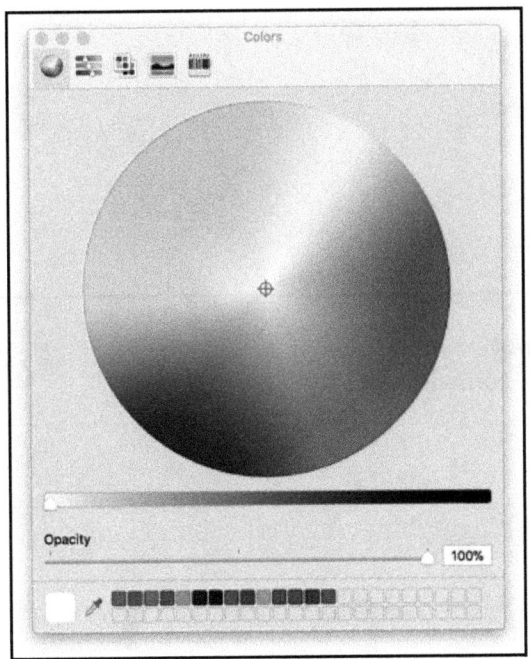

Building Our App Structure in Storyboard

6. Click the second tab, Color Slider, and change the **Hex Color** # value to AAAAAA. When you are done, you should see the following:

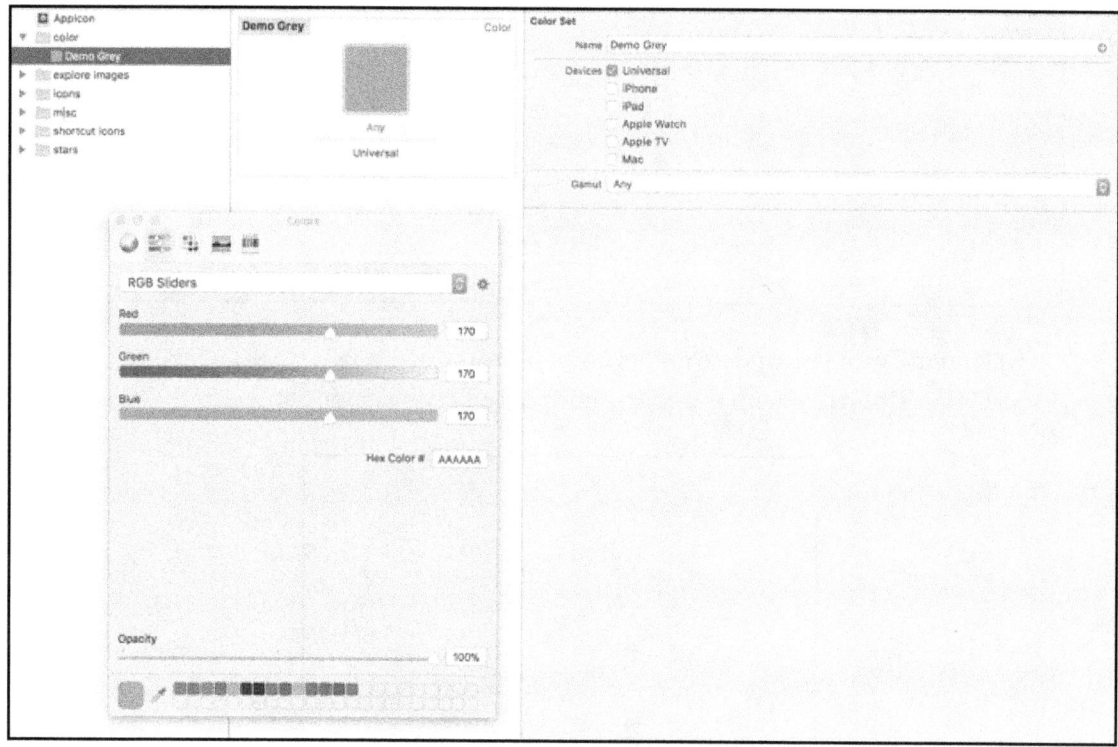

7. Now that we have a color, we will be able to find our new color in the **Color** drop-down, as you will see next.

Setting up our cell

To set up our cell, we need to perform the following steps:

1. In `Main.storyboard`, select the **Collection View** prototype cell, which is the small box inside of your **Collection View**.
2. Open the Attributes inspector in the Utilities panel:

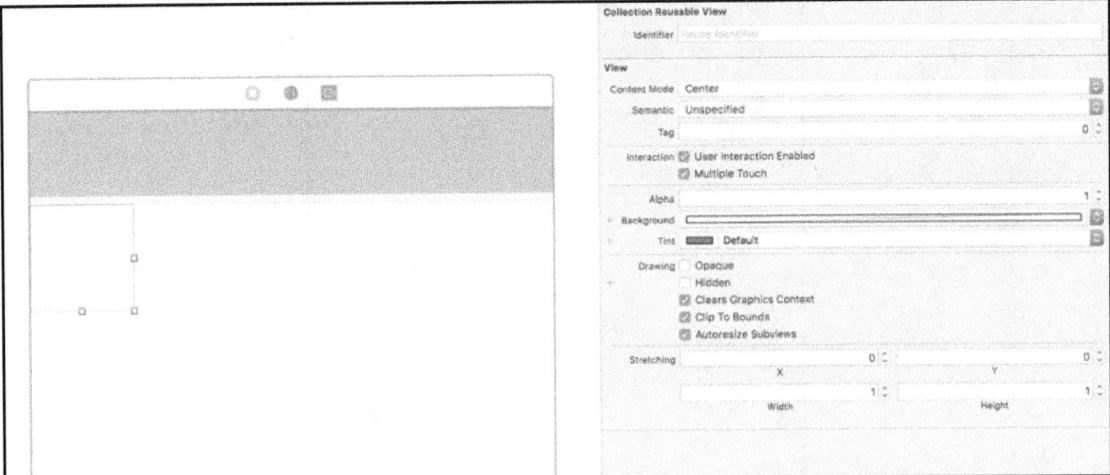

3. Update the following:

    - **Identifier**: `exploreCell`
    - **Background**: Demo Grey

Building Our App Structure in Storyboard

4. In order to update the background, you will need to click on the drop-down arrow under **Background**. You will see that our **Demo Grey** has been added:

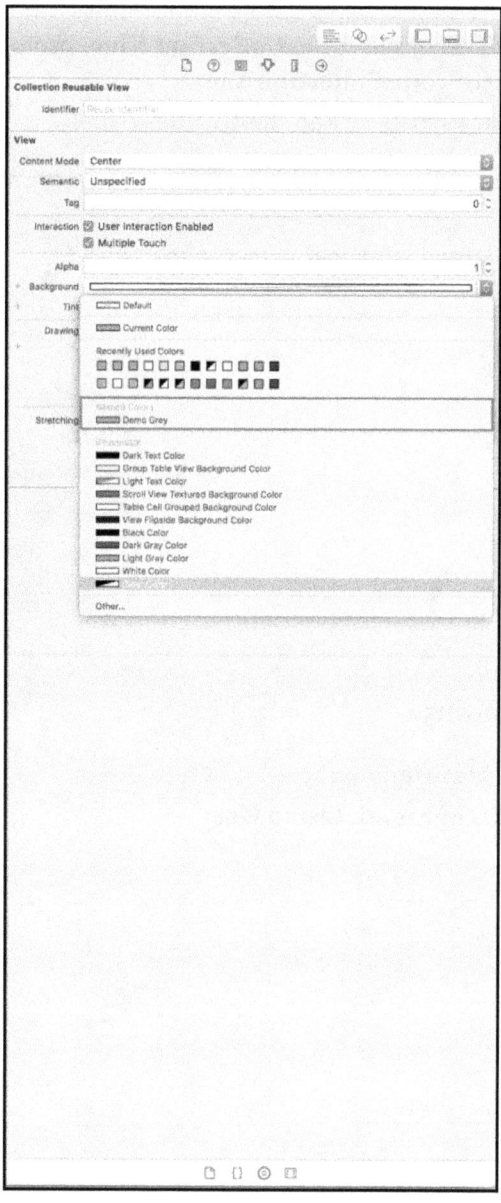

You should now see the following:

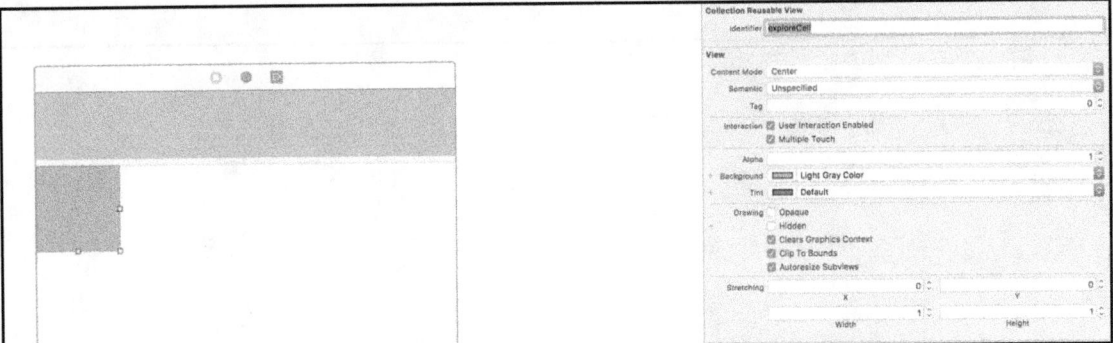

Next, we need to add a section header.

Section header

Our section header will include the page title, selected location, and a button that we will use to see the locations:

1. Select the **Collection View** in the `Main.storyboard` outline.

2. Then, in your Utilities panel, select the Attributes inspector and, under **Collection View Accessories**, select the checkbox next to **section header**:

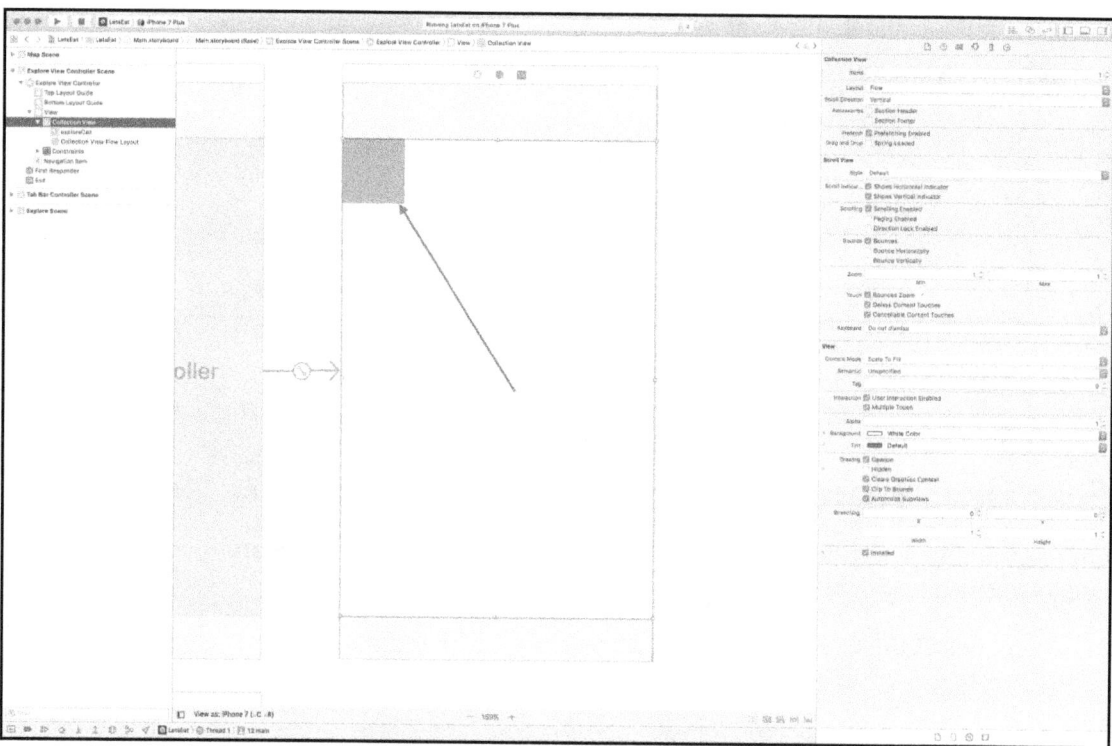

3. Next, you will see a box appear above our **Demo Grey** cell, which is our new section header; you should select this:

Chapter 8

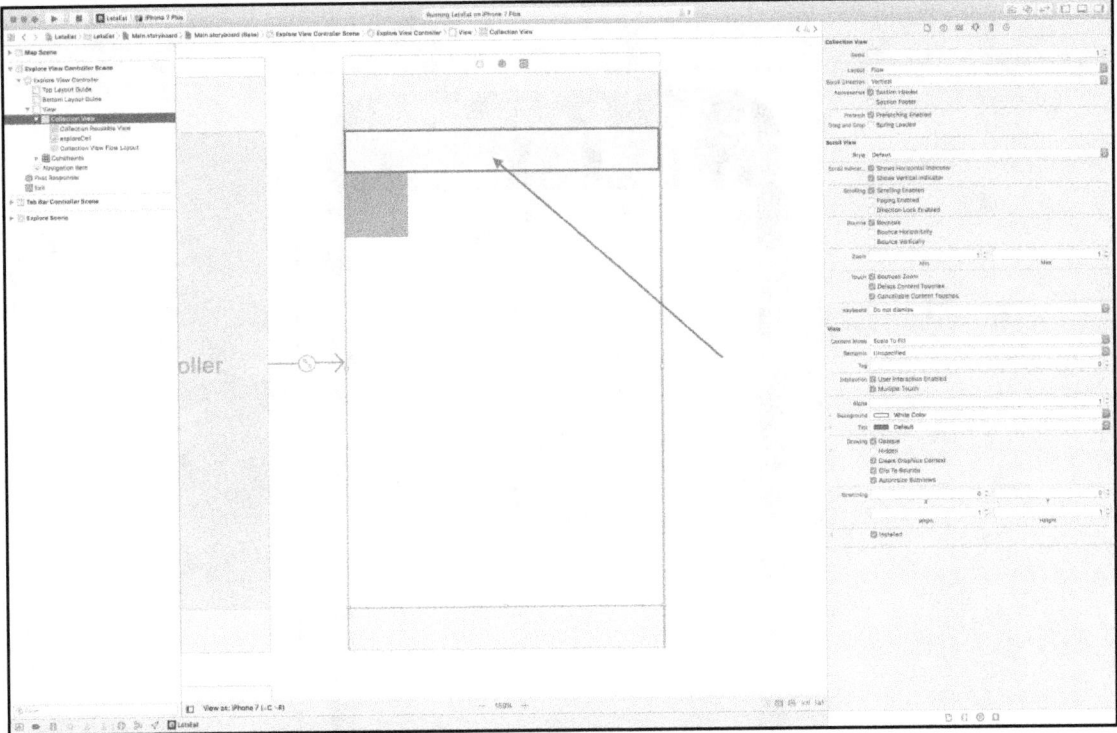

4. Finally, in the Attributes inspector in the Utilities panel, update **Identifier** to **Header**:

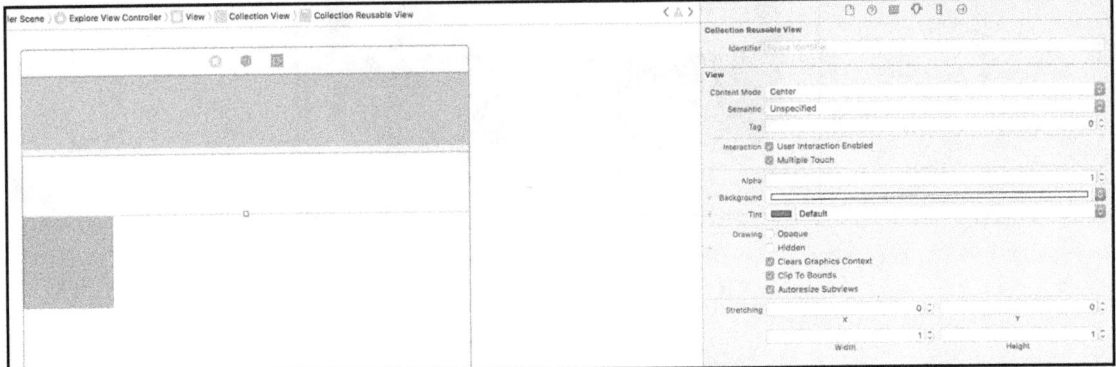

Building Our App Structure in Storyboard

Let's build and run the project by hitting the Play button (or use *cmd* + *R*):

You will see that you now have a grid of boxes and some white space (the section header) near the top of the grid. Before we work on the section header, let's update our grid to match our design of two items per row with a particular size cell.

Updating the grid

In order to update our grid, we need to take the following steps:

1. Use *cmd + Shift + O*, and in the **Open Quickly** window, type `Main.storyboard`, and then hit *Enter*.
2. Select the **Collection View**, and then, in the Utilities panel, select **Size Inspector**.
3. Update the following values, based on the simulator that you are currently using. These values may need to be changed so that your grid has two columns of cells, so feel free to alter the values:

   For iPhone 7, use the following values:

Fields	Values			
Cell Size	Width: 176	Height: 195		
Min Spacing	For Cells: 0	For Lines: 7		
Section Insets	Top: 7	Bottom: 7	Left: 7	Right: 7

   For iPhone 7 Plus, use the following values:

Fields	Values			
Cell Size	Width: 196	Height: 154		
Min Spacing	For Cells: 0	For Lines: 7		
Section Insets	Top: 7	Bottom: 7	Left: 7	Right: 7

Building Our App Structure in Storyboard

For iPhone 4/iPhone SE/iPhone 5/iPhone 5s, use the following values:

Fields	Values			
Cell Size	**Width**: 150	**Height**: 154		
Min Spacing	**For Cells**: 0	**For Lines**: 7		
Section Insets	**Top**: 7	**Bottom**: 7	**Left**: 7	**Right**: 7

This is what everything should look like when you are done:

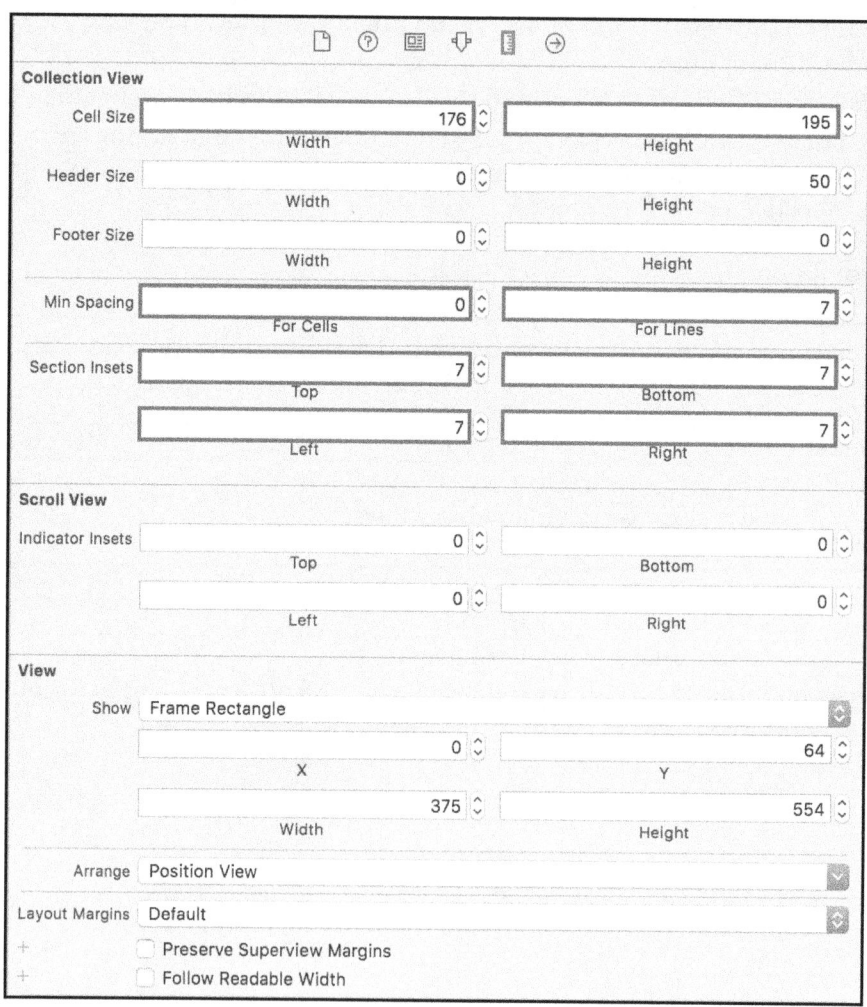

[216]

Chapter 8

For now, as we just did, we will use storyboard settings to get our cells set up. Later in the book, we will make this dynamic so that our widths and heights adjust with code. Next, we will work on our section header.

Adding a modal

Let's review the design for the section header:

Building Our App Structure in Storyboard

Notice that we have a **+ Location** button that will display our locations. Let's add that modal now:

1. While in the `Main.storyboard` file, select the object library and, in the filter field at the bottom of the Library pane, type `button`.
2. Now, drag and drop the `Button` component into the section header we created in our **Explore View Controller**:

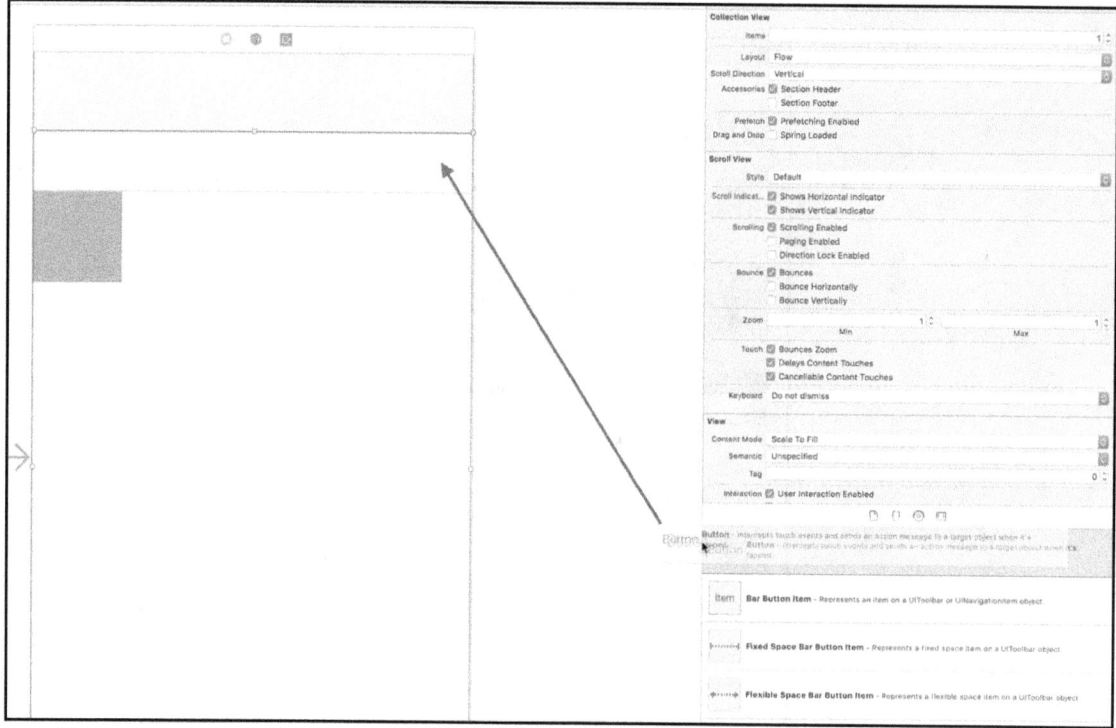

We will format the button later in terms of location and size.

Next, we need to add another View Controller to our storyboard:

1. In the filter, type `viewcontroller`, and drag and drop the `ViewController` component above the **Explore View Controller** in the `Main.storyboard`.
2. With the **View Controller** selected, navigate to **Editor | EmbedIn | NavigationController**.

[218]

3. Now, Ctrl + drag from where it says **Button** in the View Controller under the **Explore** tab to the Navigation Controller that was just created (you can also do this within Outline view by, Ctrl dragging from the button to the new Navigation Controller you just created):

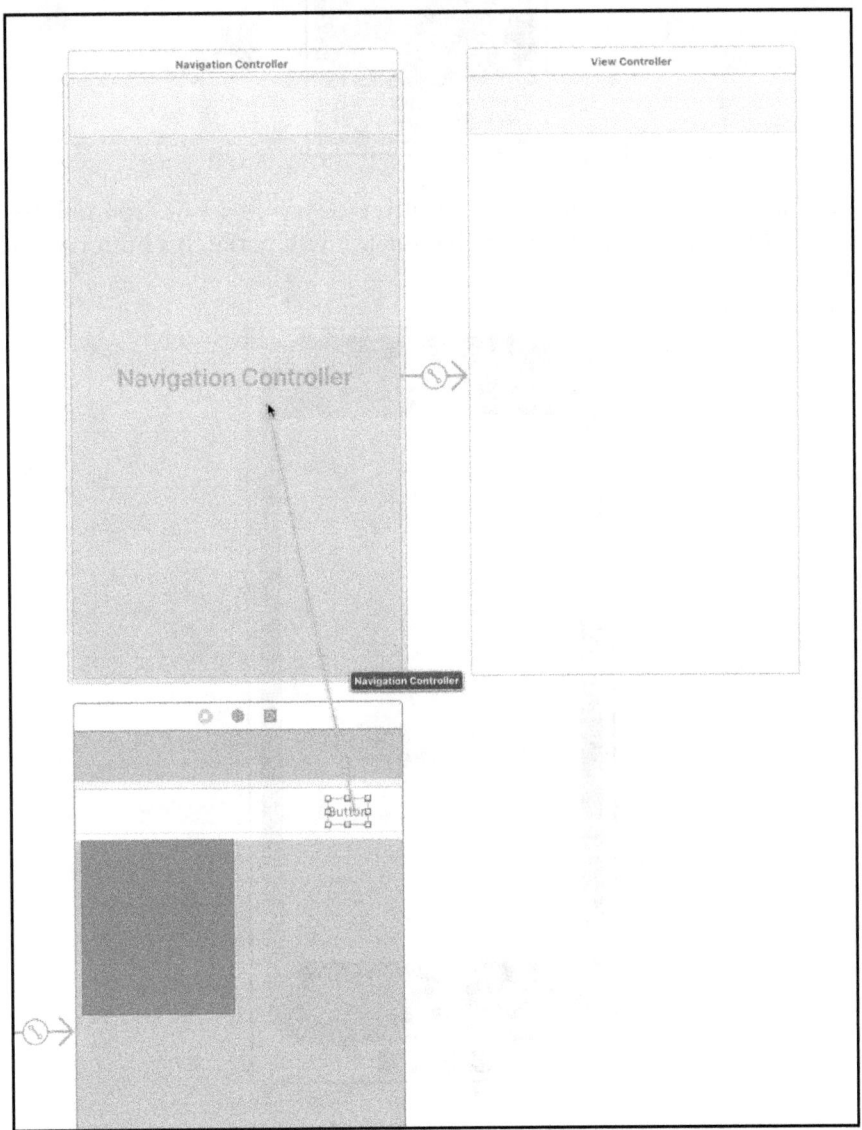

Building Our App Structure in Storyboard

4. When you let go, you will be presented with the following menu, and you should select **Present Modally**:

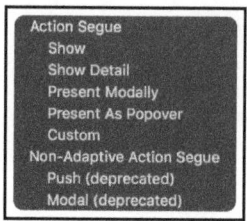

Now, let's run the project by hitting the Play button (or use *cmd* + *R*). You will see that our button now launches a modal. In the next chapter, we will make this button match our design.

Chapter 8

Currently, as you can see in the preceding screenshot, we cannot dismiss this modal. Therefore, we need a cancel button and a done button to dismiss the view. Let's fix this:

1. Open `Main.storyboard` and select the segue that is connected to the button in the header. It should now be highlighted:

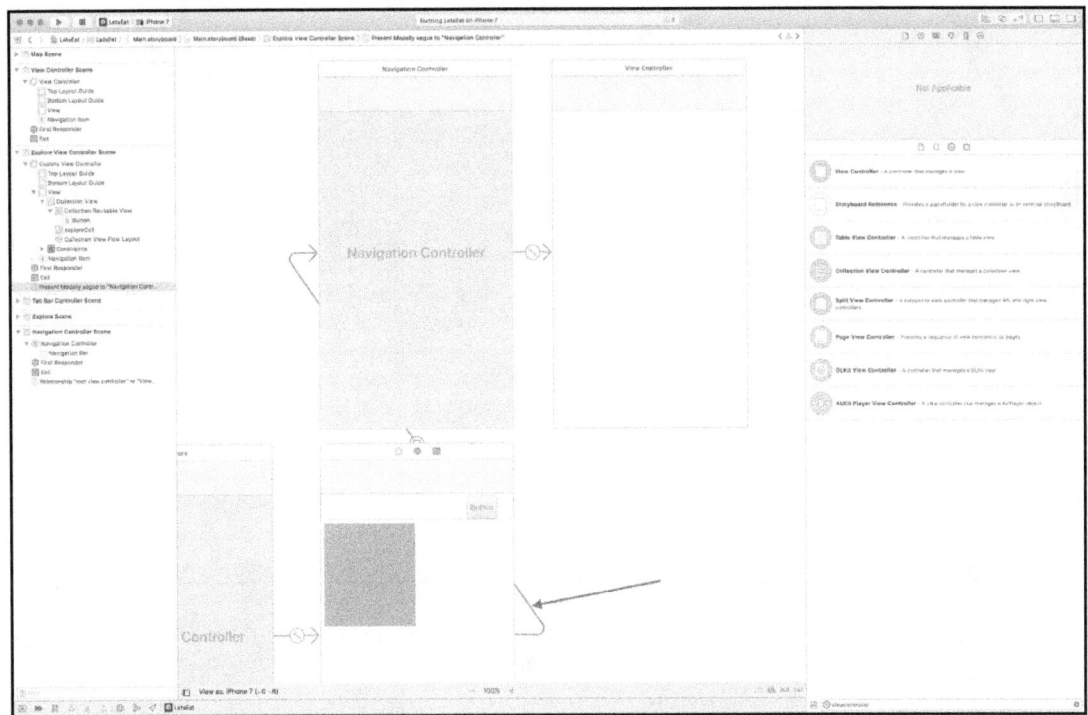

Building Our App Structure in Storyboard

2. Then, go to your **View Controller** (not the **Navigation Controller**) of your modal:

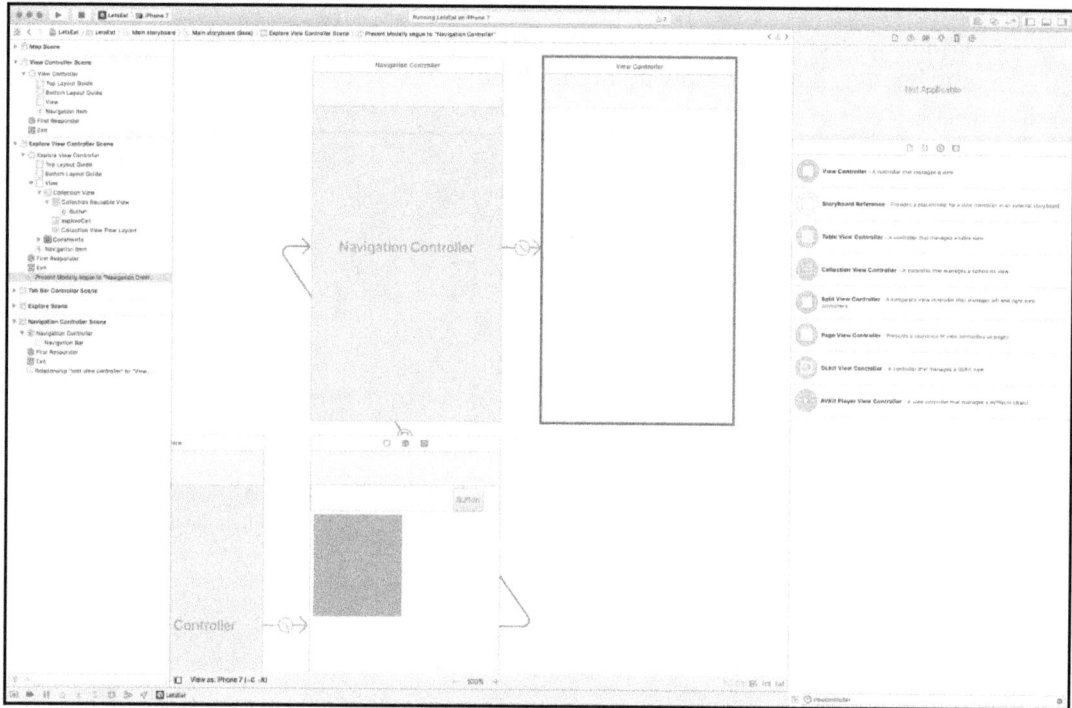

3. Next, type in `bar button` into the filter area of the objects library in the Utilities panel.

Chapter 8

4. Drag and drop a **Bar Button Item** into the right area of the **Navigation Bar** of your `View Controller Scene`:

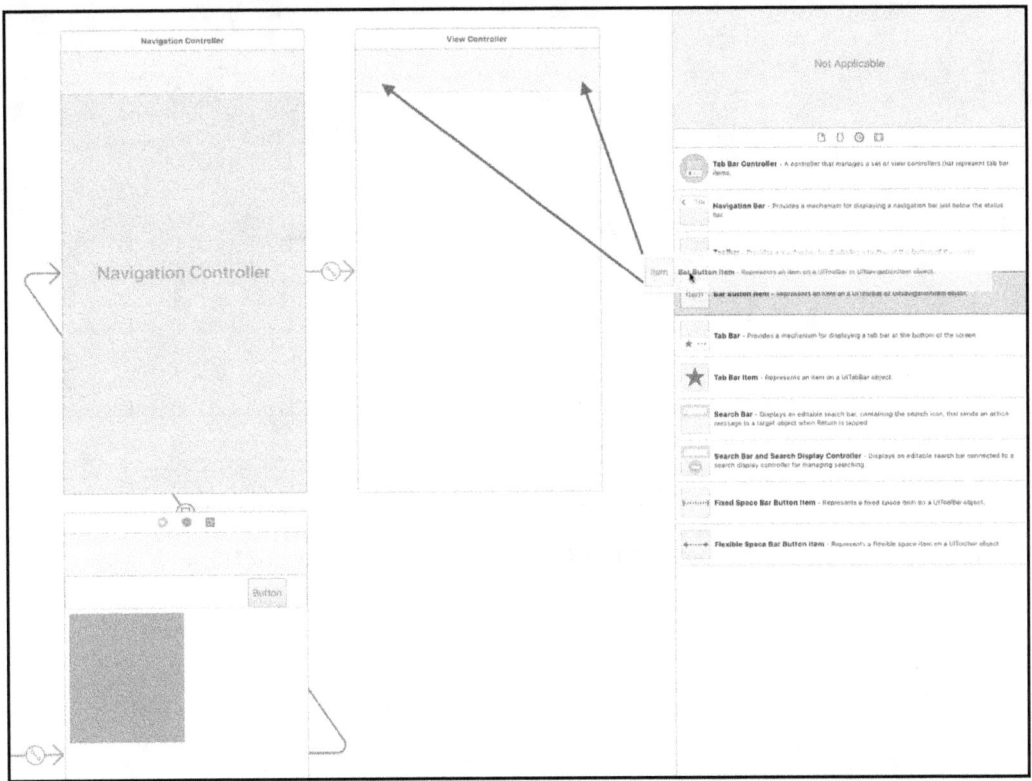

Building Our App Structure in Storyboard

5. Drag another **Bar Button Item** into the left area of the **Navigation Bar**:

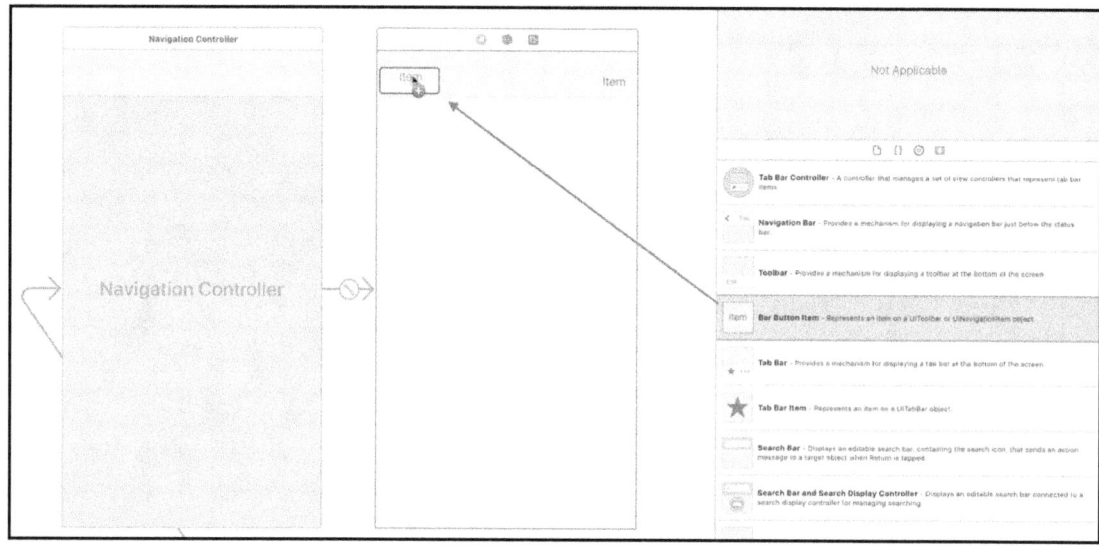

6. You should now have two **Bar Button Items** that both say **Item**:

Chapter 8

Updating Bar Button Items

Next, we need to update both of the **Bar Button Items** to say cancel and done:

1. Select the left **Bar Button Item**, and, in the Utilities panel, select the Attributes inspector.
2. Click on **System Item** and select **Cancel** in the drop-down menu.
3. Select the right **Bar Button Item**, and, while still in the Attributes inspector in the Utilities panel, update **System Item** to **Done**.

Now, you should see **Cancel** on the left and **Done** on the right:

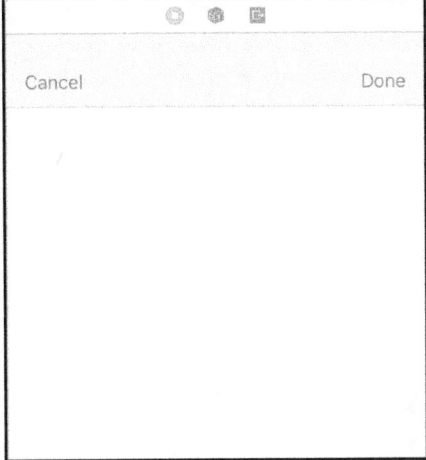

Unwinding our Cancel button

Now that we have our buttons, we want to dismiss the modal when a user hits **Cancel**:

In the `Main.storyboard`, Ctrl drag from the **Cancel** button to **Exit**:

You can also do this in the Outline view.

You will see a window popup that says **Action Segue** and **unwindLocationCancelWithSegue**. Select `unwindLocationCancelWithSegue`:

Chapter 8

Let's build and run the project by hitting the Play button (or use *cmd +R*), and test our **Cancel** button. It should now dismiss the View. We will update the **Done** button when we add code later.

Adding our first Table View

Now, let's add a `UITableView` into our `UIViewController`:

1. In the Utilities panel of `Main.storyboard`, in the filter field, type `tableview`; then, drag the Table View onto the scene:

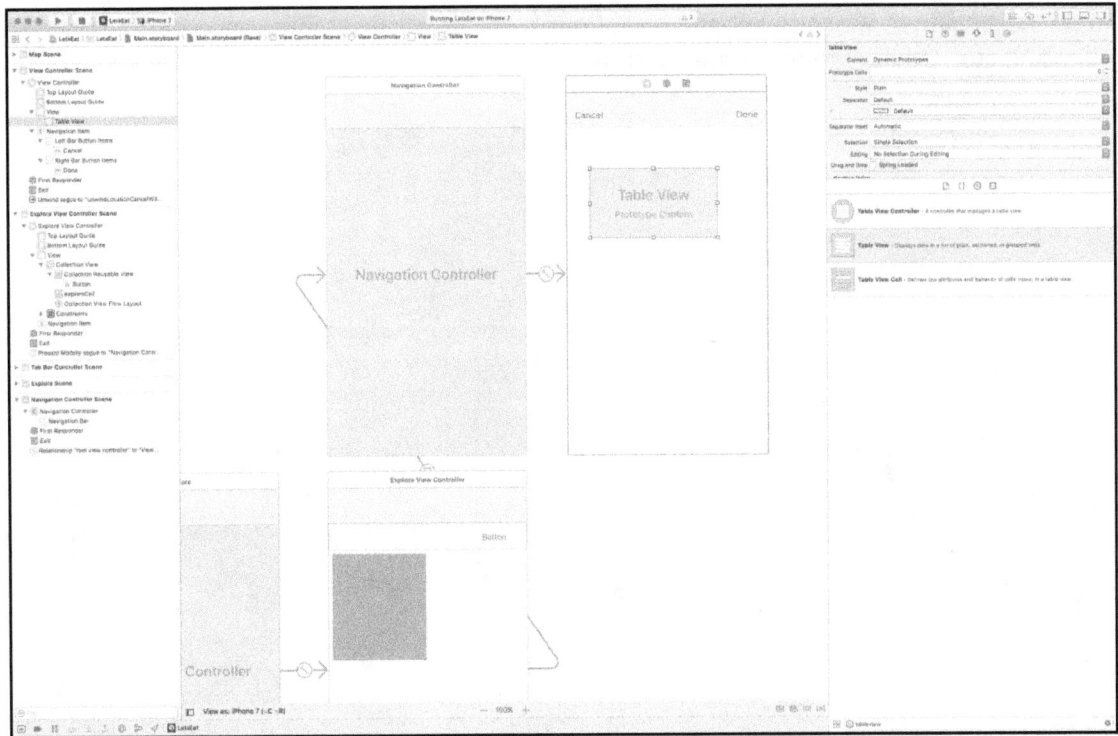

2. Select the Pin icon and enter the following values:

    - Set all values under **Add New Constraints** to 0
    - The **Constrain to margins** checkbox should be unchecked

3. Now, click on **Add 4 Constraints**.

[227]

If you build and run the project, and then launch the modal, you will see an empty Table View. We will complete this Table View later.

Summary

We are about halfway through the setup of our UI structure. In this chapter, we created our **Collection View** with a dummy cell. This allows us to continue to work on the basic structure of our app and focus on the design of the app, getting all of the assets ready to go before we add code. We also added our first prototype header, as well as presenting a modal to the user.

In the next chapter, we complete the rest of our basic structure, before concentrating on adapting our structure to match our design.

9
Finishing Up Our App Structure in Storyboard

The more we do storyboard work, the easier it gets. I remember that when I started Xcode, it was a bit overwhelming because of all the panels and it really took me time to get comfortable. Anytime I speak with someone looking to get into iOS, I always tell them to dedicate at least 10-15 minutes a day to it for the first six months. It seems like a lot, but it really makes a difference when you are trying to learn. If you step away for a week and try to come back, it is like starting from ground zero; at least, it was for me. When I finally started to catch on was when I was in Xcode everyday and was relentless.

In the last chapter, we got our **Explore** and **Location** both set up. In this chapter, we are still working on just the structure and, in the next couple of chapters, we will work on design.

We will cover the following in this chapter:

- Restaurant View Controller
- Restaurant Detail View Controller
- Reviews View Controller
- Map tab

Finishing Up Our App Structure in Storyboard

Adding our Restaurant List View

Our restaurant list will be the same basic setup we did in the last chapter. If you think you have a grasp of this, now is a good time to challenge yourself. If you think you still need more practice, keep reading and let's set up the restaurant list:

1. Select the `Main.storyboard` file, making sure that you are zoomed out and can see all of your scenes (depending on your screen resolution). In the Utilities panel, ensure that you have the object library tab selected.
2. In the filter field, you are going to type `viewcontroller`. Drag this view controller and put it next to Explore View Controller.
3. Next, in the filter field, you are going to type `collectionview`.
4. Click on and drag **Collection View** and drop it onto the new **View Controller** we just added next to the Explore View Controller.
5. After you drop it onto the scene, select the Pin icon and enter the following values:

   - All values under **Add New Constraints** are set to 0
   - Make sure to uncheck **Constrain to margins**

6. Click on **Add 4 Constraints**.

We now have our **Collection View** component set up for our Restaurant list.

Hooking up our outlets

Let's now link our file, `RestaurantViewController`, to our new `UIViewController` in storyboard:

1. Select the `UIViewController` with the **Collection View** that we just created.
2. Now, in the Utility panel, select the Identity inspector. Under **Custom Class**, in the **Class** drop-down menu, select `RestaurantViewController` and hit *Enter*.
3. After you hit *Enter*, select the **Connections Inspector** in the Utilities panel.
4. Under **Outlets**, click on the `collectionView` circle and drag from the circle to **Collection View** that we just added inside of your `UIViewController`.

[230]

Chapter 9

Now that we have our **Collection View** hooked up, we need to hook up the data source and delegate. This allows us to pass data to our **Collection View** as well as know when our **Collection View** has some kind of interaction.

1. In your scene, select your **Collection View**. Then, in your Utilities panel, select the **Connections Inspector**.
2. Click on and drag the `dataSource` property to the Restaurant View Controller in your Outline view.
3. Click on and drag the delegate property to the Restaurant View Controller in your Outline view.

Finally, let's set up our cell to have a color so we can make sure we have everything set up correctly.

Setting up our cell

In `Main.storyboard`, select the small box inside of your **Collection View**. This is your **Collection View** prototype cell.

1. Open the Attributes inspector in the Utilities panel.
2. Update the following:
   - **Identifier**: `restaurantCell`
   - **Background: Demo Grey**

Finishing Up Our App Structure in Storyboard

3. Now, CTL drag from the explore cell to Restaurant View Controller:

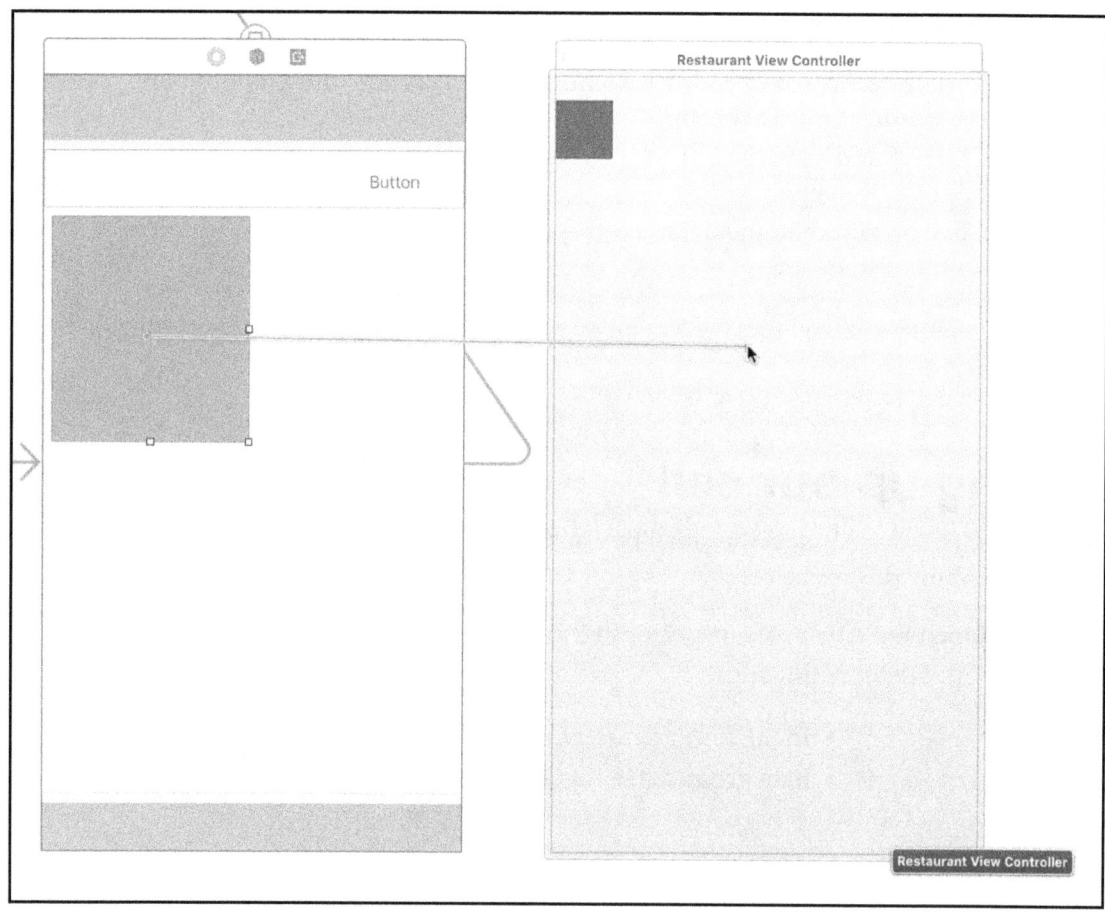

4. When you let go, you will be presented with the following menu and you should select **Show**:

Chapter 9

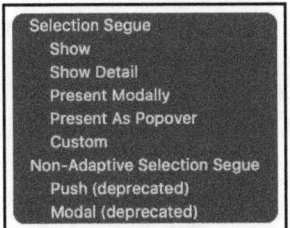

Now, let's run the project by hitting the Play button (or using *cmd* + *R*). You will now be able to tap on an explore cell and see the following:

Finishing Up Our App Structure in Storyboard

Next, we want when the user taps on a restaurant that they are presented with the restaurant details. We will use a static Table View Controller to do our detail. Using a static Table View, it allows us to create content without code. We will still have to hook up our data but, in the following chapters, you will see how static Table Views come in handy. Let's set up the restaurant detail:

1. Select the `Main.storyboard` file, making sure that you are zoomed out and can see all of your scenes (depending on your screen resolution). In the Utilities panel, ensure that you have the object library tab selected.
2. In the filter field, you are going to type: `tableviewcontroller` (make sure it's the controller—it will have a yellow icon). Drag this Table View Controller and put it next to Restaurant View Controller:

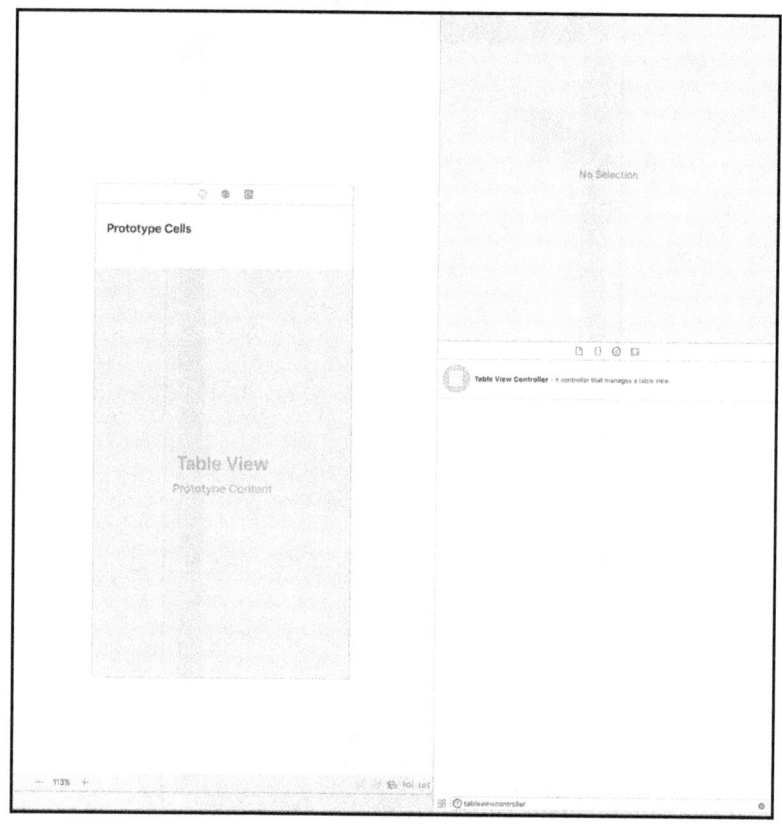

Chapter 9

3. Now, Ctrl + drag from the restaurant cell button to Restaurant Detail Table View Controller:

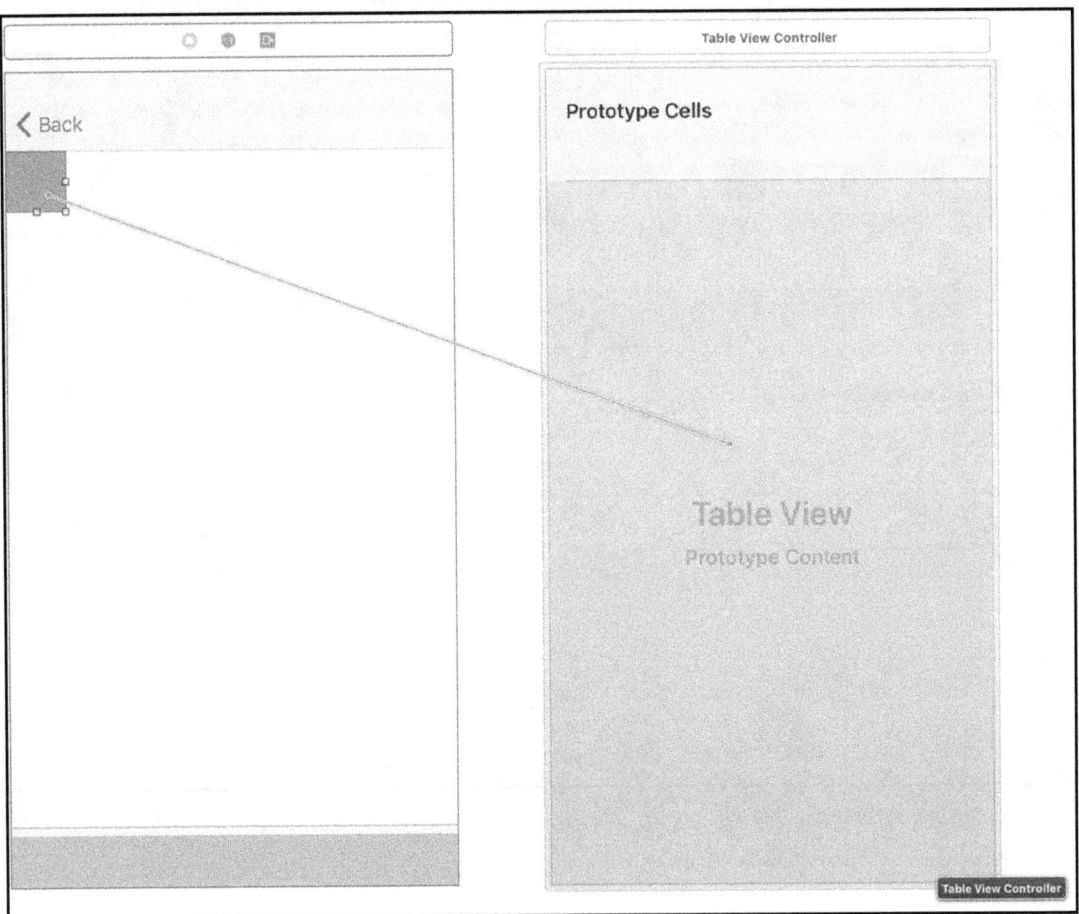

[235]

Finishing Up Our App Structure in Storyboard

4. When you let go, you will be presented with the following menu and you should select **Show**.
5. Next, click on the Table View inside of the Outline:

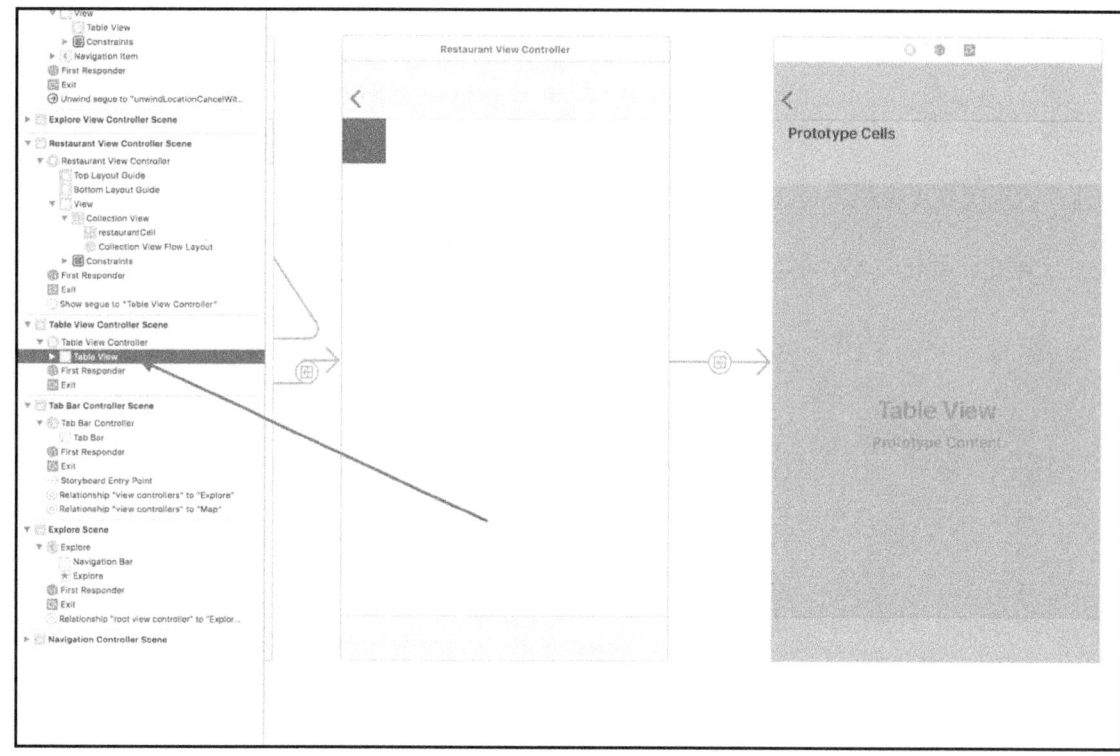

Chapter 9

6. Make sure that you have Attributes inspector opened in the Utilities panel, then change the Table View content from **Dynamic Prototypes** to **Static Cells**:

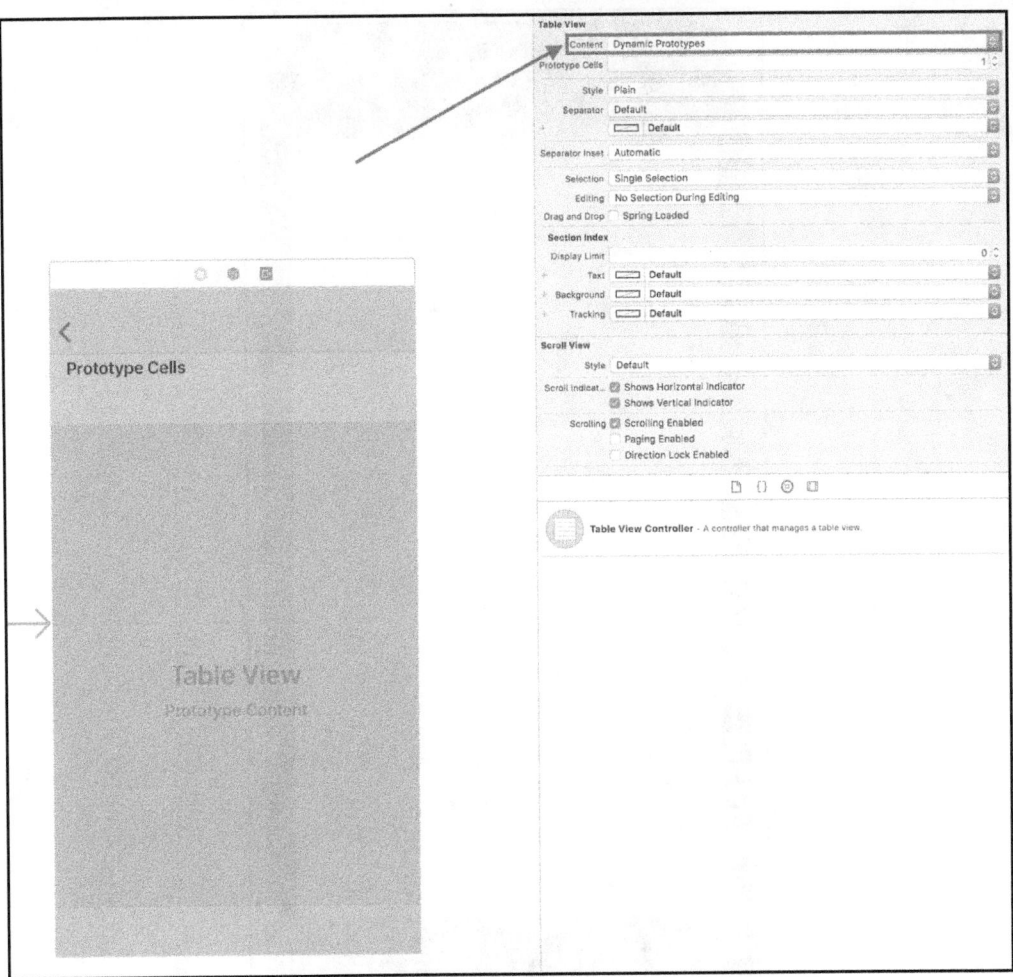

Finishing Up Our App Structure in Storyboard

Now, let's run the project by hitting the Play button (or using *cmd + R*). You will now be able to tap on a restaurant cell and see the following:

Adding Reviews View

We have our static Table View set up now, we need another view that allows us to view restaurant reviews. Let's add that next:

1. In the filter field, you are going to type: `button`. Drag this button and put it next to the one of the `tableview` cells:

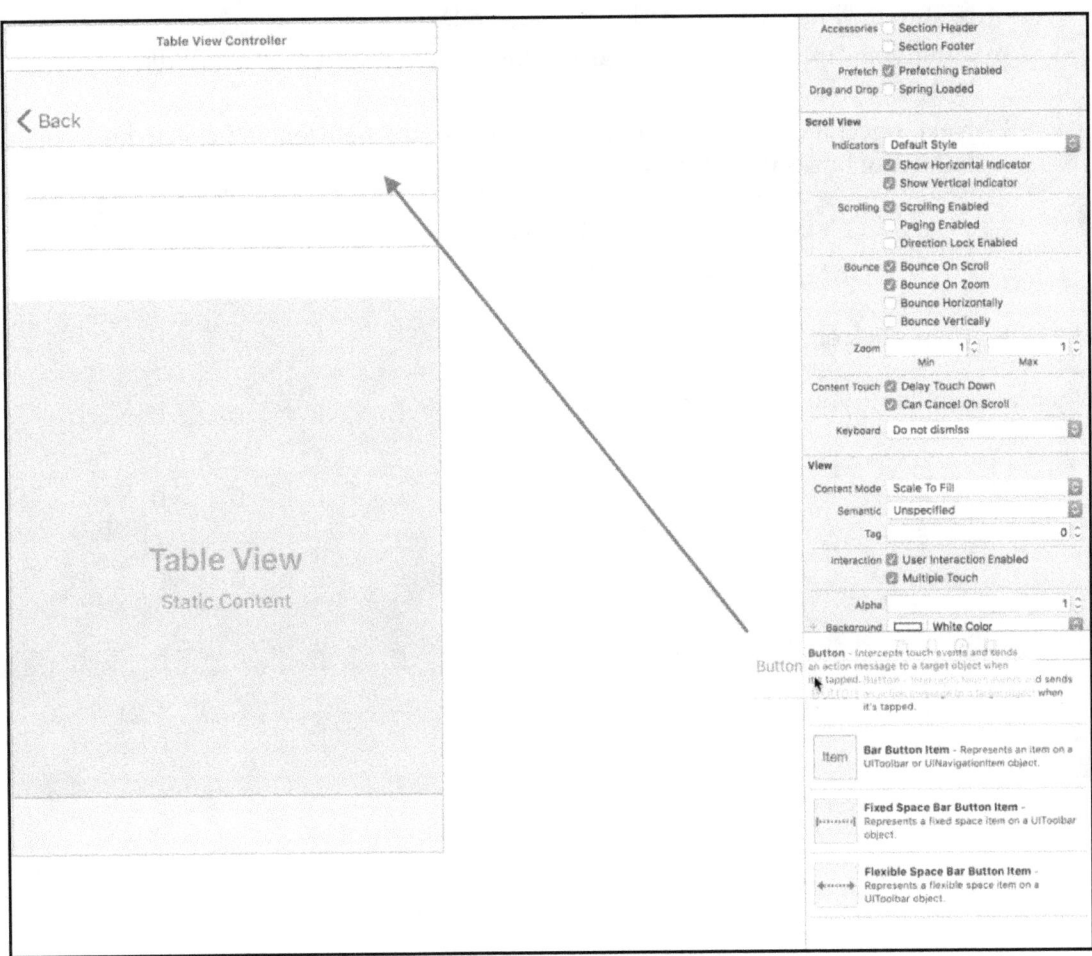

Finishing Up Our App Structure in Storyboard

2. Next, select the `Main.storyboard` file, making sure that you are zoomed out and can see all of your scenes (depending on your screen resolution). In the Utilities panel, ensure that you have the object library tab selected.
3. In the filter field, you are going to type `viewcontroller`. Drag this view controller and put it next to the Restaurant Detail View Controller.
4. Next, in the filter field, you are going to type `label`.
5. Click on and drag Label and drop it onto the new **View Controller** we just added next to the Restaurant Detail View Controller.
6. After you drop it onto the scene, double-click in the label and add the text—`Reviews`.
7. Next, select the Align icon that is to the left of the Pin icon and check the following boxes that appear:

    - Horizontally in container
    - Vertically in container

8. Then, click on **Add 2 Constraints**.

When you are done, you will see the following:

Chapter 9

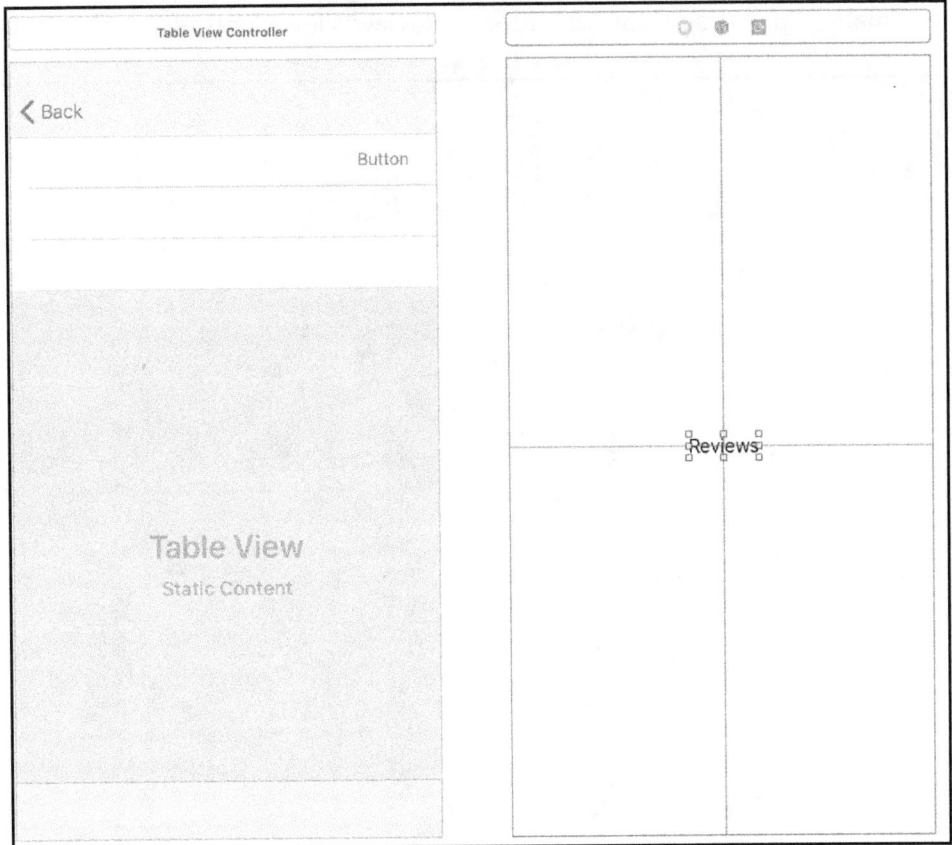

Viewing reviews

Now, we just need to add a segue to be able to get to the Reviews View Controller:

1. Back in the filter field, you are going to type `button`. Drag this button and put it in the static Table View. For now, it does not matter which cell; when we work on design, we will update this.

Finishing Up Our App Structure in Storyboard

2. Finally, Ctrl + drag from the button to Review View Controller we just added:

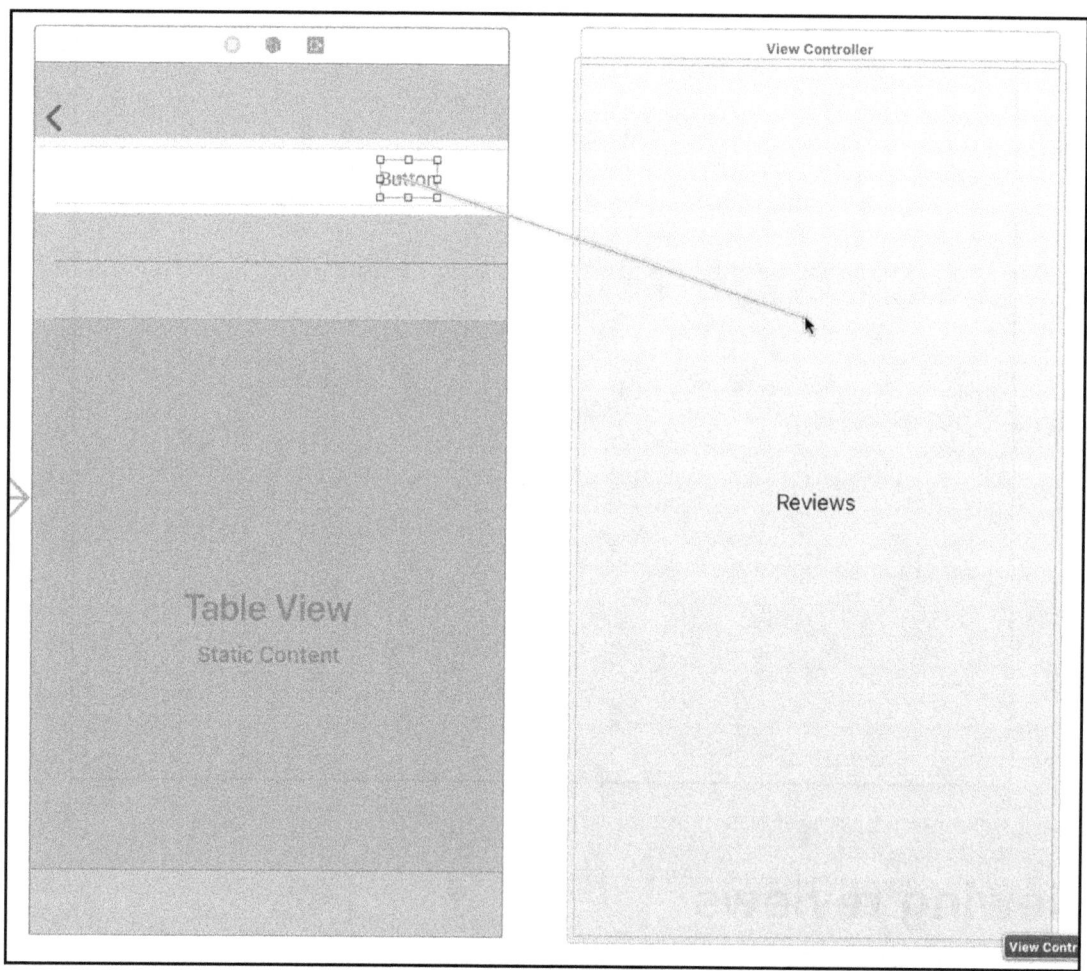

3. When you let go, you will be presented with a menu and you should select **Show**.

Chapter 9

Now, let's run the project by hitting the Play button (or using *cmd + R*). You will now be able to tap on the button in restaurant details and see the following:

Finishing Up Our App Structure in Storyboard

Map Kit View

The last thing we need to do is set up our **Map** tab. Select the `Main.storyboard` file and find the **View Controller** connected to the **Map** tab:

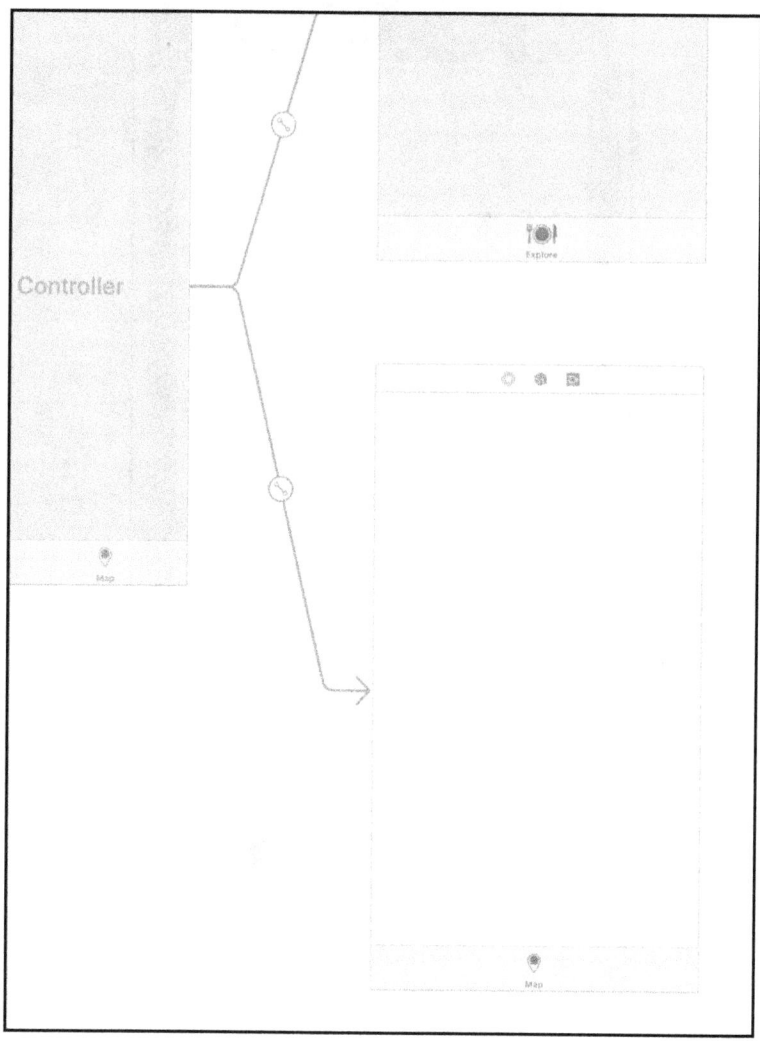

Chapter 9

Let's get started:

1. With the **View Controller** selected, navigate to **Editor | Embed In | Navigation Controller**.
2. In the Utilities panel, with the object library tab selected, type map in the filter field.
3. Drag and drop **Map Kit View** onto the **Map View Controller**:

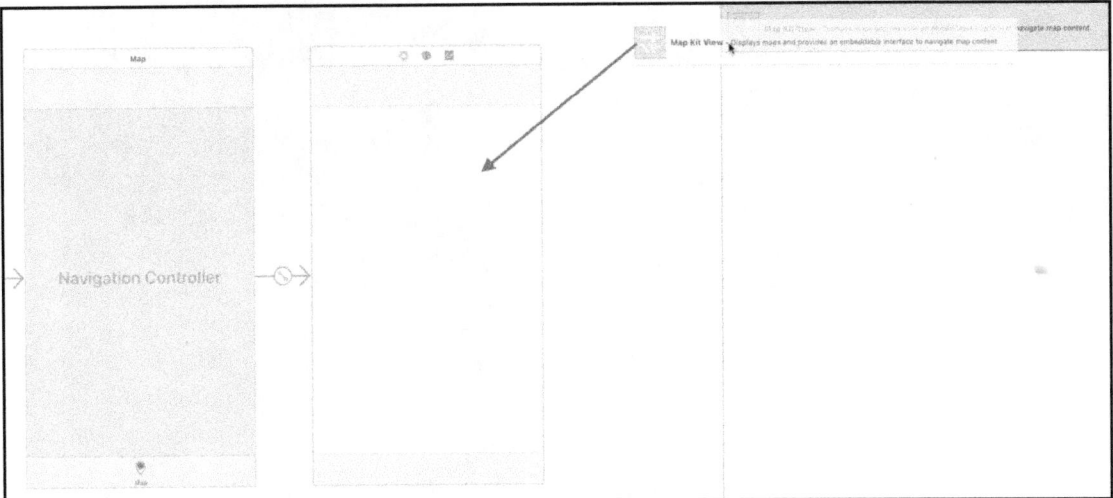

4. Next, select the Pin icon and enter the following values:

    - All values under **Add New Constraints** are set to 0
    - Uncheck the **Constrain to margins** checkbox
    - Click on **Add 4 Constraints**

Finishing Up Our App Structure in Storyboard

5. Your **View Controller** should look like the following when you are done:

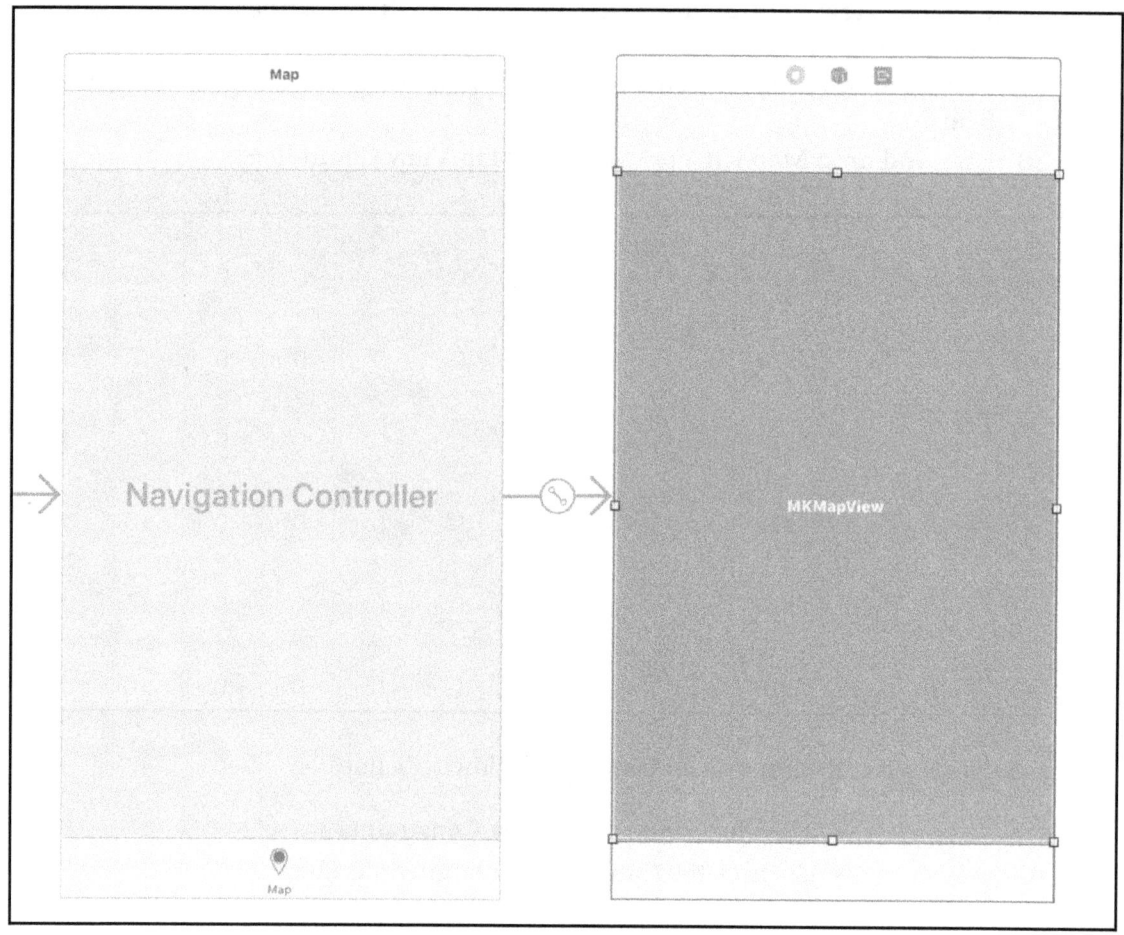

6. Let's run the project by hitting the Play button (or using *cmd + R*) and selecting the **Map** tab:

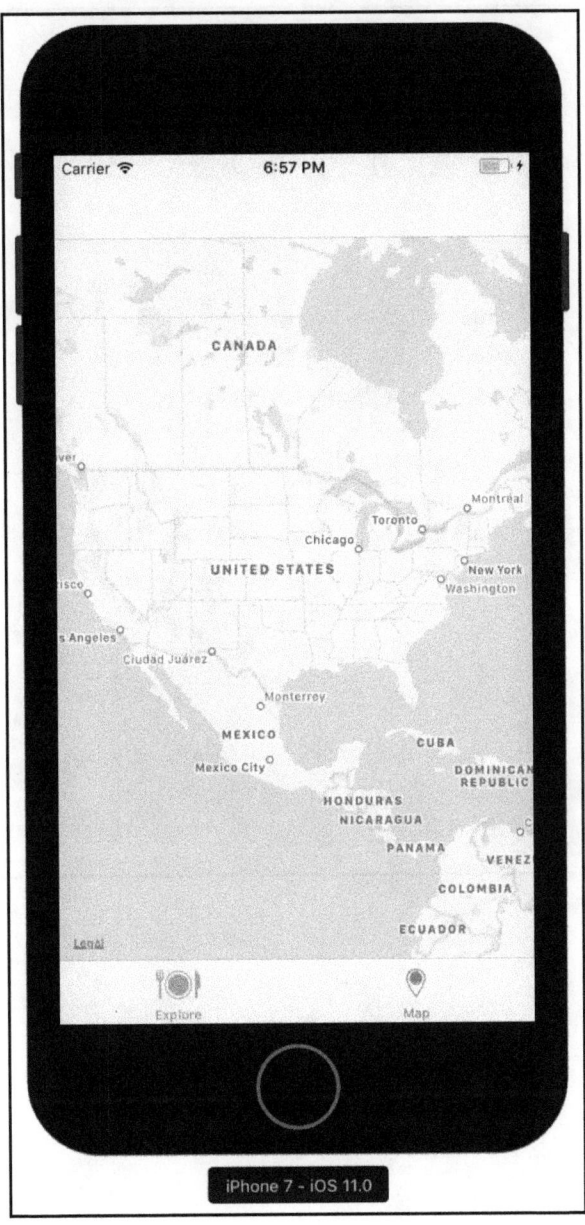

Finishing Up Our App Structure in Storyboard

We now have both tabs set up, but, as we progress through the book, we will add more scenes to the storyboard. This is what your `Main.storyboard` file should look like:

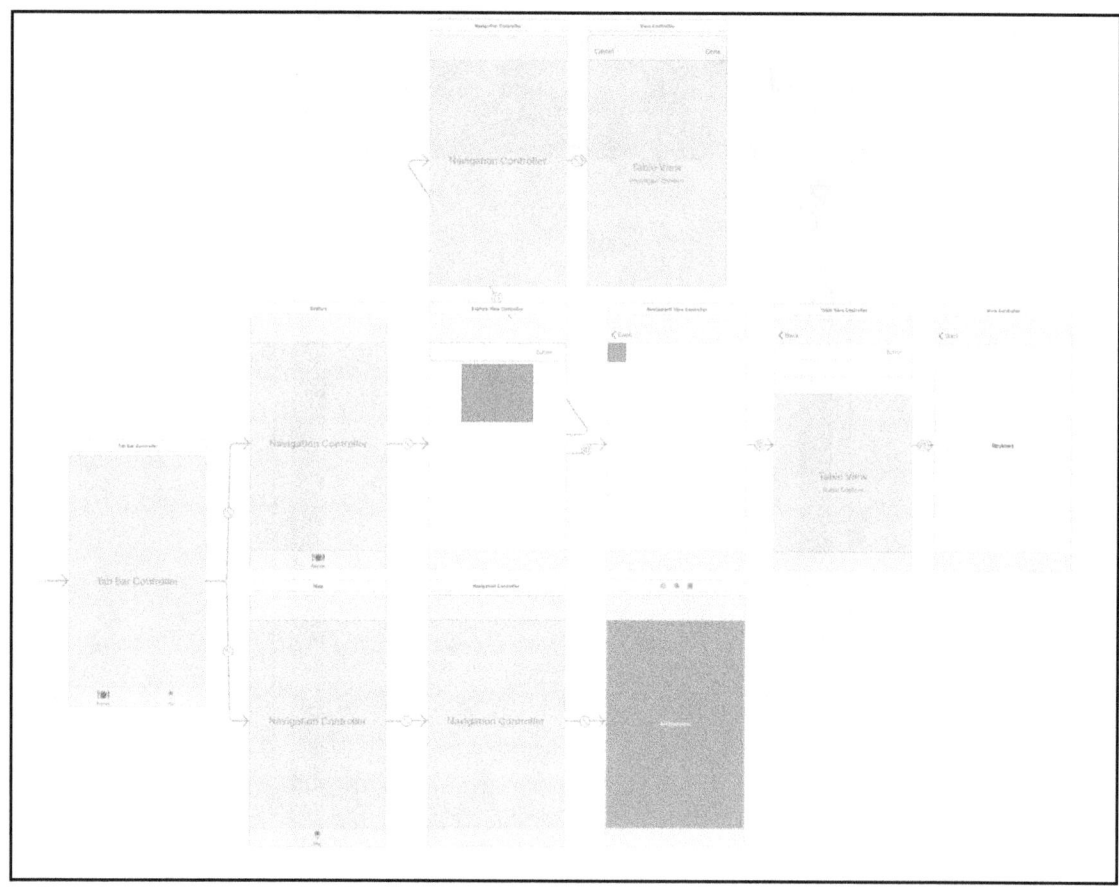

Summary

In this chapter, we have finished the application structure. We hooked up our explore cell to a restaurant list. Then, we were able to connect a restaurant to a detail. Next, we added a button in our details, which allows us to see restaurant reviews. Lastly, we added a map to our **Map** tab.

At this point, a good challenge would be to see if you can get back to this point. Starting from when we created the project towards the end of `Chapter 6`, *Starting the UI Setup*, in the *Creating a new project* section. See if you can go from that point to here without the book and without missing anything. This will really help you and it is something I like to do with those I mentor.

In the next chapter, we will start digging more into the design and getting our app to visually look like the design.

10
Designing Cells

In this chapter and throughout the book, we will adjust our app to match the design we reviewed earlier. However, the specifics of the design, such as custom fonts, are there as examples; you should feel free to change things to match your taste. By experimenting while learning, you should get a better understanding of how things work and become more comfortable using Xcode. I would recommend that you first thoroughly understand the lessons before experimenting; however, I highly encourage you to have fun and make the app your own.

In this chapter, we will be working with the following:

- Table View Cells
- Collection View Cells
- Auto Layout

Setting up the Explore header

Let's review the section header for the **Explore** tab:

In this header, we only have four elements: two `UILabels` (title and subtitle), a button, and a gray line underneath the title and button.

Designing Cells

We already have the button in the prototype header (collection reusable view) we created in an earlier chapter and now we need to add the two `UILabels` and then revise all three elements so that they match our design:

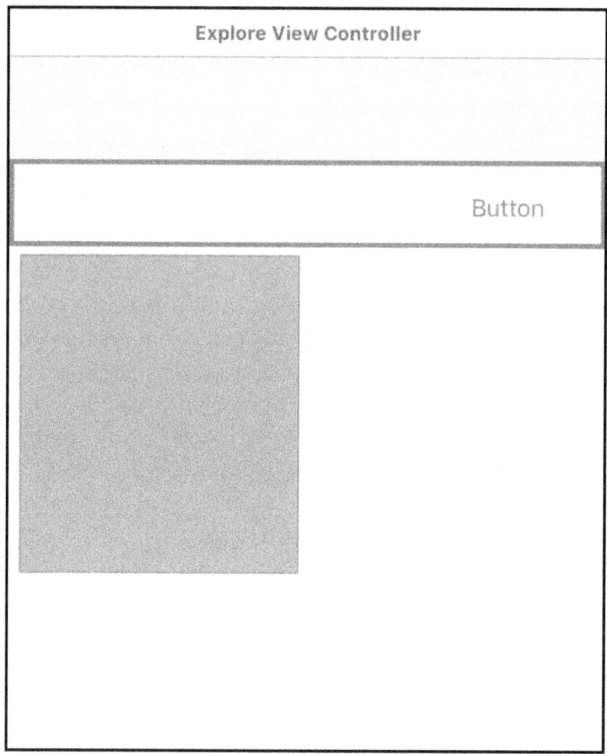

Let's get started:

1. In `Main.storyboard`, select the prototype header and, in the Size inspector, update the following values:

    - **Width**: 0
    - **Height**: 100

     When you update the size, you might experience the following:

Chapter 10

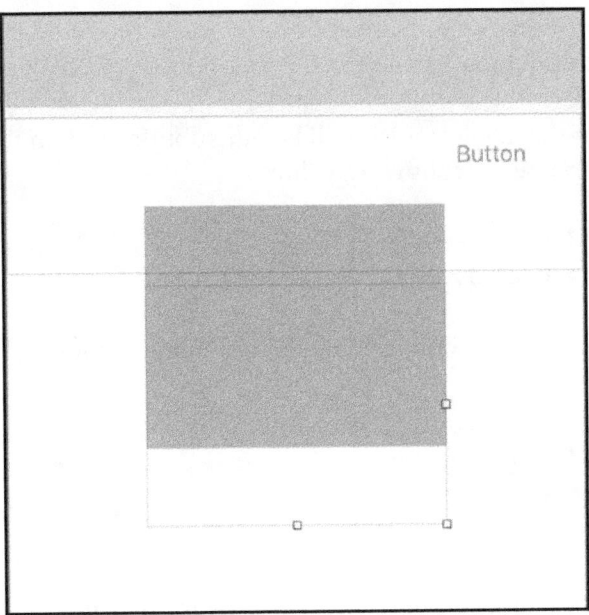

If you do, just click on a different file and come back; the storyboard should fix itself.

2. Next, in the filter field of the object library, type `view`.
3. Then, drag out a View into the prototype header.
4. Select the View (make sure you use the outline view and move this below all the other elements using the Outline view. If you do not, it will cover everything.) and, in the Size inspector, update the following values:

   - **X**: 0
   - **Y**: 0
   - **Width**: 375
   - **Height**: 90

5. Now, type `label` in the filter field of the object library.
6. Then, drag out two labels into the View of the prototype header that we just added.
7. Next, we are going to add a new color to our `Assets.xcassets` file. Name the color `LetsEat Light Grey` and set the **Hex Color** # to `AFAFB2`.

Designing Cells

8. While we are here, let's rename our `Demo Grey` to `LetsEat Dark Grey`. Our cells do not update to this new color, yet it does not break anything. We will change these colors later in the chapter.
9. Select one of the labels, which will be our subtitle, and, in the Attributes inspector, update the following values:

    - **Color**: `LetsEat Light Grey`
    - **Font**: `System Semibold 13`

10. Next, in the Size inspector, update the following values:

    - **X**: 8
    - **Y**: 24
    - **Width**: 350
    - **Height**: 21

11. Now, select the other label, which will be our title, and, in the Attributes inspector, update the value of **Font** to `System Heavy 40.0`:

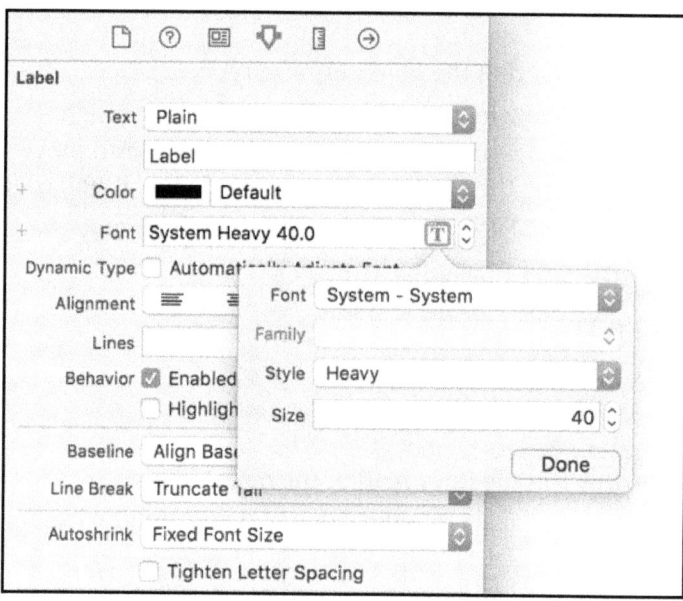

12. Then, in the Size inspector, update the following values:

    - **X**: 8
    - **Y**: 45
    - **Width**: 255
    - **Height**: 37

13. Select the button; in the Attributes inspector, update the following values:

    - **Type**: Custom
    - **Image**: btn-location
    - Remove the text button

14. Next, in the Size inspector, update the following values:

    - **X**: 271
    - **Y**: 50
    - **Width**: 96
    - **Height**: 25

15. Finally, type `view` in the filter field of the object library.
16. Then, drag a View into the prototype header.
17. Select the View (make sure you use the outline view and move this below all the other elements) and, in the Size inspector, update the following values:

    - **X**: 8
    - **Y**: 89
    - **Width**: 359
    - **Height**: 1

18. Select the button and, in the Attributes inspector, update the value of **Background** to `LetsEat Light Grey`:

Designing Cells

Now, with all of the elements placed into the prototype header, your cell should look as follows (inside your label you should have the text **Label**):

To ensure that our cells adjust to the size of different devices, we must add Auto Layout constraints.

Adding Auto Layout to the Explore header

Working with Auto Layout can be very frustrating. If it does not work correctly, I recommend that you clear all the constraints and start over.

Let's begin by adding Auto Layout to our subtitle Label, which is where we should show the current selected location:

1. Select the subtitle Label and then the Pin icon. Enter the following values:

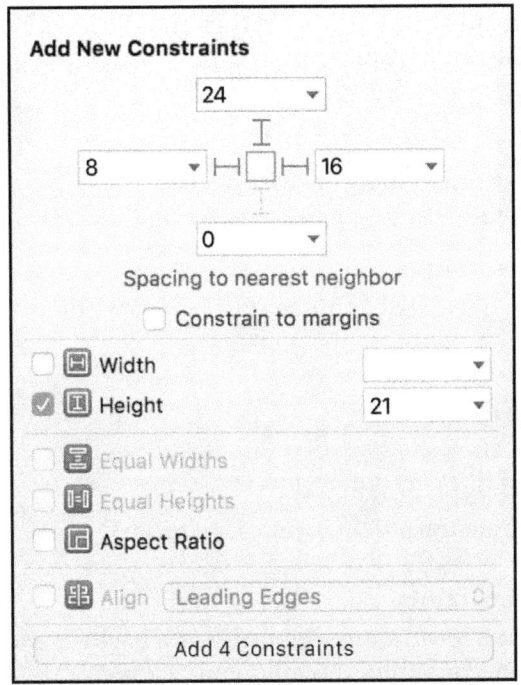

2. Click **Add 4 Constraints**.
3. Next, select the **Location** button and then the Pin icon. Enter the following values:

    - **Top**: 5
    - **Right**: 8
    - **Constrain to margins**: Unchecked
    - **Width**: 96 (should be checked)
    - **Height**: 25 (should be checked)

4. Click **Add 4 Constraints**.

Designing Cells

5. Next, select the grey line (view) and then the Pin icon. Enter the following values:
   - **Right**: 8
   - **Bottom**: 10
   - **Left**: 8
   - **Constrain to margins**: Unchecked
   - **Height**: 1 (should be checked)
6. Click **Add 4 Constraints**.
7. Now, select the title Label and then the Pin icon. Enter the following values:

   - **Top**: 0
   - **Right**: 8
   - **Left**: 8
   - **Height**: 37 (should be checked)
   - **Constrain to margins**: Unchecked

8. Click **Add 4 Constraints**.
9. Lastly, select the View that we are using as a background and just added earlier and then the Pin icon. Enter the following values:

   - **Top**: 0
   - **Right**: 0
   - **Bottom**: 10
   - **Left**: 0
   - **Constrain to Margins**: Unchecked

10. Click **Add 4 Constraints**.

We have completed adding Auto Layout to the **Explore** tab header.

Setting up the Explore cell

Next, let's work on the Explore Collection View cell:

1. Select the prototype cell, called `exploreCell`, in the Attributes inspector and update the background color to white.

2. In the Explore View Controller and, then, in the Size inspector, update the following values:

    - **Width**: 164
    - **Height**: 195

3. In the object library's filter field, type `view`.
4. Then, drag a View into the prototype cell.
5. Select the View and, in the Size inspector, update the following values:

    - **X**: 0
    - **Y**: 0
    - **Width**: 164
    - **Height**: 164

6. Next, type: `image` in the filter field.
7. Then, drag an Image view into the View we just added.
8. With the Image view still selected, update the following values in the Size inspector:

    - **X**: 0
    - **Y**: 0
    - **Width**: 164
    - **Height**: 164

9. Now, type: `label` in the filter field.
10. Then, drag a Label into the prototype cell (not the View).
11. With the Label selected, update the value of **Font** in the Attributes inspector to **Avenir Next Condensed Demibold 20**.
12. Next, in the Size inspector, update the following values:

    - **X**: 6
    - **Y**: 169
    - **Width**: 152
    - **Height**: 21

Designing Cells

The `exploreCell` is now complete. Your cell should now look like the following:

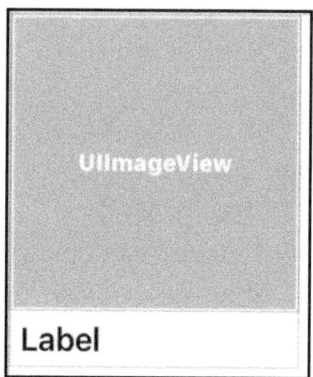

Let's add Auto Layout constraints before we move onto our Restaurant cell.

Adding Auto Layout to the Explore cell

1. In the Outline view, select the container View that is holding the Image view and, then, the Pin icon. Enter the following values:

    - **Top**: 0
    - **Right**: 0
    - **Left**: 0
    - **Constrain to margins**: Unchecked
    - **Height**: 164 (should be checked)

2. Click **Add 4 Constraints**.
3. Next, select Image view and, then, the Pin icon. Enter the following values:

    - **Top**: 0
    - **Right**: 0
    - **Bottom**: 0
    - **Left**: 0
    - **Constrain to margins**: Unchecked

4. Click **Add 4 Constraints**.

5. Finally, select the Label in this `exploreCell` and, then, the Pin icon. Enter the following values:

    - **Top**: `5`
    - **Right**: `6`
    - **Bottom**: `6`
    - **Constrain to margins**: Unchecked
    - **Height**: `21` (should be checked)

6. Click **Add 4 Constraints**.

The Explore cell now has all the necessary constraints, and we can now set up the Restaurant cell.

Setting up the Restaurant cell

The Restaurant cell that we are setting up has many elements, so make sure to take your time. Make sure that you go to the Restaurant View Controller and let's get started:

1. In the Attributes inspector, update the background color.
2. Select the restaurant list prototype cell and, in the Size inspector, update the following values:

    - **Width**: `375`
    - **Height**: `312`

3. In the filter field of the object library, type `view`.
4. Then, drag a View into the prototype cell.
5. With the View selected, update the following values in the Size inspector:

    - **X**: `75.5`
    - **Y**: `245`
    - **Width**: `224`
    - **Height**: `56`

6. Next, type `label` in the filter field.

Designing Cells

7. Then, drag a Label into the View we just added.
8. With the Label selected, update the following values in the Size inspector:

    - **X**: 0
    - **Y**: 2
    - **Width**: 224
    - **Height**: 21

9. Then, in the Attributes inspector, update the following values:

    - **Text**: Add **Available Times** into the empty text field under the Text
    - **Color**: Black
    - **Alignment**: Center
    - **Font**: **Avenir Next Condensed Bold 17**

10. Next, type button in the filter field.
11. Drag out a button into the View we just added.
12. With the button selected, update the following values in the Attributes inspector:

    - **Type**: System
    - **Title**: Plain and then add **7:30 pm** in the empty text field under the Title
    - **Font**: **Avenir Next Condensed Regular 17**
    - **Text Color**: White Color
    - **Background**: time-bg

13. Next, in the Size inspector, update the following values:

    - **Width**: 68
    - **Height**: 27

14. Now, select the button in the Outline view and hit *cmd + C* to copy.
15. Then, hit *cmd + V* two times to paste. You should now have three buttons.

16. Next, *cmd* + click each button created and click on the **Embed in Stack** icon. This is the fourth icon to the left of the filter icon:

17. Select the stack view in the Outline view and, then, update the following values in the Attributes inspector:

    - **Axis**: Horizontal
    - **Alignment**: Fill
    - **Distribution**: Equal Spacing
    - **Spacing**: 10

18. In the Size inspector, set the **X** to 0.
19. Next, in the filter field of the Object library, type `view`.
20. Then, drag a View into the prototype cell.
21. With the View selected, update the following values in the Size inspector:

    - **X**: 11
    - **Y**: 42
    - **Width**: 353
    - **Height**: 200

22. Next, type `image` in the filter field.
23. Then, drag out an Image view into the View we just added.
24. Select the Image view in the Outline view and update the value of **Image** in the Attributes inspector with `american`. We are just using this image as a placeholder to see that our cells are set up correctly. Later, we will remove this and load the images using code.

Designing Cells

25. With the Image view selected, update the following values in the Size inspector:
    - **X**: 0
    - **Y**: 0
    - **Width**: 353
    - **Height**: 200

26. Next, type: `label` in the filter field.
27. Then, drag two Labels into the prototype cell.
28. Select one of the Labels and update the value of **Font** in the Attributes inspector with **Avenir Next Condensed Demi Bold 17**.
29. Then, in the Size inspector, update the following values:
    - **X**: 10
    - **Y**: 8
    - **Width**: 355
    - **Height**: 19

30. Select the other Label and update the following values in the Attributes inspector:
    - **Color**: `LetsEat Dark Grey`
    - **Font**: **Avenir Next Condensed Regular 14**

31. Then, in the Size inspector, update the following values:
    - **X**: 10
    - **Y**: 32
    - **Width**: 355
    - **Height**: 19

We have completed our Restaurant cell setup, and now look like the following:

Now we need to add Auto Layout to all of the elements.

Adding Auto Layout to the Restaurant cell

Since we have many elements in the Restaurant cell, it means that there are more chances for errors with Auto Layout. Although you may be frustrated at times using Auto Layout, if you are a visual person like me, hopefully you will eventually appreciate using it:

1. Select the top label and then enter the following values:

    - **Top**: 8
    - **Right**: 10
    - **Left**: 10
    - **Constrain to margins**: Unchecked
    - **Height**: 19 (should be checked)

Designing Cells

2. Click **Add 4 Constraints**.
3. Now, select the Label right below the last label, then, the Pin icon. Enter the following values:

    - **Top**: 5
    - **Right**: 10
    - **Left**: 10
    - **Constrain to margins**: Unchecked
    - **Height**: 16 (should be checked)

4. Click **Add 4 Constraints**.
5. Next, select the Image container and, then, the Pin icon. Enter the following values:

    - **Top**: 4
    - **Constrain to margins**: Unchecked
    - **Width**: 353 (should be checked)
    - **Height**: 200 (should be checked)

6. Click **Add 3 Constraints**.
7. Next, click on the Align icon and enter the value of **Horizontally in Container** as 0 (this should be checked).
8. Click **Add 1 Constraint**.
9. Now, select the Image inside of the container and, then, the Pin icon. Enter the following values:

    - **Top**: 0
    - **Right**: 0
    - **Bottom**: 0
    - **Left**: 0
    - **Constrain to margins**: Unchecked

10. Click **Add 4 Constraints**.

11. Now, select the container that is holding the stack view and the available time's label and, then, the Pin icon. Enter the following values:

    - **Top**: 3
    - **Constrain to Margins**: Unchecked
    - **Width**: 224
    - **Height**: 56

12. Click **Add 3 Constraints**.
13. Next, click on the Align icon and enter the value **Horizontally in Container** as 0 (this should be checked).
14. Click **Add 1 Constraint**.
15. Now, select the stack view inside of the container and, then, the Pin icon. Enter the following values:

    - **Top**: 4
    - **Right**: 0
    - **Left**: 0
    - **Constrain to margins**: Unchecked
    - **Height**: 27

16. Click **Add 4 Constraints**.
17. Next, select the Label above the three buttons and, then, the Pin icon. Enter the following values:

    - **Top**: 2
    - **Left**: 0
    - **Right**: 0
    - **Constrain to margins**: Unchecked
    - **Height**: 21

18. Click **Add 4 Constraints**.
19. Finally, click on the Align icon and enter the value of **Horizontally in Container** as 0 (this should be checked).
20. Click **Add 1 Constraint**.

Designing Cells

Now, all of the Auto Layout for the Restaurant cell is set up. Let's build and run our project and go to the restaurant cell. Everything should look like the design we reviewed earlier in the book.

Location cell

We now need to work on the Locations cell. Find the Location View Controller and, for this cell, we are using a predefined cell that Apple provides.

1. Select the Table View, and update **Prototype Cells** to 1.
2. Next, select the prototype cell and enter the following values:

    - **Style**: Basic
    - **Identifier**: `locationCell`

That is all we need to do. Now, your cell should look as follows:

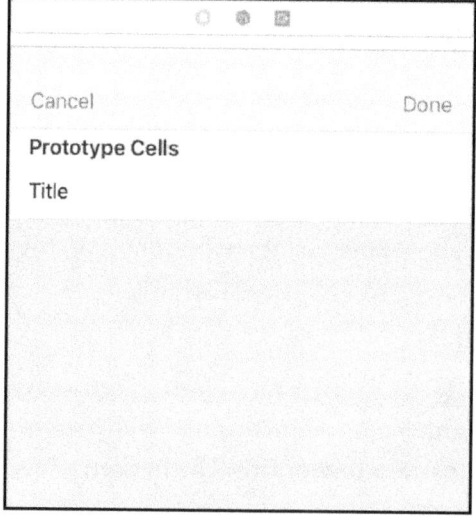

When you change the style from **Custom** to **Basic**, the word **Title** should appear in the cell. The word **Title** is just placeholder text. All of our cells are now ready for code that we address in the later chapters.

[268]

Summary

In this chapter, we formatted our cells to match our design and added Auto Layout constraints. Auto Layout can be complicated; however, as with anything, the more you practice, the easier it gets. You can write Auto Layout with code, but it is not what I prefer in storyboard. If you would like to do it in code, there are plenty of tutorials that can help you with this.

In the next chapter, we are going to work on getting the Restaurant details page looking like the design. Since a lot of this is static, you should see how using static tables can get your app up and running in no time.

11
Designing Static Tables

When storyboards were first introduced in late 2011, I was excited to use them. However, some developers did not (and still do not) like storyboards for many different reasons. I am a visual person; so, for me, storyboards give me the ability to see my app UI and be able to design it without having to run the app every time.

With the introduction of storyboards came static Table Views. For me, static Table Views changed the game, because I could create a complex layout all within storyboard without any, or with very little, code. Static Table Views can be used in many different ways, including for login screens, project settings, detail views, and so much more.

In this chapter, we are going to work with static Table Views; as you see, you can create complicated looks with very little code.

We will cover the following in this chapter:

- Creating our restaurant detail
- Understanding more UI elements
- Getting comfortable with Auto Layout
- Setting up our static Table View

Designing Static Tables

Setting up cells

The first thing we should do is set up our cells. We will have a total of nine rows in our Table View.

1. Select `Main.storyboard`.
2. In the Outline view, make sure that the disclosure arrows are down for **Table View Controller Scene**, **Table View Controller**, and **Table View**. Select **Table View Section** inside the **Table View**.

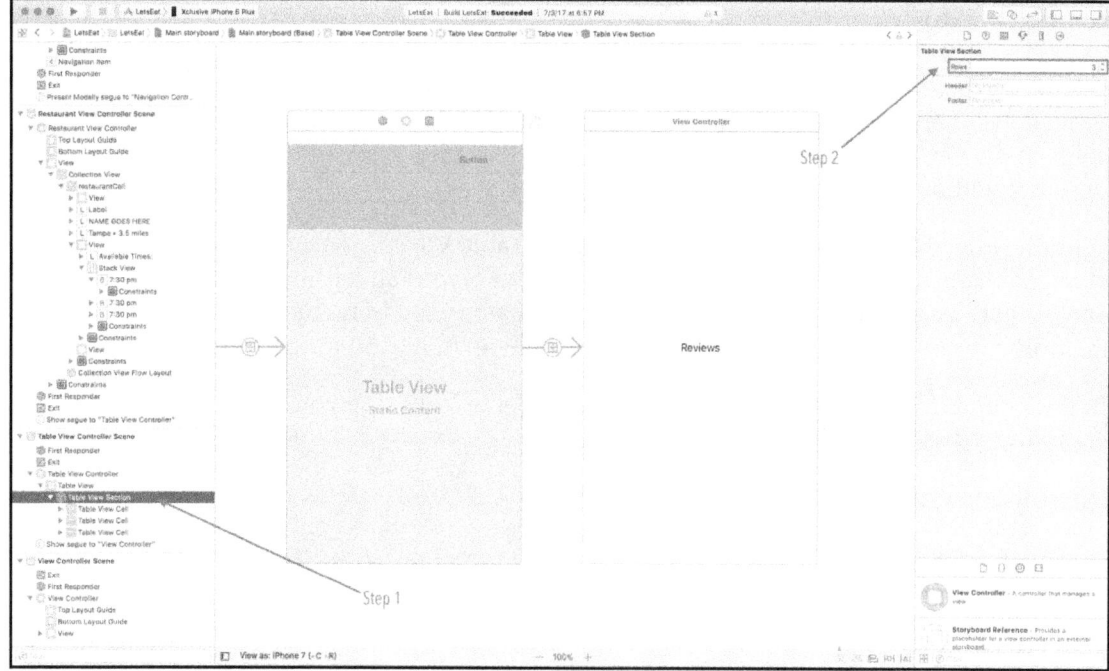

3. In the Attributes inspector of the Utilities panel, update **Rows** under **Table View Section** to 9. Then, hit *Enter*.
4. These nine cells are all we need to create our restaurant details. Let's create our section headers next.

[272]

Creating our section headers

We are going to make headers for rows 6 and 8. Let's see how we do it:

1. In the object library, **filter** field in the Utilities panel and type `label`.
2. Drag a label to the sixth row:

Designing Static Tables

3. Under the label section at the top of the Utilities panel Attributes inspector, change the word label, under **Text**, to **Photos**:

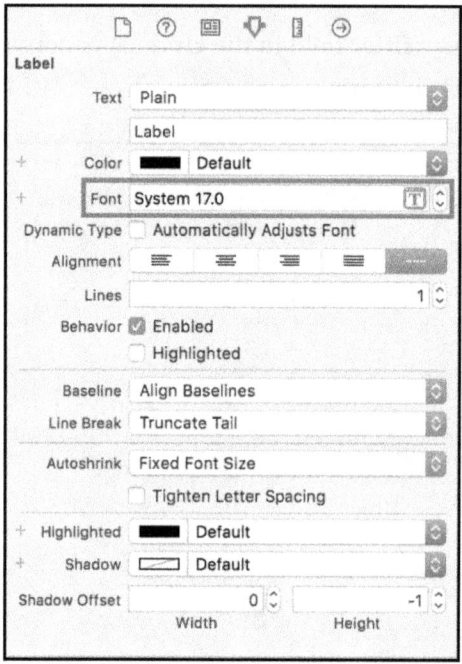

4. Now, let's update the **Font** in the Attributes inspector by selecting the **T** icon and updating the following values:

   - **Font**: Custom
   - **Family**: Avenir Next Condensed
   - **Style**: Bold
   - **Size**: 17

5. Select the Size inspector in the Utilities panel and update the following values:

   - **X**: 15
   - **Y**: 7
   - **Width**: 344
   - **Height**: 28

6. Now, we have to do the same for the next title.
7. To make it easier, select the current label and hit *cmd + C* to copy.
8. In the Outline view, select the eighth row and make sure that the disclosure arrow is down for that **Table View Cell**.
9. Then, select the **Content View** of that **Table View Cell** and hit *cmd + V* to paste:

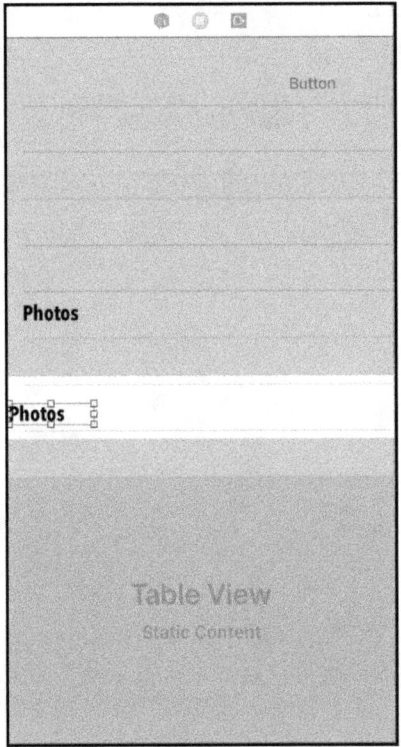

Note that, when you paste the label, it might be in the correct position. Double-click on the `UILabel` and change the label text from **Photos** to `Address`.

10. Make sure that your values match the following in the Size inspector:

- **X**: 15
- **Y**: 7
- **Width**: 344
- **Height**: 28

Designing Static Tables

11. If you copied and pasted the label, you can skip this step. If you created it by dragging it out, you can do the following. Select the **T** icon and update the following values:

    - **Font**: Custom
    - **Family**: Avenir Next Condensed
    - **Style**: Bold
    - **Size**: 17

When you are done, your `tableview` should look as follows:

We now have our headers setup. Let's move onto the rest of our Table View setup.

Creating our address section

Let's start with the address section:

In this section, we are going to add three UI elements: view, label, and an image.

1. In the **filter** field, type `label`.
2. Drag the `UILabel` into the **Content View** of the same row as our header (row 8).
3. Now, in the **filter** field, type `map`.
4. Drag a View into the **Content View** in the last row. We will use this as a container.
5. In the Utilities panel, select the Size inspector and update the following values:

    - **X**: 17
    - **Y**: 4
    - **Width**: 341
    - **Height**: 208

6. Next, drag out an **Image View** into the View container we just added.
7. In the Utilities panel, select the Size inspector, and update the following values:

    - **X**: 0
    - **Y**: 0
    - **Width**: 341
    - **Height**: 208

8. In the Outline view, select the **Table View Cell** that contains the **Image View**, and in the Size inspector, under **Table View Cell**, update **Row Height** to 217, then hit *Enter*.
9. Next, select the eighth row in the Outline view. Select the label and open the Size inspector in the Utilities panel. Update the following values:

    - **X**: 107
    - **Y**: 12
    - **Width**: 252
    - **Height**: 21

Designing Static Tables

10. With the label selected, select the **T** icon and updating the following values:

    - **Font**: `Custom`
    - **Family**: `Avenir Next Condensed`
    - **Style**: `Regular`
    - **Size**: `15`
    - **Alignment**: `Right`

We have now completed the address section. We will add text to our label in this section later in the book. Your address section should now look like mine:

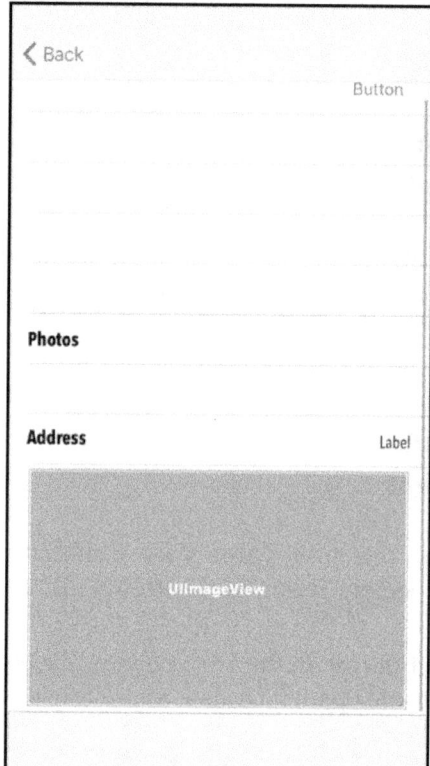

[278]

Adding Auto Layout to the headers

Let's add some Auto Layout to these new elements:

1. Select the label that says **Address** and then select the Pin icon and enter the following values:

    - **Top**: 10
    - **Left**: 15
    - **Constrain to margins**: Unchecked
    - **Height**: 28 (should be checked)
    - **Width**: 84 (should be checked)

2. Click **Add 4 Constraints**.
3. Next, select the other label in this row; this label will be used to display the actual address. Then, select the Pin icon and entering the following values:

    - **Top**: 12
    - **Right**: 15
    - **Left**: 8
    - **Constrain to margins**: Unchecked
    - **Height**: 21 (should be checked)

4. Click **Add 4 Constraints**.
5. Now, select the label that says **Photos** and then select the Pin icon and enter the following values:

    - **Top**: 9
    - **Left**: 15
    - **Right**: 15
    - **Constrain to margins**: Unchecked
    - **Height**: 28 (should be checked)

6. Click **Add 4 Constraints**.

Designing Static Tables

7. Finally, select the View holding the **Image View** in the last row and then select the Pin icon and enter the following values:

    - **Top**: 4
    - **Right**: 17
    - **Left**: 17
    - **Bottom**: 4.5
    - **Constrain to margins**: Unchecked

8. Click **Add 4 Constraints**.

With our address section completed, let's work on the photos section next.

Photos section

In this section, we are going to do something a bit different. This section has a bunch of photos that scroll from left to right. The best way to accomplish this is to use a Container View. We have not talked about Container Views yet but, they are containers that allow us to have separate View Controllers in specific areas. Right now, this will not make sense, but when we add the code later in the book, it will all make sense:

1. In the Outline view, select the Select the 7th row **Table View Cell**, and in the Size inspector, under **Table View Cell**, update **Row Height** to 214, then hit *Enter*.
2. In the object library **filter** field in the Utilities panel, type `container`.
3. Drag out a Container View into the seventh row.

    A Container View allows you to add a custom component. In this section, we add a Collection View that scrolls photos from left to right. Our reviews section does the same thing as well.

4. Select the Container View, open the Size inspector in the Utilities panel, and update the following values:

    - **X**: 0
    - **Y**: 0
    - **Width**: 375
    - **Height**: 214

When you add the Container View, you will see another window that looks like the following:

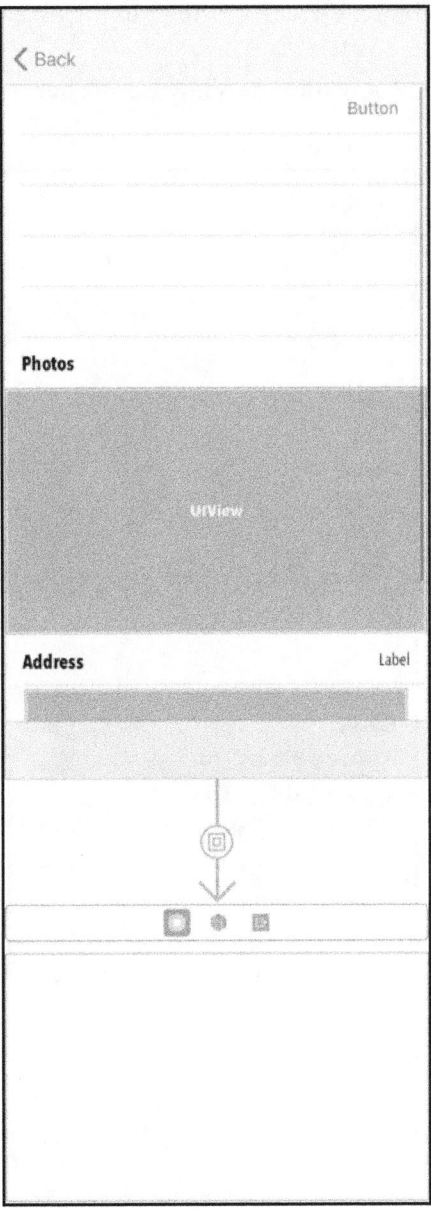

Designing Static Tables

This window is where we will add our Collection View. Before we do that, let's update the cell height as well as the height of the Container View.

1. Now, in the Container's View Controller, in the object library **filter** field in the Utilities panel, type `collection`.
2. Drag the Collection View into the View Controller.

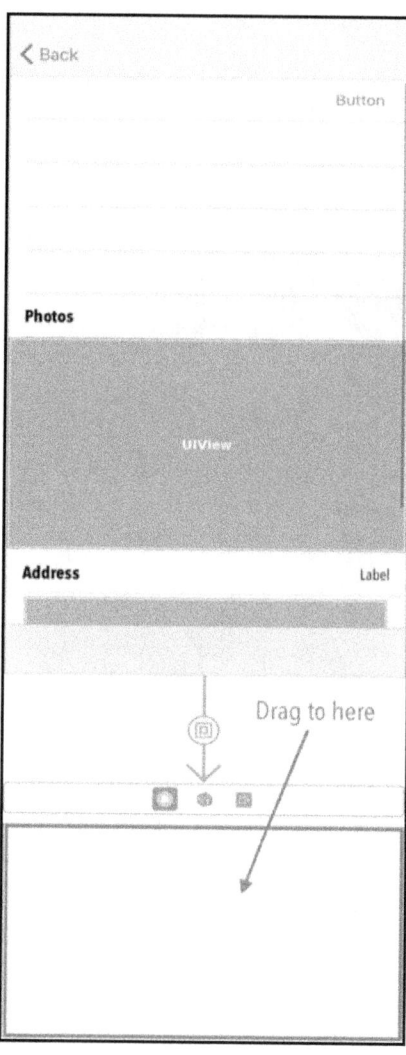

3. Select the Collection View, open the Size inspector in the Utilities panel, and update the following values:

    - **X:** 0
    - **Y:** 0
    - **Width:** 375
    - **Height:** 214

We are done with adding all of our UI elements.

Adding Auto Layout to the photos section

Let's add some Auto Layout to this section.

1. Select the Container View and then select the Pin icon and enter the following values:

    - **Top:** 0
    - **Right:** 0
    - **Bottom:** 0
    - **Left:** 0
    - **Constrain to margins:** Unchecked

2. Click **Add 4 Constraints**.
3. Next, select the Collection View that is inside of the Container View's View Container and then select the Pin icon and enter the following values:

    - **Top:** 0
    - **Right:** 0
    - **Bottom:** 0
    - **Left:** 0
    - **Constrain to margins:** Unchecked

4. Click **Add 4 Constraints**.

Designing Static Tables

Our photos section is now set up just like the following:

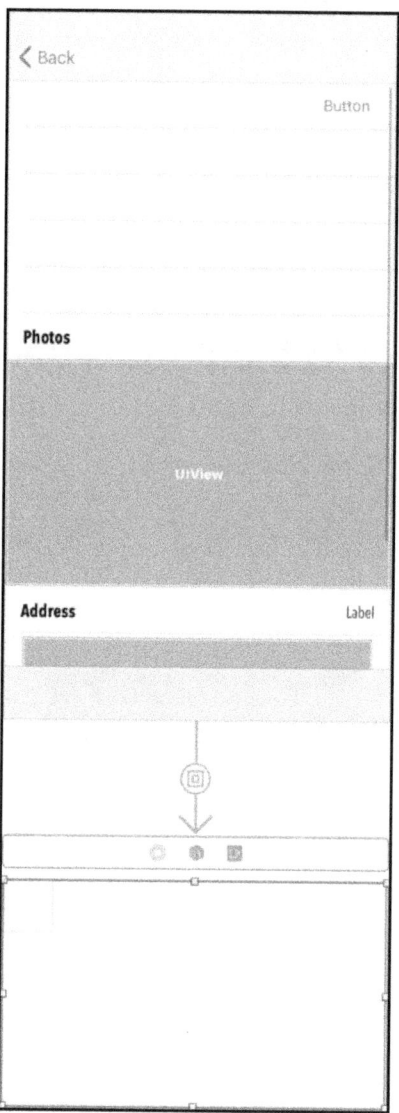

We now need to add reviews next.

Reviews section

Our review section takes up three cells (rows 3-5). The last cell shows actual reviews; the second cell has a button to add a photo and another button to add a review. Finally, the first cell has the restaurants average rating along with a title. Let's start from the bottom up.

The section that has the reviews is another Collection View and is set up the same way we set up the photos section:

1. In the Outline view, select the fifth **Table View Cell**, and in the Size inspector, under **Table View Cell**, update **Row Height** to `214`, then hit *Enter*.
2. In the object library **filter** field in the Utilities panel, type `container`.
3. Drag out the Container View into the fifth row.
4. Select the Container View, open the Size inspector in the Utilities panel, and update the following values:

   - **X**: 0
   - **Y**: 0
   - **Width**: 375
   - **Height**: 214

5. Now, in the Container's View Controller, in the object library **filter** field in the Utilities panel, type `collection`.
6. Just like we did before, drag the Collection View into the View Controller.
7. Select the Collection View, open the Size inspector in the Utilities panel, and update the following values:

   - **X**: 0
   - **Y**: 0
   - **Width**: 375
   - **Height**: 214

Designing Static Tables

Next, let's work on the next section. We are going to add some buttons to the next row, but we have to set these up a bit differently because of the design. We will create one first, and then we will copy it and just update the image and text:

1. In the Outline view, select the fourth **Table View Cell**, and in the Size inspector, under **Table View Cell**, update **Row Height** to 70, then hit *Enter*.
2. In the object library **filter** field in the Utilities panel, type `view`.
3. Drag out the View into the fourth row.
4. Select the View, open the Size inspector in the Utilities panel, and update the following values:

    - **X**: 0
    - **Y**: 0
    - **Width**: 187
    - **Height**: 70

5. Drag out another view and drag it into the View we just added. This view holds an image and a label that we will add shortly.
6. Select the View, open the Size inspector in the Utilities panel, and update the following values:

    - **X**: 33.5
    - **Y**: 4
    - **Width**: 120
    - **Height**: 62

7. Next, in the object library **filter** field in the Utilities panel, type `image`.
8. Drag the image into the View we just added. *Make sure that you add the image into the container (view).*
9. Select the image, open the Size inspector in the Utilities panel, and update the following values:

    - **X**: 47
    - **Y**: 7
    - **Width**: 27
    - **Height**: 22

10. In the Attributes inspector, update the values of **Image** with `icon-photo`.

11. Then, drag out a label into the container. *Make sure that you add the label into the container (view).*

12. In the Attributes inspector, update the following values:

    - Add photo (add into the empty text field under the `Text`)
    - Update the value of **Font** with `Avenir Next Condensed Bold 17`
    - Update the value of **Alignment** with `Center`

13. Next, in the Size inspector, update the following values:

    - **X**: `20`
    - **Y**: `34`
    - **Width**: `81`
    - **Height**: `21`

14. Finally, drag a button from the object library into the container. *Make sure that you add the button into the container (view).*

15. In the Size inspector, update the following values:

    - **X**: `0`
    - **Y**: `0`
    - **Width**: `120`
    - **Height**: `62`

Designing Static Tables

Make sure that the button is above the image and label. You will have to do this in the Outline view. Delete the text from the label. Here is what you should end up with:

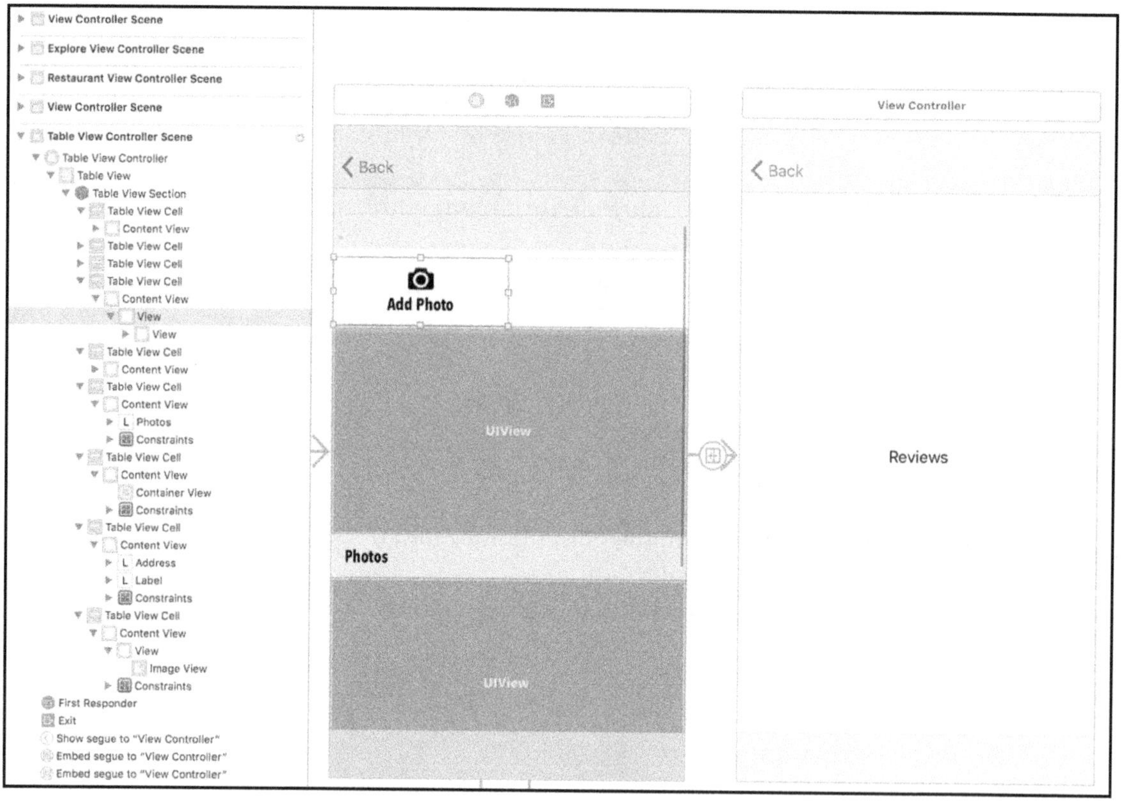

[Screenshot of Xcode Interface Builder showing the Outline view with Table View Controller Scene hierarchy on the left, and storyboard scenes showing an "Add Photo" button with camera icon, a "Photos" section, and a Reviews view controller on the right]

Notice where my button is in the Outline view. This will be important later, when we use the button. If it is on the bottom, then the icon and label will cover up some of the button.

16. Now, select the entire outer container that we just did and hit *cmd + C* and then *cmd + V*. This will copy what we just did.

17. Select the new container we just copied and in the Size inspector, update the following values:

    - **X:** 188
    - **Y:** 0

[288]

You should now have the following:

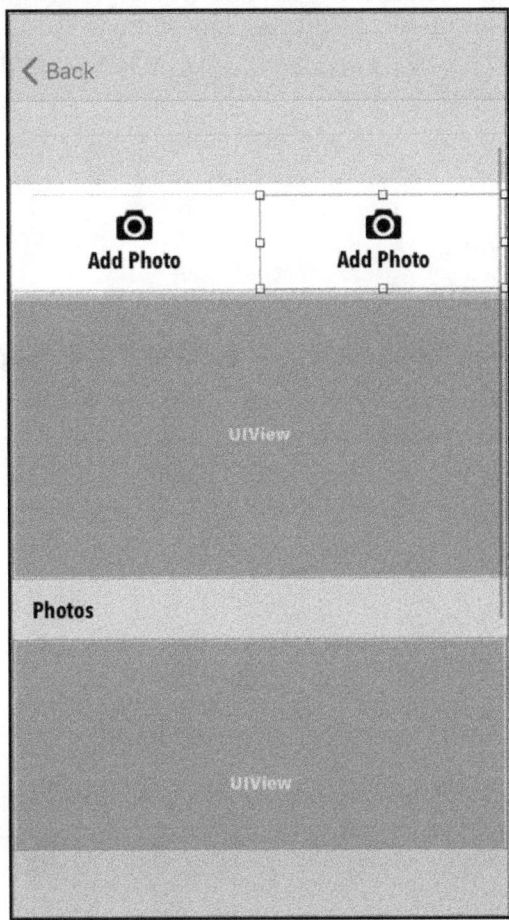

Designing Static Tables

18. Finally, using the Outline view (because the label and image are below the button, you cannot select either item in the storyboard) update the label text to say `Add Review` and select the image and update the image to `icon-review`.
19. Select the `icon-review` and open the Size inspector in the Utilities panel and update the following values:

    - **X**: 47
    - **Y**: 4
    - **Width**: 26
    - **Height**: 25

20. In the object library **filter** field in the Utilities panel, type `view`.
21. Drag it out into the same cell, but not in either container. It's easier to do this using the Outline view and not directly into the cell.
22. Open the Size inspector in the Utilities panel and update the following values:

    - **X**: 187
    - **Y**: 9
    - **Width**: 1
    - **Height**: 52

23. Select the Attributes inspector, click on the **Background**, and set it to `LetsEat Dark Grey Color`.

We are done with the first cell in the review section and it should look like the following:

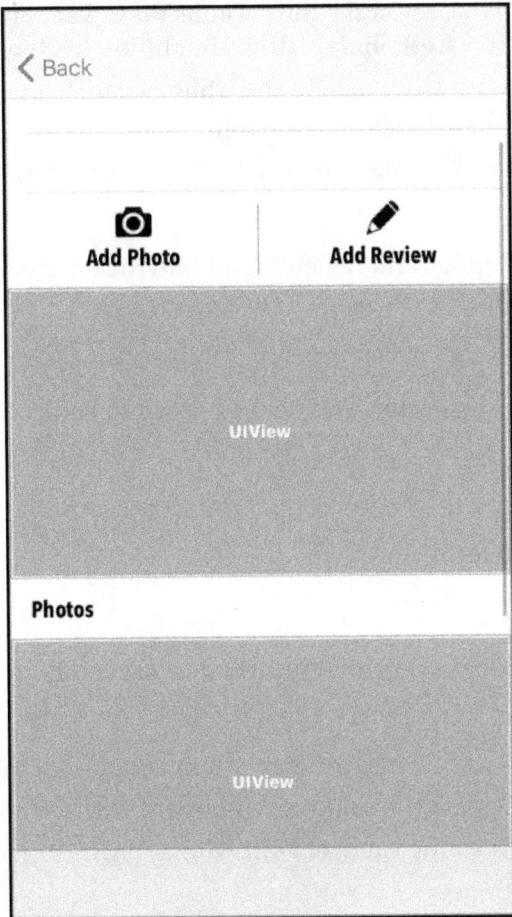

Designing Static Tables

Now that we have our first cell completed, let's continue updating the preceding cell:

1. In the Outline view, select the third **Table View Cell**, and in the Size inspector, under **Table View Cell**, update **Row Height** to `128`, then hit *Enter*.
2. In the object library **filter** field in the Utilities panel, type `label`.
3. Then, drag out three labels into the cell.
4. Select one of the labels, then in the Attributes inspector, update the following values:

    - Ratings and reviews (add into the empty text field under the **Text**)
    - Update the value of **Font** with `Avenir Next Condensed Bold 24`

5. Next, in the Size inspector, update the following values:

    - **X**: `16`
    - **Y**: `5`
    - **Width**: `220`
    - **Height**: `25`

6. Select the next label, then, in the Attributes inspector, update the following values:

    - Add `0.0` into the empty text field under the **Text**
    - Update the value of **Alignment** with `Center`
    - Next, the value of **Font** with `Avenir Next Condensed Bold 60`

7. Next, in the Size inspector, update the following values:

    - **X**: `16`
    - **Y**: `35`
    - **Width**: `97`
    - **Height**: `82`

8. Select the last label, then in the Attributes inspector, update the following values:

    - Add `out of 5` into the empty text field under the **Text**
    - Update the value of **Alignment** with `Center`
    - Next, the value of **Color** with `LetsEat Dark Grey Color`
    - Also update the value of **Font** with `Avenir Next Condensed Demi Bold 16`

9. Next, in the Size inspector, update the following values:

    - **X:** `27`
    - **Y:** `96`
    - **Width:** `71`
    - **Height:** `21`

10. In the object library **filter** field in the Utilities panel, type `image`.
11. Then, drag out an Image into the cell.
12. Select one of the labels, then in the Attributes inspector, update the value of `Image` with `0star`.

13. Next, in the Size inspector, update the following values:

    - **X:** `151`
    - **Y:** `43`
    - **Width:** `205`
    - **Height:** `34`

When you are done, you should have the following:

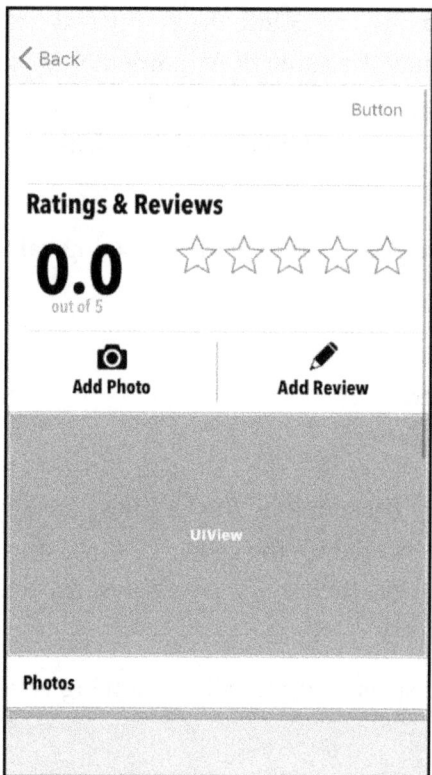

Adding Auto Layout to the Review cells

Now that we have our elements in place, let's add Auto Layout next:

1. Select the Container View that holds our **Add Photo** and then select the Pin icon and enter the following values:

    - **Top**: 0
    - **Right**: 0
    - **Bottom**: 0
    - **Left**: 0
    - **Constrain to margins**: Unchecked

2. Click **Add 4 Constraints**.
3. Next, click on the Align icon and enter the following value:

    - **Horizontally in Container**: 0 (should be checked)
    - **Vertically in Container**: 0 (should be checked)

4. Click **Add 2 Constraints**.
5. Now, select the Container that holds the image, label, and button for **Add Photo** and then select the Pin icon and enter the following values:

    - **Width**: 120
    - **Height**: 62
    - **Constrain to margins**: Unchecked

6. Next, click on the Align icon and enter the following value:

    - **Horizontally in Container**: 0 (should be checked)
    - **Vertically in Container**: 0 (should be checked)

7. Next, select the **View** that we are using as the **Add Reviews** button, and then select the Pin icon and enter the following values:

    - **Top**: 0
    - **Right**: 0
    - **Left**: 0
    - **Bottom**: 0
    - **Constrain to margins**: Unchecked

8. Click **Add 4 Constraints**.
9. Then, select the **View** that we are using as a separator (you might need to use the Outline view to select it), and then select the Pin icon and enter the following values:

    - **Constrain to margins**: Unchecked
    - **Width**: 1 (should be checked)
    - **Height**: 52 (should be checked)

Designing Static Tables

10. Click **Add 3 Constraints**.
11. Next, click on the Align icon and enter the following value:

    - **Horizontally in Container**: 0 (should be checked)
    - **Vertically in Container**: 0 (should be checked)

12. Click **Add 2 Constraints**.
13. Now, select the Container that holds our image, label, and button for the **Add Review** button and then select the Pin icon and enter the following values:

    - **Width**: 120
    - **Height**: 62
    - **Constrain to margins**: Unchecked

14. Next, click on the Align icon and enter the following value:

    - **Horizontally in Container**: 0 (should be checked)
    - **Vertically in Container**: 0 (should be checked)

15. Select the **0.0** label and then select the Pin icon and enter the following values:

    - **Top**: 5
    - **Left**: 16
    - **Width**: 97
    - **Height**: 82
    - **Constrain to margins**: Unchecked

16. Select the **Ratings and Reviews** label and then select the Pin icon and enter the following values:

    - **Top**: 5
    - **Left**: 16
    - **Right**: 16
    - **Height**: 82
    - **Constrain to margins**: Unchecked

Chapter 11

17. Select the `out of 5` label and then select the Pin icon and enter the following values:

    - **Top**: 66
    - **Left**: 27
    - **Width**: 71
    - **Height**: 21
    - **Constrain to margins**: Unchecked

18. Select the image with the empty stars and then select the Pin icon and enter the following values:

    - **Top**: 13
    - **Right**: 19
    - **Width**: 205
    - **Height**: 34
    - **Constrain to margins**: Unchecked

We have two more sections to add. Next up, we need to add the reservation times. We did this already in the restaurant listing view. To make it easier, let's copy the stack view and paste it into our cell. Go to the restaurant listing cell and select the stack view:

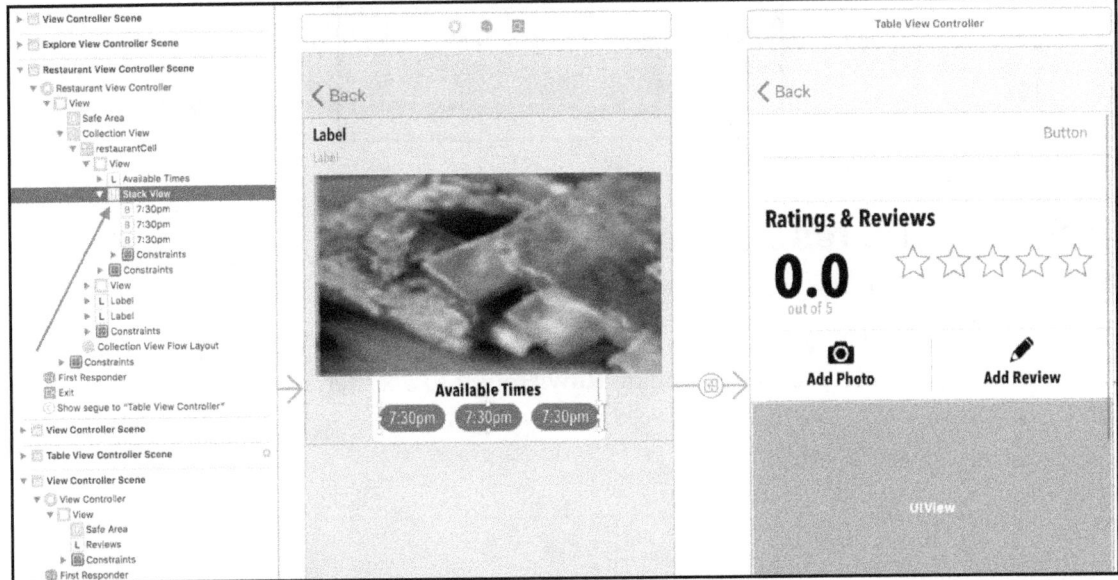

Designing Static Tables

Then, using the outline view, select the stack view and hit *cmd + C* in the online view. Then, using the Outline view, select the **Content View** for the second row and hit *cmd + V*. When you are done, you will see the following:

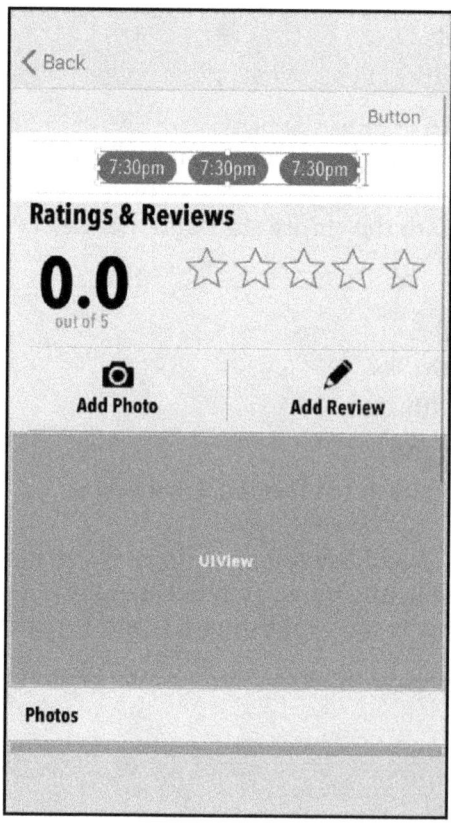

Updating the reservation times cells

Next, let's update our reservation times to match the design:

1. In the Outline view, select the second **Table View Cell**, and in the Size inspector, under **Table View Cell**, update **Row Height** to 90, then hit *Enter*.

Chapter 11

2. Select the stack view, and in the Size inspector, update the following values:
   - **X:** 15
   - **Y:** 51

3. Your reservation times section should now appear as follows:

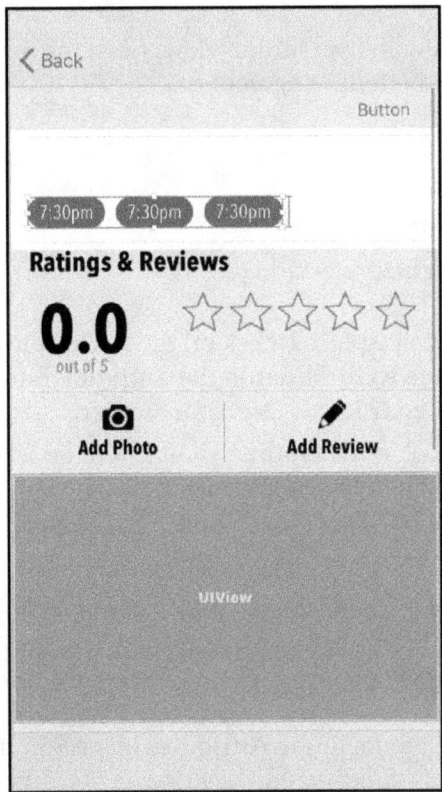

Reservation information

Now, let's move onto the reservation information section:

1. In the **filter** field of the object library, type uiview.
2. Using the Outline view, drag a UIView into the second row's **Content View**.
3. Next, in the **filter** field, type label.

Designing Static Tables

4. In the Outline view, drag a `UILabel` into the `UIView` we just added.
5. Select the Media Library icon in the Utilities panel, and in the **filter** area, type `icon-calendar`.
6. Drag and drop the `icon-calendar` into our View Container.

Now that we have all of the UI elements for this row, let's properly size and place these elements:

1. First, select the View in the Outline view, open the Size inspector in the Utilities panel and update the following values:

    - **X**: 15
    - **Y**: 8
    - **Width**: 345
    - **Height**: 34

2. Select the Attributes inspector, click on the **Background** and set the **Hex Color #** to `ECECEC` under the **RGB Slider** in the drop-down menu. You can add this color to your `Colors` in your `Asset.xcasset` folder.

3. Now, select the label in the Outline view, open the Size inspector in the Utilities panel, and update the following values:

    - **X**: 29
    - **Y**: 7
    - **Width**: 308
    - **Height**: 21

4. Select the last label; then, in the Attributes inspector, update the value of **Font** with `Avenir Next Condensed Regular 14`.

5. Finally, select the `icon-calendar` in the Outline view, and in the Size inspector, update the following values:

    - **X**: 8
    - **Y**: 9

You should now have the following:

We have finished the reservation information cleanup. Lastly, we need to update the reservation header.

Reservation header

Our first row is our reservation header; it will contain four elements, an image, and three labels. You can delete the button we added in the previous chapter:

1. Select the first row, and, in the Size inspector, update **Row Height** to 240.
2. In the object library of the Utilities panel, type uiview into the **filter** area.
3. Using the Outline view, drag a UIView into the first **Table View Cell Content View**.
4. Select the **View** and, in the Size inspector, update the following values:

    - **X**: 0
    - **Y**: 0
    - **Width**: 375
    - **Height**: 240

5. Select the Attributes inspector, click on the **Background**, and set the **Hex Color #** to 393939 under **RGB Slider** in the drop-down menu. You can also add this color to your **Color Assets**.
6. Next, in the Utilities panel, select the object library and type label in the **filter** field.
7. Drag three labels into the **View** we just created.
8. Next, select the Media Library icon in the Utilities panel, and in the filter, type detail-logo.
9. Drag a detail-logo into the same **View**.
10. Select the detail-logo in the Outline view, select the Size inspector, and update the following values:

    - **X**: 77.5
    - **Y**: 10

11. Select the first label in the Outline view and, in the Size inspector, update the following values:

    - **X**: 8
    - **Y**: 132
    - **Width**: 359
    - **Height**: 44

12. Select the Attributes inspector and change the **Alignment** to **Center**, the **Color** to **White Color**, and the **Font** to **System Heavy** size 30.

13. Next, select the second label in the Outline view and update the following values in the Size inspector:

    - **X**: 8
    - **Y**: 176
    - **Width**: 359
    - **Height**: 21

14. Open the Attributes inspector and change the **Alignment** to **Center**, the **Color** to **White Color**, and the **Font** to **System Thin** size 14.

15. Now, select the third label in the Outline view and, in the Size inspector, update the following values:

    - **X**: 8
    - **Y**: 197
    - **Width**: 359
    - **Height**: 21

16. In the Attributes inspector, change the **Alignment** to **Center**, the **Color** to **White Color**, and the **Font** to **System Thin** size 14.

Our reservation header is complete. Let's build and run the project by hitting the Play button (or use *cmd + R*) and see what our restaurant detail looks like.

Designing Static Tables

Our restaurant detail is very close to what we want, but there are a couple of remaining issues. Currently, our Table View separators have an inset, which we want, but we need an inset on both sides. By default, the inset is currently set to the left, but we need to add an inset to the right. In addition, if you select a cell in the restaurant detail view, the cell becomes highlighted, which we do not want. To correct these items, follow these steps:

1. In `Main.storyboard`, select the **Table View** in the Outline view of the restaurant detail.
2. In the Attributes inspector of the Utilities panel, change **Separator Inset** from **Automatic** to **Custom**:

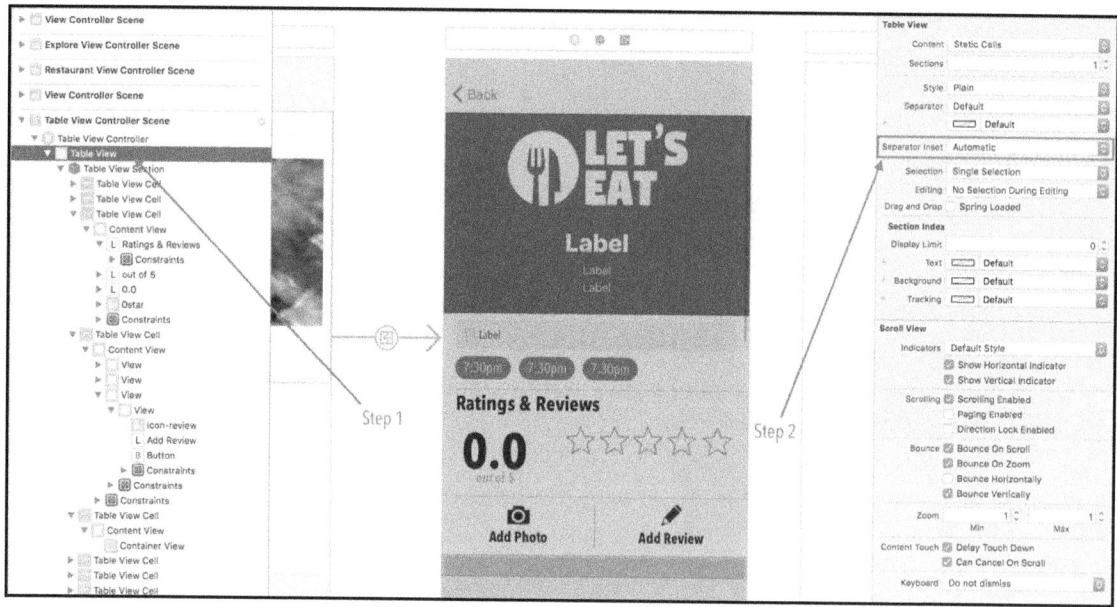

3. Then, change the **Right** inset to 15:

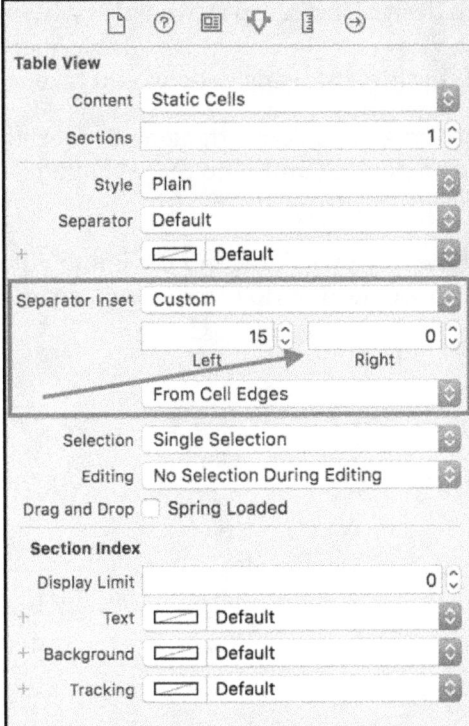

4. Then, change **Selection** from **Single Selection** to **No Selection**.

Let's build and run the project again by hitting the Play button (or use *cmd + R*); you should see those items are now corrected. We have now completed the restaurant details.

Summary

We are just about done with design and setup as we only have one more chapter. We got to see how using a static Table View can go. Using static Table Views allows us to create detail pages with minimal code. Building this using code would take a lot longer.

Hopefully, at this point, you are getting comfortable with everything we are doing. If not, get the chapter starter files and go back and redo these chapters. Getting comfortable with these things makes your life easier.

In the next chapter, we add the Reviews Form and the Photo Filter view. Our storyboard file is starting to get bigger, so we need to do some storyboard refactoring as well.

12
Designing a Photo Filter and Review Form

We have been progressing the last four chapters with our design. We wrap up the design setup in the chapter. In this chapter, we are going to set up two View Controllers. One will take care of our Photo filter and add photos to a restaurant. Our second View Controller is the form we use for users to create restaurant reviews. Finally, we will look at how to refactor storyboards. We will cover the following in this chapter:

- Creating our Photo Filter View
- Creating our Review form
- Refactoring storyboards

Setting up our View Controllers

When we set up our structure, we created a View Controller with a label that says `Review`. This was done just to see the structure, but we removed the button tapping to the review controller. We currently have two buttons on our Restaurant Detail page: **Add Photo** and **Add Review**. Both of these buttons need to have View Controllers connected to them. Our **Add Photo** hooks up to a View Controller where we launch the user's camera and our **Add Review** hooks up to a static `tableview`.

Designing a Photo Filter and Review Form

Let's work on the **Add Photo** button first:

1. Open the `Main.storyboard` and find the View Controller that has the label **Reviews** and delete the label.
2. Select the View Controller, then navigate to **Editor | Embed In | Navigation Controller**. This View Controller will now be our Photo Filter View Controller.
3. In the Restaurant Detail View, find the Table View Cell that contains the **Add Photo** label and button.
4. Open up the disclosure arrows and *Ctrl* + drag from the button that we placed inside the container to the Navigation controller we just added; under **Action Segue**, select **Present Modally**.

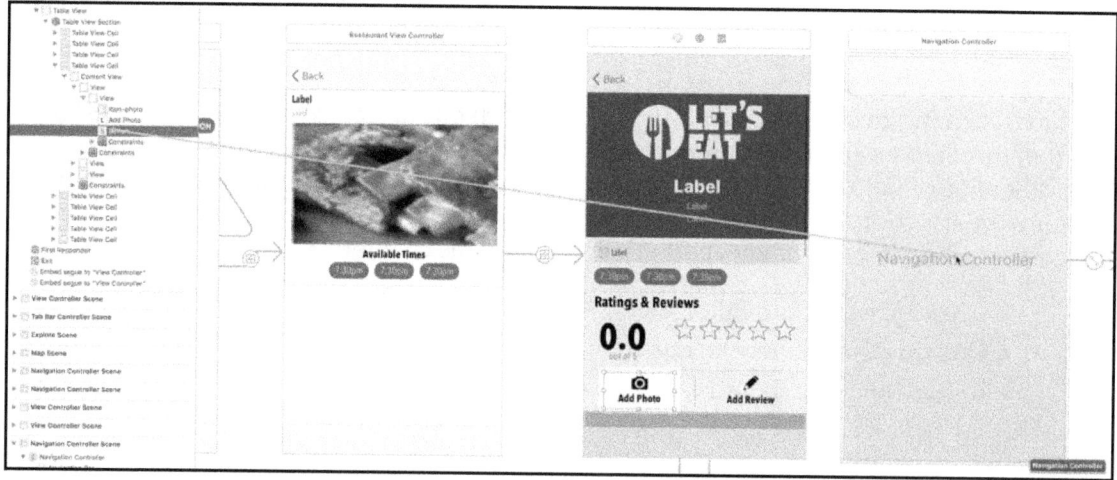

Next, let's set up this View Controller. Before we start setting up let's talk about what needs to be done next. In this controller, we want the user to be able to take a picture or pick a photo from their *Photos* app and add it. Once they select the photo, we want them to be able to apply a filter to their photo and then save it to the device. This view needs two primary things: a way to scroll the filter items and an image that displays the selected photo and filter. We could use a scroll view to do this, but later in the book we want to add drag and drop to the iPad, so collection view is the easier way. Now that you have a better idea of the direction, let's set up our UI.

Adding our Photo Filter View

The Photo Filter View is where we show the selected image and a collection view, from which the user can choose different filters to apply to the image. Let's create the Photo Filter View:

1. Select the View Controller for the Photo Filter View and, in the Attributes inspector, uncheck both **Under Top Bars** and **Under Bottom Bars**. We do not want this page to scroll, so we do not need it to go under the Top and Bottom Bars.
2. In the Main.storyboard, type bar button into the **filter** field of the object library in the Utilities panel.
3. Drag out three **Bar Button Items**. One will go to the top left and two on the top right. When you are done, you should see the following:

Designing a Photo Filter and Review Form

Our button to the left is a **Cancel** button. Our button to the right is a Camera icon and a save button. You can update each one by selecting one at a time and opening the Attributes inspector.

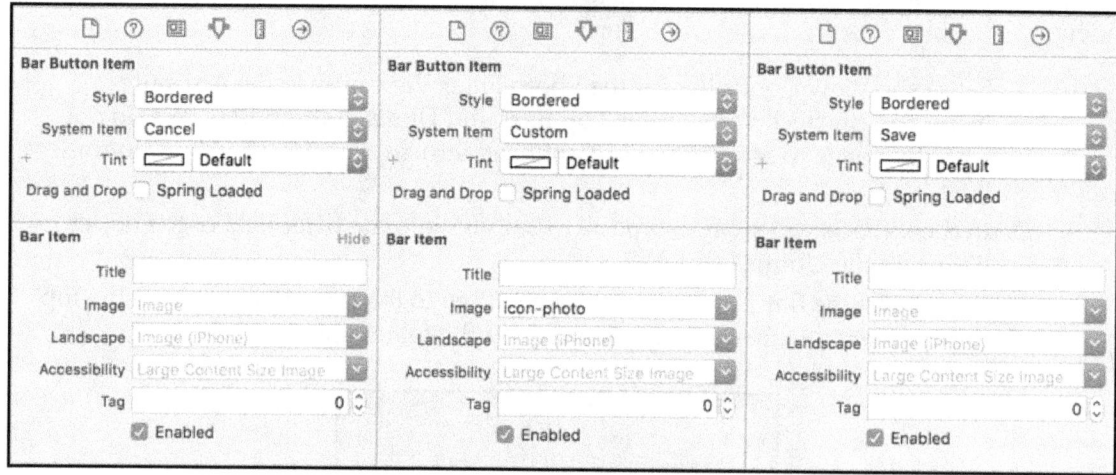

When you are done, you should see the following:

Chapter 12

4. Next, type `image` into the **filter** field of the object library in the Utilities panel.
5. Then, drag an **Image View** into the View Controller.
6. Select the Collection View in the Outline view, open the Size inspector in the Utilities panel, and then add the following values:

    - **X**: 0
    - **Y**: 0
    - **Width**: 375
    - **Height**: 400

7. Now, type `collection` into the **filter** field of the object library in the Utilities panel.
8. Then, drag a Collection View into the View Controller.
9. Select the Collection View in the Outline view, open the Size inspector in the Utilities panel, and then add the following values:

    - **X**: 0
    - **Y**: 400
    - **Width**: 375
    - **Height**: 203

Designing a Photo Filter and Review Form

When you are done, your View Controller should look like mine:

Next, let's add Auto Layout to our views.

Adding Auto Layout for the Photo Filter View

Next, let's apply Auto Layout to the Photo Filter View:

1. In the Outline view, select the **Image View** and then the Pin icon. Enter the following values:

    - **Top**: 0
    - **Left**: 0
    - **Right**: 0
    - **Constrain to margins**: unchecked
    - **Height**: 400 (checked)

2. Click **Add 4 Constraints**.
3. Next, select the **Collection View** and enter the following values:

    - **Left**: 0
    - **Bottom**: 0
    - **Right**: 0
    - **Bottom**: 0
    - **Constrain to margins**: unchecked

4. Click **Add 4 Constraints**.

We are now with the Photo Filter View Controller. Next, we need to create our cell for our Collection View. Let's set this up next.

Creating the Photo Filter View cell

Since we are using a collection view to scroll our elements, we need to add a custom cell as well.

1. Select the prototype cell inside of the Collection View:

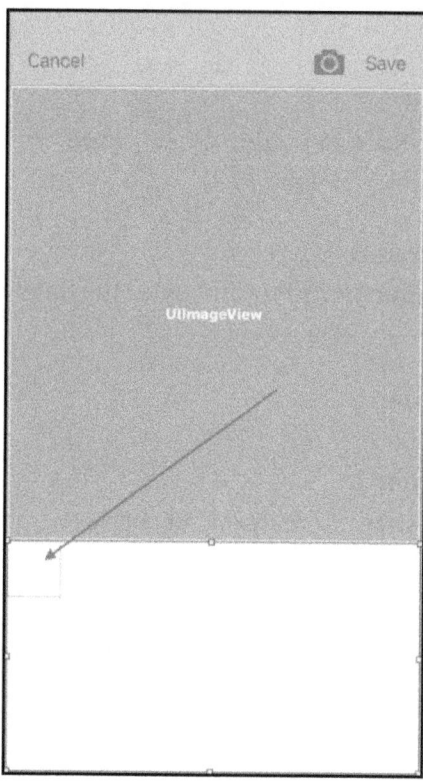

2. Under the Attributes inspector, update the **Identifier** to `filterCell`.
3. Next, select the Collection View, open the Size inspector in the Utilities panel, and under **Cell Size**, set the following values:

    - **Width**: `116`
    - **Height**: `203`

4. In the `Main.storyboard`, type `image` into the **filter** field of the Object library in the Utilities panel.

5. Drag out the image into the cell.
6. Select the **Image View** in the Outline view, open the Size inspector in the Utilities panel, and then add the following values:
    - **X**: 0
    - **Y**: 0
    - **Width**: 116
    - **Height**: 177

7. Next, type `label` into the **filter** field of the object library in the Utilities panel.
8. Drag out the label into the cell.
9. Select the label in the Outline view, open the Size inspector in the Utilities panel, and then add the following values:
    - **X**: 5
    - **Y**: 179
    - **Width**: 106
    - **Height**: 21

10. Now, with the label still selected, open the Attributes inspector; set the **Font** to **Avenir Next Condensed Regular 17**.
11. Set the **Text Alignment** to **Center**.

We are done adding elements to our cell; let's add our Auto Layout next.

Adding Auto Layout to our Photo Filter cell

Next, we want to add auto layout to our cell.

1. In the Outline view, select the **Image View** and then the Pin icon. Enter the following values:
    - **Top**: 0
    - **Left**: 0
    - **Right**: 0
    - **Constrain to margins**: unchecked
    - **Height**: 177 (checked)

2. Click **Add 4 Constraints**.
3. Next, select the label and enter the following values:
   - **Left**: 5
   - **Right**: 5
   - **Top**: 2
   - **Height**: 21
   - **Constrain to margins**: unchecked
4. Click **Add 4 Constraints**.

Our cell setup is complete. We have one more View Controller to do and that is our **Add Review** section.

Creating reviews

We have a form that users can use to write reviews. This **Create Review** form takes a title, a name, a rating, and a review.

To create this form, we use a static Table View as we did with restaurant details. Using a Table View makes it easier for us, because the static Table View comes with a lot of built-in functionality that we do not need to code. For example, keyboard dismissal and scrolling the View when a text area is tapped are all built into the static Table View.

Setting up the Review storyboard

We will be creating a form into which users can enter their name, title, rating and a review. We will need a static table view for our form so we will need to drag out a navigation controller:

1. In the `Main.storyboard`, type navigation into the filter field of the object library in the Utilities panel.
2. Drag out a navigation controller. This will have a Table View Controller attached to it and that's what we want.
3. Find the **Add Review** button in the Outline. Open up the disclosure arrows and CTL drag from the button that we placed inside the container to the Navigation Controller we just added; under **Action Segue**, select **Present Modally**.

Chapter 12

When you are done, you will see the following:

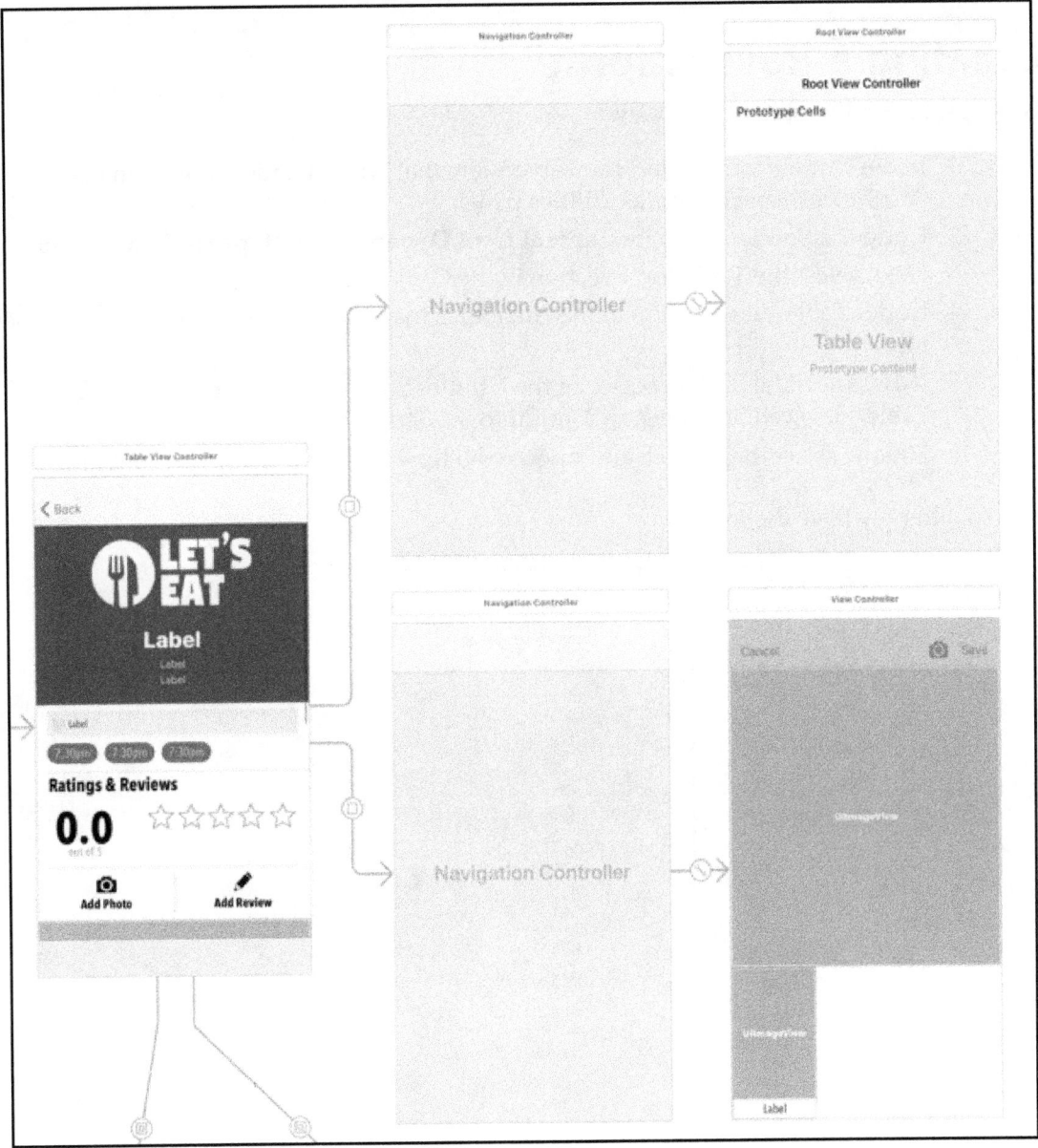

Next, we need to update our Table View.

Creating a Review form

Let's now set up this static Table View:

1. In the Outline view, select the Table View that we just added, and then open the Attributes inspector in the Utilities panel.
2. Under Table View, update **Content** from **Dynamic Prototypes** to **Static Cells**.
3. Next, select the Table View section in the Outline view.
4. Under Table View section in the Attributes inspector, update **Rows** to 4, and then hit *Enter*.
5. Now, select the Size inspector in the Utilities panel and, under select the first Table View cell, update **Row Height** to 50. Then, hit *Enter*.
6. Finally, select the last cell and update the **Row Height** to 190. Then, hit *Enter*.

You should now have the following:

Next, we need to update the inside of each Table View cell.

Updating the Review cells

To know what we need in each cell, we need to look at the design and then match our storyboard to the design. Looking at the design we discussed earlier in this chapter, in our first cell, we need an image and a label. In our second and third cells, we need a text field, and, in our last cell, we need a text view. When working with static cells, you may notice that, sometimes, you cannot drag out UI elements directly into the cell in the scene. If you encounter this issue, just drag them into the cell in the Outline view.

Updating our first cell

Let's start with updating our first cell and look into the factors involved:

1. In the object library of the Utilities panel, type label in the **filter** field and then drag a label into the first cell.
2. Then, type `image` into the filter and drag the image into the first cell.
3. Next, type text into the filter and drag one **Text Field** into the second cell and one **Text Field** into the third cell.
4. Finally, drag a Text View into the fourth cell.

Do not concern yourself with the positioning of your elements at this time, as we are going to fix their positions shortly.

We now have all the elements we need for this form and just need to position them correctly. You should be getting comfortable with positioning elements in a cell (as well as applying Auto Layout), as we have done this quite a bit in the last couple of chapters.

Positioning UI elements

Let's now place all of our elements into the correct spots:

1. In the Outline view, select the **Text Field** inside the second cell.

2. Select the Size inspector in the Utilities panel and add the following values:
    - **X**: 16
    - **Y**: 0
    - **Width**: 350
    - **Height**: 44

3. Open the Attributes inspector and, under **Text Field**, update **Placeholder** to say Title. Then, hit *Enter*. Also, set **Font** to **Avenir Next Condensed Regular 17**.
4. In the Outline view, select the **Text Field** inside the third cell.
5. Select the Size inspector in the Utilities panel and add the following values:
    - **X**: 16
    - **Y**: 0
    - **Width**: 350
    - **Height**: 44

6. Open the Attributes inspector and, under **Text Field**, update **Placeholder** to say Name. Then, hit *Enter*. Also, set **Font** to **Avenir Next Condensed Regular 17**.
7. In the first cell, update the **Image** field to say 0star and then hit *Enter*.
8. Next, in the Size inspector, add the following values:
    - **X**: 133
    - **Y**: 7
    - **Width**: 108
    - **Height**: 17

9. Update the **Image** field to 0star, and then hit *Enter*.
10. Select the label in the first cell, and update the following values in the Size inspector:
    - **X**: 97
    - **Y**: 25
    - **Width**: 181
    - **Height**: 21

11. Open the Attributes inspector and, under **Text**, update **Label** to say **Tap a Star to Rate**. Then, hit *Enter*. Also, set **Font** to **Avenir Next Condensed Regular 12**.
12. Next, in the last cell, select the **Text Field**; then, in the Size inspector, add the following values:

    - **X**: 5
    - **Y**: 5
    - **Width**: 365
    - **Height**: 179

13. Lastly, select the Attributes inspector; then, under **Text**, change **Font** to **Avenir Next Condensed Regular** size 14.

Your cells should now look as follows:

Your cells' UI elements are now positioned correctly and we just need to set up Auto Layout.

Adding Auto Layout for creating reviews

Let's now add Auto Layout to our form:

1. In the first cell, select the **Image View** and then select the Pin icon. Enter the following values:

    - **Top**: 7
    - **Width**: 108 (checked)
    - **Height**: 17 (checked)

2. Click **Add 3 Constraints**.
3. Next, select the Align icon, then check the **Horizontally** in **Container**.
4. Now, select the label under the **Image View** and then select the Pin icon. Enter the following values:

    - **Top**: 1
    - **Width**: 181 (checked)
    - **Height**: 18 (checked)

5. Click **Add 3 Constraints**.
6. Next, select the Align icon, then check the **Horizontally** in **Container**.
7. Click **Add 1 Constraint**.

8. Next, select the **Text Field** in the second cell and then the Pin icon. Enter the following values:

    - **Top**: 0
    - **Right**: 8
    - **Left**: 16
    - **Height**: 44 (checked)

9. Click **Add 4 Constraints**.
10. Now, select the **Text Field** in the third cell and then the Pin icon. Enter the following values:

    - **Top**: 0
    - **Right**: 8
    - **Left**: 16
    - **Height**: 44 (checked)

11. Click **Add 4 Constraints**.
12. Finally, select the Text View in the third cell and then the Pin icon. Enter the following values:

    - **Top**: 5
    - **Right**: 5
    - **Bottom**: 5
    - **Left**: 5

13. Click **Add 4 Constraints**.

Designing a Photo Filter and Review Form

We are now done with the adding Auto Layout to our form. Our `Main.storyboard` file has many Controllers inside of it:

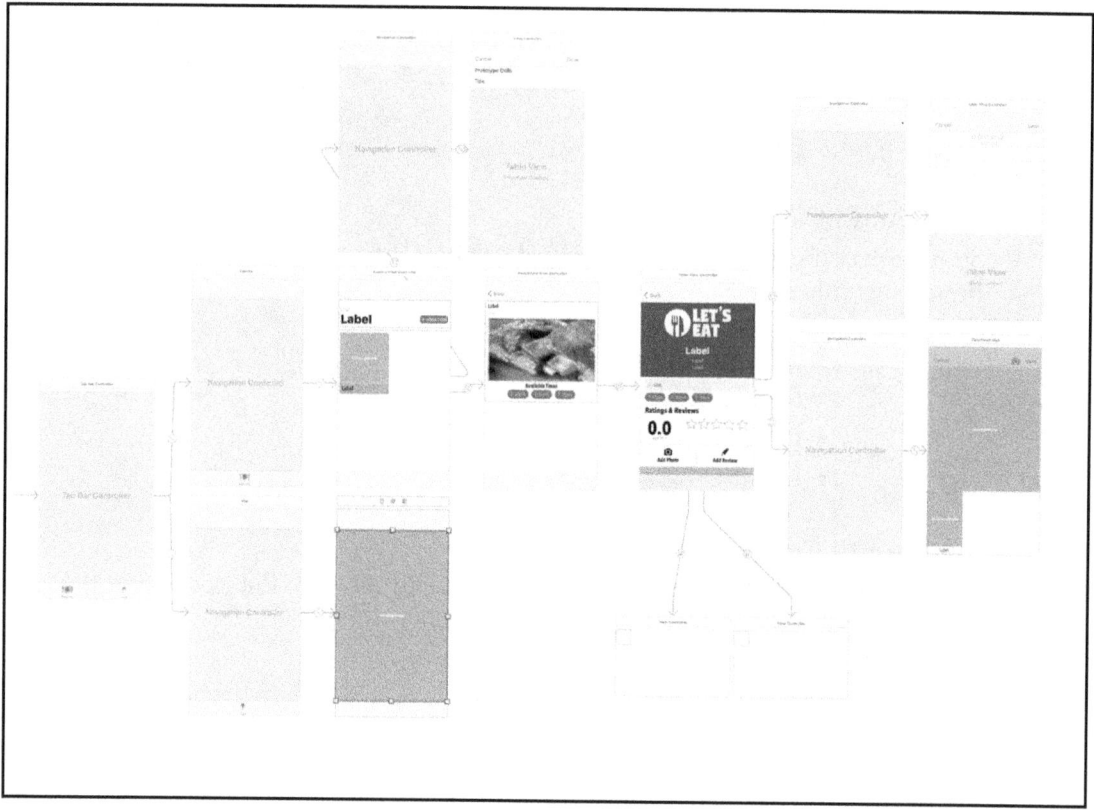

When working with a team, you do not want to have one file that controls all of your UI. You want to be able to have different people work on different sections of the app. To be able to have multiple storyboards we need to refactor our storyboard to make it more manageable. Even if you are working alone, it's good practice to have a storyboard for each part of your app. Let's see how we can refactor our storyboard.

Refactoring the storyboard

In programming, the term refactor means to take your existing code and improve on it without changing its behavior. We can apply refactoring to storyboards. We are going to refactor our storyboard so that each View Controller in our app has its own storyboard file. First we are going to separate by tabs (**Map** and **Explore**).

Chapter 12

We will be using what is called storyboard reference, which is to add references between story-boards. A storyboard reference in one storyboard can point to an area in a different storyboard. This gives us a way to organize our storyboards, rather than having one massive storyboard with which to work. Open your `Main.storyboard` file.

Creating a new storyboard for the Map tab

1. In `Main.storyboard`, click and drag over all of the scenes that go inside the **Map** tab.

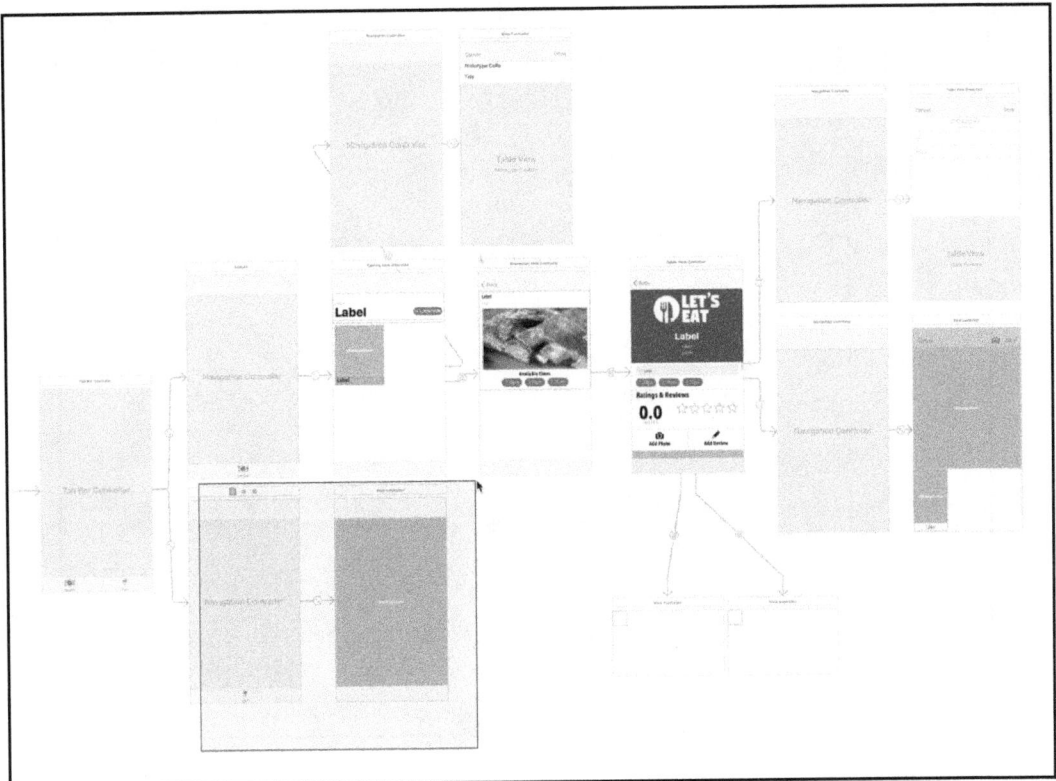

2. With the scenes selected, navigate to **Editor** | **Refactor to Storyboard**.
3. You are prompted to name the storyboard. Name this `Map.storyboard` and then hit **Save**.

Designing a Photo Filter and Review Form

4. Once you hit save, you are now inside `Map.storyboard` file; if you return to `Main.storyboard`, you should see this icon.

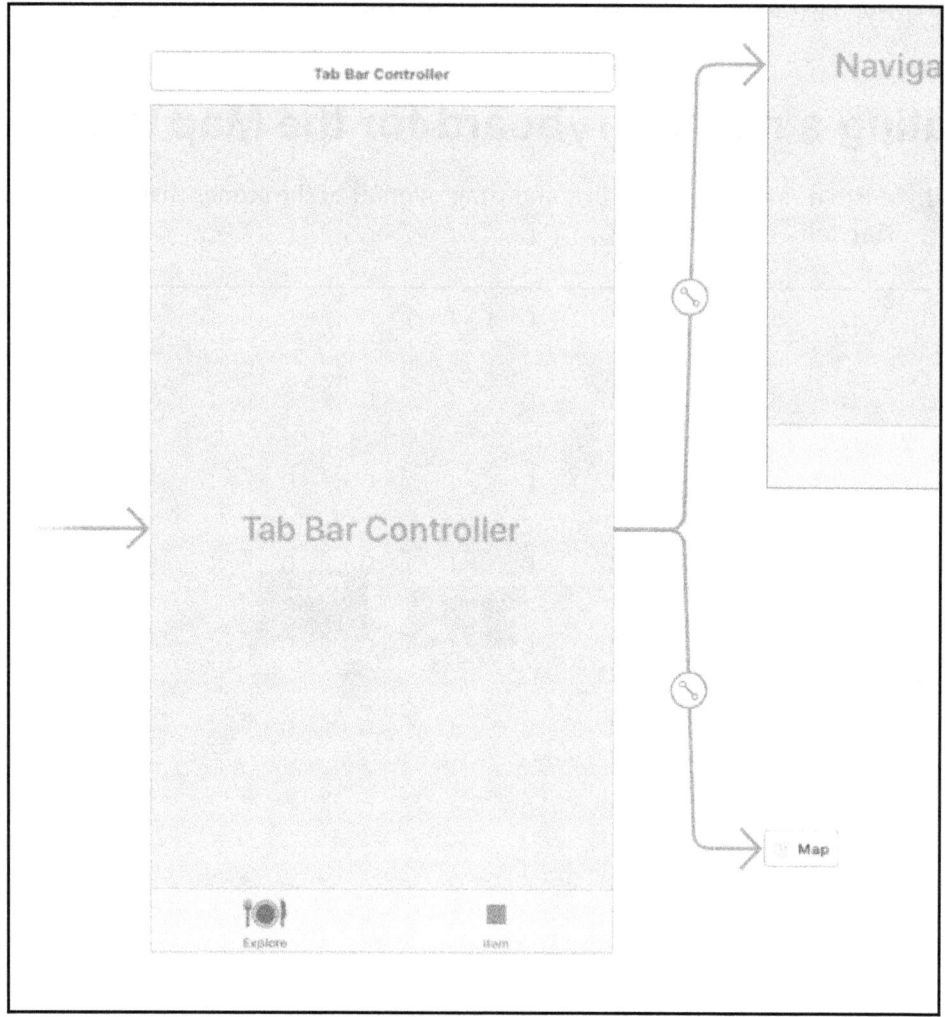

This icon is called a **storyboard reference**. You can double click on these storyboard references and be taken directly into the storyboard.

Chapter 12

Creating a new storyboard for the Explore tab

Next, we need to create our **Explore** tab. The **Explore** tab will have multiple storyboard references inside of it. Let's go ahead and create this reference now:

1. In `Main.storyboard`, you are going to click and drag over all of the scenes that are left in the scene. Note that when you click, make sure you are not clicking any scene or View Controller. You should now see the following:

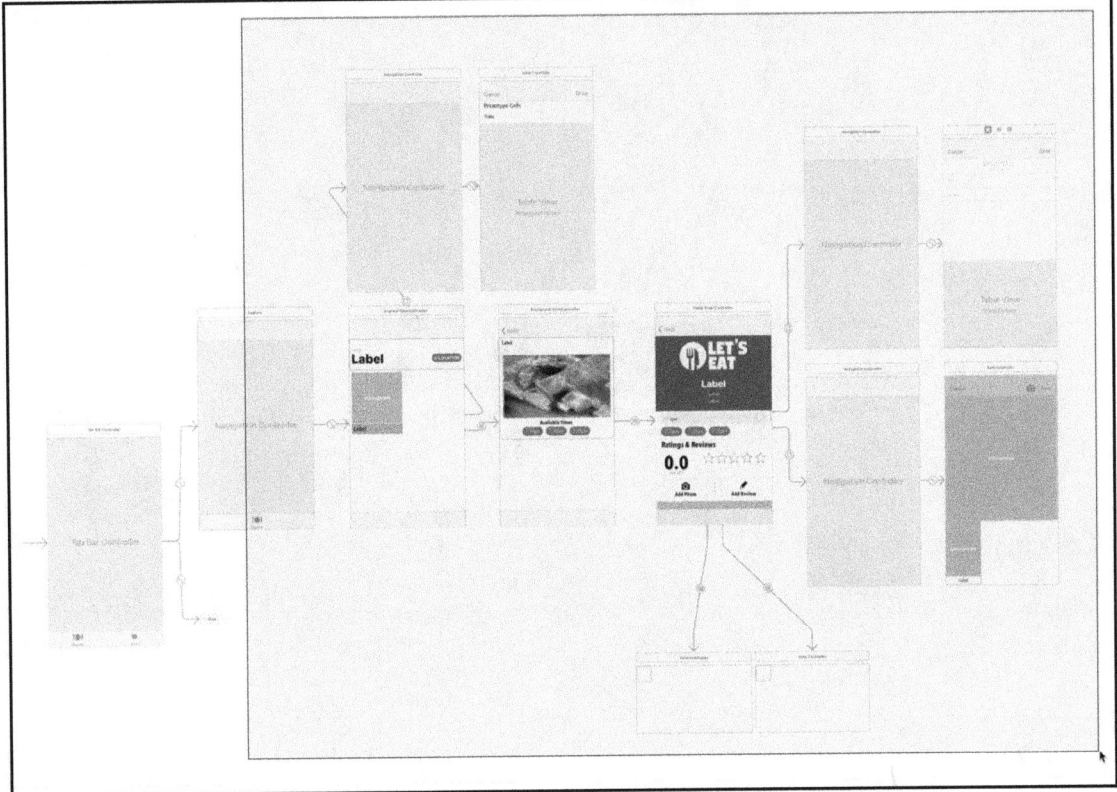

2. With the scenes selected, navigate to **Editor | Refactor to Storyboard**.
3. You will be prompted to name the storyboard. Name this `Explore.storyboard` and then hit **Save**.

Now, you will be in your new `Explore.storyboard` file.

Designing a Photo Filter and Review Form

We could stop here, but I feel like we still have way too many storyboard scenes. When you work alone doing this might not be a big deal, but when you work in a team, this makes it easier.

Let's get started by creating a location storyboard reference now:

1. Click and drag over the two controllers we are going to use for our locations:

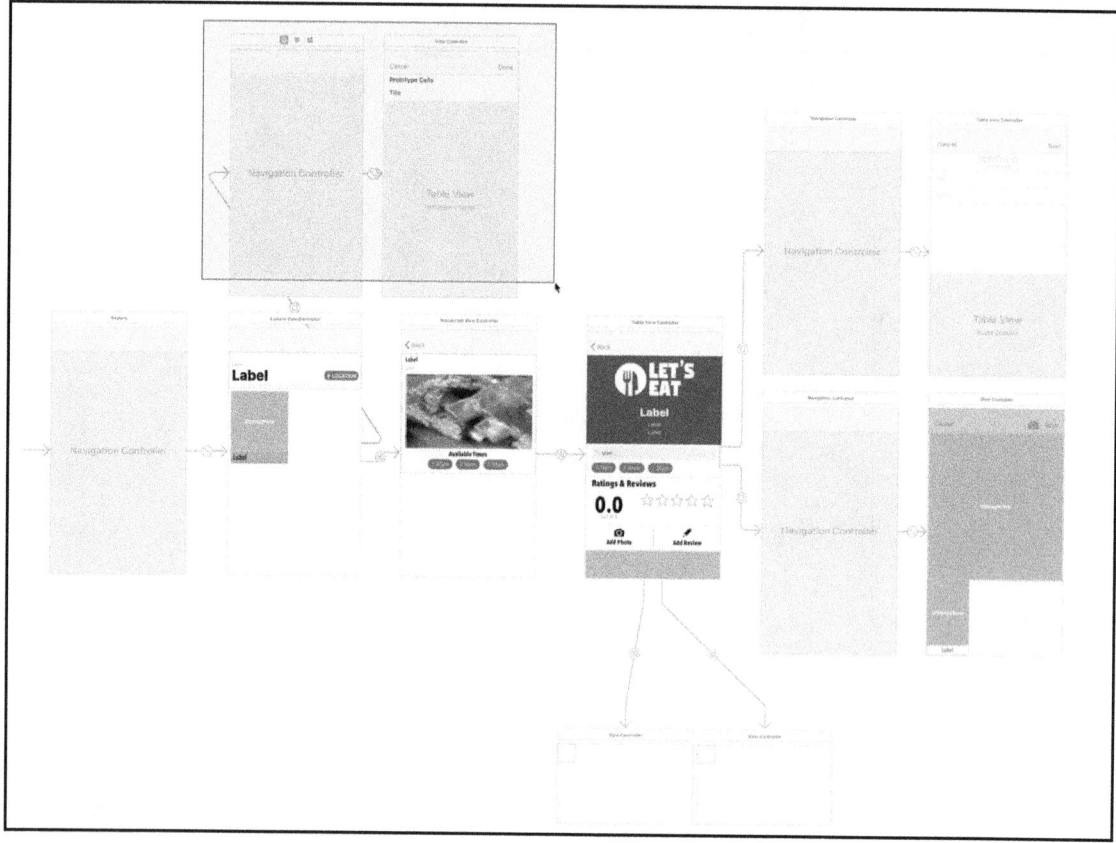

2. With the scenes selected, navigate to **Editor** | **Refactor to Storyboard**.
3. You will be prompted to name the storyboard. Name this `Locations.storyboard` and then hit **Save**.

[328]

Now, with locations set up, we need to go back to the `Explore.storyboard` file and do the following:

1. Click and drag over all of the scenes that are left in the scene. Basically you are going to need everything except for the locations storyboard reference.
2. You should now see the following:

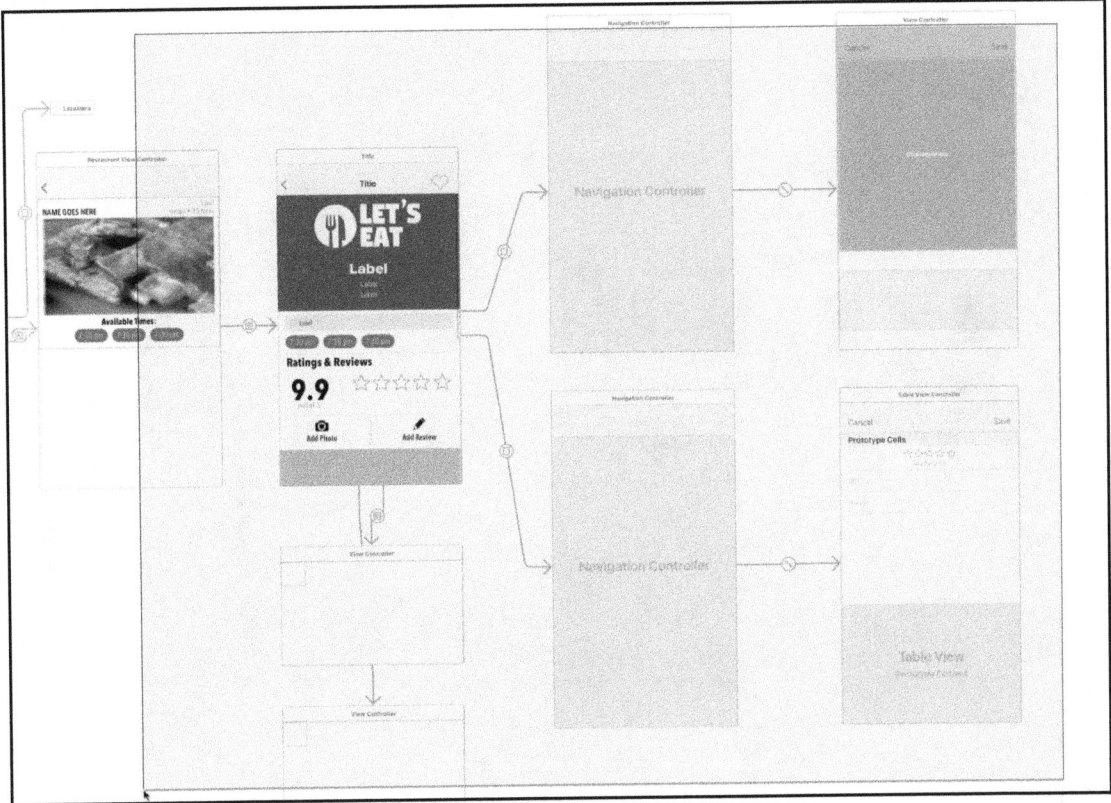

3. With the scenes selected, navigate to **Editor** | **Refactor to Storyboard**.
4. You will be prompted to name the storyboard. Name this `Restaurants.storyboard` and then hit **Save**.

Designing a Photo Filter and Review Form

Now, we have our storyboard for our restaurant list but we can still do more refactoring:

1. Inside of the `Restaurants.storyboard` file, click and drag over all of the scenes except for the restaurants list. You should now see the following:

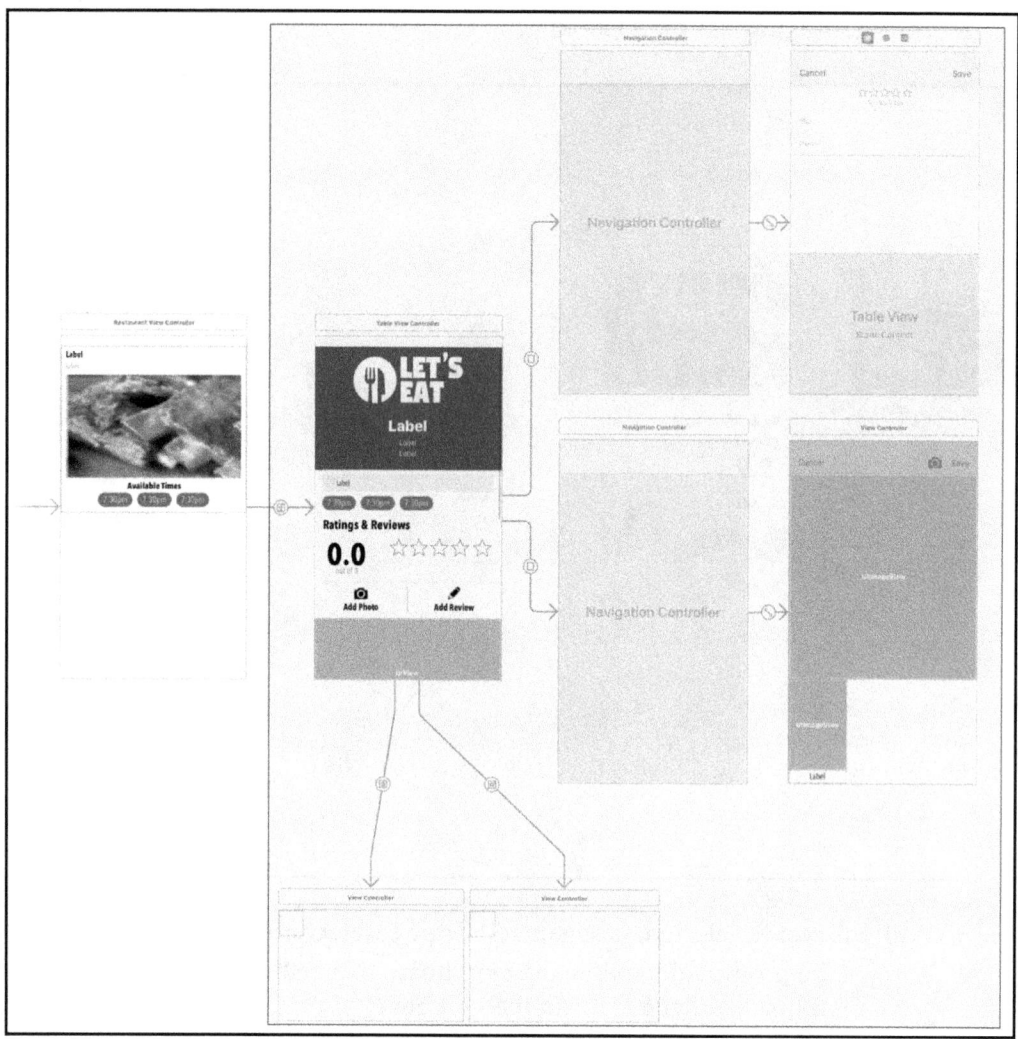

2. With the scenes selected, navigate to **Editor | Refactor to Storyboard**.
3. You will be prompted to name the storyboard. Name this `RestaurantDetail.storyboard` and then hit **Save**.

Chapter 12

Now, let's create our Photo filter storyboard reference:

1. Inside of the `RestaurantDetail.storyboard` file, click and drag over the View Controller and Navigation Controller we are using for the Photo Filter. You should now see the following:

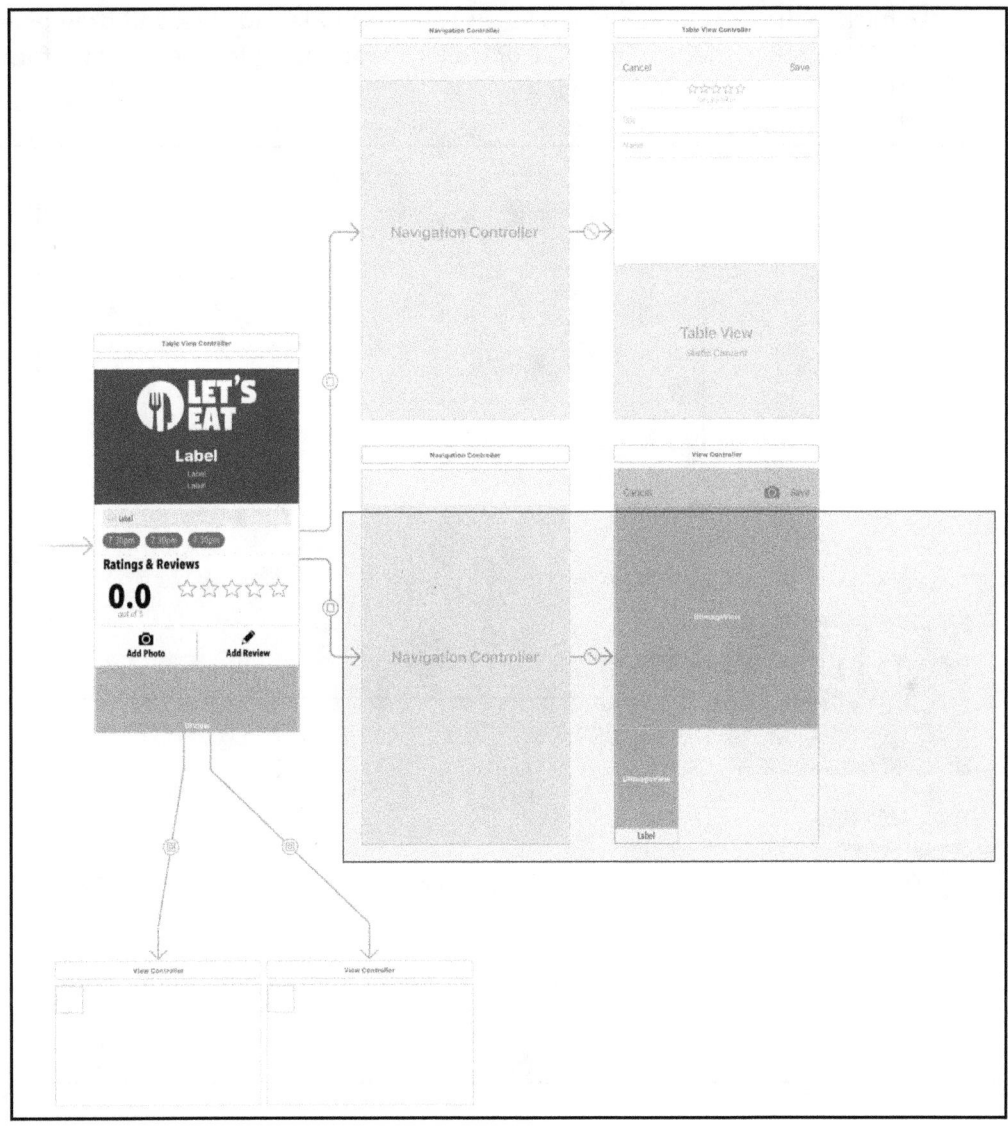

Designing a Photo Filter and Review Form

2. With the scenes selected, navigate to **Editor | Refactor to Storyboard**.
3. You will be prompted to name the storyboard. Name this PhotoFilter.storyboard and then hit **Save**.

We have one more storyboard reference to create.

1. Go back to the `RestaurantDetail.storyboard` file and click and drag over the View Controller and Navigation Controller we are using for the Reviews form. You should now see the following:

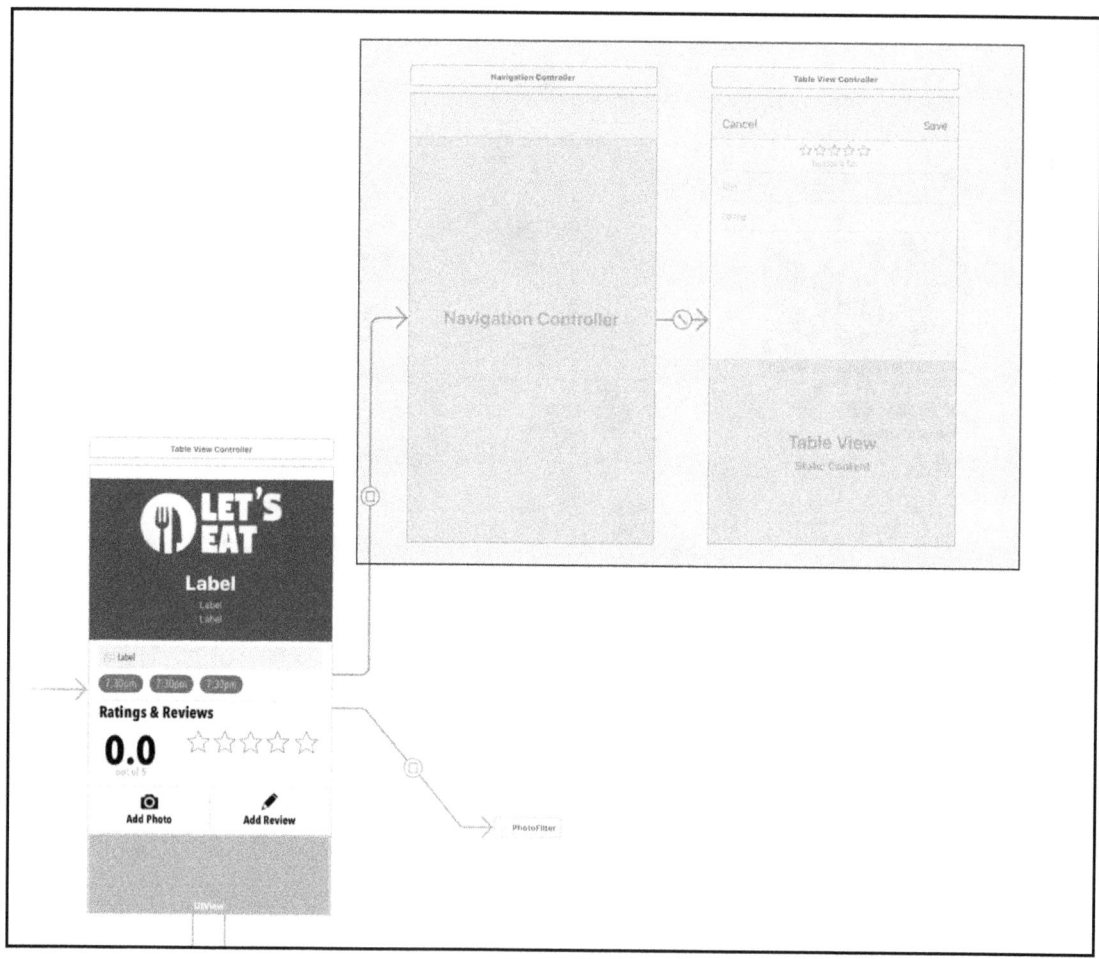

Chapter 12

2. With the scenes selected, navigate to **Editor | Refactor to Storyboard**.
3. You will be prompted to name the storyboard. Name this `ReviewForm.storyboard` and then hit **Save**.

Alright, we are finally done with creating all of our storyboards and you will now see the following in Project Navigator:

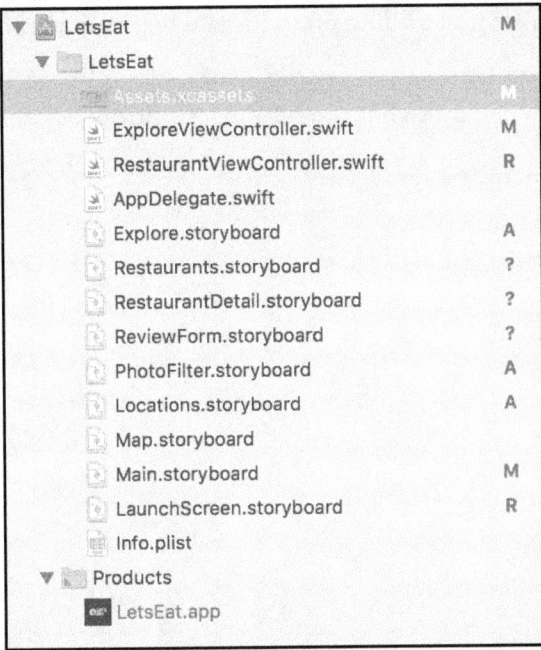

Let's build and run the project by hitting the play button (or use *cmd + R*), and you will see that nothing changed as far as navigating through the app is concerned.

Summary

We finished with storyboard and design setup. We can now focus on the code side with our UI pretty much set up. You should have a good idea of how our app should work. If you are struggling, there is nothing wrong with that. This stuff takes time to click, and as I have said before if you are struggling with anything that we have done, please go back. If you keep going when you are not comfortable, then it gets harder and harder. We will be covering a lot of new topics and adding on to them when you are not ready is not recommended.

In the next chapter, we will learn what Model View Controller is and how to work with it.

13
Getting Started with the Grid

I am a visual person; I prefer to start with the visuals and make sure that the app looks like the design. Starting with the UI helps me to identify the data structure and allows me to get familiar with the app. Therefore, I can focus my attention on the code.

In earlier chapters, we set up our app structure and developed a good understanding of the basics involved. In this chapter, you will learn about app architecture and how to create it for our *Let's Eat* app.

We will cover the following in this chapter:

- Understanding the Model View Controller architecture
- Classes and structures
- Controllers and classes

Understanding the Model View Controller architecture

Apple built iOS apps to use what is known as the **Model View Controller** (**MVC**), which is an architectural pattern that describes a way to structure the code in your app. In layman's terms, this just means breaking up our app into three distinct camps, Model, View, and Controller.

Here is a diagram of MVC to help you understand it:

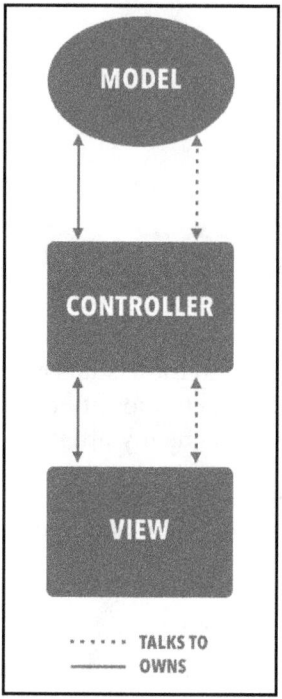

Let's discuss each camp:

- **Model**: The **Model** camp is responsible for an app's data and business logic. The Model's only job is to handle representations of data, data storage, and the operations performed on data.

- **View**: The **View** camp is responsible for all the things that you see on the screen. The View handles presenting and formatting data that results from the user's interactions.

- **Controller**: The **Controller** camp is the liaison or coordinator between the other two camps. The Controller handles a lot of setup and connections to the View. The Controller also interprets user interactions. Since the Controller is between both the View and the Model, the View and the Model should know nothing about each other.

In summary, the Controller takes user interactions and either responds back to the View or passes it onto the Model. When the Model completes a task, it passes it back to the Controller, and then the Controller talks with the View.

Getting familiar with the setup

For beginners, the MVC architecture can make you uncertain about where things should go. As we progress through the book, you will learn where to put things and why. So, you need not worry about where things should be placed as we work through this process together step by step.

As your project grows, the MVC architecture places a lot of the responsibility on the Controller. Therefore, in this book, we tweak the MVC pattern in order to not put so much pressure on the Controller.

Before we continue with our coding, we need to discuss classes and structures.

Classes and structures

Classes and structures (also known as structs) are files that contain properties and methods. You use these properties and methods to add functionality. You have been working with structs since `Chapter 1`, *Getting Familiar with Xcode*. Strings, Ints, Bools, Arrays, Dictionaries, and Sets are all structs.

Earlier in the book, we created functions. As noted in `Chapter 6`, *Starting the UI Setup*, a method is a function that lives inside a class or struct.

Classes and structs are very similar; however, Swift handles each of them a bit differently. To get a better understanding of how classes and structs work, we create a new Playground project. Working in the Playground gives us the ability to learn how to create custom classes and structs and to gain an understanding of each of their positives and negatives.

1. You can keep your project open, but let's jump back into Playgrounds. Since we have Xcode open, go to **File** | **New** | **Playground**.
2. In the options screen that appears, name your new Playground, `FunctionsStructs`, and make sure that your Platform is set to iOS. Hit **Next** and then **Create**. Now, let's delete everything inside your new Playground and toggle on the **Debug** panel, using either the toggle button or *cmd + Shift + Y*.

Getting Started with the Grid

3. In your empty Playground, add the following:

   ```
   class Cat {
   }
   struct Dog {
   }
   ```

We just created our first class and struct and defined two new custom data types (known as **Swift types**), `Cat` and `Dog`. Since we have not yet given the class or struct a property (such as a name) or created an instance of either `Cat` or `Dog`, you see nothing in the **Results** or **Debug** panels.

When you create classes and structs, it is a best practice to start with a capital letter. In addition, you must have different names for your class and for your struct. Otherwise, you will get an error. Even though one is a class and the other is a struct, each of them needs a distinct name.

Now, we need to give our `Cat` class and our `Dog` struct names. Therefore, let's give them both a property, called `name`:

```
class Cat {
   var name:String?
}

struct Dog {
   var name:String?
}
```

If you cannot set a property when it is created, then it is recommended that you set that property to an optional using the question mark (?). Using optionals, protect your code trying to access the name if you never set it. You can also set your variable as an optional unwrapped. For example, you can also do the following:

`var name:String!`.

With both `Cat` and `Dog` now having a property called `name`, let's create an instance of each of them:

```
let yellowCat = Cat()
yellowCat.name = "Whiskers"
print(yellowCat.name)
var yellowDog = Dog()
yellowDog.name = "Bruno"
print(yellowDog.name)
```

Chapter 13

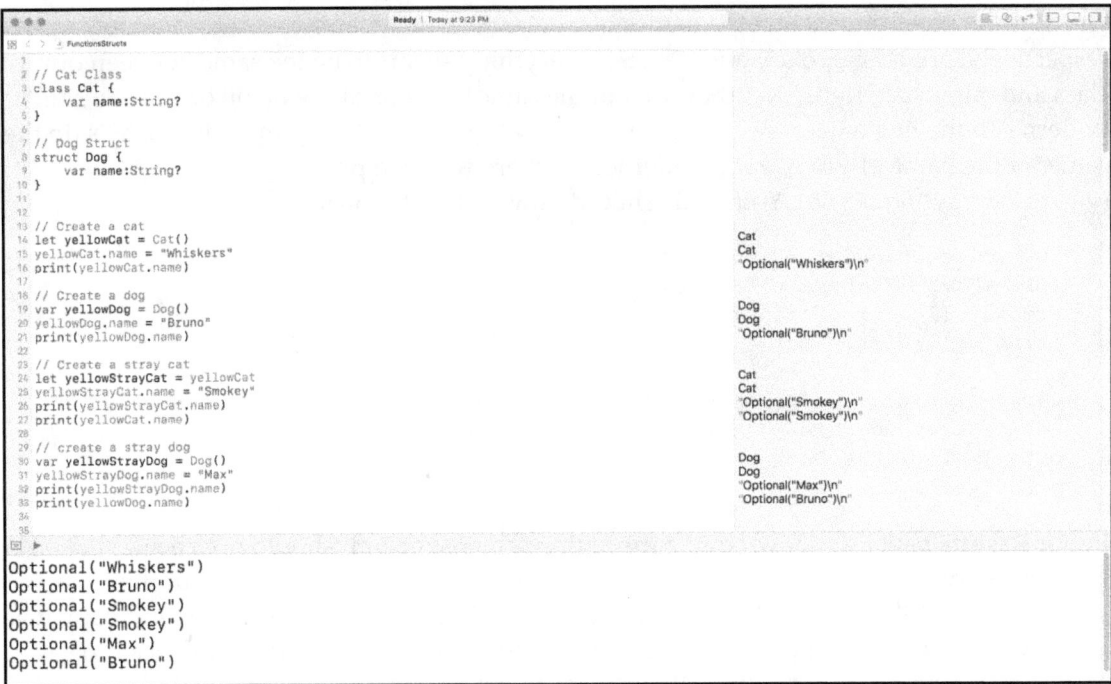

So far, everything on the surface looks the same. We created both a `Cat` and a `Dog` and gave them each names. However, let's say `Whiskers` runs away and, a few weeks later, finds a home with a new family, who decide to change his name to `Smokey`. After `Whiskers` runs away, `Bruno` becomes lonely and decides to find him, but also gets lost. `Bruno` finds a new home as well, and this new family decides to name him, `Max`.

In Playgrounds, we create a new constant called `yellowStrayCat` and set it equal to `yellowCat`, since it is still `Whiskers`. However, we change the name of `yellowStrayCat` to `Smokey`. We also create a new constant called `yellowStrayDog`, setting it equal to `yellowDog` and naming it `Max`.

```
let yellowStrayCat = yellowCat
yellowStrayCat.name = "Smokey"
print(yellowStrayCat.name)

var yellowStrayDog = yellowDog
yellowStrayDog.name = "Max"
print(yellowStrayDog.name)
```

Our **Results** panel shows that the names of `yellowStrayCat` and `yellowStrayDog`, respectively, are now `Smokey` and `Max`. So, everything seems to be the same between our class and our struct, right? No, they are not the same. Let's print the name of `yellowCat` underneath the line where we have print (`yellowStrayCat.name`). In addition, let's do the same for the name of `yellowDog` underneath where we have print (`yellowStrayDog.name`). Your code should now look as follows:

```
let yellowStrayCat = yellowCat
yellowStrayCat.name = "Smokey"
print(yellowStrayCat.name)
print(yellowCat.name)

var yellowStrayDog = yellowDog
yellowStrayDog.name = "Max"
print(yellowStrayDog.name)
print(yellowDog.name)
```

In our **Results** panel, as shown in the preceding screenshot, you should notice an unexpected result. The `yellowCat`, `Whiskers`, now has the name `Smokey`, but the `yellowDog` is still `Bruno`. Without getting too technical, when you use a class and copy it as we did, it refers back to the original instance created. This is known as a reference type. However, when structs get copied, they create a new instance and the original is not affected. This is known as a **value type**.

Before we move on, let's look at one more difference between the two. In programming, we have what is called **inheritance**, which means that we can create another object with default values and other objects can inherit from those default values. Let's create an `Animal` class that is the base class immediately below our `Cat` class:

```
class Animal {
   var age:Int?
}
```

Now, let's update our `Cat` class to inherit from it, as shown in the following code:

```
class Cat:Animal {
   ...
}
```

Note that we are only updating what goes directly after `Cat`. The rest of the class in the curly braces stays the same.

Since our class now inherits from `Animal`, we should have a new property called `age`. Underneath where we name `yellowCat` as `Whiskers` and above our `print` statement, enter the following after we set Whiskers name:

```
yellowCat.age = 3
```

Getting Started with the Grid

So, as expected, we were able to give `Whiskers` an `age`. Let's do the same for our `Dog` struct by adding `Animal` directly after `Dog`:

```
struct Dog:Animal {
   var name:String?
}
```

Once you have entered the preceding code snippet, you will see the following:

```
 2 // Cat Class
 3 class Cat:Animal {
 4    var name:String?
 5 }
 6
 7 class Animal {
 8    var age:Int?
 9 }
10
11 // Dog Struct
12 struct Dog:Animal {
13    var name:String?
14 }
15
16
17 // Create a cat
18 let yellowCat = Cat()                          Cat
19 yellowCat.name = "Whiskers"                    Cat
20 yellowCat.age = 3                              Cat
21 print(yellowCat.name)                          "Optional("Whiskers")\n"
```

```
Playground execution failed: error: FunctionsStructs.playground:6:8: error: non-class type 'Dog' cannot inherit
from class 'Animal'
struct Dog:Animal {
       ^    ~~~~~~

* thread #1: tid = 0x1939c24, 0x0000000104cf73c0 FunctionsStructs`executePlayground, queue = 'com.apple.main-
thread', stop reason = breakpoint 1.2
  * frame #0: 0x0000000104cf73c0 FunctionsStructs`executePlayground
    frame #1: 0x0000000104cf69c0 FunctionsStructs`__37-[XCPAppDelegate enqueueRunLoopBlock]_block_invoke + 32
    frame #2: 0x000000010581125c CoreFoundation`__CFRUNLOOP_IS_CALLING_OUT_TO_A_BLOCK__ + 12
    frame #3: 0x00000001057f6304 CoreFoundation`__CFRunLoopDoBlocks + 356
    frame #4: 0x00000001057f5a75 CoreFoundation`__CFRunLoopRun + 901
    frame #5: 0x00000001057f5494 CoreFoundation`CFRunLoopRunSpecific + 420
    frame #6: 0x000000010aba1a6f GraphicsServices`GSEventRunModal + 161
    frame #7: 0x000000010639fa74 UIKit`UIApplicationMain + 159
```

A red error displays and informs you that `Non-class type 'Dog' cannot inherit from class Animal`. Therefore, we need to create a struct called, `AnimalB`, since we cannot have the same name:

```
struct AnimalB {
   var age:Int?
}
```

Update your `Dog` struct from `Animal` to `AnimalB`:

```
struct Dog:AnimalB {
   var name:String?
}
```

Now, you should see an error called `Inheritance from non-protocol type 'AnimalB'`, which means that our struct cannot inherit from another struct:

```
// Cat Class
class Cat:Animal {
    var name:String?
}

class Animal {
    var age:Int?
}

// Dog Struct
struct Dog:AnimalB {
    var name:String?
}

struct AnimalB {
    var age:Int?
}

// Create a cat
let yellowCat = Cat()
```

```
Playground execution failed: error: FunctionsStructs.playground:6:8: error: inheritance from non-protocol type 'AnimalB'
struct Dog:AnimalB {
           ^

* thread #1: tid = 0x193d926, 0x00000001057893c0 FunctionsStructs`executePlayground, queue = 'com.apple.main-thread', stop reason = breakpoint 1.2
  * frame #0: 0x00000001057893c0 FunctionsStructs`executePlayground
    frame #1: 0x00000001057889c0 FunctionsStructs`__37-[XCPAppDelegate enqueueRunLoopBlock]_block_invoke + 32
    frame #2: 0x00000001062a325c CoreFoundation`__CFRUNLOOP_IS_CALLING_OUT_TO_A_BLOCK__ + 12
    frame #3: 0x0000000106288304 CoreFoundation`__CFRunLoopDoBlocks + 356
    frame #4: 0x0000000106287a75 CoreFoundation`__CFRunLoopRun + 901
    frame #5: 0x0000000106287494 CoreFoundation`CFRunLoopRunSpecific + 420
    frame #6: 0x000000010b633a6f GraphicsServices`GSEventRunModal + 161
    frame #7: 0x0000000106e31a74 UIKit`UIApplicationMain + 159
```

Inheritance is something that you can do with classes, but not with structs; this is another difference between classes and structs. There are a couple of other advanced technical differences but, for our purposes, the two described here are sufficient.

Controllers and classes

When working with `UIViewController`, `UICollectionViewController`, and `UITableViewController`, you need to create a class file for each of these elements. Each file handles all of the logic and interactions that the controller sends and receives. Along with interactions, the class file is responsible for receiving data. You should understand this more when we delve more deeply into creating each of these class files.

Getting Started with the Grid

Creating our controller

When working with our UI, we used controllers that were done for you. Now that we know that our UI is in place, we can get rid of these two files. We are going to recreate them together and understand how they work.

1. Please select the `ExploreViewController.swift` and *cmd* + click on `RestaurantViewController.swift`. When you do this you should have both files selected:

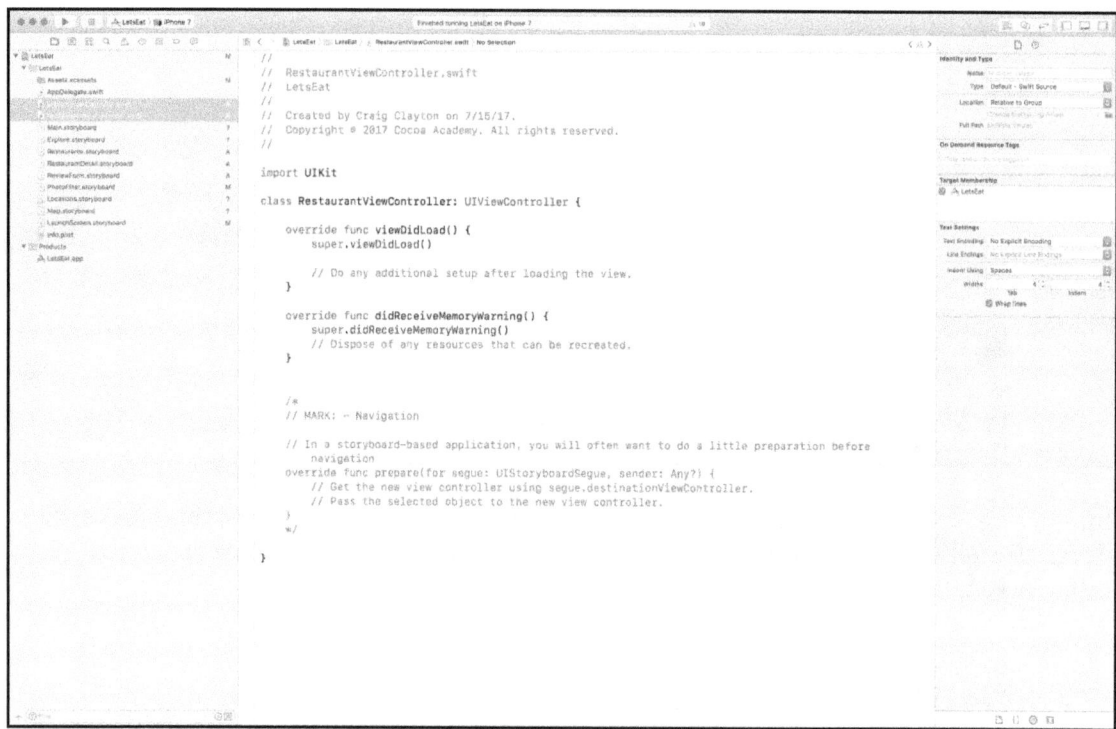

2. Next, hit *Delete* on your keyboard. You should see the following screen:

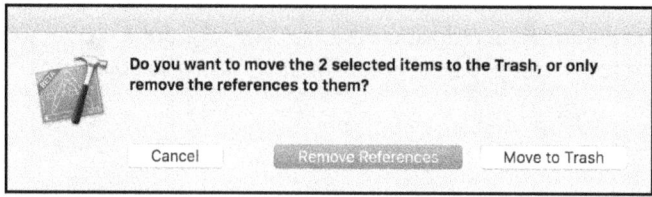

[344]

3. Click on **Move to Trash**.

4. If you select **Remove References**, it removes it from the project, but it is still in your project folder.

Next, let's create our first file:

1. Right-click inside of the `LetsEat` folder and select **New File**.
2. Inside of the **Choose a template for your new file** screen, select **iOS** at the top and, then, **Cocoa Touch Class**. Then, hit **Next**:

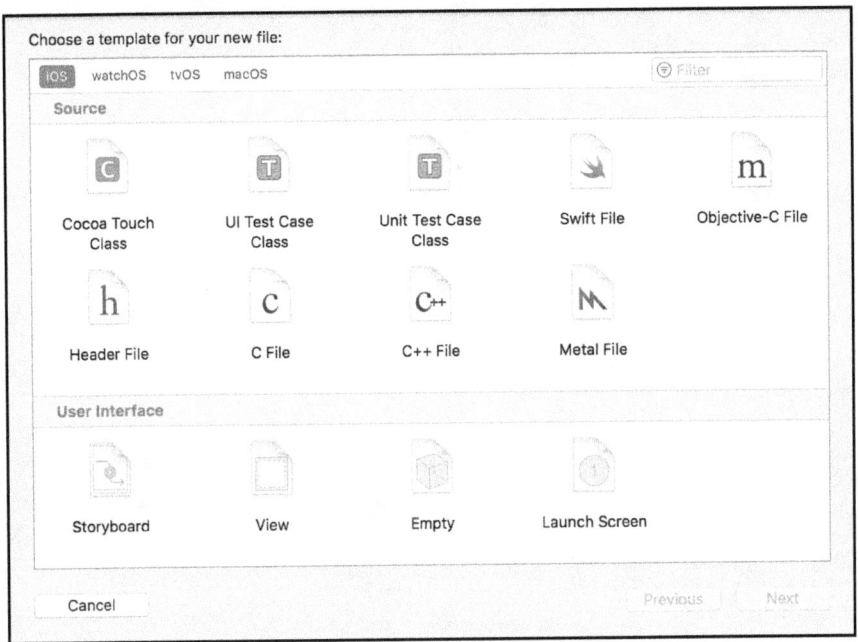

3. You should see an options screen. Add the following:

New file:

- **Class**: `ExploreViewController`
- **Subclass**: `UIViewController`
- **Also create XIB**: Unchecked
- **Language**: `Swift`

Getting Started with the Grid

4. After hitting **Next**, you are asked to create this file. Select **Create** and then your file should look like mine.

Let's review this `ExploreViewController` class file and also do some maintenance inside of the file. We created this file to use with the `UIViewController` that we created when we initially set up our UI.

Note that there are three methods in this file—`viewDidLoad()`, `didReceiveMemoryWarning()`, and `prepare()` (which is commented out). Let's delete both `didReceiveMemoryWarning()` and `prepare()`, as we do not need them at this time:

```
import UIKit

class ExploreViewController: UIViewController {

    override func viewDidLoad() {
        super.viewDidLoad()
        // Do any additional setup after loading the view.   ⊗ DELETE
    }

    override func didReceiveMemoryWarning() {
        super.didReceiveMemoryWarning()
        // Dispose of any resources that can be recreated.
    }

    /*
    // MARK: - Navigation

    // In a storyboard-based application, you will often want to do a little preparation before navigation
    override func prepare(for segue: UIStoryboardSegue, sender: Any?) {
        // Get the new view controller using segue.destinationViewController.
        // Pass the selected object to the new view controller.
    }
    */
}
```
DELETE

```
import UIKit

class ExploreViewController: UIViewController {

    override func viewDidLoad() {
        super.viewDidLoad()

    }

    override func didReceiveMemoryWarning() {
        super.didReceiveMemoryWarning()
        // Dispose of any resources that can be recreated.
    }
}
```
UPDATED

[346]

What remains is `viewDidLoad()`; this method is called only once during the life of the View Controller. Let's see what this means by updating `viewDidLoad()` to the following:

```
func viewDidLoad() {
  super.viewDidLoad()
  print("Hello Explore View Controller")
}
```

Now, run the project by hitting the Play button (or using *cmd* + *R*). Although we expected to see the above `print` statement in our **Debug** panel, we got a crash:

```
import UIKit

class ExploreViewController: UIViewController {

    override func viewDidLoad() {
        super.viewDidLoad()

        // Do any additional setup after loading the view.
    }

    override func didReceiveMemoryWarning() {
        super.didReceiveMemoryWarning()
        // Dispose of any resources that can be recreated.
    }

    /*
    // MARK: - Navigation

    // In a storyboard-based application, you will often want to do a little preparation before navigation
    override func prepare(for segue: UIStoryboardSegue, sender: Any?) {
        // Get the new view controller using segue.destinationViewController.
        // Pass the selected object to the new view controller.
    }
    */

}
```

DELETE

DELETE

```
import UIKit

class ExploreViewController: UIViewController {

    override func viewDidLoad() {
        super.viewDidLoad()

        print("Hello Explore View Controller")
    }

    override func didReceiveMemoryWarning() {
        super.didReceiveMemoryWarning()
        // Dispose of any resources that can be recreated.
    }

}
```

UPDATED

Getting Started with the Grid

This crash is telling us that it has a key `collectionView`, but it cannot find it. When we deleted our file, the storyboard still has a reference to it because it has no clue the file was deleted and recreated. To stop it from crashing, we need to either remove the reference or add the variable `collectionView` to our file.

For learning purposes, we are going to do both. Let's remove the reference and later we will add and connect it back later. The reason we are doing this is because this is one of the most common errors beginners see. You connect something and remove it but never remove it from storyboard and so your app crashes.

1. Open the `Explore.storyboard` file and, in the Utilities panel, select the **Connections inspector**.
2. Next, select the Explore View Controller in the Outline view, and you will see the problem under Outlets:

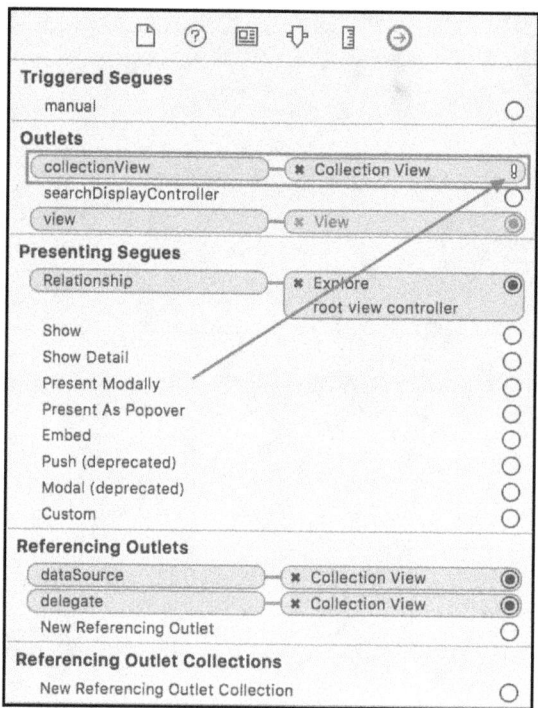

Chapter 13

This exclamation is telling us that it cannot find this variable in our `ExploreViewController.swift` file. Just click the **X** and the variable is removed from the storyboard file.

If you rerun the project now, our app crashes again. The reason is that our app is looking for data for Collection View that we have not set up yet. Let's update this so that we get rid of our crash:

1. Open the `Explore.storyboard` file.
2. Then, with the Explore View Controller still selected in the Outline view, click the **X** for both data source and delegate in the Connections inspector of the Utilities panel.

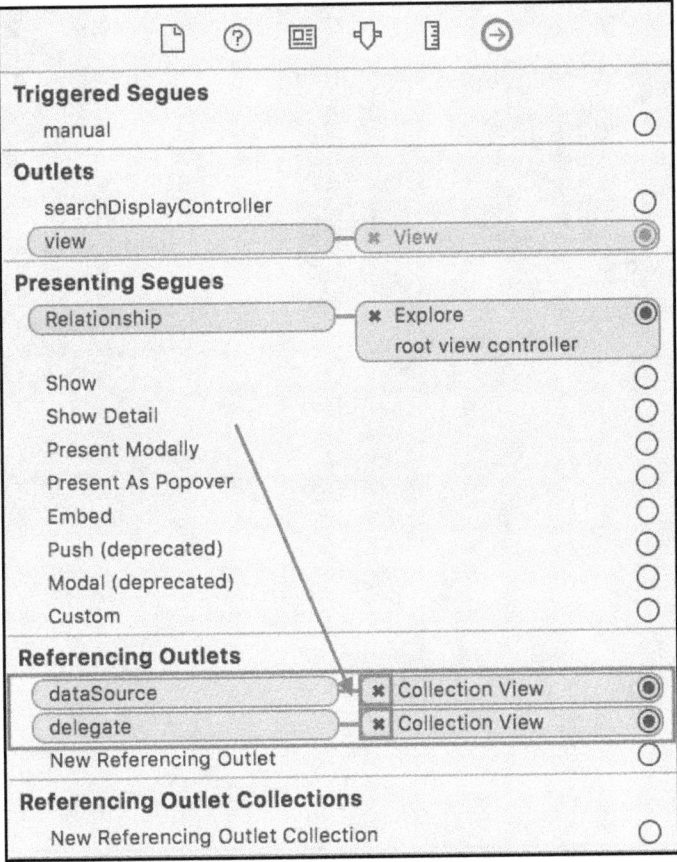

Getting Started with the Grid

Let's run the project again by hitting the Play button (or using *cmd + R*); you should now only see Hello Explore View Controller inside of the Debug panel.

Before we continue, we need to update our Restaurant View Controller as well. You are going to go into your `Restaurants.storyboard` file and, in the Outlets inspector, select the **X** for `collectionView`, `dataSource`, and `delegate` to get rid of the outlet we added earlier in the book.

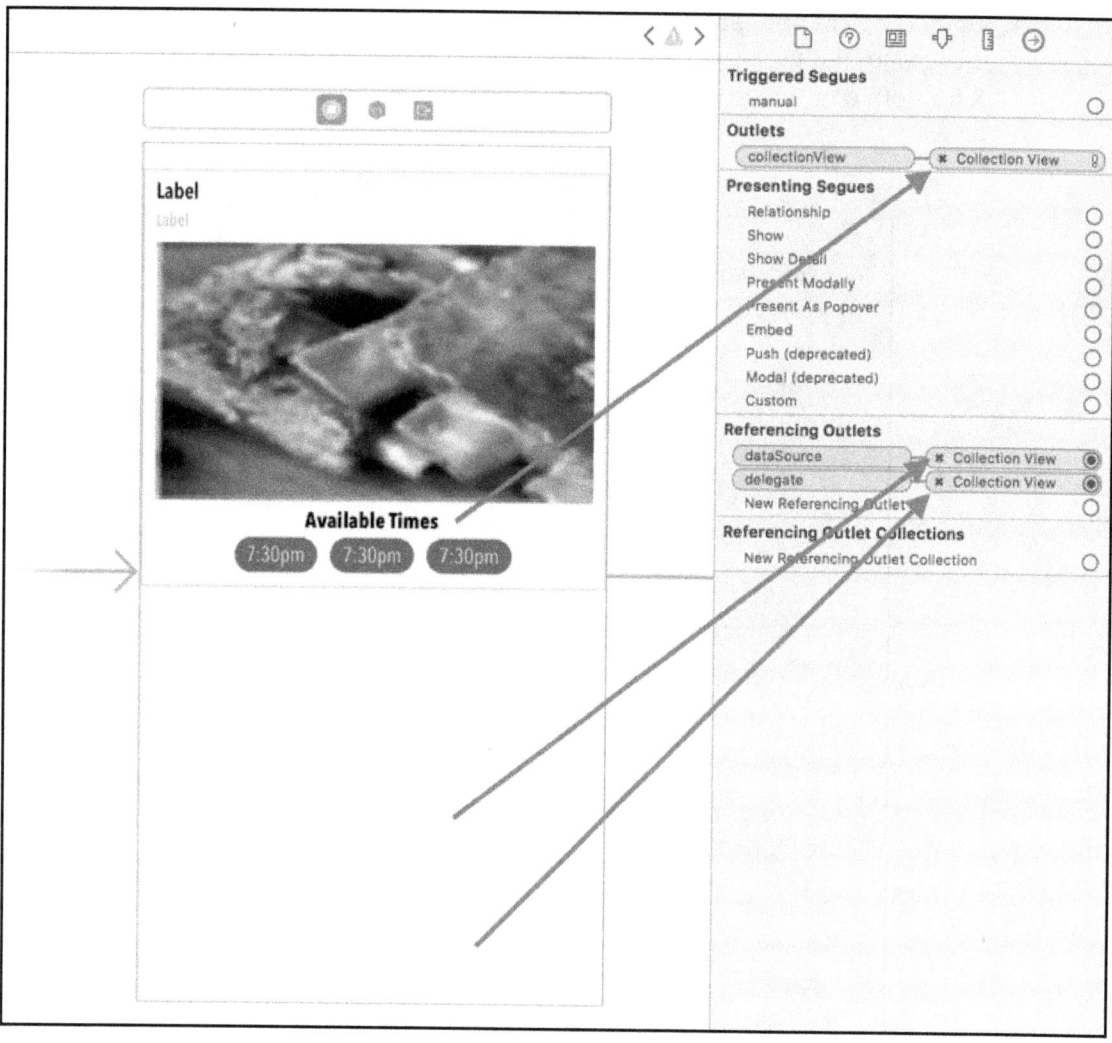

Chapter 13

Next, in the Identity inspector, delete `RestaurantViewController` inside of the custom class.

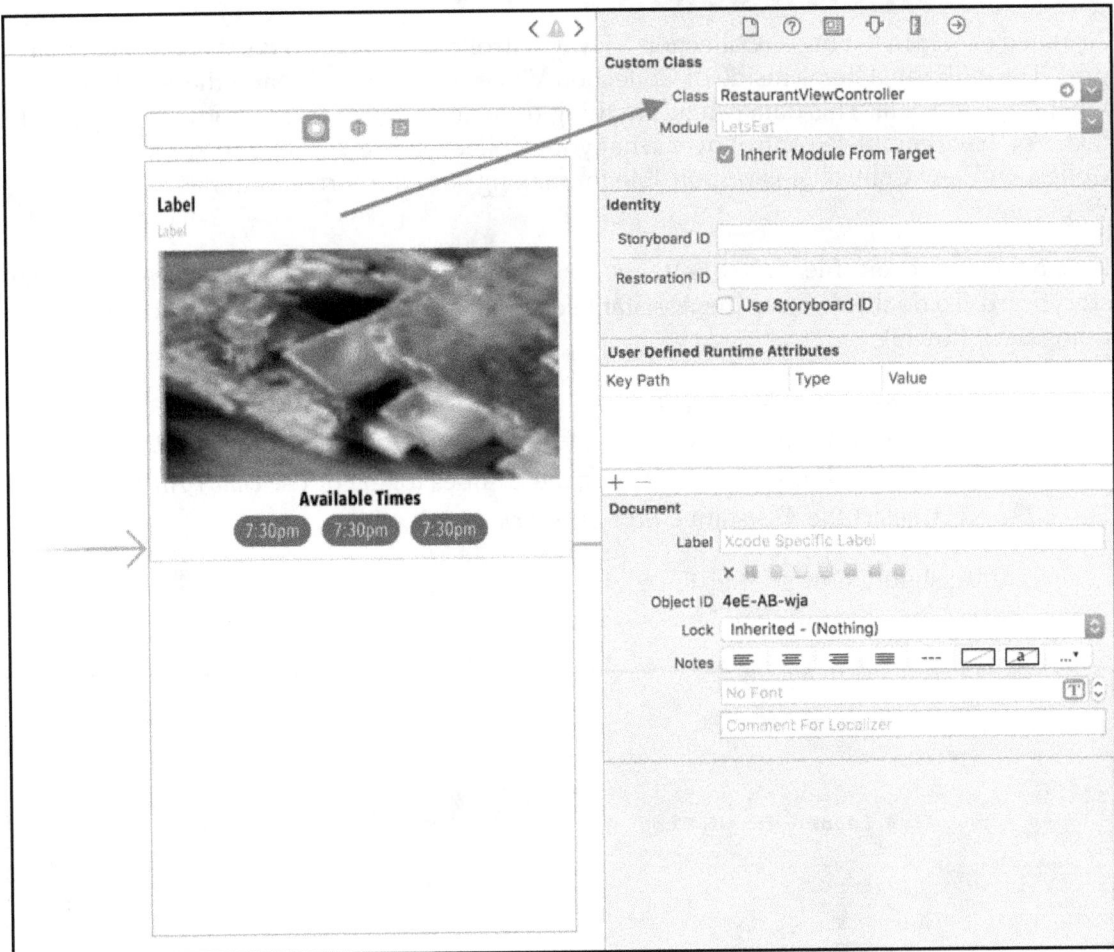

Since we deleted those files, we would have had more crashing. Now that we have our `ExploreViewController` hooked up with our `UIViewController` in the storyboard, let's start working with our `UICollectionView`.

Understanding Collection View controllers and Collection View cells

As noted earlier in the book, Collection View Controllers allow us to display our data in a grid. The individual items inside of Collection Views are called cells, and these cells are what show the data. This data can be anything from an image to text or both an image and text. You have complete control over what your Collection View cell can display. Our Collection View Controller is responsible for making sure the correct number of cells is displayed.

Let's now connect our file, `ExploreViewController`, with our `UICollectionView` in the storyboard. To do this, we use the Assistant editor (or split screen), which we access by doing the following:

1. Open `Explore.storyboard`.
2. Close the Navigator panel using the hide Navigator toggle or *cmd + 0*.
3. Close the Utilities panel by hitting the Utilities toggle or use *cmd + Alt + 0*.
4. Next, select the Assistant editor or use *cmd + Alt + Enter*.

   You should now see `Explore.storyboard` on the left and `ExploreViewController.swift` on the right:

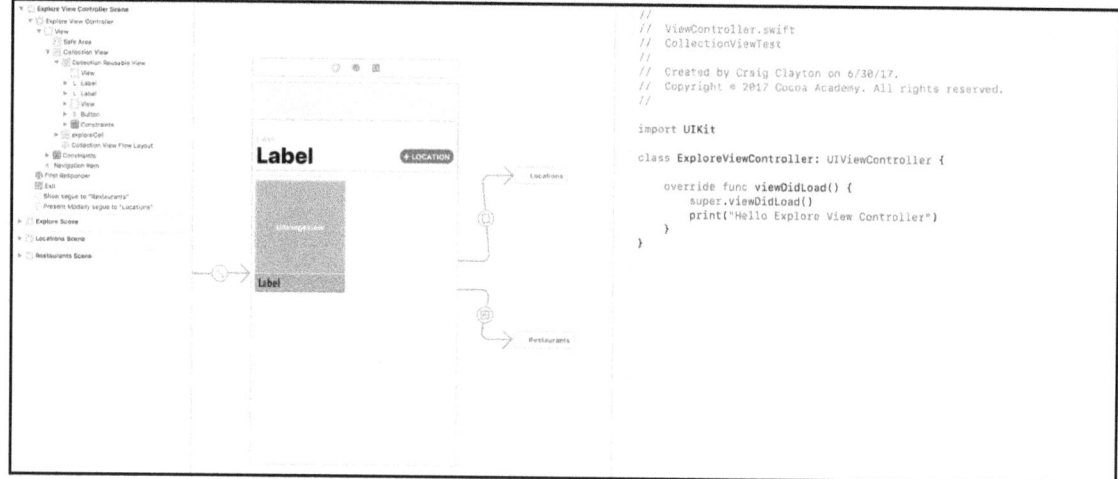

Chapter 13

5. Add the following inside of your `ExploreViewController.swift` file on the line after the following code:

   ```
   class ExploreViewController: UIViewController {
     @IBOutlet weak var collectionView:UICollectionView!
   ```

`IBOutlet` is a way to a connect to UI element. We have a Collection View on our `UIViewController`; now, we are creating a variable that allows us to hook into it.

6. After you create the variable, you should see a small circle to the left of the variable:

   ```
   ○    @IBOutlet weak var collectionView:UICollectionView!
   ```

7. When you hover over it, you should see a plus button appear inside of the circle:

   ```
   ⊕    @IBOutlet weak var collectionView:UICollectionView!
   ```

   Click on it and drag this to your Collection View inside of your `UIViewController`:

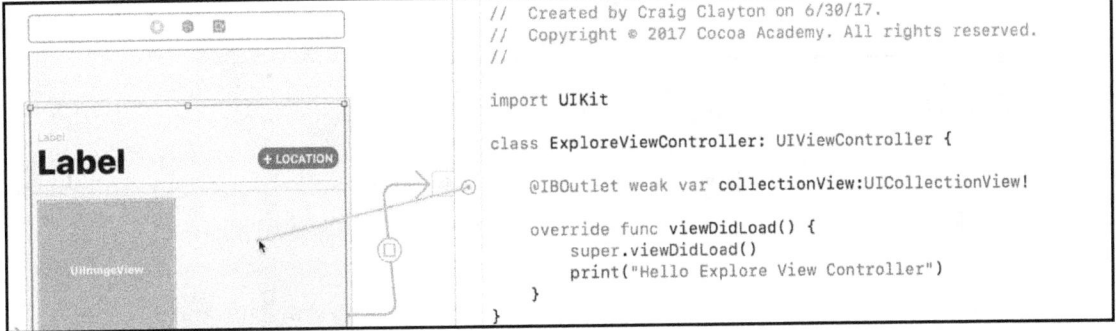

[353]

Getting Started with the Grid

8. Once you release the mouse button, you should see the circle become filled:

   ```
   @IBOutlet weak var collectionView:UICollectionView!
   ```

9. Now, select the Standard editor or use *cmd + Enter*.

   In your scene, select your Collection View. Then, in your Utilities panel, select the Connections inspector, which is the last icon on the right. Under the **Outlets** section, we now add back **dataSource** and **delegate**, the same ones we removed earlier:

   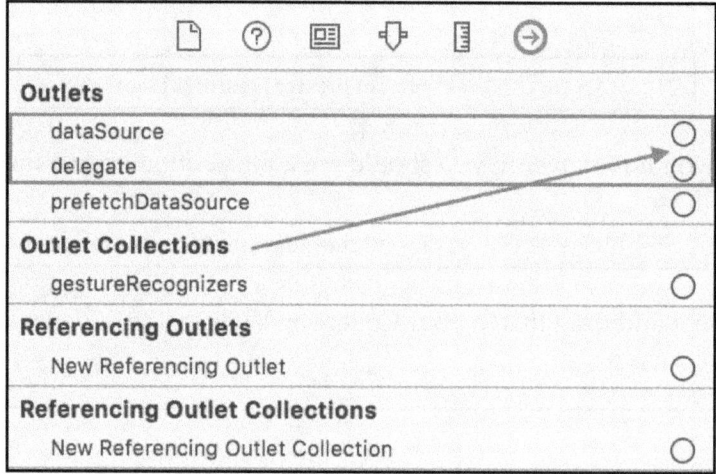

   The `dataSource` property is what is used to supply the data for our Collection View, so we need to pass whatever data we have to this property. On the other hand, the `delegate` property, which supplies the behavior, does not require us to supply anything as it receives interactions that happen within our Collection View.

   We need to update our data source for our Collection View; let's add this now:

10. Click and drag the `dataSource` property to the Explore View Controller in your Outline view.

11. Click and drag the delegate property to the Explore View Controller in your Outline view:

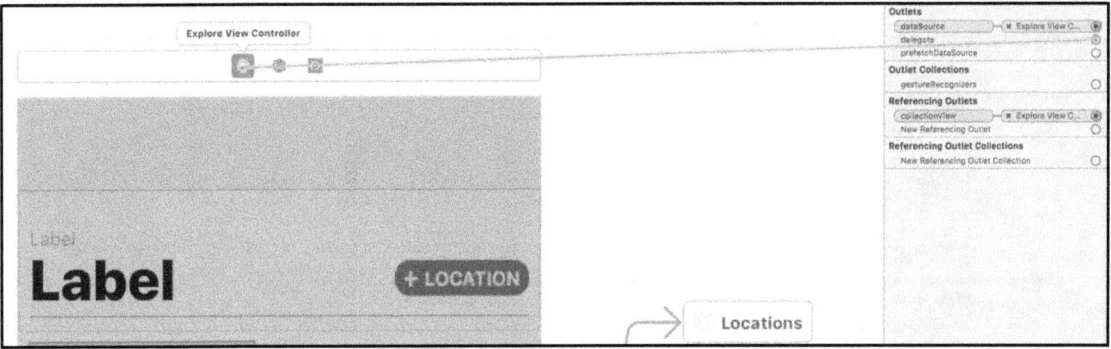

Getting data into Collection View

Having boxes is great, but having data with nice pictures is so much more appealing. Let's get some data displaying inside of our Collection View:

1. Use *cmd + Shift + O*, which opens a small window called **Open Quickly**. Inside of the window, type `ExploreView` and hit *Enter* to select the `ExploreViewController.swift` file.

2. Update our class definition from
   the `ExploreViewController:UIViewController` class to the following:

   ```
   class ExploreViewController:UIViewController,
   UICollectionViewDataSource
   ```

Understanding the data source

Whenever we use Collection View to get data, we must conform to a protocol. A protocol is a set of methods to which we have access and can either be required or optional. For Collection Views, we are required to implement three methods to get data into a Collection View. So, let's add the following four functions (each beginning with `func`) after the closing curly brace of `viewDidLoad()`:

```swift
import UIKit

class ExploreViewController: UIViewController, UICollectionViewDataSource, UICollectionViewDelegate {

    @IBOutlet weak var collectionView: UICollectionView!

    override func viewDidLoad() {
        super.viewDidLoad()
        print("Hello Explore View Controller")
    }

    func collectionView(_ collectionView: UICollectionView, viewForSupplementaryElementOfKind kind: String, at indexPath: IndexPath) -> UICollectionReusableView {
        let headerView = collectionView.dequeueReusableSupplementaryView(ofKind: kind, withReuseIdentifier: "header", for: indexPath)
        return headerView
    }

    func collectionView(_ collectionView: UICollectionView, cellForItemAt indexPath: IndexPath) -> UICollectionViewCell {
        return collectionView.dequeueReusableCell(withReuseIdentifier: "exploreCell", for: indexPath)
    }

    func numberOfSections(in collectionView: UICollectionView) -> Int {
        return 1
    }

    func collectionView(_ collectionView: UICollectionView, numberOfItemsInSection section: Int) -> Int {
        return 20
    }

    // Add Unwind here
    @IBAction func unwindLocationCancel(segue:UIStoryboardSegue) {}
}
```

Let's break down the code to better understand what we are doing:

- **Part A**: This first method is what we need to add a header to our Collection View.

  `collectionView(_:viewForSupplementaryElementOfKind:at:)`

- **Part B**: The identifier is what we added when we were designing in earlier chapters. This identifier helps Xcode know what view we are referring to:

    ```
    let headerView =
    collectionView.dequeueReusableSupplementaryView(ofKind: kind,
    withReuseIdentifier: "header", for: indexPath)
    return headerView
    ```

- **Part C**: Our next method gets called for every item we need. Therefore, in our case, it gets called 20 times:

    ```
    collectionView(_:cellForItemAt:)
    ```

- **Part D**: Here, we are creating a cell every time `collectionView(_:numberOfItemsInSection:)` is called. The identifier, exploreCell, is the name we gave it in the storyboard; so, this is the cell that is grabbed and used inside of our Collection View:

    ```
    return collectionView.dequeueReusableCell(withReuseIdentifier:
    "exploreCell", for: indexPath)
    ```

- **Part E**: This method tells our Collection View how many different sections we want to display:

    ```
    numberOfSections(in collectionView: UICollectionView)
    ```

- **Part F**: Here, we are telling our Collection View that we only want one section:

    ```
    return 1
    ```

- **Part G**: Our next method tells our Collection View how many different items we are going to display inside of the section we set up.

    ```
    collectionView(_:numberOfItemsInSection:)
    ```

- **Part H**: We are telling our Collection View that we want to display 20 items.

    ```
    return 20
    ```

- **Part I**: Finally, we add this line back as it was removed. We use this function to dismiss our location modal when you hit the **Cancel** button.

    ```
    @IBAction func unwindLocationCancel(segue:UIStoryboardSegue) {}
    ```

Let's build and run the project by hitting the Play button (or using *cmd + R*). You will see that our app is back to where it was at the end of `Chapter 11`, *Designing Static Tables*, but now we actually know what is going on the code side.

Summary

In this chapter, we covered quite a few new topics as well as a lot of code. As long as you have a basic understanding of what we covered in this chapter, you will be fine to continue. A lot of these concepts and ideas will be covered again, as these are common design patterns in iOS.

We learned about the Model View Controller architecture. Then, we covered classes and structures, their similarities and differences. Finally, we looked at Controllers and classes and how they work. We then created our Controller for our storyboard file.

In the next chapter, we will look at how to get local data into our app. We will also look at how to pass data from the **Explore** view to the restaurant list.

14
Getting Data into Our Grid

Working with data is very important, but when working with beginners, I like to do this in steps so that this process is a bit easier. In this chapter, we are going to work with data that is stored on the device. Later in the book, we will work with data that we get from a feed. Feed data means it is coming from a website URL. Using data from a feed means you can update the data without having to update the app.

We will cover the following in this chapter:

- What is a model?
- What is a plist?
- How to create a plist?
- Working with a manager class

In the last chapter, we got the **Explore** listing up, but we have no data. We need to create a model that we can use to store information that our cell can use to display data.

Model

Typically, when developing your model, the best way to start when you have a design is to look at the data associated with your view. Let's look at our app design again:

The items (`UICollectionViewCell`) displayed in the grid are each supported by some data. Looking at the design, we see that each item needs an image and a name (cuisine). Therefore, we need to create a model called `ExploreItem` with two properties, specifically `image` and `name`.

In the model camp, we have three files that we will create—`ExploreData.plist`, `ExploreItem.swift`, and `ExploreDataManager.swift`.

ExploreData.plist

The first file, `ExploreData.plist`, has already been created for you and can be found in your project files for this chapter. This file contains all the data we need to have a list of cuisines. Drag this file into your `Model` folder in the Navigator panel.

In the file, there is an array of dictionary items. Each item has a cuisine name and image for that particular cuisine. Let's take a look at the first few elements of this file:

Key	Type	Value
▼ Root	Array	(31 items)
▼ Item 0	Dictionary	(2 items)
name	String	All
image	String	all.png
▼ Item 1	Dictionary	(2 items)
name	String	Bistro
image	String	bistro.png
▼ Item 2	Dictionary	(2 items)
name	String	Bar / Lounge / Bottle Service
image	String	bar.png
▼ Item 3	Dictionary	(2 items)
name	String	Brewery
image	String	brewery.png

We will load this file into our **Explore** list, and this is what we use to filter restaurants by a specific cuisine.

ExploreItem.swift

Next, we need to create a file to represent our data. Our **Explore** list displays an image and a name that match the corresponding image and name that we see in our `Explore.plist` file. Let's create this `ExploreItem` file now:

1. Right-click on the `Model` folder and select **New File**.
2. Inside of the template screen, select **iOS** at the top and then **Swift File**. Then, hit **Next**.
3. Name the file `ExploreItem`, and then hit **Create**.

The only thing in this file is an `import` statement.

> The `import` statement allows us to import other libraries into our file, giving us the ability to see inside of these libraries and use properties from them. Foundation is one of Apple's core frameworks, and it has a bunch of tools that we can use while we program.

Since we do not need to use inheritance, we are going to make this file a `struct`. Add the following to your file:

```
struct ExploreItem {
}
```

Now that we have declared it a `struct`, let's add the two properties we need for this file—an image, and a name. For both of these properties, we are going to make them String data types. For the title, this makes sense, because it is text that we are displaying in our Collection View. However, for the image, using a String data type might not seem as obvious. The reason we are making the image a data type of String is because, to get it, we have to access it by name. For example, `american.png` is the filename for the American cuisine image. Add the following to the inside of your curly braces (`{ }`):

```
var name:String?
var image:String?
```

We have now added two properties, one for the image and one for the name, both of which are optional. Since we cannot give either of them an initial value, we have to make them optional.

Your file should look like the following:

```
struct ExploreItem {
    var name:String?
    var image:String?
}
```

We next need to add one more thing to this file.

We take the dictionary data we get from the `plist` and create an `ExploreItem` for each item. Our dictionary now looks like the following:

```
["name": "All", "image": "all.png"]
```

We need to pass this dictionary object to our `ExploreItem`. When you are passing a dictionary object, you are required to create a custom initializer. Our initializer takes a dictionary object into it. Then, we can set each item from the dictionary to the data of both of our properties, image, and name.

When you create a struct, by default, you get an `init()` method that has all the properties you created in the parameters.

For example, our `ExploreItem` will have a default initializer that looks like the following:

```
init(name:String, image:String)
```

Instead of using this initializer, we will create our own to pass a dictionary object into it.

To create a **custom initializer**, we are going to use what is called an **extension**, which gives us the ability to extend our code and add more functionality to it. Inside of your `ExploreItem` file, after the ending curly brace, add the following:

```
extension ExploreItem {
}
```

Next, let's create our custom initializer that takes a dictionary object into the parameters. Add the following between the curly braces of the extension we just added:

```
init(dict:[String:Any Object]) {
}
```

Getting Data into Our Grid

We have now created an `init()` method in the parameters, which accepts a dictionary object. As stated in the preceding section, we know that our data looks like the following:

```
["name": "All", "image": "all.png"]
```

To pass each value, we need to use the dictionary syntax, such as:

```
dict["name"]
dict["image"]
```

Let's proceed by mapping the dictionary data to our two properties. Add the following inside of the `init()` method curly braces:

```
    self.name  = dict["name"] as? String
    self.image = dict["image"] as? String
}
```

> Since our dictionary value is `AnyObject`, we have to specify that our data is a String by using the `as? String` at the end.

We now have our data item set up for our **Explore** view (cuisine list), and your file should look like the following:

```
extension ExploreItem {
  init(dict:[String:AnyObject]) {
    self.name  = dict["name"] as? String
    self.image = dict["image"] as? String
  }
}
```

Let's now focus on our data manager. We want our data manager to handle parsing the plist and giving us the data. Since our data will be coming from a plist, we need to have a method that will get the data from the plist first.

ExploreDataManager.swift

In our app, the data manager is responsible for communicating with a service (for example, the Yelp API, which we will discuss later in the book), as well as manipulating the data from the service. Once the data from the service is received, the data manager will create model objects that we can use for our app.

Chapter 14

In some apps, these two jobs are handled by the controller. However, rather than putting that responsibility on our controller, we limit the controller from talking to the manager so that it never knows anything about the service.

 As you get comfortable with programming, you will find that there are a few different types of architectures. We are sticking as closely as we can to MVC, because it is what Apple uses to build iOS apps.

Let's create the `ExploreDataManager` file now:

1. Right-click on the `Model` folder and select **New File**.
2. Inside of the template screen, select **iOS** at the top and then **Swift File**. Then, hit **Next**.
3. Name this file `ExploreDataManager`, and hit **Create**.

Since we need to define our class first, add the following under the `import` statement:

```
class ExploreDataManager {
}
```

Here, we used a `class` instead of a `struct`, because this is a file that we will inherit from later. You do not always necessarily know if you are going to inherit from another class or not; therefore, you can just default to a struct and then change to a class if you realize that you need to inherit from another class.

Now, we need to load data from the `ExploreData.plist` file. Add the following method to our `ExploreDataManager`:

```
import Foundation

class ExploreDataManager {

    fileprivate func loadData() -> [[String: AnyObject]] {
        guard let path = Bundle.main.path(forResource: "ExploreData", ofType: "plist"),
            let items = NSArray(contentsOfFile: path) else {
                return [[:]]
        }

        return items as! [[String : AnyObject]]
    }

}
```

[365]

Getting Data into Our Grid

- **Part A**: This function starts with the `fileprivate` keyword. Think of `fileprivate` as a way to give your methods an access level. If you do not use `fileprivate`, it defaults to internal, which means anyone can access or use the method outside of the class.

    ```
    private
    ```

- **Part B**: Our `loadData()` function is returning something back. The `->` states that our function has a return value. The return value for this method is an array with dictionary objects. Our dictionary will have a key of a String, and the value will be `AnyObject`.

    ```
    [[String: AnyObject]]
    ```

    `AnyObject` lets us take any data type that comes back. Therefore, we can have one item give us an Int, while another gives us back a String.

    You can also use `Any`. `Any` can represent an instance of any type at all, including functional types and optional types.

- **Part C**: Inside of the function, we are using what is known as a `guard` statement. A `guard` statement is designed for exiting a method or function early if a given statement returns `false`. Our `guard` checks two statements and both need to return `true`.

    ```
    guard let path = Bundle.main.path(forResource: "ExploreData",
        ofType: "plist")
    ```

    The first statement checks to see if the `ExploreData.plist` file exists in our app bundle. If the file is found, the statement returns `true`, and the file path is set to the constant path. Our next statement, which is separated by a comma, is discussed in *Part D*, as follows.

- **Part D**: In this statement, if the first statement returns `true`, we take the `path` constant, and then we check the contents inside of the file. Let's take a look at the data in our file again:

    ```
    let items = NSArray(contentsOfFile: path)
    ```

Chapter 14

▼ Root	Array	(31 items)
▼ Item 0	Dictionary	(2 items)
name	String	All
image	String	all.png
▼ Item 1	Dictionary	(2 items)
name	String	Bistro
image	String	bistro.png
▼ Item 2	Dictionary	(2 items)
name	String	Bar / Lounge / Bottle Service
image	String	bar.png
▼ Item 3	Dictionary	(2 items)
name	String	Brewery
image	String	brewery.png

If you look at the root of this plist, you see that its type is an array. `NSArray` has a method that we can use to get the data out of our file and put it into an array with which we can work.

Typically, plists come in two types, an array or a dictionary. Currently, neither the standard array nor dictionary gives us a method that allows us to get data out of a file, so we need to utilize `NSArray` (as we are here) or `NSDictionary`, respectively, to do that.

This statement now checks to verify that we are, indeed, working with an array, and then returns `true` if so. If both conditions return `true`, our array inside of our plist is given to us. The array is set to our constant items.

`NSArray` and `NSDictionary` come from Objective C (Apple's main programming language for building iOS apps); they have some extra features. Just know that they are similar to their Swift counterparts without the `NS`.

- **Part E**: Here, if any of the conditions are `false`, we return an array with an empty dictionary.

    ```
    else { return [[:]] }
    ```

Otherwise, we run the following `return`.

Getting Data into Our Grid

- **Part F**: This `return` gives back an array of dictionary items. Once we have our data loaded out of the plist, we can create our `ExploreItem`. Therefore, we need a method so that we can access all of our **Explore** items and return an array of items.

  ```
  return items as! [[String : AnyObject]]
  ```

Getting data

To get our data out of the plist, add the following method above `loadData()` inside of our `ExploreDataManager`:

```
func fetch() {
  for data in loadData() {
    print(data)
  }
}
```

Our `fetch()` method is going to loop through our dictionary data from the plist. Here is what your file should look like now:

```
import Foundation

class ExploreDataManager {

    func fetch() {
        for data in loadData() {
            print(data)
        }
    }

    fileprivate func loadData() -> [[String: AnyObject]] {
        guard let path = Bundle.main.path(forResource: "ExploreData", ofType: "plist"),
            let items = NSArray(contentsOfFile: path) else {
                return [[:]]
        }

        return items as! [[String : AnyObject]]
    }
}
```

Inside of your `ExploreViewController.swift` file, delete the previous `print` statement that was inside of your `viewDidLoad()` and replace it with the following:

```
let manager = ExploreDataManager()
manager.fetch()
```

Let's build and run the project by hitting the Play button (or use *cmd+ R*). You will notice that, in the **Debug** panel, every time our loop runs, it gives a dictionary object, such as the following:

```
["image": all.png, "name": All]
["image": bistro.png, "name": Bistro]
["image": bar.png, "name": Bar / Lounge]
["image": brewery.png, "name": Brewery]
["image": burgers.png, "name": Burgers]
["image": californian.png, "name": Californian]
["image": caribbean.png, "name": Caribbean]
["image": comfort.png, "name": Comfort Food]
["image": cuban.png, "name": Cuban]
["image": continental.png, "name": Continental]
["image": french.png, "name": French]
["image": international.png, "name": International]
["image": italian.png, "name": Italian]
["image": japanese.png, "name": Japanese]
["image": latin.png, "name": Latin American]
["image": mediterranean.png, "name": Mediterranean]
["image": mexican.png, "name": Mexican]
["image": organic.png, "name": Organic]
["image": panasian.png, "name": Pan-Asian]
["image": peruvian.png, "name": Peruvian]
["image": pizza.png, "name": Pizzeria]
["image": primerib.png, "name": Prime Rib]
["image": seafood.png, "name": Seafood]
["image": southamerican.png, "name": South American]
["image": southern.png, "name": Southern]
["image": spanish.png, "name": Spanish]
["image": steak.png, "name": Steakhouse]
["image": sushi.png, "name": Sushi]
["image": tapas.png, "name": Tapas / Small Plates]
["image": vietnamese.png, "name": Vietnamese]
["image": wine.png, "name": Wine Bar]
```

This is exactly what we want.

Now, inside of `ExploreDataManager`, add the following directly above our `fetch` method:

```
fileprivate var items:[ExploreItem] = []
```

Getting Data into Our Grid

Next, inside of our `fetch()`, update our `for...in` loop by replacing `print(data)` with the following:

```
items.append(ExploreItem(dict: data))
```

Your file should look like mine:

```
import Foundation

class ExploreDataManager {

    fileprivate var items:[ExploreItem] = []

    func fetch() {
        for data in loadData() {
            items.append(ExploreItem(dict: data))
        }
    }

    fileprivate func loadData() -> [[String: AnyObject]] {
        guard let path = Bundle.main.path(forResource: "ExploreData", ofType: "plist"),
            let items = NSArray(contentsOfFile: path) else {
            return [[:]]
        }

        return items as! [[String : AnyObject]]
    }
}
```

Let's build and run the project by hitting the Play button (or use *cmd* + *R*). In the **Debug** panel, you should see an array of **Explore** items.

We currently have our data, and we have cells. However, we need to get our data to our cells so that we can see the image and name. Let's open up `Explore.storyboard` and update our `exploreCell`.

Connecting to our cell

Now that we have our cell set up, we need to create a file so that we can connect to our cells:

1. Right-click on the `View` folder in the Navigator panel and select **New File**.
2. Inside of the template screen, select **iOS** at the top, and then **Cocoa Touch Class**. Then, hit **Next**.
3. You should now see an options screen. Add the following:

    New file:

    - **Class**: `ExploreCell`
    - **Subclass**: `UICollectionViewCell`
    - **Also create XIB**: Unchecked
    - **Language**: `Swift`

4. After hitting **Next**, you are asked to create this file. Select **Create** and your file should look like mine:

    ```
    import UIKit
    class ExploreCell: UICollectionViewCell {
    }
    ```

5. Next, open `Explore.storyboard` and select the `exploreCell` in the Outline view.
6. In the Utilities panel, select the Identity inspector and, under **Custom Class**, type `ExploreCell`. Then, hit *Enter*.

Getting Data into Our Grid

Hooking up our UI with IBOutlets

To access our UI elements, we need to connect them with `IBOutlets`.

1. Open the `ExploreCell.swift` file in the Navigator panel (or use *cmd* + *Shift* + *O*, type `ExploreCell`, and then hit *Enter*).
2. Inside of the class declaration, add the following:

   ```
   @IBOutlet var lblName:UILabel!
   @IBOutlet var imgExplore:UIImageView!
   ```

3. Open `Explore.storyboard` and select your `exploreCell` again.
4. In the Utilities panel, select the Connection inspector. You should see both variables we just created, **lblName** and **imgExplore**, under **Outlets**:

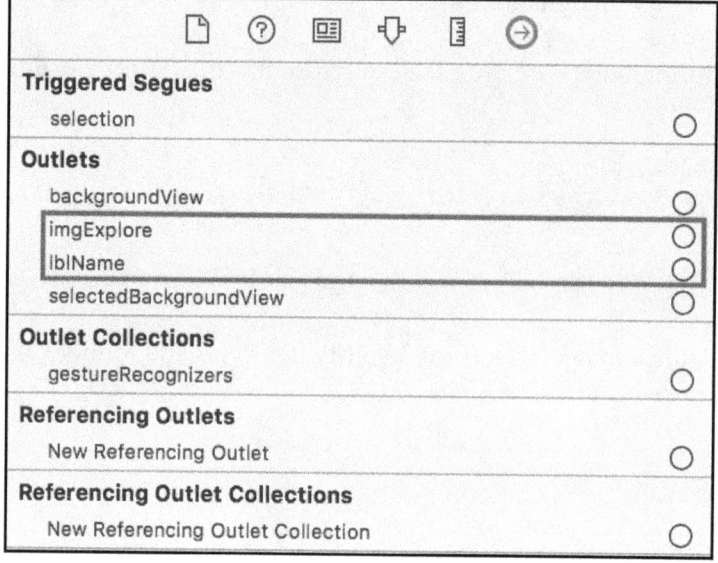

5. Now, Ctrl + drag from **imgExplore** to the **UIImageView** we put in our cell:

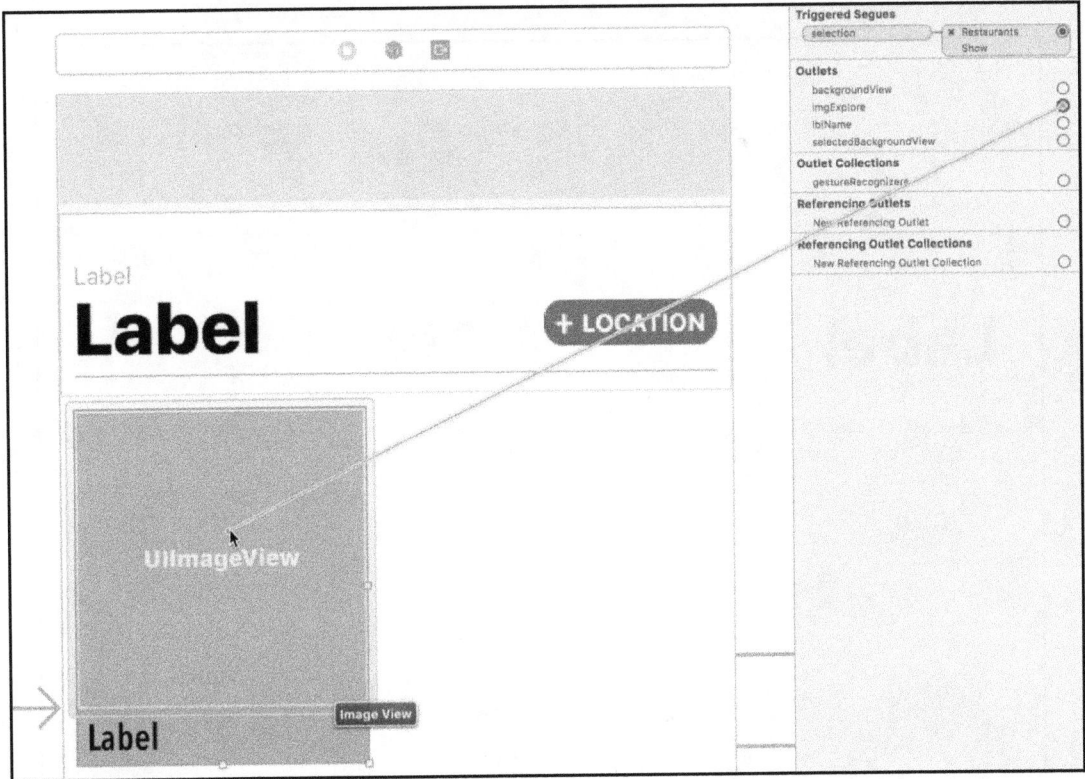

Getting Data into Our Grid

6. Repeat this step for **lblName** by CTL dragging from **lblName** to the **UILabel** in our cell:

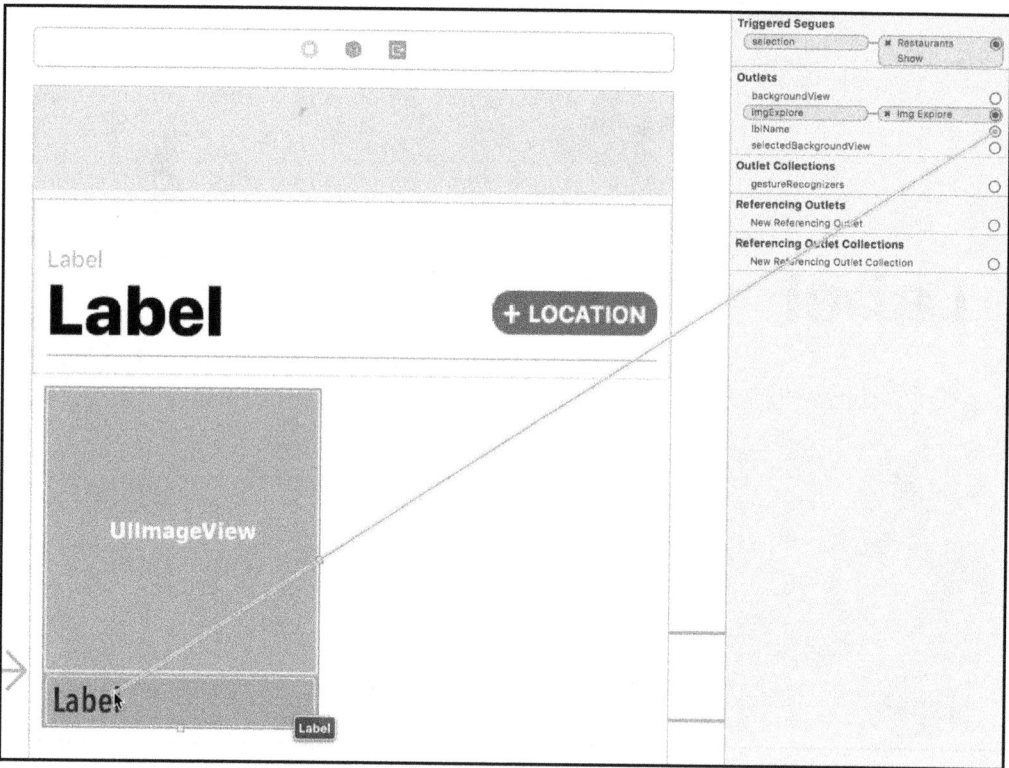

Great! Now that we have our cell set up, let's pull data into it. In our `ExploreDataManager`, add these two methods above the `loadData()` method:

```
func numberOfItems() -> Int {
   return items.count
}

func explore(at index:IndexPath) -> ExploreItem {
   return items[index.item]
}
```

We use the first method, `numberOfItems()`, to update the total number of items in our Collection View. The second method, `explore (at index:IndexPath)`, is called for each item we create in our Collection View. Then, we use this to pass the data to our cell to display the name and the image.

Now that we have these two methods added, let's open up our `ExploreViewController` file. We currently have the following inside of our `viewDidLoad()`:

```
let manager = ExploreDataManager()
manager.fetch()
```

Let's move `let manager` underneath our Collection View so that it is outside `viewDidLoad()`; and, therefore, we can access it anywhere within the class as opposed to only within the function. You should now have this before `viewDidLoad()`:

```
@IBOutlet var collectionView: UICollectionView!
let manager = ExploreDataManager()
```

Inside of `viewDidLoad()`, only `manager.fetch()` remains. Next, we need to update our `numberOfItemsInSection()` to say:

```
func collectionView(_ collectionView: UICollectionView,
numberOfItemsInSection section: Int) -> Int {
   return manager.numberOfItems()
}
```

Therefore, instead of returning 20, we are going to get the number of items from our plist.

Finally, inside of our `cellForItemAt()`, revise the `let` statement in the third required method before `return cell` by adding `as! ExploreCell`, as follows:

```
let cell = collectionView.dequeueReusableCell(withReuseIdentifier:
"exploreCell", for: indexPath) as! ExploreCell
```

Then, add the following after the code snippet you just added and before `return cell`:

```
let item = manager.explore(at: indexPath)
if let name = item.name { cell.lblName.text = name }
if let image = item.image { cell.imgExplore.image = UIImage(named: image) }
```

This gets an `ExploreItem` for each cell in our Collection View and passes the data to the cell. Finally, for your return, add the following:

```
return cell
```

Getting Data into Our Grid

Let's build and run the project by hitting the Play button (or use *cmd + R*). You should now see your Collection View come to life with images and text:

The images are not perfect, but we will fix them later. Now that we have our cells displaying content, we need to make it so that when you select a cell, it goes to our restaurant listing.

Let's build and run the project by hitting the Play button (or use *cmd* + *R*). You should now be able to select your cell, and it goes to what will be your restaurant listing page. This page will be empty for now, so let's work on this next.

Restaurant listing

Now that we have our **Explore** listing going to our restaurant listing, we need to get our Collection View connected to our `RestaurantListViewController`:

1. Right-click inside of the `LetsEat` folder and select **New File**.
2. Inside of the template screen, select **iOS** at the top and then **Cocoa Touch Class**. Then, hit **Next**.

   You should now see an options screen.

3. Add the following:

   New file:

   - **Class**: `RestaurantViewController`
   - **Subclass**: `UIViewController`
   - **Also create XIB**: Unchecked
   - **Language**: `Swift`

   After hitting **Next**, you will be asked to create this file.

4. Select **Create**.
5. Let's delete both `didReceiveMemoryWarning()` and `prepare()` (which has been commented out), as we do not need them at this time.
6. Open `Restaurants.storyboard`.
7. Then, select the `UIViewController` in the Utility panel, and select the Identity inspector, which is the third icon from the left.
8. Under **Custom Class**, and in the **Class** drop-down menu, select `RestaurantViewController` and hit *Enter*.

Getting Data into Our Grid

9. If your Navigator panel is currently open, close it by clicking on the hide navigator toggle or *cmd + 0*.
10. If your Utilities panel is currently open, close it by clicking on the Utilities toggle or use *cmd + Alt/Alt + 0*.
11. Next, select the Assistant editor or use *cmd + Alt/Alt + Enter*.
12. You should now see `Restaurants.storyboard` on the left side and `RestaurantListViewController.swift` on the right.
13. Now, add the following after:

    ```
    class RestaurantListViewController: UIViewController {
        @IBOutlet var collectionView:UICollectionView!
    ```

14. After you create the variable, you see a small circle to the left of the variable.
15. When you hover over it, you see a plus button appear inside of the circle. Click on it and drag this to your Collection View inside of your `UIViewController`:
16. Once you release, you see the circle become filled:

    ```
    @IBOutlet weak var collectionView:UICollectionView!
    ```

    Now, it is time to display something inside of our Collection View:

17. Use *cmd + Shift + O*, which opens the **Open Quickly** search box, and type `Restaurant`. Then, hit *Enter* to select the `RestaurantListViewController.swift` file.
18. In your scene, select your Collection View. Then, in your Utilities panel select the Connections inspector, which is the last icon on the right. Under the **Outlets** section, `dataSource` and `delegate`, the same ones we removed earlier, we now add them back:

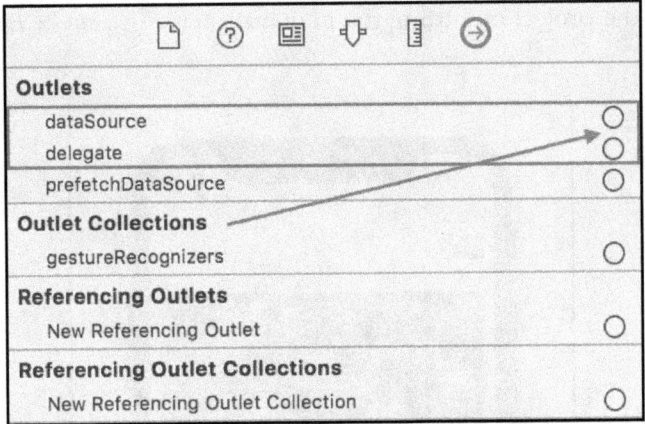

19. Next, we need to update our class definition inside of the `RestaurantListViewController`. You currently have `RestaurantListViewController:UIViewController`—update it to the following:

```
class RestaurantListViewController:UIViewController,
UICollectionViewDataSource
```

As you learned earlier with our **Explore** grid, we are required to implement `numberOfSections()`, `numberOfItemsInSection()`, and `cellForItemAt()` in order to use a Collection View. Therefore, add the following three methods inside of our `RestaurantListViewController`:

```
func collectionView(_ collectionView: UICollectionView, cellForItemAt
indexPath: IndexPath) -> UICollectionViewCell {
    return collectionView.dequeueReusableCell(withReuseIdentifier:
"restaurantCell", for: indexPath)
}

func numberOfSections(in collectionView: UICollectionView) -> Int {
    return 1
}

func collectionView(_ collectionView: UICollectionView,
numberOfItemsInSection section: Int) -> Int {
    return 10
}
```

Let's build and run the project by hitting the play button (or use *cmd + R*) to see what happens:

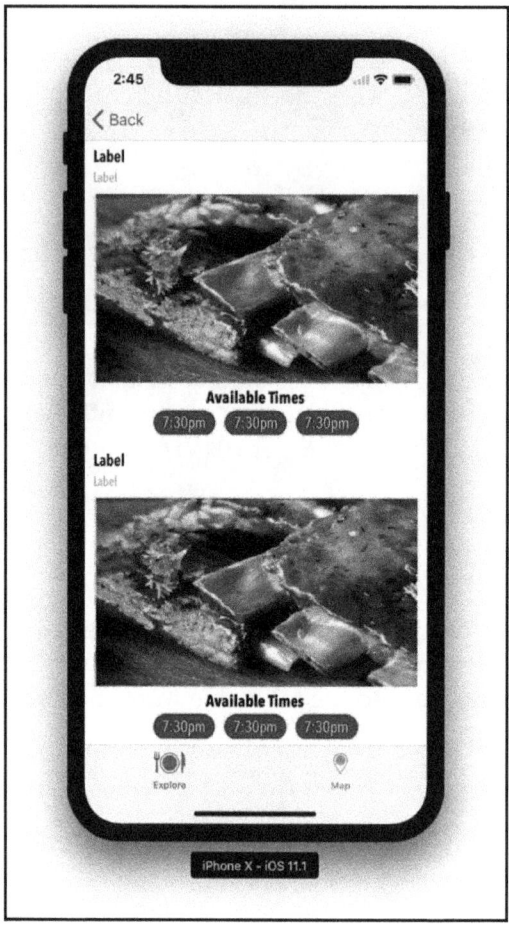

Instead of having a grid, as we did for **Explore**, our restaurant list displays a column of cells. However, when the restaurant list displays on the iPad, it shows a grid instead. This is one of the flexibilities from which we benefit by using a Collection View. We will further set up our restaurant list cells along with displaying the data later in the book.

Summary

In this chapter, we talked about what a model is and looked at what a plist is. We also learned how to create a plist as well as creating our first manager class that takes care of the data. In our data manager, we covered getting data from a plist and how to represent that data as a model object.

In the next chapter, we will look at the differences between static and prototype Table Views. You will see a lot of similarities between Table Views and Collection Views, especially concerning how we get data into them.

15
Getting Started with the List

When I started doing iOS development, I first worked with Table Views. At the time, Collection Views had not yet been introduced. As you progress in iOS development, you will work with a lot of Table and Collection Views. You begin with just the basics to get them going and then you slowly progress into more advanced Table and Collection Views.

The reason that I bring this up is that, by the end of this chapter, you may feel as though things are not clicking. It is perfectly normal. But the more you go through the steps in these chapters, the more they will become second nature to you.

For those of you that have not done iOS development, Table Views are great for presenting a list of data. The iPhone's mail app is an example of what a Table View typically looks like.

In this chapter, we are going to work with our first Table View. In our *Let's Eat* app, users select a specific location to look for restaurants.

We will cover the following in this chapter:

- Creating our first property list (plist)
- Creating our location data manager
- Cleaning up our file structure

Creating our Location View Controller class

We want to get our data to display inside our Table View. Before we start, create three new folders inside the Location folder—Controller, View, and Model. As we have previously done, right-click on the `Location` folder and hit **New Group** to create a new folder.

Getting Started with the List

Next, we need to create a Location View Controller class that we can use with our `UIViewController`:

1. Right-click on the `Controller` folder you just created and select **New File**.
2. In the **Choose a template for your new file** screen, select **iOS** at the top and **Cocoa Touch Class**. Then, hit **Next**.
3. In the **Options** screen that appears, add the following:

   New file:

   - **Class**: `LocationViewController`
   - **Subclass**: `UIViewController`
   - **Also create XIB**: Unchecked
   - **Language**: `Swift`

4. Click on **Next** and then **Create**.

Next, we need to connect our View Controller with our class:

1. Select `Locations.storyboard`.
2. Then select the **View Controller**.
3. Now, in the Utilities panel, select the Identity inspector.
4. Under **Custom Class**, in the **Class** drop-down menu, select **LocationViewController** and hit *Enter*.

Connecting our Table View with our Location View Controller

Currently, we have no way to communicate with our Table View and our Location View Controller. Let's see how we can connect these two:

1. Open the `LocationViewController.swift` file and add the following code after the class declaration:

   ```
   @IBOutlet weak var tableView:UITableView!
   ```

2. Save the file by hitting *cmd + S*. Your file should look like the following, with an empty circle next to the variable:

```
class LocationViewController: UIViewController {
    @IBOutlet weak var tableView:UITableView!
```

Before we get started, we are going to clean up our `LocationViewController.swift` file. Delete everything after `viewDidLoad()`:

```
//
//  LocationViewController.swift
//  LetsEat
//
//  Created by Craig Clayton on 11/19/16.
//  Copyright © 2016 Craig Clayton. All rights reserved.
//

import UIKit

class LocationViewController: UIViewController {

    @IBOutlet var tableView:UITableView!

    override func viewDidLoad() {
        super.viewDidLoad()

        // Do any additional setup after loading the view.
    }

    override func didReceiveMemoryWarning() {
        super.didReceiveMemoryWarning()
        // Dispose of any resources that can be recreated.
    }

    /*
    // MARK: - Navigation

    // In a storyboard-based application, you will often want to do a little preparation before navigation
    override func prepare(for segue: UIStoryboardSegue, sender: Any?) {
        // Get the new view controller using segue.destinationViewController.
        // Pass the selected object to the new view controller.
    }
    */

}
```

Delete

Next, let's connect our table view to the file.

1. Open `Explore.storyboard` again and make sure that you have the Location View Controller selected in the Outline view.

Getting Started with the List

2. Then, in the Utilities panel, select **Connections inspector**. Under the **Outlets** section, you will see an empty circle, **tableView**:

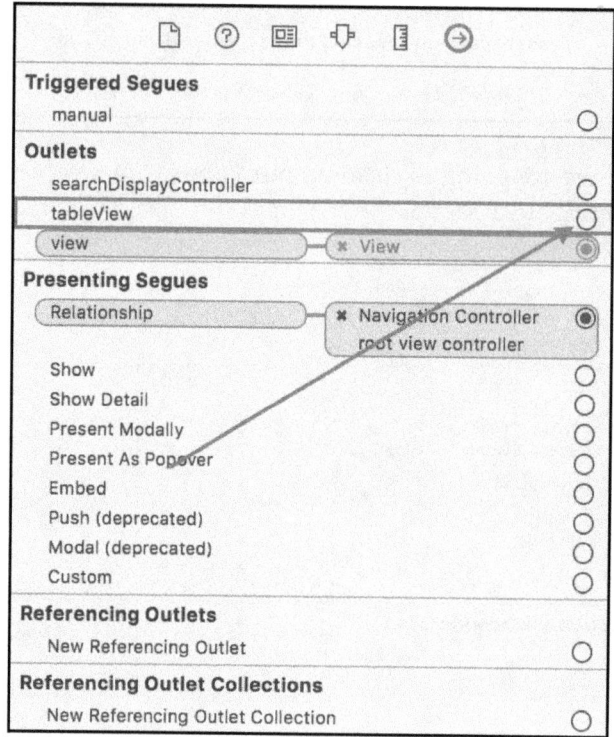

Click and drag the empty circle to the Table View in the storyboard:

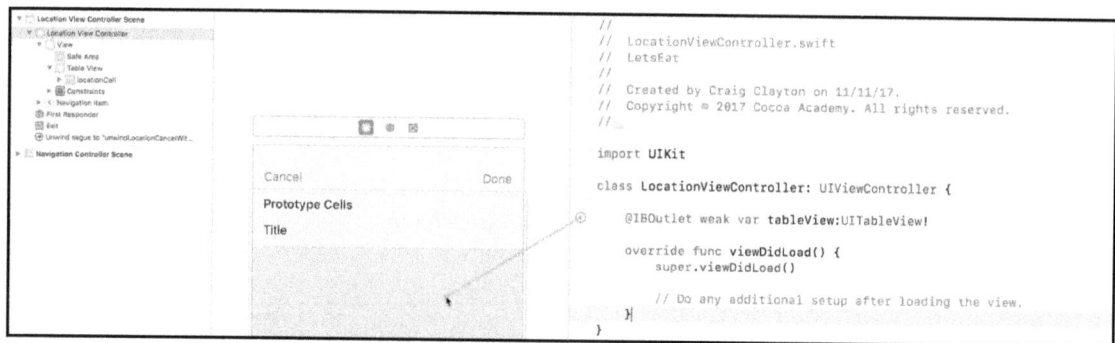

We have now connected our Table View to our Location View Controller.

[386]

Digging into our Table View code

To get data into our Table View, we must conform to a protocol as we did with the Collection View. In this case, we must implement `UITableViewDataSource`:

1. First, we need to update our `class` declaration. We currently have the following:

   ```
   class LocationViewController: UIViewController
   ```

2. We now need to add `UITableViewDataSource`, as follows:

   ```
   class LocationViewController: UIViewController,
   UITableViewDataSource
   ```

Adding the data source and delegate

As discussed in the previous chapter, we need to add a data source and delegate to our Table View. Table View uses **dynamic cells**, which we are required to add:

1. Select **Table View** in the Outline view, and then Connections inspector in the Utilities panel.
2. Click on and drag from `dataSource` to the **Location View Controller** in the Outline view:

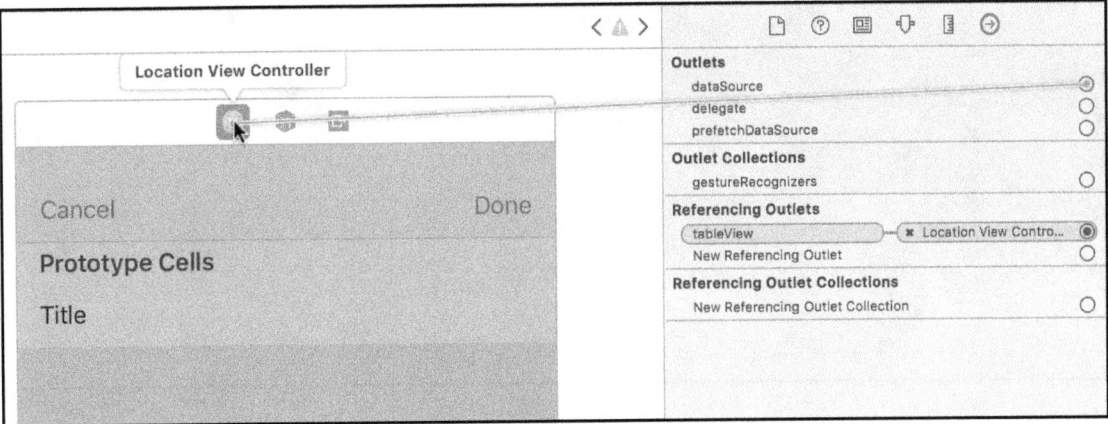

3. Repeat with the `delegate` property:

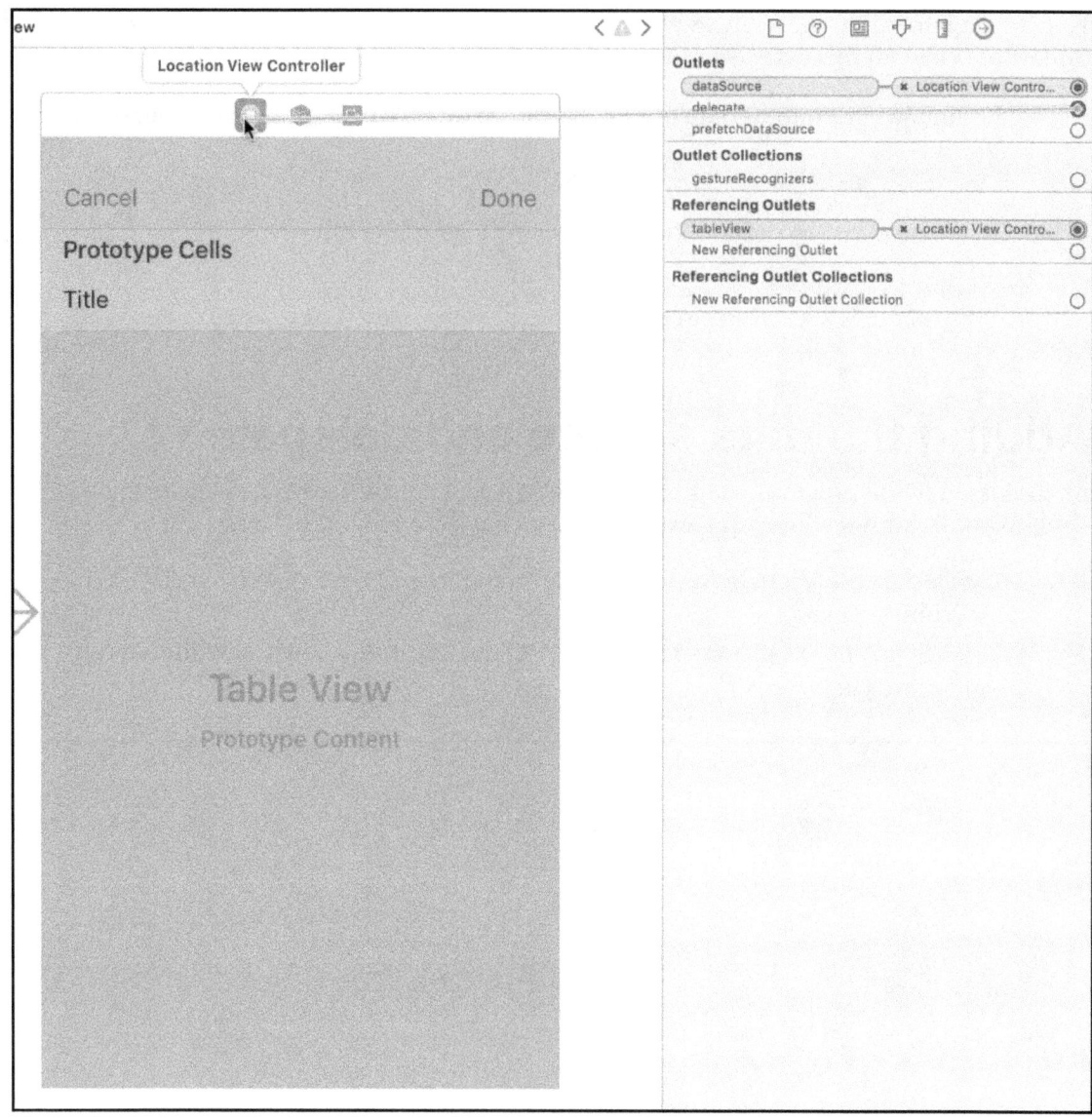

4. In the Utilities panel, select the Attributes inspector, if not already selected, and make sure you have the following values:

   - **Style**: `Basic`
   - **Identifier**: `locationCell`
   - **Selection**: `Gray`
   - **Accessory**: `Disclosure indicator`

Next, for us to display anything in `Tableview`, we need to add the `UITableViewDataSource` protocol. Our protocol requires that we implement the following three methods. Add the following after the closing curly brace of `viewDidLoad()`:

```swift
import UIKit

class LocationViewController: UIViewController, UITableViewDataSource {

    @IBOutlet weak var tableView:UITableView!

    func tableView(_ tableView: UITableView, numberOfRowsInSection section: Int) -> Int {
        return 15
    }

    func numberOfSections(in tableView: UITableView) -> Int {
        return 1
    }

    func tableView(_ tableView: UITableView, cellForRowAt indexPath: IndexPath) -> UITableViewCell {
        let cell = tableView.dequeueReusableCell(withIdentifier: "locationCell", for: indexPath) as UITableViewCell
        cell.textLabel?.text = "A cell"

        return cell
    }
}
```

Let's break down the code to understand what we are doing:

- **Part A**: This method tells our Table View how many rows we want to display.

  `tableView(_:numberOfRowsInSection:)`

- **Part B**: Here, we tell our Table View that we want to display 15 rows.

  `return 15`

- **Part C**: This method tells our Table View how many sections we want to display. Sections in Table Views are typically used as headers, but they can be used however you choose.

    ```
    numberOfSections(in:)
    ```

- **Part D**: We tell our Table View that we only want one section.

    ```
    return 1
    ```

- **Part E**: Our third and final method gets called for every item we need. Therefore, in our case, it gets called 15 times.

    ```
    tableView(_:cellForRowAt:)
    ```

- **Part F**: Here, we create a cell every time *Part E* is called, either by taking one from the queue, if available, or by creating a new cell. The identifier, `locationCell`, is the name we gave it in the storyboard. Therefore, we are telling our Table View that we want to use this cell. If we had multiple Table Views, we would reference the identifier for the row and section in which we want the cell to display.

    ```
    let cell = tableView.dequeueReusableCell(withIdentifier:
    "locationCell", for: indexPath) as UITableViewCell
    cell.textLabel?.text = "A cell"
    ```

    Since we do not have any data yet, we set our label to `A cell`. The `textLabel` variable is the default label we got when we selected a basic cell.

- **Part G**: Finally, after each time we create a new cell, we give the cell back to the Table View to display that cell.

    ```
    return cell
    ```

Chapter 15

Let's build and run the project by hitting the Play button (or using *cmd + R*) to see what happens. You should now see `A cell` repeating 15 times:

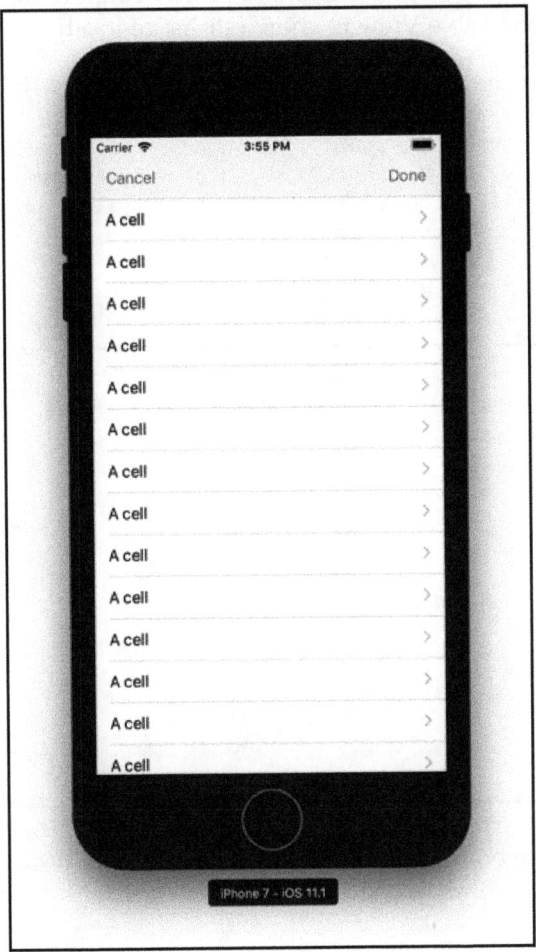

Adding locations to our Table View

We now have our Table View displaying data, but we need it to display a list of actual locations. Let's update our Table View to show our list of locations:

1. Directly under the `tableView` variable, add the following:

   ```
   let locations = ["Aspen", "Boston", "Charleston", "Chicago", "Houston", "Las Vegas", "Los Angeles", "Miami", "New Orleans", "New York", "Philadelphia", "Portland", "San Antonio", "San Francisco", "Washington District of Columbia"]
   ```

2. Your file should now look like mine:

   ```
   import UIKit

   class LocationViewController: UIViewController, UITableViewDataSource {

       @IBOutlet weak var tableView:UITableView!

       let locations = ["Aspen", "Boston", "Charleston", "Chicago", "Houston", "Las Vegas", "Los Angeles", "Miami", "New Orleans",
           "New York", "Philadelphia", "Portland", "San Antonio", "San Francisco", "Washington District of Columbia"]

       func tableView(_ tableView: UITableView, numberOfRowsInSection section: Int) -> Int {
           return 15
       }

       func numberOfSections(in tableView: UITableView) -> Int {
           return 1
       }

       func tableView(_ tableView: UITableView, cellForRowAt indexPath: IndexPath) -> UITableViewCell {
           let cell = tableView.dequeueReusableCell(withIdentifier: "locationCell", for: indexPath) as UITableViewCell
           cell.textLabel?.text = "A cell"

           return cell
       }
   }
   ```

3. Next, to update our cell to display the locations, we need to replace the `cell.textLabel?.text = "A cell"` line with the following:

   ```
   cell.textLabel?.text = locations[indexPath.item]
   ```

Let's build and run the project by hitting the Play button (or using *cmd + R*). You should see the following after clicking **Select a location in your simulator**:

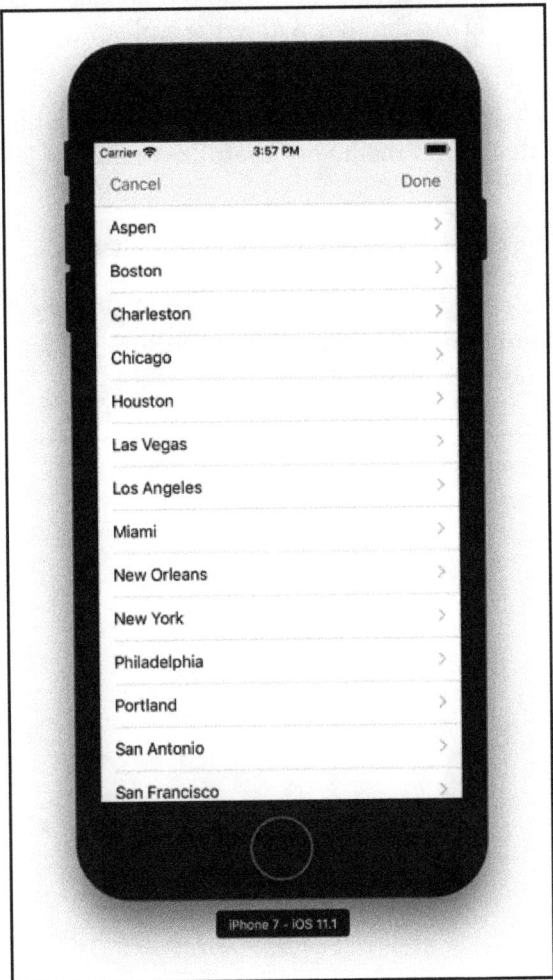

However, there are a couple of problems. If we add another location to the array, it crashes because we are manually setting the value. Also, we are just loading this list from an array we built in the app. If we decide to add more locations, we would have to update our cell number count as well as our list of locations. Therefore, we should instead pull our locations from a plist, as we did in the last chapter. Plists provide a place where we can quickly add or remove a location from our list.

Creating our first property list (plist)

In the last chapter, we used a provided plist to load our cuisine list. We will do the same in this chapter, but now that you are familiar with what a plist is, we will create one from scratch together.

I use plists all the time, from creating menus to having a file that holds app settings such as colors or social media URLs. I find them very useful, especially if I need to come back later and update or change things.

Let's learn how to create a plist from scratch. To create a plist in Xcode, do the following:

1. Right-click on the `Model` folder inside **Location** and select **New File**.
2. In **Choose a template for your new file**, select **iOS** at the top, and then type `Property` in the filter field:

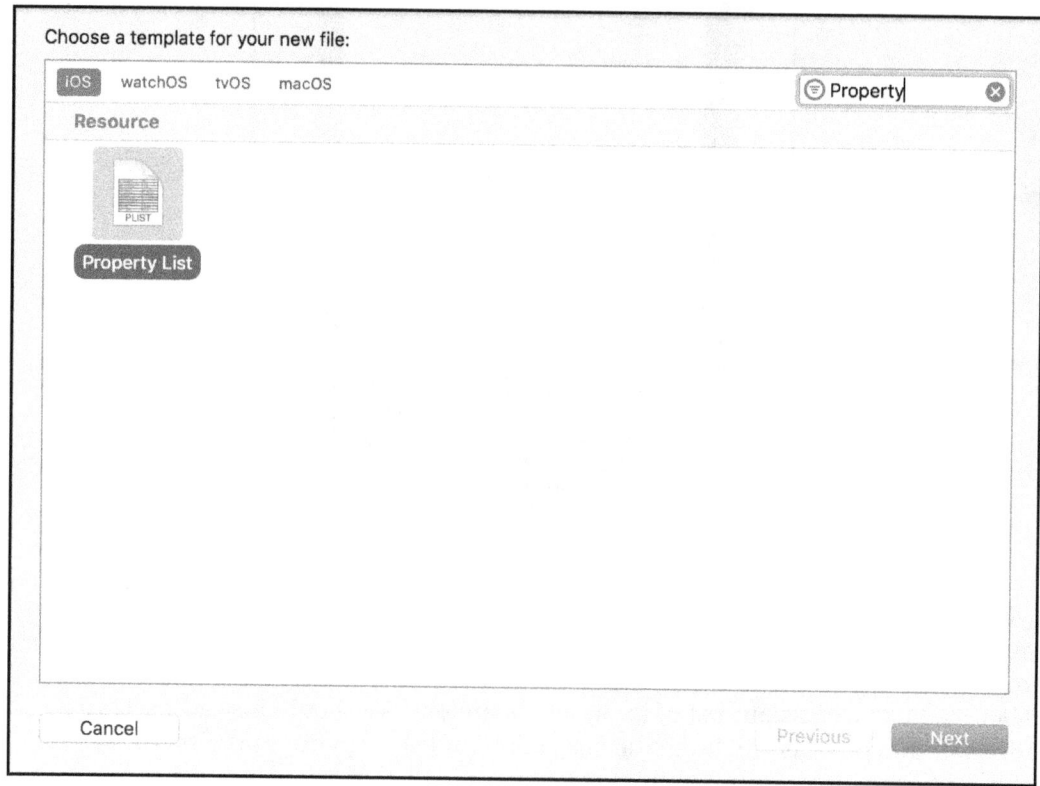

Chapter 15

3. Select **Property List** and then hit **Next**.
4. Name the file **Locations** and hit **Create**.

You should now have a file that looks like mine:

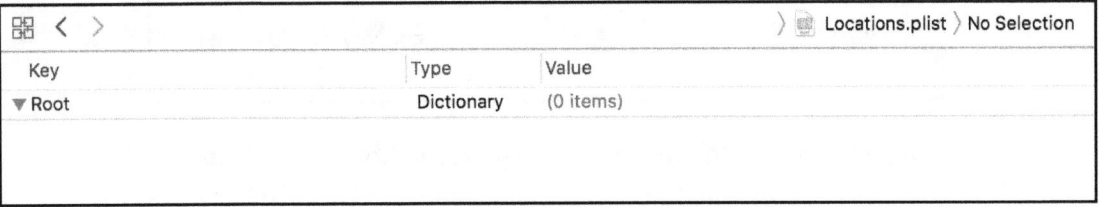

Adding data to our property list

As you learned in the previous chapter, our plist has a `Root`; for this new file, we created a `Dictionary` as our `Root` type. Since we are going to display a list of locations, we need our `Root` to be an `Array`:

1. Click on **Dictionary** in the plist and change it to **Array**:

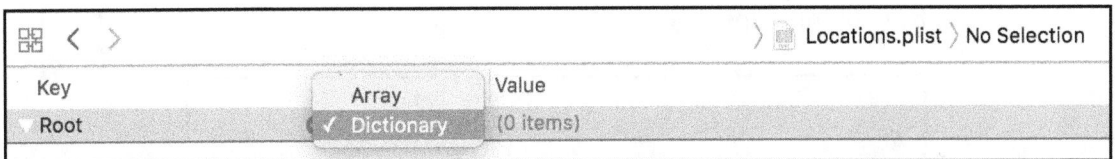

2. You should see a plus next to **Array** (if the plus button is not displaying, just hover your mouse over that line item and it will appear):

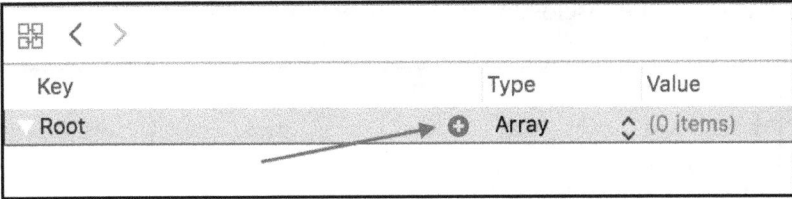

Getting Started with the List

3. Click on the plus button and it will add a new item with a String type. Change the type to **Dictionary**:

Key	Type	Value
▼ Root	Array	(1 item)
▼ Item 0	Dictionary	(0 items)

4. Click on the plus button that appears when you hover over **Item 0**.
5. We now need to update the **New Item**. Update the **Key** property to say state and update the **Value** property of the new item by entering **CO**:

Key	Type	Value
▼ Root	Array	(1 item)
▼ Item 0	Dictionary	(1 item)
state	String	CO

6. Next, click on the plus button when you hover over state.
7. Update the **Key** property to say city and update the **Value** property of the new item by entering Aspen:

Key	Type	Value
▼ Root	Array	(1 item)
▼ Item 0	Dictionary	(2 items)
state	String	CO
city	String	Aspen

8. Next, click on the disclosure arrow for **Item 0** to close it:

Key	Type	Value
▼ Root	Array	(1 item)
▶ Item 0	Dictionary	(2 items)

[396]

9. Select Item 0 and then hit *cmd + C* to copy and then *cmd + V* to paste:

Key	Type	Value
▼ Root	Array	(2 items)
▶ Item 0	Dictionary	(2 items)
▶ Item 1	Dictionary	(2 items)

10. Next, open up **Item 1** and update the **city** to **Boston** and the **state** to **MA**:

Key	Type	Value
▼ Root	Array	(14 items)
▼ Item 0	Dictionary	(2 items)
city	String	Aspen
state	String	CO
▼ Item 1	Dictionary	(2 items)
city	String	Boston
state	String	MA

11. Continue with the same process by adding the following cities and states:

Key	Type	City	State
Item 2	String	Charleston	NC
Item 3	String	Chicago	IL
Item 4	String	Houston	TX
Item 5	String	Las Vegas	NV
Item 6	String	Los Angeles	CA
Item 7	String	Miami	FL
Item 8	String	New Orleans	LA
Item 9	String	New York	NY
Item 10	String	Philadelphia	PA
Item 11	String	Portland	OR
Item 12	String	San Antonio	TX
Item 13	String	San Francisco	CA

Getting Started with the List

When you are done, your file should look like mine:

Key	Type	Value
▼ Root	Array	(14 items)
▼ Item 0	Dictionary	(2 items)
city	String	Aspen
state	String	CO
▼ Item 1	Dictionary	(2 items)
city	String	Boston
state	String	MA
▼ Item 2	Dictionary	(2 items)
city	String	Charleston
state	String	NC
▼ Item 3	Dictionary	(2 items)
city	String	Chicago
state	String	IL
▼ Item 4	Dictionary	(2 items)
city	String	Houston
state	String	TX
▼ Item 5	Dictionary	(2 items)
city	String	Las Vegas
state	String	NV
▼ Item 6	Dictionary	(2 items)
city	String	Los Angeles
state	String	CA
▼ Item 7	Dictionary	(2 items)
city	String	Miami
state	String	FL
▼ Item 8	Dictionary	(2 items)
city	String	New Orleans
state	String	LA
▼ Item 9	Dictionary	(2 items)
city	String	New York
state	String	NY
▼ Item 10	Dictionary	(2 items)
city	String	Philadelphia
state	String	PA
▼ Item 11	Dictionary	(2 items)
city	String	Portland
state	String	OR
▼ Item 12	Dictionary	(2 items)
city	String	San Antonio
state	String	TX
▼ Item 13	Dictionary	(2 items)
city	String	San Francisco
state	String	CA

Chapter 15

We just set up our data source. We now need to create a data manager similar to the one that we made in the previous chapter:

Creating our location data manager

Let's create the `LocationDataManager` file:

1. Right-click on the **Model** folder in the **Location** folder and select **New File**.
2. In **Choose a template for your new file**, select **iOS** at the top and then **Swift File**. Then hit **Next**.
3. Name this file `LocationDataManager`, and then hit **Create**.
4. We need to define our class definition now, so add the following under the `import` statement:

   ```
   class LocationDataManager {
   }
   ```

5. Inside the class declaration, add the following variable to keep our array private, as there is no reason to have to access this outside the class:

   ```
   private var locations:[String] = []
   ```

6. Now, let's add the following methods after our variable:

   ```
   init() {
       fetch()
   }

   func fetch() {
       for location in loadData() {
           if let city = location["city"] as? String,
               let state = location["state"] as? String {
               locations.append("\(city), \(state)")
           }
       }
   }

   func numberOfItems() -> Int {
       return locations.count
   }

   func locationItem(at index:IndexPath) -> String {
       return locations[index.item]
   ```

[399]

Getting Started with the List

```
    }
    private func loadData() -> [[String: AnyObject]] {
        guard let path = Bundle.main.path(forResource: "Locations",
    ofType: "plist"), let items = NSArray(contentsOfFile: path) else {
            return [[:]]
        }
        return items as! [[String : AnyObject]]
    }
```

These methods are the same as we had in `ExploreDataManager`, except that we are getting back an array of dictionary objects from our plist.

Working with our data manager

We now need to update our `LocationViewController`.

First, because we do not need it anymore, delete the following array that we created in the class:

```
let locations = ["Aspen", "Boston", "Charleston", "Chicago", "Houston",
"Las Vegas", "Los Angeles", "Miami", "New Orleans", "New York",
"Philadelphia", "Portland", "San Antonio", "San Francisco", "Washington
District of Columbia"]
```

Next, since we need to create an instance of our data manager in this class, add the following above `viewDidLoad()`:

```
let manager = LocationDataManager()
```

Inside `viewDidLoad()`, we want to fetch the data for the Table View, so add the following under `super.viewDidLoad()`:

```
manager.fetch()
```

Now, your `viewDidLoad()` should look like the following:

```
override func viewDidLoad()  {
   super.viewDidLoad()
   manager.fetch()
}
```

For the `numberOfRowsInSection()` method, instead of `15` we will use the following:

```
manager.numberOfItems()
```

Lastly, we need to update our `cellForRowAt`. Replace `cell.textLabel?.text = arrLocations[indexPath.item]` with the following:

```
cell.textLabel?.text = manager.locationItem(at:indexPath)
```

Your `cellForRowAt` should now look like this:

```
func tableView(_ tableView: UITableView, cellForRowAt indexPath: IndexPath) 
-> UITableViewCell {
    let cell = tableView.dequeueReusableCell(withIdentifier: "locationCell", 
for: indexPath) as UITableViewCell
    cell.textLabel?.text = manager.locationItem(at:indexPath)
    return cell
}
```

Let's build and run the project by hitting the Play button (or using *cmd* + *R*). We should still see our locations, but now they are coming from our plist. Before we finish this chapter, our project navigator is a mess right now. We have files just in the main folder. Putting files into the main folder without any organization is not something you want to do. Let's organize our files before we add any more.

Creating folders

Creating folders is easy: all you have to do is right-click on the `LetsEat` folder, and you can create a new group. You can also select multiple files and put all of the selected items into a new group.

Getting Started with the List

We are going to create three folders first, called `Application`, `Misc`, and `Controllers`. When you are done you should see the following:

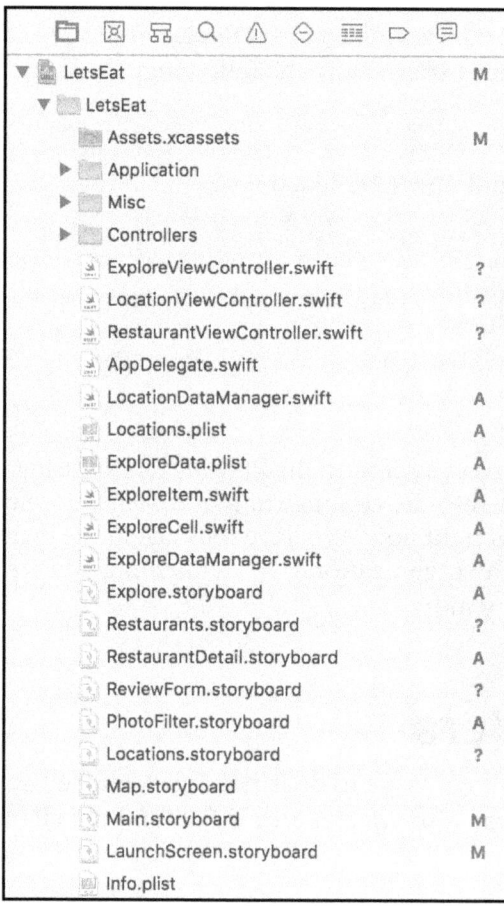

Chapter 15

We are going to move `Info.plist`, `Assets.xcasset`, `App Delegate`, `LaunchScreen.storyboard`, and `Main.storyboard` all into the `Application` folder. You can *cmd* + click each and then drag them one at a time. When you are done, you should see the following:

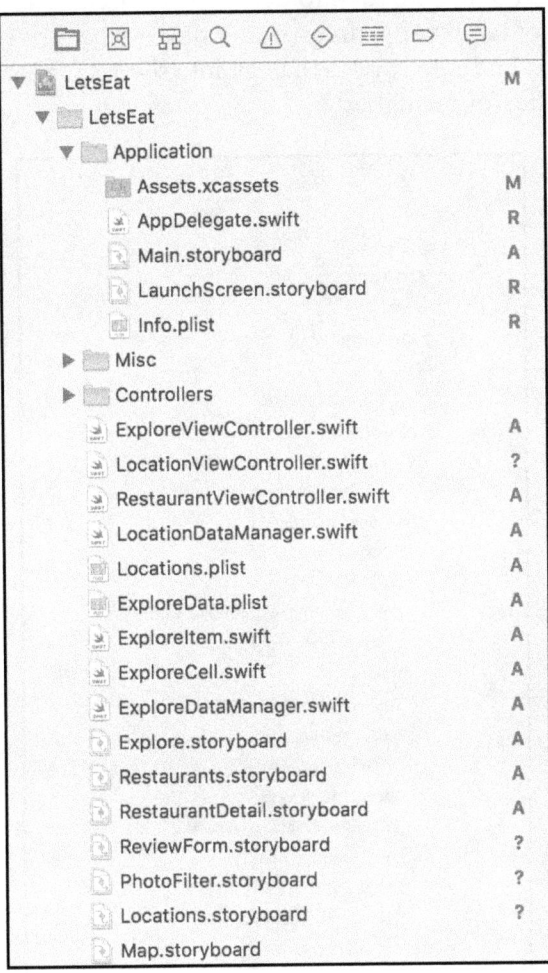

Getting Started with the List

Next, you want to create a folder for all of the View Controllers. Inside the `Controllers` folder, add the following folders: `Photo Filter`, `Restaurant Details`, `Review Form`, `Explore`, `Restaurants`, `Locations`, and `Map`. Then drag each storyboard file into each corresponding folder. Drag `ExploreData.plist`, `ExploreItem`, `ExploreCell`, and `ExploreDataManager` into the `Explore` folder. Then drag `RestaurantViewController` into the `Restaurants` folder. Finally, drag `LocationViewController`, `LocationDataManager`, and `Locations.plist` into the `Locations` folder. When you are done, you should have the following:

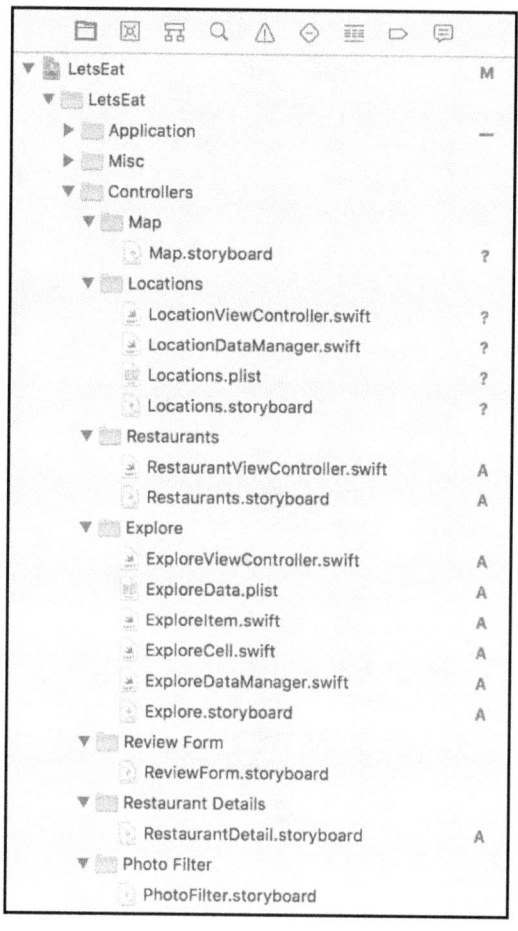

Even though we cleaned this area, I do not typically use it to open and find files because it takes way too long. To open files, I always use *cmd + O* and type the name of the file. Opening and closing folders takes forever. You should learn this shortcut as it will increase your workflow.

For now, this is good enough to move on. We could add more folders as we go, but this is a lot better than what we had before.

Summary

In this chapter, we worked with a Table View that has dynamic cells, which allows the Table View to change based on the data. We also worked with unwinding segues. Later, we passed data that we need through our segues. Along with segues, we looked at plists, learning how to create them as well as how to add data to them. Finally, we created our locations data manager, which is responsible for giving data to the View Controller.

In the next chapter, we will work with a Table View that has static cells to build out our restaurant detail. Static cells are excellent for forms or detail views. We could build out the restaurant detail using a Collection View; however, a static Table View will work well and will be less complicated.

At this point, before moving on to the next chapter, you may want to get the starter project for this chapter and try to do it again without using the book as your guide. Going back helps solidify your understanding of what you have learned.

16
Where Are We?

We have all used a map at some point in our lives, either an actual map or a map on our phone or another device. Apple Maps has come a long way from when it was first announced in 2012. Apple has made steady improvements to Apple Maps every year.

During this chapter, we will display our restaurant list using a map and custom pins. When users tap a pin on the map, they will be taken directly to the restaurant detail page that we created in the last chapter.

In this chapter, we will cover:

- What annotations are and how to add them to a map
- How to create custom annotations
- How to create a storyboard reference

Setting up map annotations

In our map, we are going to drop pins down at each restaurant location. These pins are called annotations, more specifically, `MKAnnotation`. Since we are going to create multiple `MKAnnotation` protocols, we are going to create a class that subclasses `MKAnnotation`.

What is an MKAnnotation?

`MKAnnotation` is a protocol that provides us with information related to a map view. Protocols provide a blueprint for methods, properties, and other required functionalities. The `MKAnnotation` will contain information, such as the coordinates (latitude and longitude), title, and subtitle of the annotation.

Where Are We?

To drop a pin onto a map, we must subclass the `MKAnnotation`. When we first looked at classes versus structs, we saw that classes could subclass or inherit from other classes, which means that we can get properties, methods, and additional requirements from the class that we are subclassing. Let's create an annotation that subclasses `MKAnnotation` and see how this works.

Creating a restaurant annotation

Before we jump into creating our file, we should first look at the data that we will be using. The data for the map view will be the same data that we use for our restaurant-listing page. Let's take a look at what the restaurant data will look like in plist format:

Key	Type	Value
▼ Root	Array	(5 items)
▼ Item 0	Dictionary	(16 items)
address	String	108 West 2nd Street #104
area	String	Los Angeles / Orange County
city	String	Los Angeles
▼ cuisines	Array	(2 items)
Item 0	String	Indian
Item 1	String	Gastropubs
country	String	US
id	Number	104,173
image_url	String	https://www.opentable.com/img/restimages/104173.jpg
lat	Number	34.051061
lng	Number	-118.244705
mobile_reserve_url	String	http://mobile.opentable.com/opentable/?restId=104173
name	String	Badmaash
phone	String	2132217466x
postal_code	String	90012
price	Number	2
reserve_url	String	http://www.opentable.com/single.aspx?rid=104173
state	String	CA
▶ Item 1	Dictionary	(15 items)
▶ Item 2	Dictionary	(16 items)
▶ Item 3	Dictionary	(16 items)
▶ Item 4	Dictionary	(16 items)

We need to create a file to represent this data for the map view, which will differ from the restaurant-listing page because we need to subclass `MKAnnotation`. Let's get started by creating this file now:

1. Right-click on the `Map` folder and select **New File**.
2. In the **Choose a template for your new file** screen, select **iOS** at the top and then **Cocoa Touch Class**. Then hit **Next**.
3. In the **Options** screen that appears, add the following:

   New file:
   - **Class**: `RestaurantItem`
   - **Subclass**: `NSObject`
   - **Also create XIB**: Unchecked
   - **Language**: `Swift`

4. Click **Next** and then **Create**.
5. In this new `RestaurantItem.swift` file, under `import UIKit`, add `import MapKit`. We need this `import` statement so that Xcode knows where the files are that we are going to use.
6. Next, we need to update our class declaration to make our annotation. Since this is subclassing `MKAnnotation`, we need to change what we currently have (`class RestaurantItem: NSObject`) to the following:

   ```
   class RestaurantItem: NSObject, MKAnnotation
   ```

You will see an error when you add the `MKAnnotation`. Just ignore it for now, as we will fix this error shortly.

Inside of the class declaration, add the following:

```
var name: String?
var cuisines:[String] = []
var latitude: Double?
var longitude:Double?
var address:String?
var postalCode:String?
var state:String?
var imageURL:String?
```

Where Are We?

When the user taps on the annotation, the name of the restaurant and types of cuisine will appear along with a detail icon. This detail icon will take the user to the restaurant detail page. Then, we will pass along all of this data and use it to populate the restaurant detail page we created in the last chapter.

We need to initialize all of the data passed into the object. Therefore, let's create a custom `init()` method to which we can pass a dictionary object through its parameters:

```
import Foundation
import MapKit

class RestaurantItem: NSObject, MKAnnotation {     ⊙ Type 'RestaurantItem' does not conform to protocol 'MKAnnotation'
    var name: String?
    var cuisines:[String] = []
    var latitude: Double?
    var longitude:Double?           Ignore this error
    var address:String?
    var postalCode:String?
    var state:String?
    var imageURL:String?

    init(dict:[String:AnyObject]) {
        if let lat = dict["lat"] as? Double { self.latitude = lat }
        if let long = dict["lng"] as? Double { self.longitude = long }
        if let name = dict["name"] as? String { self.name = name }
        if let cuisines = dict["cuisines"] as? [String] { self.cuisines = cuisines }
        if let address = dict["address"] as? String { self.address = address }
        if let postalCode = dict["postal_code"] as? String { self.postalCode = postalCode }
        if let state = dict["state"] as? String { self.state = state }
        if let image = dict["image_url"] as? String { self.imageURL = image }
    }
}
```

This method is large, but it is nothing you have not seen before. We are using the `if...let` statement to check for data in each element. If something is missing, it will not be sent.

Let's address the error now. The reason we are getting an error is because we are subclassing `MKAnnotation` and have not yet declared the coordinates, which is a required property. We also have two other optional properties—`title` and `subtitle`—that we are using for our map and that we need to declare. What we want to be able to do is pass the data that we have over to these three properties so that we can use them on our map.

To get rid of the error, we need to add the coordinates first. We need to set up the latitude and longitude, so add the following after the `init()` method:

```
var coordinate: CLLocationCoordinate2D {
   guard let lat = latitude, let long = longitude else { return CLLocationCoordinate2D() }
   return CLLocationCoordinate2D(latitude: lat, longitude: long )
}
```

`CLLocationCoordinate2D` is a class that is used by `MapKit` to set the exact location of a pin.

Note that we are using curly braces for this property. It is defined in `MKAnnotation`, and we are using the computed property to set the value. For the `coordinate` property, we will pass a latitude and longitude to it using a `CLLocationCoordinate2D`. In our `init()` method, we created the data that sets the latitude and longitude, and now, we are passing those coordinates over to the `coordinate` property.

Let's do the same with `subtitle` by adding the following above the variable coordinate:

```
var subtitle: String? {
   if cuisines.isEmpty { return "" }
   else if cuisines.count == 1 { return cuisines.first }
   else { return cuisines.joined(separator: ", ") }
}
```

The variable `subtitle` is a computed property, but this time we are using an `else...if` statement. We first check to see whether the array is empty; if so, nothing displays. If we only have one item in the array, we just return that item. Finally, if we have multiple items in our array, we take each item and put them in one string, separating each item with a comma. For example, if your array had the items `["American," "Bistro," "Burgers"]`, then we would create a string that looks like *American, Bistro, Burgers*.

Finally, we need to add the title. Enter the following above the `subtitle` variable:

```
var title: String? {
   return name
}
```

Your file should no longer have an error, and should now look as follows:

```swift
import Foundation
import MapKit

class RestaurantItem: NSObject, MKAnnotation {
    var name: String?
    var cuisines:[String] = []
    var latitude: Double?
    var longitude:Double?
    var address:String?
    var postalCode:String?
    var state:String?
    var imageURL:String?

    init(dict:[String:AnyObject]) {
        if let lat = dict["lat"] as? Double { self.latitude = lat }
        if let long = dict["lng"] as? Double { self.longitude = long }
        if let name = dict["name"] as? String { self.name = name }
        if let cuisines = dict["cuisines"] as? [String] { self.cuisines = cuisines }
        if let address = dict["address"] as? String { self.address = address }
        if let postalCode = dict["postal_code"] as? String { self.postalCode = postalCode }
        if let state = dict["state"] as? String { self.state = state }
        if let image = dict["image_url"] as? String { self.imageURL = image }
    }

    var title: String? {
        return name
    }

    var subtitle: String? {
        if cuisines.isEmpty { return "" }
        else if cuisines.count == 1 { return cuisines.first }
        else { return cuisines.joined(separator: ", ") }
    }

    var coordinate: CLLocationCoordinate2D {
        guard let lat = latitude, let long = longitude else { return
            CLLocationCoordinate2D() }
        return CLLocationCoordinate2D(latitude: lat, longitude: long )
    }
}
```

Next, we want to create a manager that will take our data and create annotations for our map.

Creating our Map Data Manager

In the next chapter, we will deal with data, but for now, we can mock up some data to set up our structure. We will use a plist to load our data, just like we did in the last chapter.

Let's create the `MapDataManager` file now:

1. Right-click on the `Map` folder and select **New File**.
2. In the **Choose a template for your new file** screen, select **iOS** at the top and then **Swift File**. Then hit **Next**.
3. Name this file `MapDataManager` and then hit **Create**.
4. Next, we need to define our class definition, so add the following under the `import` statement:

   ```
   class MapDataManager {}
   ```

5. Inside of the class declaration, add the following variables:

   ```
   fileprivate var items:[RestaurantItem] = []

   var annotations:[RestaurantItem] {
       return items
   }
   ```

   Note that we are keeping our array private since there is no reason to have to access this outside of the class.

6. Now, let's add the following methods inside of our class declaration, after our variables:

   ```
   func fetch(completion:(_ annotations:[RestaurantItem]) -> ()) {

       if items.count > 0 { items.removeAll() }
           for data in loadData() {
                       items.append(RestaurantItem(dict: data))
           }

           completion(items)
   }

   fileprivate func loadData() -> [[String:AnyObject]] {
           guard let path = Bundle.main.path(forResource: "MapLocations", ofType: "plist"),
               let items = NSArray(contentsOfFile: path) else { return [[:]] }
   ```

```
            return items as! [[String : AnyObject]]
    }
```

Your file should now look as follows:

```
import Foundation

class MapDataManager {

    fileprivate var items:[RestaurantItem] = []

    var annotations:[RestaurantItem] {
        return items
    }

    func fetch(completion:(_ annotations:[RestaurantItem]) -> ()) {
        if items.count > 0 { items.removeAll() }

        for data in loadData() {
            items.append(RestaurantItem(dict: data))
        }
        completion(items)
    }

    fileprivate func loadData() -> [[String:AnyObject]] {
        guard let path = Bundle.main.path(forResource: "MapLocations", ofType: "plist"),
            let items = NSArray(contentsOfFile: path) else { return [[:]] }

        return items as! [[String: AnyObject]]
    }
}
```

7. The `fetch()` and `loadData()` methods are the same as those that we had in the `ExploreDataManager` file. However, the `fetch()` method here has something new inside of its parameters, specifically:

   `completion:(_ annotations:[RestaurantItem]) -> ()`

This is called a **closure block**, which allows us to signify when we have completed the method, and it then dictates an action to occur (here, returning an array of annotations). We will use these annotations to load pins on our map. We are looping through the `for...in` loop; when we are done, we call `completion()`. When we get to our `MapViewController`, you will see how we write this.

Now, let's take a look at our `MapLocations.plist` file:

Key	Type	Value
▼ Root	Array	(5 items)
▶ Item 0	Dictionary	(16 items)
▶ Item 1	Dictionary	(16 items)
▶ Item 2	Dictionary	(16 items)
▶ Item 3	Dictionary	(16 items)
▶ Item 4	Dictionary	(16 items)

This file is the same structure as our `ExploreData.plist` file. Our `Root` is an array, and each item inside of our `Root` is a dictionary item. There is an acronym that many programmers call **DRY** (**don't repeat yourself**). Since both plist files have an array of dictionary objects, we can update our code so that we can use the same method in multiple places.

Creating a base class

To keep from repeating ourselves, we are going to create a base class. This base class will have a new method called `load(file name:)`, but we will add a parameter to pass the file name. Let's create a `DataManager` file now under our `Common` folder:

1. Right-click on the `Misc` folder and select **New File**.
2. In the **Choose a template for your new file** screen, select **iOS** at the top and then **Swift File**. Then hit **Next**:
3. Name this file `DataManager`, and then hit **Create**.

4. In this new file, we need to define our class definition; therefore, add the following under the `import` statement:

   ```
   protocol DataManager {}
   ```

5. Inside of the protocol declaration, add the following method:

   ```
   func load(file name:String) -> [[String:AnyObject]]
   ```

6. Now, create an extension under the protocol:

   ```
   extension DataManager {}
   ```

7. Inside of the `extension` declaration, add the following:

   ```
   func load(file name:String) -> [[String:AnyObject]] {
       guard let path = Bundle.main.path(forResource: name, ofType: "plist"),   let items = NSArray(contentsOfFile: path) else { return [[:]] }
       return items as! [[String : AnyObject]]
   }
   ```

8. When you are done, your file should look like mine:

```
import Foundation

protocol DataManager {
    func load(file name:String) -> [[String:AnyObject]]
}

extension DataManager {
    func load(file name:String) -> [[String:AnyObject]] {
        guard let path = Bundle.main.path(forResource: name, ofType: "plist"),
            let items = NSArray(contentsOfFile: path) else { return [[:]] }

        return items as! [[String : AnyObject]]
    }
}
```

Other than changing the function name to include parameters, we created the same function as we have in our `Explore` and `Map Data Manager` files. However, this function here is no longer a `private` method, because we want it to be accessible to any class that wants to use it.

By creating a protocol, we are using what is known as protocol-oriented programming. We will not get too heavily into the detail of this since there are plenty of books and videos on this topic. The central concept that you will want to understand is that we can use this in any class we want and have access to the `load(name:)` method.

This is all we need to do in this file.

Refactoring code

Now that we have created this new protocol, we can access it anywhere we need it. Let's first update our `MapDataManger` class to use our newly created protocol:

1. Delete the `loadData()` function, because we will not need it anymore. You will see an error after you delete the `loadData()` method. This error is happening because we need to give the `fetch()` method a filename to load whenever we call the `loadData()` method. We will fix this shortly.
2. Next, we need to update our class declaration to say:

   ```
   class MapDataManager: DataManager
   ```

3. We now have our `MapDataManager` class using our `DataManager` protocol, which means that we will use the `load(name:)` method from our `DataManager` inside of our `MapDataManager`.
4. Now, let's fix the error by updating our `fetch()` method from our data in `loadData()` to the following:

   ```
   for data in load(file: "MapLocations")
   ```

Where Are We?

Your updated file should now look like the following:

```swift
import Foundation

class MapDataManager {
    
    fileprivate var items:[RestaurantItem] = []
    
    var annotations:[RestaurantItem] {
        return items
    }
    
    func fetch(completion:(_ annotations:[RestaurantItem]) -> ()) {
        if items.count > 0 { items.removeAll() }
        for data in loadData() {
            items.append(RestaurantItem(dict: data))
        }
        completion(items)
    }
    
    fileprivate func loadData() -> [[String:AnyObject]] {
        guard let path = Bundle.main.path(forResource: "MapLocations", ofType: "plist"), let items =
            NSArray(contentsOfFile: path) else { return [[:]] }
        
        return items as! [[String : AnyObject]]
    }
}
```

We removed the error in our `MapDataManager`, but we need to do some refactoring of our `ExploreDataManager` file to do the same.

Refactoring ExploreDataManager

Because our `loadData()` was written the same in both the `ExploreDataManager` and `MapDataManager` files, we need to update our `ExploreDataManager` in the same way we just did for the `MapDataManager`. Open `ExploreDataManager` and do the following:

1. Delete the private `loadData()` function, because we will not need it anymore. Again, ignore the error as we are going to fix this shortly.
2. Next, update our class declaration to now say:

   ```
   class ExploreDataManager: DataManager
   ```

3. Now, let's fix the error by updating our `fetch()` method from for data in `loadData()` to the following:

[418]

```
            for data in load(file: "ExploreData")
```

4. Your updated function should now look like the following:

```
func fetch() {
    for data in load(file: "ExploreData") {
        items.append(ExploreItem(dict: data))
    }
}
```

We have completed refactoring our files, and we can now use the same method any time we need to load a plist that has an array of dictionary items.

Refactoring is something with which you will become more comfortable the more you write code. Understanding when to refactor is a bit harder when you first start out because you are still learning. The most prominent indicator that you need to refactor is when you have written something more than once. However, refactoring does not always work for everything; at times, writing the same code more than once can be unavoidable. Just being aware of when refactoring may be useful is a good sign, and half the battle to a greater understanding of this method. I have been coding for years; there will be times when I copy and paste something I wrote to see if it works and then never refactor. Then, months later, I will wonder why I did not write a method to handle it in both places.

Creating and adding annotations

Now, we need to get our map hooked up and start getting the annotations displaying on the map. Then, we will customize our annotations to look like those in our design.

Creating our Map View Controller

We need to create our `MapViewController` file and then connect it with our `UIViewController` and map view in storyboard. First, let's create this file:

1. In the Navigator panel, right-click on the `Controller` folder in the `Map` folder and select **New File**.
2. In the **Choose a template for your new file** screen, select **iOS** at the top and then **Cocoa Touch Class**. Then hit **Next**.

Where Are We?

3. Add the following to the **Options** screen that appears:

   New file:
   - **Class**: `MapViewController`
   - **Subclass**: `UIViewController`
   - **Also create XIB**: Unchecked
   - **Language**: `Swift`

4. Click **Next** and then **Create**.
5. Under the `import UIKit` statement, add `import MapKit`.
6. Update your class declaration to include the following subclass:

   ```
   class MapViewController: UIViewController, MKMapViewDelegate
   ```

Let's now connect this file with our `UIViewController` and our map view in storyboard:

1. Add the following after the class declaration:

   ```
   @IBOutlet var mapView: MKMapView!
   ```

2. Open your `Map.storyboard` file.
3. In the Outline view, select the View Controller that contains the map view.
4. Now, in the Utilities panel, select the Identity inspector.
5. Under **Custom Class**, in the **Class** drop-down menu, select `MapViewController` and hit *Enter* in order to connect the View Controller to the class.
6. Now, select the Connections inspector.
7. Under the Outlets section, you will see an empty circle next to `mapView`. Click and drag the outlet to the map view in the View Controller in the Outline view.

Chapter 16

We are going to start working with our map, but first we need to add some things to our `MapDataManager`:

1. Open the `MapDataManager.swift` file in the Navigator panel; underneath the `import Foundation` statement, add `import MapKit`.
2. Next, add the following method to our `MapDataManager`:

   ```
   func currentRegion(latDelta:CLLocationDegrees,
   longDelta:CLLocationDegrees) -> MKCoordinateRegion {
       guard let item = items.first else { return MKCoordinateRegion() }

       let span = MKCoordinateSpanMake(latDelta, longDelta)
       return MKCoordinateRegion(center: item.coordinate, span: span)
   }
   ```

Before we delve into the particular sections of this function, we need to understand what this function does. When you use a map and drop pins down onto it, you want the map to zoom into a particular area. To zoom in on a map, you need a latitude and longitude. What this method is doing is grabbing the first pin (or annotation) in the array and zooming in on the area:

```
                                      A
func currentRegion(latDelta:CLLocationDegrees, longDelta:CLLocationDegrees) -> MKCoordinateRegion {
    guard let item = items.first else { return MKCoordinateRegion() }  B
    let span = MKCoordinateSpanMake(latDelta, longDelta)  C

    return MKCoordinateRegion(center: item.coordinate, span: span)  D
}
```

Let's break down the code:

- **Part A**: Our method has two parameters, both of which are `CLLocationDegrees`. It is just a class that represents a latitude or longitude coordinate in degrees:

  ```
  func currentRegion(latDelta:CLLocationDegrees,
  longDelta:CLLocationDegrees) -> MKCoordinateRegion {
  ```

- **Part B**: This `guard` statement obtains the first item in the array. If there are no items in the array, it will just return an empty coordinate region. If there are items in the array, it will return the coordinate region:

  ```
  guard let item = items.first else { return MKCoordinateRegion() }
  ```

- **Part C**: Here, we are creating an `MKCoordinate` with the latitude and longitude that we passed into the function. `MKCoordinateSpan` defines a span, in the latitude and longitude directions, to show on the map:

    ```
    let span = MKCoordinateSpanMake(latDelta, longDelta)
    ```

- **Part D**: Lastly, we are setting the center and the span of our region and returning them so that when the pins drop, the map can zoom in on the area:

    ```
    return MKCoordinateRegion(center: item.coordinate, span: span)
    ```

Now, let's set up our `MapViewController` to display annotations:

1. Open the `MapViewController.swift` file in the Navigator panel and delete both `didReceiveMemoryWarning()` and `prepare()` (which has been commented out), as we do not need them for our purposes.
2. Directly under our `IBOutlet` statement, add the following:

    ```
    let manager = MapDataManager()
    ```

3. Then, inside of the class definition, add the following method after `viewDidLoad()`:

    ```
    func addMap(_ annotations:[RestaurantItem]) {
        mapView.setRegion(manager.currentRegion(latDelta: 0.5,
    longDelta: 0.5), animated: true)
        mapView.addAnnotations(manager.annotations)
    }
    ```

In this method, we are doing a couple of things. We first pass annotations through the parameter. When we call `fetch()` and it is completed, it will return the array of annotations. We will pass that array over to our `addMap(_ annotations:)` to use. Next, we set the region by obtaining it from our `MapDataManager`, thus setting the latitude and longitude delta. This will set our zoom and region for our map. Once we have that, we then pass all of our annotations for the map to display.

Therefore, we need to have our manager fetch the annotations:

Add the following method above `addMap(_ annotations:)`:

```
func initialize() {
    mapView.delegate = self
    manager.fetch { (annotations) in
        addMap(annotations)
    }
}
```

Inside of the `initialize()` method, we are setting the map delegate to the class. In previous chapters, we did this using storyboard; however, you can also do this with code. This line allows us to be notified when the user taps on an annotation or taps the disclosure indicator in the annotation.

Earlier in this chapter, we created a `fetch()` method in the `MapDataManager`, wherein we used a closure block. This closure block requires that we wrap it in curly braces. Once the `completion()` block is called in the manager, everything inside of the curly braces will run. For our purposes in building this app, we are going to have a small number of pins or annotations ; therefore, we do not need a completion block. However, if you have 100 or 500 annotations, for instance, a closure block would be more efficient. We will do more with this later so that you can get more practice with closure blocks.

Add `initialize()` inside of `viewDidLoad()` so that everything will run when the view loads.

Before you build, make sure that you add the `MapLocations.plist` file into the `maps` folder. This file is in the book `assets` folder for this chapter.

Where Are We?

Let's build and run the project by hitting the Play button (or use *cmd + R*):

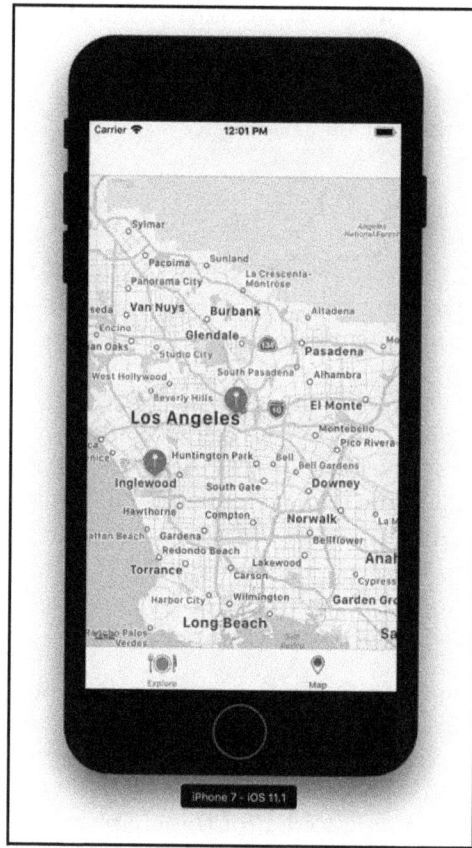

We now have pins on our map, but we need to update them so that they look more like the ones in our design. Let's learn how to customize the annotations in our map.

Creating custom annotations

If you have ever owned an iPhone and used Apple Maps, you will be familiar with pins. When you have a map inside of your app, having custom pins (annotations) gives your app a bit more polish. Let's create our custom annotations.

Open up `MapViewController` in the Navigator panel and add the following directly under the `addMap(_ annotations:)` method:

Chapter 16

```swift
func mapView(_ mapView: MKMapView, viewFor annotation: MKAnnotation) -> MKAnnotationView? {
    let identifier = "custompin"
    guard !annotation.isKind(of: MKUserLocation.self) else { return nil }
    var annotationView: MKAnnotationView?
    if let customAnnotationView = mapView.dequeueReusableAnnotationView(withIdentifier: identifier) {
        annotationView = customAnnotationView
        annotationView?.annotation = annotation
    }
    else {
        let av = MKAnnotationView(annotation: annotation, reuseIdentifier: identifier)
        av.rightCalloutAccessoryView = UIButton(type: .detailDisclosure)
        annotationView = av
    }
    if let annotationView = annotationView {
        annotationView.canShowCallout = true
        annotationView.image = UIImage(named: "custom-annotation")
    }
    return annotationView
}
```

Let's break down this code so we can better understand what we are doing. We will break the function down into the following sections:

[425]

Let's start with A:

- **Part A**: This method will call the `mapView.delegate` we set up earlier, when annotations need to be placed. We will use this method to grab the annotations before they are placed and replace the default pins with custom pins:

    ```
    mapView(_:viewFor:)
    ```

- **Part B**: Here, we set an identifier, similar to those that we set when using Collection Views and Table Views:

    ```
    let identifier = "custompin"
    ```

- **Part C**: This guard will ensure that our annotation is not the user location. If the annotation is the user location, the `guard` will return `nil`. Otherwise, it will move on through the method:

    ```
    guard !annotation.isKind(of: MKUserLocation.self) else {
        return nil
    }
    ```

- **Part D**: `MKAnnotationView` is the class name for the pin; here, we create a variable that we can use to set our custom image:

    ```
    var annotationView:MKAnnotationView?
    ```

- **Part E**: In this statement, we are checking to see whether there are any annotations already created that we can reuse. If so, we point them to the variable we just added previously. Otherwise, we create the annotation in the next `else` statement:

    ```
    if let customAnnotationView =
    mapView.dequeueReusableAnnotationView(withIdentifier: identifier) {
        annotationView = customAnnotationView
        annotationView?.annotation = annotation
    }
    ```

- **Part F**: If there are no annotations to reuse, we create a new `MKAnnotationView` and give it a callout with a button. A callout is a bubble that appears above the annotation when you tap it to display the title (restaurant name) and subtitle (cuisines) associated with that annotation. If the user selects this callout button, the user is taken to the restaurant detail view:

    ```
    else {
        let av = MKAnnotationView(annotation: annotation,
    reuseIdentifier: identifier)
            av.rightCalloutAccessoryView = UIButton(type: .detailDisclosure)
                    annotationView = av
    }
    ```

- **Part G**: Here is where we make sure that our custom annotation will show a callout. We also set our custom image for our annotation:

    ```
    if let annotationView = annotationView {
        annotationView.canShowCallout = true
        annotationView.image = UIImage(named: "custom-annotation")
    }
    ```

- **Part H**: Once we are finished going through the method, we return our custom annotation to the map. This method is called for every annotation that appears on the map:

    ```
    return annotationView
    ```

Where Are We?

Let's build and run the project by hitting the Play button (or use *cmd + R*):

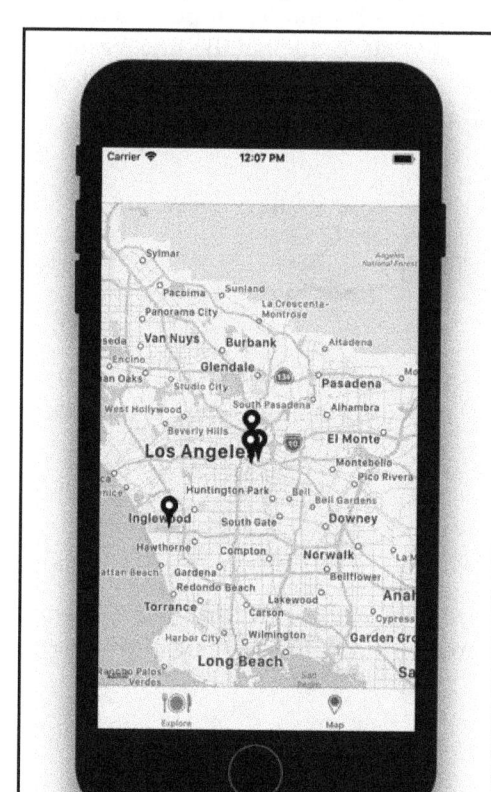

We now have custom annotations displaying on our map. Each pin's callout shows the restaurant name as well as the cuisines for the restaurant associated with that particular pin. If you tap on the callout, the restaurant detail disclosure does not yet work. Let's now set that up.

Map to restaurant detail

For us to go to the restaurant detail from the callout, we need to update our app so that our map can also open the restaurant detail. To do this, we must first create a storyboard reference.

Chapter 16

Creating a storyboard reference

In order to link to the restaurant detail from the map, we need to create a storyboard reference:

1. Open the `Map.storyboard`, and in the object library of the Utilities panel, drag a **Storyboard Reference** into the `Map.storyboard` scene:

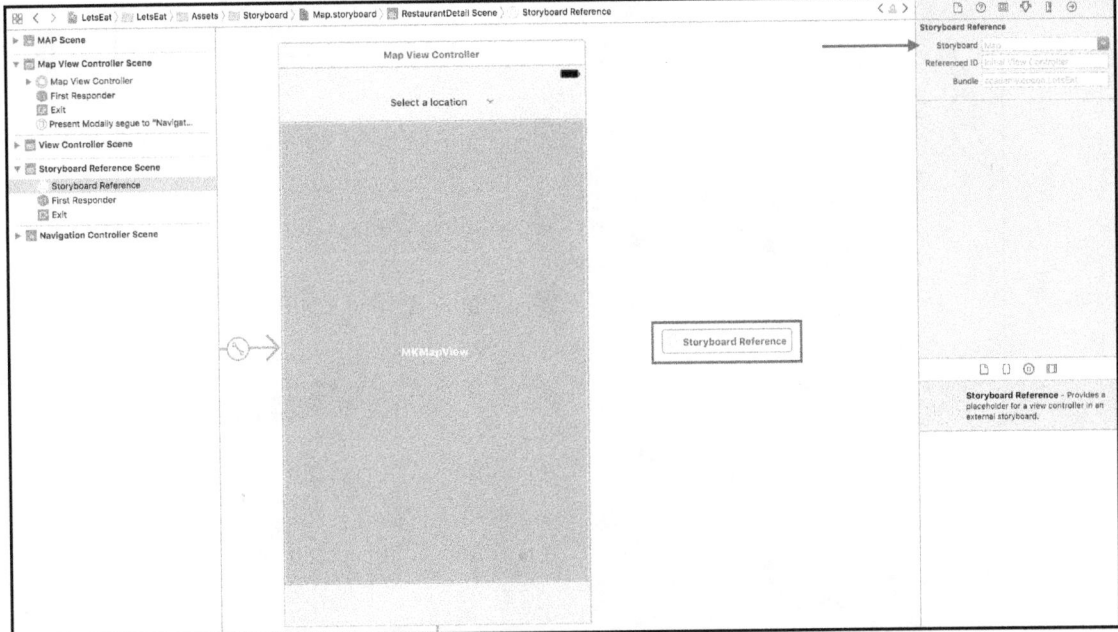

2. Next, select the Attributes inspector in the Utilities panel, and update the storyboard under **Storyboard Reference** to say `RestaurantDetail`. Then, hit *Enter*:

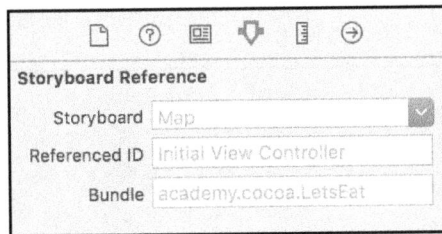

[429]

3. *Ctrl* + drag from the Map View controller to the storyboard reference we just created and select **Show** on the screen that appears. Note that you can *Ctrl* + drag from either the Map View controller in the Outline view or the Map View controller icon in the scene, as shown in the following screenshot:

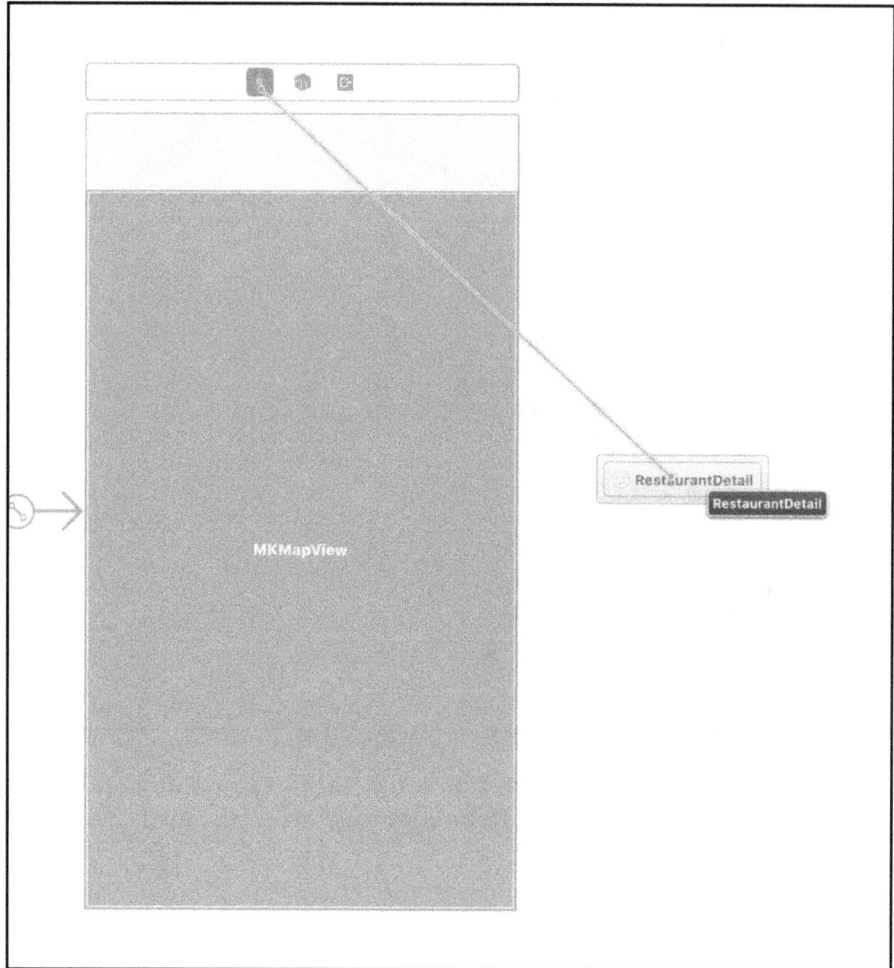

4. Select the segue connecting the Map View controller to the storyboard reference:

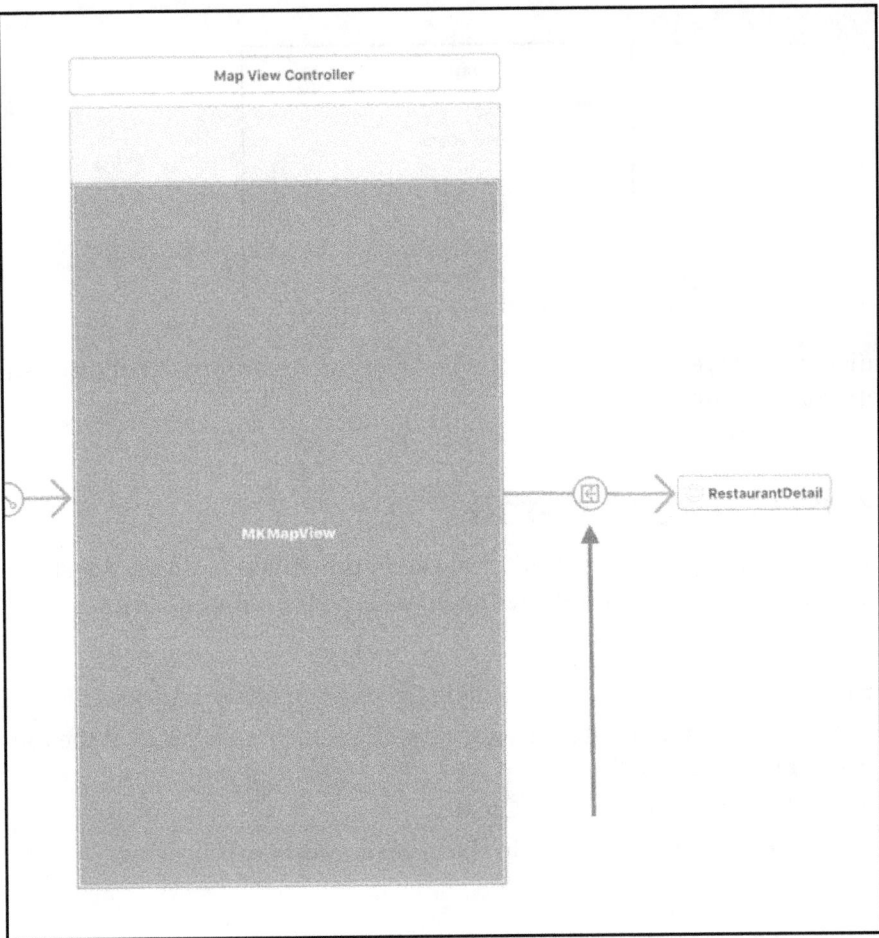

Where Are We?

5. In the Attributes inspector, update the **Identifier** under **Storyboard Segue** to say `showDetail`. Then, hit *Enter*:

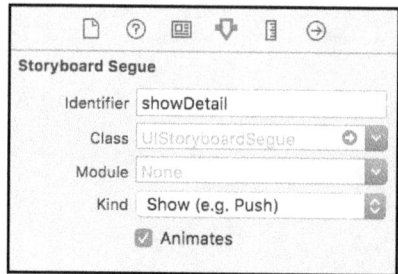

This identifier is what we are going to call whenever the restaurant detail disclosure is tapped. Let's connect our segue next.

Map to restaurant detail

Before we connect our segue, we should create an enumeration (an `enum` for short) to keep track of our segues. An `enum` is a user-defined data type that consists of a set of related values:

1. Right-click on the `Misc` folder inside the `Common` folder and select **New File**.
2. In the **Choose a template for your new file** screen, select **iOS** at the top and then **Swift File**. Then hit **Next**.
3. Name this file `Segue` and hit **Create**.
4. Under `import Foundation` in the new file, add the following:

```
enum Segue:String {
   case showDetail
   case showRating
   case showReview
   case ShowAllReviews
   case restaurantList
   case locationList
   case showPhotoReview
}
```

We will eventually need all of these segues, so we can add them once. Whenever we use a new one, I will refer back to this file. The next thing we need is to know when the user taps the detail disclosure of the callout.

In the `MapViewController.swift` file, add the following under the `addMap(_ annotations:)` method:

```
func mapView(_ mapView: MKMapView, annotationView view: MKAnnotationView,
    calloutAccessoryControlTapped control: UIControl) {
        self.performSegue(withIdentifier: Segue.showDetail.rawValue, sender:
self)
}
```

We are using `performSegue()` to call our custom segue. Now, when you tap the annotation and then the callout, you will go to the restaurant-detail view:

```
        mapView.delegate = self

        manager.fetch { (annotations) in
            addMap(annotations)
        }
    }

    func addMap(_ annotations:[RestaurantAnnotation]) {
        mapView.setRegion(manager.currentRegion(latDelta: 0.5, longDelta: 0.5), animated: true)
        mapView.addAnnotations(annotations)
    }

    func mapView(_ mapView: MKMapView, annotationView view: MKAnnotationView,
        calloutAccessoryControlTapped control: UIControl) {
            self.performSegue(withIdentifier: Segue.showDetail.rawValue, sender: self)
    }

    func mapView(_ mapView: MKMapView, viewFor annotation: MKAnnotation) -> MKAnnotationView? {
        let identifier = "custompin"

        guard !annotation.isKind(of: MKUserLocation.self) else {
            return nil
        }

        var annotationView:MKAnnotationView?
```

Let's build and run the project by hitting the Play button (or use *cmd* + *R*). We can now get to the restaurant detail view from the map.

Passing data to restaurant detail

In the next chapter, we are going to display the data in our restaurant detail. For now, we want to pass the data over to the detail view.

Where Are We?

To make this work, we need to update both our `RestaurantDetailViewController` (which we have not created yet) and the `MapViewController`. Let's create the `RestaurantDetailViewController`:

1. Right-click on the `Restaurant` folder and create a new group named `Restaurant Detail`.
2. Then, right-click on the new `Restaurant Detail` folder and create a new group named `Controller`.
3. Next, right-click on the new `Controller` folder and select **New File**.
4. In the **Choose a template for your new file** screen, select **iOS** at the top and then **Cocoa Touch Class**. Then hit **Next**.
5. In the **Options** screen, add the following:

    New file:

    - **Class**: `RestaurantDetailViewController`
    - **Subclass**: `UITableViewController`
    - **Also create XIB**: Unchecked
    - **Language**: `Swift`

6. Click **Next** and then **Create**.
7. Delete everything after the `viewDidLoad()` method, as we do not need all of the other code.

    Your file should now look as follows:

    ```swift
    //
    //  RestaurantDetailViewController.swift
    //  LetsEat
    //
    //  Created by Craig Clayton on 11/15/16.
    //  Copyright © 2016 Craig Clayton. All rights reserved.
    //

    import UIKit

    class RestaurantDetailViewController: UITableViewController {
        override func viewDidLoad() {
            super.viewDidLoad()
        }
    }
    ```

8. Next, inside of the class declaration, add the following:

    ```
    var selectedRestaurant:RestaurantItem?
    ```

9. Then, add the following code inside of `viewDidLoad()`:

    ```
    dump(selectedRestaurant as Any)
    ```

10. Your file should now look like the following:

    ```
    //
    //  RestaurantDetailViewController.swift
    //  LetsEat
    //
    //  Created by Craig Clayton on 11/12/17.
    //  Copyright © 2017 Cocoa Academy. All rights reserved.
    //

    import UIKit

    class RestaurantDetailViewController: UITableViewController {

        var selectedRestaurant:RestaurantItem?

        override func viewDidLoad() {
            super.viewDidLoad()
            dump(selectedRestaurant as Any)
        }
    }
    ```

11. Open your `RestaurantDetail.storyboard` file.
12. In the Outline view, select the Table View Controller.
13. In the Utilities panel, select the Identity inspector.
14. Under **Custom Class**, in the **Class** drop-down menu, select **RestaurantDetailViewController** and hit *Enter* in order to connect the View Controller to the class.

    This is all we need to do in `RestaurantDetailViewController`. Next, we need to update our `MapViewController`:

15. Open the `MapViewController.swift` file.
16. Directly under where we declare our manager, add the following code:

    ```
    var selectedRestaurant:RestaurantItem?
    ```

Where Are We?

17. Then, add the following code into the `calloutAccessoryControlTapped()` method above `performSegue`:

    ```
    guard let annotation = mapView.selectedAnnotations.first else {
    return }
    selectedRestaurant = annotation as? RestaurantItem
    ```

    Your file should now look as follows:

    ```
    func mapView(_ mapView: MKMapView, annotationView view: MKAnnotationView, calloutAccessoryControlTapped control: UIControl) {
        guard let annotation = mapView.selectedAnnotations.first else { return }
        selectedRestaurant = annotation as? RestaurantItem

        self.performSegue(withIdentifier: Segue.showDetail.rawValue, sender: self)
    }
    ```

18. Next, add the following code after `viewDidLoad()`:

    ```
    override func prepare(for segue: UIStoryboardSegue, sender: Any?) {
        switch segue.identifier! {
            case Segue.showDetail.rawValue:
                showRestaurantDetail(segue: segue)
            default:
                print("Segue not added")
        }
    }
    ```

You will see an error, but ignore it as we are going to fix this in the next step.

Whenever we transition with a segue, this method gets called. First, we check for the `showDetail` identifier; if this identifier is called, we want to do something (in this case, get the selected restaurant and pass it to the detail view) before we transition.

Add the following code after the `addMap(_ annotations:)` method:

```
func showRestaurantDetail(segue:UIStoryboardSegue) {
    if let viewController = segue.destination as? RestaurantDetailViewController, let restaurant = selectedRestaurant {
        viewController.selectedRestaurant = restaurant
    }
}
```

Here, we are checking to make sure that the segue destination is the `RestaurantDetailViewController`; if so, we make sure that we have a selected restaurant. When it is confirmed that the segue destination is the `RestaurantDetailViewController` and we have a selected restaurant, we use the `selectedRestaurant` variable that we created in `RestaurantDetailViewController` and set it to the selected restaurant in `MapViewController`.

Your file should now look like the following with the two new methods we just added:

```swift
override func viewDidLoad() {
    super.viewDidLoad()
    
    initialize()
}

override func prepare(for segue: UIStoryboardSegue, sender: Any?) {
    switch segue.identifier! {
    case Segue.showDetail.rawValue:
        showRestaurantDetail(segue: segue)
    default:
        print("Segue not added")
    }
}

func initialize() {
    mapView.delegate = self
    
    manager.fetch { (annotations) in
        addMap(annotations)
    }
}

func addMap(_ annotations:[RestaurantAnnotation]) {
    mapView.setRegion(manager.currentRegion(latDelta: 0.5, longDelta: 0.5), animated: true)
    mapView.addAnnotations(annotations)
}

func showRestaurantDetail(segue:UIStoryboardSegue) {
    if let viewController = segue.destination as? RestaurantDetailViewController, let restaurant = selectedRestaurant {
        viewController.selectedRestaurant = restaurant
    }
}
```

Where Are We?

Let's build and run the project by hitting the Play button (or using *cmd + R*) and test whether we can pass data to our `RestaurantDetailViewController`. You should see the following in your Debug panel, if everything worked:

```
2017-11-12 12:32:42.020113-0500 LetsEat[11094:1811464] Could not inset legal attribution from corner 4
Optional(<LetsEat.RestaurantItem: 0x608000391c60>)
  some: <LetsEat.RestaurantItem: 0x608000391c60> #0
    - super: NSObject
    name: Optional("Maria\'s Italian Kitchen - Downtown")
      - some: "Maria\'s Italian Kitchen - Downtown"
    cuisines: 2 elements
      - "Indian"
      - "Gastropubs"
    latitude: Optional(34.04934200000001)
      - some: 34.04934200000001
    longitude: Optional(-118.258174)
      - some: -118.258174
    address: Optional("615 S. Flower Street")
      - some: "615 S. Flower Street"
    postalCode: Optional("90017")
      - some: "90017"
    state: Optional("CA")
      - some: "CA"
    imageURL: Optional("https://www.opentable.com/img/restimages/19183.jpg")
      - some: "https://www.opentable.com/img/restimages/19183.jpg"
2017-11-12 12:32:45.572309-0500 LetsEat[11094:1811464] [Warning] Warning once only: Detected a case where constraints ambiguously suggest
a height of zero for a tableview cell's content view. We're considering the collapse unintentional and using standard height instead.
```

We now have our `RestaurantDetailViewController` capable of receiving data; in the next chapter, we will display that data. However, before we write any more code, we should organize our code a bit better.

Organizing your code

Earlier, we wrote an extension for our `DataManager`; extensions are useful for adding your functionality onto standard libraries, structs, or classes—such as arrays, ints, and strings—or onto your data types.

Here is an example. Let's say that you wanted to know the length of a string:

```
let name = "Craig"
name.characters .count
```

For us to access the count of the string, we would need to access the characters and then get a count.

Let's simplify this by creating an extension:

```
extension String {
    var length: Int {
            return self.characters.count
    }
}
```

With this newly created `String` extension, we can now access the count by writing the following:

```
let name = "Craig"
name.length
```

As you can see, extensions are very powerful by enabling us to add extra functionality without having to change the main class or struct.

Up until now, we have paid very little attention to file structure and more attention to understanding what we are writing. Organizing your code is also very important, which is why we are going to refactor our code. The refactoring will mostly consist of copying and pasting code that you have already written. Extensions can help us organize our code better and stay away from cluttering our View Controllers. Also, we can extend the functionality of View Controllers through extensions. We are going to update four classes: `ExploreViewController`, `RestaurantListViewController`, `LocationViewController`, and `MapViewController`.

Refactoring ExploreViewController

We are going to divide our View Controller into distinct sections using what is known as a `MARK` comment. Let's start with our `ExploreViewController`:

1. In the `ExploreViewController` file, after the last curly brace, hit *Enter* a couple of times and add the following code (remember this should be outside of the class, not inside):

   ```
   // MARK: Private Extension
   private extension ExploreViewController {
     // code goes here
   }
   // MARK: UICollectionViewDataSource
   extension ExploreViewController: UICollectionViewDataSource {
     // code goes here
   }
   ```

   Here, we are creating two extensions. Our first one will be private and will be where we add any methods that we create that we need for this controller. Our second one is an extension that just deals with our `collectionview` data source. Let's keep going for now.

Where Are We?

2. We currently have an error because we are using `UICollectionViewDataSource` in two places.
   Delete `UICollectionViewDataSource` (including the comma) from the class definition at the top of the file:

   ```
   class ExploreViewController: UIViewController, UICollectionViewDataSource {
       @IBOutlet weak var collectionView:UICollectionView!
       let manager = ExploreDataManager()
       override func viewDidLoad() {
           super.viewDidLoad()
   ```
   ← delete (the `, UICollectionViewDataSource` portion)

3. Now, let's move all of our `CollectionViewDataSource` methods into our extension. You should be moving the following:

```
import UIKit

class ExploreViewController: UIViewController {
    @IBOutlet weak var collectionView:UICollectionView!
    let manager = ExploreDataManager()

    override func viewDidLoad() {
        super.viewDidLoad()
        manager.fetch()
    }

    func collectionView(_ collectionView: UICollectionView, viewForSupplementaryElementOfKind kind: String, at indexPath: IndexPath) -> UICollectionReusableView {
        let headerView = collectionView.dequeueReusableSupplementaryView(ofKind: kind, withReuseIdentifier: "header", for: indexPath)
        return headerView
    }

    func collectionView(_ collectionView: UICollectionView, cellForItemAt indexPath: IndexPath) -> UICollectionViewCell {
        let cell = collectionView.dequeueReusableCell(withReuseIdentifier: "exploreCell", for: indexPath) as! ExploreCell
        let item = manager.explore(at: indexPath)
        if let name = item.name { cell.lblName.text = name }
        if let image = item.image { cell.imgExplore.image = UIImage(named: image) }
        return cell
    }

    func numberOfSections(in collectionView: UICollectionView) -> Int {
        return 1
    }

    func collectionView(_ collectionView: UICollectionView, numberOfItemsInSection section: Int) -> Int {
        return manager.numberOfItems()
    }

    @IBAction func unwindLocationCancel(segue:UIStoryboardSegue) {}
}

// MARK: Private Extension
private extension ExploreViewController {
    // code goes here
}

// MARK: UICollectionViewDataSource
extension ExploreViewController: UICollectionViewDataSource {
    // code goes here      ←——— Move all the code marked above to here
}
```

Your file, including the extension, should now look as follows:

```swift
import UIKit

class ExploreViewController: UIViewController {

    @IBOutlet weak var collectionView:UICollectionView!

    let manager = ExploreDataManager()

    override func viewDidLoad() {
        super.viewDidLoad()

        manager.fetch()
    }


    @IBAction func unwindLocationCancel(segue:UIStoryboardSegue) {}
}
// MARK: Private Extension
private extension ExploreViewController {
    // code goes here
}
// MARK: UICollectionViewDataSource
extension ExploreViewController: UICollectionViewDataSource {
    func collectionView(_ collectionView: UICollectionView, viewForSupplementaryElementOfKind kind: String, at indexPath: IndexPath) -> UICollectionReusableView {
        let headerView = collectionView.dequeueReusableSupplementaryView(ofKind: kind, withReuseIdentifier: "header", for: indexPath)
        return headerView
    }

    func collectionView(_ collectionView: UICollectionView, cellForItemAt indexPath: IndexPath) -> UICollectionViewCell {
        let cell = collectionView.dequeueReusableCell(withReuseIdentifier: "exploreCell", for: indexPath) as! ExploreCell

        let item = manager.explore(at: indexPath)
        if let name = item.name { cell.lblName.text = name }
        if let image = item.image { cell.imgExplore.image = UIImage(named: image) }

        return cell
    }

    func numberOfSections(in collectionView: UICollectionView) -> Int {
        return 1
    }

    func collectionView(_ collectionView: UICollectionView, numberOfItemsInSection section: Int) -> Int {
        return manager.numberOfItems()
    }
}
```

Now, you are probably wondering why we created the `private` extension. Well, one thing that I try to do is keep `viewDidLoad()` as clean as possible. Instead of writing a ton of code inside of `viewDidLoad()`, I like to create an `initialize()` method and call that instead. This way, it's clear to anyone going into my code what I am doing. Let's add the following to our `private` extension:

```
func initialize() {
  manager.fetch()
}

@IBAction func unwindLocationCancel(segue:UIStoryboardSegue){}
```

Where Are We?

Now we can call `initialize()` inside of `viewDidLoad()`. When you are done, you should see the following:

```
class ExploreViewController: UIViewController {
    @IBOutlet weak var collectionView:UICollectionView!
    let manager = ExploreDataManager()
    override func viewDidLoad() {
        super.viewDidLoad()
        initialize()
    }
}

// MARK: Private Extension
private extension ExploreViewController {
    func initialize() {
        manager.fetch()
    }

    @IBAction func unwindLocationCancel(segue:UIStoryboardSegue){}
}
```

Now, this might seem like we wrote extra code for nothing, but as your classes grow, you will see the benefit of doing this. Before we clean up the other files, let's look at what the `MARK` comment does.

Using the MARK comment

Currently, our `MARK` comment may seem like a useless comment in our code, but it is more powerful than you think. Look at the bottom bar that is located to the right of the Play and Stop buttons in Xcode and look for the last arrow. Mine says `No Selection`, but if you have your cursor on a method you might see that instead:

```
LetsEat > LetsEat > Controllers > Explore > ExploreViewController.swift > No Selection
//
//  Created by Craig Clayton on 6/30/17.
//  Copyright © 2017 Cocoa Academy. All rights reserved.
//
```

Click on this last item and you will see the following:

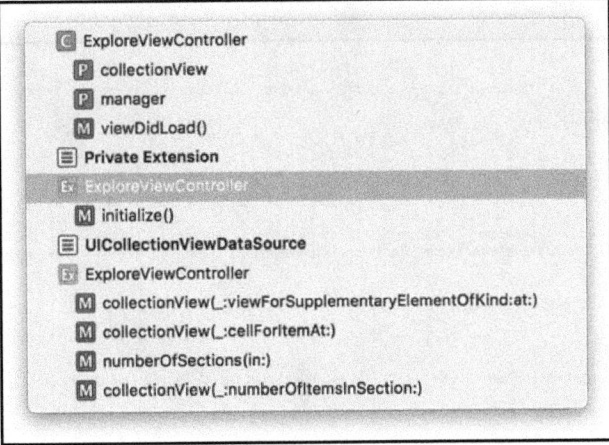

This shows all of your code divided just like our file. You can click on any method and the file will jump right to that method. Even if your file is long and you are looking for a method, you can use this technique to get where you need to be. We are done cleaning up our `ExploreViewController`.

Refactoring RestaurantViewController

We now know our structure, so let's update our `RestaurantViewController`. Even though we do not currently have anything to put in our `private` extension, we will add it anyway as good practice:

1. Inside our `RestaurantViewController`, after the last curly brace, hit *Enter* a couple of times and add the following code (remember, this should be outside of the class, not inside):

    ```
    // MARK: Private Extension

    private extension RestaurantViewController {}
        // MARK: UICollectionViewDataSource

    extension RestaurantViewController: UICollectionViewDataSource {}
    ```

2. Next, delete the `UICollectionViewDataSource` subclass from the main class.

Where Are We?

3. Now, let's move all of our `CollectionViewDataSource` methods into our extension. You should be moving the following:

```swift
import UIKit

class RestaurantViewController: UIViewController, UICollectionViewDataSource {

    @IBOutlet var collectionView:UICollectionView!

    override func viewDidLoad() {
        super.viewDidLoad()
    }

    func collectionView(_ collectionView: UICollectionView, cellForItemAt indexPath: IndexPath) -> UICollectionViewCell {
        return collectionView.dequeueReusableCell(withReuseIdentifier: "restaurantCell", for: indexPath)
    }

    func numberOfSections(in collectionView: UICollectionView) -> Int {
        return 1
    }

    func collectionView(_ collectionView: UICollectionView, numberOfItemsInSection section: Int) -> Int {
        return 10
    }
}

// MARK: Private Extension
private extension RestaurantListViewController {

}

// MARK: UICollectionViewDataSource
extension RestaurantListViewController: UICollectionViewDataSource {

}
```

← Move all the code marked above to here

4. Your file, including the extension, should now look as follows:

```swift
import UIKit

class RestaurantViewController: UIViewController {

    @IBOutlet var collectionView:UICollectionView!

    override func viewDidLoad() {
        super.viewDidLoad()
    }
}

// MARK: Private Extension
private extension RestaurantViewController {

}

// MARK: UICollectionViewDataSource
extension RestaurantViewController: UICollectionViewDataSource {
    func collectionView(_ collectionView: UICollectionView, cellForItemAt indexPath: IndexPath) -> UICollectionViewCell {
        return collectionView.dequeueReusableCell(withReuseIdentifier: "restaurantCell", for: indexPath)
    }

    func numberOfSections(in collectionView: UICollectionView) -> Int {
        return 1
    }

    func collectionView(_ collectionView: UICollectionView, numberOfItemsInSection section: Int) -> Int {
        return 10
    }
}
```

We successfully updated our `RestaurantListViewController`.

Next, let's take a look at our `LocationViewController`:

1. Inside of our `LocationViewController`, after the last curly brace, hit *Enter* a couple of times and add the following code (remember, this should be outside of the class, not inside):

   ```
   // MARK: Private Extension
   private extension LocationViewController {}

   // MARK: UITableViewDataSource
   extension LocationViewController: UITableViewDataSource {}
   ```

2. Next, remove the `UITableViewDataSource` subclass from the main class.
3. Now, let's move all of our `TableViewDataSource` methods into our extension. You should be moving the following:

```
class LocationViewController: UIViewController {

    @IBOutlet weak var tableView:UITableView!

    let manager = LocationDataManager()

    override func viewDidLoad() {
        super.viewDidLoad()
        manager.fetch()
    }

    func tableView(_ tableView: UITableView, numberOfRowsInSection section: Int) -> Int {
        return manager.numberOfItems()
    }

    func numberOfSections(in tableView: UITableView) -> Int {
        return 1
    }

    func tableView(_ tableView: UITableView, cellForRowAt indexPath: IndexPath) -> UITableViewCell {
        let cell = tableView.dequeueReusableCell(withIdentifier: "locationCell", for: indexPath) as UITableViewCell
        cell.textLabel?.text = manager.locationItem(at:indexPath)

        return cell
    }
}

// MARK: Private Extension
private extension LocationViewController {

}

// MARK: UITableViewDataSource
extension LocationViewController: UITableViewDataSource {           ←──── Move all the code marked above to here

}
```

Where Are We?

Your file, including the extension, should now look as follows:

```swift
import UIKit

class LocationViewController: UIViewController {

    @IBOutlet weak var tableView:UITableView!

    let manager = LocationDataManager()

    override func viewDidLoad() {
        super.viewDidLoad()
        manager.fetch()
    }
}
// MARK: Private Extension
private extension LocationViewController {

}

// MARK: UITableViewDataSource
extension LocationViewController: UITableViewDataSource {
    func tableView(_ tableView: UITableView, numberOfRowsInSection section: Int) -> Int {
        return manager.numberOfItems()
    }

    func numberOfSections(in tableView: UITableView) -> Int {
        return 1
    }

    func tableView(_ tableView: UITableView, cellForRowAt indexPath: IndexPath) -> UITableViewCell {
        let cell = tableView.dequeueReusableCell(withIdentifier: "locationCell", for: indexPath) as UITableViewCell
        cell.textLabel?.text = manager.locationItem(at:indexPath)

        return cell
    }
}
```

4. Now, just like we did in our `ExploreViewController`, we want to create an `initialize()` method in our `private` extension and update `viewDidLoad()` to call `initialize()`. When you are done, your file should look like mine:

```
class LocationViewController: UIViewController {

    @IBOutlet weak var tableView:UITableView!

    let manager = LocationDataManager()

    override func viewDidLoad() {
        super.viewDidLoad()
        initialize()
    }
}

// MARK: Private Extension
private extension LocationViewController {
    func initialize() {
        manager.fetch()
    }
}
```

We finish by cleaning up our `LocationViewController`. Finally, let's take a look at our `MapViewController`.

Refactoring MapViewController

We are just about done refactoring our files. The last file we need to refactor is our `MapViewController`. Let's get started:

1. Inside of our `MapViewController`, after the last curly brace, hit *Enter* a couple of times and add the following code (remember, this should be outside of the class, not inside):

   ```
   // MARK: Private Extension
   private extension MapViewController {}

    // MARK: MKMapDelegate
    extension MapViewController: MKMapDelegate {}
   ```

2. Next, remove the `MKMapViewDelegate` subclass from the main class and move it into our extension.

Where Are We?

3. Now, let's move all of our `MKMapViewDelegate` methods into the extension. You should be moving the following:

```swift
import UIKit
import MapKit

class MapViewController: UIViewController {

    @IBOutlet var mapView: MKMapView!

    let manager = MapDataManager()
    var selectedRestaurant:RestaurantItem?

    override func viewDidLoad() {
        super.viewDidLoad()
        initialize()
    }

    override func prepare(for segue: UIStoryboardSegue, sender: Any?) {
        switch segue.identifier! {
        case Segue.showDetail.rawValue:
            showRestaurantDetail(segue: segue)
        default:
            print("Segue not added")
        }
    }

    func initialize() {
        mapView.delegate = self
        manager.fetch { (annotations) in
            addMap(annotations)
        }
    }

    func addMap(_ annotations:[RestaurantItem]) {
        mapView.setRegion(manager.currentRegion(latDelta: 0.5, longDelta: 0.5), animated: true)
        mapView.addAnnotations(manager.annotations)
    }

    func showRestaurantDetail(segue:UIStoryboardSegue) {
        if let viewController = segue.destination as? RestaurantDetailViewController, let restaurant = selectedRestaurant {
            viewController.selectedRestaurant = restaurant
        }
    }
```

```
    func mapView(_ mapView: MKMapView, viewFor annotation: MKAnnotation) -> MKAnnotationView? {
        let identifier = "custompin"

        guard !annotation.isKind(of: MKUserLocation.self) else { return nil }
        var annotationView: MKAnnotationView?

        if let customAnnotationView = mapView.dequeueReusableAnnotationView(withIdentifier: identifier) {
            annotationView = customAnnotationView
            annotationView?.annotation = annotation
        }
        else {
            let av = MKAnnotationView(annotation: annotation, reuseIdentifier: identifier)
            av.rightCalloutAccessoryView = UIButton(type: .detailDisclosure)
            annotationView = av
        }

        if let annotationView = annotationView {
            annotationView.canShowCallout = true
            annotationView.image = UIImage(named: "custom-annotation")
        }

        return annotationView
    }

    func mapView(_ mapView: MKMapView, annotationView view: MKAnnotationView, calloutAccessoryControlTapped control: UIControl) {
        guard let annotation = mapView.selectedAnnotations.first else { return }
        selectedRestaurant = annotation as? RestaurantItem

        self.performSegue(withIdentifier: Segue.showDetail.rawValue, sender: self)
    }
}

// MARK: Private Extension
private extension MapViewController {

}

// MARK: MKMapViewDelegate
extension MapViewController: MKMapViewDelegate {

}
```

⬅ Move all the code marked above to here

Your extension should now look as follows:

```swift
// MARK: MKMapViewDelegate
extension MapViewController: MKMapViewDelegate {
    func mapView(_ mapView: MKMapView, viewFor annotation: MKAnnotation) -> MKAnnotationView? {
        let identifier = "custompin"

        guard !annotation.isKind(of: MKUserLocation.self) else { return nil }
        var annotationView: MKAnnotationView?

        if let customAnnotationView = mapView.dequeueReusableAnnotationView(withIdentifier: identifier) {
            annotationView = customAnnotationView
            annotationView?.annotation = annotation
        }
        else {
            let av = MKAnnotationView(annotation: annotation, reuseIdentifier: identifier)
            av.rightCalloutAccessoryView = UIButton(type: .detailDisclosure)
            annotationView = av
        }

        if let annotationView = annotationView {
            annotationView.canShowCallout = true
            annotationView.image = UIImage(named: "custom-annotation")
        }

        return annotationView
    }

    func mapView(_ mapView: MKMapView, annotationView view: MKAnnotationView, calloutAccessoryControlTapped control: UIControl) {
        guard let annotation = mapView.selectedAnnotations.first else { return }
        selectedRestaurant = annotation as? RestaurantItem

        self.performSegue(withIdentifier: Segue.showDetail.rawValue, sender: self)
    }
}
```

4. Next, let's update our `private` extension by moving the following:

```swift
import UIKit
import MapKit

class MapViewController: UIViewController {

    @IBOutlet var mapView: MKMapView!

    let manager = MapDataManager()
    var selectedRestaurant:RestaurantItem?

    override func viewDidLoad() {
        super.viewDidLoad()
        initialize()
    }

    override func prepare(for segue: UIStoryboardSegue, sender: Any?) {
        switch segue.identifier! {
        case Segue.showDetail.rawValue:
            showRestaurantDetail(segue: segue)
        default:
            print("Segue not added")
        }
    }

    func initialize() {
        mapView.delegate = self
        manager.fetch { (annotations) in
            addMap(annotations)
        }
    }

    func addMap(_ annotations:[RestaurantItem]) {
        mapView.setRegion(manager.currentRegion(latDelta: 0.5, longDelta: 0.5), animated: true)
        mapView.addAnnotations(manager.annotations)
    }

    func showRestaurantDetail(segue:UIStoryboardSegue) {
        if let viewController = segue.destination as? RestaurantDetailViewController, let restaurant = selectedRestaurant {
            viewController.selectedRestaurant = restaurant
        }
    }
}

// MARK: Private Extension
private extension MapViewController {
                        ⟵────────────── Move all the code marked above to here
}
```

When you are done, you should have the following:

```swift
import UIKit
import MapKit

class MapViewController: UIViewController {

    @IBOutlet var mapView: MKMapView!

    let manager = MapDataManager()
    var selectedRestaurant:RestaurantItem?

    override func viewDidLoad() {
        super.viewDidLoad()
        initialize()
    }

    override func prepare(for segue: UIStoryboardSegue, sender: Any?) {
        switch segue.identifier! {
        case Segue.showDetail.rawValue:
            showRestaurantDetail(segue: segue)
        default:
            print("Segue not added")
        }
    }
}

// MARK: Private Extension
private extension MapViewController {
    func initialize() {
        mapView.delegate = self
        manager.fetch { (annotations) in
            addMap(annotations)
        }
    }

    func addMap(_ annotations:[RestaurantItem]) {
        mapView.setRegion(manager.currentRegion(latDelta: 0.5, longDelta: 0.5), animated: true)
        mapView.addAnnotations(manager.annotations)
    }

    func showRestaurantDetail(segue:UIStoryboardSegue) {
        if let viewController = segue.destination as? RestaurantDetailViewController, let restaurant = selectedRestaurant {
            viewController.selectedRestaurant = restaurant
        }
    }
}
```

I did not include the `MKMapViewDelegate` extension because the file is too long. The extension is under our `private` extension. Why did I not move the `prepare()` method? The `prepare()` and `viewDidLoad()` methods are methods that are overrides for `UIViewController` in this case. We want to keep these methods inside of our main class declaration. The more we do this, the clearer it will become.

We finished cleaning up the four View Controllers. You might be wondering what the benefits of this are. In this project, it may not seem like these updates are very important, because we are not doing a lot in our View Controllers. However, as a project grows, there will be some cases where multiple protocols and delegates are adopted; thus, these updates will be beneficial.

Here is an example:

```
class NewsListingView: UIViewController, NewsListingViewProtocol,
UICollectionViewDelegate, UICollectionViewDataSource,
LiveGameNewsViewDelegate, UIGestureRecognizerDelegate
```

This class is subclassing a View Controller and adopting one protocol, three delegates, and one data source. If you have two methods for each one that you need, you would have 12 functions in your class that would need certain methods. Separating out our code makes it really easy to find where things are located.

Summary

In this chapter, we discussed what `MKAnnotations` are and how to add and subclass them in order to use them on our map. We also learned how to customize our annotations. Our app now takes us from tapping on an annotation to a restaurant detail page. We also learned that extensions help to organize code as well as add functionality without having to change the main class or struct with which we are working.

In the next chapter, we are going to display data on our restaurant list. We will also set up our restaurant detail page to display data.

17
Working with an API

When building iOS apps, data can be the most critical part. Typically, the apps you make require getting data from an online data source, known as an **Application Programming Interface** (**API**). In the previous chapters, we have only worked with a plist to supply our data. Using a plist bridges the gap to understanding how to work with an API, as you will see shortly. In this chapter, we will work with an API that is in **JavaScript Object Notation** (**JSON**) format. This format is typical no matter which backend service was used to create the JSON. In this chapter, we will cover:

- What a JSON file is and the different components of this data feed
- Passing data using segues
- What extensions are and how to use them to clean up your code

For our app, we need one class to handle our data, but we need to share it with both our Explore View Controller and Map View Controller. Let's first understand the responsibility of our API Manager.

Creating an API Manager

In this chapter, we will be building an API Manager. This manager will be responsible for anything that has to do with getting data from online. When dealing with data online, you will typically get it in a particular format, which you then need to convert into something that your app can read.

What is an API?

A RESTful API is a web service from which an app can receive data. Typically, when you are dealing with APIs, such as YELP, they tend to change often. For our purposes, we want to use static files so that we can work on this project without having to be concerned about changes to the API. Therefore, most of the data we are going to use comes from the site, `http://opentable.herokuapp.com/`, which is not managed full time and does not change often. The site's API, however, is missing some data that we need; therefore, I have updated these files (which are in the project files for this chapter) to include that missing data.

APIs are typically in JSON format, and working with them is similar to working with plists. The transition from one to the other should be pretty seamless. Let's get familiar with the JSON format.

Understanding a JSON file

Before we write any code, we need to take a look at the structure of a simple JSON file. Let's create a new group inside the `Misc` folder in the `Navigator` panel called `JSON`. Then, drag and drop all of the JSON files found in the project files for this chapter into the new `JSON` folder, by clicking on **Finish** in the screen that appears. Lastly, open up the `Charleston.json` file and let's review the first part of it, including the first restaurant listing:

```
{
    "total_entries": 67,
    "per_page": 25,
    "current_page": 1,
    "restaurants": [
        {
            "id": 147475,
            "name": "Union Provisions",
            "address": "513 King Street",
            "city": "Charleston",
            "state": "SC",
            "area": "South Carolina",
            "postal_code": "29403",
            "country": "US",
            "phone": "8436410821x",
            "lat": 32.790291,
            "lng": -79.93936,
            "price": 2,
            "reserve_url": "http://www.opentable.com/single.aspx?rid=147475",
            "mobile_reserve_url": "http://mobile.opentable.com/opentable/?restId=147475",
            "image_url": "https://www.opentable.com/img/restimages/147475.jpg",
            "cuisines": [
                {
                    "cuisine": "American"
                },
                {
                    "cuisine": "Bar"
                }
            ]
        },
```

This file has four nodes inside it, `total_entries`, `per_page`, `current_page`, and `restaurants`. When you work with a feed, it will split items up into pages so that you are not trying to load all the data at once. This feed tells us that there are 67 total pages with 25 restaurants per page and that we are currently on page one. We do not need the first three nodes in this book since we are just going to load 25 restaurants.

The `restaurant`'s node, on the other hand, is essential for the purposes of this book. The restaurant's node is an array of data, recognizable as such by the brackets ([ ]) used in the node. If you review the individual items in the restaurant's node, you will notice that everything needed for our app's name, address, city, and so on, is covered. This structure is the same as that which we saw in the plists earlier in this book. If you look at cuisines, you will notice that it is wrapped inside brackets ([ ]). Again, this is what we had in our plist data previously. We have an idea of what a JSON file looks like; let's see how we can work with it.

Working with an API

Exploring the API Manager file

We just created our `API Manager` folder; now, let's create the `API Manager` file:

1. Right-click on the `Misc` folder in the `Common` folder of the Navigator panel and select **New File**.
2. Inside the **Choose a template for your new file** screen, select **iOS** at the top. Then, select **Swift File**. Hit **Next** after.
3. Name this file `RestaurantAPIManager`, and hit **Create**.

We need to define our class definition first; therefore, add the following to the `import` statement:

```
import Foundation
struct RestaurantAPIManager {   (A)
    static func loadJSON(file name:String) -> [[String:AnyObject]] {
        var items = [[String : AnyObject]]()
                                            (C)
        guard let path = Bundle.main.path(forResource: name, ofType: "json"),
            let data = NSData(contentsOfFile: path) else {
            return [[:]]
        }
        do {
            let json = try JSONSerialization.jsonObject(with: data as Data, options: .allowFragments) as AnyObject
            if let restaurants = json["restaurants"] as? [[String: AnyObject]] {
                items = restaurants as [[String : AnyObject]]
            }
        }
        catch {
            print("error serializing JSON: \(error)")
            items = [[:]]
        }

        return items  (G)
    }
}
```

- **Part A**: Here, we defined the class.

    ```
    struct RestaurantAPIManager {
    ```

- **Part B**: The `loadJSON()` method is known as a type method because it has the `static` keyword in front of it. Type methods are called using the dot syntax. Static functions cannot be overridden.

    ```
    static func loadJSON(file name:String) -> [[String:AnyObject]] {
    ```

[456]

The next bullet list explains what we need to write when we want to call the `loadJSON` method inside the `RestaurantAPIManager` file.

- **Part C**: Calling this method will return an array of dictionary objects. If this sounds familiar, it is because our plist data returns the same thing.

    ```
    var items = [[String: AnyObject]]()
    ```

- **Part D**: On this line, we are declaring an array of dictionary objects.

    ```
    guard let path = Bundle.main.path(forResource: name, ofType:
    "json"), let data = NSData(contentsOfFile: path) else {
        return [[:]]
    }
    ```

- **Part E**: Since we are not loading from the internet, we need to make sure to call the right filename. If the path is found and there is nothing wrong with the data, we will use the data. Otherwise, we will return an empty array with no dictionary objects.

Here, we are using a `do...catch`. To employ it, we must utilize it with what is known as a try. We first try to serialize or convert the data from the JSON file; if that is successful, we can then access the information inside that file. To obtain the restaurant items in the JSON file (all of which are located inside the restaurant's node), we used `json["restaurants"]`.

Next, we cast this using the `as?` as an array of dictionary objects. Also, since our data types are mixed, we used `AnyObject` to accept the dictionary of mixed data types. Finally, we set our data to the array of items. We now have the same structure, an array of dictionary objects that we had in the `Map` section.

```
do {
let json = try JSONSerialization.jsonObject(with: data as Data,
options: .allowFragments) as AnyObject
if let restaurants = json["restaurants"] as? [[String: AnyObject]]
{
        items = restaurants as [[String : AnyObject]]
    }
}
```

- **Part F**: This `catch` will run only if there is a problem serializing the data from the file. If there is a problem, we will return an empty array with no dictionary objects. This allows for our app to keep running without crashing.

    ```
    catch {
      print("error serializing JSON: \(error)")
      items = [[:]]
    }
    ```

- **Part G**: Finally, if all goes well, we return the array of dictionary items back.

    ```
    return items
    ```

This entire class is built so that we can pass any name we want; it will return data if it finds the file.

Location list

Let's review how our app will work. A user will select a cuisine and location. Then, the location is passed to the Explore view. The user will get restaurants from the selected location filtered by the selected cuisine.

If this were online, we would pass the location to the API, and the API would return the JSON data. As you can see, we are doing the same. When you eventually deal with an API, the transition of working with online data will be seamless.

Selecting a location

Therefore, as stated earlier, to get data, we need a location. To get the location, we need to get it from the `LocationViewController`. When a location is selected, we will show a checkmark. We will need this checkmark to update each time a new item is set. Finally, when the **Done** button is tapped, we need to pass this location to `ExploreViewController`.

Let's update our `LocationViewController` first. We need a variable to keep track of the selected location. Add the following inside the `LocationViewController.swift` file, under the constant manager:

```
var selectedCity:String?
```

Then, we need to create a new extension for `UITableViewDelegate`, as follows. Add the following after our `UITableViewDataSource` extension:

```
//MARK: UITableViewDelegate
extension LocationViewController: UITableViewDelegate {
}
```

As we discussed earlier in the book, delegates supply the behavior. Here, we want a behavior for when the user selects a Table View row and another behavior for when the user deselects the row. First, let's add the selection behavior into our new extension by adding the following code:

```
func tableView(_ tableView: UITableView, didSelectRowAt indexPath:IndexPath) {
    if let cell = tableView.cellForRow(at: indexPath) {
        cell.accessoryType = .checkmark
        selectedCity = manager.locationItem(at:indexPath)
        tableView.reloadData()
    }
}
```

Here, we will get the cell of the selected row and set its `accessoryType` to a `checkmark`. Then, we will get the location and set it to the `selectedCity` variable. To only see the `checkmark` in our Table View cell, we need to remove the disclosure arrow and gray cell selection. Let's update this by doing the following:

1. Open `Explore.storyboard`.
2. Select the Table View `locationCell` in the **Location View Controller**.
3. Select the Attributes inspector in the Utilities panel, and update the **Selection** field from **Gray** to **None**.
4. Next, update the **Accessory** field from **Disclosure Indicator** to **None**.

Adding a Header view

Our **Explore** has a header, and we need to pass data over to it. To do that, we need to create a header class for it:

1. Right-click on the **Explore** folder and select **New File**.
2. Inside the **Choose a template for your new file** screen, select **iOS** at the top. Then, select **Cocoa Touch Class**. Hit **Next** after.
3. In the options screen that appears, add the following:

   New file:
   - **Class**: `ExploreHeaderView`
   - **Subclass**: `UICollectionReusableView`
   - **Also create XIB**: Unchecked
   - **Language**: `Swift`

4. Click **Next** and then **Create**.
5. Add the following to this file:

   ```
   import UIKit
   class ExploreHeaderView: UICollectionReusableView {
       @IBOutlet weak var lblLocation:UILabel!
   }
   ```

6. Next, open the `Explore.storyboard` file and under the Identity inspector in the Utilities panel, update the **Class** to `ExploreHeaderView`.

Now, let's work on passing data from a location to explore and display the selected location in our header.

Chapter 17

Passing a selected location back to Explore View

Now, we need to be able to send the selected city back to our `ExploreViewController`. Therefore, we need a selected city, as well as an unwind for the **Done** button inside `ExploreViewController`. First, let's get our selected city to display in our **Explore** view:

1. Add the following variable under the constant manager in our `ExploreViewController.swift` file:

   ```
   var selectedCity:String?
   var headerView: ExploreHeaderView!
   ```

2. Next, open `Explore.storyboard` and select the **Explore Header View** in the Outline view.

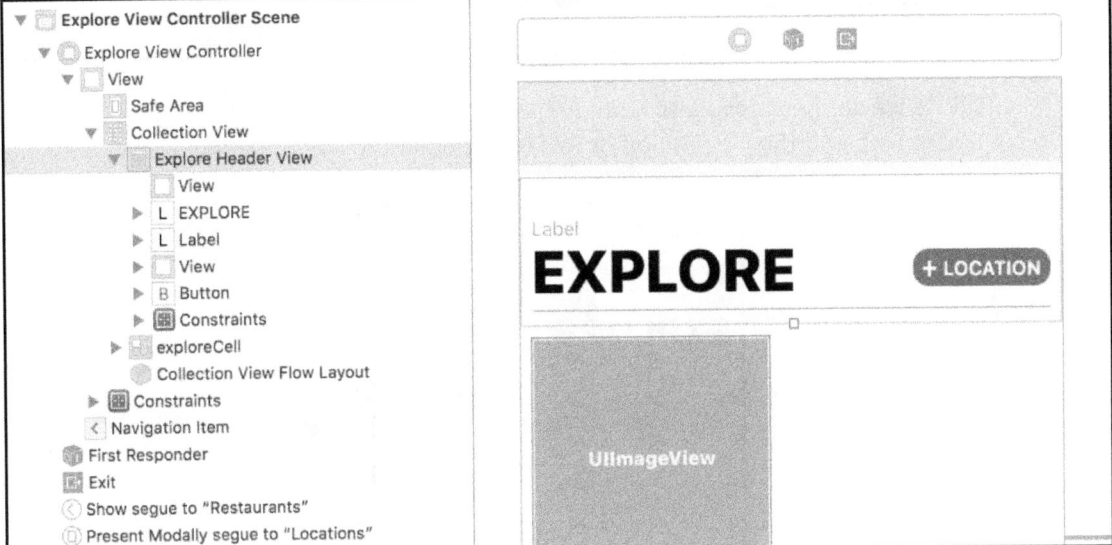

Working with an API

3. Then, select the Connections inspector in the Utilities panel, and click and drag from the empty circle `lblLocation` under Outlets to the label in the **Explore View Controller Header** scene:

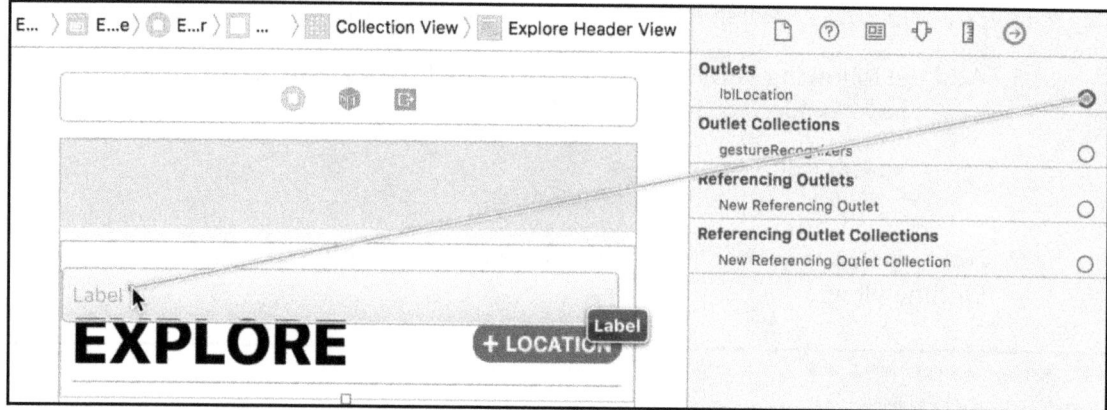

4. While we are here, let's also update this label to say, `PLEASE SELECT A LOCATION`, and the label below it to say `EXPLORE`:

Next, let's unwind our **Done** button in our **Explore View Controller**.

Unwinding our Done button

Earlier in the book, we added an unwind for our **Cancel** button. Now we need to make it so that our **Done** button can also dismiss the modal, but we also want to capture the selected location when the user is done. Let's add this code next:

1. Open the `ExploreViewController.swift` file again and, in the `private` extension under the `unwindLocationCancel()` function, add the following code:

    ```
    @IBAction func unwindLocationDone(segue:UIStoryboardSegue) {
        if let viewController = segue.source as? LocationViewController {
            selectedCity = viewController.selectedCity
            if let location = selectedCity {
                headerView.lblLocation.text = location
            }
        }
    }
    ```

    The code we just added is checking the source of the segue. If its source is a class of `LocationViewController`, then we want to grab the selected city and set the `selectedCity` variable inside `ExploreViewController` to that city. We then use an `if...let` statement to make sure that `selectedCity` is not `nil`; if it is not, then we set the label in the header to the currently selected city. Now, we need to hook up this `IBAction`.

2. In your `UICollectionViewDataSource` extension, update `collectionView:viewForSupplementaryElementOfKind:atIndexPath:` with the following:

    ```
    func collectionView(_ collectionView: UICollectionView,
    viewForSupplementaryElementOfKind kind: String, at indexPath:
    IndexPath) -> UICollectionReusableView {
        let header =
    collectionView.dequeueReusableSupplementaryView(ofKind: kind,
    withReuseIdentifier: "header", for: indexPath)
        headerView = header as! LocationHeaderView
        return headerView
    }
    ```

Working with an API

3. Next, open `Locations.storyboard`.
4. Now, *Ctrl* + drag from the **Done** button in the **Location View Controller** to **Exit** in the **Location View Controller** scene:

5. When you let go, select `unwindLocationDoneWithSegue:` in the menu that appears:

Let's build and run the project by hitting the Play button (or use *cmd* + *R*). You should now be able to select a location; when you hit **Done**, the Explore Header view should show you the selected location:

Getting the last selected location

We have a couple of issues that we need to correct under **Select a location**. You will notice that when you click on **Select a location**, you can check multiple locations. We only want the user to be able to select one location. Also, the checkmark next to your selected location disappears if you click on **Done** in **Location View** and then click to choose a location again. We need to set the last selected location so that it is saved when you go back to your location list. We can address these issues at the same time:

1. Open `Explore.storyboard`:
2. Select the segue that is connected to the `LocationViewController`.
3. Then, select the Attributes inspector in the Utilities panel and set **Identifier** under **Storyboard Segue** to **locationList**. Then, hit *Enter*:

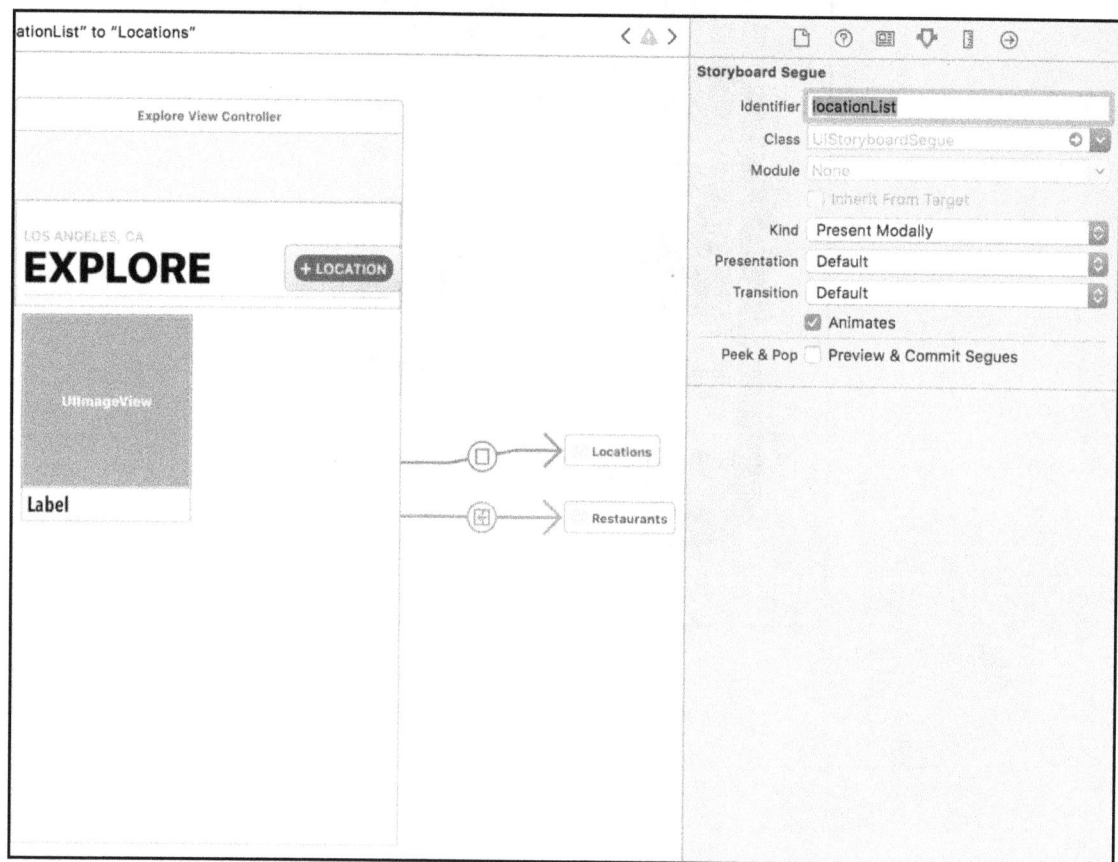

Chapter 17

4. Now, select the segue that is connected to the `RestaurantViewController` and set **Identifier** to `restaurantList`. Then, hit *Enter*:

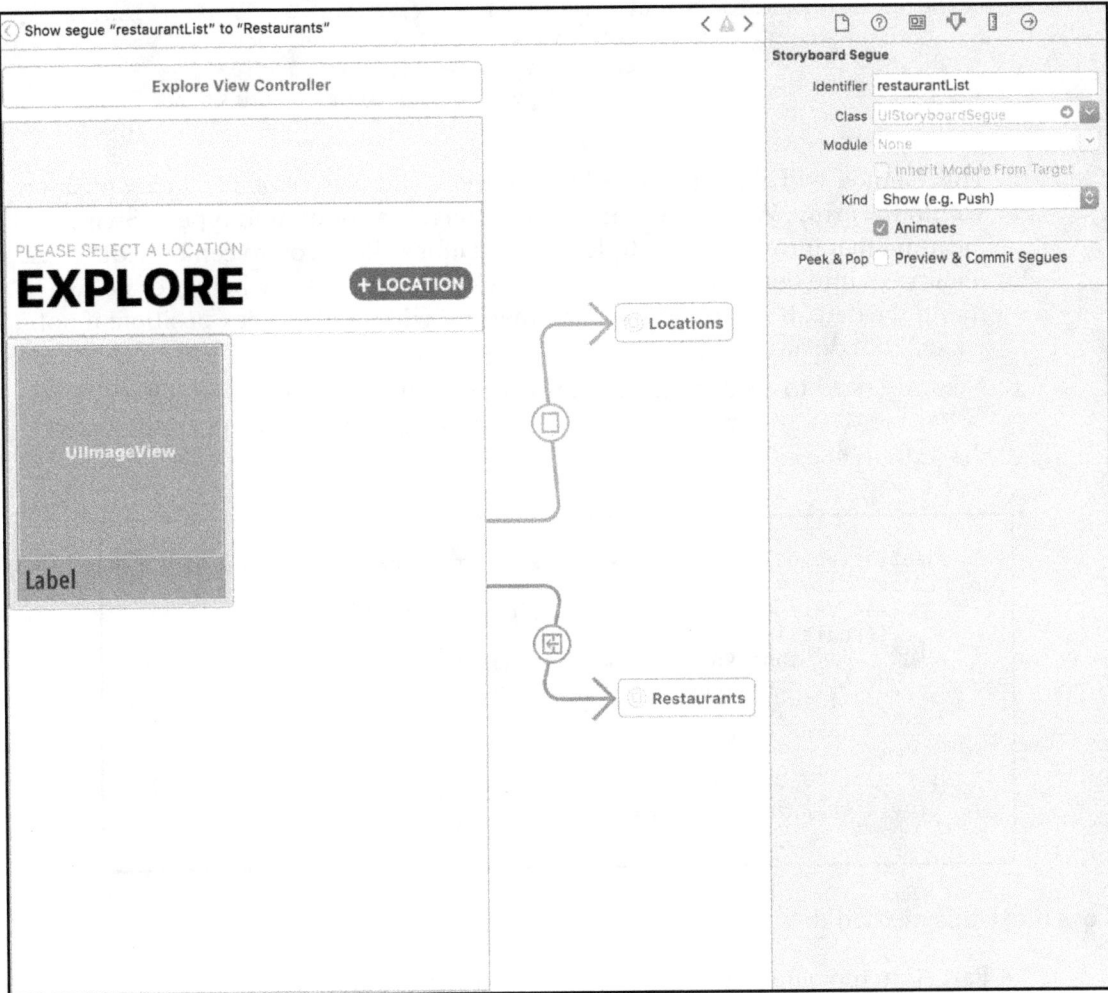

5. Next, we need to set up these identifiers. We are going to update the segue enum, which we created in the last chapter. Add the following code inside the `Segue.swift` file under the `Misc` folder in the `Common` folder:

```
case restaurantList
case locationList
```

Working with an API

6. Then, open up the `LocationDataManager.swift` file and add the following code before the last curly brace:

   ```
   func findLocation(by name:String) -> (isFound:Bool, position:Int) {
           guard let index = arrLocations.index(of: name) else
           { return (isFound:false, position:0) }
           return (isFound:true, position:index)
   }
   ```

7. This method will allow us to find the location, and then obtain its index position within the array. We will return a tuple, which is a compound type in Swift, meaning that it can hold multiple values. Tuples allow you to combine different data types into one. The method will check the tuple to see whether or not we found the data. If we found the data, then we will use the index position; if not, we will not do anything.

8. Next, we need to check whether or not a previous location was set. Open up the `LocationViewController.swift` file and create the following method after the `viewDidLoad()` method:

   ```
   func set(selected cell:UITableViewCell, at indexPath:IndexPath) {   A
       if let city = selectedCity {                                     B
           let data = manager.findLocation(by: city)                    C
           if data.isFound {                                            D
               if indexPath.row == data.position {
                   cell.accessoryType = .checkmark
               }
               else { cell.accessoryType = .none }
           }
       }
       else { cell.accessoryType = .none }                              E
   }
   ```

Let's break this method down:

- **Part A**: In the parameters of this method, we are taking in a cell and an index path:

   ```
   set(cell:at)
   if let city = selectedCity
   ```

[468]

- **Part B**: Here, we are checking to make sure that the selected city is set.

  ```
  let data = manager.findLocation(by: city)
  ```

- **Part C**: Then, we are calling the method we created in `LocationDataManager`, passing the selected city into the manager, and getting back a tuple of data.

  ```
  if data.isFound {
      if indexPath.row == data.position {
          cell.accessoryType = .checkmark
      }
      else { cell.accessoryType = .none }
  }
  ```

- **Part D**: Next, we are checking to see if data was found in the tuple; if so, we are checking to see if the selected row is the same as the position in the array. If the row and position are the same, we are directing the cell to set its accessoryType to a checkmark; otherwise, the accessoryType will be set to none.

  ```
  else { cell.accessoryType = .none }
  ```

- **Part E**: Finally, if no data is found, we are setting `accessoryType` to none. Add the following inside `cellForRowAt()` after we set the text for the cell:

  ```
  set(selected: cell, at: indexPath)
  ```

Build and run the project by hitting the Play button (or use *cmd* + *R*). You should see that you can only select one location now. However, after you select the location, if you click on **Done** in the **Location** view and then click to show locations again, your last selected location is not saved. We still need to address that issue, which we will do next.

Passing location and cuisine to the restaurant list

Open the `ExploreViewController.swift` file, and inside the `private` extension add the following method above the `unwindLocationCancel()` method:

```
func showLocationList(segue:UIStoryboardSegue) {
    guard let navController = segue.destination as? UINavigationController,
        let viewController = navController.topViewController as? LocationViewController else {
            return
    }
}
```

```
        guard let city = selectedCity else { return }
        viewController.selectedCity = city
}
```

Our `showLocationList()` method will be called whenever our destination view has a Navigation Controller. Then, it checks to see if the `topViewController` is of the class `LocationViewController`. If either of these two statements is `false`, we do nothing. If both are `true`, we check the `selectedCity;`. If it is `nil`, then we also do nothing. If the `selectedCity` has a location, we set the `selectedCity` variable inside the `LocationViewController` to the `selectedCity` in the `ExploreViewController`. This will save the last selected location if we return to the locations list after having selected a location earlier.

We also need to pass the selected city over to the `RestaurantViewController`. Therefore, add the following variables inside the `RestaurantViewController.swift` file above your `@IBOutlet var collectionView:`

```
var selectedRestaurant:RestaurantItem?
var selectedCity:LocationItem?
var selectedType:String?
```

While still in the `RestaurantViewController.swift` file, add the following code under the `viewDidLoad()` method:

```
override func viewDidAppear(_ animated: Bool) {
  super.viewDidAppear(animated)
  print("selected city \(selectedCity as Any)")
  print("selected type \(selectedType as Any)")
}
```

The `viewDidAppear()` method will get called every time we load the View Controller, whereas the `viewDidLoad()` method only gets called once. We can print the `selectedCity` variable to verify that we are, in fact, passing the location over correctly.

Next, open the `ExploreViewController.swift` file again and add the following under the `showLocationList()` method inside:

```
func showRestaurantListing(segue:UIStoryboardSegue) {
    if let viewController = segue.destination as? RestaurantViewController,
let city = selectedCity,
        let index = collectionView.indexPathsForSelectedItems?.first, let type = manager.explore(at: index).name {
            viewController.selectedType = type
            viewController.selectedCity = city
    }
}
```

We now check to see if the segue destination is `RestaurantViewController`, and we make sure that `selectedCity` is set in `ExploreViewController`. Next, we get the selected `indexPath` of the Collection view. Once we have that, we then get the item from the `ExploreDataManager` at the `index` position. Finally, we get the name from the item. If we get all those items back, then we pass the `selectedCity` and `selectedType` variables to the `RestaurantViewController`. If we do not, then we will display an alert, letting the user know that they need to select a location first. Let's create the three methods that will display such an alert:

1. First, we will create the actual alert. While still in the `ExploreViewController`, add the following code before `unwindLocationCancel()`:

    ```
    func showAlert() {
                    let alertController = UIAlertController(title: "Location Needed", message:"Please select a location.", preferredStyle: .alert)
                    let okAction = UIAlertAction(title: "OK", style: .default, handler: nil)
                    alertController.addAction(okAction)
                    present(alertController, animated: true, completion: nil)
    }
    ```

2. Then, we need to check that we have a location; if not, we want to make sure that the user cannot go to the restaurant list. Inside the `ExploreViewController`, add the following method after the `viewDidLoad()` method:

    ```
    override func shouldPerformSegue(withIdentifier identifier: String, sender: Any?) -> Bool {
        if identifier == Segue.restaurantList.rawValue {
            guard selectedCity != nil else {
                showAlert()
    ```

Working with an API

```
            return false
        }
        return true
    }
    return true
}
```

Here, we check whether the segue equals `restaurantList;`. If it does, we check to see if the `selectedCity` variable is set. If we return `true`, then the segue will be performed, and we will go to the restaurant list. If we return `false`, then we display our alert, letting the users know that they need to select a location first.

3. Lastly, we need to show either the location list or restaurant list, depending on whether or not the user chose a location before trying to see the restaurant list. Add the following method after `viewDidLoad()`, and before the `shouldPerformSegue` method we just added:

```
override func prepare(for segue: UIStoryboardSegue, sender: Any?) {
    switch segue.identifier! {
        case Segue.locationList.rawValue:
            showLocationList(segue: segue)
        case Segue.restaurantList.rawValue:
            showRestaurantListing(segue: segue)
        default:
            print("Segue not added")
    }
}
```

The `prepare()` method checks which identifier is called. If it is the location list, then we call the `showLocationList()` method; if it is the restaurant list, then we call the `showRestaurantListing()` method.

Now, build and run the project by hitting the Play button (or use *cmd* + *R*). If you try to select a cuisine first, you should not be able to go to the restaurant list. Instead, you should receive an alert, stating that you need to select a location:

If you pick a location, hit **Done**, and then tap the locations list again, you should see your location still selected. Now, if you select a cuisine, you should be directed to the restaurant listing and see the selected location printing in the Debug panel. If you do not see that panel, you can open it using the toggle or *cmd + Shift + Y*.

```
selected city Optional(LetsEat.LocationItem(state: Optional("NC"), city: Optional("Charleston")))
selected type Optional("Bistro")
```

Now that we have the location, we need to check our `RestaurantAPIManager` for data. Therefore, let's update our `print` statement inside the `RestaurantViewController` by revising the `viewDidAppear()` method to the following:

```
override func viewDidAppear(_ animated: Bool) {
    guard let location = selectedCity?.city, let type = selectedType else {
        return
    }
    
    print("type \(type)")
    print(RestaurantAPIManager.loadJSON(file: location))
}
```

Working with an API

You should now see the type selected, along with an array of dictionary objects, in the Debug panel:

```
type Bistro
[[["state": SC, "city": Charleston, "country": US, "name": Union Provisions, "address": 513 King Street, "lat":
32.790291, "price": 2, "reserve_url": http://www.opentable.com/single.aspx?rid=147475, "long":
-79.93935999999999, "id": 147475, "phone": 8436410821x, "image_url": https://www.opentable.com/img/restimages/
147475.jpg, "mobile_reserve_url": http://mobile.opentable.com/opentable/?restId=147475, "area": South
Carolina, "postal_code": 29403, "cuisines": <__NSArrayI 0x608000232e80>(
{
    cuisine = Pizza;
},
{
    cuisine = Italian;
}
)
], ["state": SC, "city": Charleston, "country": US, "name": McCrady's, "address": 2 Unity Alley, "lat":
32.778, "price": 4, "reserve_url": http://www.opentable.com/single.aspx?rid=3751, "long": -79.92700000000001,
"id": 3751, "phone": 8435770025x1, "image_url": https://www.opentable.com/img/restimages/3751.jpg,
"mobile_reserve_url": http://mobile.opentable.com/opentable/?restId=3751, "area": South Carolina,
"postal_code": 29401, "cuisines": <__NSArrayI 0x6080002311c0>(
{
```

Now that we have our data, let's get that data to display in our `RestaurantViewController`. To do this, we need to set up our cell as well as a restaurant data manager. The restaurant data manager, rather than the `RestaurantViewController`, will be the class that uses our `RestaurantAPIManager`.

Creating our restaurant cell class

Now, we need to create a file so that we can connect to the cell:

1. Inside the `Restaurants` folder in the Navigator panel, right-click on the `View` folder and select **New File**.
2. Inside the **Choose a template for your new file** screen, select **iOS** at the top and then **Cocoa Touch Class**. Then, hit **Next**.

3. In the options screen that appears, add the following:

   New file:

   - **Class**: `RestaurantCell`
   - **Subclass**: `UICollectionViewCell`
   - **Also create XIB file**: Unchecked
   - **Language**: `Swift`

4. Click **Next** and then **Create**. Your file should look like the following:

   ```
   import UIKit
   class RestaurantCell: UICollectionViewCell {
   }
   ```

5. Inside the class declaration, add the following:

   ```
   @IBOutlet weak var lblTitle:UILabel!
   @IBOutlet weak var lblCuisine:UILabel!
   @IBOutlet weak var imgRestaurant: UIImageView!
   ```

6. Save the file.

Now that our file is set up, let's get our outlets connected.

Setting up restaurant list cell outlets

We need to set up our `restaurantCell` outlets:

1. Open `Explore.storyboard` and select our `restaurantCell` again in the Outline view.
2. Now, in the Utilities panel, select the Identity inspector.
3. Under **Custom Class**, in the **Class** drop-down menu, select **RestaurantCell** and hit *Enter* in order connect the **Cell** to the class.
4. Now, select the Connections inspector.

5. Click on and drag from the empty circle `lblTitle` under Outlets to the top label in our `restaurantCell`:

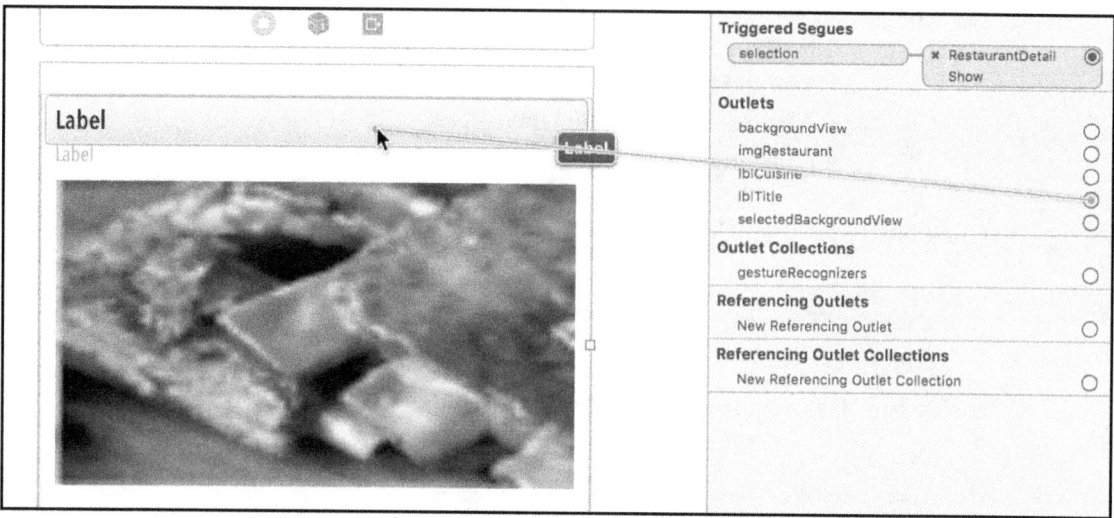

6. Click on and drag from the empty circle `lblCuisine` under Outlets to the other label in our `restaurantCell`:

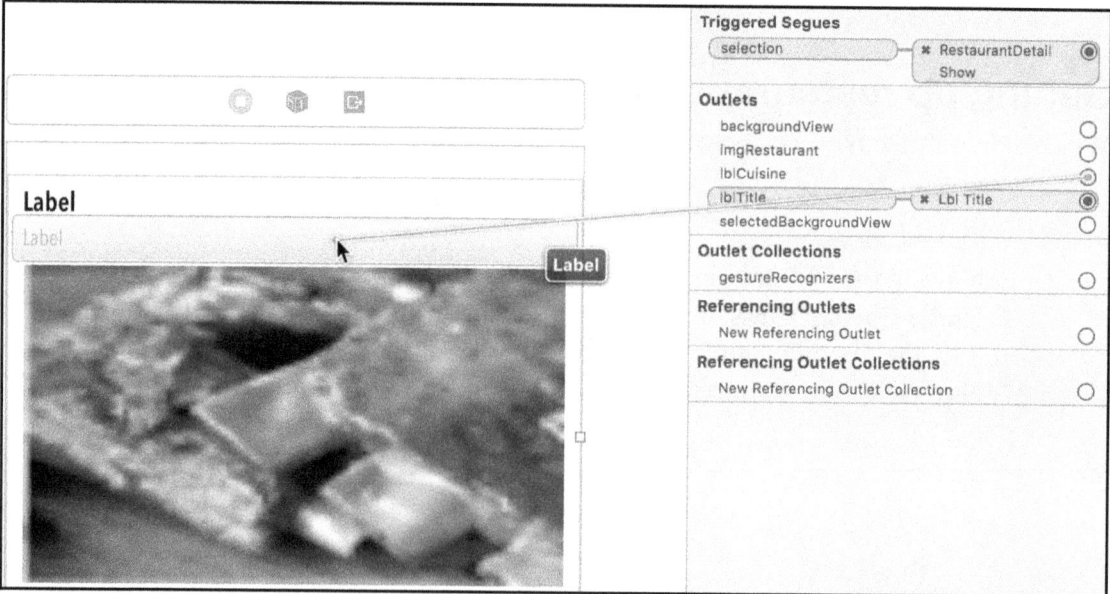

Chapter 17

7. Click on and drag from the empty circle `imgRestaurant` under Outlets to the image in our `restaurantCell`:

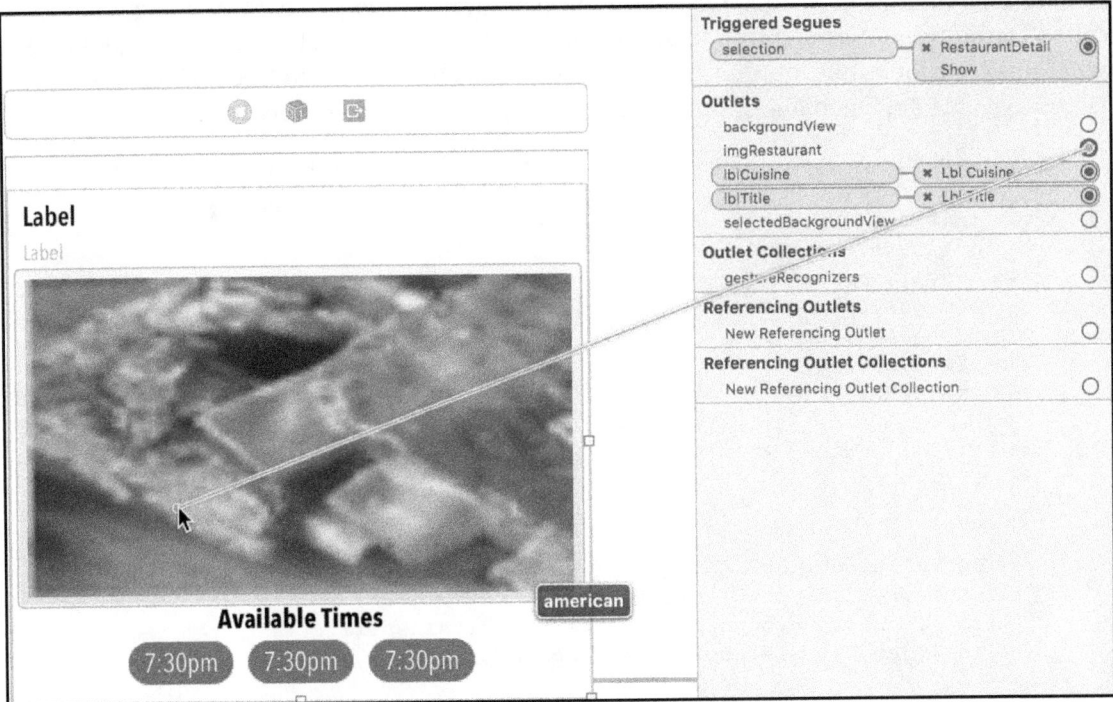

Now that we have our `restaurantListCell` outlets set up, let's get some data into our cell. We previously created our `RestaurantItem.swift` file; we will use this in our restaurant list.

Creating a restaurant data manager

We need to create a data manager for our restaurants, but before we do that we need to update a few things. In Swift 4, we have a more natural way to parse JSON using what is called **Decodable**. We need first to update our `RestaurantItem`, but before we get into what this code looks like, our `RestaurantItem` needs to conform to Decodable. Open `RestaurantItem`. Open `RestaurantItem` and update it to the following:

```swift
class RestaurantItem: NSObject, MKAnnotation, Decodable {
    var name: String?
    var cuisines:[String] = []
    var latitude: Double?
    var longitude:Double?
    var address:String?
    var postalCode:String?
    var state:String?
    var imageURL:String?
    
    var title: String? {
        return name
    }
    
    var subtitle: String? {
        if cuisines.isEmpty { return "" }
        else if cuisines.count == 1 { return cuisines.first }
        else { return cuisines.joined(separator: ", ") }
    }
    
    var coordinate: CLLocationCoordinate2D {
        guard let lat = latitude, let long = longitude else {
            return CLLocationCoordinate2D() }
        return CLLocationCoordinate2D(latitude: lat, longitude: long )
    }
}
```

Now we have a `Location` object that returns an `RestaurantItems` array, just like our JSON data.

Let's create the `RestaurantDataManager` file now:

1. Right-click on the `Restaurants` folder and select **New File**.
2. Inside the **Choose a template for your new file** screen, select **iOS** at the top and then **Swift File**. Then, hit **Next**:
3. Name this file `RestaurantDataManager`, and hit **Create**.

We need to define our class definition first, so add the following under the `import` statement in this new file:

```
class RestaurantDataManager {
}
```

Inside the class declaration, add the following variable:

```
private var items:[RestaurantItem] = []
```

Here, we keep our array `private`, since there is no reason to have to access this outside of the class.

Now, let's add the following three methods:

```
func fetch(by location:String, withFilter:String="All",
completionHandler:() -> Swift.Void) {
    var restaurants:[RestaurantItem] = []
    for restaurant in RestaurantAPIManager.loadJSON(file: location) {
        restaurants.append(RestaurantItem(dict: restaurant))
    }

    if withFilter != "All" {
        items = restaurants.filter({ $0.cuisines.contains(withFilter) })
    }
    else { items = restaurants }
    completionHandler()
}
func numberOfItems() -> Int {
    return items.count
}

func restaurantItem(at index:IndexPath) -> RestaurantItem {
    return items[index.item]
}
```

[479]

Working with an API

The first method here differs from the one we looked at in `ExploreDataManager`, whereas the last two methods here are the same as those in `ExploreDataManager`.

```
import Foundation

class RestaurantDataManager {
    private var items:[RestaurantItem] = []         ── A

    func fetch(by location:String, withFilter:String="All",  completionHandler:() -> Swift.Void) {
        var restaurants:[RestaurantItem] = []                    C                                                    B

        for restaurant in RestaurantAPIManager.loadJSON(file: location) {
            restaurants.append(RestaurantItem(dict: restaurant))     D
        }

        if withFilter != "All" {
            items = restaurants.filter({ $0.cuisines.contains(withFilter) })  ── E
        }
        else { items = restaurants }

        completionHandler()  F
    }
G   func numberOfItems() -> Int {
        return items.count
    }

H   func restaurantItem(at index:IndexPath) -> RestaurantItem {
        return items[index.item]
    }
}
```

Let's break these methods down to better understand what we are doing:

- **Part A**: In the parameters of this method, we are passing in a cell and an index path.

    ```
    private var items:[RestaurantItem] = []
    ```

- **Part B**: This function is pretty long; however, we are simply fetching restaurants with a location as a filter. We have a closure block, which will allow us to let the function run until it is complete.

    ```
    fetch(location:withFilter:completionHandler)
    ```

- **Part C**: In this parameter, we are setting a default. If we do not pass anything into this parameter, it will use `All`; otherwise, it will use whatever we give it.

    ```
    withFilter:String="All"
    ```

As you type your code, Xcode will provide code hints (choices) that it believes that you might want. When you type this method, Xcode gives you two hints, one that includes the `withFilter` parameter, and one that does not:

```
M    Void fetch(by: String, completionHandler: () -> Void)
M    Void fetch(by: String, withFilter: String, completionHandler: () -> Void)
     Int numberOfItems()
     RestaurantItem restaurantItem(at: IndexPath)
```

- **Part D**: Here, we get restaurants from the JSON file.

    ```
    for restaurant in RestaurantAPIManager.loadJSON(file: location) {
        restaurants.append(RestaurantItem(dict: restaurant))
    }
    ```

- **Part E**: Here, we are filtering the restaurants by cuisine. Since our restaurants have multiple cuisines, we must check each cuisine, which is why we use contains.

    ```
    if withFilter != "All" {
        items = restaurants.filter({ $0.cuisines.contains(withFilter) })
    }
    else { items = restaurants }
    ```

- **Part F**: This is used to tell our method that we are finished.

    ```
    completionHandler()
    ```

- **Part G**: This method tells us how many restaurant items we have.

    ```
    numberOfItems()
    ```

- **Part H**: This method allows us to get the restaurant at the index position at which it is located.

    ```
    restaurantItem(at:)
    ```

Now we have a greater understanding of our restaurant data manager. We have done a lot of code, and some of it may not make full sense, but as long as you have a basic understanding then you will be fine.

Working with an API

Now we need to get the data displaying in our restaurant list. One of the most common things when displaying data is how to handle a Table View or Collection View when there is no data. Some of the filtering we are doing may return no results, so we should handle both cases. We are going to do this next.

Handling no data

It is common to want to create a custom view that you can reuse, but also have a visual representation of it as well. There are two common ways to do this; the first way we will do now, and the other we will do later in the book. You can create a `UIView` that comes with a **XIB** (pronounced zib or nib). This was the common way to create elements before storyboards, and it is still effective today. Let's create one now:

1. Right-click on the `Misc` folder and select **New Group** and call it `No Data`.
2. Then, right-click on the `No Data` folder and create a new file.
3. Inside the **Choose a template for your new file** screen, select **iOS** at the top. Then, select **Cocoa Touch Class**. Hit **Next** after.
4. In the options screen that appears, add the following:

    New file:

    - **Class**: `NoDataView`
    - **Subclass**: `UIView`
    - **Language**: `Swift`

5. Click **Next** and then **Create**.
6. Next, right-click on the `No Data` folder again and create a new file.
7. Inside the **Choose a template for your new file** screen, select **iOS** at the top. Then, select **View** under **User Interface**. Hit **Next** after.
8. Name the file `NoDataView` and hit **Create**.
9. First, open the `NoDataView.swift` file and add the following into this file:

```
class NoDataView: UIView {
    var view: UIView!
    @IBOutlet var lblTitle: UILabel!
    @IBOutlet var lblDesc: UILabel!

    override init(frame: CGRect) {
        super.init(frame: frame)
        setupView()
```

```swift
        }

        required init?(coder aDecoder: NSCoder) {
            super.init(coder: aDecoder)!
            setupView()
        }

        func loadViewFromNib() -> UIView {
            let nib = UINib(nibName: "NoDataView", bundle: Bundle.main)
            let view = nib.instantiate(withOwner: self, options: nil)[0] as! UIView
            return view
        }

        func setupView() {
            view = loadViewFromNib()
            view.frame = bounds
            view.autoresizingMask = [.flexibleWidth, .flexibleHeight]
            addSubview(view)
        }

        func set(title: String) {
            lblTitle.text = title
        }

        func set(desc: String) {
            lblDesc.text = desc
        }
    }
```

Our two `init` methods are required; just simply call `setupView()`. The `loadViewFromNib()` method is used to get our XIB file. Our `setupView()` is used to take the NIB and add it to the `UIView()`. Finally, we have two methods that set up our two labels. The first four methods are boilerplate code that you will write every time you want to create a `UIView` with a NIB (XIB) file. Next, let's get this set up:

1. Open `NoDataView.xib`.
2. Select **Files Owner** in the Outline. Then, open the Identity inspector and update **Class** to `NoDataView` and hit *Enter*.
3. Next, in the filter field of the object library, type `label`.
4. Then, drag out two labels into the view.

5. Select one of the labels; then, in the Attributes inspector, update the following values:

    - **Text**: Add `TITLE GOES HERE` into the empty text field under the text
    - **Color**: `Black`
    - **Alignment**: `Center`
    - **Font**: `Avenir Next Condensed Bold 26`

6. Then in the Size inspector, update the following values:

    - **Width**: `355`
    - **Height**: `36`

7. Select one of the labels; then, in the Attributes inspector, update the following values:

    - **Text**: Add `TITLE GOES HERE` into the empty text field under the text
    - **Color**: `Black`
    - **Alignment**: `Center`
    - **Font**: `Avenir Next Condensed Regular 17`

8. Then in the Size inspector, update the following values:

    - **Width**: `355`
    - **Height**: `21`

9. Select both labels and then the Pin icon. Enter the value of **Height** (should be checked).

10. Now with both labels selected, hit the Stack View icon or you can go to **Editor | Embed In | Stack View**.

11. Select the Stack View in the Outline view, and then the Pin icon. Enter the following values:

    - **Right**: `10`
    - **Left**: `10`

12. Then, the Align icon. Enter the following values:

    - **Horizontally in container**: (should be checked)
    - **Vertically in container**: (should be checked)

13. Select the **Files Owner** in the Outline view.
14. Then, open the Identity inspector and connect `lblTitle` to the label that says `TITLE GOES HERE`.
15. Connect `lblDesc` to the other label.

When you are done, you should see the following:

Working with an API

Now, let's finally connect everything. Open the `RestaurantViewController.swift` file.

1. Above the `selectedRestaurant` variable, add the following:

   ```
   var manager = RestaurantDataManager()
   ```

2. Next, add the following method inside the `private` extension:

   ```
   func createData() {
       guard let location = selectedCity?.city, let filter = selectedType else { return }
       manager.fetch(by: location, with: filter) { _ in
           if manager.numberOfItems() > 0 {
               collectionView.backgroundView = nil
           }
           else {
               let view = NoDataView(frame: CGRect(x: 0, y: 0, width: collectionView.frame.width, height: collectionView.frame.height))
               view.set(title: "Restaurants")
               view.set(desc: "No restaurants found.")
               collectionView.backgroundView = view
           }
           
           collectionView.reloadData()
       }
   }
   ```

This method is checking to see if we have a selected location and a filter. Then, we run the fetch method we created earlier. If we have items, we make sure our background view is `nil`. If not, we will create our `NoDataView` and set it to display `No restaurants found`. Finally, we reload the Collection View.

3. Next, lets update -collectionView:cellForItemAtIndexPath: by adding the following:

```swift
func collectionView(_ collectionView: UICollectionView,
cellForItemAt indexPath: IndexPath) -> UICollectionViewCell {
    let cell = collectionView.dequeueReusableCell(withReuseIdentifier: "restaurantCell", for: indexPath) as! RestaurantCell
    let item = manager.restaurantItem(at: indexPath)
    if let name = item.name { cell.lblTitle.text = name }
    if let cuisine = item.subtitle { cell.lblCuisine.text = cuisine
}
    if let image = item.imageURL {
        if let url = URL(string: image) {
            let data = try? Data(contentsOf: url)
            if let imageData = data {
                DispatchQueue.main.async {
                    cell.imgRestaurant.image = UIImage(data: imageData)
                }
            }
        }
    }
    return cell
}
```

Here, we are just passing data into our cell. We are displaying the title, cuisine, and the image.

4. Finally, update -collectionView:numberOfItemsInSection: to the following:

```swift
func collectionView(_ collectionView: UICollectionView,
numberOfItemsInSection section: Int) -> Int {
    return manager.numberOfItems()
}
```

5. Build and run the project, and you should now see the following either with data or without:

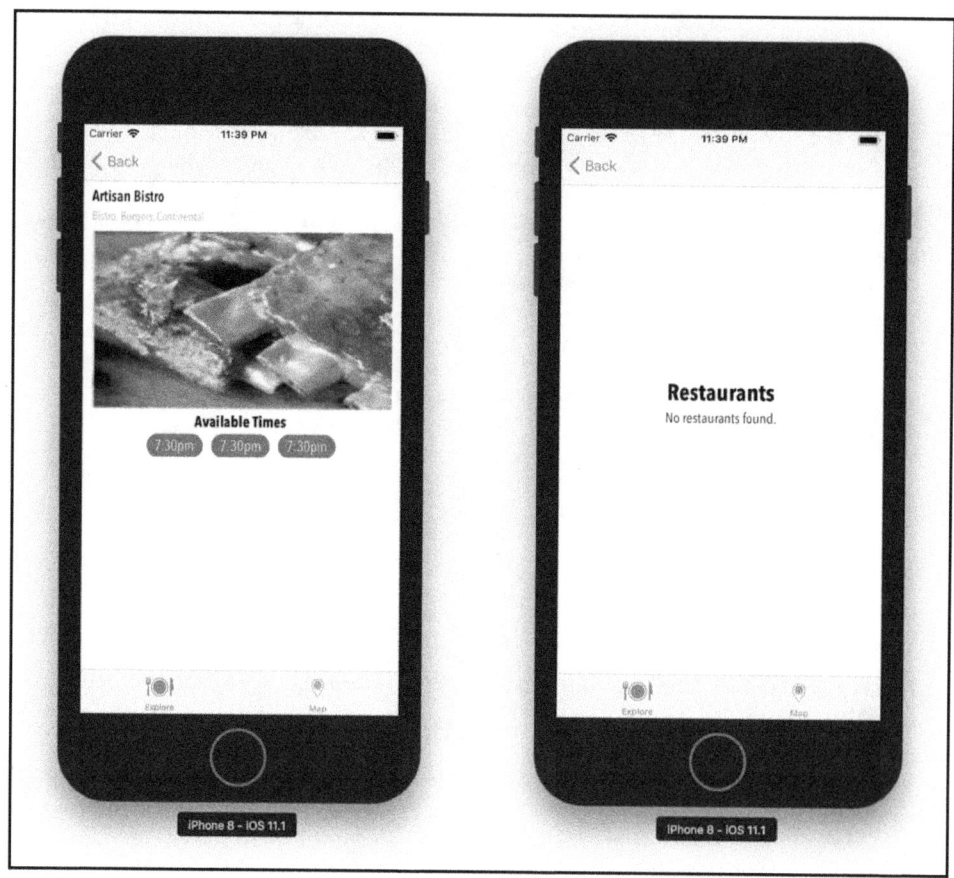

Before we wrap it up, let's add one more thing. When you select a location, let's display it on this view using the new iOS 11 large titles. Add the following into the private extension under `createData()`:

```
func setupTitle() {
    navigationController?.setNavigationBarHidden(false, animated: false)
    if let city = selectedCity?.city, let state = selectedCity?.state {
        title = "\(city.uppercased()), \(state.uppercased())"
    }
    navigationController?.navigationBar.prefersLargeTitles = true
}
```

Then, call `setupTitle()` after `createData` in the `viewDidAppear()` method. Build and run the project again, and you should now see the selected city. When you scroll, the large title will appear in the title view:

We are done with this chapter; good work. We did a lot, but you should be starting to see this app coming to life.

Summary

Well, we finally have data working in our app. We are not using a service, but if we wanted to, it would not be hard to add it. Working with local JSON files is the same as working with an API feed. You should feel confident having to do either. One thing I love to do is when I know what the feed is like, but I do not want to write that portion yet, I will create static JSON files of the feed and work with those. This allows me to focus on getting the app to where it needs to be, and not be stopped because of the API data layer.

In this chapter, we learned what JSON is and how to use that JSON feed to make data for our app. We also looked at how to pass data using segues. Finally, we looked at extensions and how they are useful for cleaning up and organizing code.

In the next chapter, we will look at how to display even more data.

18
Displaying Data in Restaurant Detail

Our app is coming together nicely, but we have one more section to do before we can start adding features. We have data in all of our views except for in our restaurant detail. In the last chapter, we passed data using segues, and we are going to do this again in this chapter. We have a few other things in this view that we need to set up before we move on to some of the features of the app; so in this chapter, we will cover:

- Passing data using segues
- Connecting IBOutlet to display data
- Displaying one annotation in a Map view

Let's set up our `RestaurantDetailViewController` by adding the following:

1. Add the following variables after the class declaration and before the `selectedRestaurant` variable:

    ```
    // Nav Bar
    @IBOutlet weak var btnHeart: UIBarButtonItem!

    // Cell One
    @IBOutlet weak var lblName: UILabel!
    @IBOutlet weak var lblCuisine: UILabel!
    @IBOutlet weak var lblHeaderAddress: UILabel!

    // Cell Two
    @IBOutlet weak var lblTableDetails: UILabel!

    // Cell Three
    @IBOutlet weak var lblOverallRating: UILabel!
    ```

Displaying Data in Restaurant Detail

```
// Cell Eight
@IBOutlet weak var lblAddress: UILabel!
@IBOutlet weak var imgMap: UIImageView!
```

2. Make sure you save the file.

Now that we've created our `IBOutlet`, we need to connect them:

1. Open the `RestaurantDetail.storyboard`, select the Restaurant Detail View Controller in the Outline view, and then open the Connections inspector in the Utilities panel.
2. Now click on and drag from the empty circle of each of the following variables we just added under Outlets to their respective elements listed as follows in either the scene or Outline view.
3. An empty circle for `imgMap` to the Map View in the Outline view:

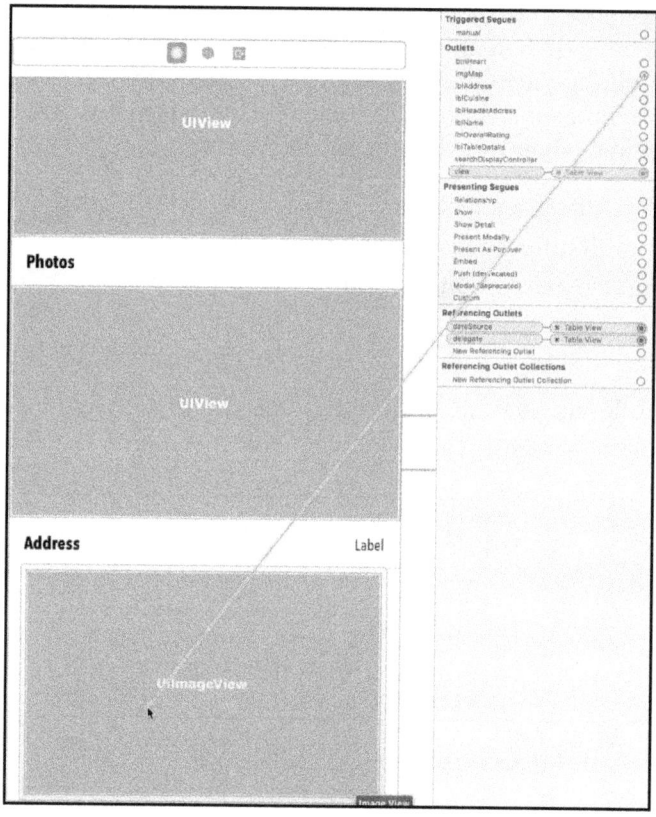

4. An empty circle for `lblAddress` to the address **Label** above the map:

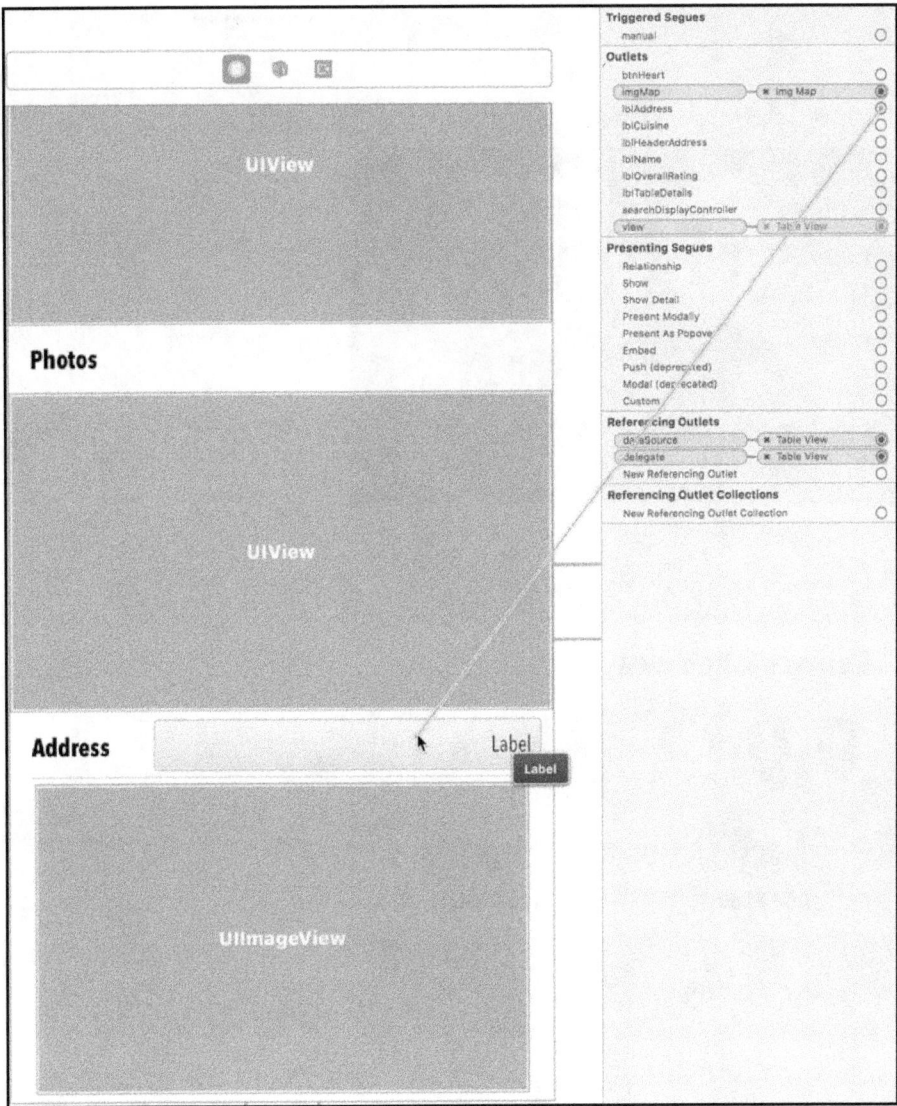

Displaying Data in Restaurant Detail

5. An empty circle for `lblOverallRating` to the **Label** inside the **Reviews** cell:

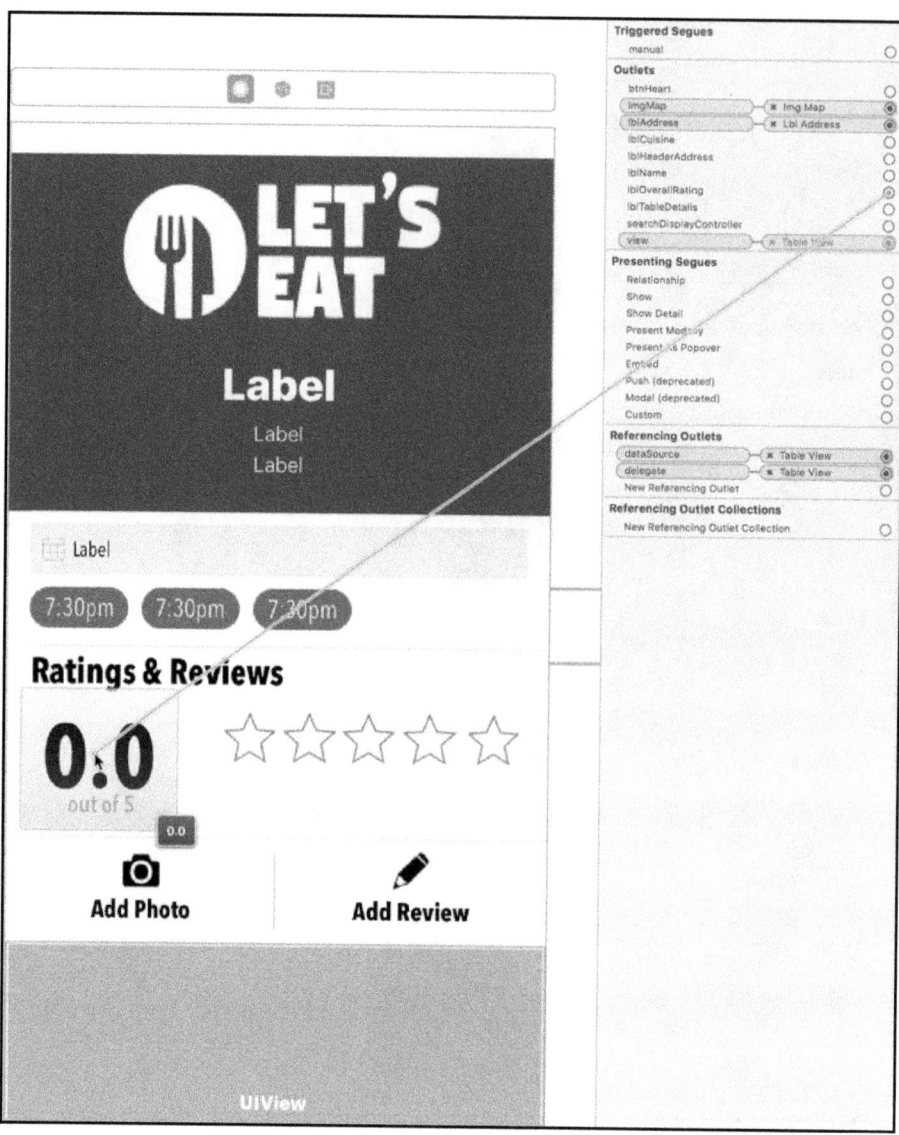

Chapter 18

6. An empty circle for `lblTableDetails` to the **Label** under the header in the scene:

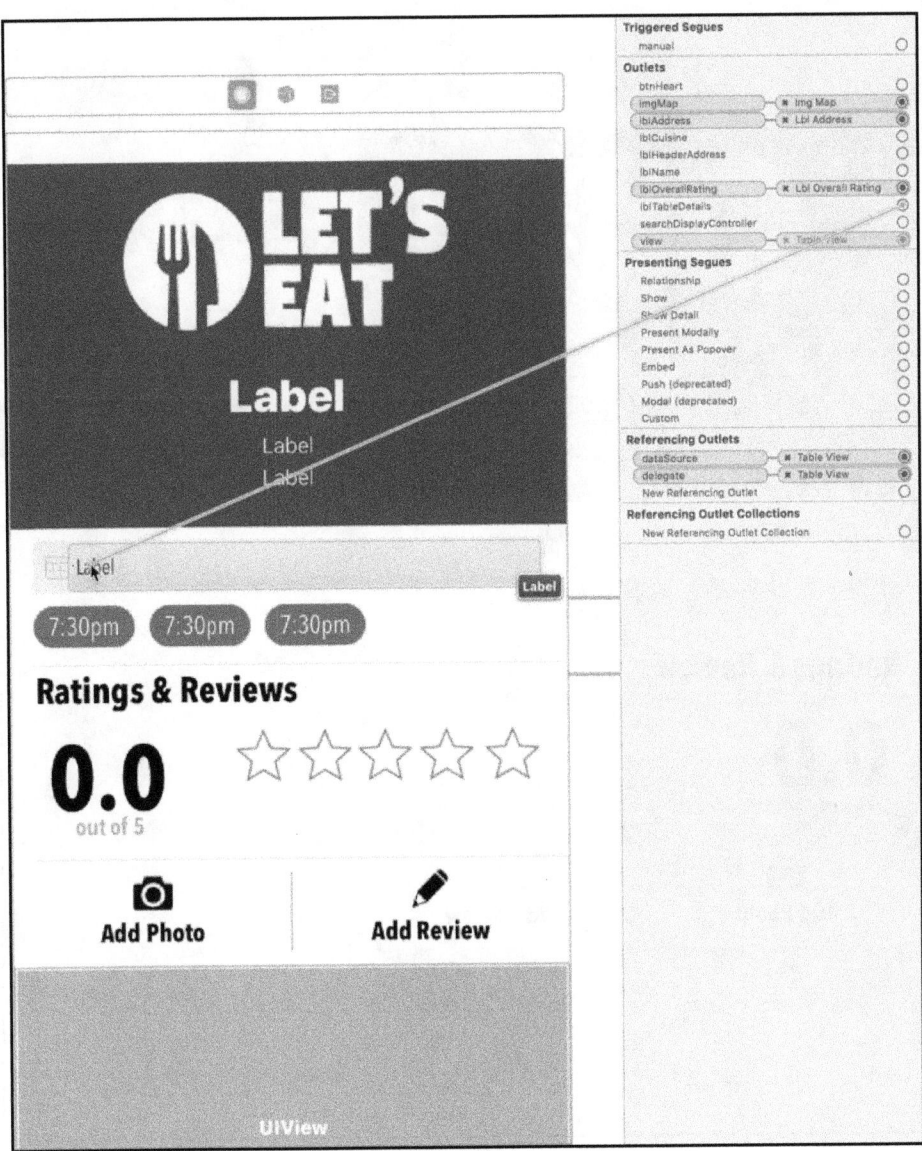

[495]

Displaying Data in Restaurant Detail

7. An empty circle for `lblName` to the **Label** under the logo in the scene:

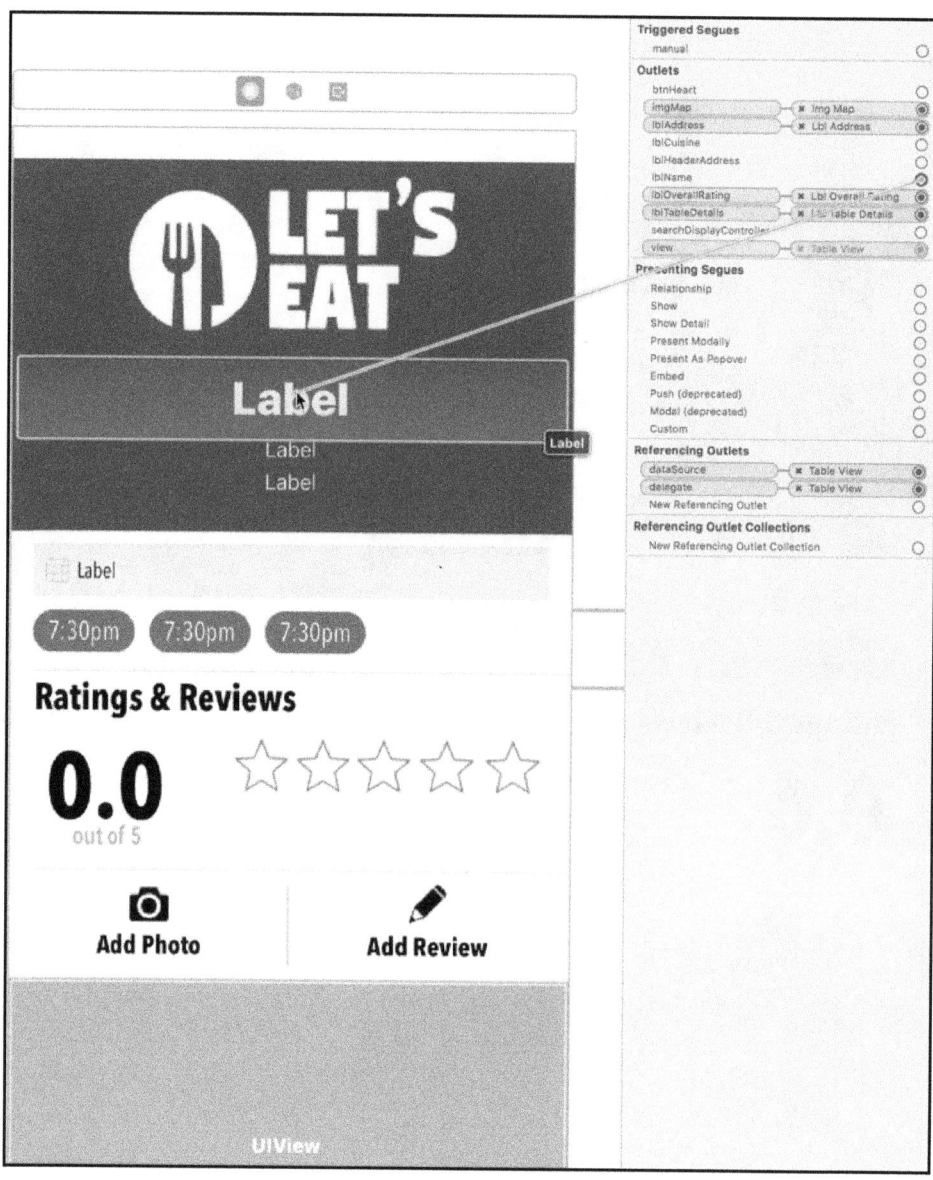

Chapter 18

8. An empty circle for `lblCuisine` to the **Label** under `lblName` in the scene:

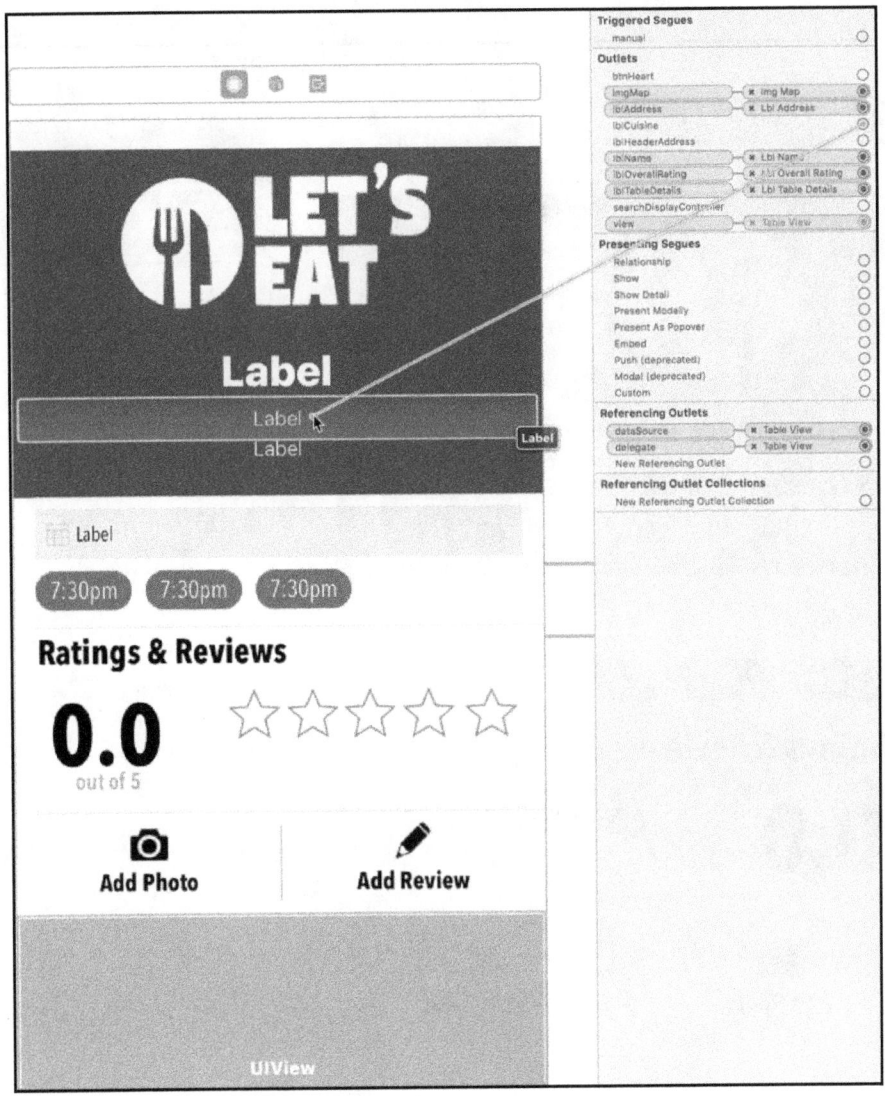

[497]

Displaying Data in Restaurant Detail

9. An empty circle for `lblHeaderAddress` to the **Label** under `lblCuisine` in the scene:

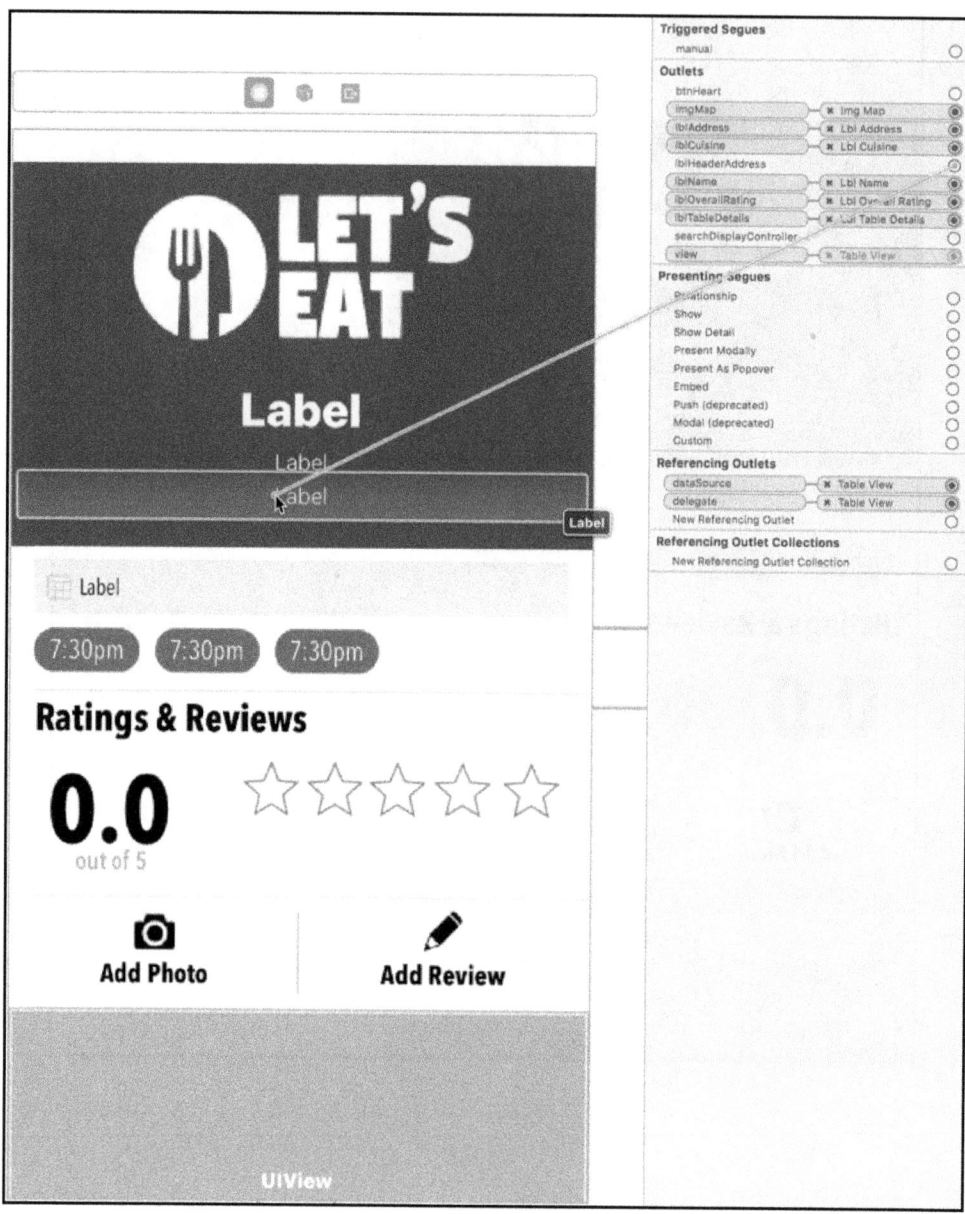

Adding a navigation button

Adding a navigation button used to be as simple as just dragging out the button; however, for some reason that isn't the case anymore. To display a heart in the navigation bar, we will have to do the following:

1. Select the Restaurant Detail View Controller in the Outline view.
2. Next, go to **Editor** | **Embed In** | **Navigation Controller**.

When complete, you should see the following:

Displaying Data in Restaurant Detail

3. Next, open the Utilities panel, and in the filter bar of the object library, type `bar`; drag a bar button item to the top-right of the Restaurant Detail View Controller. You will see an outline appear in this area, as follows:

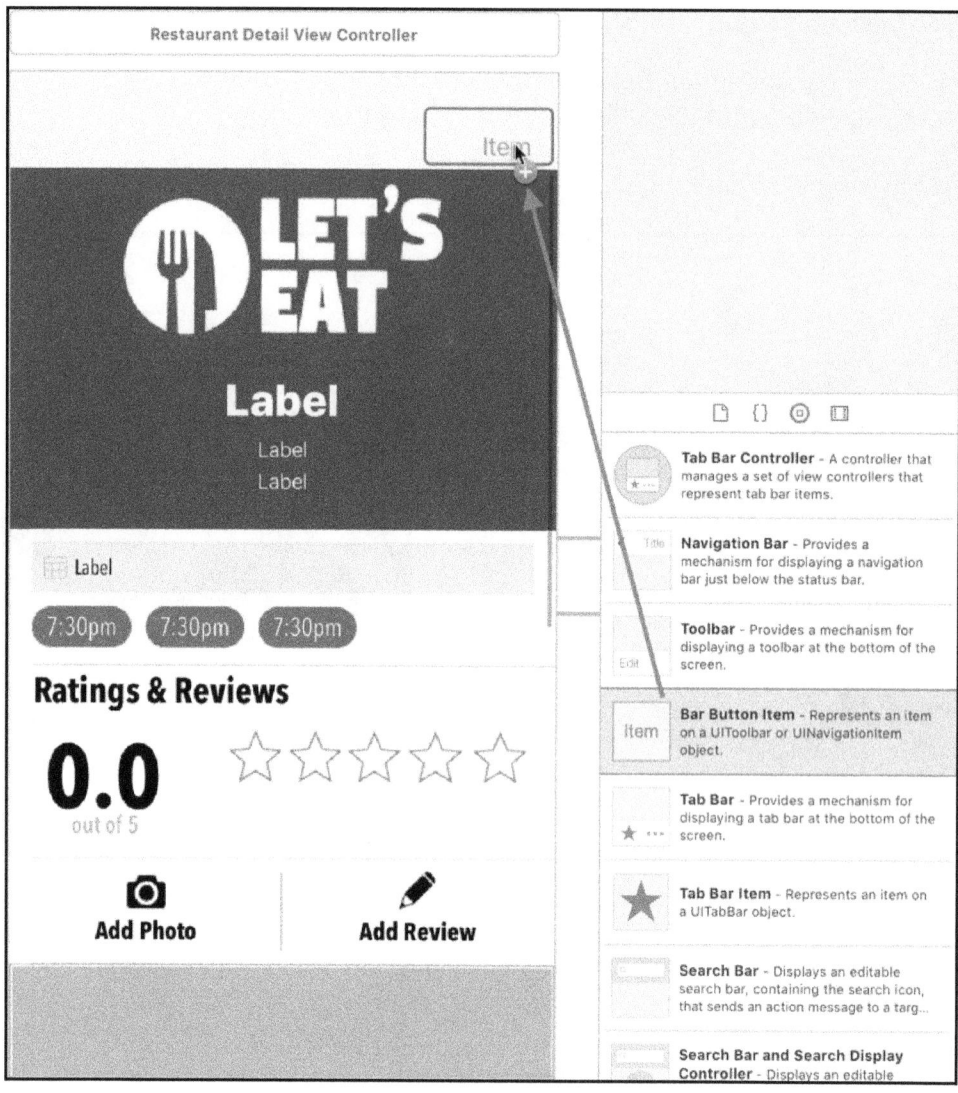

Chapter 18

In the Attributes inspector, under **Bar Item**, delete the text **Item** for **Title** and **Image** and update the image value to heart-unselected. When complete, you should see the following:

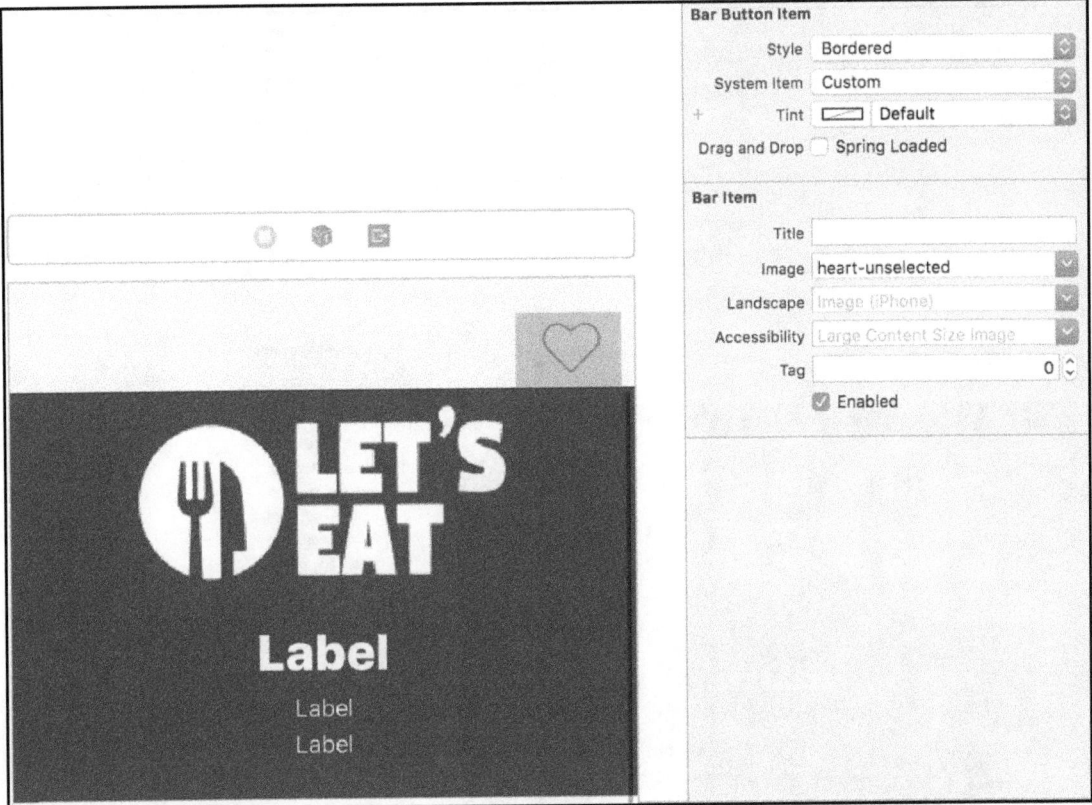

Displaying Data in Restaurant Detail

4. Now we need to connect our favorite icon in the navigation bar. Select the Restaurant Detail View Controller in the Outline view. Then, in the Outlet inspector, click and drag `btnHeart` to our newly created button, as follows:

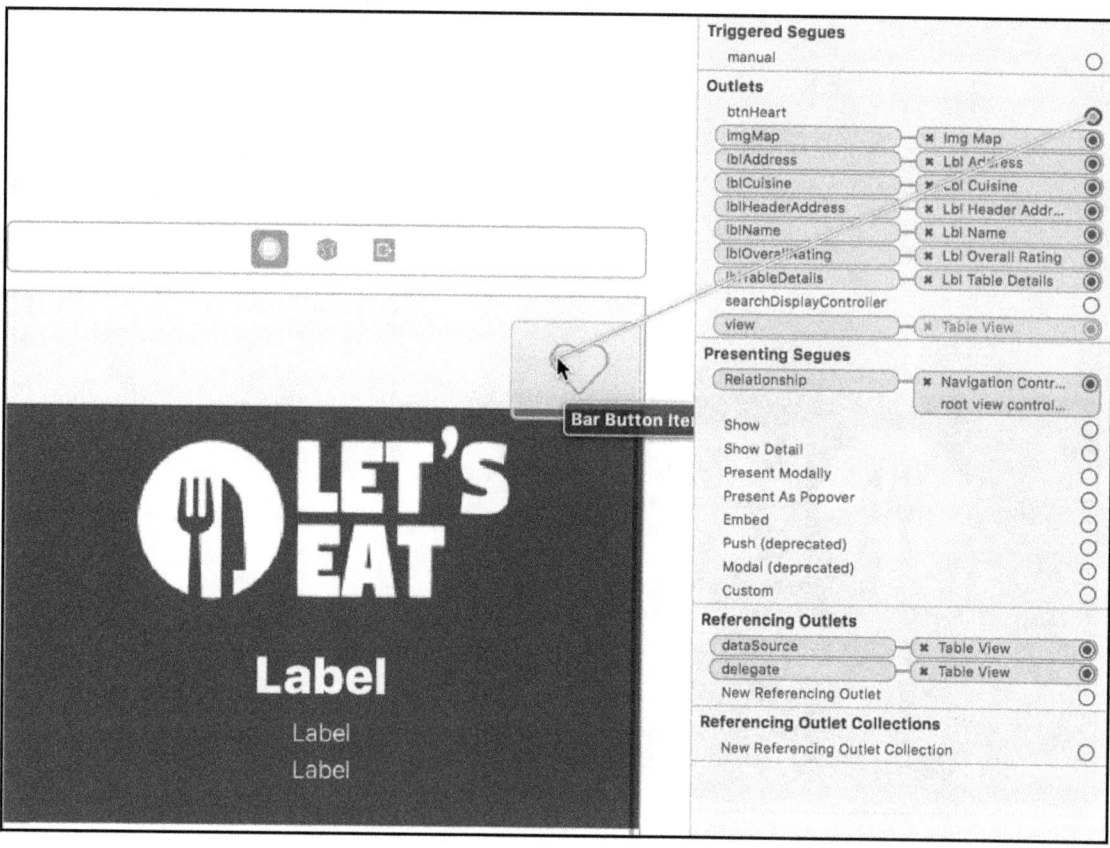

5. Next, with the View Controller still selected, in the Attributes inspector click on the checkbox next to **Is Initial View Controller**. When complete, you should see the following:

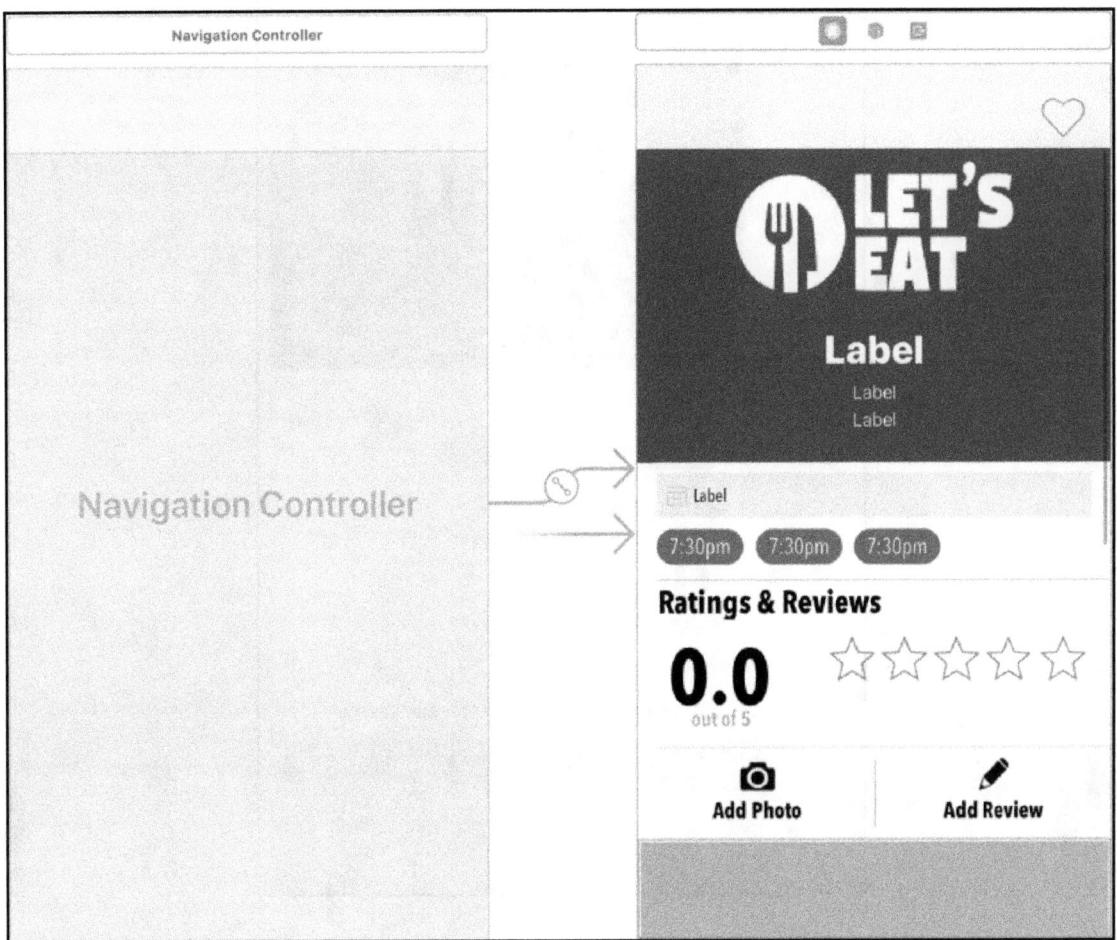

Displaying Data in Restaurant Detail

6. Now select the Navigation Controller and delete it. When you are done, you should see the following:

For some reason, we had to go through all of that just to add the bar button item, even though typically we could just drag it and drop it. Now that we have everything connected, we can now jump into coding and get our detail page displaying data.

Displaying data in our static Table View

Next, we need to create a method that will display all of our data in our labels.

So, open the `RestaurantDetailViewController.swift` file and add the following before the last curly brace:

```
func setupLabels() {
    guard let restaurant = selectedRestaurant else { return }
    if let name = restaurant.name {
        lblName.text = name
        title = name
    }

    if let cuisine = restaurant.subtitle { lblCuisine.text = cuisine }
    if let address = restaurant.address {
        lblAddress.text = address
        lblHeaderAddress.text = address
    }

    lblTableDetails.text = "Table for 7, tonight at 10:00 PM"
}
```

This method will now get the data and display it inside our labels. Next, we want to display a map of the restaurant location at the bottom of our Detail view. Now, you might be wondering why we are using an image and not a map. Using a map uses a lot more resources, whereas an image makes things a lot smoother. Let's arrange for an image of a map to display, and also show our custom annotation in the image. Add the following method under the `setupLabels()` method and before the last curly brace:

```
func createMap() {
    guard let annotation = selectedRestaurant, let long = annotation.longitude, let lat = annotation.latitude else { return }
    let location = CLLocationCoordinate2D(
        latitude: lat,
        longitude: long
    )

    takeSnapShot(with: location)
}
```

Displaying Data in Restaurant Detail

In this method, we get the longitude and latitude and enter the values into a `CLLocationCoordinate2D` object. We then pass the location to a method called `takeSnapShot(with:)`. Add the following method under the `createMap()` method:

```
func takeSnapShot(with location: CLLocationCoordinate2D) {
    let mapSnapshotOptions = MKMapSnapshotOptions()
    var loc = location
    let polyLine = MKPolyline(coordinates: &loc, count: 1)
    let region = MKCoordinateRegionForMapRect(polyLine.boundingMapRect)
    mapSnapshotOptions.region = region
    mapSnapshotOptions.scale = UIScreen.main.scale
    mapSnapshotOptions.size = CGSize(width: 340, height: 208)
    mapSnapshotOptions.showsBuildings = true
    mapSnapshotOptions.showsPointsOfInterest = true

    let snapShotter = MKMapSnapshotter(options: mapSnapshotOptions)
    snapShotter.start() { snapshot, error in
        guard let snapshot = snapshot else {
            return
        }

        UIGraphicsBeginImageContextWithOptions(mapSnapshotOptions.size, true, 0)
        snapshot.image.draw(at: .zero)

        let identifier = "custompin"
        let annotation = MKPointAnnotation()
        annotation.coordinate = location

        let pinView = MKPinAnnotationView(annotation: annotation, reuseIdentifier: identifier)
        pinView.image = UIImage(named: "custom-annotation")!
        let pinImage = pinView.image
        var point = snapshot.point(for: location)

        let rect = self.imgMap.bounds
        if rect.contains(point) {
            let pinCenterOffset = pinView.centerOffset
            point.x -= pinView.bounds.size.width / 2
            point.y -= pinView.bounds.size.height / 2
            point.x += pinCenterOffset.x
            point.y += pinCenterOffset.y
            pinImage?.draw(at: point)
        }

        if let image = UIGraphicsGetImageFromCurrentImageContext() {
            UIGraphicsEndImageContext()
```

```
                DispatchQueue.main.async {
                    self.imgMap.image = image
                }
            }
        }
    }
```

This method is long, but it allows us to create a map at the size we need. We then pass all of our settings to our snapshotter to create a picture. Once we have created our image, we then add our custom annotation to it. Although this requires a lot of code, it is the best way to understand it in its entirety. Here, we would recommend changing values line-by-line to see how it affects the image.

Now that we have created our functions, we just need to call them, as follows:

Add the following after the `viewDidLoad()` method in the `RestaurantDetailViewController.swift` file:

```
func initialize() {
    setupLabels()
    createMap()
}
```

This method now needs to be called inside your `viewDidLoad()` method. Replace the `dump` statement in the `viewDidLoad()` method with the following:

```
initialize()
```

Now we have finished with our Restaurant Detail View Controller. Let's build and run the project by hitting the Play button (or using *cmd* + *R*). When you select a restaurant, you should see all of the restaurant's information on the details page.

Displaying Data in Restaurant Detail

Also, you should see a pin dropped at the restaurant's location on the map, which is actually an image:

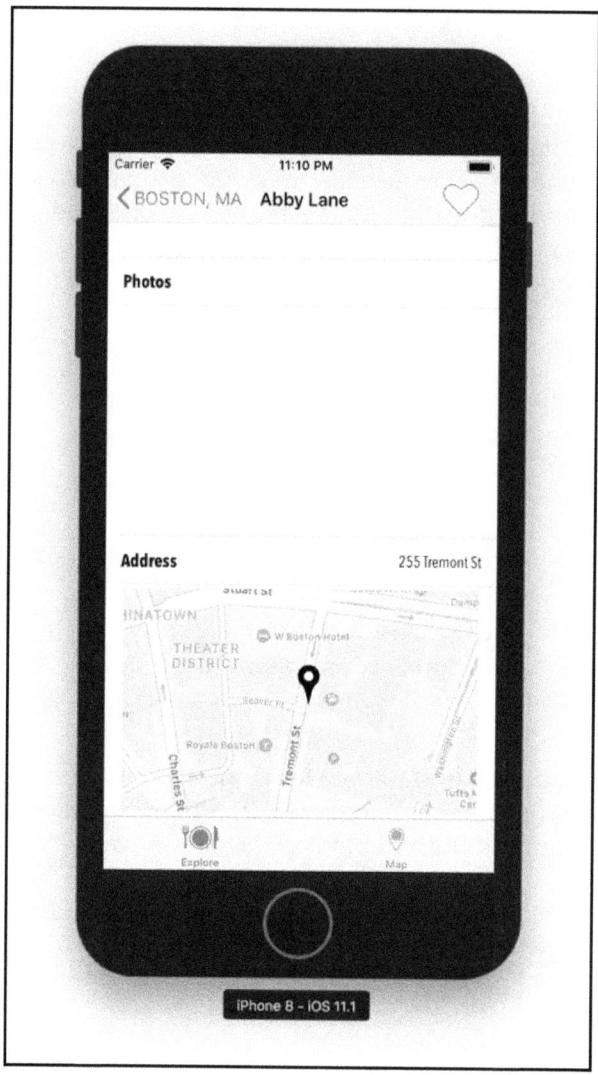

We are done with the restaurant detail for now, but we still need to be able to show ratings, reviews, and photos. We will work on all of these features in upcoming chapters.

Chapter 18

Summary

We now have JSON data loading into our app. As you can see, going from a plist to a JSON file was not a huge step. Our app is now looking more and more like it should be available on the App Store. In the following chapters, we will turn our attention to adding features that you might want to use in your app. These features will enhance the user experience, and therefore learning them will be invaluable. Even if the features don't seem like something you want or need, it will be beneficial in the long run to understand what they are and how they work.

In the next chapter, you will work with the camera and learn how to apply filters and save images to the Camera Roll.

19
Foodie Reviews

We are all familiar with reviews, from food reviews to App Store reviews. Seeing reviews for websites and apps is common place. In this chapter, we will create a review form that has a custom five-star rating component that we will add to it. We will learn about `UIControls` and how powerful they are. We will also look at literals and how to use them in our code.

In this chapter, you will learn about:

- Creating a form that users can use to write a review
- Creating a custom star rating
- Image and color literals

Getting started with reviews

Our review form UI is set up, but we need to make a slight change to it. Right now, we have an image displayed for ratings. We are going to build a custom rating component that we will use in both restaurant details and our Review form.

We add it to our restaurant details first, then once we are finished, we add it to the Review form. We want our ratings view to be able to show ratings from zero stars to five stars. We also want the user to be able to select half stars when rating, so it will also need to show half stars.

Foodie Reviews

The first thing we do is start creating our custom `UIControl`. `UIButtons` and `UISwitches` are sub-classes of `UIControls`, and without getting super technical, we are going to create our control:

1. Right click the `Reviews Form` folder and select **New File**.
2. Inside of the **Choose a template for your new file** screen, select **iOS** at the top, and then **Cocoa Touch Class**. Then, hit **Next**.
3. In the options screen that appears, add the following:

   New file:

   - **Class**: `RatingsView`
   - **Subclass**: `UIControl`
   - **Language**: `Swift`

4. Click **Next**, and then **Create**.

Now that we have created our file, we want to be able to hook it up to a `UIView` in storyboard. Let's do the following:

1. Open up `RestaurantDetail.storyboard`.
2. In the object library of the Utilities panel, type `view` in the **filter** field.
3. Delete the image with the five empty stars.
4. Then, drag out a View into the cell with the empty stars.
5. Select the View and, in the Size inspector, update the following values:

   - **X**: `151`
   - **Y**: `43`
   - **Width**: `205`
   - **Height**: `34`

6. Select the **View**, and then the Pin icon. Enter the following values:

   - **Top**: `13`
   - **Left**: `0`

- **Width**: 205 (checked)
- **Height**: 34 (checked)
- **Constrain to margins**: Unchecked

7. Click **Add 4 Constraints**.
8. Next, select the Restaurant View Controller, then in the Identity inspector, update the **Custom Class** to RatingsView and hit *Enter*.

Now, we are set up to get started. Open up the RatingsView.swift file and let's get started.

Displaying ratings in our custom UIControl

Inside the RatingsView.swift file, we first need to create all of the variables we will need to work with. Add the following under the class declaration:

```
let imgFilledStar = #imageLiteral(resourceName: "filled-star")
let imgHalfStar = #imageLiteral(resourceName: "half-star")
let imgEmptyStar = #imageLiteral(resourceName: "empty-star")
let shouldBecomeFirstResponder = true
var rating:CGFloat = 0.0
var totalStars = 5
```

If you are having trouble using an image literal, you can use UIImage(named:) instead.

We are doing something in this file. We are using image literals as our variables. If you type Image Literal in your file and hit return, you will see a small icon:

```
import UIKit

class RatingView: UIControl {

    let imgFilledStar = 🌟
}
```

Double-click this icon and a modal appears that shows you an image to choose:

```
import UIKit

class RatingView: UIControl
    let imgFilledStar = 
}
```

You can look and find the three images using this window, or you can just type everything you see here, and the image appears. When done you should see the following:

```
import UIKit

class RatingView: UIControl {
    let imgFilledStar = ★
    let imgHalfStar = 
    let imgEmptyStar = ☆

    let shouldBecomeFirstResponder = true
    var rating:CGFloat = 0.0
    var totalStars = 5
}
```

The first three variables created are used for drawing our ratings view. The next variable, `showBecomeFirstResponder`, is a variable to let us be able to respond and handle events as they happen. Next, the rating variable is used for keeping track of our current rating. Finally, we have a variable to keep track of the total number of stars.

Now let's add our `init` methods:

```
override init(frame: CGRect) {
    super.init(frame: frame)
}
required init?(coder aDecoder: NSCoder) {
    super.init(coder: aDecoder)
}
override func setNeedsLayout() {
    super.setNeedsLayout()
    self.setNeedsLayout()
}
```

These are just boilerplate code that you need when creating views. There's nothing really to explain here other than that you need them. Next, we need to create a few methods that will handle creating our stars. We need three of them for each type of star (full, half, and empty). Add the following after the last curly bracket:

```
private extension RatingView {
    func drawStar(with frame:CGRect, highlighted:Bool) {
        let image = highlighted ? imgFilledStar :imgEmptyStar
        draw(with: image, and: frame)
    }

    func drawHalfStar(with frame:CGRect) {
        draw(with: imgHalfStar, and: frame)
    }

    func draw(with image:UIImage, and frame:CGRect) {
        image.draw(in: frame)
    }
}
```

These methods just create a full, half, or empty star. We now need to be able to draw these stars. `UIView` has a draw method we can use to draw stars. Before the `drawStar(frame:highlighted:)` method, add the following method inside of the class:

```
override func draw(_ rect: CGRect) {
    let context = UIGraphicsGetCurrentContext()
    context!.setFillColor( colorLiteral(red: 1, green: 1, blue: 1, alpha: 0).cgColor)
    context!.fill(rect)

    let availWidth = rect.size.width
    let cellWidth = availWidth / CGFloat(totalStars)
    let starSide = (cellWidth <= rect.size.height) ? cellWidth : rect.size.height

    for index in 0...totalStars {
        let value = cellWidth*CGFloat(index) + cellWidth/2
        let center = CGPoint(x: value+1, y: rect.size.height/2)
        let frame = CGRect(x: center.x - starSide/2, y: center.y - starSide/2, width: starSide, height: starSide)
        let highlighted = (Float(index+1) <= ceilf(Float(self.rating)))

        if highlighted && (CGFloat(index+1) > CGFloat(self.rating)) {
            drawHalfStar(with: frame)
        } else {
            drawStar(with: frame, highlighted: highlighted)
        }
```

```
        }
    }
```

Here is all the code we need to create our stars. Let's break down the code and see what is happening. First, we get a graphics context, and we set its fill color to be clear. We are using a **Color Literal** this time, and this allows us to create colors and see those colors directly in our Swift file. You can either type `Color Literal` and hit *Enter*. You will see a white box has been created for you, and if you double-click this box, you can edit the color just like you would in storyboard.

Next, we create three variables: `availWidth`, `cellWidth`, and `starSide`. Since we are using `UIView` in the storyboard, we check to see the size of this container. We then determine the size of each star based on the width and the number of stars. Finally, we calculate the height of the star.

Then, we loop through each star and create them based on the rating value. Our rating can be 0-5, with increments of `0.5`. We also set up the positioning of each star using the center point. Finally, we determine, based on the value, whether the star should be an empty star, a half star, or a full star. That is our setup method and you do not have to get what is going on entirely, just have a basic understanding, and the more you code, the more it starts to make sense.

Before we build the project, open `RestaurantDetailViewController`, and under import `UIKit`, add the following import:

```
import MapKit
Then, after imgMap, add the following outlet:
@IBOutlet weak var ratingView: RatingView!
```

Let's do some cleaning up by moving the `createMap()`, `setupLabels()`, and `takeSnapshot(:location)` methods into a private extension. When you are done, you should see the following:

```
private extension RestaurantDetailViewController {
    func setupLabels() {
        guard let restaurant = selectedRestaurant else { return }
        if let name = restaurant.name {
            lblName.text = name
            title = name
        }
        if let cuisine = restaurant.subtitle { lblCuisine.text = cuisine }
        if let address = restaurant.address {
            lblAddress.text = address
            lblHeaderAddress.text = address
        }
```

```swift
            lblTableDetails.text = "Table for 7, tonight at 10:00 PM"
    }
    func createMap() {
        guard let annotation = selectedRestaurant, let long = annotation.longitude, let lat = annotation.latitude else { return }
        let location = CLLocationCoordinate2D(
            latitude: lat,
            longitude: long
        )
        takeSnapShot(with: location)
    }

    func takeSnapShot(with location: CLLocationCoordinate2D) {
        let mapSnapshotOptions = MKMapSnapshotOptions()
        var loc = location
        let polyLine = MKP olyline(coordinates: &loc, count: 1)
        let region = MKCoordinateRegionForMapRect(polyLine.boundingMapRect)
        mapSnapshotOptions.region = region
        mapSnapshotOptions.scale = UIScreen.main.scale
        mapSnapshotOptions.size = CGSize(width: 340, height: 208)
        mapSnapshotOptions.showsBuildings = true
        mapSnapshotOptions.showsPointsOfInterest = true
        let snapShotter = MKMapSnapshotter(options: mapSnapshotOptions)
        snapShotter.start() { snapshot, error in
            guard let snapshot = snapshot else {
                return
            }
            UIGraphicsBeginImageContextWithOptions(mapSnapshotOptions.size, true, 0)
            snapshot.image.draw(at: .zero)
            let identifier = "custompin"
            let annotation = MKPointAnnotation()
            annotation.coordinate = location
            let pinView = MKPinAnnotationView(annotation: annotation, reuseIdentifier: identifier)
            pinView.image = UIImage(named: "custom-annotation")!
            let pinImage = pinView.image
            var point = snapshot.point(for: location)
            let rect = self.imgMap.bounds
            if rect.contains(point) {
                let pinCenterOffset = pinView.centerOffset
                point.x -= pinView.bounds.size.width / 2
                point.y -= pinView.bounds.size.height / 2
                point.x += pinCenterOffset.x
                point.y += pinCenterOffset.y
                pinImage?.draw(at: point)
            }
```

```
                if let image = UIGraphicsGetImageFromCurrentImageContext() {
                    UIGraphicsEndImageContext()
                    DispatchQueue.main.async {
                        self.imgMap.image = image
                    }
                }
            }
        }
    }
}
```

Next, add the following method into the private method:

```
func createRating() {
    ratingView.rating = 3.5
}
```

Next, open `RestaurantDetail.storyboard` and select the Restaurant View Controller, then in the Outlet inspector click and drag from `ratingView` to the `UIView` we created earlier. Let's build and run the project by hitting the Play button (or use *cmd + R*). When you get to the restaurant details, you will see that we now have 3.5 stars:

This is precisely what we want, but we also need our control be able to handle touch events.

Adding our touch events

Adding touch events will be used to change the rating to the desired rating. Open `RatingView` and let's add the methods we need to get our control to accept touch events by adding the following inside the main class:

```
override var canBecomeFirstResponder: Bool {
    return shouldBecomeFirstResponder
}
override func beginTracking(_ touch: UITouch, with event: UIEvent?) -> Bool
{
    if self.isEnabled {
        super.beginTracking(touch, with: event)
        if (shouldBecomeFirstResponder && self.isFirstResponder) {
            becomeFirstResponder()
        }
        handle(with: touch)
        return true
    }
    else { return false }
}
```

Then, add the following into the private extension:

```
func handle(with touch: UITouch) {
    let cellWidth = self.bounds.size.width / CGFloat(totalStars)
    let location = touch.location(in: self)
    var value = location.x / cellWidth
    
    if (value + 0.5 < CGFloat(ceilf(Float(value)))) {
        value = floor(value) + 0.5
    }
    else {
        value = CGFloat(ceilf(Float(value)))
    }
    
    updateRating(with: value)
}
// Update Rating
func updateRating(with value:CGFloat) {
    if (self.rating != value && value >= 0 && value <= CGFloat(totalStars))
    {
        self.rating = value
```

```
            setNeedsDisplay()
    }
}
```

The following code is used to handle touch. First, we set the `canBecomeFirstResponder` variable. Next, we have the `beginTracking(touch:event:)`. In this method, we set whether our control can accept touch events. If the control is enabled, then we allow touches, and we call the `handle()` method and pass it the `UITouch` location. Let's discuss the `handle()` method.

In our handle method, we start with three variables. We first get the width of the entire rating view. Next, we get the value of the touch location, then finally we take the x value of the location and divide it by the width. We then check the value, figure out whether it is less than 0.5 or greater than 0.5, and round appropriately. Last, we update the rating with the value we calculate.

In the `updateRating(value:)` method, we check to make sure that our value is not equal to the current value and whether the value is greater than zero and less than the total number of stars. If these conditions pass, then we set the rating to the new value and call the `setNeedsDisplay()` method. This method makes sure that our control is redrawn.

Open `RestaurantDetailsViewController` and in the `createRating()` method, add the following:

```
ratingView.isEnabled = true
```

We now have a rating, and by setting the rating to 3.5, we should now see 3.5 stars. We also set the `isEnabled` value to `true`, which means we can touch and change the rating. If we set it to `false`, then the value cannot change. In the restaurant details, we want to turn off touch, but in the `ReviewFormViewController` we want that to be enabled. You can play with this, and when done set the `isEnable` value to `false` and remove the rating.

We set the rating later in the book when we start saving reviews:

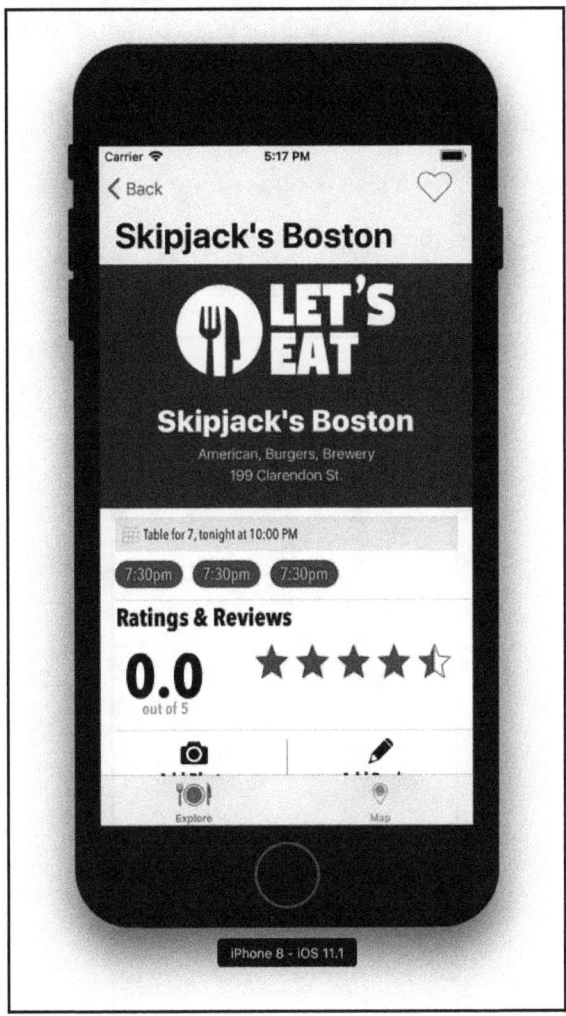

You can now change the rating from 3.5 to 4.5 by tapping on the view. Now that we have this set up, let's get our review form set up.

Foodie Reviews

Setting up the unwind segues

As we have done before, we need to add code for us to unwind (dismiss) a View Controller:

1. Open the `RestaurantDetailsViewController.swift` file and add the following into the private extension:

   ```
   @IBAction func unwindReviewCancel(segue:UIStoryboardSegue) {}
   ```

2. Save the file and open the `ReviewForm.storyboard`.
3. CTL drag the **Cancel** button to the Exit icon inside of the same View Controller:

4. In the screen that appears, under **Action Segue**, select `unwindReviewCancelWithSegue`.

If you build and run the project by hitting the Play button (or use *cmd + R*), you should now be able to dismiss the **Ratings View**.

Chapter 19

Setting up our rating control

We are now going to set up our rating control:

1. Open up `ReviewForm.storyboard`.
2. In the object library of the Utilities panel, type `view` in the **filter** field.
3. Delete the image with the five empty stars.
4. Then, drag out a View into the cell with the empty stars.
5. Select the View and, in the Size inspector, update the following values:

    - **X**: `133`
    - **Y**: `7`
    - **Width**: `108`
    - **Height**: `17`

6. Next, in the Identity inspector, update the **Custom Class** to `RatingsView` and hit *Enter*.
7. Next, select the view inside of the view and then select the Pin icon and enter the following values:

    - **Top**: `7`
    - **Constrain to margins**: Unchecked
    - **Width**: `108` (should be checked)
    - **Height**: `17` (should be checked)

8. Click **Add 3 Constraints**.
9. Next, click the Align icon and enter the value of **Horizontally in Container** as 0 (should be checked).
10. Click **Add 1 Constraint**.
11. Select the label that says **Tap a Star to Rate**.
12. Then, select the Pin icon and enter the value of **Top** as `1`.
13. Click **Add 1 Constraints**.
14. Next, select the Restaurant View Controller, then in the Identity inspector, update the **Custom Class** to `RatingsView` and hit *Enter*.

Our form is now updated; let's create our controller next.

Creating our review form controller

1. Right-click the `Review Form` folder again and select **New File**.
2. Inside of the **Choose a template for your new file** screen, select **iOS** at the top, and then **Cocoa Touch Class**. Then, hit **Next**.
3. In the options screen that appears, add the following:

   New file:
   - **Class**: `ReviewFormViewController`
   - **Subclass**: `UITableViewController`
   - **Also create XIB**: Unchecked
   - **Language**: `Swift`

4. Click **Next**, and then **Create**.

Delete everything after the `viewDidLoad()` method, as we do not need all of the other code. Next, let's set up our `ReviewFormViewController` by adding the following after the class declaration:

```
@IBOutlet weak var ratingView: RatingView!
@IBOutlet weak var tfTitle: UITextField!
@IBOutlet weak var tfName: UITextField!
@IBOutlet weak var tvReview: UITextView!
```

We also need to add a method when our save button is tapped by adding the following:

```
@IBAction func onSaveTapped(_ sender: Any) {
  print(ratingView.rating)
  print(tfTitle.text as Any)
  print(tfName.text as Any)
  print(tvReview.text)
  dismiss(animated: true, completion: nil)
}
```

Chapter 19

Let's now connect this file with our `UIViewController` and our review form in storyboard:

1. In the Utilities panel, select the Identity inspector.
2. Under **Custom Class**, in the **Class** drop-down menu, type/select **ReviewFormViewController** and hit *Enter* in order connect the View Controller to the class.
3. Now, select the Connections inspector in the Utilities panel.
4. Now, click and drag from the empty circle of each of the following variables we just added under Outlets to their respective elements in either the scene or Outline view.
5. Click and drag from the empty circle for `ratingView` to the `UIView` in the storyboard:

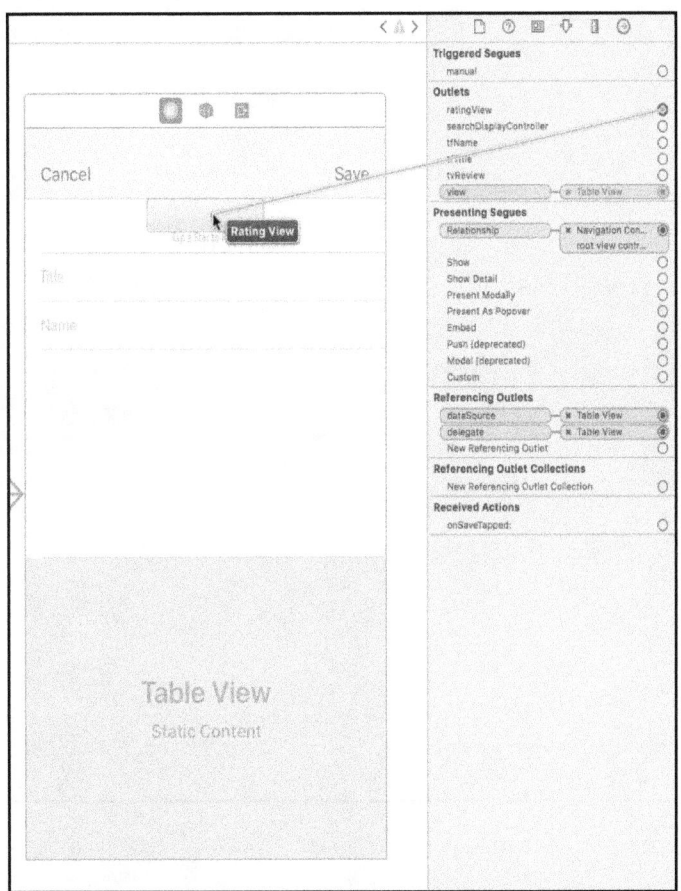

6. Click and drag from the empty circle for `tfTitle` to the `Textfield` in the storyboard:

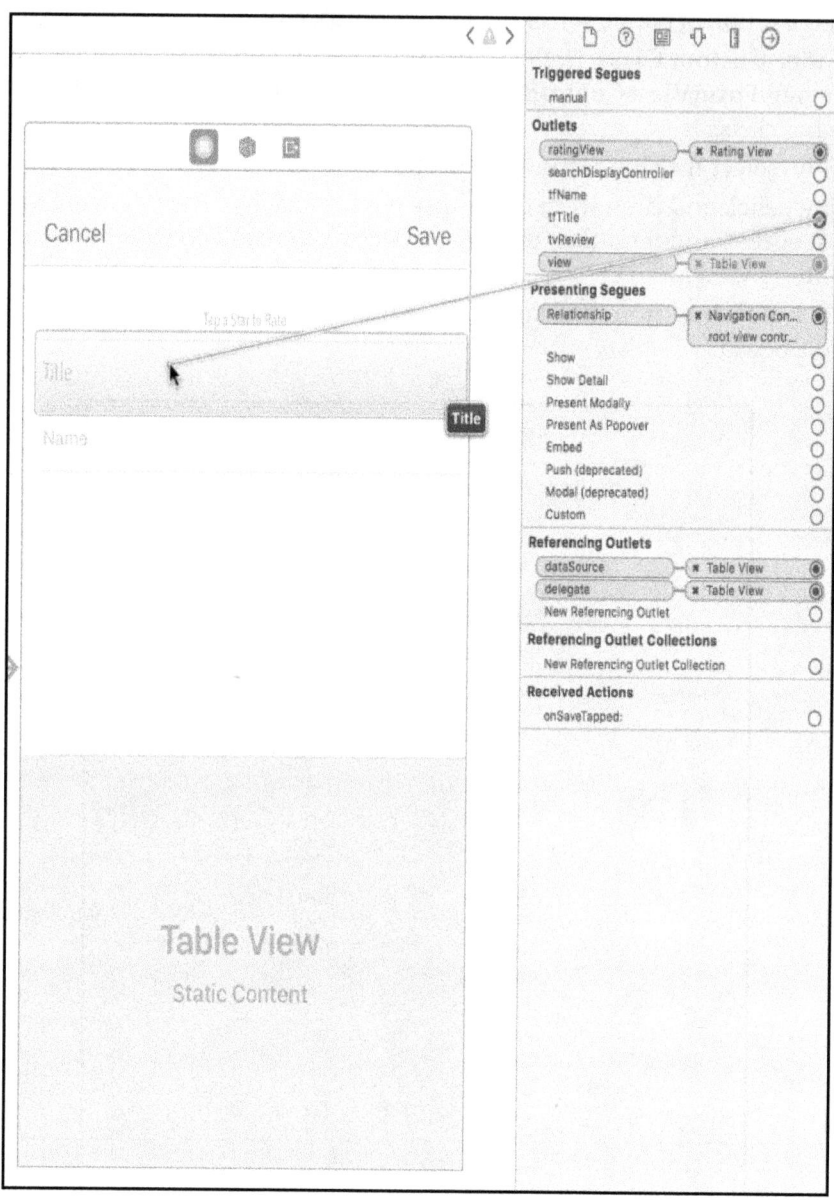

7. Click and drag from the empty circle for `tfName` to the `Textfield` in the storyboard:

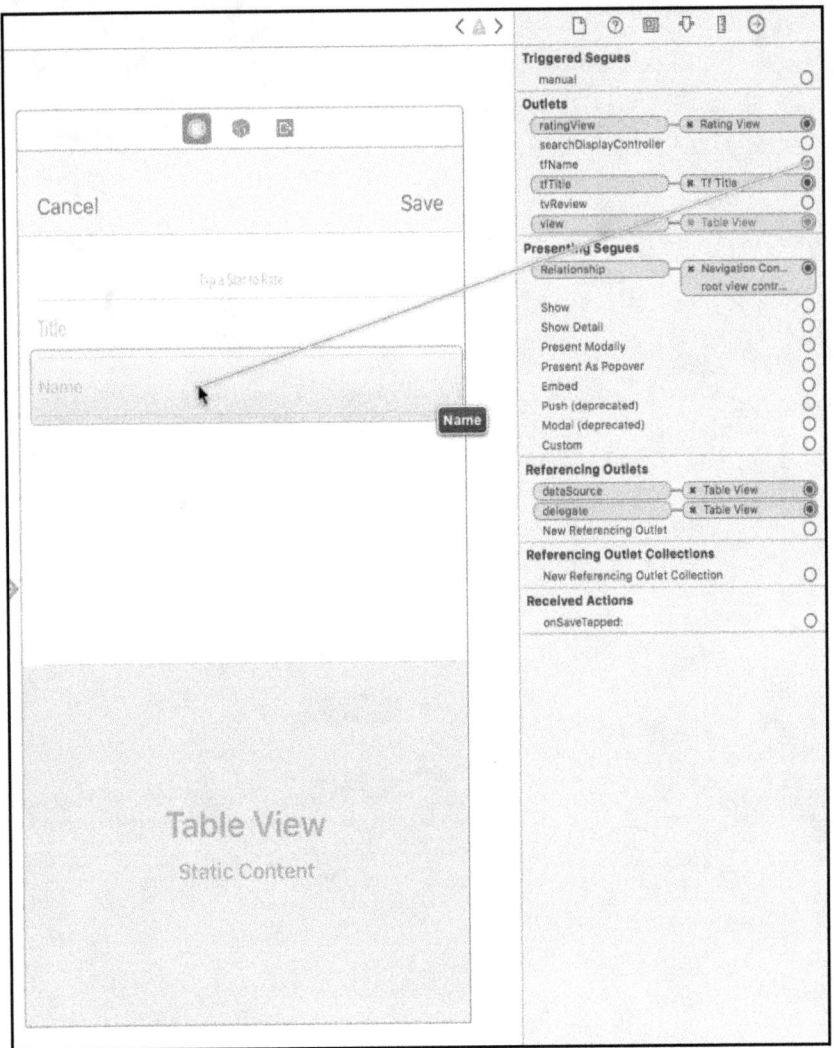

8. Click and drag from the empty circle for `tvReview` to the `Text View` in the storyboard:

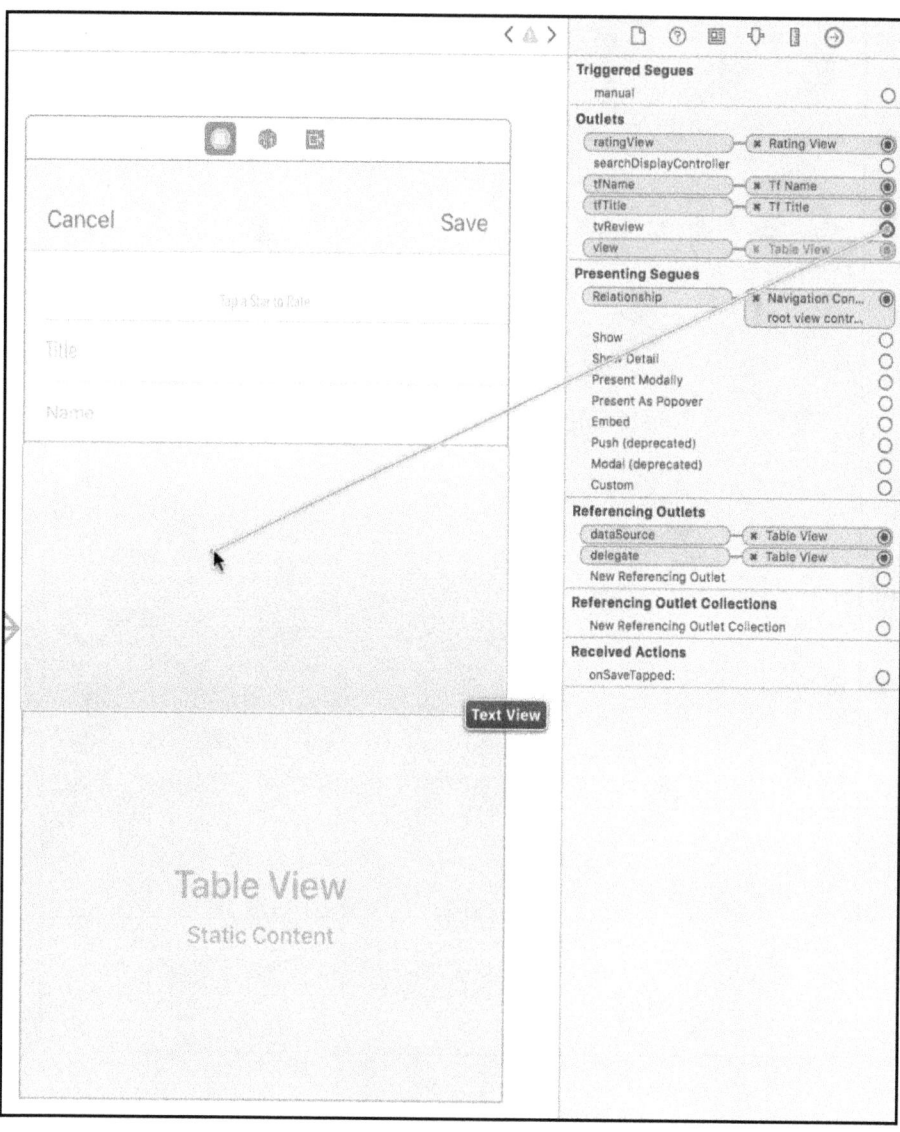

9. Finally, click and drag from the empty circle for `onSaveTapped` to the **Save** button in the Navigation controller:

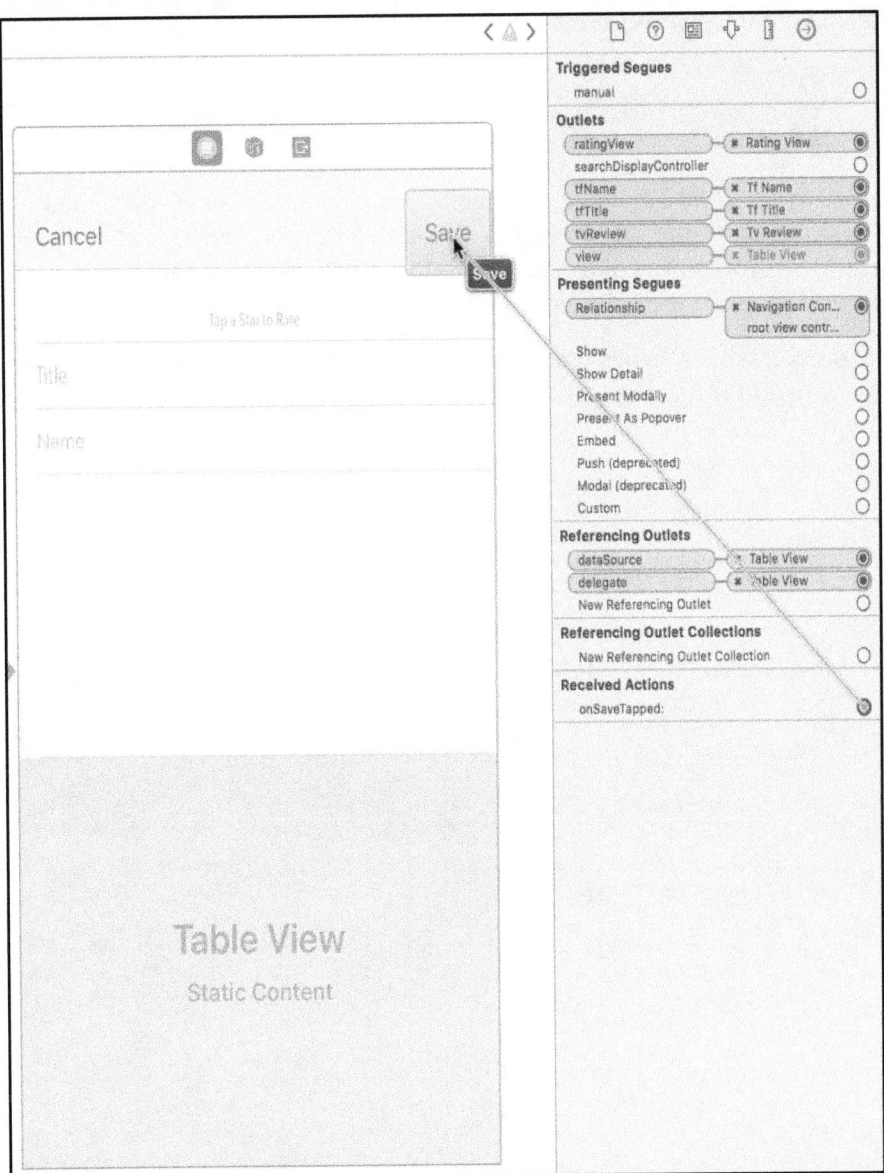

Now, that we have an outlet connected to our form, let's build and run the project by hitting the Play button (or use *cmd + R*). If you go to your form, enter the information and hit save so you can see that information in your Output panel. Our reviews are now ready to go. Next, we'll create photos with filters.

Summary

In this chapter, we created a Review form using a static table view. We worked with Text View and Text Fields for the first time. We also set up our first custom `UIControl` with our star rating, and we got to use color and **Image Literals** in this chapter. Literals are a great way to see your image or the color you are working with visually.

In the next chapter, we will work on creating a way to add a photo to a restaurant. We will also learn how to add filters to our photos.

20
Working with Photo Filters

In this chapter, we focus on creating photos for a restaurant and how to use the camera and camera roll. We give the user the ability to take a picture and apply a filter to that picture. In the next chapter, we tie the last chapter and this chapter all together by completing the work on the review form and enabling users to save their reviews. We will also learn how to save photos as well.

In this chapter, you will learn:

- How to use the camera roll to get pictures
- How to use the camera to take pictures and bring them into our app
- How to apply filters to our pictures and get them ready to save to the device

Understanding filters

Based on our design, we know that we are going to need to apply filters to a photo. Instead of just creating an array of filters, we are going to use a plist to load in a set of filters that we want. You can find the `FilterData.plist` file inside this chapter's `asset` folder. Drag and drop this file into the `Model` folder that is inside the `Review` folder. Make sure that `Copy` items if needed is checked and then hit **Finish**.

Working with Photo Filters

Let's take a look at the plist and see what it contains:

Key	Type	Value
▼ Root	Array	(10 items)
▼ Item 0	Dictionary	(2 items)
filter	String	None
name	String	None
▼ Item 1	Dictionary	(2 items)
filter	String	CIPhotoEffectMono
name	String	Mono
▼ Item 2	Dictionary	(2 items)
filter	String	CISepiaTone
name	String	Sepia
▼ Item 3	Dictionary	(2 items)
filter	String	CIPhotoEffectTonal
name	String	Tonal
▼ Item 4	Dictionary	(2 items)
filter	String	CIPhotoEffectNoir
name	String	Noir
▼ Item 5	Dictionary	(2 items)
filter	String	CIPhotoEffectFade
name	String	Fade
▼ Item 6	Dictionary	(2 items)
filter	String	CIPhotoEffectChrome
name	String	Chrome
▼ Item 7	Dictionary	(2 items)
filter	String	CIPhotoEffectProcess
name	String	Process
▼ Item 8	Dictionary	(2 items)
filter	String	CIPhotoEffectTransfer
name	String	Transfer
▼ Item 9	Dictionary	(2 items)
filter	String	CIPhotoEffectInstant
name	String	Instant

This list only has 10 of over 170 filters and effects that you can use. If you would like to see a full list of filters, you can find the list at `http://tinyurl.com/coreimage-ios`. Feel free to add, remove, or update any filters. Now that we have seen what our plist looks like, we need to create a model that represents this data. We also need to create a `Manager` class to manage our items. Let's create the model first:

1. Right-click the `Model` folder in the `Review` folder and select **New File**.
2. Inside the **Choose a template for your new file** screen, select **iOS** at the top, and then **Swift File**. Then, hit **Next**.
3. Name this file `FilterItem` and hit **Create**.
4. Next, we need to define our struct; therefore, add the following under the `import` statement:

```
class FilterItem: NSObject {
    let filter:String
    let name:String
    init(dict:[String:AnyObject]) {
        name   = dict[name] as! String
        filter = dict[filter] as! String
    }
}
```

The `filter` property will be the class passed to apply the filter; and the `name` property will be used as a display.

Let's create our `FilterManager` file next:

1. Right-click the `Photo Filter` folder and select **New File**.
2. Inside of the **Choose a template for your new file** screen, select **iOS** at the top, and then **Swift File**. Then, hit **Next**.
3. Name this file `FilterManager` and hit **Create**.

Working with Photo Filters

4. Next, we need to define our class definition; therefore, add the following under the `import` statement:

```
class FilterManager: DataManager {
    func fetch(completionHandler:(_ items:[FilterItem]) -> Swift.Void) {
        var items:[FilterItem] = []
        for data in load(file: "FilterData") {
            items.append(FilterItem(dict: data))
        }
        completionHandler(items)
    }
}
```

This file uses our `DataManager` base class, which converts our plist data into an array of dictionary objects. Once that is complete, we create `FilterItems` from that.

Next, we need to create a file that takes a `FilterItem` and apply a filter to an image. Since we are going to do this in numerous places, it is best to have all of this code in one place. Therefore, we are going to create a file that handles all of this processing for us. Let's create our `ImageFiltering` file:

1. Right-click the `Photo Filter` folder and select **New File**.
2. Inside the **Choose a template for your new file** screen, select **iOS** at the top, and then **Swift File**. Then, hit **Next**.
3. Name this file `ImageFiltering`, and hit **Create**.
4. Update your file to the following:

```
import UIKit
import CoreImage

protocol ImageFiltering {
    func apply(filter:String, originalImage:UIImage) -> UIImage
}

protocol ImageFilteringDelegate:class {
    func filterSelected(item:FilterItem)
}

extension ImageFiltering {
    func apply(filter:String, originalImage:UIImage) -> UIImage {
        let initialCIImage = CIImage(image: originalImage, options: nil)
        let originalOrientation = originalImage.imageOrientation
        guard let ciFilter = CIFilter(name: filter) else {
```

```
            print("filter not found")
            return UIImage()
        }
        ciFilter.setValue(initialCIImage, forKey: kCIInputImageKey)
        let context = CIContext()
        let filteredCIImage = (ciFilter.outputImage)!
        let filteredCGImage =
context.createCGImage(filteredCIImage, from:
filteredCIImage.extent)
            return UIImage(cgImage: filteredCGImage!, scale: 1.0,
orientation: originalOrientation)
        }
    }
```

Let's break down each section so that we can understand what we are doing with this code:

```
import UIKit
import CoreImage
```

`CoreImage` give us access to the image processing we need for filtering.

```
protocol ImageFiltering {
    func apply(filter:String, originalImage:UIImage) -> UIImage
}
```

Creating this protocol allows us to have other classes conform to it, therefore giving us access to the method and allowing us to use it wherever we want.

```
protocol ImageFilteringDelegate:class {
    func filterSelected(item:FilterItem)
}
```

This protocol is used when a filter is selected, and when we need the selected filter, is passed from one View or View Controller to another. The extension has the `apply(filter:originalImage:)` method in it. In this method, we are creating an extension and adding all of the code that we are going to use for applying filters to images.

Creating our filter scroller

After a user selects a photo to use, we present the user with a screen, which contains that image. In the following image, we have a scroller, also known as a `UIScrollView`, which allows us to create content that scrolls either horizontally or vertically. The `UIScrollView` displays an image (thumbnail) with the filter applied to it as well as the name of the filter. This image and name represent our filters visually to our users.

When the user taps on the image, the user sees the selected filter change the primary image. Let's look at an example:

We are now going to create the elements inside the `UIScrollView`. Since we have created a lot inside storyboard, let's create the `PhotoItem` entirely in code:

1. Right-click the `Review` folder and select **New File**.
2. Inside the **Choose a template for your new file** screen, select **iOS** at the top, and then **Swift File**. Then, hit **Next**.
3. Name this file `PhotoItem` and hit **Create**.
4. Update your file to the following:

```
import UIKit

class PhotoItem: UIView, ImageFiltering {
}
```

5. Next, add your variables inside of the class declaration:

   ```
   var imgThumb:UIImageView?
   var lblTitle:UILabel?
   var data:FilterItem?
   weak var delegate: ImageFilteringDelegate?
   ```

   Here, we are creating a delegate, which is used to let any class know when something happens. We use this delegate when someone taps on the object itself, which allows us to pass the `FilterItem` data to a parent class.

   You have used this pattern already plenty of times. Table Views and Collection Views both have delegates to which you conform.

6. Now, we need to add our `init` methods. Add the following after your variables:

   ```
   required init?(coder aDecoder: NSCoder) {
       fatalError(init(coder:) has not been implemented)
   }

   init(frame:CGRect, image:UIImage, item:FilterItem) {
       super.init(frame: frame)
       setDefaults(item: item)
       createThumbnail(image: image, item: item)
       createLabel(item: item)
   }
   ```

   Whenever you create a `UIView`, you are required to add this method. If you do not, it gives you an error, and then you have to add it.

   This is a custom `init()` method, which allows us to pass data (here, the frame, image, and filter items) when the item gets created. We have a few errors because we have not created the methods we added to our `init()` method.

7. Next, let's create an extension and add the following methods:

   ```
   private extension PhotoItem {
     func setDefaults(item:FilterItem) {
       data = item
       let tap = UITapGestureRecognizer(target: self,
       action:#selector(thumbTapped))
       self.addGestureRecognizer(tap)
       self.backgroundColor = .clear
     }
   ```

Working with Photo Filters

```
    func createThumbnail(image:UIImage, item:FilterItem) {
      if item.filter != "None" {
        let filteredImg = apply(filter: item.filter, originalImage:
image)
        imgThumb = UIImageView(image: filteredImg)
      }
      else { imgThumb = UIImageView(image: image) }

      guard let thumb = imgThumb else {
        return
      }

      thumb.contentMode = .scaleAspectFill
      thumb.frame = CGRect(x: 0, y: 22, width: 102, height: 102)
      thumb.clipsToBounds = true
      addSubview(thumb)
    }

    func createLabel(item:FilterItem) {
      lblTitle = UILabel(frame: CGRect(x: 0, y: 0, width: 102,
height: 22))

      guard let label = lblTitle else {
        return
      }

      label.text = item.name
      label.font = UIFont.systemFont(ofSize: 12.0)
      label.textAlignment = .center
      label.backgroundColor = .clear


      addSubview(label)
    }
}
```

Our `setDefaults()` method is used to create a tap gesture. When the item gets tapped, we call the `thumbTapped` method. We also set the data and the background color of this method.

The `createThumbnail(image: item:)` is used to create an image and apply a filter to the image. Then, we are setting its frame and adding the image to the View.

With our final method, `createLabel(item:)`, we are creating a label and passing in the name of the filter. Then, we are setting its frame and adding the label to the View. We have two more methods we need to add to our extension.

8. Add the following after the `createLabel(item:)` method:

```
@objc func thumbTapped() {
   if let data = self.data {
     filterSelected(item: data)
   }
}

func filterSelected(item:FilterItem) {
   delegate?.filterSelected(item: item)
}
```

The `thumbTapped()` method is used to detect taps. When the user taps the item, it calls `filterSelected`.

The `filterSelected(item:)` method is the protocol we created earlier; and all we are doing is calling the `delegate` method, `filterSelected`. We see what happens next when the selected filter gets called.

Our `PhotoItem` is complete; now we need to work on our cell for our `Filter` collection view.

Creating a filter cell

We already created our cell that we need in the storyboard. However, before we create our View Controller, we need to create a filter cell. This cell is used to display all of the available filters.

1. Right-click the `Photo Filter` folder in the `Controller` folder in the `Review` folder and select **New File**.
2. Inside the **Choose a template for your new file** screen, select **iOS** at the top, and then **Cocoa Touch Class**. Then, hit **Next**.

Working with Photo Filters

3. In the options screen that appears, add the following:

   New file:
   - **Class**: `FilterCell`
   - **Subclass**: `UICollectionViewCell`
   - **Also create XIB**: Unchecked
   - **Language**: `Swift`

4. Click **Next**, and then **Create**.
5. Update your file to the following:

```swift
class FilterCell: UICollectionViewCell {
  @IBOutlet var lblName:UILabel!
  @IBOutlet var imgThumb: UIImageView!
}

extension FilterCell: ImageFiltering {
  func set(image:UIImage, item:FilterItem) {
    if item.filter != "None" {
      let filteredImg = apply(filter: item.filter, originalImage: image)
      imgThumb.image = filteredImg
    }
    else { imgThumb.image = image }

    lblName.text = item.name

    roundedCorners()
  }

  func roundedCorners() {
    imgThumb.layer.cornerRadius = 9
    imgThumb.layer.masksToBounds = true
  }
}
```

Our cell is pretty basic: we are setting an image and giving it rounded corners.

6. Open `PhotoFilter.storyboard`.
7. In the Outline view, select the **Collection View** cell. Then, in the Utilities panel, under the Identity inspector set the **Custom Class** to **FilterCell**.
8. In the Attributes inspector, set the **Identifier** to **filterCell**.

9. Next, connect your outlets for both `lblName` and `imgThumb`.
10. We need to make sure we can dismiss our modal when we click the **Add Photo** button. We already added the method we needed, but we just need to add this to the storyboard. CTL drag from **Cancel** to the **Exit** icon:

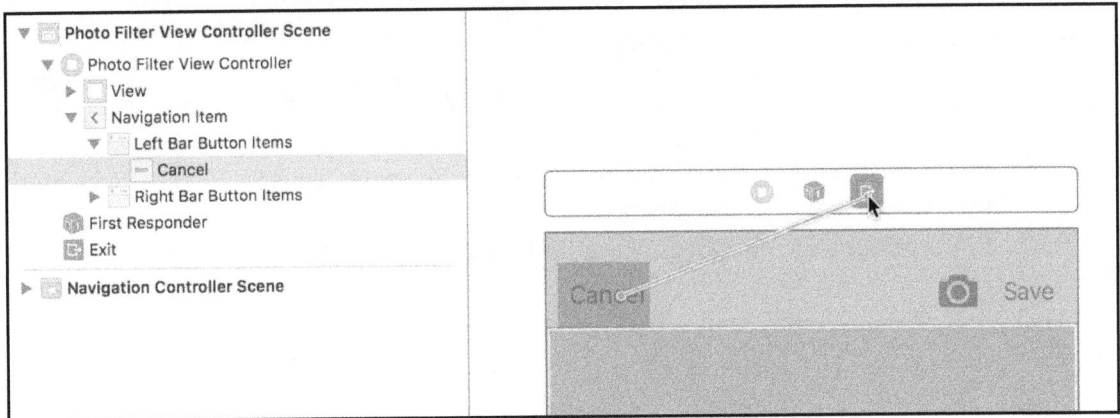

11. In the popup, select `unwindReviewCancelWithSegue`:

12. In the Navigation controller, select the Navigation bar in the Outline view. Then, in the Attributes inspector, uncheck **Translucent**:

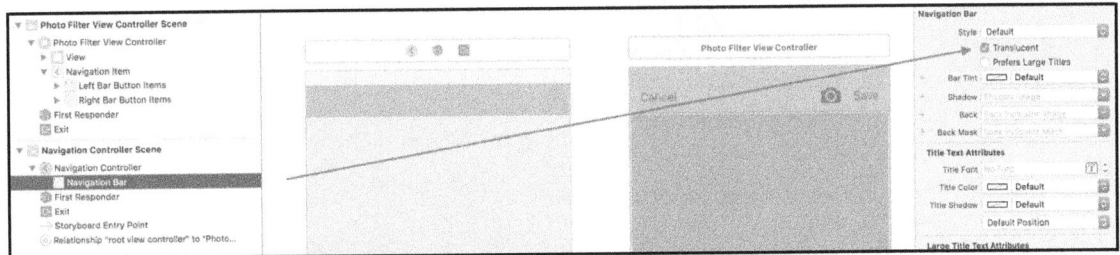

Adding this makes sure our navigation bar is a solid white color and not translucent.

Working with Photo Filters

We are done with setting up the cell and storyboard setup. Let's move to creating our View Controller.

Creating our apply filter view controller

Now we need to create our `PhotoFilterViewController`:

1. Right-click the `Photo Filter` folder in the `Controller` folder in the `Review` folder and select **New File**.
2. Inside the **Choose a template for your new file** screen, select **iOS** at the top, and then **Cocoa Touch Class**. Then, hit **Next**.
3. In the options screen that appears, add the following:

    New file:

    - **Class**: `PhotoFilterViewController`
    - **Subclass**: `UIViewController`
    - **Also create XIB**: Unchecked
    - **Language**: `Swift`

4. Click **Next** and then **Create**.

    When the file opens, delete everything after the `viewDidLoad()` method.

5. Then, add the following:

    ```
    class PhotoFilterViewController: UIViewController {
        var image: UIImage?
        var thumbnail: UIImage?
        let manager = FilterManager()
        var selectedRestaurantID:Int?
        var data:[FilterItem] = []
        @IBOutlet var collectionView: UICollectionView!
        @IBOutlet weak var imgExample: UIImageView!

        override func viewDidLoad() {
            super.viewDidLoad()
            initialize()
        }
    }
    ```

Chapter 20

Here, we are setting up our variables and our `initialize()` method. You can ignore the error, as we fix this next by creating an extension after our class definition.

6. Add the following extension:

```
// MARK: - Private Extension
private extension PhotoFilterViewController {

  func initialize() {
    requestAccess()
    setupCollectionView()
    checkSource()
  }
}
```

We are creating some basic functions that we need. Our first function is our `initialize()` method, which calls three new methods. Let's create those three methods next.

7. Add the following methods after the `initialize()` method:

```
func requestAccess() {
  AVCaptureDevice.requestAccess(for: AVMediaType.video) { granted in
    if granted {}
  }
}

func setupCollectionView() {
  let layout = UICollectionViewFlowLayout()
  layout.scrollDirection = .horizontal
  layout.sectionInset = UIEdgeInsets(top: 7, left: 7, bottom: 7, right: 7)
  layout.minimumInteritemSpacing = 0
  layout.minimumLineSpacing = 7

  collectionView?.collectionViewLayout = layout
  collectionView?.delegate = self
  collectionView?.dataSource = self
}

func checkSource() {
  let cameraMediaType = AVMediaType.video
  let cameraAuthorizationStatus = AVCaptureDevice.authorizationStatus(for: cameraMediaType)
```

[543]

Working with Photo Filters

```
        switch cameraAuthorizationStatus {
          case .authorized:
          showCameraUserInterface()
          case .restricted, .denied:
          break
          case .notDetermined:
          AVCaptureDevice.requestAccess(for: cameraMediaType) { granted
    in
            if granted {
              self.showCameraUserInterface()
            }
          }
        }
      }
```

Our next method, `setupCollectionView()` method, is our basic setup for our collection view. We are doing something different with the `delegate` and `dataSource`. In the previous chapters, we set this up using the Outlet inspector. This time, I am setting them up in code. Either can be done; there is no right or wrong way, but pick one way and stick with it in the entire app. I did both only for demonstration purposes.

The next method requests user access to their camera or the photo library. The `checkSource()`, checks whether you are running this in the simulator or phone. If you are running the simulator, you automatically get the photo library since there is no camera. If you are on a device, then the user has access to their camera. Now, we need to add two more helper methods. Let's add them first and then discuss after.

8. Add the following methods:

```
      func showApplyFilter() {
        manager.fetch { (items) in
          if data.count > 0 { data.removeAll() }
          data = items
          if let image = self.image {
            imgExample.image = image
            collectionView.reloadData()
          }
        }
      }

      func filterItem(at indexPath: IndexPath) -> FilterItem{
        return data[indexPath.item]
      }
```

Chapter 20

The first method `showApplyFilter()` is used to create the filter content inside of our collection view. The `filterItem(at:)` is used when the user selects a `filter` item. We will pass the index position of the Collection View and create a filter item from it. This item is used to display the currently selected filter in the larger image above our Collection View.

Let's work on getting items displayed in our Collection View. As we have done in the past, we have a few methods that are required for our Collection View to display cells. Add the following extension under our private extension:

```
extension PhotoFilterViewController: UICollectionViewDataSource {
    func collectionView(_ collectionView: UICollectionView,
numberOfItemsInSection section: Int) -> Int {
        return data.count
    }

    func numberOfSections(in collectionView: UICollectionView) -> Int {
        return 1
    }

    func collectionView(_ collectionView: UICollectionView, cellForItemAt indexPath: IndexPath) -> UICollectionViewCell {
        let cell = collectionView.dequeueReusableCell(withReuseIdentifier: "filterCell", for: indexPath) as! FilterCell
        let item = self.data[indexPath.row]
        if let img = self.thumbnail {
            cell.set(image: img, item: item)
        }
        return cell
    }
}
```

We have done this before, but let's go over the methods again. Our -`collectionView:numberOfItemsInSection:` is responsible for the number of items in each section. For this collection view, it means the number of filter items we are going to display. Next, we have -`numberOfSectionsInCollectionView:`, which tells our Collection View how many sections we have; in our case, we only have one. Finally, we have the -`collectionView:cellForItemAtIndexPath:` this is the method that gets run for every cell we need to create. In this method, we are creating a filter cell.

Working with Photo Filters

Now that we have our basic collection view set up, we need to make sure our Collection View is laid out correctly. Let's add another extension in this file that is responsible for the layout of items for our Collection View. Add the following extension and method after the last extension we just added:

```
extension PhotoFilterViewController: UICollectionViewDelegateFlowLayout {
    func collectionView(_ collectionView: UICollectionView, layout
collectionViewLayout: UICollectionViewLayout, sizeForItemAt indexPath:
IndexPath) -> CGSize {
        let screenRect = collectionView.frame.size.height
        let screenHt = screenRect - 14
        return CGSize(width: 150, height: screenHt)
    }
}
```

This extension just sets up our cell size and spacing. Save the file. Next, let's hook up our two `IBOutlets`:

1. Open the `PhotoFilter.storyboard`.
2. Select the View Controller in the Outline view, and then the Identity inspector in the Utilities panel.
3. Under **Custom Class**, in the **Class** drop-down menu, select or type `PhotoFilterViewController` and hit *Enter*.
4. Then, select the Connections inspector in the Utilities panel.
5. Under Outlets, click and drag from the empty circle of each of the components, `imgExample`, `collectionView`, and `onPhotoTapped:`, to the `Image View`, `CollectionView View`, `Camera Icon (inside Navigation Bar at the top)`, respectively, in the scene. Now, please open the `PhotoFilterViewController.swift` file again, and let's add some more code.

Our Collection View is set up, but we need to add some more code before we can get everything else working. Next, we need to add two more extensions that handle when a user uses the camera and photo library and the second one that is for our custom protocol we created earlier. We will need to use `AVFoundation` and `MobileCoreServices` in our app. `AVFoundation` is a framework that gives us access to the camera and `MobileCoreServices` gives us access to the filters. At the top of the file under import `UIKit`:

```
import AVFoundation
import MobileCoreServices
```

6. Now, let's add the first extension we will need for access to the camera and photo library:

```swift
extension PhotoFilterViewController:
UIImagePickerControllerDelegate, UINavigationControllerDelegate {

    func imagePickerControllerDidCancel(_ picker:
UIImagePickerController) {
        picker.dismiss(animated: true, completion: nil)
    }

    func imagePickerController(_ picker: UIImagePickerController,
didFinishPickingMediaWithInfo info: [String : Any]) {
        let image = info[UIImagePickerControllerEditedImage] as?
UIImage
        if let img = image {
            self.thumbnail = generate(image: img, ratio:
CGFloat(102))
            self.image = generate(image: img, ratio: CGFloat(752))
        }
        picker.dismiss(animated: true, completion: {
            self.showApplyFilter()
        })
    }

    func showCameraUserInterface() {
        let imagePicker = UIImagePickerController()
        imagePicker.delegate = self
        #if (arch(i386) || arch(x86_64)) && os(iOS)
            imagePicker.sourceType =
UIImagePickerControllerSourceType.photoLibrary
        #else
            imagePicker.sourceType =
UIImagePickerControllerSourceType.camera
            imagePicker.showsCameraControls = true
        #endif
        imagePicker.mediaTypes = [kUTTypeImage as String]
        imagePicker.allowsEditing = true
        self.present(imagePicker, animated: true, completion: nil)
    }

    func generate(image:UIImage, ratio:CGFloat) -> UIImage {
        let size = image.size
        var croppedSize:CGSize?
        var offsetX:CGFloat = 0.0
        var offsetY:CGFloat = 0.0
        if size.width > size.height {
```

Working with Photo Filters

```
            offsetX = (size.height - size.width) / 2
            croppedSize = CGSize(width: size.height, height:
size.height)
        }
        else {
            offsetY = (size.width - size.height) / 2
            croppedSize = CGSize(width: size.width, height:
size.width)
        }
        guard let cropped = croppedSize, let cgImage =
image.cgImage else {
            return UIImage()
        }
        let clippedRect = CGRect(x: offsetX * -1, y: offsetY * -1,
width: cropped.width, height: cropped.height)
        let imgRef = cgImage.cropping(to: clippedRect)
        let rect = CGRect(x: 0.0, y: 0.0, width: ratio, height:
ratio)
        UIGraphicsBeginImageContext(rect.size)
        if let ref = imgRef {
            UIImage(cgImage: ref).draw(in: rect)
        }
        let thumbnail = UIGraphicsGetImageFromCurrentImageContext()
        UIGraphicsEndImageContext()
        guard let thumb = thumbnail else { return UIImage() }
        return thumb
    }
}
```

This extensions that we created for `UIImagePickerControllerDelegate` and `UINavigationControllerDelegate` have two methods we need to implement. We also have some custom helper methods that we use. The `-imagePickerControllerDidCancel: method()` is called when the user hit the **Cancel** button; therefore, we just dismiss the `Controller` and do nothing.

The `-imagePickerController:didFinishPickingMediaWithInfo: method()` is used when we get the image from the `Picker` once it is dismissed. We set our thumbnail and image values here; then, we apply the `generate()` method in order to get them in a smaller size. Finally, we dismiss the `Controller` and then call `showApplyFilter()` to add our selected image to our filter view.

Chapter 20

The `showCameraUserInterface()` is used to show the camera interface along with the camera controls. As I mentioned earlier, the code first checks to see if you are running the simulator and, if so, it shows the photo library. If you are running on a device, you see the camera interface. The `generate(image:ratio:)` method is what we use to take the images and crop them to the size we need and return an image in a smaller size. The photo library and camera images are quite large. Therefore, if we did not use this method, it would take a long time for UI to go through and do everything we need.

We just have one more extension to add, and that is for the custom protocols we created earlier. Add the following extension at the bottom of your `PhotoFilterViewController`:

```
extension PhotoFilterViewController: ImageFiltering, ImageFilteringDelegate
{
    func filterSelected(item: FilterItem) {
        let filteredImg = image
        if let img = filteredImg {
            if item.filter != "None" {
                imgExample.image = self.apply(filter: item.filter, originalImage: img)
            }
            else {
                imgExample.image = img
            }
        }
    }
}
```

The `filterSelected(item:)` gets the selected filter item and applies the filter to our `imgExample`. We have an `if` statement that checks to see if the user selected `None` and, if so, shows the image without any filters. Before we can run it, we need to get the user's permission to use the camera or access the user's photo library.

Getting permission

Apple requires that, if we use the camera or access the camera roll, we must let the user know that we are doing so and why. If you fail to do this, your code regarding the camera will not work and your app will be rejected when you submit it. Let's take care of this now.

Open the `Info.plist` file and add the following two keys by hovering over any key and hitting the plus icon for the first key and then repeating for the second key:

- `- NSPhotoLibraryUsageDescription`
- `- NSCameraUsageDescription`

For each key's value, enter anything you want as an alert that the user will see. In the following example, the value is set as `The app uses your camera to take pictures`:

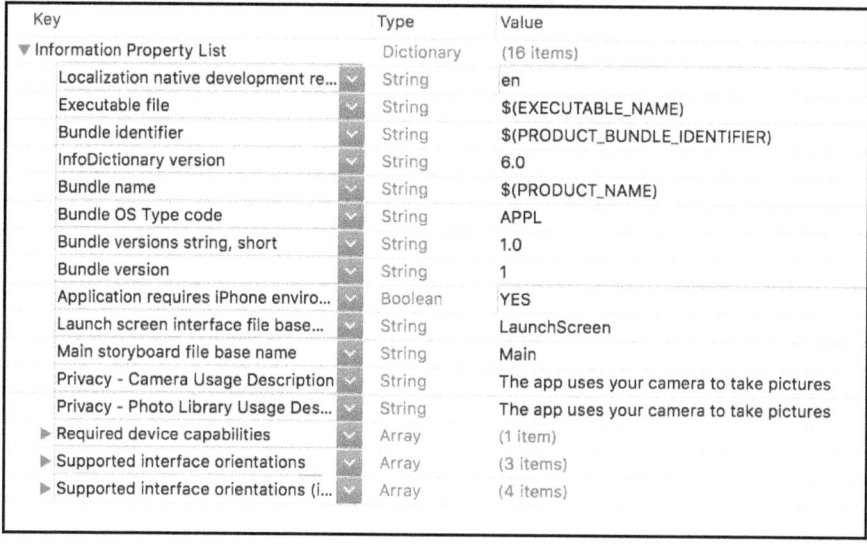

Chapter 20

Please make sure if you are submitting this to the store that you put in the appropriate verbiage. This verbiage is seen by the user as well as Apple. Let's build and run the project by hitting the Play button (or using *cmd + R*). You should now be able to get a photo from the photo library or use the camera.

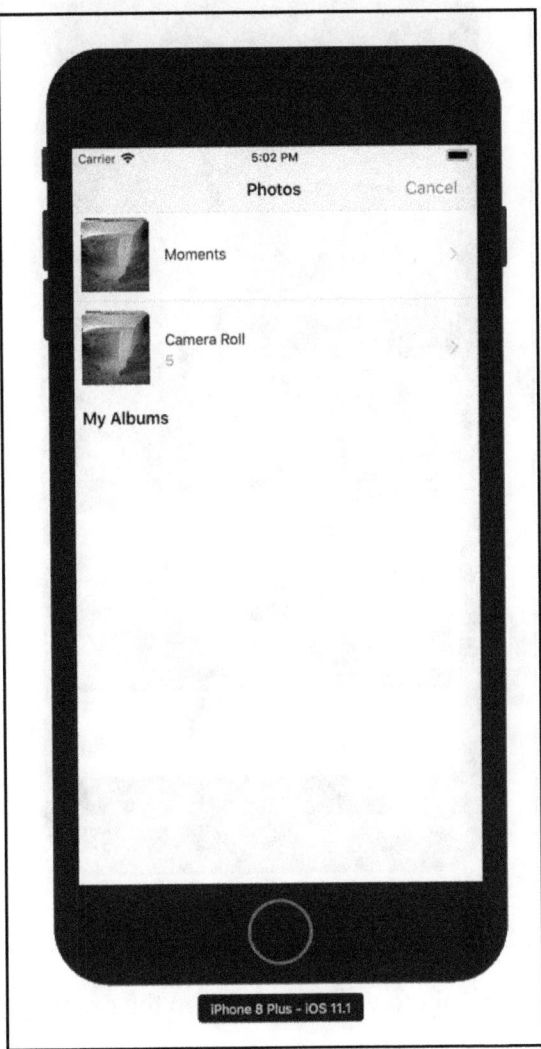

Working with Photo Filters

Once you have a photo, the window dismisses and you can apply a filter and save it.

We are not actually saving the photo yet. We do this in the next chapter.

Summary

In this chapter, we covered a lot of new things. You learned how to use the camera and how to integrate the camera roll when a camera is not available. We used a `UICollectionView` horizontally for the first time, to put in a row of images. This chapter had a lot of code and there may be some parts that were confusing. Review these parts and make sure that you fully understand them. There are numerous things in this chapter that you can reuse in many other apps.

In the next chapter, we will be able to save photos and reviews to restaurants.

21
Understanding Core Data

Our app is coming along nicely and we are close to wrapping it up. In the previous chapter, we created a restaurant review form, the Create Review form, which allows us to take pictures or use photos from our library. We can apply filters to photos and even add more filters quickly by updating our plist file.

In this chapter, we finish up working on the Create Review form. We get the form fully working where we can save the data entered into the form to what is known as Core Data. Core Data is a framework that handles persistent data using what is known as **Object-Relational Mapping** (**ORM**). We go much deeper into what Core Data is and how to use it in this chapter.

In this chapter we will cover the following topics:

- What is Core Data?
- What are `NSManagedObjectModel`, `NSManagedObjectContext`, and `NSPersistentStoreCoordinator`?
- Creating our first Core Data model

What is Core Data?

Let's start by taking a quote directly from Apple: *"Core Data is a framework for managing and persisting an object graph."* Apple does not call Core Data a database, even though, behind the scenes, it saves data to a SQLite file in iOS. Core Data is very hard to explain to someone new to programming or to someone who has come from a different programming language. However, in iOS 10, Core Data has been dramatically simplified. Having a general understanding of what Core Data does and how it works is sufficient for our purposes in this book.

Understanding Core Data

When using the Core Data framework, you should be familiar with the **managed object model**, the managed object context, and the **persistent store coordinator**. Let's look at a diagram to get a better understanding of how they interact with each other:

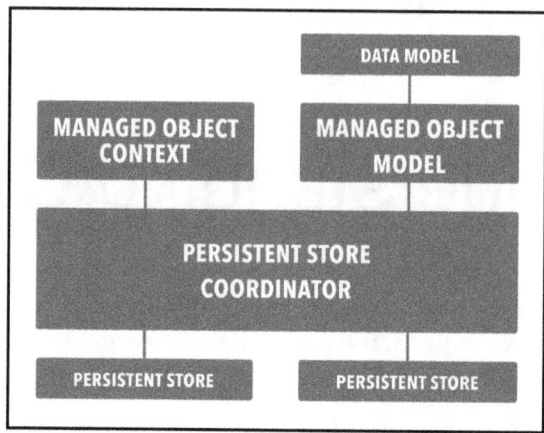

- `NSManagedObjectModel`: The managed object model represents the data model of your Core Data application. The managed object model interacts with all of the data models (also known as entities) that you create within your app. This model is known for any relationships that your data may have in your app. The managed object model interacts with your data model as well as with the persistent store coordinator.
  Entities are just objects that represent your data. In our app, since we are going to be saving customer reviews for restaurants, we need to create a review entity.
- `NSManagedObjectContext`: The managed object context manages a collection of model objects, which it receives from the persistent store coordinator. The managed object context is responsible for creating, reading, updating, and deleting models. The context is what you interact with the most.
- `NSPersistentStoreCoordinator`: The persistent store coordinator has a reference to the managed object model, as well as the managed object context. The persistent store coordinator communicates with the persistent object store. The persistent store coordinator interacts with an object graph. This graph is where you create your entities and set up relationships within your app.

Core Data is not an easy topic, so you do not need to worry about the finer details. The more you work with Core Data, the easier it becomes to understand it. In this chapter, focus on obtaining a high-level understanding and the rest will come.

Chapter 21

Before iOS 10, you had to create an instance of each of the following: the managed object model, the managed object context, and the persistent store coordinator. Now, in iOS 10, these have been consolidated into what is called `NSPersistentContainer`. We cover this shortly but, first, we need to create our data model.

Creating a data model

The data model is where you create your app's model objects and their properties. For our project, we only need to create one model object, called **Review**. Let's create a managed object model now:

1. In the Navigator panel, right-click on the `Misc` folder and create a new group, called `Core Data`.
2. Next, right-click this new `Core Data` folder and click **New File**.
3. Inside the **Choose a template for your new file screen**, select **iOS** at the top and then scroll down to the **Core Data** section and select **Data Model**. Then, hit **Next**:

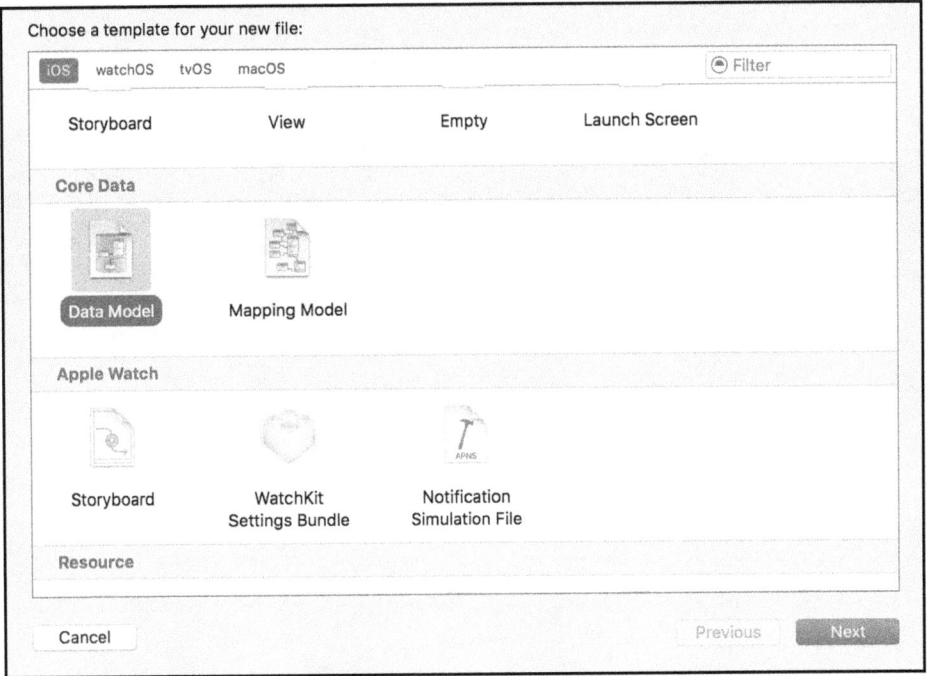

[557]

Understanding Core Data

4. Name the file `LetsEatModel` and click **Create**.
5. Click **Add Entity** in the screen that appears:

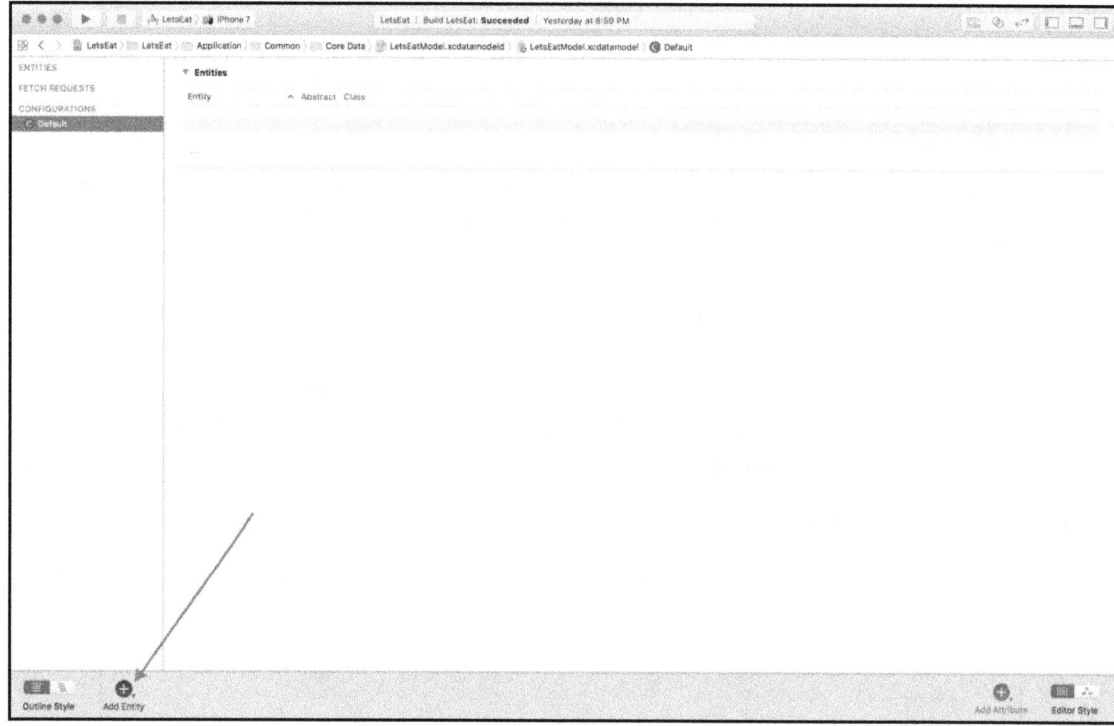

Chapter 21

Then, in the bottom-right corner of the new screen, change the **Editor Style** to the **Graph Style**:

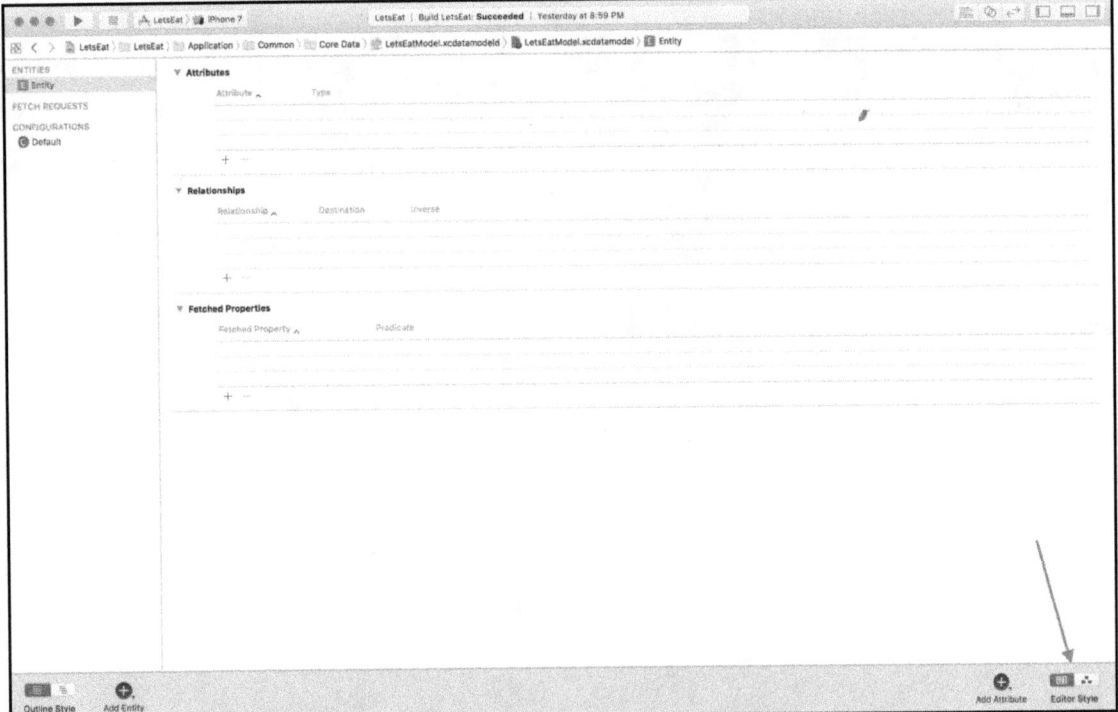

Understanding Core Data

In the **Graph Style**, double-click on **Entity** in the box in the middle of the graph to change our entity's name:

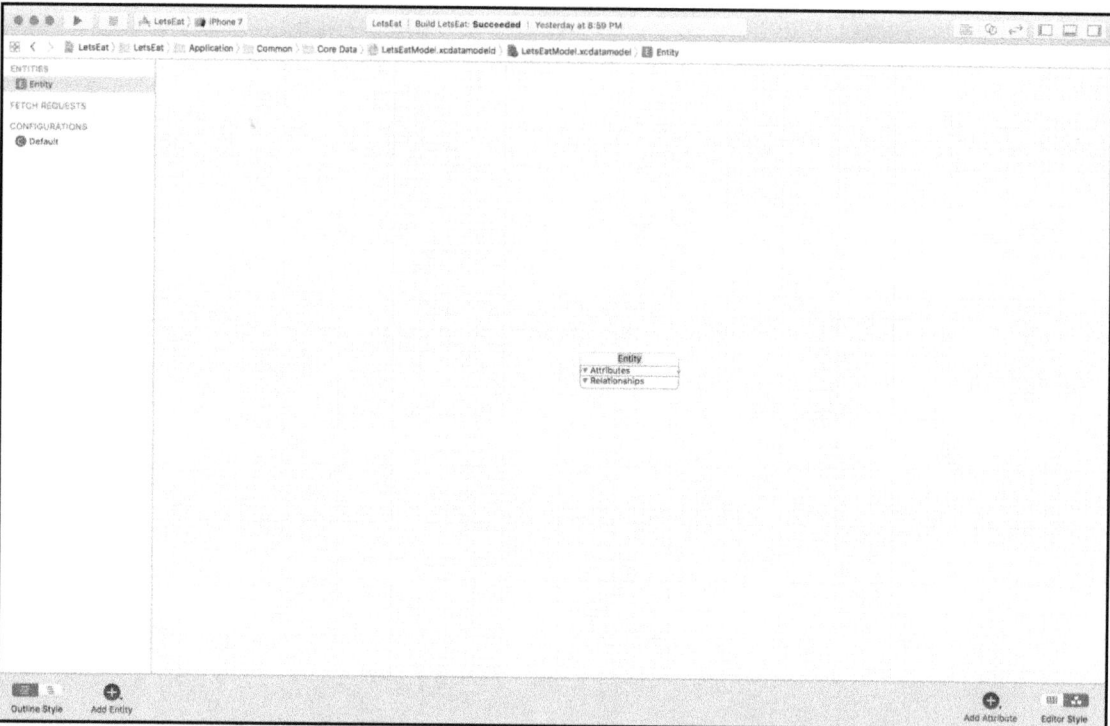

6. Update the text to say **Review** and then hit *Enter*.
7. Now that we have our first entity created, let's add our first attribute. Select our **Review Entity** and click the **Add Attribute** button in the bottom-right corner of the screen. The word attribute is under **Attributes** in the box in the middle of the screen:

Chapter 21

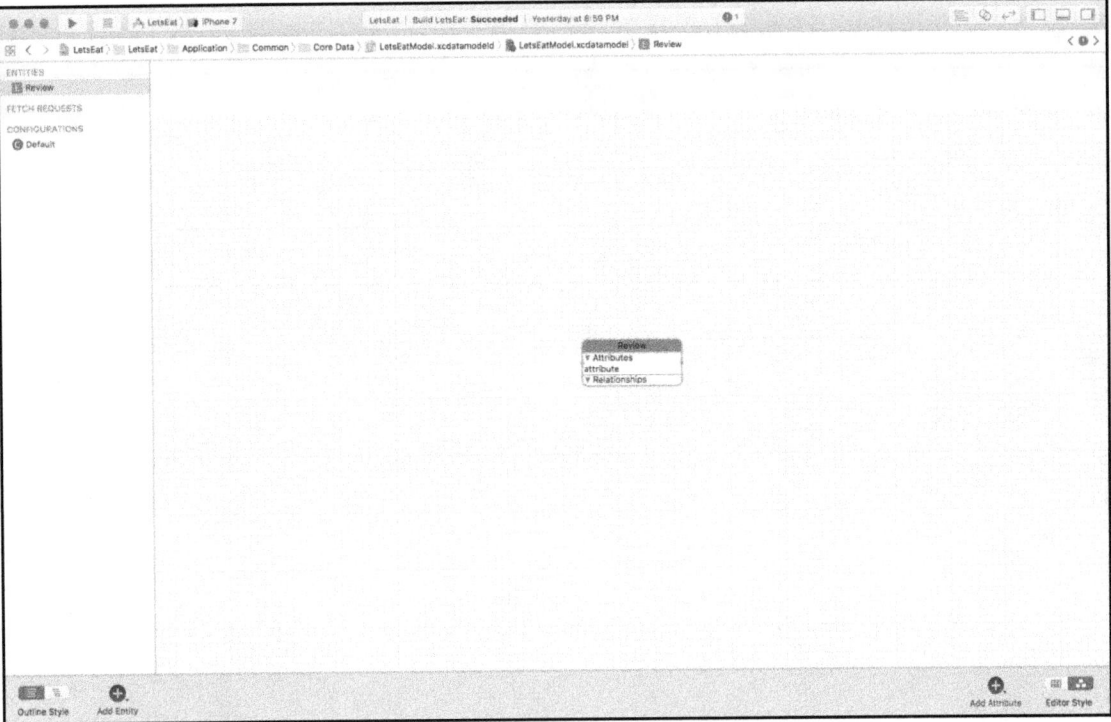

8. You see that Xcode has given you an error. The reason for the error is that we created an attribute without giving it a type yet. Let's do this now.
9. Select the word attribute and open your Utilities panel. You only see three icons: the File inspector, the Quick Help inspector, and the Data Model inspector.
10. Select the last icon, the Data Model inspector, and, under **Attribute**, click on the drop-down for **Attribute Type** and change it from **Undefined** to **String**. The error should now disappear.
11. Next, under **Attribute** in the Data Model inspector, change the **Name** from attribute to name and hit *Enter*.

Understanding Core Data

Your first attribute should now look as follows:

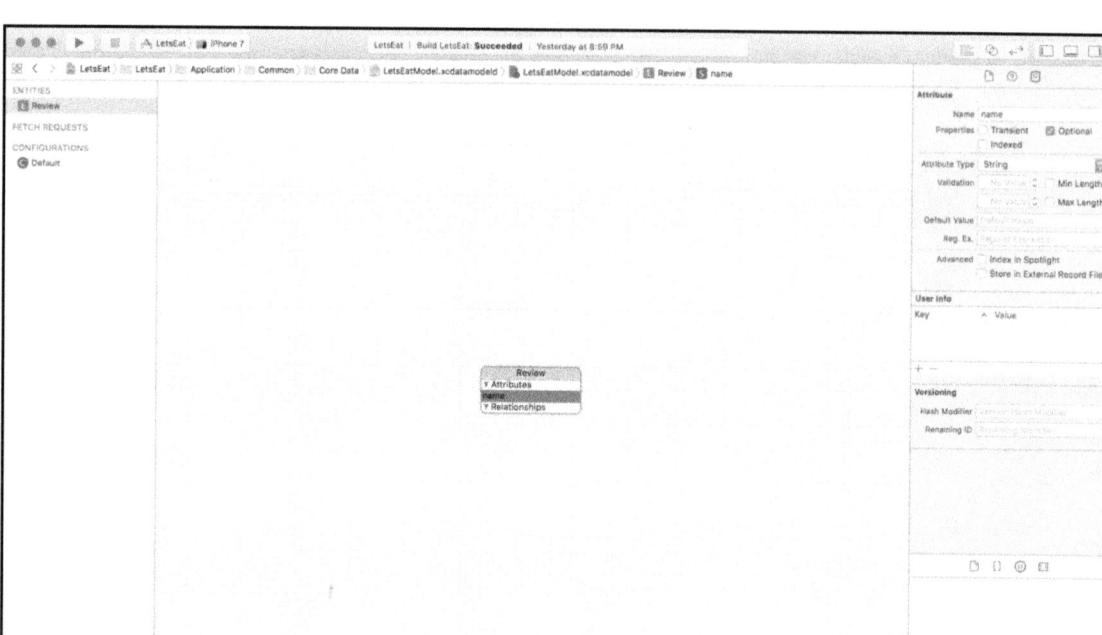

We have created our first attribute in the **Graph Style** and now need to set up the rest of our attributes, which we do in the **Table Style**:

1. Switch the **Editor Style** to the **Table Style** and then click **Add Attribute**:
2. Update the attribute to date and set its data type to **Date**. You do not have to do anything in the Data Model inspector for this attribute.
3. Next, select the + button in the **Attributes** section of the **Table Style** screen under the two attributes we just added.
4. Update this third attribute to `customerReview` and set its data type to **String**.
5. Next, add a fourth attribute, named rating with a data type of **Float**.
6. Now, add a fifth attribute, named `restaurantID` with a data type of **Integer 32**.

Chapter 21

7. When we save reviews, we save them with their `restaurantID`. Whenever we go to a restaurant detail page, we get all of the reviews just for that specific restaurant and then display them. If we do not have any reviews, then we display a default message.
8. Lastly, add a sixth attribute, named `uuid` with a data type of **String** and, under **Attribute** in the Data Model inspector, uncheck the **Optional** checkbox. This attribute is our unique ID for each review.

Your **Attributes** table should now look like the following:

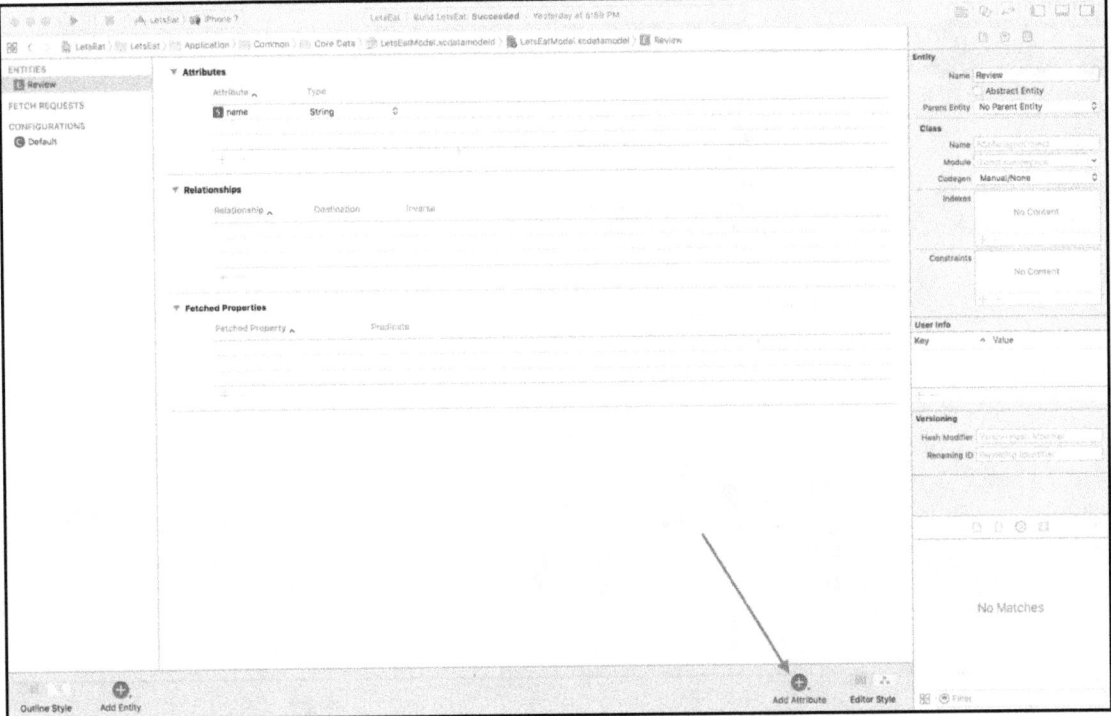

Now that we have our attributes set, we need to do a few more things before we start working on some code.

[563]

Understanding CORE Data

Entity auto-generation

We could have Xcode create a file for our **Review Entity**; however, if we wanted to add more attributes, we would have to generate more code. Core Data offers the ability to auto-generate our code for us. To take advantage of this feature:

1. In in the list of entities in the left panel, select our only **Entity**, **Review**.
2. After you select the entity, select the Data Model inspector in the Utilities panel. You should notice that your Data Model inspector panel has changed from when we were working on our **Attributes**.

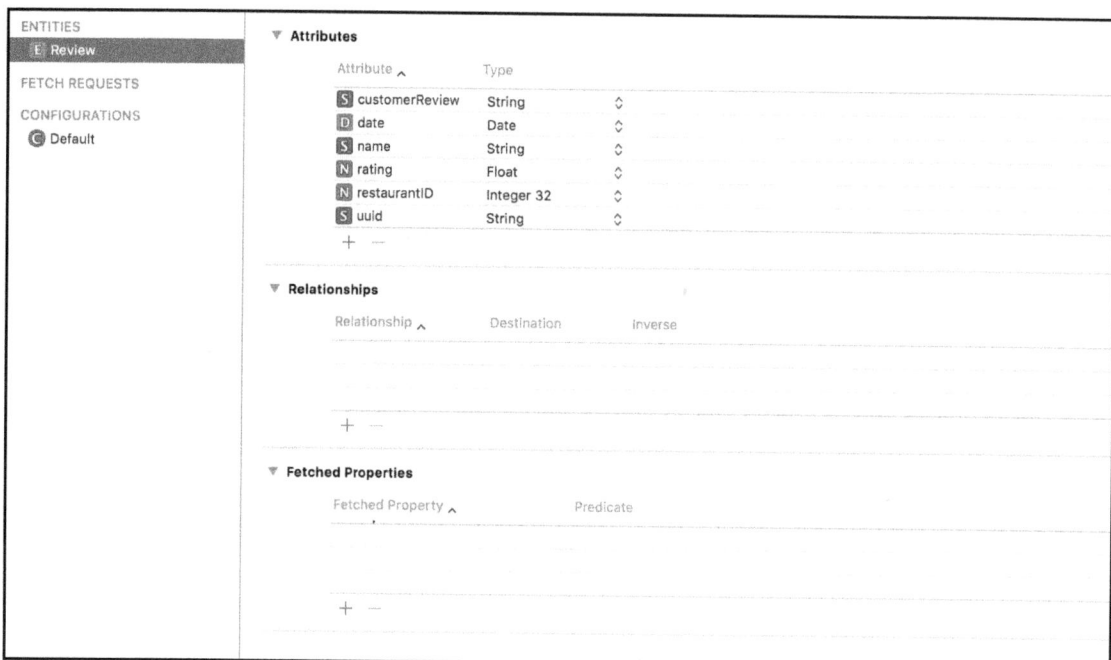

3. Now, hit cmd + B to build the project. This will create the **Review** class that we created in **Core Data**. You will not see the file anywhere, but it has been created.

We now need to create another entity called `RestaurantPhoto`.

Restaurant Photo Entity

Using the same steps as in the previous section, create a photo entity with the following values:

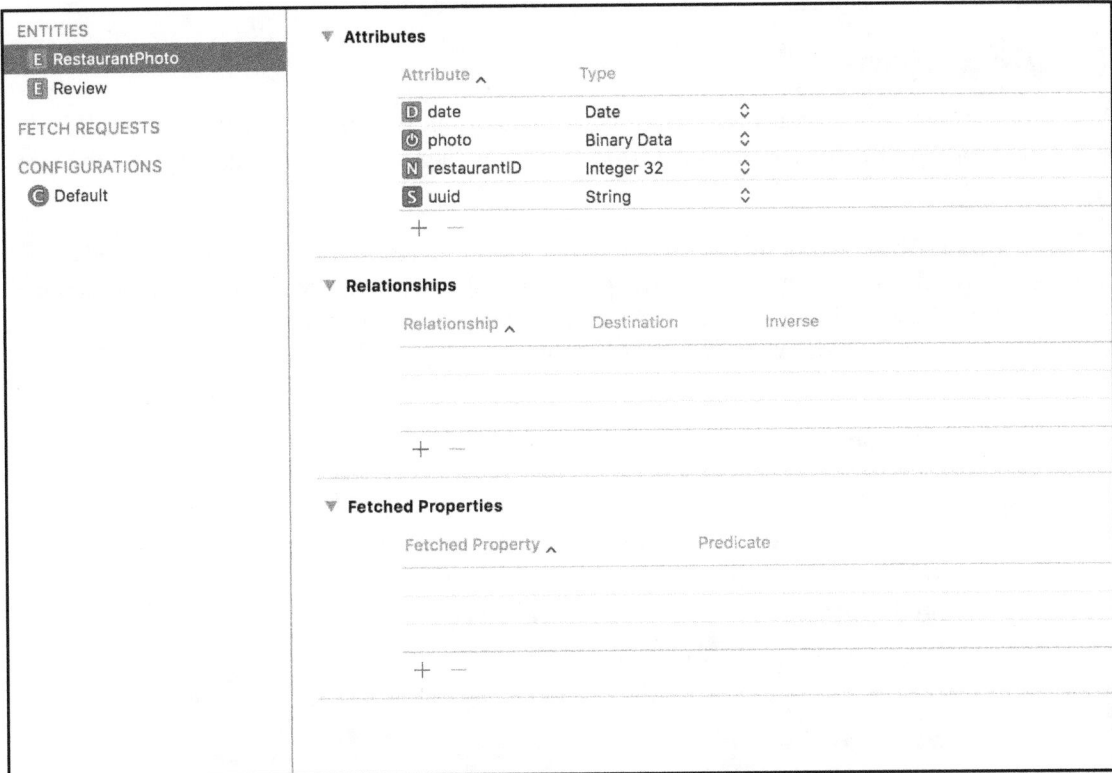

Now, hit *cmd + B* to build the project; this creates the `Photo` class that we created in **Core Data**.

We cannot just store images in Core Data, as they have to be converted to data first. Therefore, we take the image used in the review and convert it to binary data for Core Data to save. Then, when we pull the review out of the Core Data, we convert it back to an image to display it.

Understanding Core Data

For learning, we store images in Core Data. I would stay away from doing this as much as possible, because images can be large and you can quickly fill up the user's storage. If you are using a feed, you can save the URL path to the image instead of the actual image. If the user is not online, then you can just display a placeholder in its place.

Review item

We get this new `Review` class back from Core Data when we need to fetch items from it. Instead of passing the `Review` class around, we create a generic data object that we can use instead.

When I work with stored data, I typically like to have two model objects: one used when storing data and the other generic. In the past, passing around Core Data objects caused a lot of technical issues. These issues were addressed in iOS 10; however, in an overabundance of caution, I typically get the items from Core Data and then convert those objects into a struct.

Let's create this file now:

1. Right-click the `Review Form` folder and select **New File**.
2. Inside **Choose a template for your new file screen**, select **iOS** at the top and then **Swift File**. Then hit **Next**.
3. Name this file `ReviewItem` and hit **Create**.
4. Update your file to the following:

```swift
import UIKit
struct ReviewItem {
    var rating:Float?
    var name:String?
    var customerReview:String?
    var date:NSDate?
    var restaurantID:Int?
    var uuid = UUID().uuidString
    var displayDate:String {
        let formatter = DateFormatter()
        formatter.dateFormat = "MMMM dd, yyyy"
        return formatter.string(from: self.date as! Date)
    }
}

extension ReviewItem {
    init(data:Review) {
        self.date = data.date
```

```
            self.customerReview = data.customerReview
            self.name = data.name
            self.restaurantID = Int(data.restaurantID)
            self.rating = data.rating
            if let uuid = data.uuid { self.uuid = uuid }
        }
    }
```

This file is not doing anything special, other than using a variable to handle dates.

The extension in this file allows us to take the Review from Core Data and map it to a `ReviewItem`. Our custom `init()` method allows us just to pass the `Review` object into the `init` parameters.

We need to create another item for our photos that we are saving. This file has the same basic structure as the `ReviewItem` does. Let's create this file now:

1. Right-click `Controllers` to create a new group called `Photo Reviews`.
2. Right-click the `Photo Filter` folder and select **New File**.
3. Inside the **Choose a template for your new file screen**, select **iOS** at the top and then **Swift File**. Then hit **Next**.
4. Name this file `RestaurantPhotoItem` and hit **Create**.
5. Update your file to the following:

```
struct RestaurantPhotoItem {
    var photo:UIImage?
    var date:NSDate?
    var restaurantID:Int?
    var uuid = UUID().uuidString
    var photoData:NSData {
        guard let image = photo else {
            return NSData()
        }
        return NSData(data: UIImagePNGRepresentation(image)!)
    }
}
extension RestaurantPhotoItem {
    init(data:RestaurantPhoto) {
        self.date = data.date
        self.restaurantID = Int(data.restaurantID)
        self.photo = UIImage(data:photo as Data, scale:1.0)
        if let uuid = data.uuid { self.uuid = uuid }
    }
}
```

Understanding Core Data

The first part of this file is exactly what we did for the review item, except for the `photoData` variable. Since we cannot store an image directly into Core Data, we need to convert it into binary data. The `photoData` variable handles this for us and makes it easier when we save an item just to pass `photoData` to Core Data.

Now that we have our `ReviewItem` and `RestaurantPhotoItem`, we need to set up our manager next.

Core Data manager

As we have done throughout the book, we are going to create a `Manager` class. This class will be responsible for getting data in and out of Core Data. Let's get started:

1. Right-click the `Core Data` folder in the `Common` folder and select **New File**.
2. Inside the **Choose a template for your new file screen**, select **iOS** at the top and then **Cocoa Touch Class**. Then hit **Next**.
3. In the options screen that appears, add the following:

    New file:

    - **Class**: `CoreDataManager`
    - **Subclass**: `NSObject`
    - **Also create XIB**: Unchecked
    - **Language**: `Swift`

4. Click **Next** and then **Create**.

When the file opens, under your `import UIKit`, add the following:

```
import CoreData
```

This import allows us to have access to the Core Data library. Next, inside the class definition, add the following:

```
let container:NSPersistentContainer
```

This constant, which is an `NSPersistentContainer`, gives us everything we need within a Core Data stack. As we discussed earlier, the `NSPersistentContainer` is composed of three things; a persistent store coordinator, a managed object context, and a managed object model.

You may have noticed an error after adding this variable. The reason for the error is that we do not have an `init()` method created.

Let's add this `init()` method after the constant we just added:

```swift
override init() {
    container = NSPersistentContainer(name: "LetsEatModel")
    container.loadPersistentStores { (storeDesc, error) in
        guard error == nil else {
            print(error?.localizedDescription as Any)
            return
        }
    }
    super.init()
}
```

This code is initializing the container and grabbing the managed object model we created earlier. The model is now able to see all of our entities and attributes therein.

Our `CoreDataManager` needs to do two things for us. We need to be able to add new a `ReviewItem` and fetch it. When we save a restaurant review, we want to be able to save the review with the restaurant. We do not need to save all of the restaurant information, since we can simply use the `restaurantID`. When we go to restaurant details, we can check Core Data for any reviews for a particular restaurant by its `restaurantID`. Let's add the following method after our `init()` method to accomplish this task for us:

```swift
func fetchReviews(by identifier:Int) -> [ReviewItem] {
    let moc = container.viewContext
    let request:NSFetchRequest<Review> = Review.fetchRequest()
    let predicate = NSPredicate(format: "restaurantID = %i",
Int32(identifier))
    var items:[ReviewItem] = []
    request.sortDescriptors = [
      NSSortDescriptor(key: "date", ascending: false)]
    request.predicate = predicate
    do {
        for data in try moc.fetch(request) {
            items.append(ReviewItem(data: data))
        }
        return items
```

Understanding Core Data

```
    } catch {
        fatalError("Failed to fetch reviews: \(error)")
    }
}
```

Let's review this code. Our `fetchReviews(by:)` method takes an ID and we use it to find reviews for a particular restaurant.

```
let moc = container.viewContext
let request:NSFetchRequest<Review> = Review.fetchRequest()
let predicate = NSPredicate(format: "restaurantID = %i", Int32(identifier))
```

In the first line, we are creating an instance of the **managed object context** (**moc**). This variable allows us to interact with Core Data. In the next line, we are creating a fetch request. This request is passed to the managed object context and tells it what we need. Finally, we are creating a predicate, which allows us to apply some search parameters. Specifically, we are saying that we want every `ReviewItem` that has the ID that we pass it.

```
request.sortDescriptors = [NSSortDescriptor(key: "date", ascending: false)]
request.predicate = predicate
```

Here, we are applying a sort descriptor to our request. Instead of getting reviews back in a random order, we sort all of the reviews by date.

```
do {
   for data in try moc.fetch(request) {
        items.append(ReviewItem(data: data))
   }
   return items
} catch {
   fatalError("Failed to fetch reviews: \(error)")
}
```

Finally, we are wrapping everything into a `do...catch` block. When the search occurs, it returns an array of `ReviewItems` or, if there were no `ReviewItems`, an empty array. If there was a problem with your setup, then you get a fatal error. When the fetch is complete, we then loop through the items and create our `ReviewItems`.

Here, we are applying a sort descriptor to our request. Instead of getting reviews back in a random order, we sort all of the reviews by date.

We have added our method to get reviews; we need to do the same for fetching photos. Add the following after the `fetchReviews(identifier:)` method:

```
func fetchPhotos(by identifier:Int) -> [RestaurantPhotoItem] {
    let moc = container.viewContext
    let request:NSFetchRequest<Review> = RestaurantPhoto.fetchRequest()
    let predicate = NSPredicate(format: "restaurantID = %i", Int32(identifier))
    var items:[RestaurantPhotoItem] = []
    request.sortDescriptors = [NSSortDescriptor(key: "date", ascending: false)]
    request.predicate = predicate
    do {
        for data in try moc.fetch(request) {
            items.append(ReviewItem(data: data))
        }
        return items
    } catch {
        fatalError("Failed to fetch photos: \(error)")
    }
}
```

Everything is the same as what we did to fetch review items, except we are fetching `RestaurantPhoto` items instead. Now we need to add a method to save our data into Core Data. Let's add the next two methods by adding the following after our `init()` method:

```
func addReview(_ item:ReviewItem) {
    let review = Review(context: container.viewContext)
    review.name = item.name
    review.date = NSDate()
    if let rating = item.rating { review.rating = rating }
    review.customerReview = item.customerReview
    review.uuid = item.uuid

    if let id = item.restaurantID {
        review.restaurantID = Int32(id)
        print("restaurant id \(id)")
            save()
    }
}

func addPhoto(_ item:RestarauntPhotoItem) {
    let photo = RestarauntPhoto(context: container.viewContext)
    photo.date = NSDate()
    photo.photo = item.photoData
    photo.uuid = item.uuid
```

Understanding Core Data

```
        if let id = item.restaurantID {
            photo.restaurantID = Int32(id)
            print("restaurant id \(id)")
                save()
        }
    }
```

You will get an error, because we have not created the `save()` method yet. Ignore it for now, as it will be created next.

This `addReview()` method takes a `ReviewItem` in the parameters. We convert the `ReviewItem` into a `Review` and then call the `save()` method.

Now, let's add the `save()` method after the `addReview()` method we just created:

```
    fileprivate func save() {
        do {
            if container.viewContext.hasChanges {
                try container.viewContext.save()
            }
        }
        catch let error {
            print(error.localizedDescription)
        }
    }
```

Once again, we are wrapping everything into a `do...catch` block. Inside of the do, we check to see if the managed object context has changed. If it has changed, then we call the `save()` method. We have now completed our Core Data manager.

Next, we need to create another manager class. This manager is responsible for making calls to the Core Data manager, similar to how the corresponding manager in the explore manager is responsible for getting the data from the plist; this gets us photos and reviews. Let's create this manager file now:

1. Right-click the `Misc` folder and select **New File**.
2. Inside the **Choose a template for your new file screen**, select **iOS** at the top and then **Cocoa Touch Class**. Then hit **Next**.

Chapter 21

3. In the options screen that appears, add the following:

New file:

- **Class**: `ReviewDataManager`
- **Subclass**: `NSObject`
- **Also create XIB**: Unchecked
- **Language**: `Swift`

4. Hit **Next** and then **Create**. Update your file to the following:

```
import Foundation
class ReviewDataManager: NSObject {
    private var reviewItems:[ReviewItem] = []
    private var photoItems:[RestaurantPhotoItem] = []
    let manager = CoreDataManager()
    func fetchReview(by restaurantID:Int) {
        if reviewItems.count > 0 { reviewItems.removeAll() }
        for data in manager.fetchReviews(by: restaurantID) {
            reviewItems.append(data)
        }
    }
    
    func fetchPhoto(by restaurantID:Int) {
        if photoItems.count > 0 { photoItems.removeAll() }
        for data in manager.fetchPhotos(by: restaurantID) {
            photoItems.append(data)
        }
    }
    
    func numberOfReviewItems() -> Int {
        return reviewItems.count
    }
    
    func numberOfPhotoItems() -> Int {
        return photoItems.count
    }
    
    func reviewItem(at index:IndexPath) -> ReviewItem {
        return reviewItems[index.item]
    }
```

```
        func photoItem(at index:IndexPath) -> RestaurantPhotoItem {
            return photoItems[index.item]
        }
    }
```

This manager class is similar to the other managers that we have created so far. In this manager, our fetch method takes an ID in the parameter. This ID represents the `restaurantID` that we use to search for `ReviewItems` in Core Data. If we find any `ReviewItems`, we add them to our array.

Summary

In this chapter, you learned about what Core Data is and how to use it. We also looked at `NSManagedObjectModel`, `NSManagedObjectContext`, and `NSPersistentStoreCoordinator` and how they work together inside Core Data. Even if they all do not make sense, and they did not work for me the first time, it is all right because it eventually clicks. Finally, we created two Core Data models, one for reviews and one for photos.

In the next chapter, we work on actually saving the data we create as well as getting it back out. We take our reviews and photos and display them inside our restaurant details.

22

Saving Reviews

We are just about done with our app. In this chapter, we will finally start saving reviews and photos into Core Data. We will then learn how to pull data from Core Data and display them in our app. A lot of the setup is already done for us and most of what we are doing is calling methods we created earlier in the book.

In this chapter, you will learn how to:

- Save items to Core Data
- Fetch items from Core Data
- Display items from Core Data into a Table View

Saving reviews

First, we will start with saving reviews into Core Data. Open up `ReviewFormViewController.swift` and above the `@IBOutlets` add the following variable:

```
var selectedRestaurantID:Int?
```

Next, delete everything inside your `onSavedTapped(:)` method and then add the following:

```
@IBAction func onSaveTapped(_ sender: Any) {
    
    var item = ReviewItem()
    item.name = tfName.text
    item.customerReview = tvReview.text
    item.restaurantID = selectedRestaurantID
    item.rating = Float(ratingView.rating)
```

Saving Reviews

```
let manager = CoreDataManager()
manager.addReview(item)
dismiss(animated: true, completion: nil)
}
```

This code is all we need to do to save an item into Core Data using our `CoreDataManager`. To display reviews for a particular restaurant, we need to save all reviews with a restaurant identifier. Then, when we go to a certain restaurant, we will use the restaurant identifier to search Core Data to see if there are any saved reviews. We pass this identifier using a segue.

1. Open `RestaurantDetail.storyboard` and select the segue we are using to go to the `ReviewForm`.
2. In the Attributes inspector of the Utilities panel, update **Identifier** under **Storyboard Segue** to say `showReview`. Then, hit *Enter*.
3. Next, we need to make sure that, when a user creates a review, we pass `restaurantID` to the **Review Form View Controller**. We need to update our `RestaurantItem` so it has an ID. Open `RestaurantItem` after var `imageURL:String?` and add the following:

    ```
    var restaurantID:String?
    ```

4. Next, inside the enum `CodingKeys:String` add the new case:

    ```
    case restaurantID = "id"
    ```

5. Open `RestaurantDetailViewController.swift` and add this method after the `viewDidLoad()` method (ignore the errors for now):

    ```
    override func prepare(for segue: UIStoryboardSegue, sender: Any?) {
        if let identifier = segue.identifier {
            switch identifier {
            case Segue.showReview.rawValue:
                showReview(segue: segue)
            default:
                print("Segue not added")
            }
        }
    }
    ```

The `prepare()` method inside the `RestaurantDetailViewController` will check for the `showReview` segue identifier. If successful, it will call the `showReview()` method, which will take you to the Reviews list.

6. Next, add the following method above the `createRating()` method inside the private extension:

    ```
    func showReview(segue:UIStoryboardSegue) {
        guard let navController = segue.destination as? UINavigationController,
            let viewController = navController.topViewController as? ReviewFormViewController else {
                return
        }
        viewController.selectedRestaurantID = selectedRestaurant?.restaurantID
    }
    ```

7. While we are cleaning up, move the `initialize()` method into the `private` extension.

8. Next, open `ReviewFormViewController`; let's create a `private` extension and move `onSaveTapped(_:)` into it. Then, delete everything inside the method and update the method with the following:

    ```
    private extension ReviewFormViewController {
        @IBAction func onSaveTapped(_ sender: Any) {
            var item = ReviewItem()
            item.name = tfName.text
            item.customerReview = tvReview.text
            item.restaurantID = selectedRestaurantID
            item.rating = Float(ratingView.rating)
            let manager = CoreDataManager()
            manager.addReview(item)
            dismiss(animated: true, completion: nil)
        }
    }
    ```

    Let's make sure we are passing the `restaurantID` by adding a `print` statement inside `ReviewFormViewController`.

9. Inside the `-viewDidLoad()` method, add the following `print` statement:

    ```
    print(selectedRestaurantID as Any)
    ```

Let's build and run the project by hitting the Play button (or use ⌘ + R). You should now be able to see `restaurantID` in the console. You can create a review and, after you save the review, you are brought back to the restaurant detail view, but we are still missing displaying our reviews in restaurant details. We will work on this later in this chapter. Before we do that, let's look at how we can save photos into Core Data.

Saving photos

Saving reviews was pretty simple and there is essentially no difference in saving photos. Our code will be pretty similar to what we did with reviews. Open the `PhotoFilterViewController`, delete everything inside the `checkSavedPhoto()` method, and update it with the following:

```
func checkSavedPhoto() {
    if let img = self.imgExample.image {
        var item = RestaurantPhotoItem()
        item.photo = generate(image: img, ratio: CGFloat(102))
        item.date = NSDate() as Date
        item.restaurantID = selectedRestaurantID
        let manager = CoreDataManager()
        manager.addPhoto(item)
    }
}
```

This method will make sure that we have an image and then save it to Core Data with its restaurant ID. We need to add a method for when **Save** is tapped. Add the following method inside the private extension:

```
@IBAction func onSaveTapped(_ sender: AnyObject) {
    DispatchQueue.main.async {
        self.checkSavedPhoto()
    }
}
```

Now, when a user taps the Save button, this will make sure that an image is saved; if so, it will save the data to Core Data. Before we can save, we need to pass the restaurant identifier to the PhotoFilterViewController.swift.

1. Open RestaurantDetail.storyboard and select the segue we are using to go to the Photo Filter View.
2. In the Attributes inspector of the Utilities panel, update **Identifier** under **Storyboard Segue** to say `showPhotoFilter`. Then, hit *Enter*.
3. Finally, open the `Segue.swift` file in the `Misc` folder under the `Common` folder and verify that the following `case` statement is included; if not, add it:

   ```
   case showPhotoFilter
   ```

4. Inside the `RestaurantDetailViewController.swift`, update your prepare method with the following:

```
override func prepare(for segue: UIStoryboardSegue, sender: Any?) {
    if let identifier = segue.identifier {
        switch identifier {
        case Segue.showReview.rawValue:
            showReview(segue: segue)
        case Segue.showPhotoFilter.rawValue:
            showPhotoFilter(segue: segue)
        default:
            print("Segue not added")
        }
    }
}
```

5. Next, add the following method after the `showReview()` method inside your `private` method:

```
func showPhotoFilter(segue:UIStoryboardSegue) {
    guard let navController = segue.destination as? UINavigationController,
        let viewController = navController.topViewController as? PhotoFilterViewController else {
            return
    }
    viewController.selectedRestaurantID = selectedRestaurant?.restaurantID
}
```

We are passing the restaurant identifier to our photos and we now have our photos saved in Core Data. After you save a photo, you are brought back to the restaurant detail view but next we need to display the photos in our **Detail** section.

We are missing one last thing. The photo review and review sections need to pull data from the database for it to be displayed. We need to create a class for each one, so let's start by adding this class now:

1. Create a new folder called `Reviews`.
2. Now, right-click the folder and select **New File**.
3. Inside the **Choose a template for your new file screen**, select **iOS** at the top and then **Cocoa Touch Class**. Then, hit **Next**.

Saving Reviews

4. In the options screen that appears, add the following:
   New file:

   - **Class**: `ReviewsViewController`
   - **Subclass**: `UIViewController`
   - **Also create XIB**: Unchecked
   - **Language**: `Swift`

5. Hit **Next** and then **Create**. When the file opens, replace everything with the following code:

   ```swift
   import UIKit
   class ReviewsViewController: UIViewController {
       @IBOutlet weak var collectionView: UICollectionView!
       var selectedRestaurantID:Int?
       let manager = CoreDataManager()
       var data: [ReviewItem] = []
       override func viewDidLoad() {
           super.viewDidLoad()
           initialize()
       }

       override func viewDidAppear(_ animated: Bool) {
           super.viewDidAppear(animated)
           setupDefaults()
       }
   }
   ```

6. Next, let's add our `private` extension by adding the following:

   ```swift
   private extension ReviewsViewController {
       func initialize() {
           setupCollectionView()
       }

       func setupDefaults() {
           checkReviews()
       }

       func setupCollectionView() {
           let flow = UICollectionViewFlowLayout()
           flow.sectionInset = UIEdgeInsets(top: 7, left: 7, bottom: 7, right: 7)
           flow.minimumInteritemSpacing = 0
           flow.minimumLineSpacing = 7
   ```

```
            flow.scrollDirection = .horizontal
            collectionView?.collectionViewLayout = flow
    }

    func checkReviews() {
        let viewController = self.parent as? RestaurantDetailViewController
        if let id = viewController?.selectedRestaurant?.restaurantID {
            if data.count > 0 { data.removeAll() }
            data = manager.fetchReviews(by: id)
            if data.count > 0 {
                collectionView.backgroundView = nil
            }
            else {
                let view = NoDataView(frame: CGRect(x: 0, y: 0, width: collectionView.frame.width, height: collectionView.frame.height))
                view.set(title: "Reviews")
                view.set(desc: "There are currently no reviews")
                collectionView.backgroundView = view
            }
            collectionView.reloadData()
        }
    }
}
```

We are doing the basic setup that we did before. Our `checkReviews()` method is a bit different, because we are first checking to see if there are any reviews at all. If there are not, we display a message that says `There are currently no reviews`. If there are, we do not display anything.

7. Next, let's add our Collection View extensions by adding the following to our data source:

```
extension ReviewsViewController: UICollectionViewDataSource {
    func collectionView(_ collectionView: UICollectionView, numberOfItemsInSection section: Int) -> Int {
        return data.count
    }

    func numberOfSections(in collectionView: UICollectionView) -> Int {
        return 1
    }

    func collectionView(_ collectionView: UICollectionView,
```

Saving Reviews

```
cellForItemAt indexPath: IndexPath) -> UICollectionViewCell {
        return
collectionView.dequeueReusableCell(withReuseIdentifier:
"reviewCell", for: indexPath)
    }
}
```

8. Next, let's add our Collection View extensions by adding the following to our layout:

```
extension ReviewsViewController: UICollectionViewDelegateFlowLayout
{
    func collectionView(_ collectionView: UICollectionView, layout
collectionViewLayout: UICollectionViewLayout, sizeForItemAt
indexPath:IndexPath) -> CGSize {
        if data.count == 1 {
            let width = collectionView.frame.size.width - 14
            return CGSize(width: width, height: 200)
        }
        else {
            let width = collectionView.frame.size.width - 21
            return CGSize(width: width, height: 200)
        }
    }
}
```

Next, for our Collection View to work, we need to create our cell and an extension of this class:

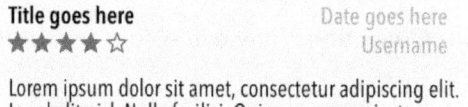

1. Right-click the `Review` folder and select **New File**.

2. Inside the **Choose a template for your new file screen**, select **iOS** at the top and then **Cocoa Touch Class**. Then, hit **Next**.
3. In the options screen that appears, add the following:

    New file:

    - **Class**: `ReviewCell`
    - **Subclass**: `UICollectionViewCell`
    - **Also create XIB**: Unchecked
    - **Language**: `Swift`

4. Click **Next** and then **Create**.
5. In this new file, add the following code:

    ```
    @IBOutlet weak var lblTitle: UILabel!
    @IBOutlet weak var lblDate: UILabel!
    @IBOutlet weak var lblName: UILabel!
    @IBOutlet weak var lblReview: UILabel!
    @IBOutlet weak var ratingView: RatingView!
    ```

6. Save the file and open up `RestaurantDetail.storyboard`.
7. Locate the `Container` that we created for `Reviews` and select the cell inside the Collection View. Select the View Controller and in the Identity inspector and under **Custom Class** set **Class** to **ReviewsViewController**.
8. Then hit *Enter*.
9. Now, in the Utilities panel, under the Size inspector, update the **Size** to **Custom**.
10. Next, set **Width** to `350` and **Height** to `200`.
11. Under the Attributes inspector, set the **Identifier** to `reviewCell` and the background color to `#F2F2F2`. You can add this color to your **Color** set.
12. Then under Identity inspector, update the class to `ReviewCell`.
13. Select the Collection View, and in the Identity inspector click and drag from dataSource and delegate to the View Controller.

Saving Reviews

Setting up the cell UI

Now, let's get all of our UI elements into the `reviewCell` (the example shown earlier):

1. In the object library of the Utilities panel, type label in the **filter** field.
2. Then, drag out four **Labels** into the **Cell**.
3. Select one of the **Labels** and, in the Size inspector, update the following values:

    - **X**: 8
    - **Y**: 5
    - **Width**: 116
    - **Height**: 5

4. Then, select the Attributes inspector in the Utilities panel; update the **Font** to **Avenir Next Condensed Demi Bold** and set the **Size** to 16.
5. Select another label and update the following values in the Size inspector:

    - **X**: 245
    - **Y**: 5
    - **Width**: 97
    - **Height**: 21

6. Then, select the Attributes inspector in the Utilities panel; update the **Font** to **Avenir Next Condensed Medium**, set the **Size** to 16, and set **Color** to **LetsEat Light Grey**.
7. Select another label and update the following values in the Size inspector:

    - **X**: 245.5
    - **Y**: 21
    - **Width**: 97
    - **Height**: 21

8. Then, select the Attributes inspector in the Utilities panel; update the **Font** to **Avenir Next Condensed Medium**, set the **Size** to 16, and set color to **LetsEat Light Grey**.

9. Select the last label and update the following values in the Size inspector:
    - **X**: 8
    - **Y**: 54
    - **Width**: 334
    - **Height**: 137

10. Then, select the Attributes inspector in the Utilities panel; update the **Font** to **Avenir Next Condensed Regular** and set the **Size** to 16. Now, set **Lines** to 6.

We are done with setting up our cell, but we just need to add Auto Layout to our cells.

Adding Auto Layout

If we do not add Auto Layout to our cells, they will not look correct; so, let's do that now:

1. Open `RestaurantDetail.storyboard`.
2. Next, select the Container View, the one used for reviews, and then the Pin icon. Enter the following values:
    - **Top**: 0
    - **Right**: 0
    - **Bottom**: 0
    - **Left**: 0
    - **Constrain to margins**: Unchecked
3. Click **Add 4 Constraints**.
4. Now, select the Collection View, the one used for reviews, and then the Pin icon. Enter the following values:
    - **Top**: 0
    - **Right**: 0
    - Bottom: 0

- **Left**: 0
- **Constrain to margins**: Unchecked

5. Click **Add 4 Constraints**.

Build and run your project and add a couple of reviews; you should now see reviews appearing in your restaurant details:

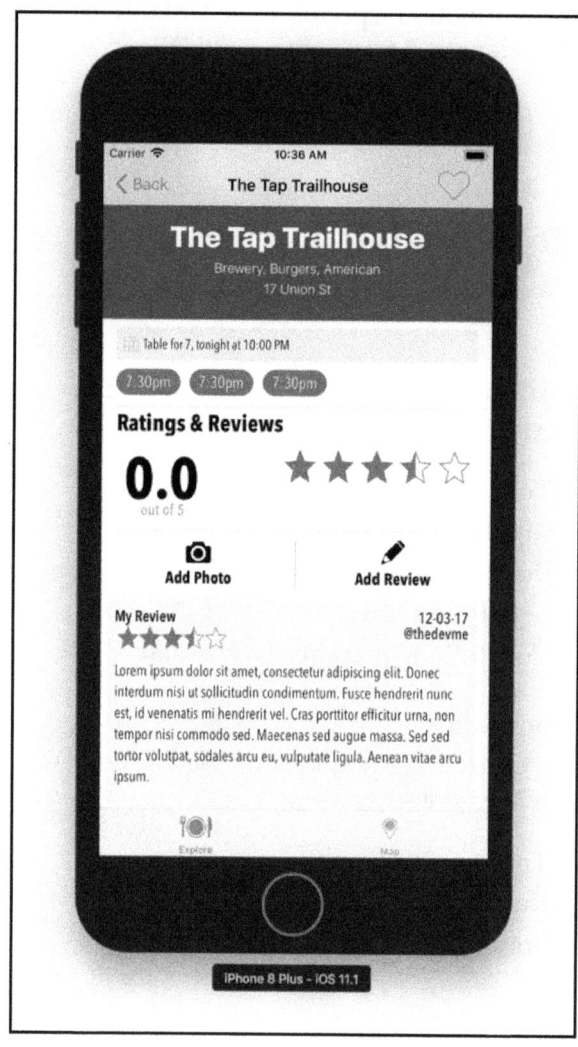

We have two more things I would like to update before the end of this chapter. Now that we are saving reviews, we have an overall rating for restaurants. Let's add this next.

Adding an overall rating

To add an overall rating, we need to pull all of the reviews from Core Data, add them all together, and get an average. Let's add a new method to our Core Data manager to handle this. Please add the following inside `CoreDataManager.swift`:

```
func fetchRestaurantRating(by identifier:Int) -> Float {
    let reviews = fetchReviews(by: identifier).map({ $0 })
    let sum = reviews.reduce(0, {$0 + ($1.rating ?? 0)})
    return sum / Float(reviews.count)
}
```

In this method, we fetch all of the reviews for a restaurant by their ID. Then, we use the `reduce` method to add them all together, and then finally we calculate the average. Now let's use this newly created method. Open up `RestaurantDetailViewController.swift`. Under our `selectedRestaurant` variable add the following:

```
let manager = CoreDataManager()
```

Next, under the `createRating()` method, we just set our rating to 3.5 stars. Update this method to the following:

```
func createRating() {
    if let id = selectedRestaurant?.restaurantID {
        let value = manager.fetchRestaurantRating(by: id)
        ratingView.rating = CGFloat(value)
        if value.isNaN { lblOverallRating.text = "0" }
        else { lblOverallRating.text = "\(value)" }
    }
}
```

Saving Reviews

Now our method is checking to make sure we have a restaurant ID. If we do, then we set the rating for `ratingView`. We also update the overall label to display the average. Build and run your project and you should now see a rating for restaurants that have them:

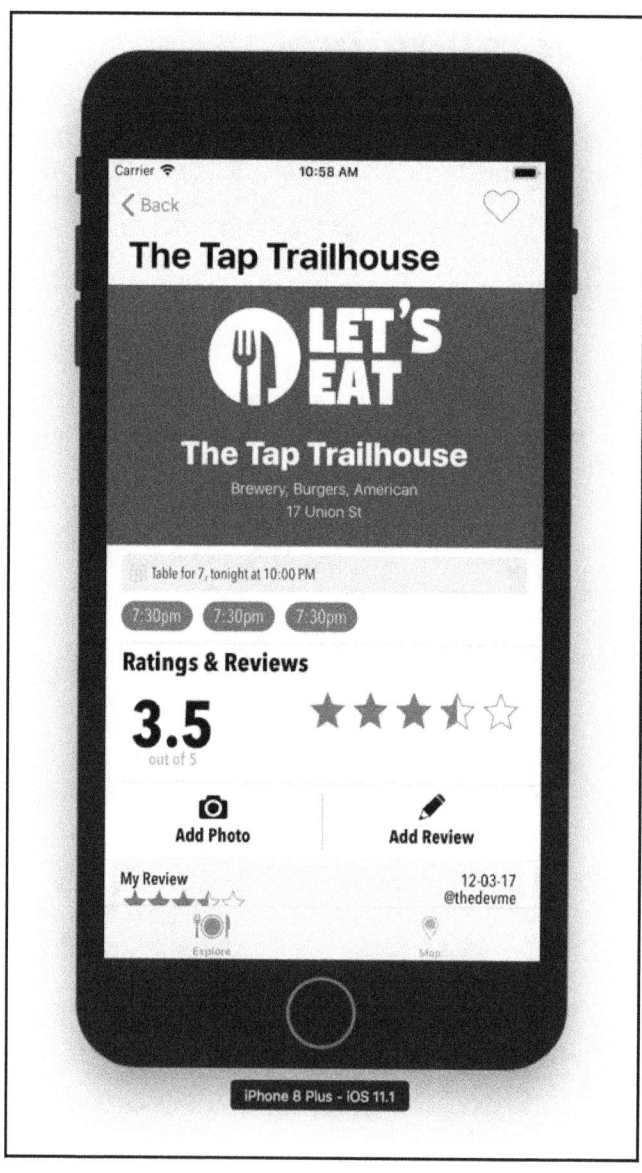

We are finished with this chapter, but there is one section left that we did not do and that's Photo Reviews. Your challenge is to add photo reviews and get them displayed in the Collection View. We covered everything in the chapter, and all of the code is the same. If you get stuck, feel free to use the project files in the next chapter.

Summary

We covered a lot in this chapter and we've now finished building our main app's primary functionality. Our app is starting to take shape. We were able to create a Core Data model and can now save reviews to the Core Data. We also can display all the reviews for a restaurant or pull out the last review and display it.

In the next chapter, we will work on putting the final touches to our app to make it more of a universal app. Once we do that, our main app is finished and we can focus on adding some cool features, such as an iMessage app, notifications, and 3D Touch.

23
Universal

We have spent most of this entire book focusing on logic for our app and getting the app to work on the iPhone. We have not paid much attention to the app working on iPads or other devices. During this chapter, we will look at the app on an iPad, as well as updating the app on all iPhone devices. You will be surprised at how much is already working and that only minor changes will need to be made to get our app to look how we want. We will also take the time to clean up some of our design elements to match the design more closely.

In this chapter, we will cover the following:

- Updating our app to be supported on all devices
- Learning about multitasking and how to code for it
- Cleaning up design elements and using global settings

Explore

Let's do some design tweaks before we jump into making our layout work for every device and start to get this app more polished.

Let's compare what we see on the iPhone 8 with the original design:

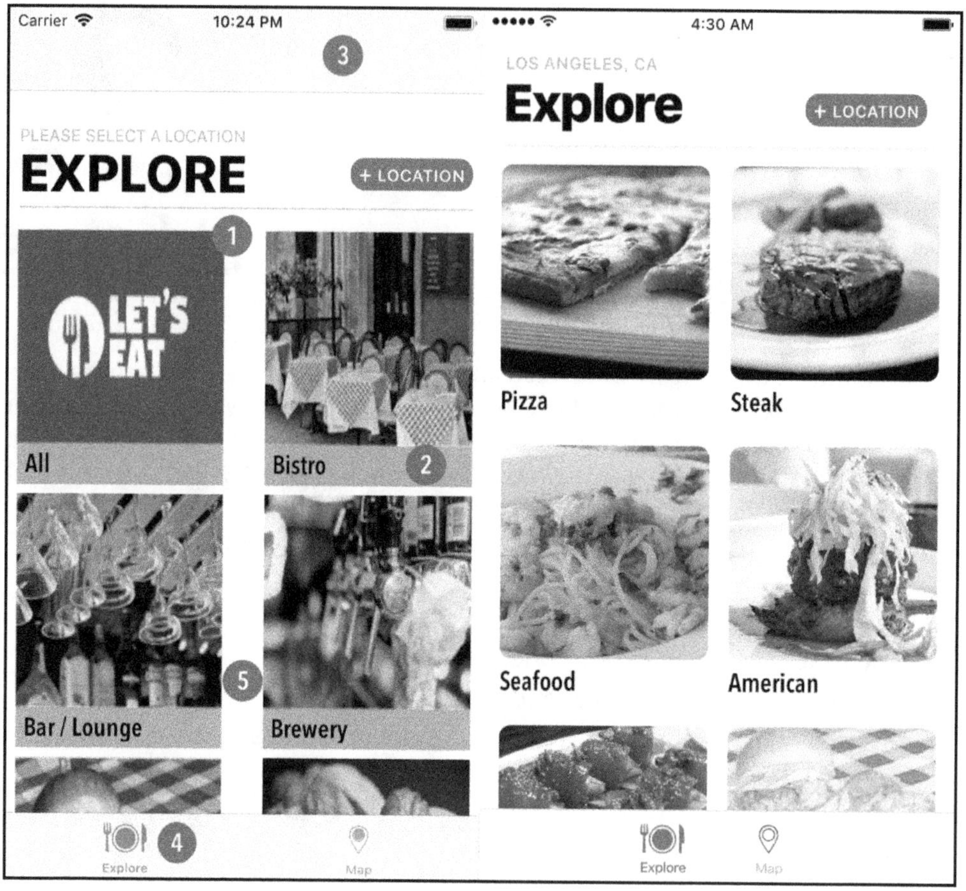

There are a few things we need to fix:

- Implement rounded corners
- Remove the grey background
- Navigation bar appears
- Fix spacing
- Tab bar color

We will fix all of these, but we will focus on first four right now. We have rounded corners in our photo filter list. We can implement these here. Open the `ExploreCell.swift` file by hitting *cmd* + *Shift* + *o*, type `ExploreCell`, and hit *Enter*. Add the following extension:

```
private extension ExploreCell {
    func roundedCorners() {
        imgExplore.layer.cornerRadius = 9
        imgExplore.layer.masksToBounds = true
    }
}
```

Add a `roundedCorners()` call inside the `-layoutSubviews` method.

Now that we have fixed the first issue let's fix the second by removing the background color. Open `Explore.storyboard` and select the `exploreCell` in the Outline view. Under the Utility panel, in the Attributes inspector update the **Background** from **LetsEat Dark Grey** to **White Color**. The third issue, that the navigation bar is displayed, is pretty easy to fix as well. Open the `ExploreViewController.swift` file by hitting *cmd* + *Shift* + *o* and type `ExploreViewController` and hit *Enter*. After `viewDidLoad()` add the following method:

```
override func viewWillAppear(_ animated: Bool) {
    super.viewWillAppear(animated)
    navigationController?.setNavigationBarHidden(true, animated: false)
}
```

That is all we need to do; now, every time we go to this view, we will always hide the Navigation bar at the top. Finally, let's update our app so that our tab bar buttons are the correct color. We need to add a new color to our **Color Set** called **LetsEat Red** and set the **Hex** value to D0021B. Now, open up the `AppDelegate.swift` file at the bottom of the file after the last curly brace adds the following:

```
private extension AppDelegate {
    func initialize() {
        setupDefaultColors()
    }

    func setupDefaultColors() {
        guard let red = UIColor(named: "Lets Eat Red") else { return }
        UITabBar.appearance().tintColor = red
        UITabBar.appearance().barTintColor = .white
        UITabBarItem.appearance()
            .setTitleTextAttributes(
                [NSAttributedStringKey.foregroundColor: UIColor.black],
                for: UIControlState.normal)
```

```
            UITabBarItem.appearance()
                .setTitleTextAttributes(
                    [NSAttributedStringKey.foregroundColor: red],
                    for: UIControlState.selected)
            UINavigationBar.appearance().tintColor = red
            UINavigationBar.appearance().barTintColor = .white
            UITabBar.appearance().isTranslucent = false
            UINavigationBar.appearance().isTranslucent = false
        }
    }
```

Now inside the `-application:didFinishLaunchingWithOptions:` add the `initialize()` method call. Build and run the project by hitting the Play button (or using ⌘ + R).

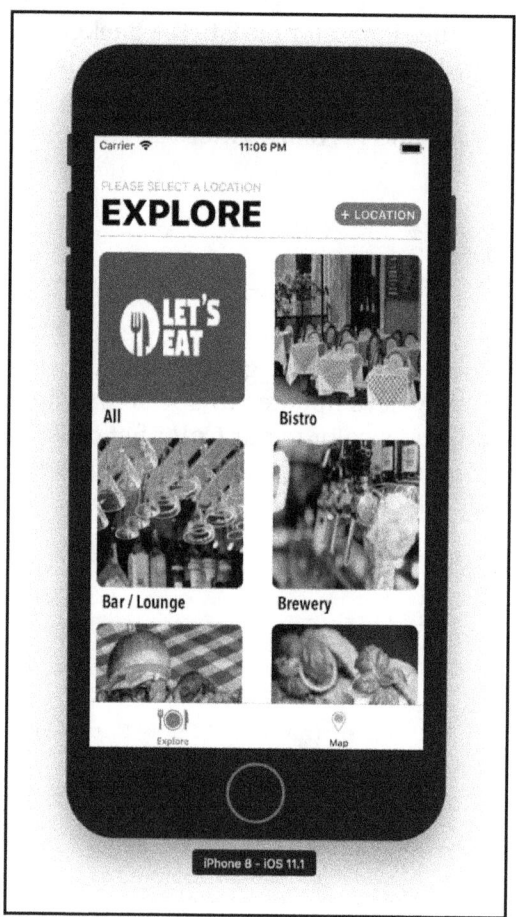

You should now see we have completed the first four items. Let's address the spacing issue next. Before we do, let's first switch our device to any iPad (I typically use the iPad Air 2, but you can pick whatever one you like). Then build and run the project by hitting the Play button (or using ⌘ + R). You will see that it is not too bad currently, but the spacing is different on each device. Now, we have set up values that only work for one device. However, we need this to work on all devices.

Let's start with our `Explore.storyboard`. First, we need to update some Auto Layout for our explore cells. Right now, we have a width set up for our image that needs to be more dynamic:

1. Open up `Explore.storyboard`.
2. Select the image inside the `exploreCell`.
3. Then, in the Utilities panel, select the Attributes inspector and change the **Content Mode** under the **View** section to **Aspect Fill**. This will keep the images from looking stretched, while still filling the entire area.

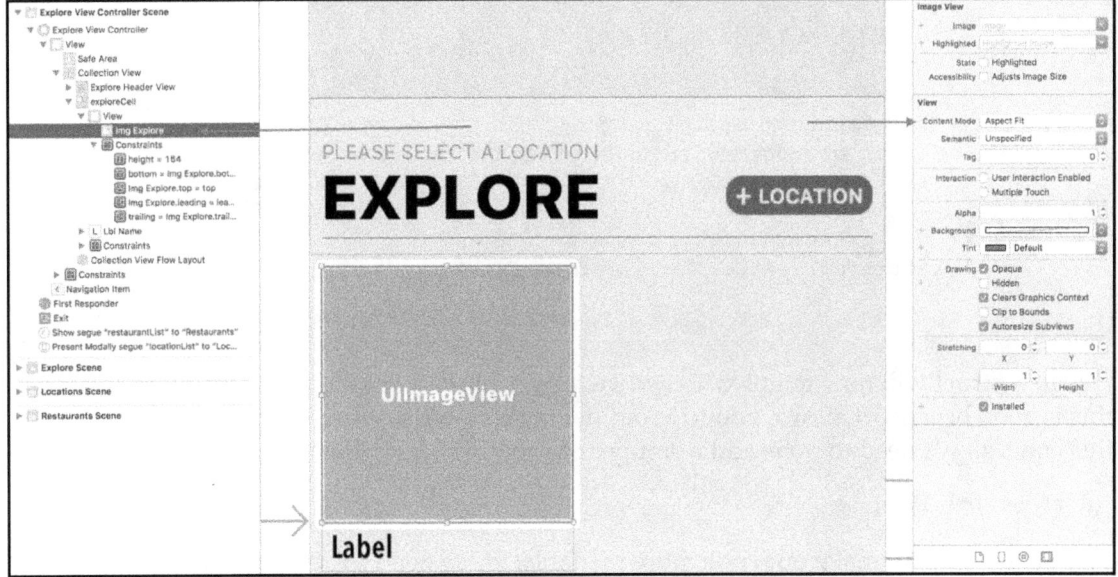

Universal

These are the only updates we need to make to our explore cell. Next, we are going to create a file that will let us know which device is used. We can then use this to set up different looks, depending on the device. Let's create this file:

4. Right-click the `Misc` folder and select **New File**.
5. Inside of the **Choose a template for your new file screen**, select **iOS** at the top and then **Swift File**. Then, hit **Next**.
6. Name this file `Device` and then hit **Create**.

First, we need to update our `import` statement from `import Foundation` to `import UIKit`.

Next, add the following to the `import` statement:

```
struct Device {
    static var currentDevice: UIDevice {
        struct Singleton {
            static let device = UIDevice.current
        }
        return Singleton.device
    }

    static var isPhone: Bool {
        return currentDevice.userInterfaceIdiom == .phone
    }

    static var isPad: Bool {
        return currentDevice.userInterfaceIdiom == .pad
    }
}
```

Our new struct will now tell us whether we are on an iPad or an iPhone. Having a file like this is good because it allows you to avoid having to rewrite the same code. To implement this code, all we need to do is add a snippet of code like the following:

```
if Device.isPhone{ }
```

This statement will make our code more readable; if we need to add any more checks for particular devices, we can do it all in the same file. One more great use of putting code like this into its file is that, when you build the next app, you can just add this file to your project and continue.

Next, let's open the `ExploreViewController.swift` file and make some more updates to our code. We need to create a variable that we will use for the spacing we want between items. Add the following before our `viewDidLoad()` method:

```
fileprivate let minItemSpacing: CGFloat = 7
```

Now, we need to create a function to set up some default Collection View values. We also need to create an `initialize()` method to call our setup function. Add the following method call inside of the `initialize()` method:

```
setupCollectionView()
```

Next, add the following inside of the `private` extension after the `initialize()` method:

```
func setupCollectionView() {
    let flow = UICollectionViewFlowLayout()
    flow.sectionInset = UIEdgeInsets(top: 7, left: 7, bottom: 7, right: 7)
    flow.minimumInteritemSpacing = 0
    flow.minimumLineSpacing = 7
    collectionView?.collectionViewLayout = flow
}
```

This method will make sure that we have seven pixels of spacing all the way around. We finally need to create an extension that will let us handle all of the spacing programmatically. After the last curly brace add the following extension:

```
extension ExploreViewController: UICollectionViewDelegateFlowLayout {
    func collectionView(_ collectionView: UICollectionView, layout collectionViewLayout: UICollectionViewLayout, sizeForItemAt indexPath: IndexPath) -> CGSize {
        if Device.isPad {
            let factor = traitCollection.horizontalSizeClass == .compact ? 2:3
            let screenRect = collectionView.frame.size.width
            let screenWidth = screenRect - (CGFloat(minItemSpacing) * CGFloat(factor + 1))
            let cellWidth = screenWidth / CGFloat(factor)
            
            return CGSize(width: cellWidth, height: 195)
        }
        else {
            let screenRect = collectionView.frame.size.width
            let screenWidth = screenRect - 21
            let cellWidth = screenWidth / 2.0
            
            return CGSize(width: cellWidth, height: 195)
        }
```

Universal

```
    }

        func collectionView(_ collectionView: UICollectionView, layout
    collectionViewLayout: UICollectionViewLayout,
    referenceSizeForHeaderInSection section: Int) -> CGSize {

            return CGSize(width: self.collectionView.frame.width, height: 100)
        }
    }
```

Adding the `UICollectionViewDelegateFlowLayout` allows us to update our cell item size in code. Let's discuss each part of this extension we just added. The -`collectionView:layout:sizeForItemAtIndexPath:` method is used to set the size of the cell. Inside of this method, we are using the struct we created. We are checking to see if we are using an iPad or an iPhone.

In the if part of the `if...else` statement, we are checking whether the screen is compact or not. If the screen is compact, then we want a two-column grid; otherwise, we want a three-column grid. We are also distributing our items evenly across the width of the screen.

In the else part of the `if...else` statement, we are just setting up a two-column grid on all phones. We get the screen width then subtract `21`, and then we divide the result by 2 to distribute the cells evenly.

If you run the project, everything will look good.

There is one more thing that's broken if you attempt to rotate the device by using ⌘ + right arrow or ⌘ + left arrow. Then, you will see that our layout spacing does not update.

In order to fix this, we need to make one more update. After -`shouldPerformSegueWithIdentifier:sender:`, add the following:

```
    override func viewWillTransition(to size: CGSize, with coordinator:
    UIViewControllerTransitionCoordinator) {
        collectionView.reloadData()
    }
```

Now, build and run your project again by hitting the Play button (or using ⌘ + R) and rotate the device. You will see that our layout spacing now updates.

Explore is now complete; let's move to our locations list.

Universal

Location listing

Let's compare our current location listing with the design:

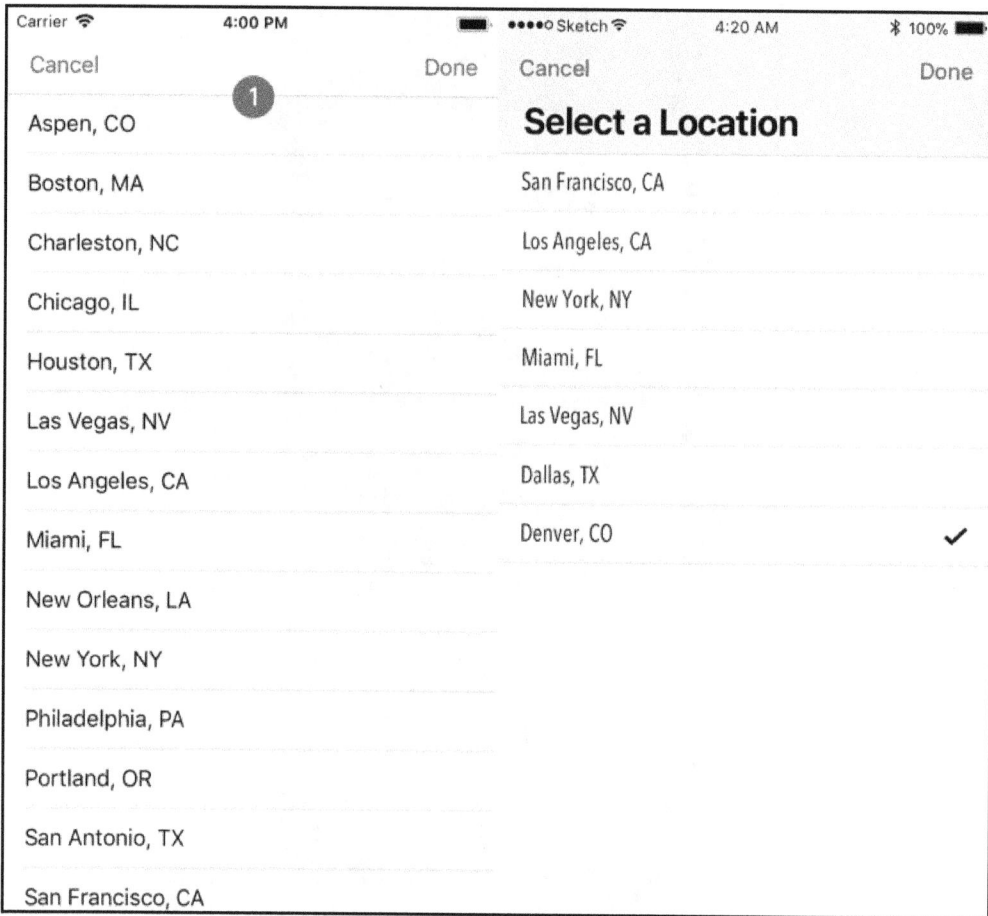

We have one thing that needs fixing: the large title. This is a simple update. Open up the `LocationViewController` and, inside of the `initialize()` method, add the following code after `manager.fetch()`:

```
title = "Select a Location"
navigationController?.navigationBar.prefersLargeTitles = true
```

Chapter 23

In this code, we are setting a new iOS 11 feature `prefersLargeTitles` to `true`. If you build and run, you will see that we are good here now. Next, we will direct our attention to the restaurant listing page and go into more detail on the iPad and multitasking.

Restaurant listing

For our restaurant listing page, we want a one-column grid on all phones and a two-column grid on all iPads. If you build and run the project by hitting the Play button (or using ⌘ + *R*) and go to a restaurant listing page, you will see that we need to fix the spacing on the iPad to show two columns correctly:

Let's see how we can fix this. Remember that we still want one column on the iPhone and a grid on the iPad. Open the `RestaurantViewController.swift` file and add the following above the `createData()` method inside of the `private` extension:

```
func initialize() {
    createData()
    setupTitle()
    if Device.isPad{ setupCollectionView() }
}
```

You will get an error for the `setupCollectionView()` method. Ignore it for now, as we will fix it shortly. This method checks if the device is an iPad; if it is, it calls the method `setupCollectionView()`. Next, add the following under the `initialize()` method we just added:

```
func setupCollectionView() {
    let flow = UICollectionViewFlowLayout()
    flow.sectionInset = UIEdgeInsets(top: 7, left: 7, bottom: 7, right: 7)
    flow.minimumInteritemSpacing = 0
    flow.minimumLineSpacing = 7
    collectionView?.collectionViewLayout = flow
}
```

The preceding method is the same thing we previously added in the storyboard regarding spacing between items, but here we are implementing it programmatically.

We have a couple of more things that we need to address. First, we are going to have the size of the screen calculated for us programmatically. Just like we did in `ExploreViewController`, we are going to a new extension to handle our Collection View layout. Add the following before our `viewDidLoad()` method:

```
fileprivate let minItemSpacing: CGFloat = 7
```

Now, add the following at the bottom of the file after the last curly brace:

```
extension RestaurantViewController: UICollectionViewDelegateFlowLayout {

    func collectionView(_ collectionView: UICollectionView, layout collectionViewLayout: UICollectionViewLayout, sizeForItemAt indexPath: IndexPath) -> CGSize {
        if Device.isPad {
            let factor = traitCollection.horizontalSizeClass == .compact ? 2:3
            let screenRect = collectionView.frame.size.width
            let screenWidth = screenRect - (CGFloat(minItemSpacing) * CGFloat(factor + 1))
            let cellWidth = screenWidth / CGFloat(factor)
            return CGSize(width: cellWidth, height: 325)
        }

        else {
            let screenRect = collectionView.frame.size.width
            let screenWidth = screenRect - 21
            let cellWidth = screenWidth / 2.0

            return CGSize(width: cellWidth, height: 325)
        }
    }
}
```

This code states that, if the device is an iPhone, a one-column grid will be shown; if it is an iPad, a two-column grid will be shown. Now, we need to update our `viewDidAppear()` method. Currently, we are calling both `createData()` and `setupTitle()`. We need to remove both of these calls and just call `initialize()` instead. When you are finished, `viewDidAppear()` should look like the following:

```
override func viewDidAppear(_ animated: Bool) {
    super.viewDidAppear(animated)
    initialize()
}
```

[603]

Universal

Let's build and run the project for the iPad by hitting the Play button (or using ⌘ + R):

The two-column grid is what we want for the iPad for our restaurant listing page, but we need to verify that we did not change the one-column grid on the iPhone. Switch the device back to any iPhone simulator and, after building and rerunning the project, you should still see a one-column grid on the iPhone.

There are still issues with the iPad setup. Switch back to the iPad and build and rerun the project by hitting the Play button (or using ⌘ + R). When the project launches, hit ⌘ + right arrow to rotate the device. Then, return to your restaurant listing page. The first issue is that, if you turn the device, the cell spacing does not update. Another problem is that, if you multitask, your app resizes and you need to make sure that your layout adjusts accordingly.

To see multitasking, swipe up from the bottom:

Then, drag the app to the right side of our app:

Grab the small tab that will be in the middle of this new screen and pull it to the left. This tab will split the screen with our app and allow you to take over more (or less, if you move it back to the right) of the screen :

Chapter 23

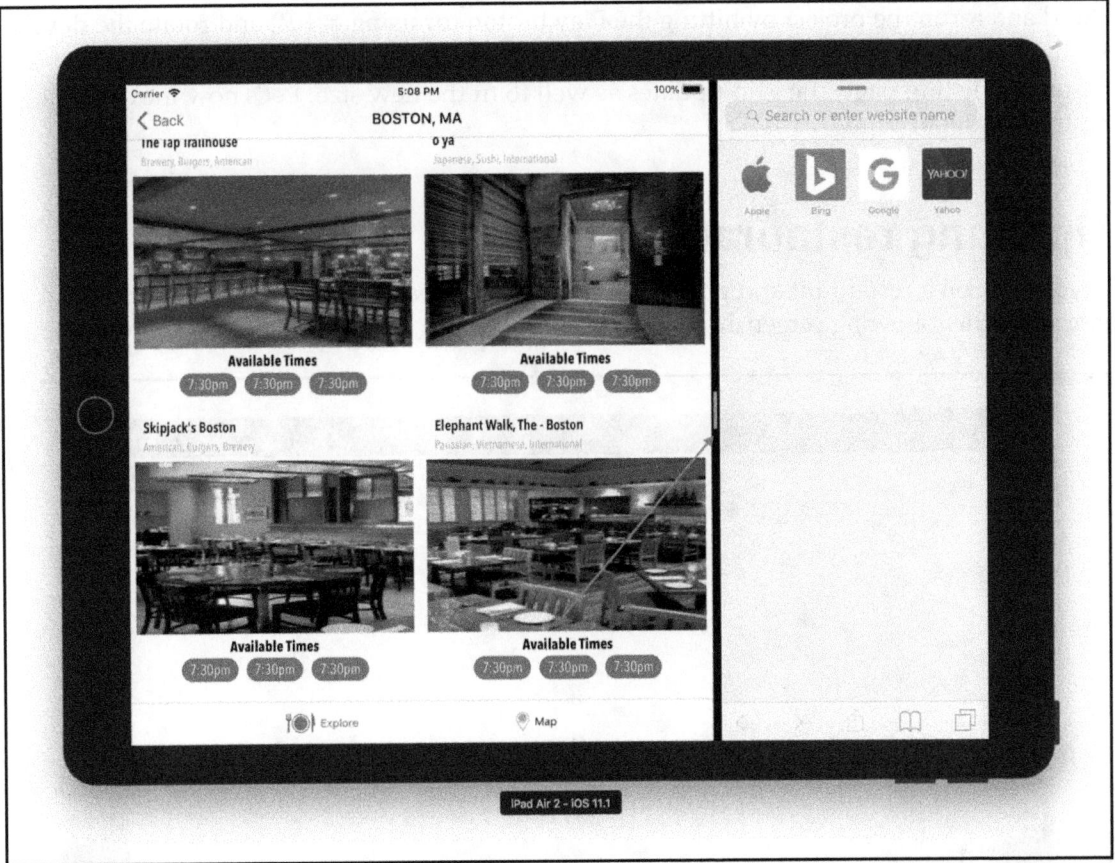

When you move the tab to the left, you will notice that the *Let's Eat* app does not resize the cells and instead shows one column. Our app needs to adjust no matter the size it has available when splitting the screen between our app and another app.

Resolving these problems is a really simple fix. In your `RestaurantViewController`, before the last curly brace, add the following code:

```
override func viewWillTransition(to size: CGSize, with coordinator
: UIViewControllerTransitionCoordinator) {    collectionView.reloadData()
}
```

Universal

Build and rerun the project by hitting the Play button (or using ⌘ + R) and rotate the device by using ⌘ + right arrow. You will now see that, every time you update the size of the restaurant listing page, the grid updates as well to fit the new size. Let's now move to the restaurant detail page.

Updating restaurant details

If you click on a restaurant and go to a restaurant detail page, you should see something similar to the following screenshot:

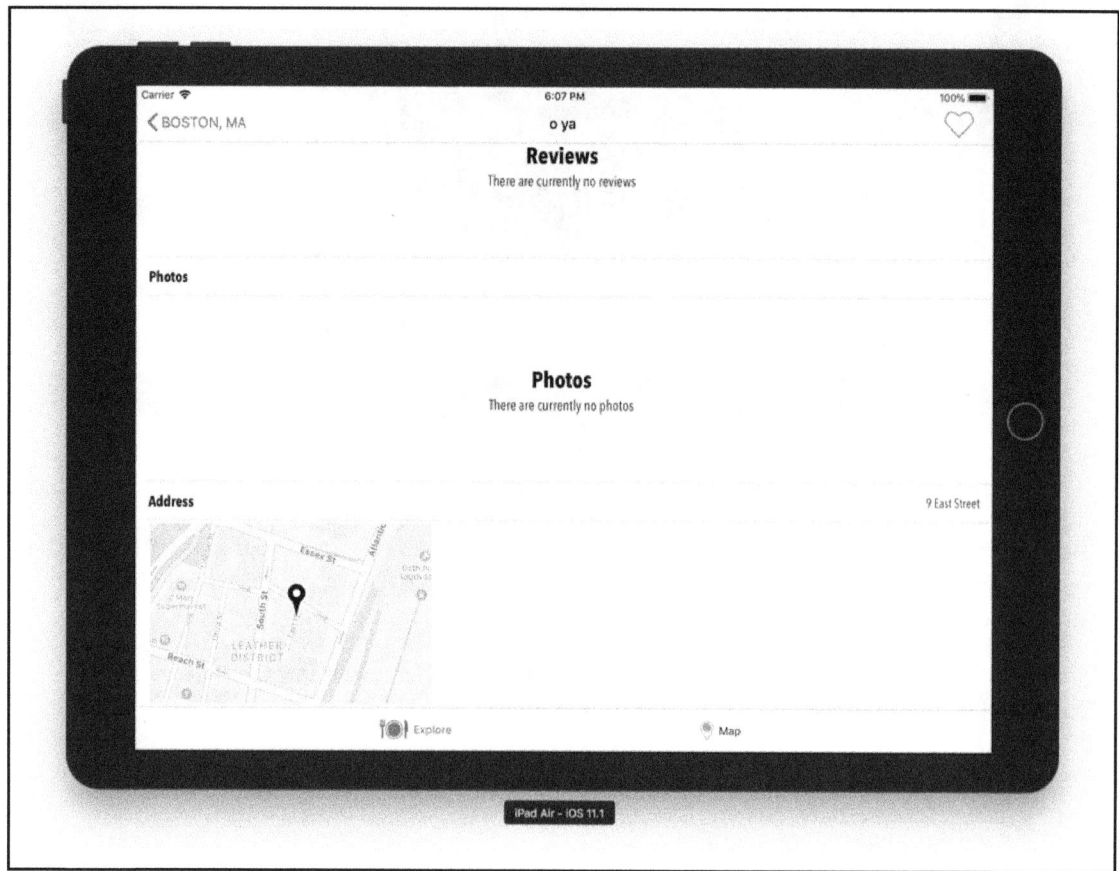

Chapter 23

We do not have much to fix on this screen. If you scroll down to the bottom, you will see that the image we create is not sized correctly. We need to update this so that, depending on the device, we render the appropriate image size. We also need to update the Auto Layout. You can try other device sizes; you should see the same display on all the screens.

1. Open `RestaurantDetail.storyboard`.
2. Select the image map using the Outline view and in the Attributes inspector update the **Content Mode** to **Aspect Fill**.

If you build and run now, you will see that our map now fills the area, but our image is stretched. We can leave this but, if this were being submitted, making our image size based off device would be a much better way to handle this. We are done with cleaning up and making our app ready for the iPad. You should now be able to see how powerful Collection Views are and how they make it easy to have a custom look with very little code.

Summary

You now have an app that functions perfectly on all devices. You can see how using the Collection View gives your app some variety on different devices with very little code. As you get more and more comfortable with this, you will find other ways to make your app look unique on various devices.

We could submit the app as-is right now and it would be perfectly fine, but why not take advantage of some additional features you can implement?

In the next chapter, we will do just that by creating an iMessage app for our app.

24
iMessages

Text messaging started with just simple text and the creation of faces using special characters. As smartphones began to become more and more commonplace, so did text messaging. Messages are now a significant form of communication for the vast majority of people. People find it easier to respond to a text message than to answer a phone call.

When Apple announced iMessage apps and stickers, it took messaging to another level. We had stickers before this announcement, but now we had a fully integrated system. iMessages does not only allow you to send a sticker to express a feeling or an emotion more effectively than words; you can now use messages to send the score of a game or even play games through text messages.

In this chapter, we are going to create an *iMessage* app. This app will allow the user to look for restaurants and send reservations to others. We will build our UI to look similar to what our phone looks like. To create the *iMessages* app, we need to add a message extension to our app.

We will cover the following in this chapter:

- Building a custom message app UI
- Creating a framework
- Sharing code between multiple targets
- Learning how to send a reservation to others

iMessages

Understanding iMessages

Starting with the UI is always my preferred way to begin building an app, because you can get a feel for what you need to code. We are going to implement a single screen that will be a list of restaurants (accessible by hitting the sticker icon next to where a user writes his or her message). The user can choose a restaurant for which he or she has a reservation and send it via messages to another person. Once that other person receives the message, that person will be able to tap on the reservation and see all of the details.

In a message View Controller, there are two types of presentation styles: compact and expanded.

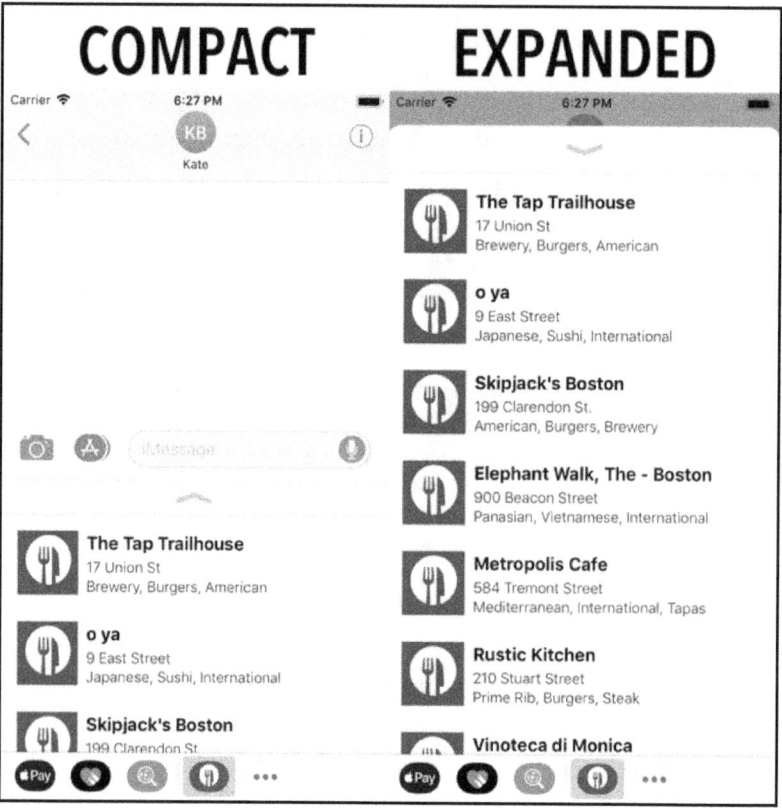

Chapter 24

Apple recommends that you have two different View Controllers for each style. However, since our screen is simple, we will use just one. Keep in mind, however, that, if you want to do a more complicated layout, you should use two controllers.

Creating our extension

Let's get started by working on the UI now:

1. In the Navigator panel, select the Project navigator and, then, your project:

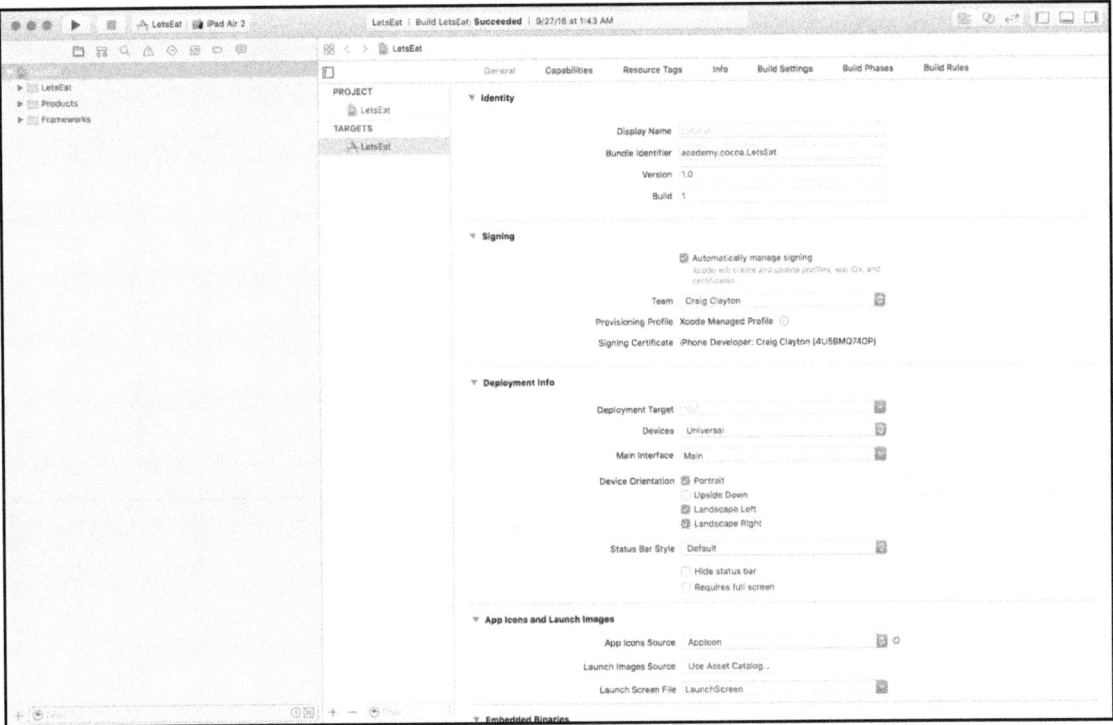

iMessages

2. In the Standard Editor, locate the **TARGETS** area and then the **+** (plus button) at the bottom of the **TARGETS** area. (If your **TARGETS** area is not displaying, hit the icon highlighted in blue to the left of **General** in the following screenshot):

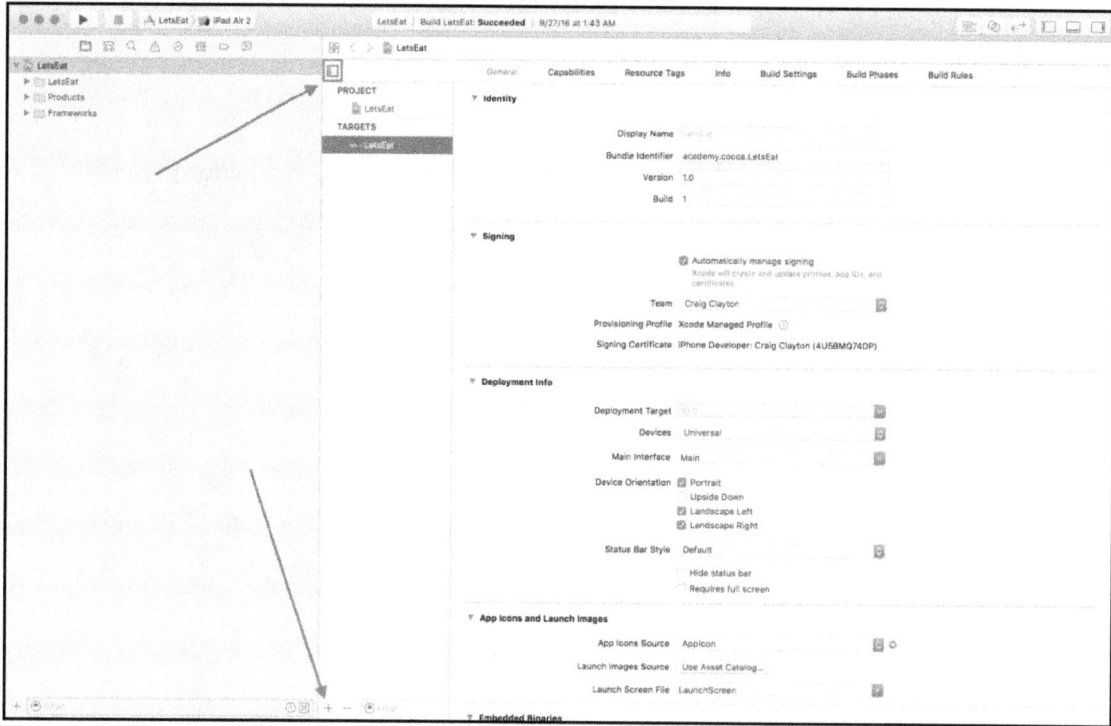

Chapter 24

3. Click the + (plus button) and, then, select **iMessage Extension**:

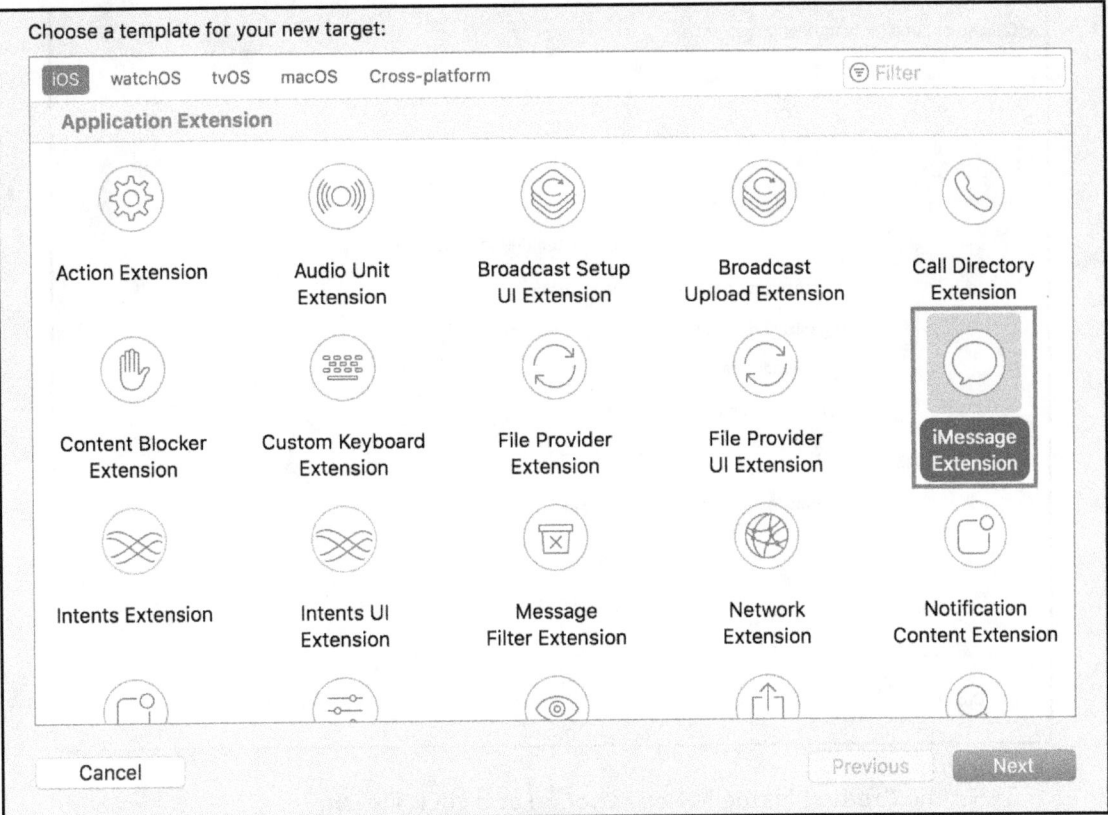

iMessages

4. Click **Next** and, then, you will see the following screen:

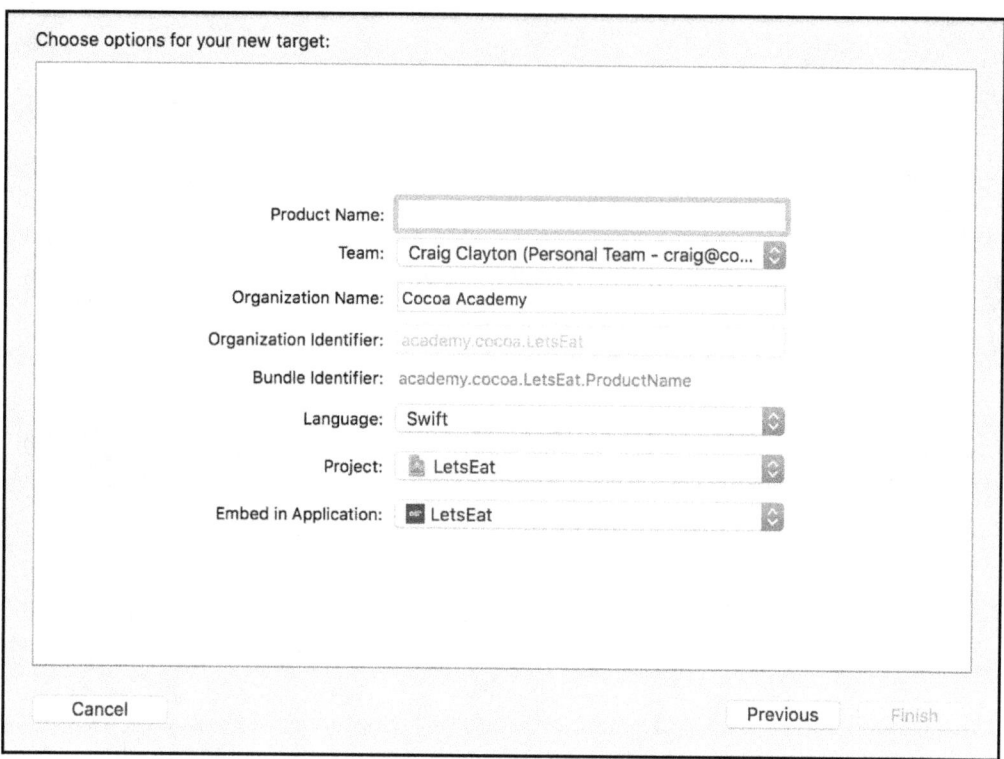

5. Set the **Product Name** to `MessageApp` and click **Finish**.
6. You will receive the following message after you click **Finish**. Select **Activate**:

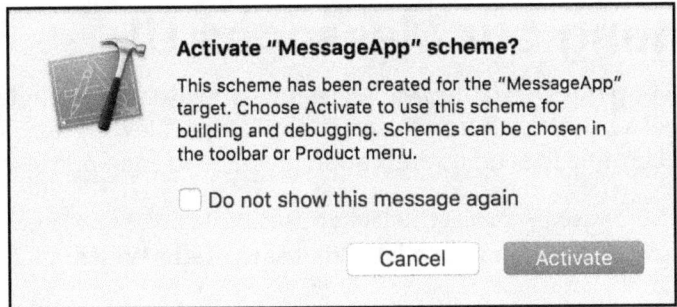

By activating the `MessageApp` scheme, we will be able to build and run iMessages from the simulator. Now, you will have the choice of running either our *Let's Eat* app or our *iMessages* app.

Updating our assets

Next, we need to add assets that are necessary for our *iMessages* app:

1. In the `MessageApp` folder in the Navigator panel, select the `Assets.xcassets` folder.
2. Hit the *Delete* button and, then, select **Move to Trash** in the screen that appears.
3. Then, open the project's `assets` folder downloaded from Packt's website (https://www.packtpub.com/).
4. Open `Chapter24` and drag the `Assets.xcassets` folder into your `MessageApp` folder inside the Navigator panel. Do not do this in Xcode; you will need to open this up in finder just like we did at the beginning of the book.
5. In the options screen that appears, ensure that **Copy items if needed** and **Create groups** are both selected and then select **Finish**.

If you open the `Assets.xcassets` folder, you will see that you now have an icon and two other image assets that we will need for our *iMessages* app.

Implementing our Messages UI

Next, we need to set up our UI. In our *iMessages* app, we will have a single screen; in this screen, we will show a list of restaurants using a Collection View. When you tap on the restaurant, you will be able to send a reservation message to someone else. Let's get started:

1. In your `MessageApp` project, select your `MainInterface.storyboard`. You will see a single storyboard with a label that says **Hello World**:

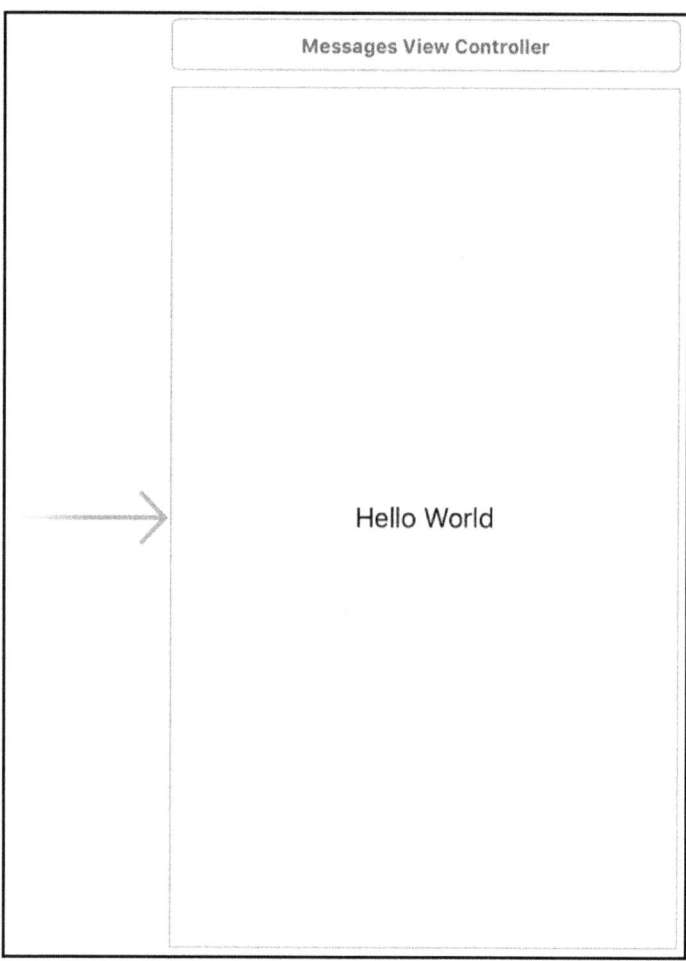

2. Delete the label that says **Hello World** by selecting it in the Outline view and, then, hitting *Delete*.
3. Select the Messages View Controller and, then, the Attributes inspector in the Utilities panel and change the status bar under **Simulated Metrics** from **Inferred** to **None**.
4. Next, in the Object library of the Utilities panel, type `collectionview` in the filter and then drag a Collection View into the View Controller in the scene.
5. With the Collection View selected, select the Pin icon and enter the following values:

    - All values under **Add New Constraints** are set to 0
    - **Constrain to margins** is unchecked
    - **Update Frames** is set to **Items of New Constraints**

6. Click **Add 4 Constraints**.
7. Next, with the Collection View still selected, open the Attributes inspector in the Utilities panel.
8. Select Background in the Attributes inspector and, under the **Color Sliders** tab, set the **Hex Color** # to `ECECEC` under **RGB Sliders** in the drop-down menu.
9. Next, select the Collection View cell and, then, the Size inspector in the Utilities panel.
10. Change the **Size** from **Default** to **Custom**. Then, set the **Width** to 320 and the **Height** to 78.
11. Then, select **Background** in the Attributes inspector and, under the **Color Sliders** tab, set the **Hex Color** # to `FFFFF` under **RGB Sliders** in the drop-down menu.
12. In the Utilities panel, select the **Media Library** and type restaurant-list into the filter field.
13. Drag a `restaurant-list-img` into your Collection View cell.
14. With the image still selected, go to the Size inspector in the Utilities panel and update the following values:

    - **X**: 8
    - **Y**: 9
    - **Width**: 60
    - **Height**: 60

iMessages

15. Next, select the object library in the Utilities panel and type `label` into the filter.
16. Drag three labels into the cell.
17. Select the first label and, in the Size inspector, update the following values:

    - **X**: `76`
    - **Y**: `10`
    - **Width**: `236`
    - **Height**: `21`

18. Next, select the Attributes inspector; update the **Font** to **Bold** and verify that the **Font size** is `17`.
19. Select the second label and, in the Size inspector, update the following values:

    - **X**: `76`
    - **Y**: `35`
    - **Width**: `236`
    - **Height**: `16`

20. Then, in the Attributes inspector, update the **Font** to **Light**, size `14`.
21. Select the last label and, in the Size inspector, update the following values:

    - **X**: `76`
    - **Y**: `53`
    - **Width**: `236`
    - **Height**: `16`

22. Lastly, in the Attributes inspector, update the **Font** to **Light**, size `14`.

When you are done, your cell should look like the following:

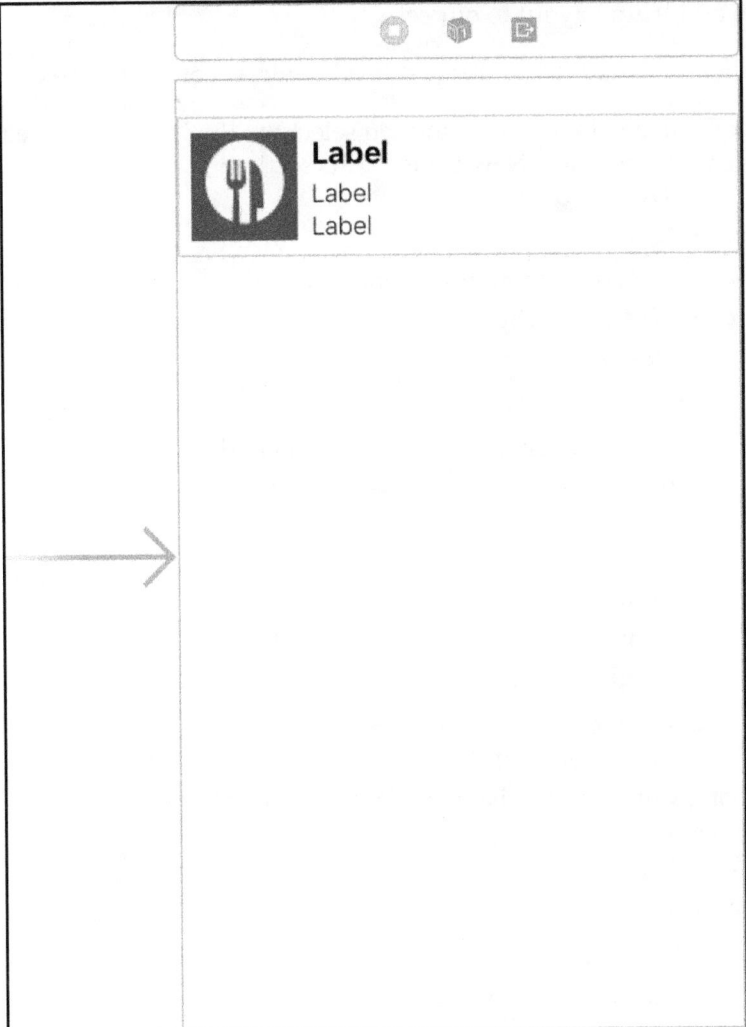

Now that we have our items in place, we need to add some Auto Layout to our elements.

iMessages

Adding Auto Layout to our cell

Let's see how to add Auto Layout to our cell.

Auto Layout will allow our layout to adjust to all devices. Let's get started:

1. Select the image in our cell and then select the Pin icon. Enter the following values under the **Add New Constraints** section:
     - **Top**: 9
     - **Left**: 8
     - **Constrain to margins**: unchecked
     - **Width**: 60 (checked)
     - **Height**: 60 (checked)
2. Click **Add 4 Constraints**.
3. Next, select the first label in our cell and, then, the Pin icon. Enter the following values under the **Add New Constraints** section:
     - **Top**: 10
     - **Left**: 8
     - **Right**: 8
     - **Constrain to margins**: unchecked
     - **Height**: 21 (checked)
4. Click **Add 4 Constraints**.
5. Next, select the second label in our cell and, then, the Pin icon. Enter the following values under the **Add New Constraints** section:
     - **Top**: 4
     - **Left**: 8
     - **Right**: 8
     - **Constrain to margins**: unchecked
     - **Height**: 16 (checked)
6. Click **Add 4 Constraints**.

7. Finally, select the last label in our cell and, then, the Pin icon. Enter the following values under the **Add New Constraints** section:
   - **Top**: 2
   - **Left**: 8
   - **Right**: 8
   - **Constrain to margins**: unchecked
   - **Height**: 16 (checked)
8. Click **Add 4 Constraints**.

We have completed setting up our UI and can now proceed to get data into our app and display it.

Creating a framework

Since all of our code for data is created in our iOS app, it does not make sense to rewrite our code for our *iMessages* app. We can create what is known as a framework to share our data between our iOS and iMessage apps.

Using frameworks along with app extensions allows us to put shared code in one place. That means less code and more efficiency, because you will not need to update code in multiple places when you have to make a change. Let's get started creating our framework:

1. In the Navigator panel, select the Project navigator and, then, your project again as we did earlier.
2. Find the **TARGETS** area and click on the **+** button at the bottom of that area.

iMessages

3. Under the **iOS** tab, scroll to the bottom to **Framework & Library**, select **Cocoa Touch Framework**, and then hit **Next**:

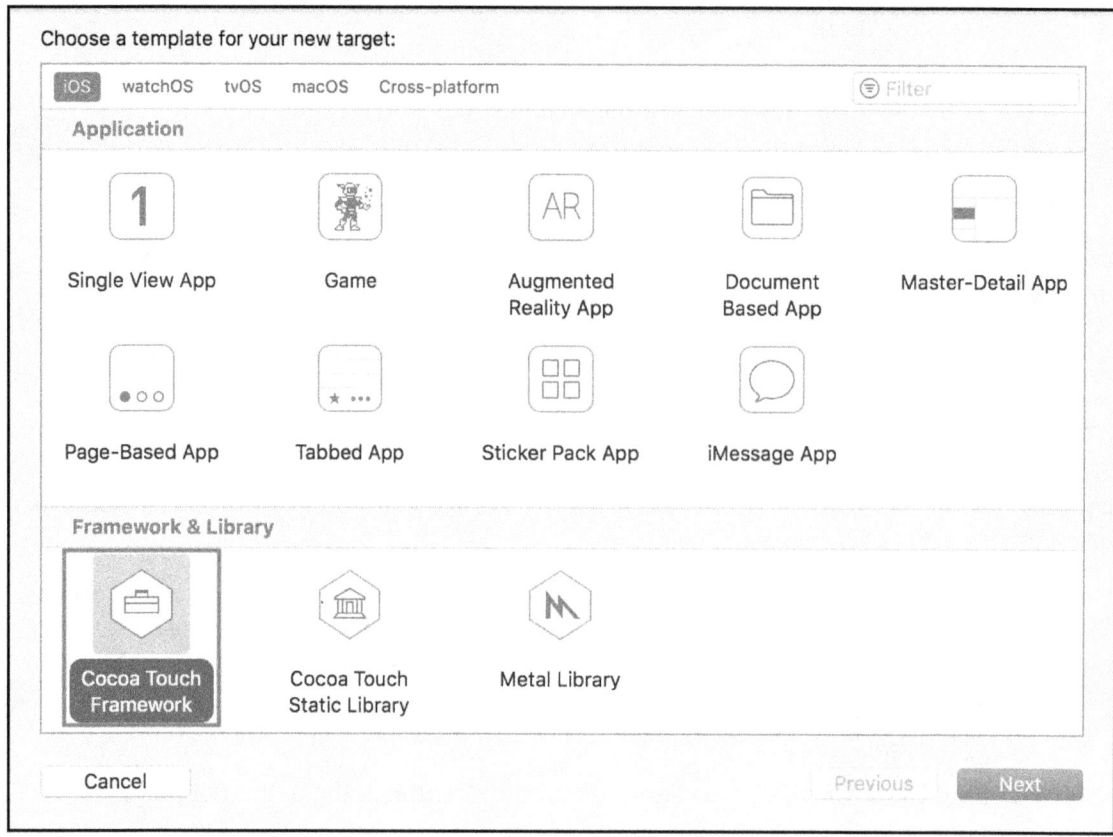

4. Under **Product Name**, type `LetsEatDataKit` and then hit **Finish**.

Chapter 24

You should now see the following folder and files in the `Products` folder in your Navigator panel:

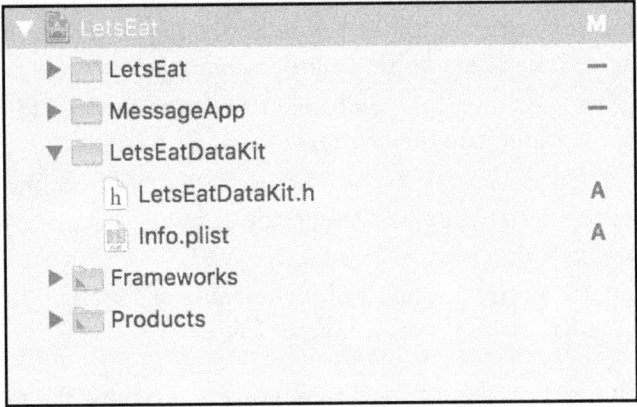

5. Select the `LetsEatDataKit` target and ensure that, under **Deployment Info**, your **Deployment Target** is set to `10.0` and **App Extensions** is checked:

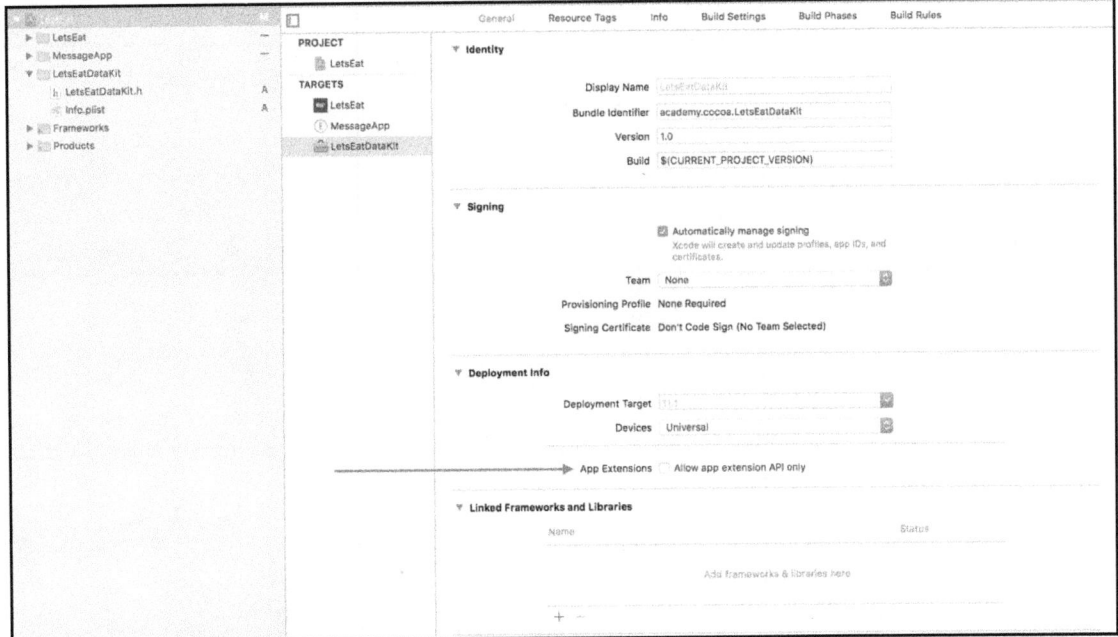

6. Right-click the `LetsEatDataKit` folder in the Navigator panel and create a new group named `Restaurant`.
7. Now, from your *Let's Eat* app, please drag the `RestaurantDataManager.swift` file from the `Restaurant` folder inside of the `Controllers` folder into the newly created `LetsEatDataKit` folder's `Restaurant` folder.
8. Next, drag the `RestaurantItem.swift` file from the `Map` folder inside of the `Controllers` folder into the `LetsEatDataKit` folder's `Restaurant` folder.
9. Then, drag the `RestaurantAPIManager.swift` file from the `Restaurant` folder inside of the `Controllers` folder into the `LetsEatDataKit` folder's `Restaurant` folder.
10. Finally, drag the entire `JSON` folder from inside of the `Misc` folder into the `LetsEatDataKit` folder's `Restaurant` folder.

When you have completed these steps, you should have the following files in your `LetsEatDataKit` folder:

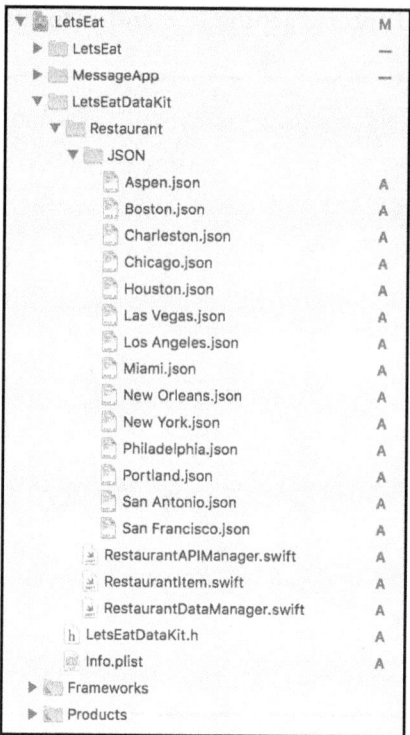

Chapter 24

11. Next, open the `API Manager` folder we just moved and, in the `json` subfolder, select the `Aspen.json` file.
12. In the Utilities panel, select the File inspector and locate the **Target Membership** section:

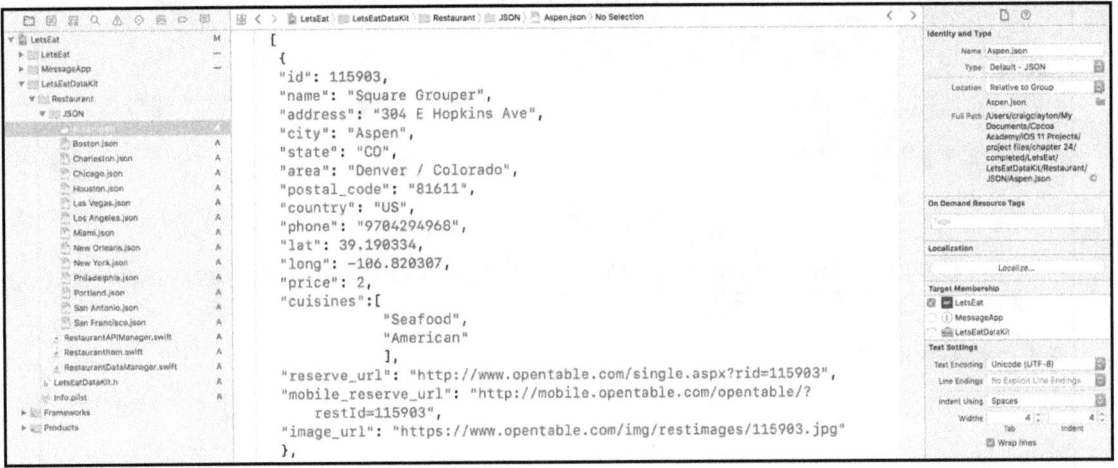

[627]

iMessages

13. To set the target of this file not only to our app but also to our `MessageApp` and `LetsEatDataKit`, check **MessageApp** and **LetsEatDataKit** under **Target Membership**. Therefore, our *Let's Eat* app, **MessageApp**, and **LetsEatDataKit** should all be checked:

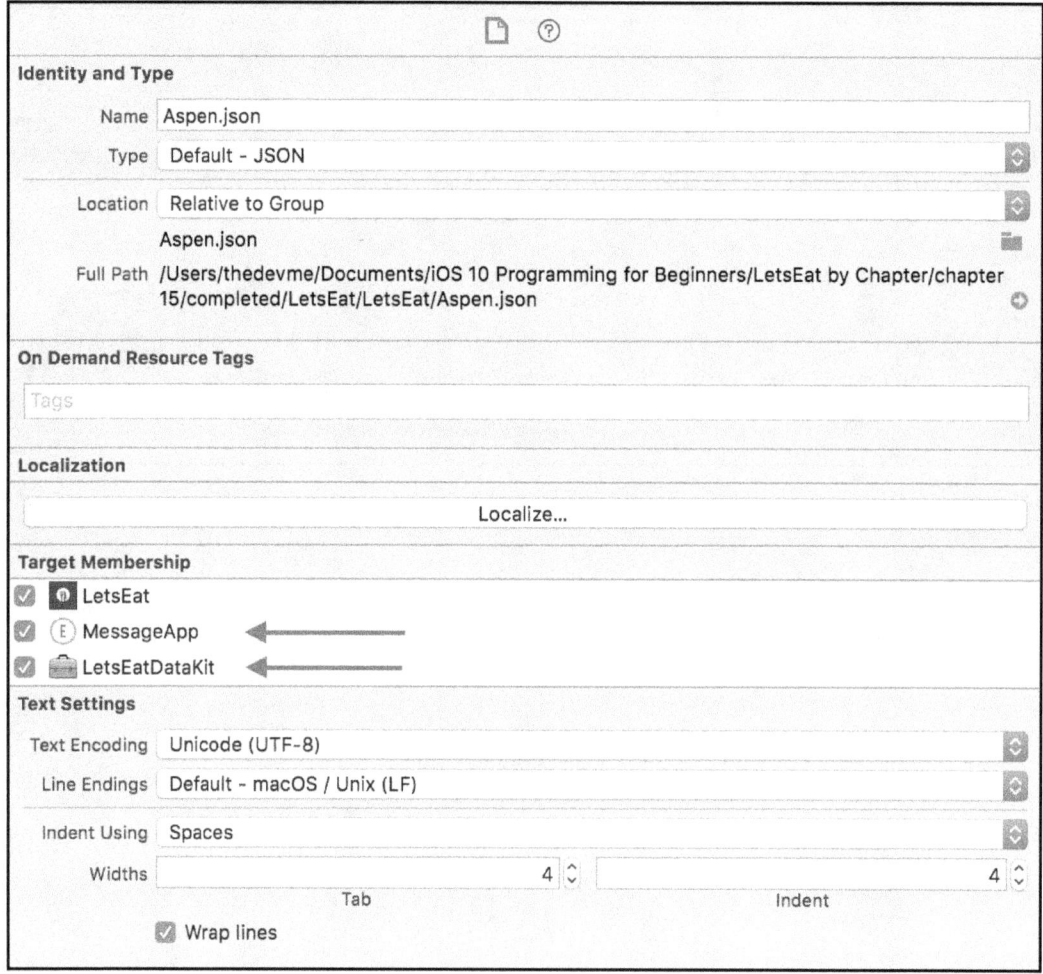

14. Next, select each JSON file inside of the `json` folder and update all of the files so that they are all targeted to `LetsEat`, `MessageApp`, and `LetsEatDataKit`.

[628]

15. Then, select each of the remaining three files inside of the `LetsEatDataKit` folder's `Restaurant` folder and update them so that each one is targeted to `LetsEatDataKit` only.
16. Now, change your target from `MessageApp` to `LetsEatDataKit`:

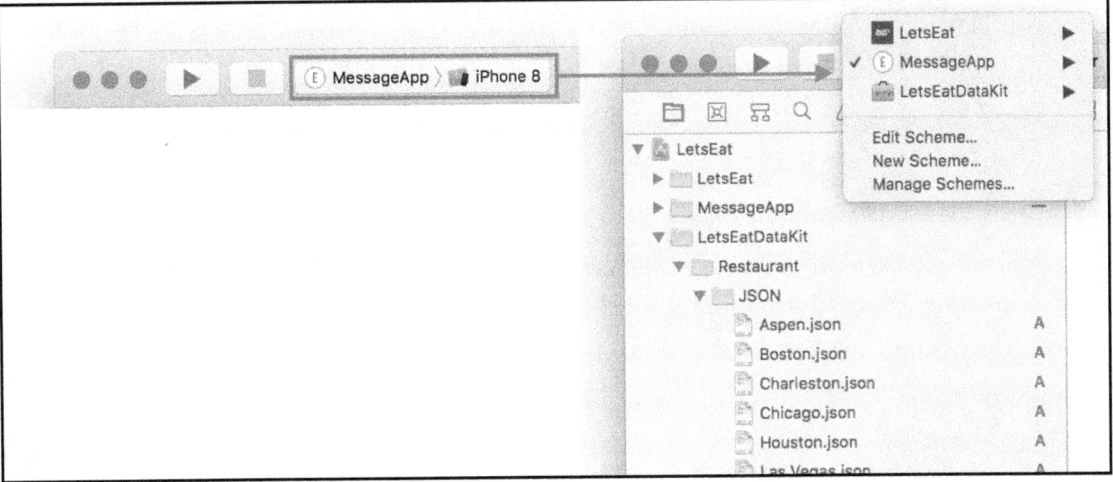

Hit ⌘ + B to build the app without running it and your build should be successful as long as you updated the target of all of your files.

Now, switch back to the *Let's Eat* app and hit ⌘ + B. You will notice some errors. These errors are expected and are easy to fix:

1. Inside of the `MapViewController.swift` file, add the following `import` at the top of the file:

   ```
   import LetsEatDataKit
   ```

2. Then, continue by updating your `RestaurantItem`. We need to make this file public so that it is seen by other files. Therefore, inside of the `RestaurantItem.swift` file, update our struct declaration to add `public` before the class so that it looks like the following:

   ```
   public class RestaurantItem
   ```

Similarly, we need to make each of our variables `public`, since we are using them all as data. Update all variables by adding the keyword `public` in front of them and then save the file. When you add `public` to the annotation variable, you will see another error occur. This error is complaining because we are trying to make the variable `public` while the class is not `public`.

3. Therefore, open your `RestaurantItem` class and update the class, each of the following variables, and the `init()` method with `public` access:

```
public class RestaurantItem: NSObject, MKAnnotation
public var name: String?
public var cuisines:[String] = []
public var latitude: Double?
public var longitude:Double?
public var address:String?
public var postalCode:String?
public var state:String?
public var imageURL:String?
public var restaurantID:Int?
public var title: String?
public var subtitle: String?
public var coordinate: CLLocationCoordinate2D
public enum CodingKeys: String, CodingKey
```

4. Save the file and now your `RestaurantItem` errors will disappear.

We still have more minor updates to make. We need to make both our `RestaurantAPIDataManager` and `RestaurantDataManager` public as well. Let's start with the `RestaurantAPIDataManager` and update the following `struct` and method with `public` access:

```
public struct RestaurantAPIManager
public static func loadJSON(file name:String) -> [[String:AnyObject]]
```

Next, update the class and each of the following methods inside of `RestaurantDataManager` with `public` access:

```
public class RestaurantDataManager
public func fetch(by location:String, withFilter:String="All", completionHandler:() -> Swift.Void)
public func numberOfItems() -> Int
public func restaurantItem(at index:IndexPath) -> RestaurantItem
```

We also need to make our `init()` method for our `RestaurantDataManager` class `public`; so, after the class declaration, add the following:

```
public init() {}
```

Having this `init()` method allows us to write the following:

```
let manager = RestaurantDataManager()
```

When we make it `public`, we are calling the `init()` method when we have `RestaurantDataManager()`.

Now, change the target to the `LetsEatDataKit` and build it again by hitting ⌘ + B. The build should be successful again at this point. If you, open the `MapViewController` file, you should see that all of the errors are fixed in this file.

However, we still have more errors to address inside of `MapDataManager`, `LocationViewController`, `RestaurantViewController`, `ExploreViewController`, `RestaurantDetailViewController`, and `MessagesViewController`. Therefore, inside of each of these three files, add the following at the top of each file in the `import` statement section:

```
import LetsEatDataKit
```

Next, hit ⌘ + B again, and there should be no errors inside of any of these three files or in your entire project.

Now, if you switch the target back to our *Let's Eat* app and build and run it by hitting the Play button (or using ⌘ + R), you should see that everything is working as expected. We can now start using this data in our *iMessages* app.

Connecting our message cell

Now that we have our files in order, we can start connecting everything. Earlier, we created our cell and now we need to create a cell class with which to connect it:

1. Right-click the `MessageApp` folder in the Navigator panel and select **New File**.
2. Inside of the **Choose a template for your new file screen**, select **iOS** at the top and, then, **Cocoa Touch Class**. Then, hit **Next**.

iMessages

3. You will now see an options screen. Please add the following in the new file section:

    - **Class**: `RestaurantMessageCell`
    - **Subclass**: `UICollectionViewCell`
    - **Also create XIB**: Unchecked
    - **Language**: `Swift`

4. Click **Next** and, then, **Create**.
5. In the new file, add the following inside of the class declaration:

    ```
    @IBOutlet var lblTitle:UILabel!
    @IBOutlet var lblCity:UILabel!
    @IBOutlet var lblCuisine:UILabel!
    ```

6. Save the file and then open `MainInterface.storyboard` in the `MessageApp` folder in the Navigator panel.
7. In the Outline view, select the **Collection View Cell**.
8. Then, select the Identity inspector in the Utilities panel; and, under **Custom Class** in the **Class** drop-down menu, select **RestaurantMessageCell** and hit *Enter*.
9. Next, switch to the Attributes inspector in the Utilities panel and update the identifier to `restaurantCell` and then hit *Enter*.
10. Now, switch to the Connections inspector in the Utilities panel, and click and drag from the empty circle next to each outlet listed to the corresponding `UILabel` in the screen shown in the following screenshot:

    ```
    lblTitle
    lblCity
    lblCuisine
    ```

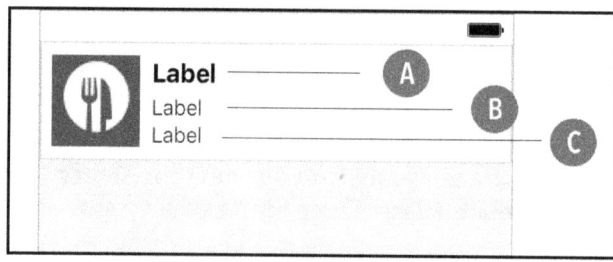

We now have our cell set up. Let's continue getting our *iMessages* app working.

Showing restaurants

We will be showing a list of restaurants just like in our app, but we will not be doing the entire interface. Most of this code will be familiar to you as we have done it before.

1. Open up the `MessagesViewController.swift` file in the Navigator panel and add the following code inside of the class declaration:

   ```
   @IBOutlet var collectionView: UICollectionView!
   let manager = RestaurantDataManager()
   var selectedRestaurant:RestaurantItem?
   ```

2. Next, we need to set up our Collection View defaults. Add the following method inside of a `private` extension:

   ```
   private extension MessagesViewController {
       func setupCollectionView() {
           let flow = UICollectionViewFlowLayout()
           flow.sectionInset = UIEdgeInsets(top: 7, left: 7, bottom: 7, right: 7)
           flow.minimumInteritemSpacing = 0
           flow.minimumLineSpacing = 7
           collectionView.collectionViewLayout = flow
           collectionView.delegate = self
           collectionView.dataSource = self
       }
   }
   ```

   You will see errors once you add the preceding code. Ignore them for now as we will fix them shortly. Now, we will create an `initialize()` method that will set up the Collection View and fetch our data.

3. Add the following method above the `createMessage()` method:

   ```
   func initialize() {
      setupCollectionView()
      manager.fetch(by: "Chicago", completionHandler: {
           self.collectionView.reloadData()
      })
   }
   ```

iMessages

Since this tab does not contain a location list, we will just pass a city in manually. Here, we use Chicago, but you can change it to any city of your choice.

4. Next, call the `initialize()` method inside of the `viewDidLoad()` method, so that your `viewDidLoad()` method now looks as follows:

```
override func viewDidLoad() {
    super.viewDidLoad()
    initialize()
}
```

5. Then, let's create another extension for our Collection View delegates and data source. After the last curly brace in the `MessagesViewController.swift` file, add the following `extension` declaration:

```
extension MessagesViewController:UICollectionViewDelegate, UICollectionViewDataSource, UICollectionViewDelegateFlowLayout {
}
```

6. Now that we have our `extension` set up, let's add all of the methods we need to get our Collection View showing data. Please add the following inside of our extension (which will get rid of our earlier errors):

```
func numberOfSections(in collectionView: UICollectionView) -> Int {
    return 1
}

func collectionView(_ collectionView: UICollectionView,
numberOfItemsInSection section: Int) -> Int {
    return manager.numberOfItems()
}

func collectionView(_ collectionView: UICollectionView,
cellForItemAt indexPath: IndexPath) -> UICollectionViewCell {
```

```
        let cell =
collectionView.dequeueReusableCell(withReuseIdentifier:
"restaurantCell", for: indexPath) as! RestaurantMessageCell
        let item = manager.restaurantItem(at: indexPath)
        if let name = item.name { cell.lblTitle.text = name }
        if let address = item.address { cell.lblCity.text = address }
        if let cuisine = item.subtitle { cell.lblCuisine.text = cuisine }
}
        return cell
}

    func collectionView(_ collectionView: UICollectionView, layout
collectionViewLayout: UICollectionViewLayout, sizeForItemAt
indexPath: IndexPath) -> CGSize {
        let cellWidth = self.collectionView.frame.size.width - 14
        return CGSize(width: cellWidth, height: 78)
}

    func collectionView(_ collectionView: UICollectionView,
didSelectItemAt indexPath: IndexPath) {
        selectedRestaurant = manager.restaurantItem(at: indexPath)
        guard let restaurant = selectedRestaurant else { return }
        createMessage(with: restaurant)
}
```

You should be very familiar with what we just added. We are setting up our Collection View data source as well as making sure our cells have a spacing of 14 pixels (7 on each side).

Lastly, before we build our app, we need to connect our Collection View in the storyboard:

1. Open up `MainInterface.storyboard` in the `MessageApp` folder in the Navigator panel.
2. Select the **Message View Controller** and, then, the Connections inspector in the Utilities panel.
3. Then, under **Outlets**, click and drag from the empty circle next to `collectionView` to the **Collection View** in our scene.

iMessages

Let's change the target *Message App* and build and run our *iMessages* app by hitting the Play button (or using ⌘ + R). Your app should look similar to the following after clicking the stickers button:

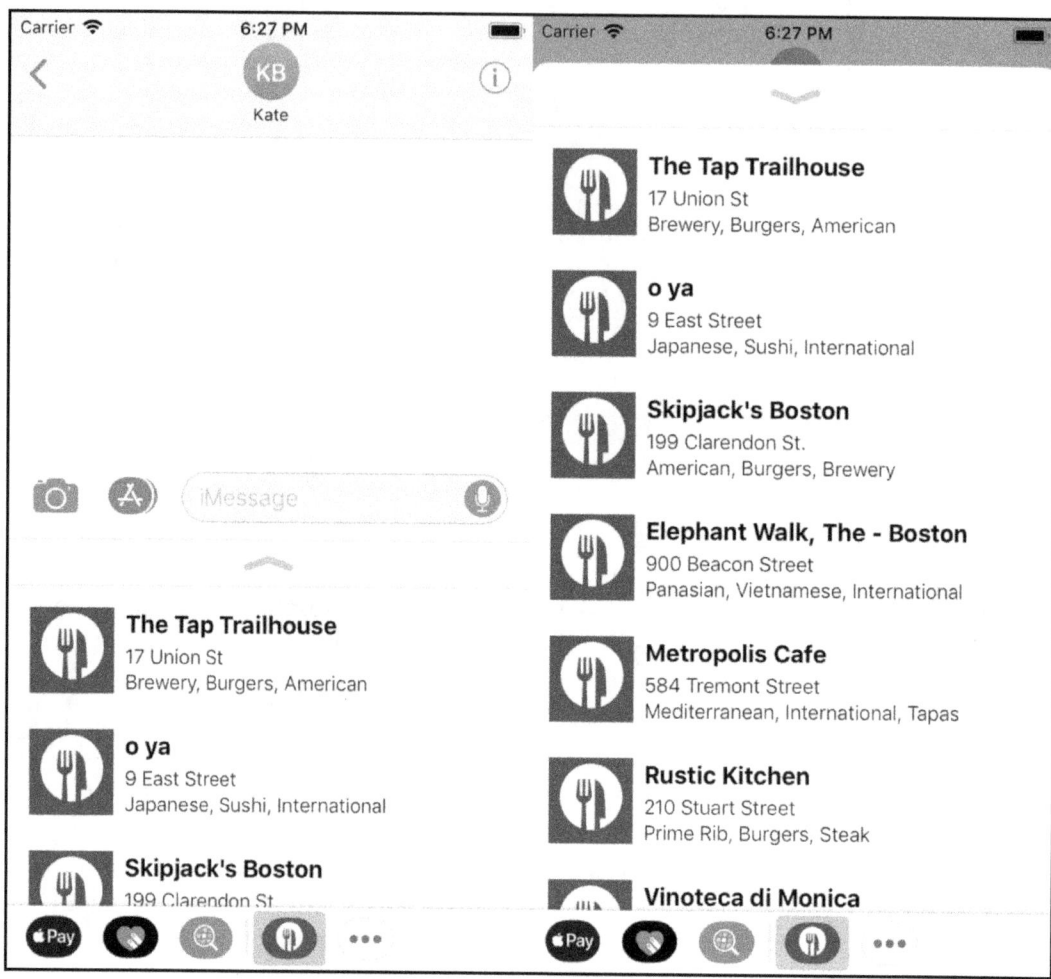

Hitting the arrow (highlighted by the red boxes) will expand the screen to expanded mode from compact mode and back again. Now that we have our restaurants displaying, we need to be able to send the restaurant reservation to other people. Let's add that next.

iMessage crashing

If you just tried to launch the app and it crashed, there is a fix for this.

1. In the simulator, open the `Messages` app.
2. Select **Kate**.
3. Then click on the icon with the three dots:

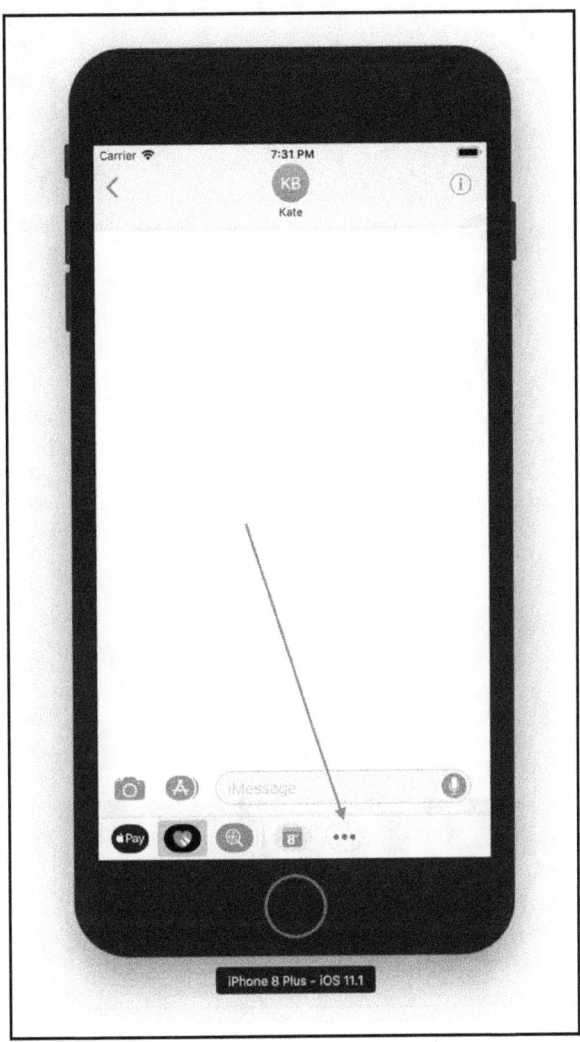

4. Then click **Edit**:

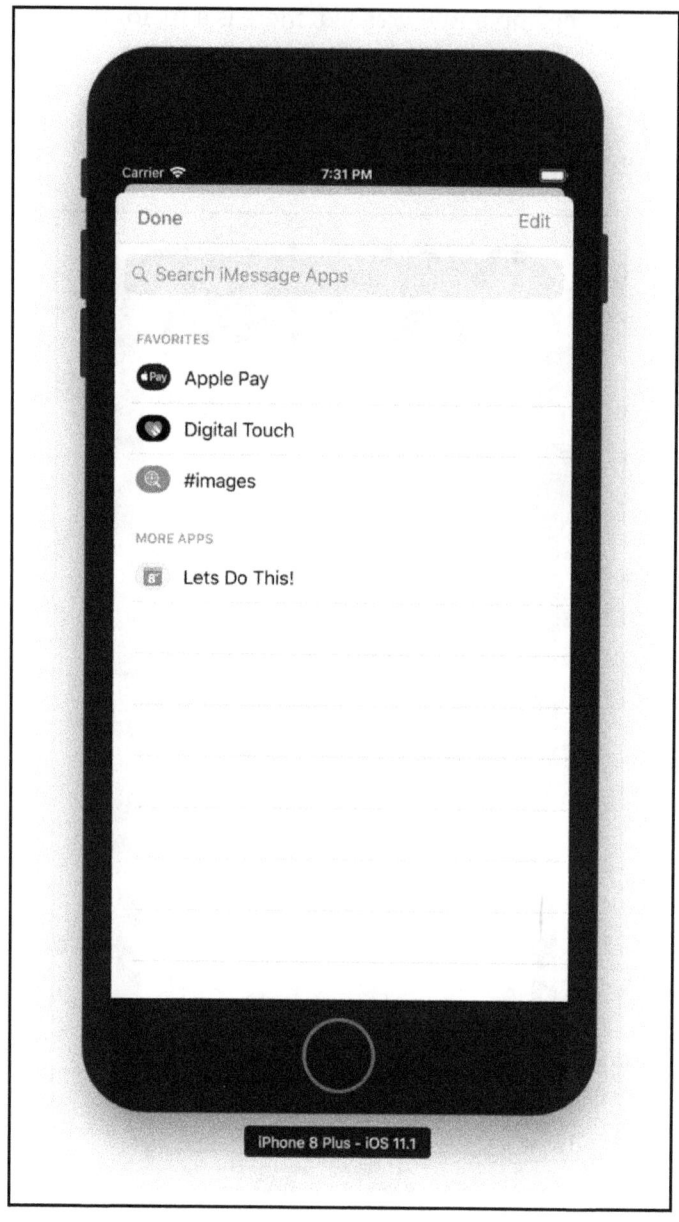

5. Click the switch for `MessageApp`:

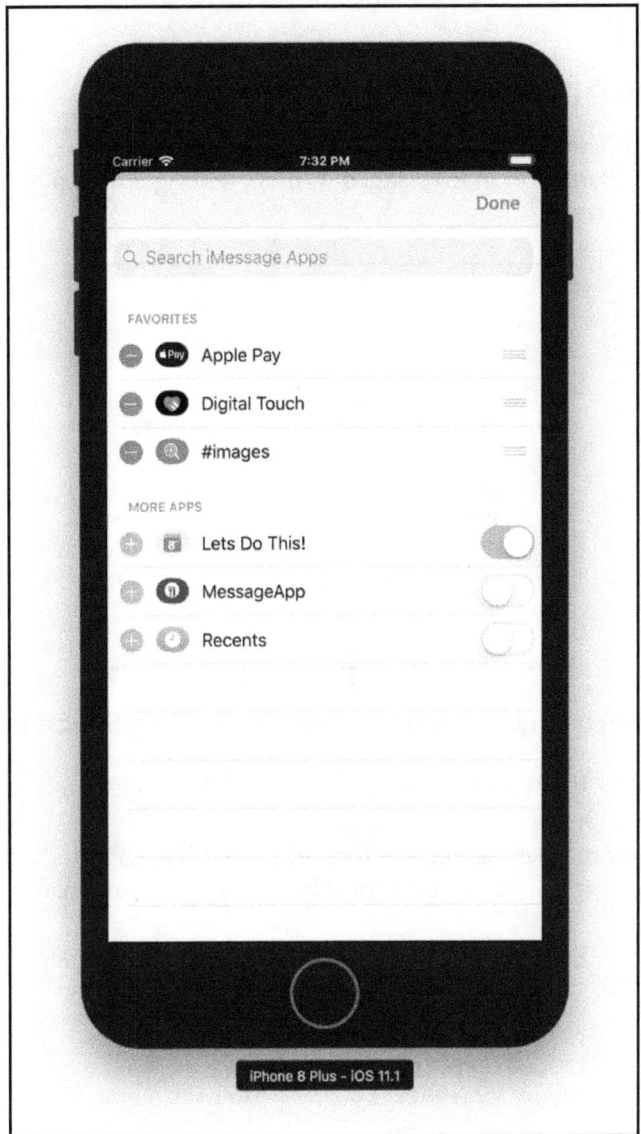

6. Click **Done**.

iMessages

Build and rerun the app, and you should be fine. This error is an Apple bug and performing these steps is the only way to fix this issue. Let's move on to sending reservations.

Sending reservations

We need to set up our Collection View so that, when the user taps on a cell, it will add the reservation to the conversation in iMessages. When creating a message to send, we have the following things we can set:

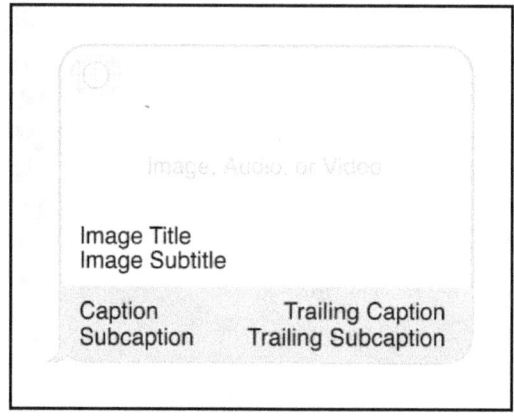

We will use everything but the **Trailing Caption** and **Trailing Subcaption**.

1. Open up `MessagesViewController` in the `MessageApp` folder in the Navigator panel.
2. Then, in our main class declaration, add the following method after the `setupCollectionView()` method in the `private` extension:

```
func createMessage(with restaurant:RestaurantItem) {
    if let conversation = activeConversation {
        let layout = MSMessageTemplateLayout()
        layout.image = UIImage(named: "restaurant-detail")
        layout.caption = "Table for 7, tonight at 10:00 PM"
        layout.imageTitle = restaurant.name
        layout.imageSubtitle = restaurant.cuisine
        let message = MSMessage()
        message.layout = layout
        message.url = URL(string: "emptyURL")
        conversation.insert(message, completionHandler: { (error: Error?) in
            if error != nil {
```

```
                    print("there was an error \(error)")
                }
                else {
                    self.requestPresentationStyle(.compact)
                }
            })
        }
    }
```

In this method, we are setting up an `MSMessage`. We check for an active conversation first. If `true`, we then set up our layout. Here, we are just using an image from our assets to create an image background (we could have also used a video, for example). Also, we set the caption `Table for 7, tonight at 10:00PM`. This allows the receiver to see all of the relevant information for the reservation. Next, we set the restaurant name as the image title and the restaurant's cuisine as the image subtitle. Then, we create an instance of the `MSMessage`, pass it the layout we created, and give it a URL (which, in our case, is just an empty string, since we do not have an URL). Finally, we insert the message into the conversation. We need to make sure that, when we want to send a message, we are in compact mode; otherwise, the user will think that the app does not work.

Lastly, we just need to add the code that calls our `createMessage()` method. Add the following method in our extension, but before the last curly brace:

```
func collectionView(_ collectionView: UICollectionView, didSelectItemAt indexPath: IndexPath) {
    selectedRestaurant = manager.restaurantItem(at: indexPath)
    guard let restaurant = selectedRestaurant else { return }
    createMessage(with: restaurant)
}
```

Here, we are checking for when the user taps a cell; then, we get `selectedRestaurant` and pass it to our `createMessage()` method.

iMessages

Let's build and run the project by hitting the Play button (or using ⌘ + R). Select a restaurant and you will now see a message with the selected restaurant in the message area:

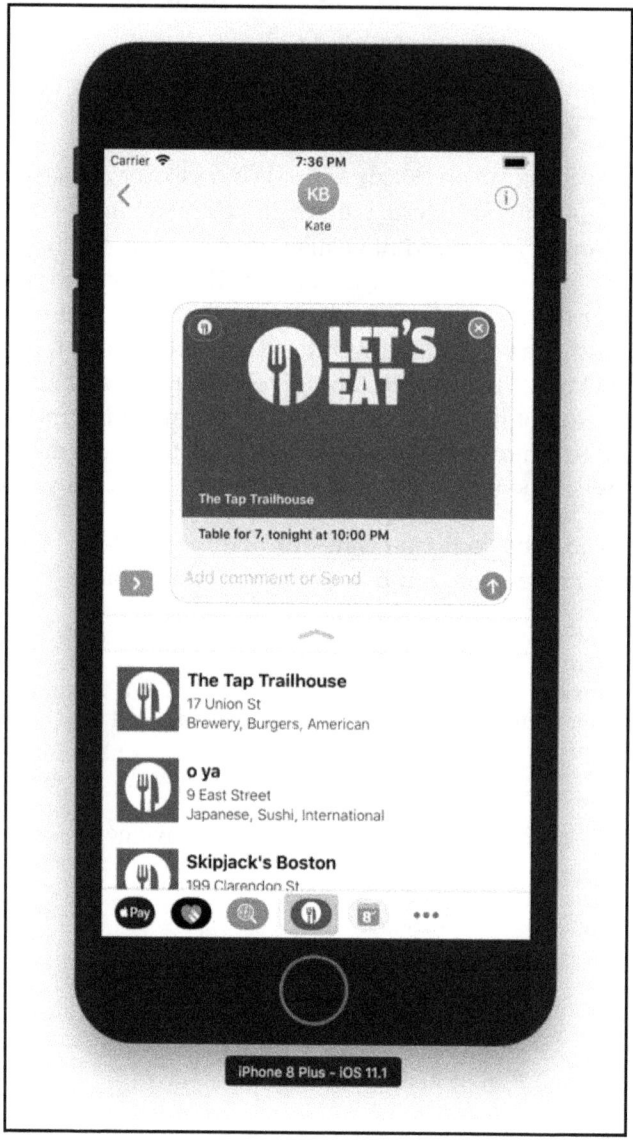

You can see that, with a little bit of work, you can add a nice *iMessages* app to your app.

Summary

In this chapter, we looked at how to add an *iMessage* app to our app. We also created a framework that allowed us to use data in both our apps without having to duplicate code. We looked at what is involved with creating an `MSMessage` and how we can pass an `MSMessageTemplateLayout` to an `MSMessage`. We now know that we can also send embedded videos as well as images when we send messages. Also, we can now send reservations through the *iMessages* app with relevant data for a reservation.

In the next chapter, we will go back to our *Let's Eat* app and we will learn how to work with notifications in our app.

25
Notifications

Notifications were first launched in 2009 and are a staple of the iOS system. Whether from your favorite app or a text message, you have encountered a notification at some point while using a smartphone. Pre-iOS 10, if you had to work with notifications in iOS, you had two types of push notifications: remote (from a server) and local.

iOS 10 made changes to notifications that simplified them, but also made them more robust. In iOS 10, there is now one notification that covers both remote and local notifications, which is great for those who have worked with them in the past. Concerning breadth of functionality, notifications now allow you to embed rich media (such as images, video, and audio), as well as having custom UI content.

In this chapter, we are going to learn how to create basic notifications, as well as notifications with embedded images. After we look at both of these examples, we also look at how to create a custom UI for our notifications.

What we will cover in this chapter:

- Learning how to build basic notifications
- Learning how to embed images into notifications
- Learning how to build a custom notification UI

Starting with the basics

Let's begin by getting our app to send us basic notifications. Inside of our restaurant details page, we have three buttons (**9:30 PM**, **10:00 PM**, and **10:30 PM**) that currently do not do anything. We are going to update those buttons so that, when you tap on one of them, it creates a restaurant reservation notification. If this were a real reservations app, we would want to store these reservations. When the reservation date and time neared, we would then post a notification to the user as a reminder. Doing all of that is beyond the scope of this book; so, we will just address creating a restaurant reservation notification.

Getting permission

Before we can send any notifications, we must get the user's permission. Therefore, open the `AppDelegate.swift` file and add the following method after the `didFinishLaunchingWithOptions()` method:

```
func checkNotifications() {
   UNUserNotificationCenter.current().requestAuthorization(options: [.alert, .sound, .badge]) { (isGranted, error) in
   }
}
```

This method here checks for the user's authorization. If the user has not been asked, it displays a message to the user for permission to use notifications. When you add this method, you will get an error. The reason for this error is that we need to `import UserNotifications`. At the top of the file, under `import UIKit`, add the following:

```
import UserNotifications
```

Next, the method we just added needs to run inside of the `applicationDidFinishLaunching(application:launchOptions)` method. Add the following after `setupDefaultColors()`:

```
checkNotifications()
```

Your `applicationDidFinishLaunching(application:launchOptions)` method should now look like the following:

```
func application(_ application: UIApplication,
didFinishLaunchingWithOptions launchOptions:
[UIApplicationLaunchOptionsKey: Any]?) -&gt; Bool {
   setupDefaultColors()
```

```
        checkNotifications()
        return true
}
```

Build and run the project by hitting the Play button (or using ⌘ + R), and you should see the following message:

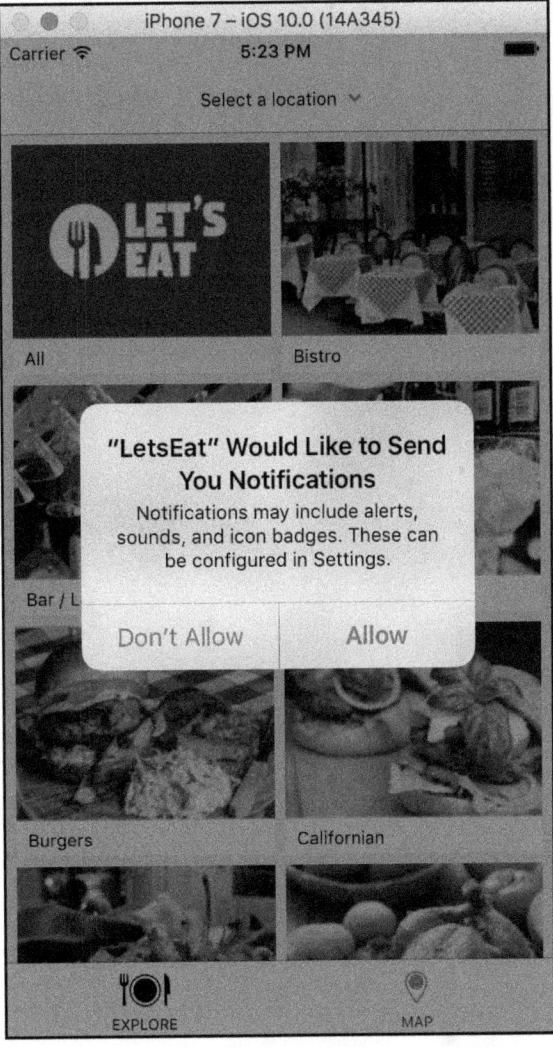

Notifications

Setting up notifications

Now that we have permission, we need to set up notifications. We start setting up our buttons:

1. Open the `RestaurantDetailViewController.swift` file and add the following method after our `showAllReviews()` method and before the last curly brace of our class file:

   ```
   @IBAction func onTimeTapped(sender: UIButton) {
   }
   ```

2. Save the file, and you see an empty circle appear next to this new `@IBAction`.
3. Now, open the `RestaurantDetail.storyboard` and select the `RestaurantDetailViewController`.
4. Select the Connections inspector in the Utilities panel and, under `Received Actions`, you see `onTimeTappedWithSender:`.

Chapter 25

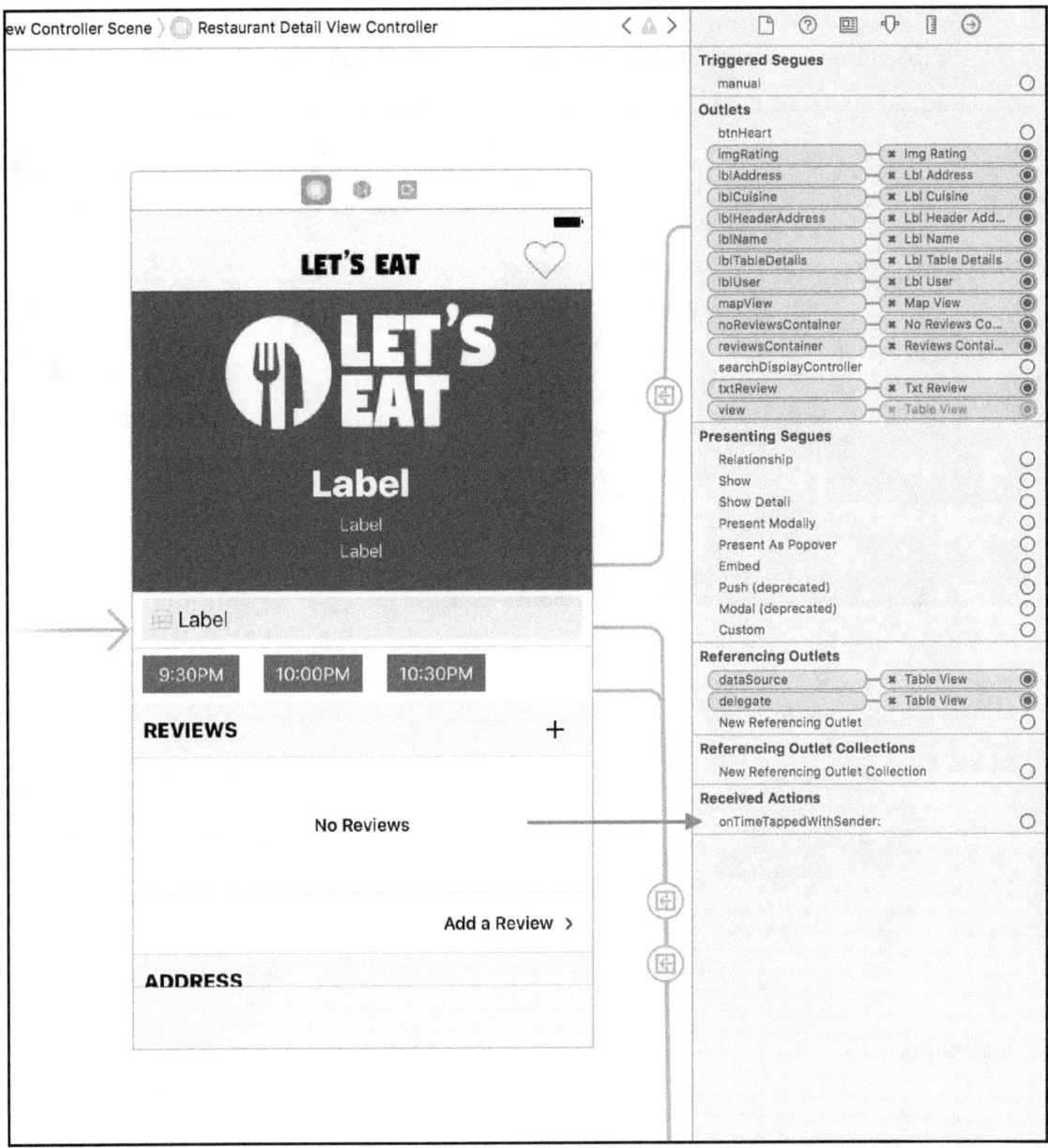

[649]

Notifications

5. Click and drag from the empty circle next to `onTimeTappedWithSender` to the first button (marked **9:30 PM**) in the restaurant detail scene.

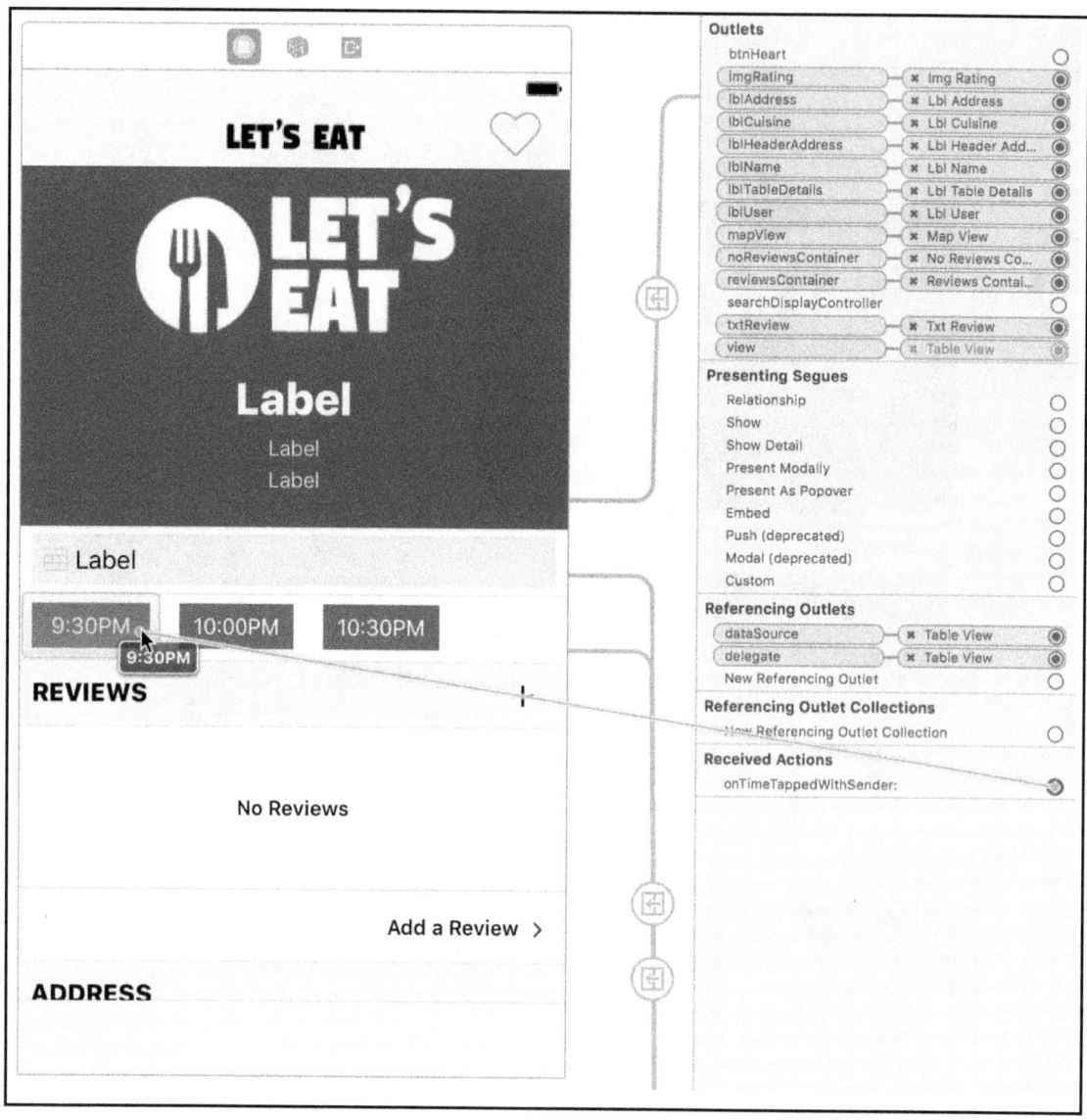

6. In the prompt, select **Touch Up Inside**.

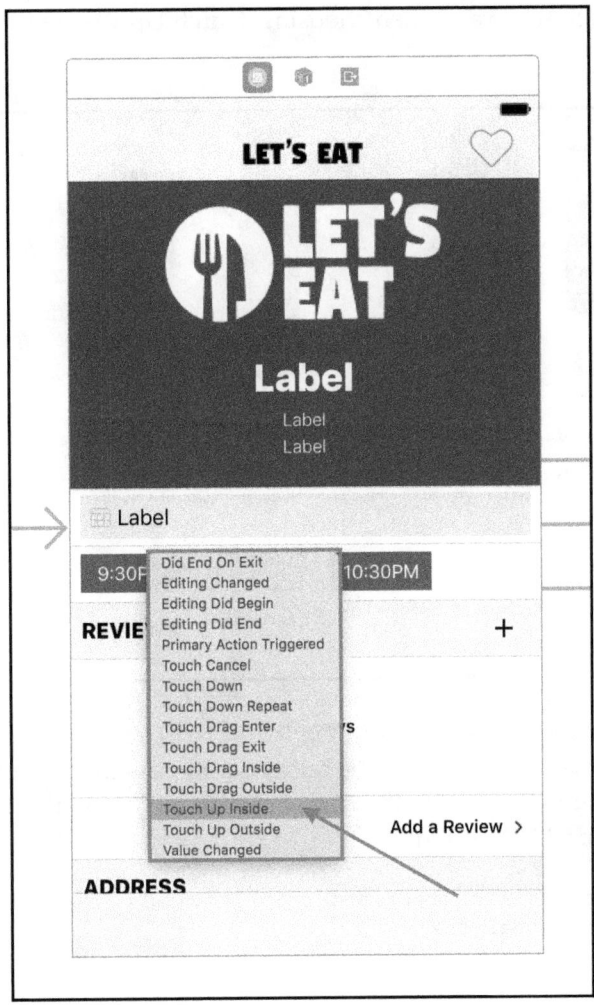

Notifications

7. Repeat these steps for the remaining two buttons (**10:00 PM** and **10:30 PM**), clicking and dragging the same circle (now filled) to each of the remaining buttons in the scene and then choosing **Touch Up Inside** for each prompt that follows.

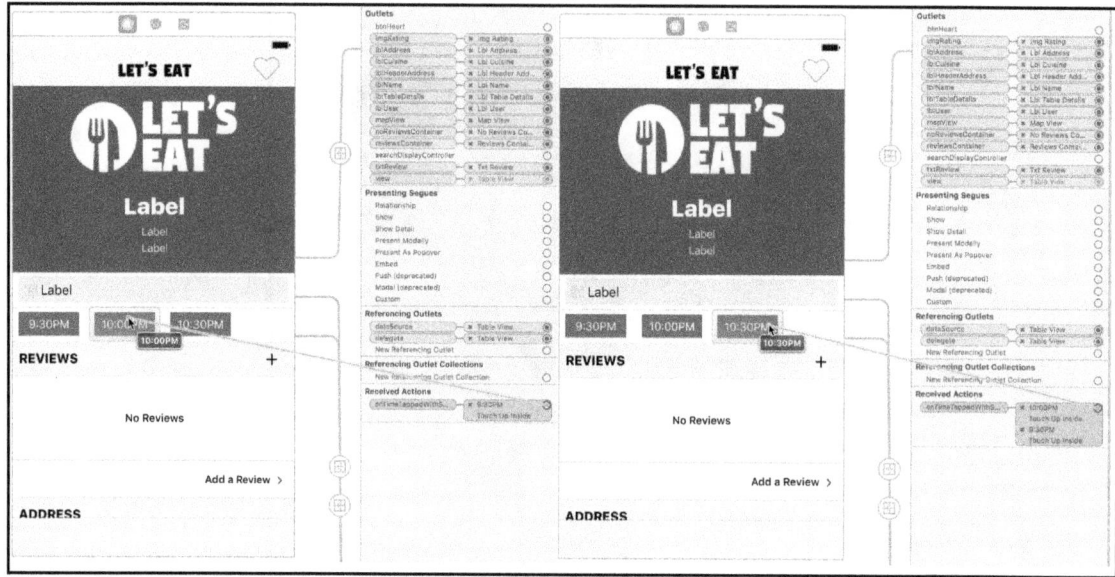

8. Now, open `RestaurantDetailViewController.swift`; this is where we need to get the time from inside of the buttons and pass them to our notifications. Add the following method after the `showAllReviews()` method and above the `onTimeTapped()` method:

```
func showNotification(sender:String?) {
   print(sender as Any)
}
```

9. Inside of the `onTimeTapped()` method, add the following:

```
showNotification(sender: sender.titleLabel?.text)
```

Chapter 25

We are now passing the time value to our `showNotification()` method. Build and run the project by hitting the Play button (or using ⌘ + R). You should now see the time of each selected button in the console.

Showing notifications

Now that we have a time, let's show our notification along with the time selected:

1. In the `RestaurantDetailViewController.swift` file, after `import LetsEatDataKit`, add the following:

    ```
    import UserNotifications
    ```

2. Next, inside of the `showNotification()` method, add the following:

    ```
    let content = UNMutableNotificationContent()
    if let name = selectedRestaurant?.name { content.title = name }
    if let time = sender { content.body = "Table for 7, tonight at \(time) " }
    content.subtitle = "Restaurant Reservation"
    content.badge = 1
    content.sound = UNNotificationSound.default()
    let trigger = UNTimeIntervalNotificationTrigger(timeInterval: 5, repeats: false)
    let identifier = "letsEatReservation"
    let request = UNNotificationRequest(identifier: identifier, content: content, trigger: trigger)
    UNUserNotificationCenter.current().add(request, withCompletionHandler: { error in
        // handle error
    })
    ```

In the preceding code, we are creating a notification content object. In this object, we are going to set the title, the body, the subtitle, the badge, and the sound.

3. After the `initialize()` method, add the following method:

   ```
   func setupNotificationDefaults() {
       UNUserNotificationCenter.current().delegate = self
   }
   ```

   This method is our `delegate` method for notifications. We get an error for our `delegate`, because we have not yet implemented the required functions.

4. Let's do that now by creating an extension at the end of this file, after the last curly brace. You may already have an extension in this file for our map if you tackled the challenges at the end of Chapter 11, *Designing Static Tables*; if so, add this new extension after the last curly brace of that Map extension. In either case, add the following code:

   ```
   extension RestaurantDetailViewController: UNUserNotificationCenterDelegate {
       func userNotificationCenter(_ center: UNUserNotificationCenter,
   willPresent notification: UNNotification, withCompletionHandler
   completionHandler: @escaping (UNNotificationPresentationOptions) -
   &gt; Void) {
             completionHandler([.alert, .sound])
         }
   }
   ```

5. Finally, we just need to call the `setupNotificationDefaults()` method inside of our `initialize()` method. Your updated `initialize()` method should now look like the following:

   ```
   func initialize() {
      setupLabels()
      setupMap()
      setupNotificationDefaults()
   }
   ```

Chapter 25

6. Build and run the project by hitting the Play button (or using ⌘ + R). Open a restaurant detail page, tap the time button, and wait five seconds. You should see the following:

Notifications

7. Then, if you click and pull down on the notification, you should see the following:

We just implemented a basic notification; however, we can do so much more. Next, let's get an image inside of our notification.

Customizing our notifications

Before we can embed an image, we need a test image. In the `Assets` folder of the Navigator panel, create a new group, called `Images`. Then, in the project folder for this book, open the `asset` folder for this chapter and drag the image assets into the `Images` folder that we just created.

Embedding images

Next, let's embed our images. First, return to the `RestaurantDetailViewController.swift` file and, in the `showNotification()` method we created, remove the following code:

```
let trigger = UNTimeIntervalNotificationTrigger(timeInterval: 5, repeats: false)
let identifier = "letsEatReservation"
let request = UNNotificationRequest(identifier: identifier, content: content, trigger: trigger)
UNUserNotificationCenter.current().add(request, withCompletionHandler: { error in
    // handle error
})
```

Replace the deleted section of code with the following code:

```
do {
    let url = Bundle.main.url(forResource: "sample-restaurant-img@3x", withExtension: "png")
    if let imgURL = url {
        let attachment = try UNNotificationAttachment(identifier: "letsEatReservation", url: imgURL, options: nil)
        content.attachments = [attachment]
        let trigger = UNTimeIntervalNotificationTrigger(timeInterval: 5, repeats: false)
        let identifier = "letsEatReservation"
        let request = UNNotificationRequest(identifier: identifier, content: content, trigger: trigger)
        UNUserNotificationCenter.current().add(request, withCompletionHandler: { error in
            // handle error
        })
    }
}
catch {
    print("there was an error with the notification")
}
```

In this do...catch, we are getting the image URL from our project and creating an attachment. We attach the rich media (here, an image) to the notification. The rest of the code is what we removed and just added back inside of the do...catch.

Notifications

Build and rerun the project by hitting the Play button (or using ⌘ + R). When you get to a restaurant detail page, tap the time button and wait five seconds. You should now see a thumbnail image in the notification:

Also, if you click and pull down on the notification, you should see the following:

Notifications

Thus far, we have been receiving notifications while inside of the app. If you want to test notifications outside of the app, take the following steps. Build and run the project by hitting the Play button (or using ⌘ + R). When you get to a restaurant detail page, tap the time button and, then, immediately hit ⌘ + *Shift* + *H*. This takes you out of the app, and you will then see the following:

Chapter 25

If you click and pull down on the notification, you will see the following :

Our notifications are looking good, but you really cannot do anything with them. It would be nice to confirm your reservation with a yes or no, for example. We need to add some buttons for the notifications to do this.

Adding buttons

We only need to add a few things to add buttons to our notifications. First, we need to update our restaurant detail:

1. Inside of the `RestaurantDetailViewController.swift` file, add the following into the `showNotification()` method after `content.sound = UNNotificationSound.default()`:

   ```
   content.categoryIdentifier = "reservationCategory"
   ```

2. Next, we need to create a file for our button identifiers. Right click the `Misc` folder inside of the `Common` folder and select **New File**.
3. Inside of the **Choose a template for your new file screen**, select **iOS** at the top and, then, **Swift File**. Then, hit **Next**.
4. Name this file `Identifier` and hit **Create**.

It is good practice to eliminate as many strings from your app as you can. Adding this file will not only eliminate strings, but it also keeps you from accidentally typing the wrong value. For example, we could easily misspell identifier. Therefore, it is a protective measure to have it in an `enum`. Add the following to the `import` statement in this new file:

```
enum Identifier:String {
    case reservationCategory
    case reservationIdentifier = "letsEatReservation"
}
enum Option:String {
    case one = "optionOne"
    case two = "optionTwo"
}
```

We will use this to create our button options for our notification. Open the `AppDelegate.swift` file. In the `checkNotifications()` method, add the following code:

```
let optionOne = UNNotificationAction(identifier: Option.one.rawValue,
title: "Yes", options: [.foreground])
let optionTwo = UNNotificationAction(identifier: Option.two.rawValue,
title: "No", options: [.foreground])
let category = UNNotificationCategory(identifier:
Identifier.reservationCategory.rawValue, actions: [optionOne, optionTwo],
intentIdentifiers: [], options: [])
UNUserNotificationCenter.current().setNotificationCategories([category])
```

Add this code inside of the `requestAuthorization` block:

```
func checkNotifications() {
    UNUserNotificationCenter.current().requestAuthorization(options: [.alert, .sound, .badge]) { (isGranted, error) in
        // Add code here
    }
}
```

In this code, we are setting up two actions: one for yes and one for no. We are creating a category and setting it to our notification category, which defines the type of notification that we want to use.

Lastly, we need to write code to handle when we receive a notification. Return to the `RestaurantDetailViewController.swift` file and add the following inside of your new extension for notifications after the `willPresent()` method:

```
func userNotificationCenter(_ center: UNUserNotificationCenter, didReceive response: UNNotificationResponse, withCompletionHandler completionHandler: @escaping () -&gt; Void) {
    if let identifier = Option(rawValue: response.actionIdentifier) {
        switch identifier {
        case .one :
            print("User selected yes")
        case .two:
            print("User selected no")
        }
    }
    completionHandler()
}
```

Notifications

Build and run the project by hitting the Play button (or using ⌘ + R). When you get the notification and pull down on it, you will see that you now have button options:

Inside of our `didReceive()` method, we are printing out what the user selected, but you can choose whatever `print` statement you would like.

Chapter 25

Up until this point, we have looked at how to create basic notifications as well as notifications with images embedded in them. Next, we can take our app a step further by adding our custom UI into our notifications.

Custom UI in notifications

To add custom UI to our notifications, we need to add an extension. Let's get started by doing the following:

1. In the Navigator panel, select the Project navigator and, then, your project.
2. At the bottom of the **TARGETS** area, click the + button.
3. Select **Notification Content Extension** under **Application Extension** and, then, click **Next**:

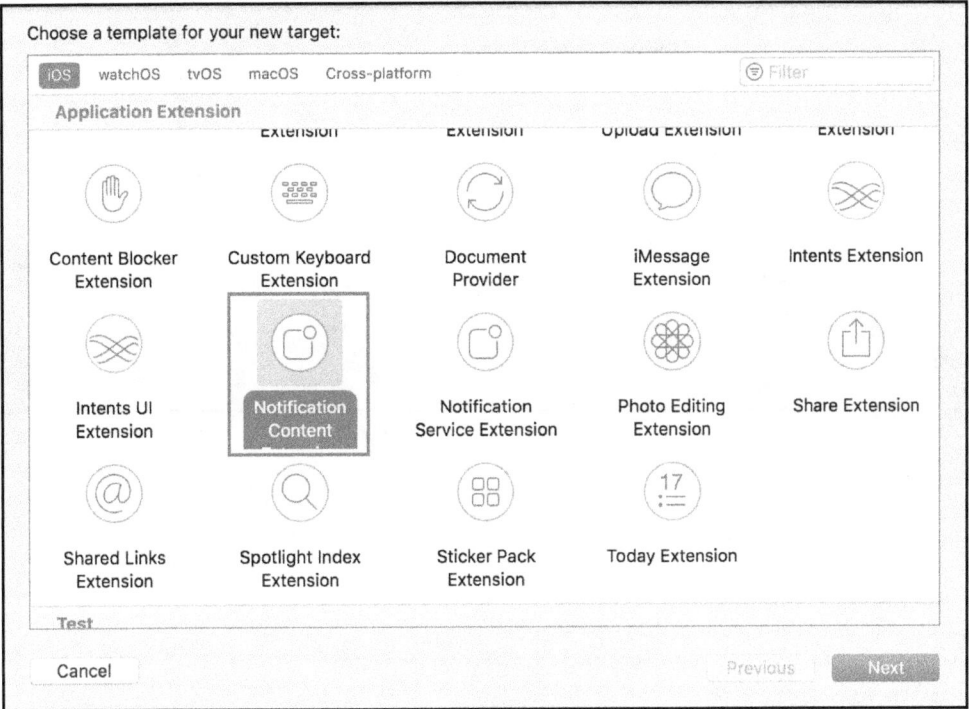

Notifications

4. In the options screen that appears, set **Product Name** to
   `LetsEatContentExtension` and click **Finish**:

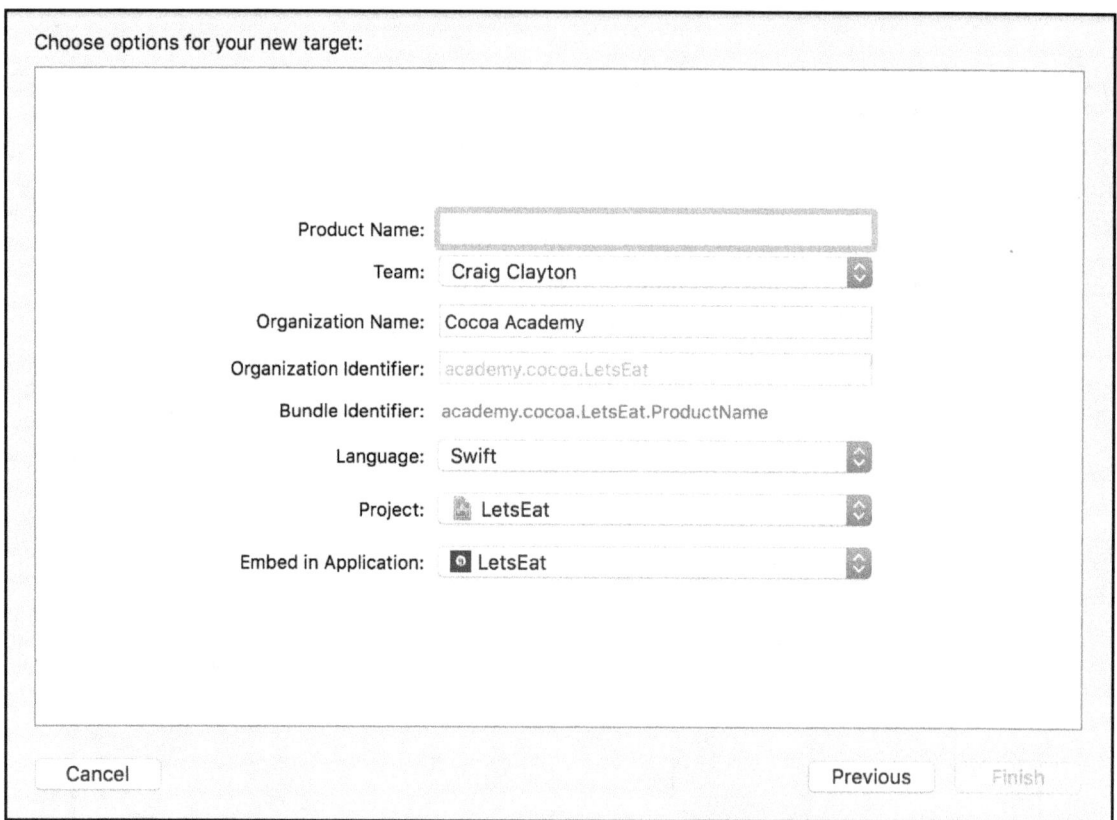

5. Next, select **Activate** on the screen that appears:

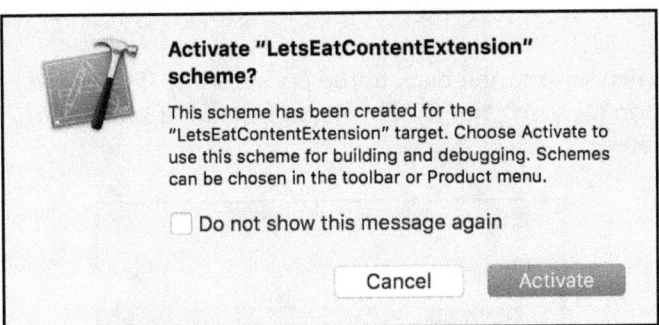

This activation allows us to build and run our custom UI extension in the simulator. Now, you have a choice of running our app, the *iMessages* app, our kit or our custom UI extension.

Now that our extension is created, we need to be able to use it.

1. Open the `info.plist` file in our `LetsEatContentExtension` folder.
2. Tap the `NSExtension` disclosure arrow to open up that key.
3. Then, tap the disclosure arrow to open `NSExtensionAttributes`, under which you can see `UNNotificationExtensionCategory`:

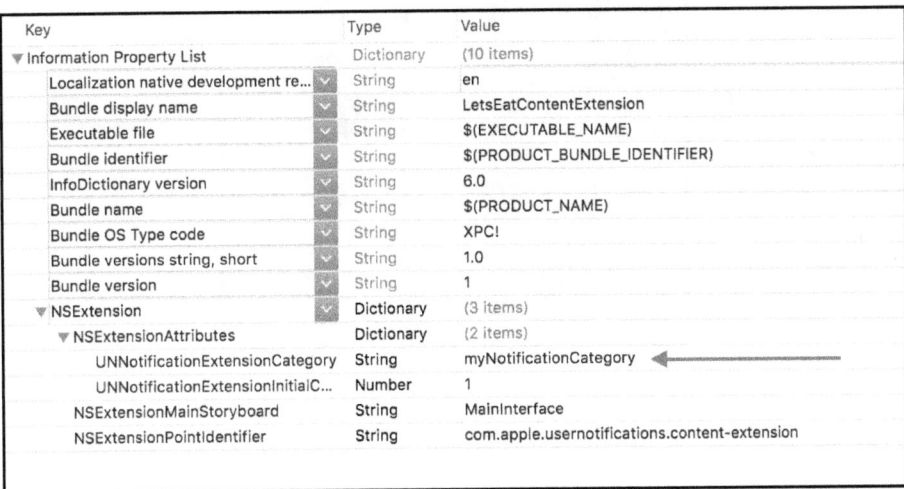

[667]

This category is the name of the category of our notification we set earlier.

4. Update `myNotificationCategory` to `reservationCategory`.

Save the file and switch your target back to the *Let's Eat* app. Build and run the project by hitting the Play button (or using ⌘ + R). This time, instead of seeing our custom image, we now have the following:

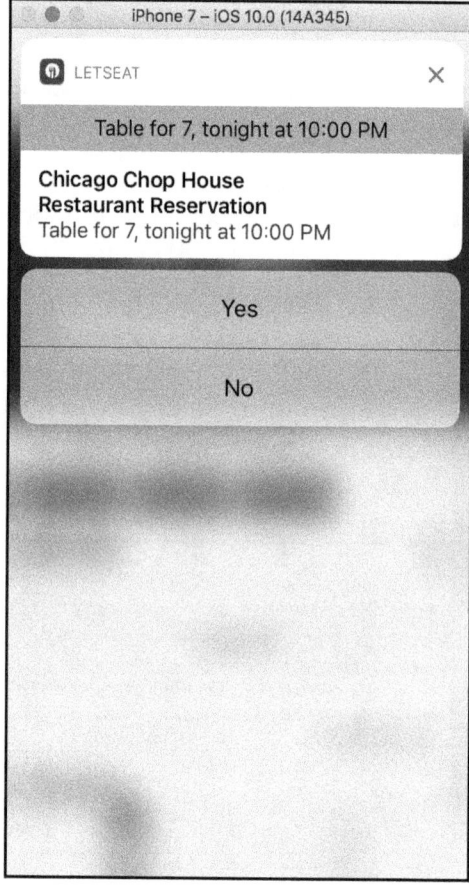

Chapter 25

You might have noticed something slightly off when you pulled down on the notification. The notification starts out large and then shrinks down. Inside of your `Info.plist` file, there is a property, `UNNotificationExtensionInitialContentSizeRatio`, that is currently set to 1. Changing it to 0.25 makes this less obvious.

Currently, this custom notification is showing us the custom and default content together. We can fix this by returning to our `Info.plist` inside of the `LetsEatContentExtension`:

Inside of `NSExtensionAttributes`, add a new item called `UNNotificationExtensionDefaultContentHidden` and set the type as **Boolean** and the value to **YES**:

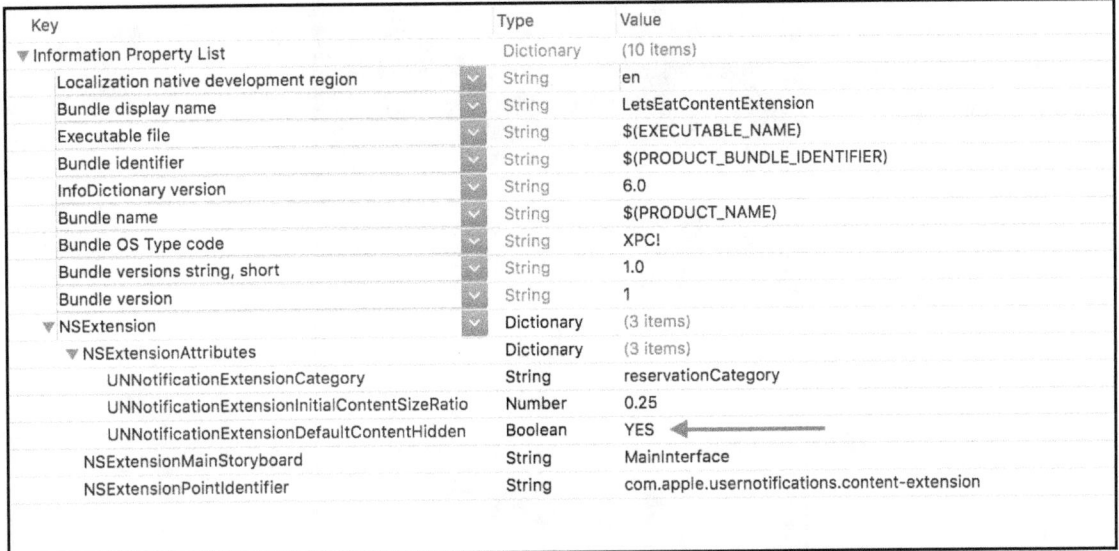

Notifications

Save the file and build and run the project by hitting the Play button (or using ⌘ + R). Once you pull down on the notification, you see that the default content is hidden:

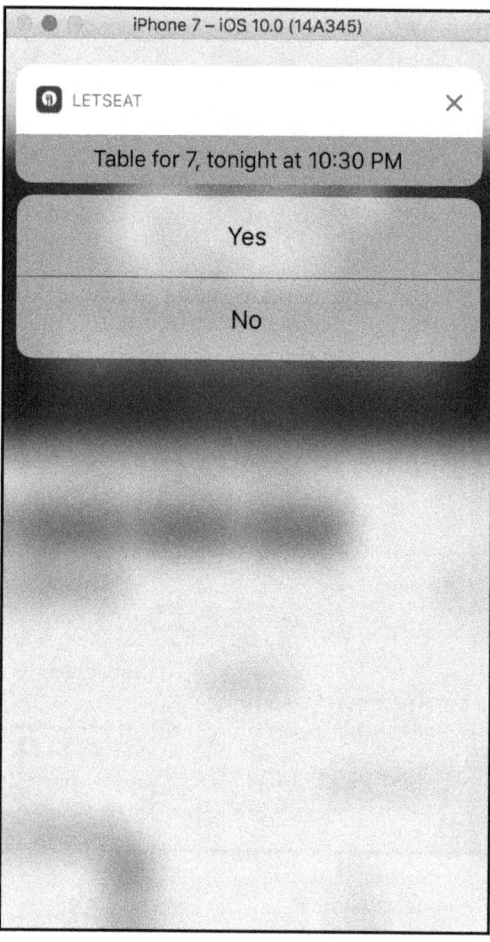

You can now update the `MainInterface.storyboard` inside of your `LetsEatContentExtension` folder. In this book, we are not going to do this as we have done plenty of storyboarding, and this gives you an opportunity to practice what you have learned in this book to create a custom interface for this.

Summary

Notifications in iOS 10 are now even more powerful and really give you the flexibility to create rich custom content with very little work. In this chapter, we learned how to build basic notifications and then we stepped it up a bit more by adding embedded images into our notifications. Lastly, we briefly looked at how to add a custom notification using an extension.

In the next chapter, we will address how we can integrate 3D Touch into our app. 3D Touch allows users to jump into our app using shortcuts.

26
Just a Peek

In 2015, when the iPhone 6S and 6S Plus were announced, Apple also introduced 3D Touch. 3D Touch uses a Taptic Engine with haptic feedback, which allows the device to sense the pressure of a touch, thereby triggering specific actions. For example, pressing hard on an icon will enable us to quickly open an action menu.

This chapter will cover the following topics:

- Adding 3D Touch quick actions
- Understanding the difference between static and dynamic quick actions
- Adding 3D Touch support inside of a Collection View

The first thing we will do for our app is to add quick actions for our app icon.

Adding 3D Touch quick actions

For our app, we are going to add four quick actions (which is the maximum amount that you can have). These actions will do the following:

- Launch the map
- Launch the locations
- Select **Los Angeles** as a location
- Select **Las Vegas** as a location

Just a Peek

There are two types of quick actions: static and dynamic. Static means that they cannot be changed and dynamic means that they can. For example, Apple has 3D Touch on their *Messages* app. If you press hard on the *Messages* app, you will see one static quick action, **New Message**, and three dynamic quick actions, the three most-texted contacts. In our app, we will have two static quick actions, launching the **Map** tab and the locations list, and two dynamic quick actions, launching Los Angeles and Las Vegas as locations. Let's start setting up our quick actions:

1. Right-click the `Misc` folder and select **New File**.
2. Inside of the **Choose a template for your new file screen**, select **iOS** at the top and then **Swift File**. Then, hit **Next**.
3. Name this file **Shortcut** and hit **Create**.

Inside of this file, add the following `enum` after the `import` statement:

```
enum Shortcut: String {
    case openMap
    case openLocations
    case openLosAngeles
    case openLasVegas

    init?(with identifier: String) {
        guard let shortIdentifier = identifier.components(separatedBy: ".").last else { return nil }
        self.init(rawValue: shortIdentifier)
    }

    var type: String {
        guard let identifier = Bundle.main.bundleIdentifier else { return "" }
        return identifier + ".\(self.rawValue)"
    }
}
```

This `enum` is used for our quick actions. As we discussed, we will have four quick actions for our app.

4. Now, open your `AppDelegate.swift` file. After the `window` variable, add the following:

```
var launchedShortcutItem: UIApplicationShortcutItem?
static let applicationShortcutUserInfoIconKey =
"applicationShortcutUserInfoIconKey"
```

Here, we have a variable for our shortcut item and a constant for our user info key. When the application launches, we need to check to see if the app was launched using a quick action.

Next, we need to create a method to handle our shortcuts. Add the following after the `checkNotifications()` method:

```
func checkShortCut(_ application: UIApplication, launchOptions: [UIApplicationLaunchOptionsKey: Any]?) -> Bool {
    var isPerformingAdditionalDelegateHandling = true                    (A)
    if let shortcutItem = launchOptions?[UIApplicationLaunchOptionsKey.shortcutItem] as? UIApplicationShortcutItem {
        launchedShortcutItem = shortcutItem
        isPerformingAdditionalDelegateHandling = false
    }
    if let shortcutItems = application.shortcutItems, shortcutItems.isEmpty {
        let laShortcut = UIMutableApplicationShortcutItem(type: Shortcut.openLosAngeles.type, localizedTitle: "Los
(B)     Angeles", localizedSubtitle: "", icon: UIApplicationShortcutIcon(templateImageName: "shortcut-city"),
            userInfo:nil
        )
(C)     let lvShortcut = UIMutableApplicationShortcutItem(type: Shortcut.openLasVegas.type, localizedTitle: "Las Vegas",
            localizedSubtitle: "", icon: UIApplicationShortcutIcon(templateImageName: "shortcut-city"), userInfo: nil
        )
        application.shortcutItems = [laShortcut, lvShortcut]
    }                                                   (D)
    return isPerformingAdditionalDelegateHandling
}
```

Just a Peek

Now, let's break down our code and have a look at each part:

- **Part A**: Here is where we check for a shortcut item. If we have a shortcut item, then the rest of the code inside of this `if...let` statement will run:

    ```
    if let shortcutItem =
    launchOptions?[UIApplicationLaunchOptionsKey.shortcutItem] as?
    UIApplicationShortcutItem
    ```

- **Part B**: This is our first dynamic shortcut. This will set our current selected location to **Los Angeles**. We will also set the icon image here to a custom image that is in our image assets:

    ```
    let laShortcut = UIMutableApplicationShortcutItem(type:
    Shortcut.openLosAngeles.type, localizedTitle: "Los Angeles",
    localizedSubtitle: "", icon:
    UIApplicationShortcutIcon(templateImageName: "shortcut-city"),
    userInfo:nil)
    ```

- **Part C**: This is our second dynamic shortcut. This will set our current selected location to **Las Vegas**. We will also set the icon image here to a custom image that is in our image assets:

    ```
    let lvShortcut = UIMutableApplicationShortcutItem(type:
    Shortcut.openLasVegas.type, localizedTitle: "Las Vegas",
    localizedSubtitle: "", icon:
    UIApplicationShortcutIcon(templateImageName: "shortcut-city"),
    userInfo: nil)
    ```

- **Part D**: Finally, when we are done, we will return `true` or `false`. True will be sent if a shortcut icon was not selected, and `false` will be sent if one was selected:

    ```
    return isPerformingAdditionalDelegateHandling
    ```

Now that we have our method created, let's update our return value inside of `didFinishLaunchingWithOptions`. Update the return from the current value of `true` to the following:

```
return checkShortCut(application, launchOptions: launchOptions)
```

Next, we need to add a few more methods for our application to handle shortcuts. Let's add a method that will handle any shortcut links that are selected. Add the following method after the `checkShortCut()` method:

```swift
func handleShortCut(_ item: UIApplicationShortcutItem) -> Bool {
    var isHandled = false
    guard Shortcut(with: item.type) != nil, let shortCutType = item.type as String?, let tabBarController = self.window?.rootViewController as? UITabBarController else { return false }

    switch (shortCutType) {

    case Shortcut.openLocations.type:

        tabBarController.selectedIndex = 0
        let navController = self.window?.rootViewController?.childViewControllers.first as! UINavigationController
        let viewController = navController.childViewControllers.first as! ExploreViewController
        viewController.performSegue(withIdentifier: "locationList", sender: self)

        isHandled = true

        break

    case Shortcut.openMap.type:

        tabBarController.selectedIndex = 1
        isHandled = true

        break

    case Shortcut.openLosAngeles.type:

        let navController = self.window?.rootViewController?.childViewControllers.first as! UINavigationController
        let viewController = navController.childViewControllers.first as! ExploreViewController
        viewController.selectedCity = LocationItem(state: "CA", city: "Los Angeles")

        tabBarController.selectedIndex = 1
        tabBarController.selectedIndex = 0
        isHandled = true

        break

    case Shortcut.openLasVegas.type:

        let navController = self.window?.rootViewController?.childViewControllers.first as! UINavigationController
        let viewController = navController.childViewControllers.first as! ExploreViewController
        viewController.selectedCity = LocationItem(state: "NV", city: "Las Vegas")

        tabBarController.selectedIndex = 1
        tabBarController.selectedIndex = 0
        isHandled = true

        break

    default:
        break
    }

    return isHandled
}
```

Just a Peek

Let's break down this code, so that you can better understand the different parts of the code:

- **Part A**: Here, we are ensuring that we have a shortcut item, shortcut type, and a Tab Bar controller. If we do not have any of these things, we will return `false` and not go any further:

    ```
    guard Shortcut(with: item.type) != nil, let shortCutType =
    item.type as String?, let tabBarController =
    self.window?.rootViewController as? UITabBarController else {
    return false }
    ```

- **Part B**: This shortcut will allow us to launch the location list view. We are setting the selected index of the Tab Bar controller and then using the `performSegue` to enable the modal to appear:

    ```
    tabBarController.selectedIndex = 0
    let navController =
    self.window?.rootViewController?.childViewControllers.first as!
    UINavigationController
    let viewController = navController.childViewControllers.first as!
    ExploreViewController
    viewController.performSegue(withIdentifier: "locationList", sender:
    self)
    ```

- **Part C**: This shortcut will allow us to go directly to the **Map** tab:

    ```
    tabBarController.selectedIndex = 1
    isHandled = true
    ```

- **Part D**: This shortcut will allow us to launch the explore view with **Los Angeles** already selected:

    ```
    let navController =
    self.window?.rootViewController?.childViewControllers.first as!
    UINavigationController
    let viewController = navController.childViewControllers.first as!
    ExploreViewController
    viewController.selectedCity = LocationItem(state: "CA", city: "Los
    Angeles")

    tabBarController.selectedIndex = 1
    tabBarController.selectedIndex = 0
    isHandled = true
    ```

- **Part E**: This shortcut will allow us to launch the explore view with **Las Vegas** already selected.

  ```
  let navController =
  self.window?.rootViewController?.childViewControllers.first as!
  UINavigationController
  let viewController = navController.childViewControllers.first as!
  ExploreViewController
  viewController.selectedCity = LocationItem(state: "NV", city: "Las
  Vegas")

  tabBarController.selectedIndex = 1
  tabBarController.selectedIndex = 0
  isHandled = true
  ```

Now that we can have a method for handling any shortcut links, add the following method after the `applicationWillTerminate()` method:

```
func application(_ application: UIApplication, performActionFor
shortcutItem: UIApplicationShortcutItem, completionHandler: @escaping
(Bool) -> Void) {
    let handledShortCutItem = handleShortCut(shortcutItem)
    completionHandler(handledShortCutItem)
}
```

This method gets called every time a shortcut action is performed.

Finally, we need to add code to check when the app becomes active. Find the `applicationDidBecomeActive()` method and add the following inside of the curly braces:

```
guard let item = launchedShortcutItem else { return }
_ = handleShortCut(item)

launchedShortcutItem = nil
if (application.applicationIconBadgeNumber != 0) {
  application.applicationIconBadgeNumber = 0
}
```

Just a Peek

Here, we are handling any shortcut actions. Also, we are checking whether the badge icon is set to a number other than 0, and, if so, we reset it to 0.

If you are keeping track, you will see that we have only added two items so far—our dynamic items. We still need to add our static items; however, these will actually be added to your `Info.plist`.

Open the `Info.plist` in the `Assets` folder of the Navigator panel. Hover over **Privacy - Camera Usage Description** and then click on the + button to add the key `UIApplicationShortcutItems`. Make the type an array:

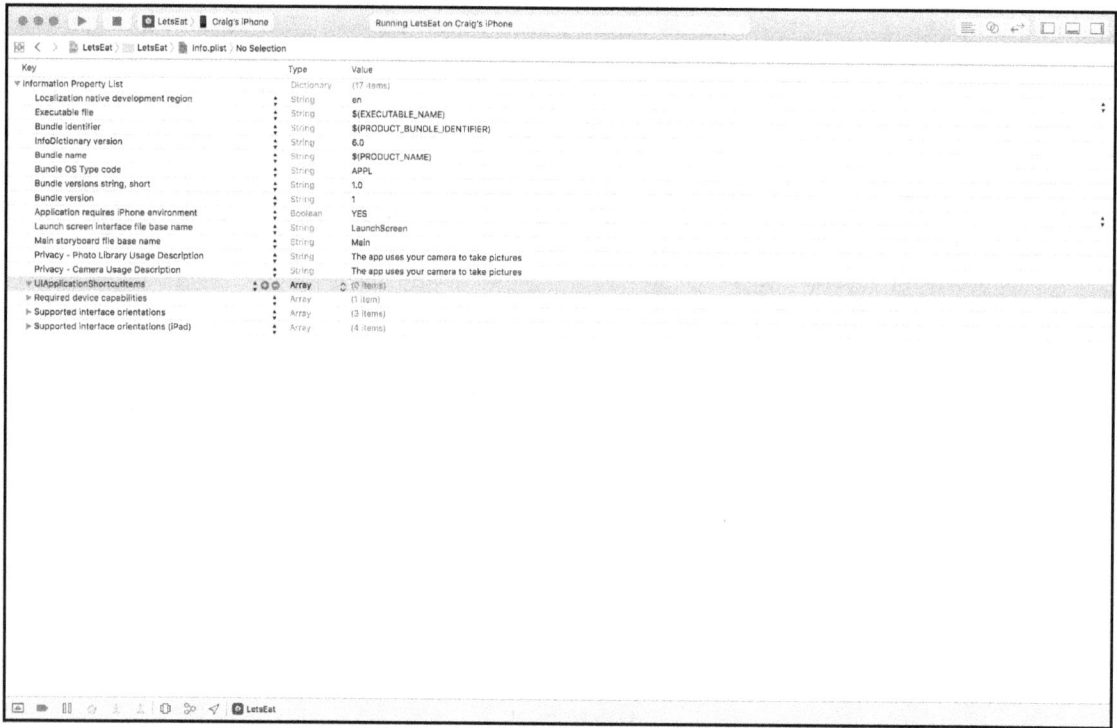

Chapter 26

Next, hover over `UIApplicationShortcutItems` and click on the **+** button to add an item to this array. Change the type to **Dictionary**:

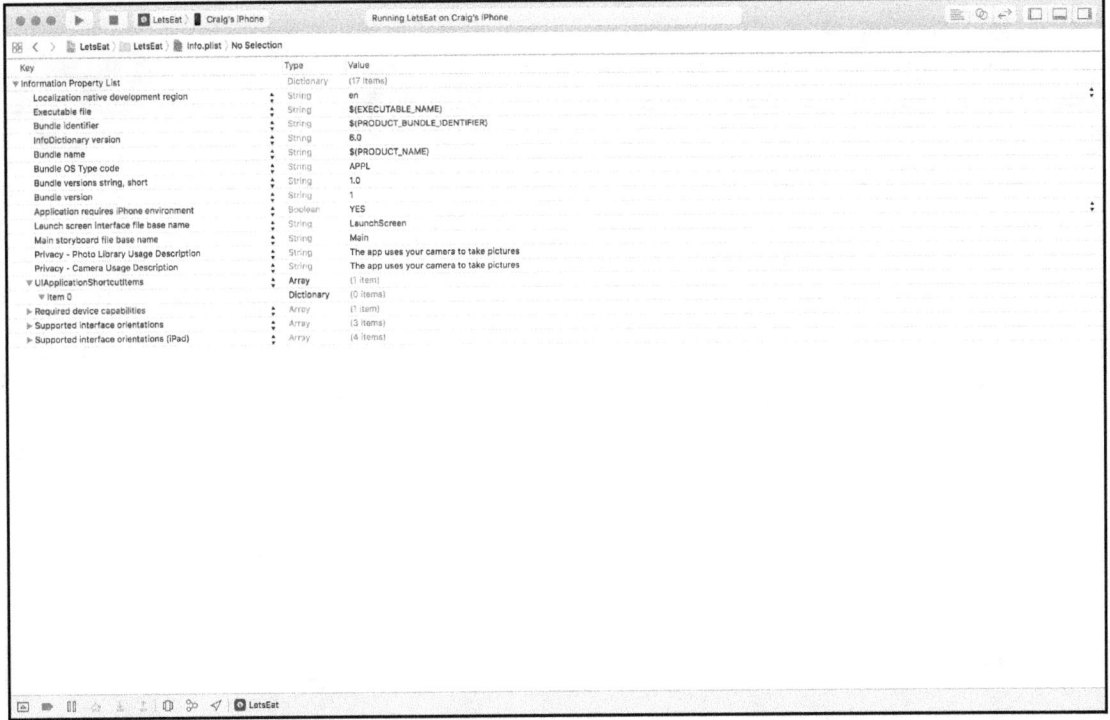

Just a Peek

Hover over **Item 0** and click on the + button three times to add three strings. Give the three keys the following names:

    UIApplicationShortcutItemIconFile
    UIApplicationShortcutItemTitle
    UIApplicationShortcutItemType

Now, copy **Item 0** (⌘ + C) and paste it (⌘ + V) into `UIApplicationShortcutItems`. You should now have **Item 0** and **Item 1**, each with the same three Strings:

Chapter 26

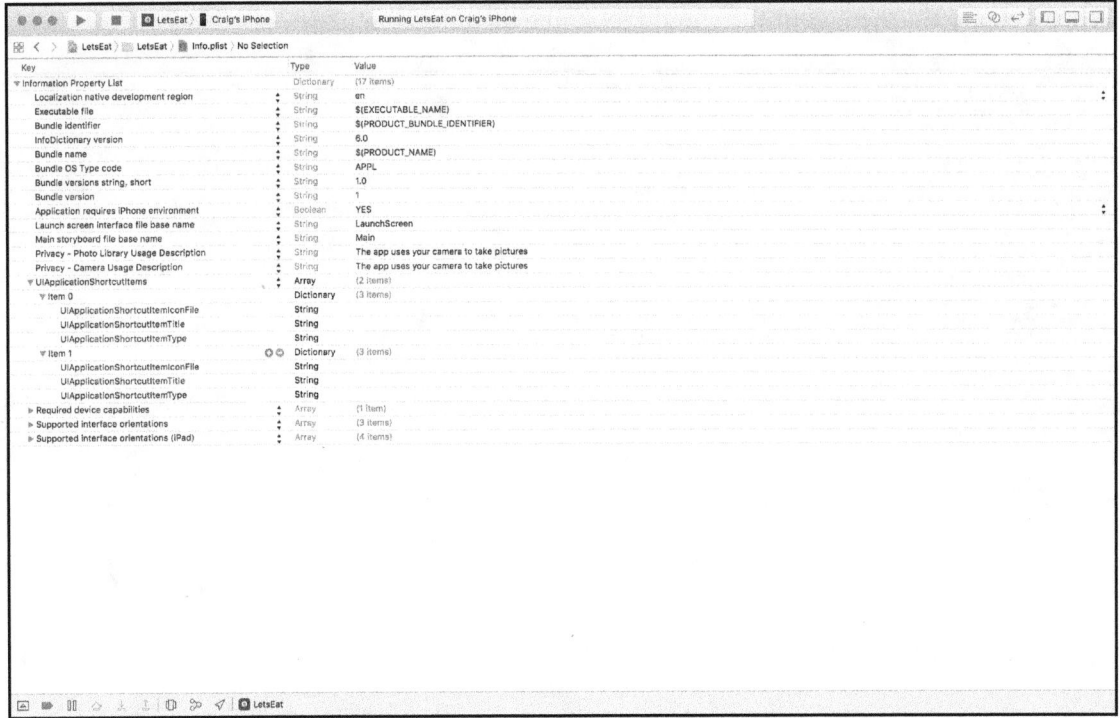

Next, set their values to the following for **Item 0**:

- **UIApplicationShortcutItemIconFile**: `shortcut-map`
- **UIApplicationShortcutItemTitle**: `Map`
- **UIApplicationShortcutItemType**: `$(PRODUCTBUNDLEIDENTIFIER).openMap`

For **Item 1**, set their values as follows:

- **UIApplicationShortcutItemIconFile**: `shortcut-location`
- **UIApplicationShortcutItemTitle**: `Locations`
- **UIApplicationShortcutItemType**: `$(PRODUCTBUNDLEIDENTIFIER).openLocations`

Just a Peek

When you are finished, your file should look like the following:

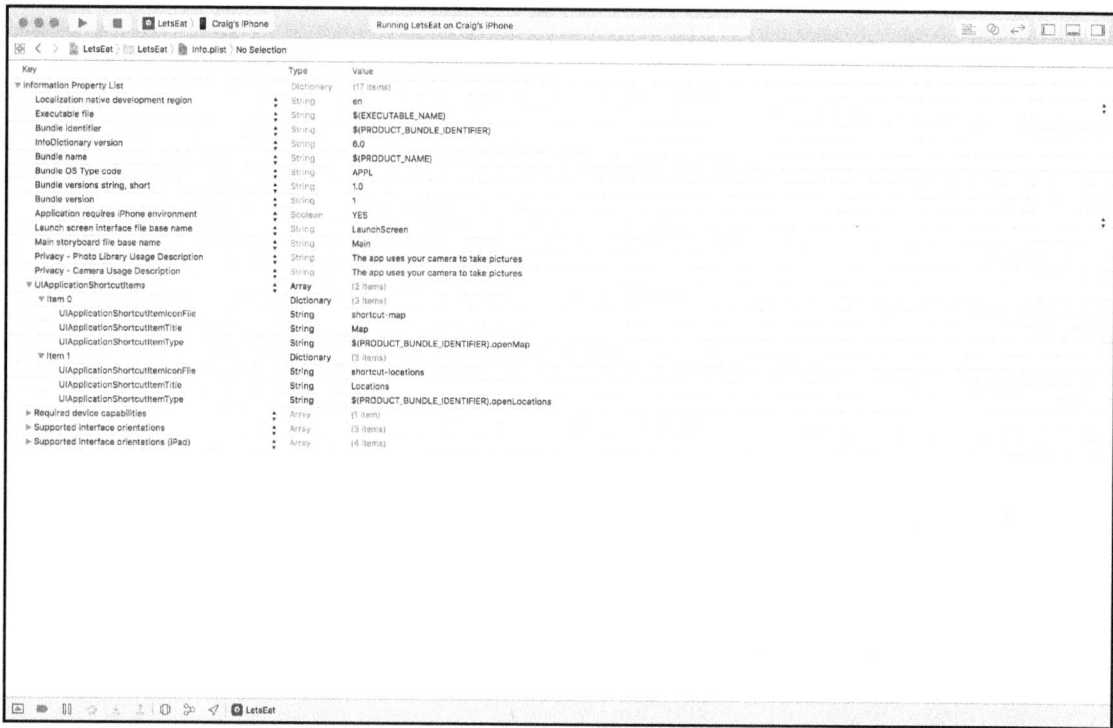

Save your file, and build and run the project on your device. If you have a MacBook or a MacBook Pro with a Force Touch mouse, you can run this in the simulator.

If you are building your phone, you might encounter errors. These errors occur because you have not built the framework for your phone. Just switch to the framework, then hit ⌘ + B, then switch to your *iMessages* app and do the same again. Then, build and run the project on your device.

Once your app launches, hit ⌘ + H (if you are in a simulator) or the home button on your device. 3D Touch the *Let's Eat* app icon, and you should now see the following:

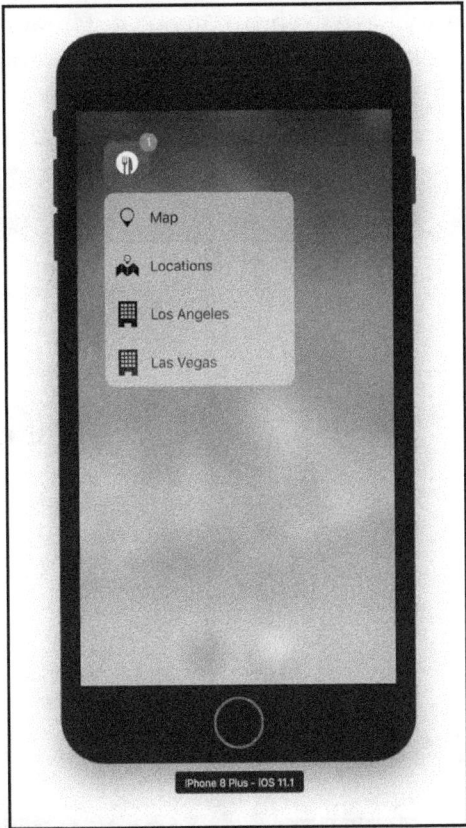

If you select **Los Angeles** or **Las Vegas**, you will see that the location is now set for you at the top. If you select the **Map** shortcut, you will be taken to the **Map** tab. If you select the **Locations** shortcut, you will be taken to the **Locations** list. We have now added 3D Touch quick actions to our app. Let's add 3D Touch to one more place.

Adding favorites

A nice feature for our app would be to use 3D Touch to allow users to add favorites to our restaurant list view. We already have the heart in our restaurant detail page. Therefore, let's add 3D Touch to the heart to add favorites. This is how we want it to look when we are finished:

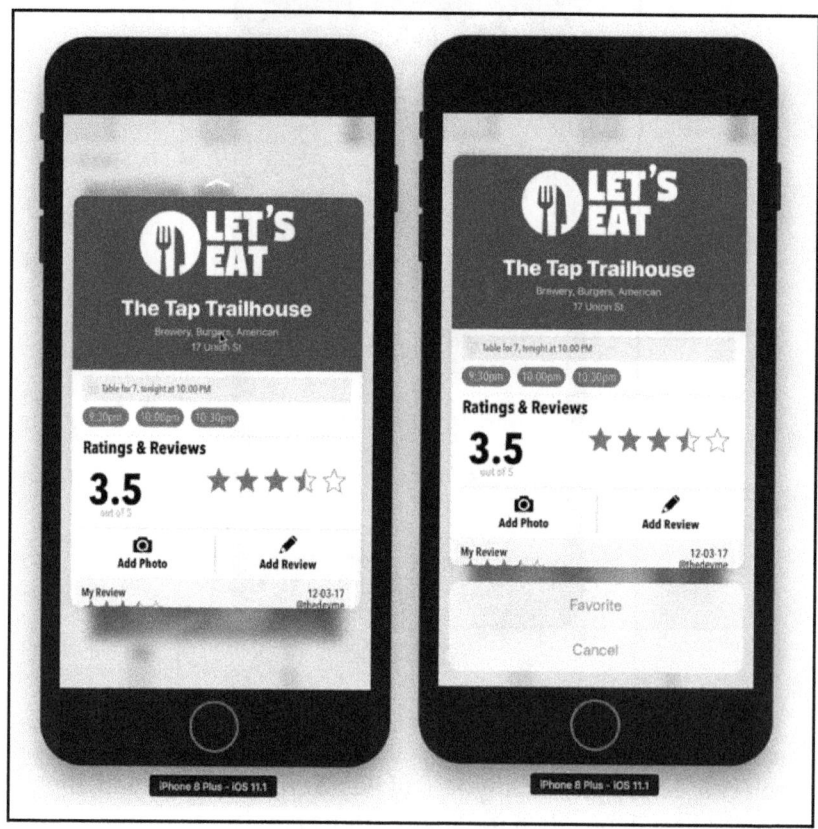

The first thing we need to do is add a new model object so that we can save our restaurant favorites to Core Data.

Chapter 26

Creating a new model object

Let's look at how to create a new model object:

1. In the Navigator panel, open the `LetsEatModel.xcdatamodel` file, which can be found in the Core Data folder in the `Common` folder.
2. Make sure that you have the **Graph Style** selected:

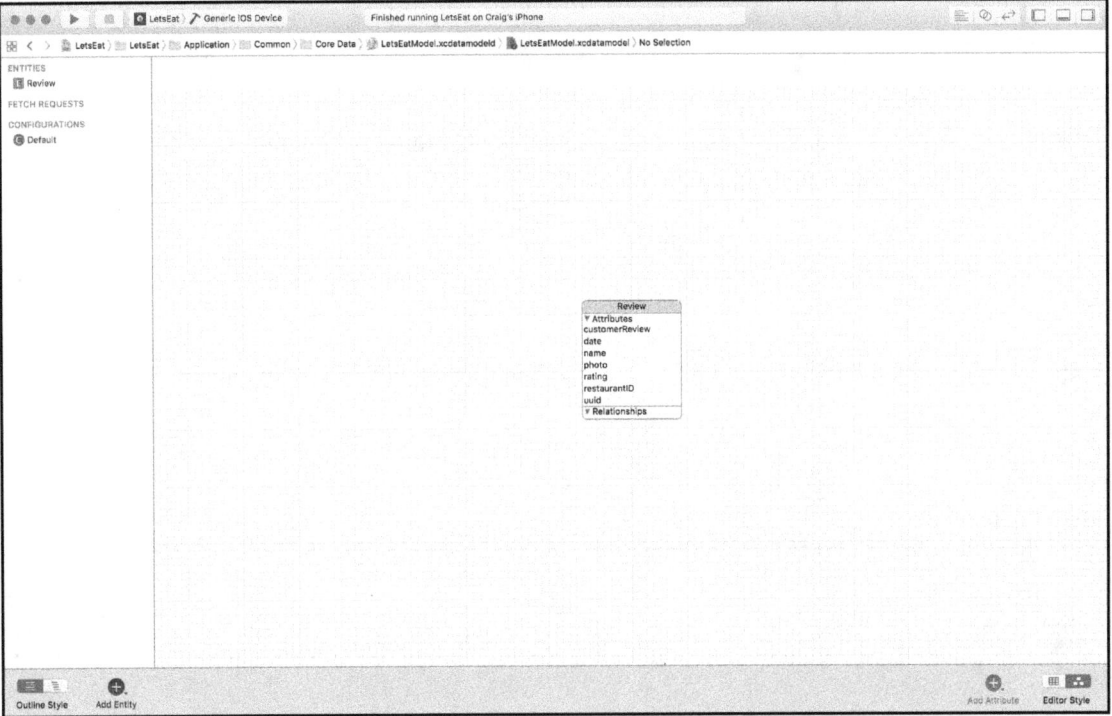

Just a Peek

3. Click the **+** button for **Add Entity** and then double-click on **Entity**, and update it to **Favorite**:

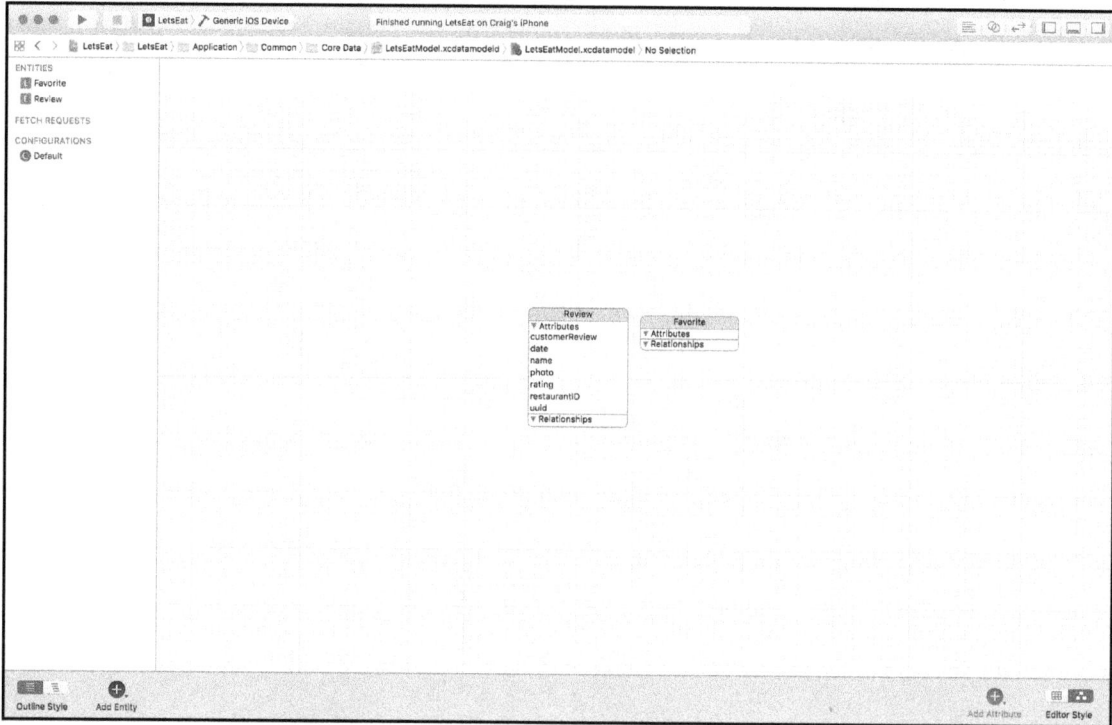

Chapter 26

4. Next, ensure that the **Favorite** entity is selected and click the + button for **Add Attribute**:

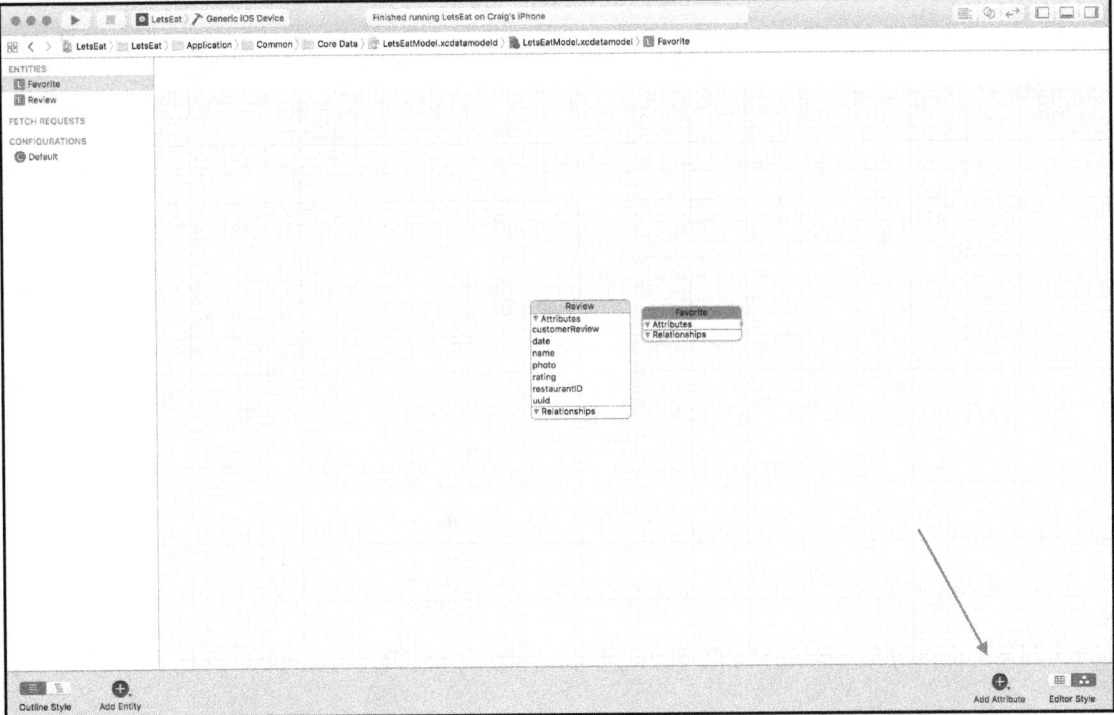

Just a Peek

5. In the box in the center of the screen, under **Attributes**, you should now see the word attribute. Double-click on **Attributes** and change it to `restaurantID`:

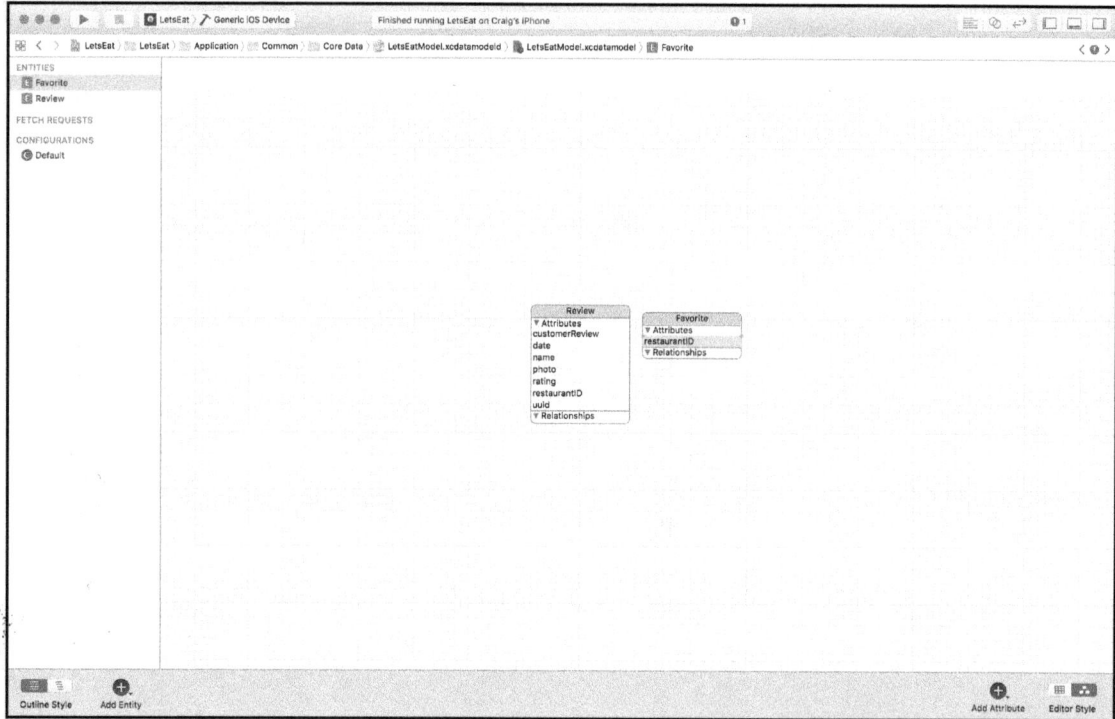

6. Next, select the favorite entity again and then the Data Model inspector in the Utilities panel.

7. Under **Class**, update the following:

    - **Name:** `Favorite`
    - **Codegen:** `Class definition`
    - **Constraints:** `restaurantID` (you add this constraint by hitting the + button in **Constraints** and then replacing the default constraint, which autopopulates, with this new constraint)

Your entity settings should now look like the following:

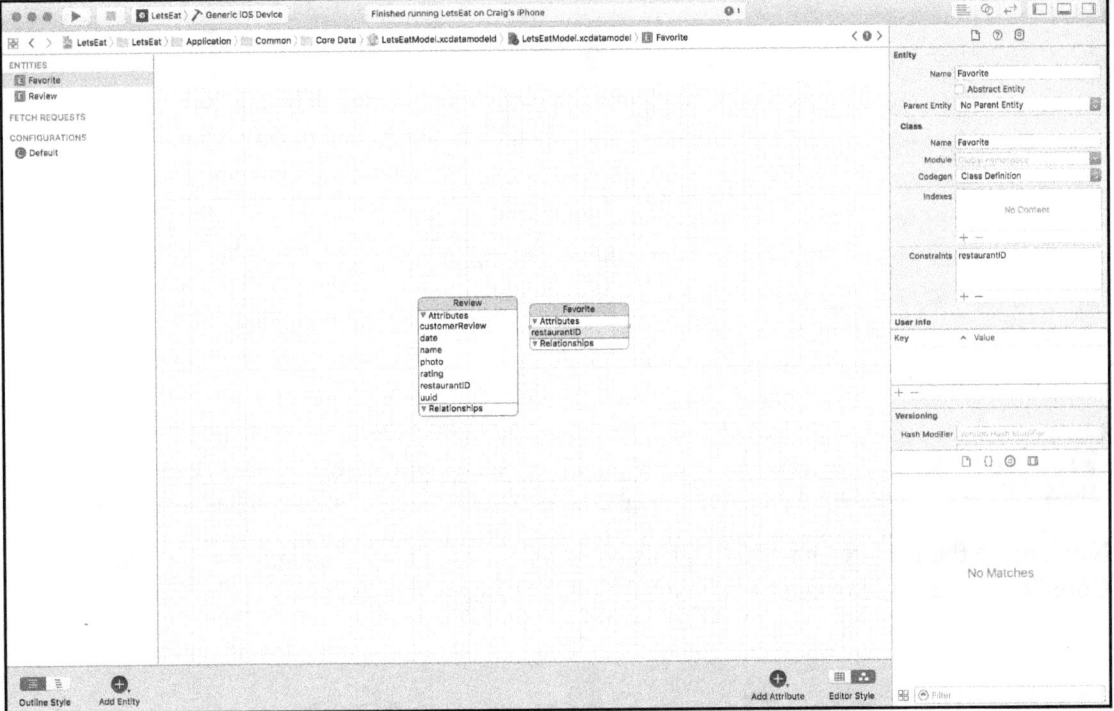

Just a Peek

8. Finally, select the `restaurantID` attribute, and under the Data Model inspector in the Utilities panel, select **Integer 32** under **Attribute Type**. The error regarding this attribute should now disappear:

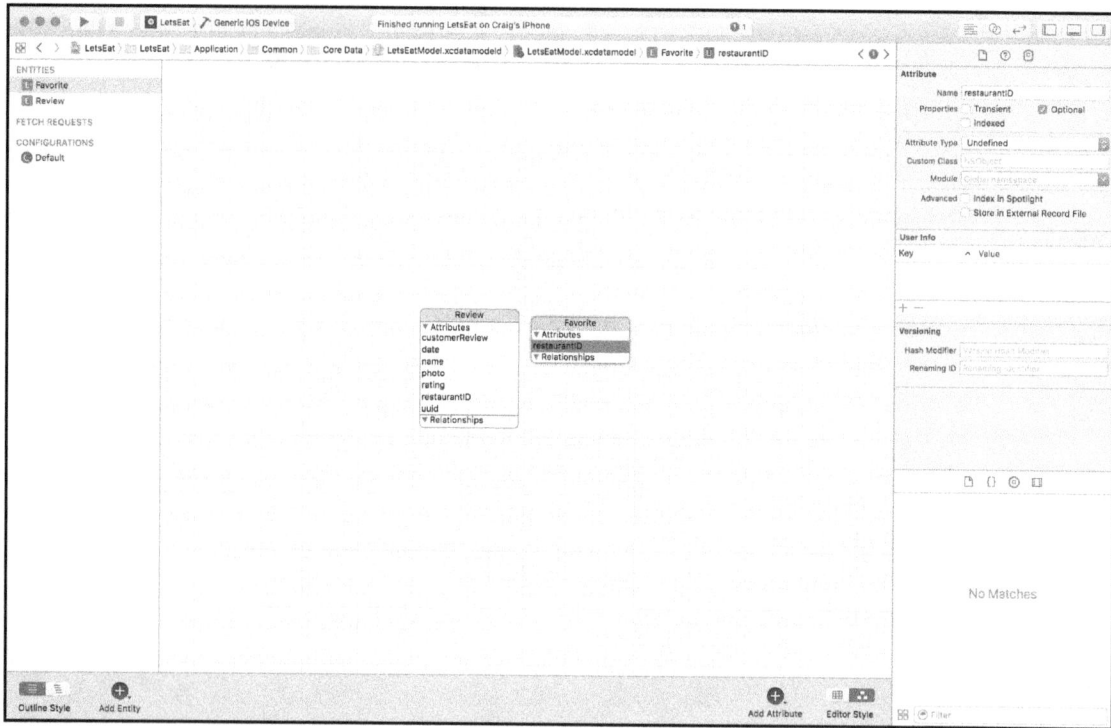

Now, build the project using ⌘ + B. This will create our `Favorite` class that we created in Core Data. You will not see the file anywhere, but it has been created.

Updating our Core Data manager

Now that we have our favorite entity created, we need to update our Core Data manager to actually save restaurants as favorites. Inside of the `CoreData-Manager.swift` file, add the following before the last curly brace:

```
func addFavorite(by restaurantID:Int) {
    let item = Favorite(context: container.viewContext)
    item.restaurantID = Int32(restaurantID)
```

```
    save()
}
```

This method creates a `Favorite` object and then calls the `save()` method.

Now, let's add one more method to this file by adding the following before the last curly brace:

```
func isFavorite(with identifier:Int) -> Bool {
    let moc = container.viewContext
    let request:NSFetchRequest<Favorite> = Favorite.fetchRequest()
    let predicate = NSPredicate(format: "restaurantID = %i", Int32(identifier))
    request.predicate = predicate

    do {
        let count = try moc.count(for: request)
        if count == 0 { return false }
        else { return true }
    } catch {
        fatalError("Failed to fetch reviews: \(error)")
    }
}
```

In this method, we are going to fetch a favorite restaurant by passing a `restaurantID`. The method will check Core Data, and if we get data back, that restaurant will be set as a favorite. Otherwise, if we get back no data, we return `false`. We can now save favorite restaurants.

Next, open the `RestaurantViewController.swift` file and define a new extension after the extension we created for our Collection View by adding the following code:

```
extension RestaurantViewController: UIViewControllerPreviewingDelegate {
    func previewingContext(_ previewingContext: UIViewControllerPreviewing, viewControllerForLocation location: CGPoint) -> UIViewController? {
        let restaurantDetail : UIStoryboard = UIStoryboard(name: "RestaurantDetail", bundle: nil)
        Ⓐ
        guard let indexPath = collectionView?.indexPathForItem(at: location), let cell = collectionView?.cellForItem(at: indexPath), let detailVC = restaurantDetail.instantiateViewController(withIdentifier: "RestaurantDetail") as? RestaurantDetailViewController else { return nil }

        selectedRestaurant = manager.restaurantItem(at: indexPath)
        detailVC.selectedRestaurant = selectedRestaurant
        Ⓑ detailVC.preferredContentSize = CGSize(width: 0.0, height: 528)
        previewingContext.sourceRect = cell.frame

        return detailVC
    }

    Ⓒ func previewingContext(_ previewingContext: UIViewControllerPreviewing, commit viewControllerToCommit: UIViewController)
    {
        show(viewControllerToCommit, sender: self)
    }
}
```

Just a Peek

Let's discuss what we just added:

- **Part A**: First, we are getting an instance of our `RestaurantDetail.storyboard`. Then, we are obtaining a current index path. Once we have an index path, we are checking that we have a cell. Finally, we are creating an instance to our `RestaurantDetailViewController`:

    ```
    let restaurantDetail : UIStoryboard = UIStoryboard(name:
    "RestaurantDetail", bundle: nil)
    guard let indexPath = collectionView?.indexPathForItem(at:
    location), let cell = collectionView?.cellForItem(at: indexPath),
    let detailVC =
    restaurantDetail.instantiateViewController(withIdentifier:
    "RestaurantDetail") as? RestaurantDetailViewController else {
    return nil }
    ```

- **Part B**: Here, we are setting our `selectedRestaurant`, and then, we are passing the `selectedRestaurant` over to the detail view. We are then setting the height that we want and passing the cell frame to the previewing context:

    ```
    selectedRestaurant = manager.restaurantItem(at: indexPath)
    detailVC.selectedRestaurant = selectedRestaurant
    detailVC.preferredContentSize = CGSize(width: 0.0, height: 450)
    previewingContext.sourceRect = cell.frame
    ```

- **Part C**: This method is called so that we can prepare the presentation of the view controller, which here is the commit view controller. In our case, we are preparing the `RestaurantDetailViewController` to be shown (or popped):

    ```
    func previewingContext(_ previewingContext:
    UIViewControllerPreviewing, commit viewControllerToCommit:
    UIViewController) {
        show(viewControllerToCommit, sender: self)
    }
    ```

Next, open the `RestaurantDetail.storyboard` and select the `RestaurantDetailViewController`. Open the Identity inspector in the Utilities panel and, in storyboard ID under **Identity**, add `RestaurantDetail`.

Then, hit *Enter*:

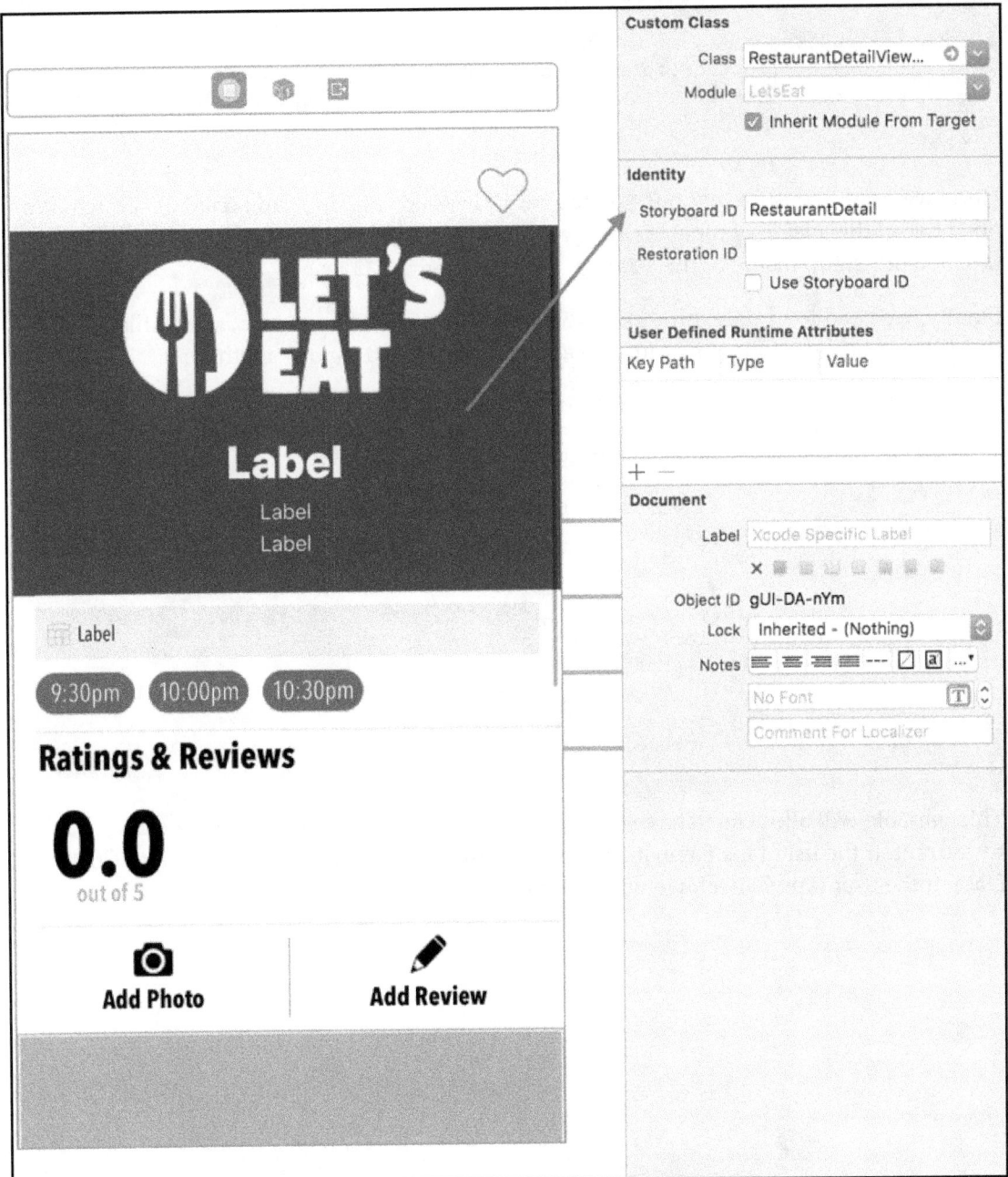

Now, return to the `RestaurantViewController.swift` file and add the following code after the `showRestaurantDetail()` method:

```
func setup3DTouch() {
    if( traitCollection.forceTouchCapability == .available){
        registerForPreviewing(with: self, sourceView: view)
    }
}
```

Here, we need to ensure that our `RestaurantViewController` can accept 3D Touch. We need to call this inside of the `initialize()` method after our `if` statement. We have finished our setup inside of the `RestaurantViewController`.

Finally, we need to update our `RestaurantDetailViewController.swift` file. Open this file and add the following variable above the `viewDidLoad()` method:

```
override var previewActionItems: [UIPreviewActionItem] {
    let favorite = UIPreviewAction(title: "Favorite", style: .default) {
(action, viewController) -> Void in
        let manager = CoreDataManager()
        if let id = self.selectedRestaurant?.restaurantID {
manager.addFavorite(by: id) }
    }

    let cancel = UIPreviewAction(title: "Cancel", style: .destructive) {
(action, viewController) -> Void in
        print("You hit cancel")
    }

    return [favorite, cancel]
}
```

This variable will allow us to have two actions, **Favorite** and **Cancel**, when we peek at a restaurant. If the user taps **Favorite**, we will get the `restaurantID` and save it to Core Data. If the user taps **Cancel**, we will dismiss the view.

Next, add the following code above the `createRating()` method:

```
func checkFavorites() {
    let manager = CoreDataManager()
    if let id = selectedRestaurant?.restaurantID {
        let isFavorite = manager.isFavorite(with: id)
        let btnImage = UIButton()
        btnImage.frame = CGRect(x: 0, y: 0, width: 30, height: 30)
        btnImage.addTarget(self, action: #selector(getter: UIDynamicBehavior.action), for: .touchUpInside)


        if isFavorite {
            btnImage.setImage(UIImage(named: "heart-selected"), for: .normal)
            btnHeart.customView = btnImage
        }
        else {
            btnImage.setImage(UIImage(named: "heart-unselected"), for: .normal)
            btnHeart.customView = btnImage
        }
    }
}
```

This method will now be run whenever we go to a detail view. First, we check Core Data to see if the current restaurant is a favorite. If it is a favorite, we will show a filled-in heart, and if it is not, we will show a heart with just an outline. This method will be called after the `createRating()` method inside of the `initialize()` method.

Build and run the project by hitting the Play button (or use ⌘ + R). When you get to the restaurant list, touch one of the restaurant items and you will see the following:

If you swipe up while touching, you will see that we now have two buttons:

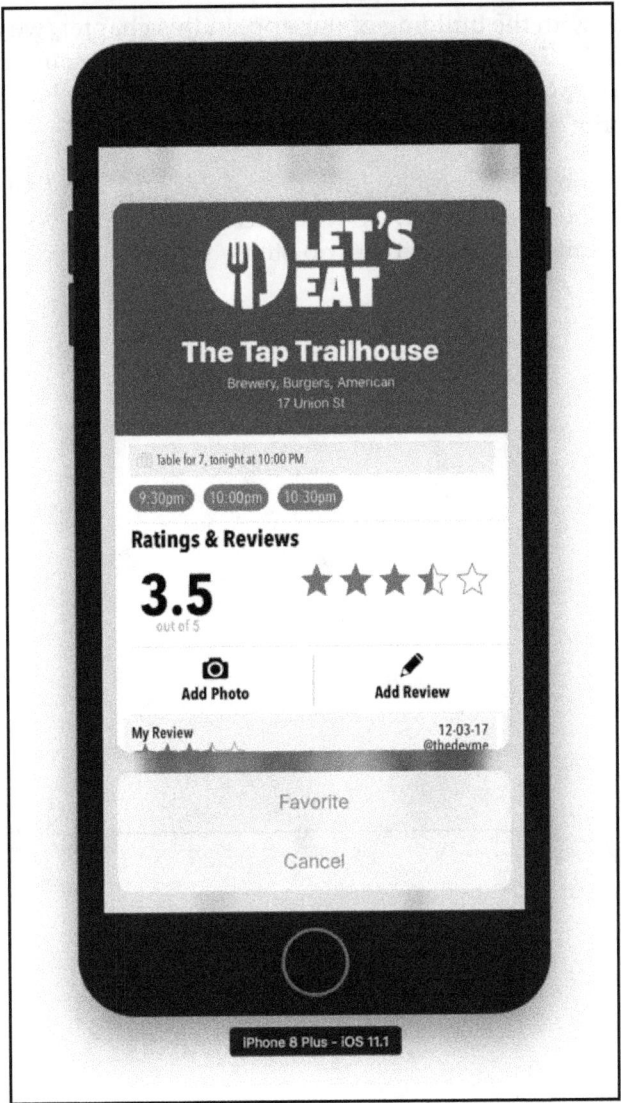

If you tap **Cancel**, it will dismiss the view. If you tap **Favorite** and select the same restaurant, you will now see that the heart will change to a filled-in one.

Summary

We are officially done with the building of our app. In this chapter, we learned about the two different types of 3D Touch quick actions that we can add to our app. We also added 3D Touch support to our Collection View. Our restaurant list now has 3D Touch support so that we can add favorite restaurants from the restaurants list.

It is now time to move on to the most exciting part of this app, and that is getting our app into the App Store. In the next chapter, we will discuss everything you will need to know regarding how to submit your app to the App Store.

27
Drag and Drop

Drag and drop was introduced in June 2017 at WWDC and it intrigued me in different ways. I love using my iPad and I felt like this would make it easier to do things. As I have had time to use iOS 11, I think that I was right about my assumption and I cannot wait until more apps have this feature.

We are going to add drag and drop to our iPad app by letting users drag filter items we use in our filter scroller. We will also accept drag and drop from the *Photos* app. Users will be able to drag from the *Photos* app and drop it into our scroller when on the iPad.

We will cover the following in this chapter:

- How to drag from a Collection View
- How to create custom drag elements
- How to accept drag and drop from the *Photos* app

There is a lot of code in this chapter, mainly because we will be doing quite a few things. The first thing we want to do is drag photos from the *Photos* app or any app that has photos and drop it into our filter view area. Drag and drop is an alternative to using the picker control to add a photo.

Accepting drag from other apps

Let's get started in accepting drag and drop from other apps:

- Add drag and drop to our photo view from *Photos* apps
- Add drag and drop from filter scroller

Drag and Drop

The first thing we want to do is enable dragging for our filter items. We need to create a new extension to our `PhotoFilterViewController` called `PhotoFilterViewController+UIDropInteraction`. Inside this file, add the following:

```
import UIKit
import Foundation
extension PhotoFilterViewController: UIDropInteractionDelegate {
}
```

Next, we need to add all of the methods needed to accept drop interaction. We will write this to allow dropping within the app as well as outside of the app. When you start to drag an element, Apple calls this a **session**. There are two primary sessions we will need to watch out for, local sessions or non-local sessions. Local sessions mean that we are dragging within our app and if that is not happening then it means that the session is coming from a different app. Let's handle this by first adding the first method – `dropInteraction:canHandleSession:`

```
func dropInteraction(_ interaction: UIDropInteraction, canHandle session:
UIDropSession) -> Bool {
    if session.localDragSession == nil {
        return session.canLoadObjects(ofClass: UIImage.self)
    }
    else { return false }
}
```

This method is where we give permission for items to be dropped into our app as well as the local dragging of objects. For a local drag, we are accepting an image and for now we are not accepting drops from within the app. We will add this later. Let's add the next method that we need to implement, `-dropInteraction:sessionDidUpdate::`

```
func dropInteraction(_ interaction: UIDropInteraction, sessionDidUpdate
session: UIDropSession) -> UIDropProposal {
    let operation: UIDropOperation
    if session.localDragSession == nil {
        operation = .copy
    }
    else { operation = .copy }
    return UIDropProposal(operation: operation)
}
```

This method is telling our app how we want to consume data and in both cases we are going to copy it. Let's add the next method, -dropInteraction:performDrop:

```
func dropInteraction(_ interaction: UIDropInteraction, performDrop session: UIDropSession) {
    if session.localDragSession == nil {
        for dragItem in session.items {
            loadImage(dragItem.itemProvider)
        }
    }
}
```

This method gets called after the user lifts their finger from the screen. This indicates the user's intent to drop the item and this is your opportunity to request the data for the drag item. We simply take this data and display it in our Image View; we also create filter thumbnails. This behavior is the same behavior we have for selecting an image in the picker. Finally, we add our last method to - dropInteraction:previewForDroppingItem:withDefault:

```
func dropInteraction(_ interaction: UIDropInteraction, previewForDropping item: UIDragItem, withDefault defaultPreview: UITargetedDragPreview) -> UITargetedDragPreview? {
    if item.localObject == nil {
        return nil
    } else {
        let target = UIDragPreviewTarget(container: view, center: imgExample.center)
        return defaultPreview.retargetedPreview(with: target)
    }
}
```

This last method is creating a preview for the image being dragged into our view. When you are done your extension should look like the following:

```
import UIKit
import Foundation

extension PhotoFilterViewController: UIDropInteractionDelegate {
    
    func dropInteraction(_ interaction: UIDropInteraction, canHandle session: UIDropSession) -> Bool {
        if session.localDragSession == nil {
            return session.canLoadObjects(ofClass: UIImage.self)       }
        else { return false }
    }
    
    func dropInteraction(_ interaction: UIDropInteraction, sessionDidUpdate
```

```
    session: UIDropSession) -> UIDropProposal {
        let operation: UIDropOperation
        if session.localDragSession == nil {
            operation = .copy
        }
        else { operation = .copy }
        return UIDropProposal(operation: operation)
    }

    func dropInteraction(_ interaction: UIDropInteraction, performDrop
session: UIDropSession) {
        if session.localDragSession == nil {
            for dragItem in session.items {
                loadImage(dragItem.itemProvider)
            }
        }
    }

    func dropInteraction(_ interaction: UIDropInteraction,
previewForDropping item: UIDragItem, withDefault defaultPreview:
UITargetedDragPreview) -> UITargetedDragPreview? {
        if item.localObject == nil {
            return nil
        } else {
            let target = UIDragPreviewTarget(container: view, center:
imgExample.center)
            return defaultPreview.retargetedPreview(with: target)
        }
    }
}
```

We are now done with implementing dragging from other applications. Now that our drop implementation is added, we just need to make sure that our view will accept it. Add the following method inside the `PhotoFilterViewController`:

```
func addDropInteraction() {
    view.addInteraction(UIDropInteraction(delegate: self))
}
```

Here, we are implementing the `UIDropInteraction` we just created in our extension. We just need to call this method. Add `addDropInteraction()` into the `initialize()`. It should now look like the following:

```
func initialize() {
    requestAccess()
    addDropInteraction()
    setupCollectionView()
    checkDevice()
}
```

Launch the iPad Air simulator and open the *Photos* app at the same time. You can now drag from the *Photos* app directly into our filter area:

Drag and Drop

We can also drag from Safari and drop into our filter area:

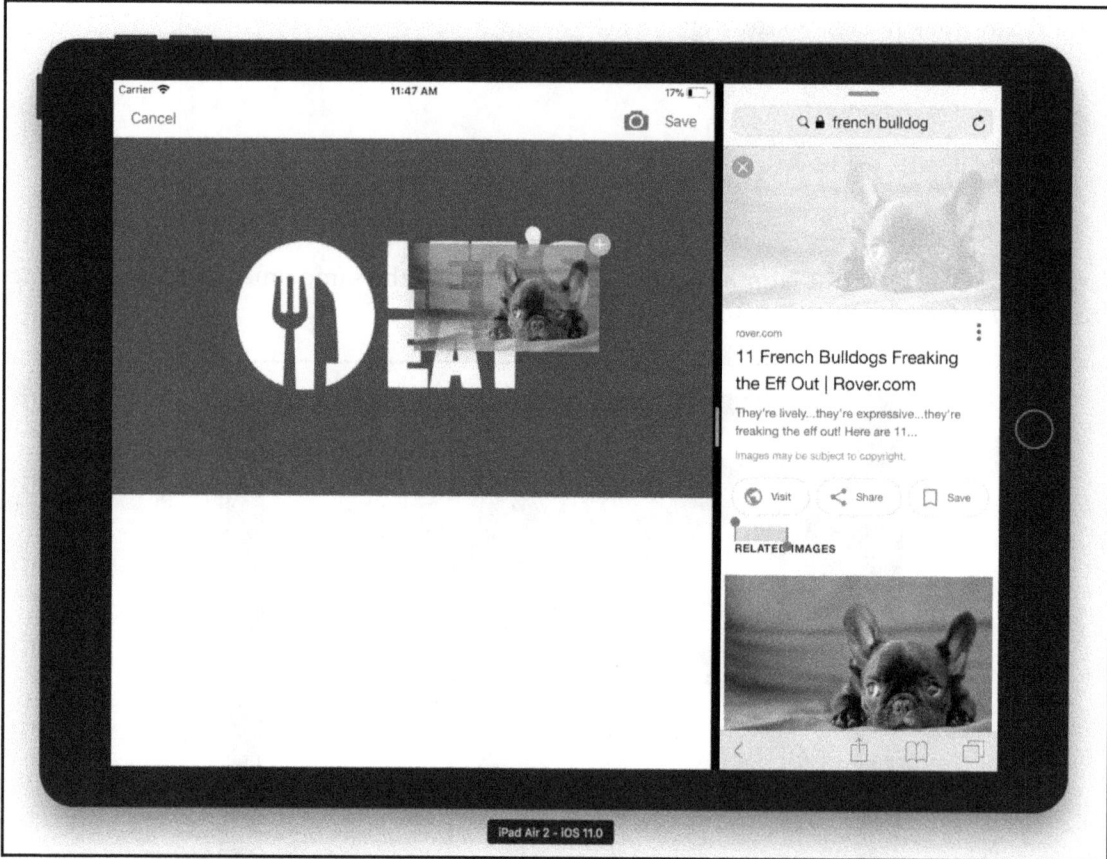

We can drag our filter items to our Photo, but it currently does not do anything at this time. We have some work to do to get this in.

Dragging and dropping filter items

In order to make our filter items draggable, we have quite a few things to do. First, we need to update our `PhotoFilterViewController+UIDropInteraction` file. Open it up, look for the `-dropInteraction:canHandleSession:` method, and update the `else` statement from `false` to the following:

```
else { return session.canLoadObjects(ofClass: FilterItem.self) }
```

When you are done, your method will look like the following:

```
func dropInteraction(_ interaction: UIDropInteraction, canHandle session:
UIDropSession) -> Bool {
    if session.localDragSession == nil {
        return session.canLoadObjects(ofClass: UIImage.self)
    }
    else { return session.canLoadObjects(ofClass: FilterItem.self) }
}
```

You can ignore the error for now. Here, we are just making sure that our `FilterItem` class can be dropped and loaded. Now, we need to do one more update in this class: find the -`dropInteraction:performDrop:` method. After the `if` statement we are going to add an `else`:

```
else {
    for dragItem in session.items {
        let itemProvider = dragItem.itemProvider
        itemProvider.loadObject(ofClass: FilterItem.self) { (object, error) in
            if let error = error {
                print(error.localizedDescription)
            } else {
                DispatchQueue.main.async {
                    if let item = object as? FilterItem {
                        print("filter \(item.filter)")
                        self.filterSelected(item: item)
                    }
                }
            }
        }
    }
}
```

This `else` statement we just added will loop through each item that is being dragged and load the object. Our app does not support multiple draggable items, but this is where it is handled. When we add this code we will have another error but we will address this soon. The -`dropInteraction:performDrop:` method should now look like the following:

```
func dropInteraction(_ interaction: UIDropInteraction, performDrop session:
UIDropSession) {
    if session.localDragSession == nil {
        for dragItem in session.items {
            loadImage(dragItem.itemProvider)
        }
    }
}
```

Drag and Drop

```
        else {
            for dragItem in session.items {
                let itemProvider = dragItem.itemProvider
                itemProvider.loadObject(ofClass: FilterItem.self) { (object,
    error) in
                    if let error = error {
                        print(error.localizedDescription)
                    } else {
                        DispatchQueue.main.async {
                            if let item = object as? FilterItem {
                                print("filter \(item.filter)")
                                self.filterSelected(item: item)
                            }
                        }
                    }
                }
            }
        }
    }
}
```

We still have two errors that we need to fix; let's fix those next by opening the `FilterItem` class inside your `Photo Filter` folder. Add the following under the `init` method:

```
required init(itemProviderData data: Data, typeIdentifier: String) throws {
    if typeIdentifier == FilterItem.typeIdentifier {
        let item = try? JSONDecoder().decode(FilterItem.self, from: data)
        if let i = item {
            self.name = i.name
            self.filter = i.filter
            return
        }
    }

    throw ParseError.decodingFailed("Invalid type!")

}
```

We are adding our a `init` method that we need for dragging. This allows us to pass the data around. We have two errors because we need to conform to `NSItemProviderReading` and `NSItemProviderWriting`. We will write them both in the same file. In the `Photo Filter` folder, create a new `Swift` class and add the first extension:

```
import UIKit
import MobileCoreServices

extension FilterItem: NSItemProviderReading {
```

```
    static var readableTypeIdentifiersForItemProvider: [String] {
        return [FilterItem.typeIdentifier]
    }

    static func object(withItemProviderData data: Data,
      typeIdentifier: String) throws -> Self {
        switch typeIdentifier {
        case FilterItem.typeIdentifier:
            return try! JSONDecoder().decode(self, from: data)
        default:
            throw ParseError.decodingFailed("Invalid type!")
        }
    }
}
```

This extension is to conform to `NSItemProviderReading`, which decodes the data that we are passing so that we can read it. Next, add the last extension by adding the following after our first extension:

```
extension FilterItem: NSItemProviderWriting {
    static var writableTypeIdentifiersForItemProvider: [String] {
        return [FilterItem.typeIdentifier, kUTTypeUTF8PlainText as String]
    }

    func loadData(withTypeIdentifier typeIdentifier: String,
forItemProviderCompletionHandler completionHandler: @escaping (Data?, Error?) -> Void) -> Progress? {
        let data: Data?
        switch typeIdentifier {
        case FilterItem.typeIdentifier:
            data = try? JSONEncoder().encode(self)
        case kUTTypeUTF8PlainText as NSString as String:
            data = "\(name), \(filter)".data(using: .utf8)
        default:
            data = nil
        }
        completionHandler(data, nil)
        return nil
    }
}
```

Drag and Drop

This extension allows us to export our data into a binary representation by first making sure the class type is of `FilterItem`. We are just about done with all the setup we need. We now need to make sure that our Collection View allows dragging. Currently, if you try to drag, nothing will happen. Open the `PhotoFilterViewController` and, in the `setupCollectionView()` method, add the following at the bottom of the method:

```
collectionView?.dragDelegate = self
```

Adding this line will show an error, but you can ignore it, as we are about to fix it. When you finish, the entire method will look like the following:

```
func setupCollectionView() {
    let layout = UICollectionViewFlowLayout()
    if Device.isPhone { layout.scrollDirection = .horizontal }
    else { layout.scrollDirection = .vertical }
    layout.sectionInset = UIEdgeInsets(top: 7, left: 7, bottom: 7, right: 7)
    layout.minimumInteritemSpacing = 0
    layout.minimumLineSpacing = 7

    collectionView?.collectionViewLayout = layout
    collectionView?.dragDelegate = self
}
```

This now enables dragging from a Collection View, but we now implement the drag delegate code for it all to work. Before we create another extension, let's create a new folder inside the `Photo Filter` folder and name this folder `Extensions`. Then drag both files we created earlier, `Filter-Item+NSItemProvider` and `PhotoFilterViewController+UIDropInteraction`, into the `Extensions` folder.

Now that we have that folder set up right, click the `Extensions` folder inside the `Photo Filter` folder and create a new file called `PhotoFilterViewController+UICollectionViewDrag`. Once you have created the file, add the following:

```
import UIKit

extension PhotoFilterViewController: UICollectionViewDragDelegate {
    func collectionView(_ collectionView: UICollectionView,
    itemsForBeginning session: UIDragSession, at indexPath: IndexPath) -> [UIDragItem] {
        let itemProvider = NSItemProvider(object: data[indexPath.item])
        let dragItem = UIDragItem(itemProvider: itemProvider)
        return [dragItem]
    }
}
```

This method `-collectionView:itemsForBeginningDragSession:atIndexPath:` we are getting the data for the item at index path as a drag is being made. If the array is empty, the drag session will not begin. We are finished; if you build and run the project, you will now be able to drag filter items onto the selected photo. Let's drag from our filter list:

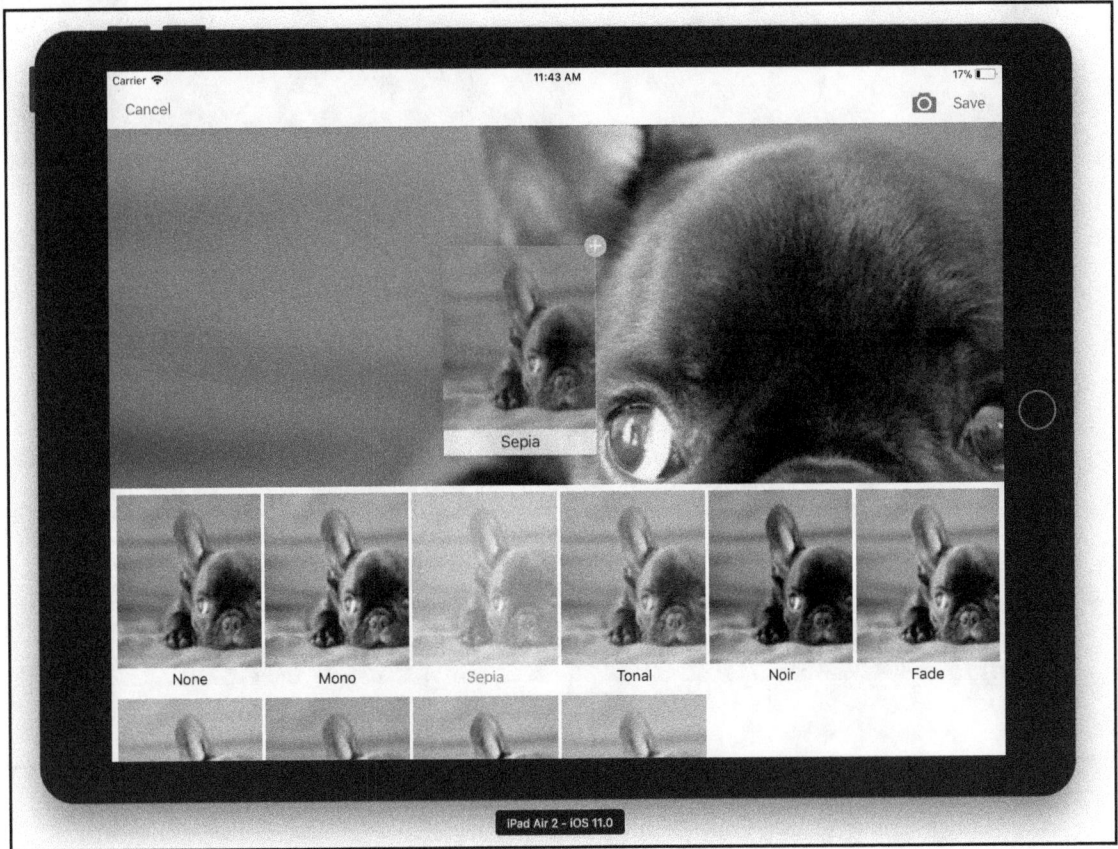

Drag and Drop

After dropping the filter item, you should see the following:

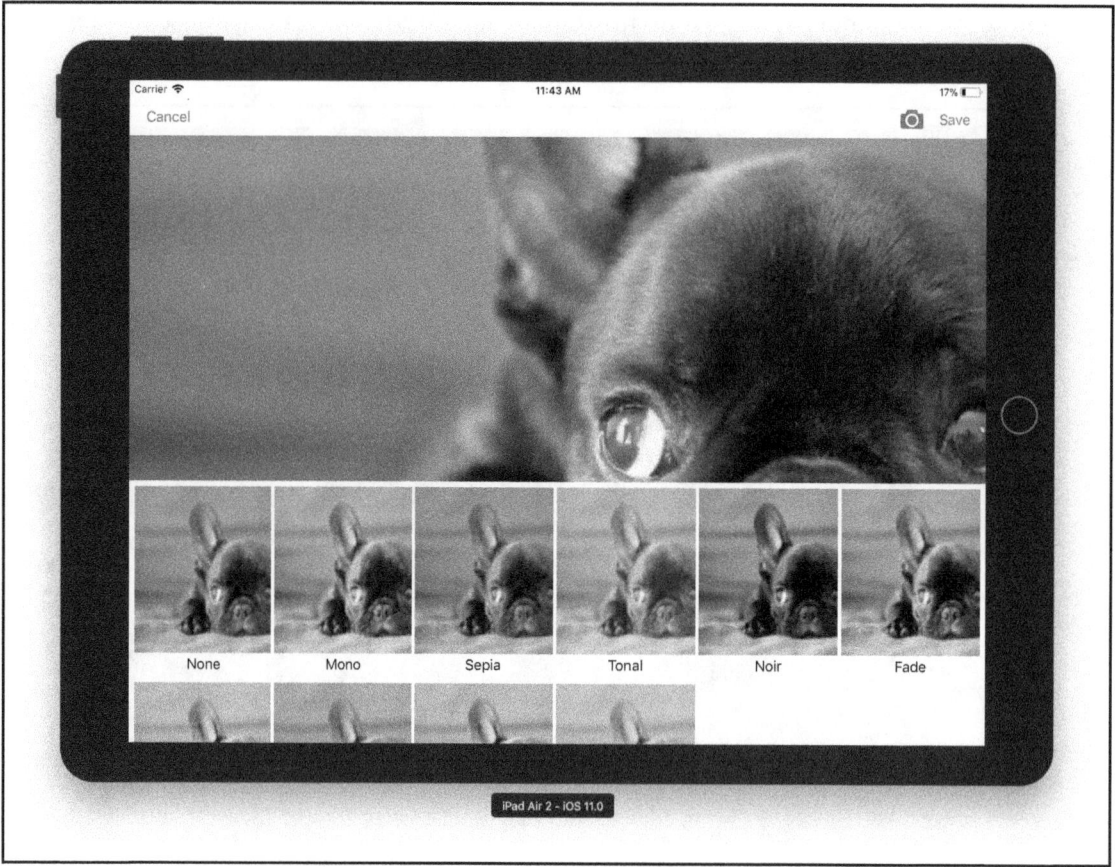

Summary

In this chapter, we looked at how to accept drag and drop from other applications. We also looked at how to create custom drag items using a Collection View. Now, we can use drag and drop on the iPad as a way to quickly add photos whereas the iPhone will use the *Camera Roll* only. Drag and drop is only supported for the iPad at this time, but hopefully soon Apple will open this up to us to use in our apps. In the next chapter, we will look at how to use Siri to request payments for friends for dinner.

28
SiriKit

Last year, Apple announced the addition of a new framework called **SiriKit**. This framework allows developers to leverage Siri in their apps. For the last year, SiriKit has been slowly adopted by developers. This year, Apple added even more supported domains. In this chapter, we are going to add SiriKit support to our app.

My original goal was to have Siri set up restaurant reservations, but unfortunately, Apple software requires this feature to be done using MapKit. Using MapKit is not the real issue, though. The real issue is that you have to work with Apple to get this set up so that we cannot make restaurant reservations. If you are working on an app that needs this feature, then you need to contact Apple support. In this chapter, we are going to set up the framework so that we have the ability to request money from someone. The setup for SiriKit is quite similar, so once you are comfortable doing this chapter, you should not have a problem working through the others. Please note that to use SiriKit, you must have a developer license to run Siri on your device.

We will cover the following topics in this chapter:

- Understanding SiriKit
- Working with SiriKit extensions
- Working with SiriKit UI extensions

Understanding SiriKit

We first need to understand how Siri interacts with our app before we get started. Have a look at how it works through this diagram:

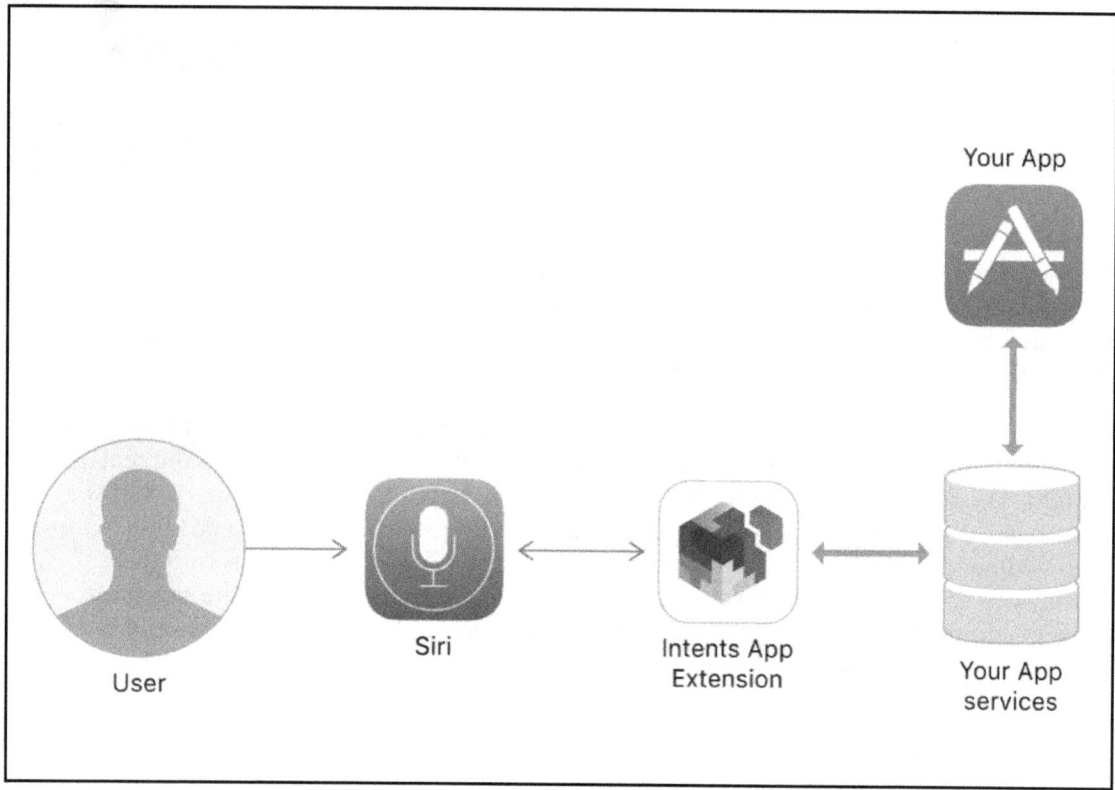

A user interacts with Siri to compose a request. Siri takes the request and looks through the intents for the requesting app. If the app is not found, Siri lets you know. If the app is found, but cannot do what was requested, Siri will notify you that the request cannot be done at this time. If the intent can be handled by the app, it will pass the information to your app. Your app does what it needs to do with that information and reports back to Siri. If the app needs further information, it lets Siri know what to request until the app has everything it needs or the user cancels the request.

Supported intents

As of iOS 11, Apple currently supports the following intents:

- VoIP Calling (initiate calls and search the user's call history)
- Messaging (send messages and search the user's received messages)
- Payments (send payments between users or pay bills)
- Lists and notes (create and manage notes and to-do list items)
- Visual Codes (convey contact and payment information using Quick Response (QR) codes)
- Photos (search for and display photos)
- Workouts (start, end, and manage fitness routines)
- Ride booking (book rides and report their status)
- Car commands (manage vehicle door locks and get the vehicle's status)
- CarPlay (interact with a vehicle's CarPlay system)
- Restaurant reservations (create and manage restaurant reservations with help from the *Maps* app)

This API requires you to work with Apple Maps before your app can use it. For information on how to get started, go to `http://mapsconnect.apple.com`.

We are going to use the Payment intent, which allows us to send payments between users or pay bills. When we are done, we can just say *Hey Siri! Send $100 to Jason Clayton for dinner last night using LetsEat*. We can hook this up to any banking system, but at the moment, we have everything else set up for this. Let's get started.

Enable Siri capabilities

The first thing we need to do is enable SiriKit:

1. In Xcode, go to your app and select the **LetsEat** target:

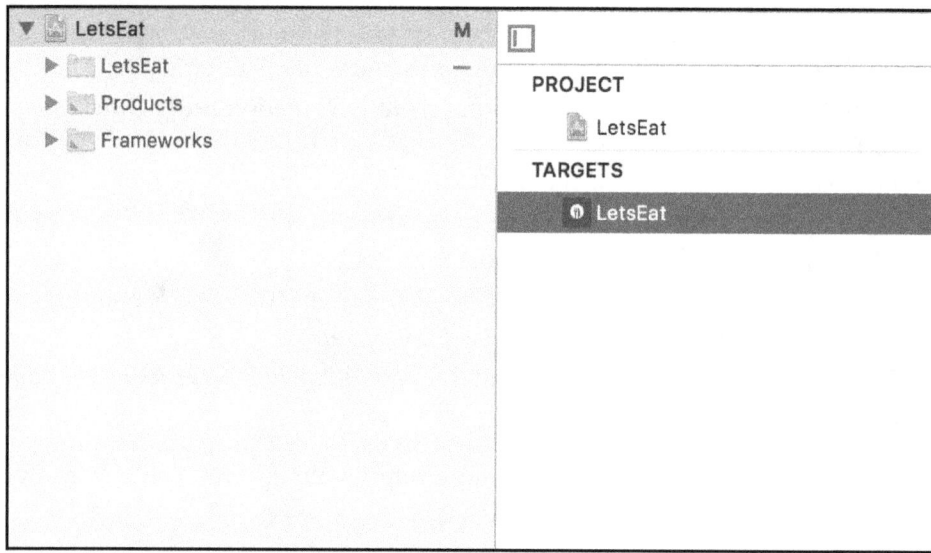

2. Next, click on the **Capabilities** tab:

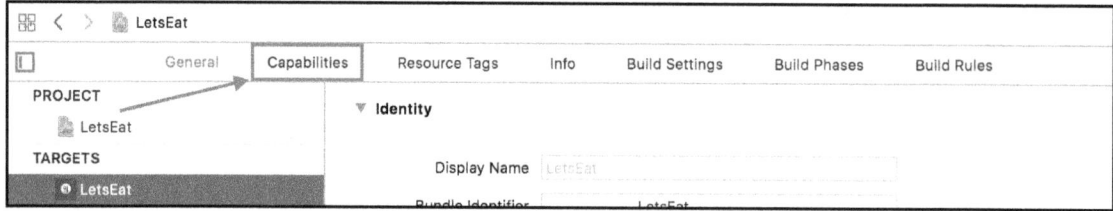

Chapter 28

3. Then, hit the switch for Siri to switch it to **ON**:

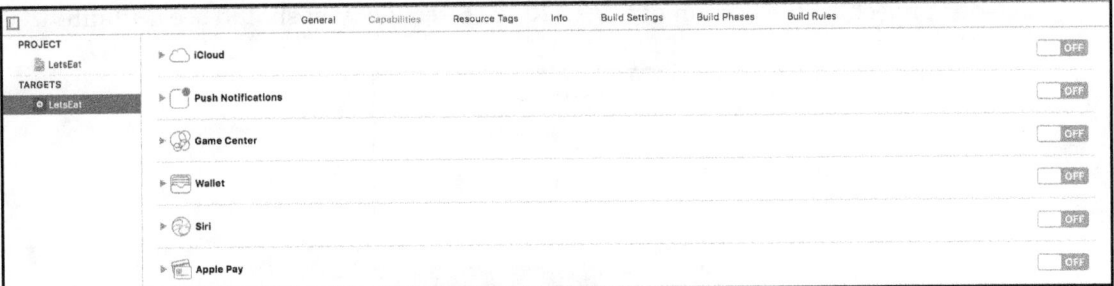

4. You should see the following when you are done:

[717]

SiriKit

5. You need a working developer account to do the following steps. Otherwise, you will see errors when trying to follow along. Next, we need to add a new target to our project. At the bottom of the **TARGETS** section, you should see a + button.

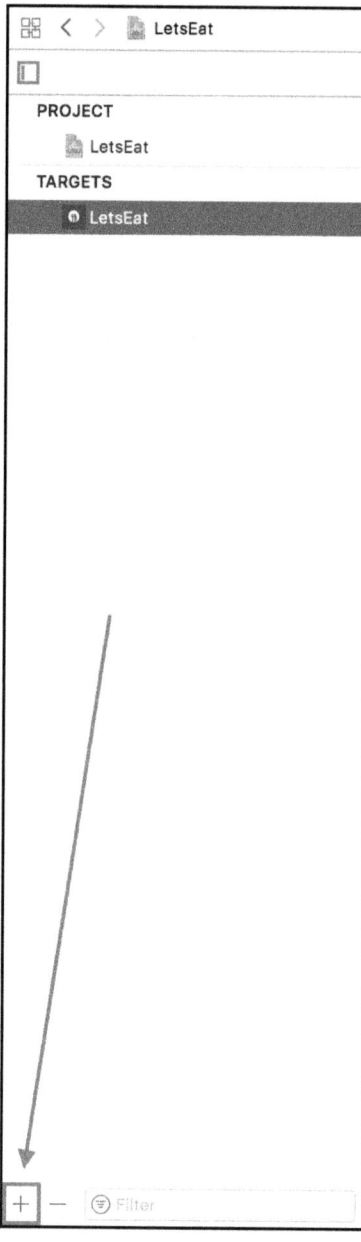

[718]

6. Click the + button, and you will see the following screen:

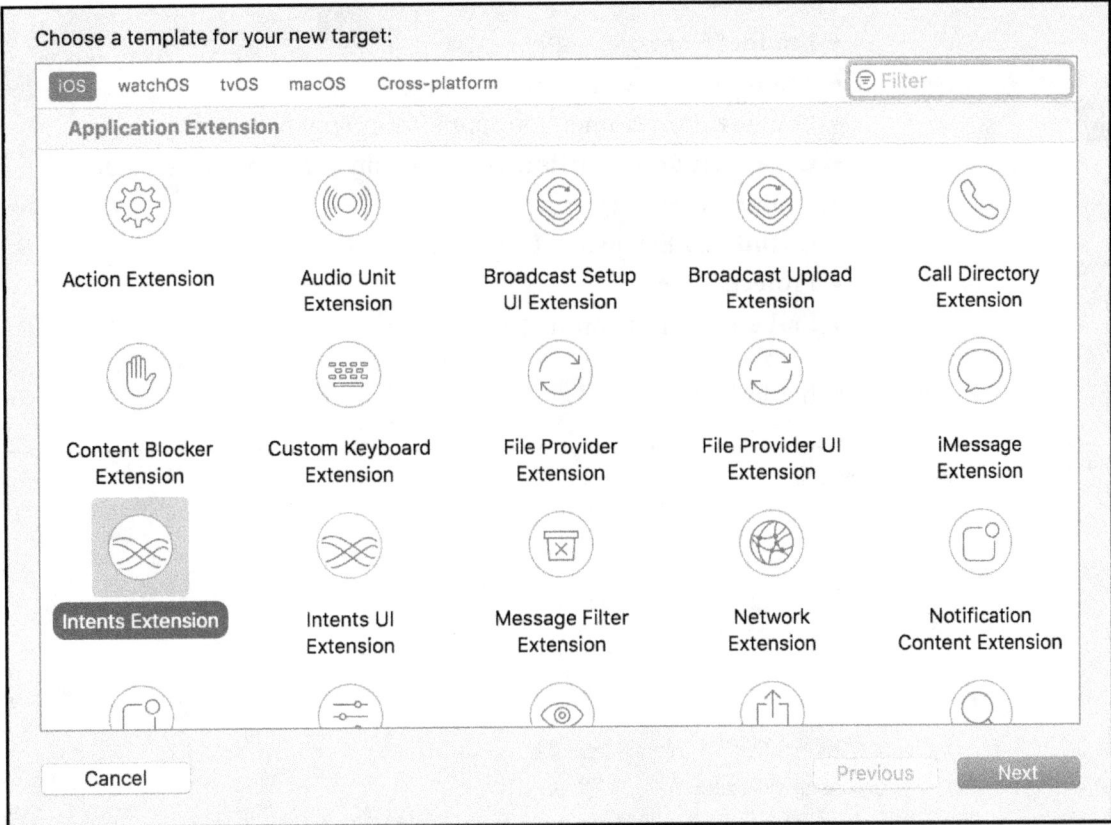

7. Next, select **Intents Extension** under the **iOS** tab. Then hit **Next**.

SiriKit

8. In the **Options** screen that appears, there are some fields to fill out or choose. Add the following to the **Options** screen and then hit **Next**:

    - **Product Name**: `MakePayment`
    - **Team**: Must have a team
    - **Organization Name**: Your name/company name
    - **Organization Identifier**: Your domain name in reverse order
    - **Language**: `Swift`
    - **Include UI Extension**: Checked
    - **Project**: `LetsEat`
    - **Embed in Application**: `LetsEat`

This is how it should look:

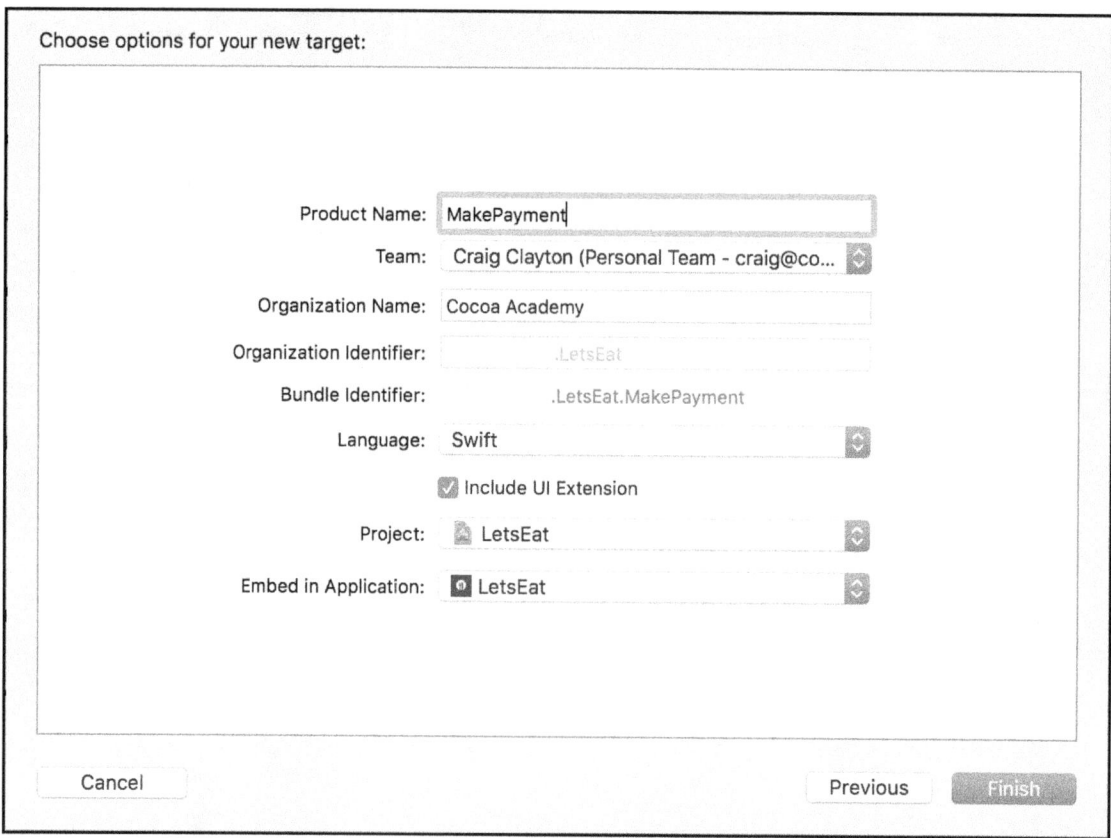

When you have finished, we will have two extensions added to our project: the `MakePayment` and `MakePaymentUI` extensions. These extensions are what we will use to add SiriKit to your project. We need to edit these extensions so that they can accept payments:

1. Open the `MakePayment` folder and select the `Info.plist` file.
2. Open all of the disclosure arrows under `NSExtension`. When they are all open, you should see the following:

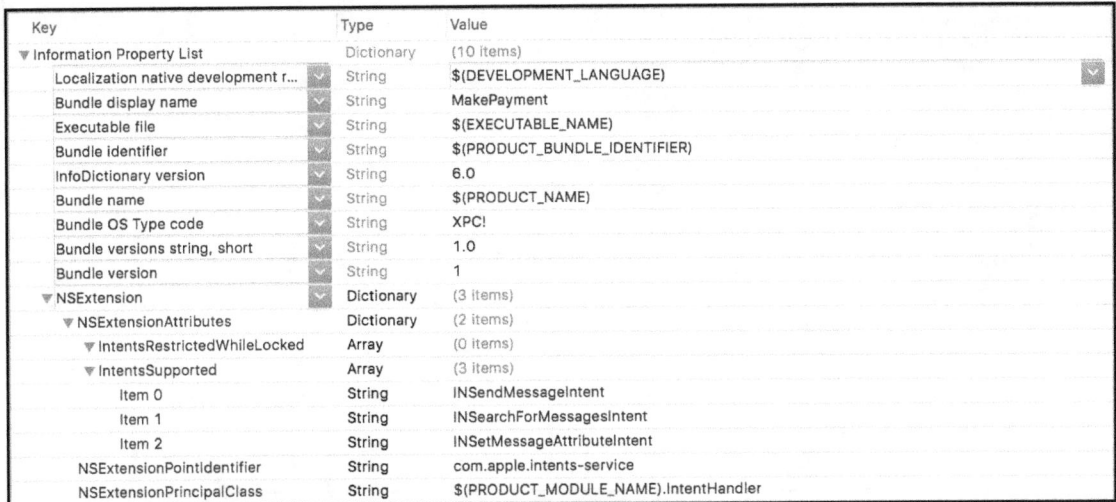

Currently, the app is set up to use the **Send Message** intent, and we want to use the **Send Payment** intent.

SiriKit

3. Under `IntentsSupported`, delete Item 1 (`INSearchForMessagesIntent`) and Item 2 (`INSetMessageAttributeIntent`):

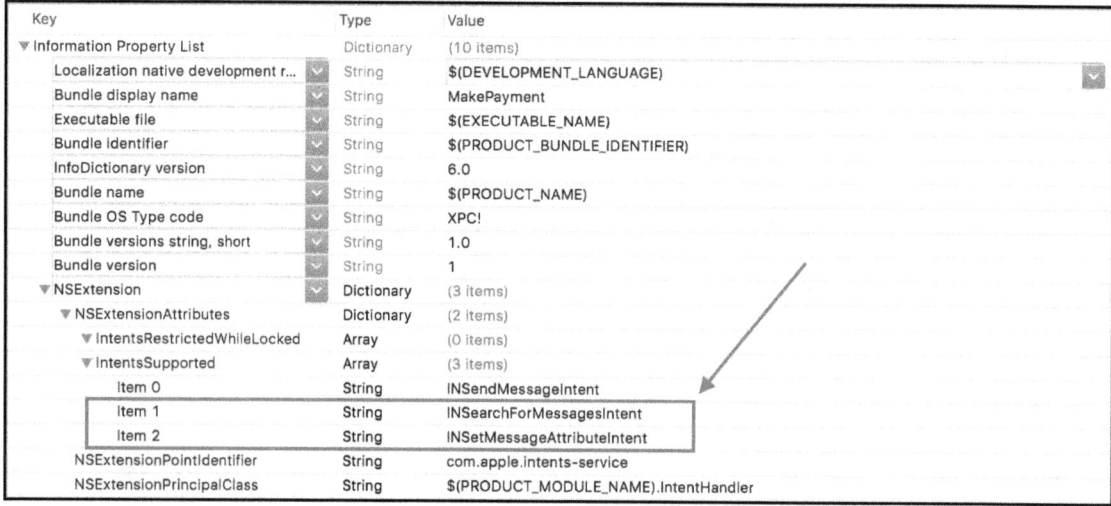

4. Now, for `Item 0`, change `INSendMessageIntent` to `INSendPaymentIntent`.
5. Under `IntentsRestrictedWhileLocked`, add `INSendPaymentIntent` by clicking the + button:

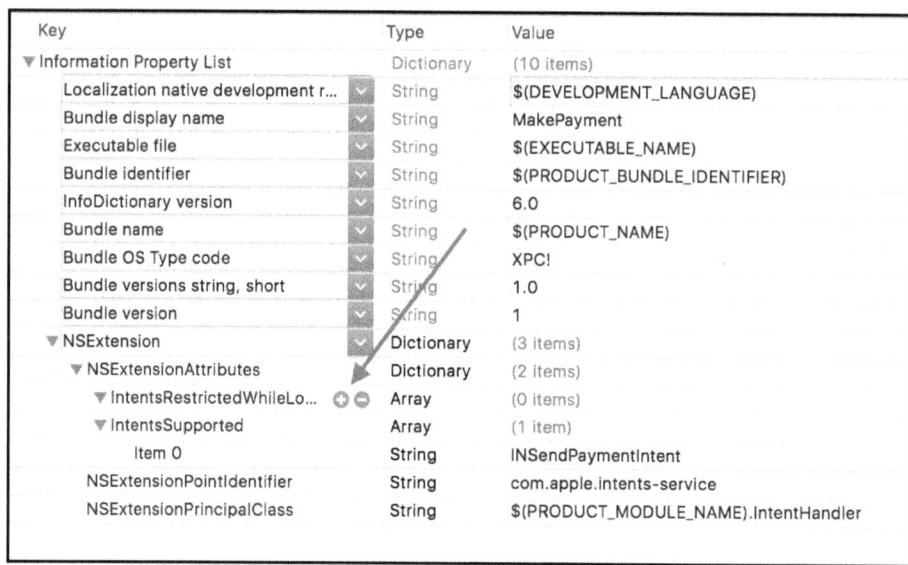

[722]

Chapter 28

6. When finished, you should see the following:

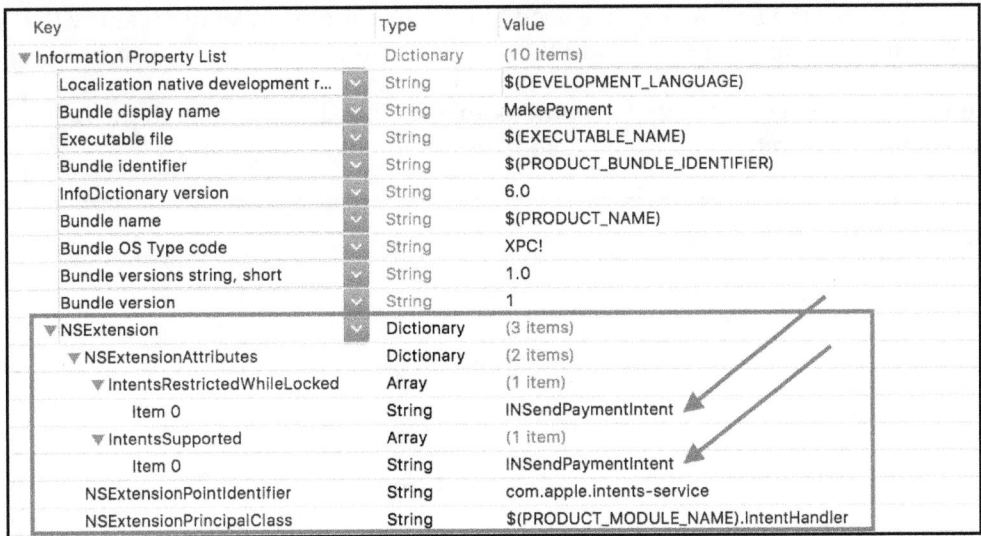

7. Next, open up `Info.plist` under the `MakePaymentUI` folder, open all the disclosure arrows under `NSExtension`, and change `INSendMessageIntent` under `IntentsSupported` to `INSendPaymentIntent`:

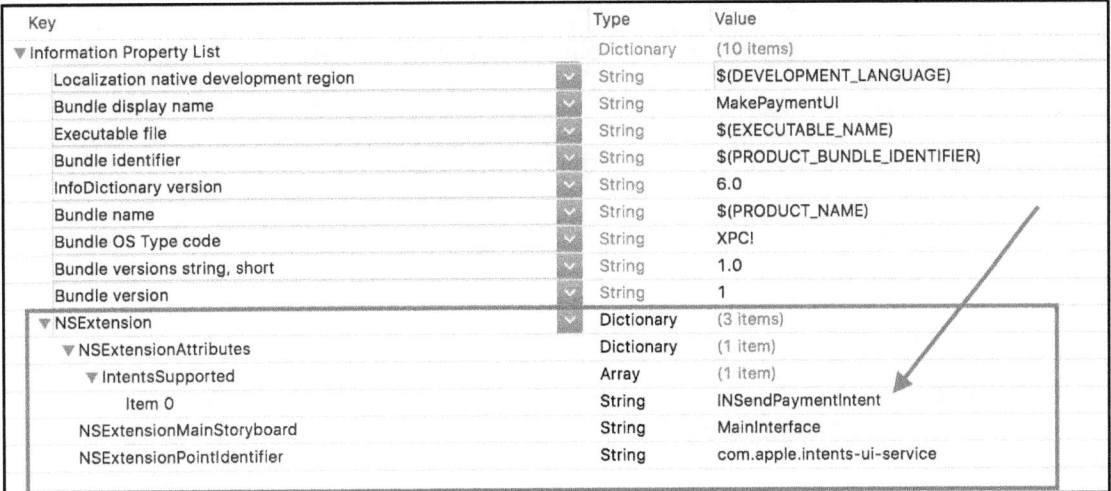

[723]

SiriKit

We have finished setting up our plist. Whenever we access something, we always have to ask permission, just like we did earlier when we accessed the user's photos. In the `Info.plist` file of the *LetsEat* app, we need to update our plist to let users know that we need access for Siri and our reason. Add the `NSSiriUsageDescription` key.

For the key value, enter anything you want as an alert that the user sees. In the following example, the value is set as `This app uses Siri to send payments.`:

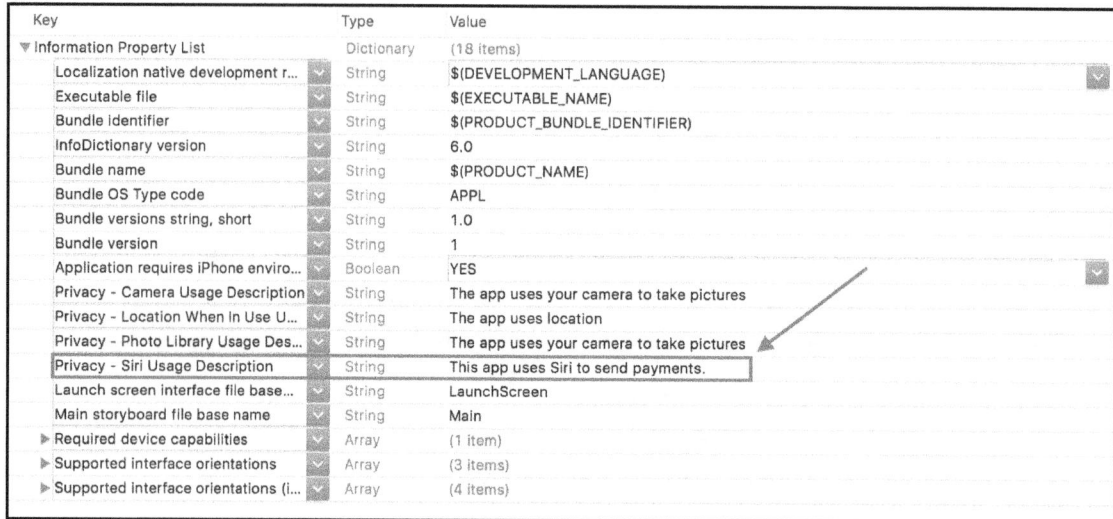

Now, inside of your `AppDelete`, add the following import after `import UIKit`:

```
import Intents
```

Next, after `setupDefaultColors()`, add the following method:

```
func requestSiriPermissions() {
    INPreferences.requestSiriAuthorization({ (status) in
        print(status)
    })
}
```

Then, in your `-application:didFinishLaunchingWithOptions:` under `setupDefaultColors()`, add `requestSiriPermissions()`.

Adding this asks the user for permission to use Siri. Now, if you are going to use this in a real app, I would say that you should add a **Settings** section where users can use a switch to turn Siri on or off. You do not want to force users to use something without really giving them a reason. In iOS, once you ask a user for permission and they decline, they have to go into the **Settings** section. If you want to ask, then it is better to have another dialog box that asks for permission; if they say yes, then run the request, and if the users say no, then you do nothing. This way you do not have to force your users to go to the phone settings to turn this feature on. Now that we have our permissions set up, we need to create users that we can send money to.

Creating users

When using SiriKit, it needs to have an `INPerson` object. An `INPerson` object is used by Siri to send users things—money in our case. Let's create this new file:

1. Right-click the `Misc` folder and select **New File**.
2. Inside of the **Choose a template for your new file** screen, select **iOS** at the top, and then **Swift**. Then, hit **Next**.
3. Save the file as `RestaurantContact`.
4. Click **Create**.
5. Add the following code to this file:

```
import Intents

struct RestaurantContact {
    let name: String
    let email: String
    static func allContacts() -> [RestaurantContact] {
        return [
            RestaurantContact(name: "Jason Clayton", email: "jason@mac.com"),
            RestaurantContact(name: "Joshua Clayton", email: "joshua@texas.edu"),
            RestaurantContact(name: "Teena Harris", email: "teena@gmail.com")
        ]
    }
    func inPerson() -> INPerson {
        let formatter = PersonNameComponentsFormatter()
        let handle = INPersonHandle(value: email, type: .emailAddress)
        if let components = formatter.personNameComponents(from: name) {
            return INPerson(personHandle: handle, nameComponents:
```

```
            components, displayName: components.familyName, image: nil,
contactIdentifier: nil, customIdentifier: nil)
        }
        else {
            return INPerson(personHandle: handle, nameComponents: nil,
displayName: nil, image: nil, contactIdentifier: nil, customIdentifier:
nil)
        }
    }
}
```

Here, we are creating contacts that we can use to ask Siri to send money. We have set up three people to accept money at this time: Jason Clayton, Joshua Clayton, and Teena Harris. When we request with Siri, these are the names that it looks for to see if the person exists. If the name is not in this list, Siri lets you know that the name is not found. This list can have any name you wish to have, so if you want to change the names to something else, you can do that now. Just make sure that when we get to the requesting section, you change the name there as well. Our `inPerson()` method is just formatting into a format that SiriKit needs to be able to read the object. We now need to add code that runs when the send payment intent is invoked.

Updating our intent handler

We can now finally add our code that runs when the **Send Payment** intent is invoked. Open the `IntentHandler` class inside of the `MakePayment` extension folder. After the import intents line deletes everything else from this file, add the following code:

```
class IntentHandler: INExtension{
    override func handler(for intent: INIntent) -> Any {
        if intent is INSendPaymentIntent {
            return SendMoneyIntent()
        }
        return self
    }
}
```

Here, we are creating a custom intent handler. When the intent is to send payment, we want to run our `SendMoneyIntent` class. We need to create this file next. In the same file direction under the `IntentHandler` class, add the following:

```
class SendMoneyIntent: NSObject, INSendPaymentIntentHandling {
    func handle(intent: INSendPaymentIntent, completion: @escaping (INSendPaymentIntentResponse) -> Void) {
        if let person = intent.payee, let amount = intent.currencyAmount {
            //handle payment
            print("person (person.displayName) - amount (String(describing: amount.amount))")
            completion(INSendPaymentIntentResponse(code: .success, userActivity: nil))
        }
        else {
            completion(INSendPaymentIntentResponse(code: .failure, userActivity: nil))
        }
    }
}
```

In this class, the `handle()` method responds to a `SendPaymentIntent`. We are printing the person's display name and amount. We pass a completion block here, but in real production code, you would run whatever API you are using to verify the payment. Add the following inside of the `SendMoney` intent under the `handle()` method:

```
func resolvePayee(for intent: INSendPaymentIntent, with completion: @escaping (INPersonResolutionResult) -> Void) {
    if let payee = intent.payee {
        let contacts:[RestaurantContact] = RestaurantContact.allContacts()
        var result: INPersonResolutionResult?
        var matchedContacts:[RestaurantContact] = []
        for contact in contacts {
            print("checking existing: (contact.name) - (payee.displayName)")
            if contact.name == payee.displayName {
                matchedContacts.append(contact)
            }
            switch matchedContacts.count {
            case 0:
                print("no matches")
                result = .unsupported()
            case 1:
                print("best matched")
                let person = matchedContacts[0].inPerson()
                result = INPersonResolutionResult.success(with: person)
```

```
                default:
                    print("more than one match")
                    let person:[INPerson] = matchedContacts.map { contact in
                        return contact.inPerson()
                    }
                    result = INPersonResolutionResult.disambiguation(with: person)
                }
            }
            completion(result!)
        } else {
            completion(INPersonResolutionResult.needsValue())
        }
    }
}
```

In this method, we are getting the payee information and checking to see if the person matches within our contacts. We are looping through the contacts and looking for a match. When completed, we return the result to Siri. If the user is not found, then Siri will tell you that the person is not found. If Siri finds the person, then `PaymentIntent` continues. Lastly, inside of the `IntentViewController`, update the `desiredSize` variable to the following:

```
var desiredSize: CGSize {
    return CGSize(width: self.desiredSize.width, height: 150)
}
```

Here, we are setting the size of the UI to a `height` of `150`. Let's look at how we can test this.

Testing Siri

We can test Siri on a device or in the simulator. If you want to test on a device, just change the target to the `MakePayment` target and plug in your iOS 11 device. If you want to test this in the simulator, we need to do the following:

1. First, go to `Settings` in the iPhone Simulator.
2. Next, select **Siri**.
3. Click the switch to enable **Press Home for Siri**.

4. Select **Enable Siri**.

   Now, you have two options. You can run the app and Siri in the simulator. At this point, you can say `Send $100 to Jason Clayton for dinner last night using LetsEat` (or you use the name of whomever you added to the contacts we created earlier). Option two is that you can enter text that you want to display each time. To set up this text, every time you run the app, select the `MakePayment` scheme:

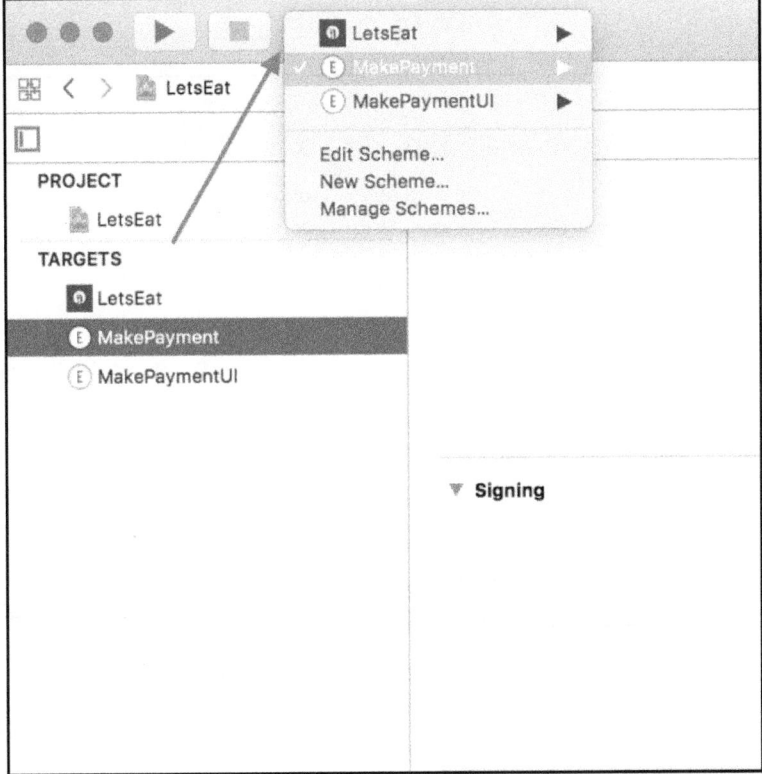

SiriKit

5. Then, hit the **Scheme** dropdown again and select **Edit Scheme...**:

6. Then, under **Siri Intent Query**, put in the desired text, such as `Send $100 to Jason Clayton for dinner last night using LetsEat`, and then hit **Close**:

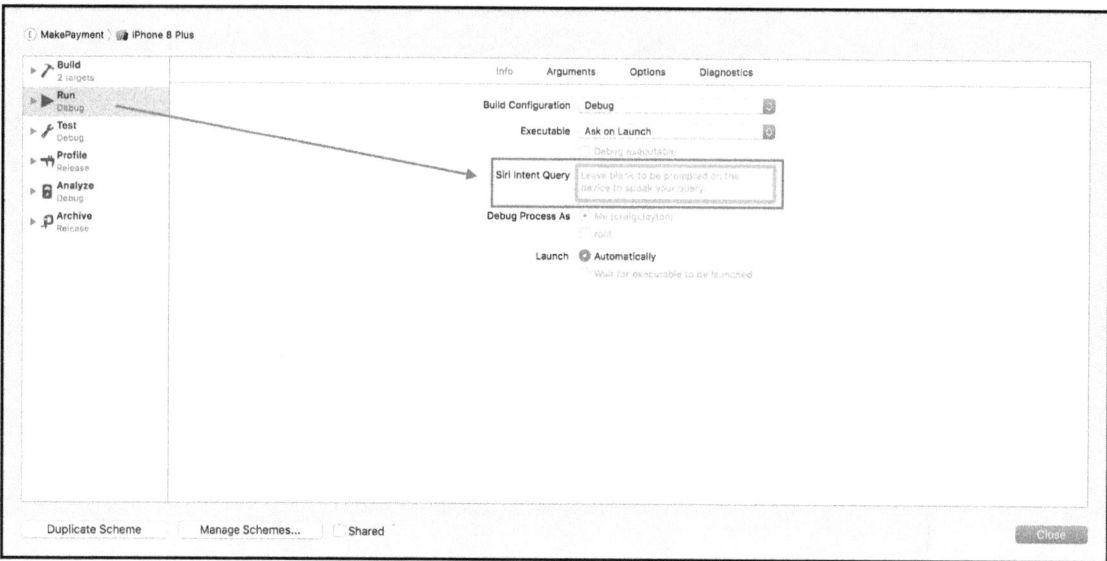

Chapter 28

Remember that we have the `MakePayment` scheme. Run the `MakePayment` scheme, and the first thing that will happen is that Siri will first ask you for permission:

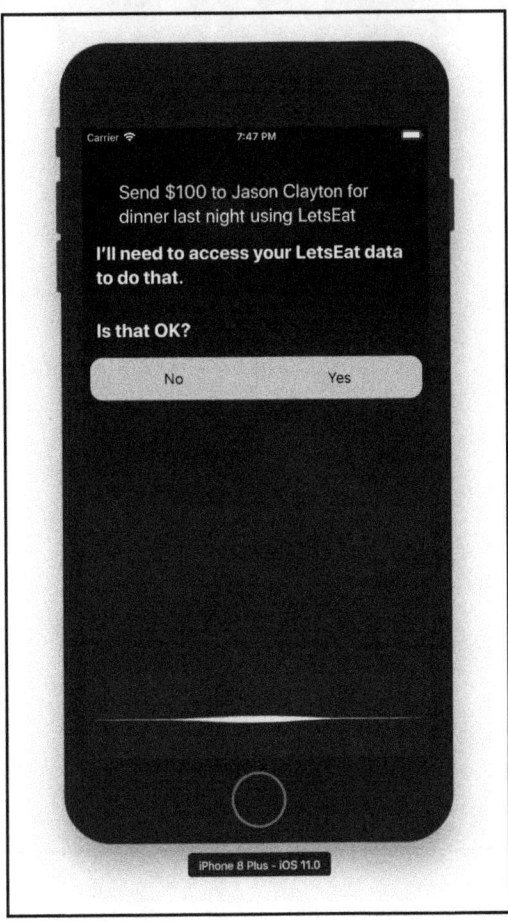

SiriKit

7. When you accept, Siri will show you your request and ask if you accept it:

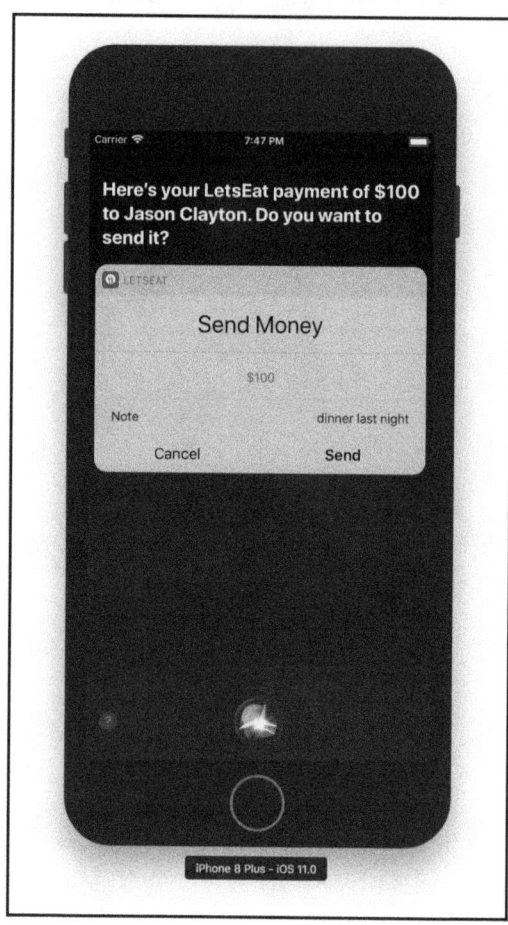

When you accept, you will see that your money's been sent. In our example, we are not actually sending money, so this step will always goes through:

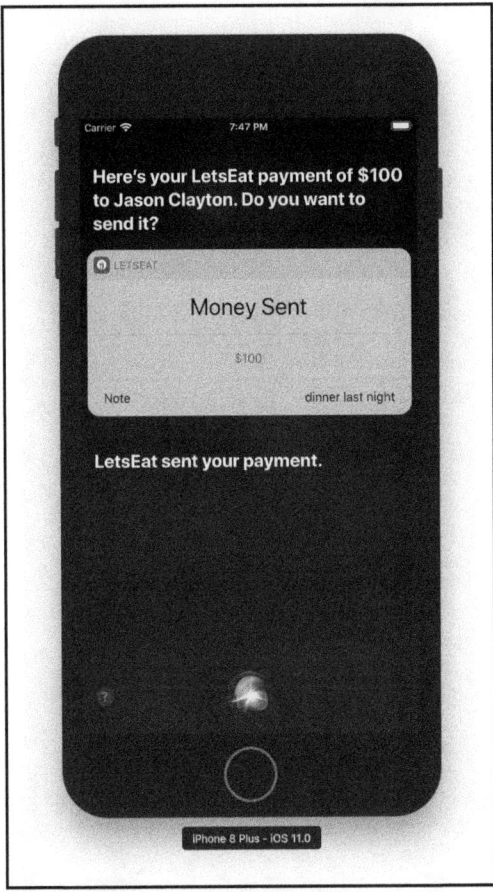

Note that the reason Siri is asking for permission is that we are running Siri first instead of the app. If we ran the app, we would get the following:

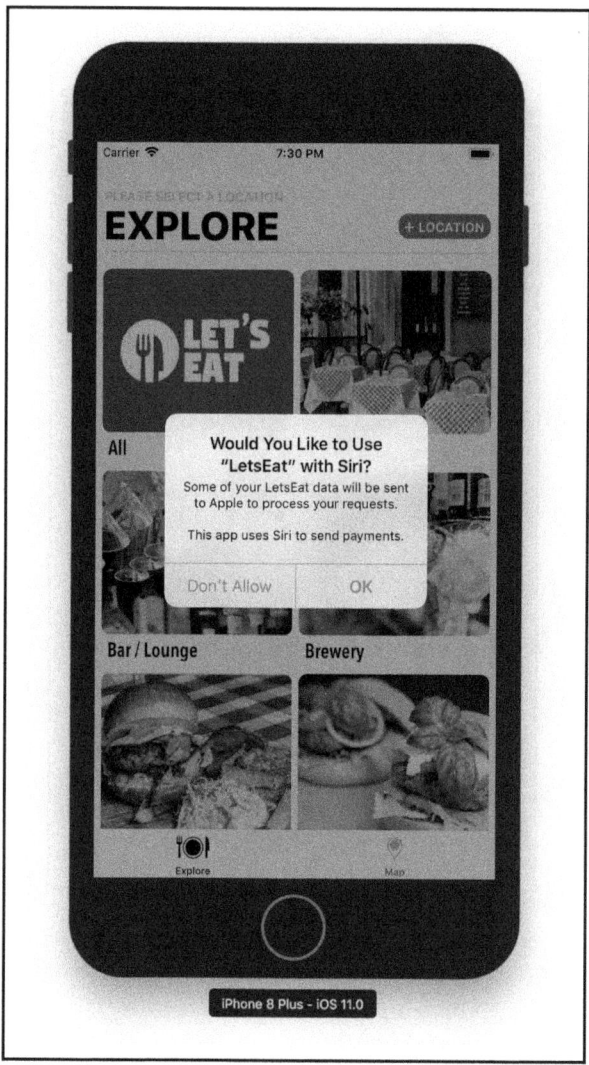

We are now done. We did not do anything with our UI, but you can add anything you want to your UI, such as a logo, a view or display to show to the payee, or whatever you decide. Have fun with it and make it your own.

Summary

In this chapter, we looked at how to integrate Siri into our app. Even though Siri is limited to specific intents, we can still find unique ways to use it, such as using it for messaging, notes, and lists. The overall setup for each intent is the same—the only difference is what you do once the intent hits your app. In the next chapter, we will look at how to distribute our app to others for testing, as well as how to submit our app to the App Store.

29
Beta and Store Submission

Throughout this book we've come a long way, from learning about Xcode to how to build an entire app. This process would not be complete, however, without actually learning how to submit the app to the App Store. This process may seem like a lot when doing it for the first time, but it becomes easier and even second nature after a while.

When I submitted my first app, I was extremely nervous. I remember the relief I felt after submitting the app, but I was soon repeatedly checking the site and my inbox for that approval email. I'd heard many stories of people who spent a lot of time working on an app only to have it rejected; these fears are understandable, but know that Apple wants you to succeed. Even if your app gets rejected (and my first one did), it's not necessarily a bad thing.

My first app was a sports app, and it was rejected for two reasons. First, in Apple's eyes, the logo for my app was too similar to the NFL logo. To address this, I simply made a generic logo with the initials of the app. Second, the quality of my images was considered not up to standard; therefore, I obtained better images. I then resubmitted my app, and within a couple of days my app was approved. It is almost a certainty that you will encounter rejections, even if you have been doing this for a while. Take comfort in the fact that you can address any issues with your app and resubmit it for approval from the App Store.

Beta and Store Submission

In this chapter, we will cover everything you need to know about getting your app into the App Store. In Xcode 9, a lot of things are done for you behind the scenes; however, the goal of this chapter is to show you how you can set up things on your own. You will need a developer account in order to follow along with these steps. Go to `https://developer.apple.com/programs/` if you would like to purchase a developer account.

We will cover the following topics in this chapter:

- Creating a bundle identifier
- Creating a certificate signing request
- Creating production and development certificates
- Creating production and development provisioning profiles
- Creating an App Store listing
- Making the release build and submitting to the App Store
- Conducting internal and external testing

This chapter is set up for you to use as you need it. It is not meant for you to follow in order, as with the other chapters in this book. For example, you may need to create a bundle identifier and then need to know how to add external testers. Use this chapter as a resource for when you need to do one of these tasks.

Chapter 29

Creating a bundle identifier

When we created our project, we talked about the bundle identifier (also known as your App ID). This bundle identifier is used to identify your app, and therefore must be unique. Let's proceed with the following steps:

1. Log in to your Apple developer account, and you will see the following screen:

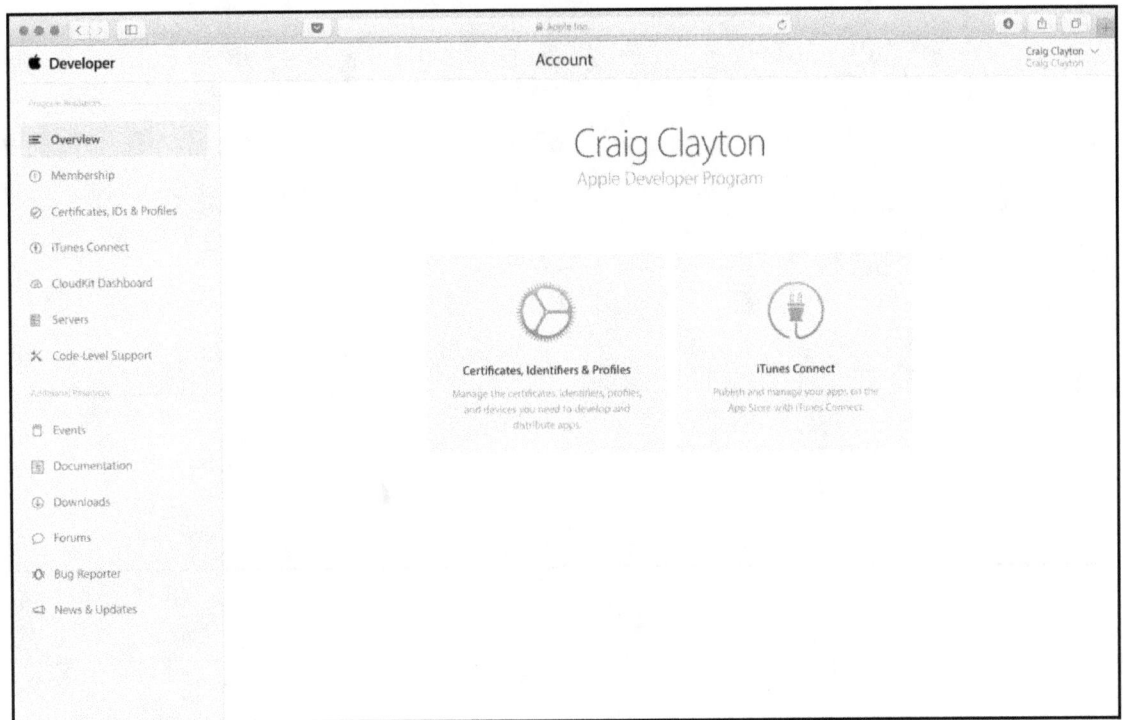

Beta and Store Submission

2. Click **Certificates, Identifiers & Profiles**.
3. Then, under **Identifiers**, click **App IDs**:

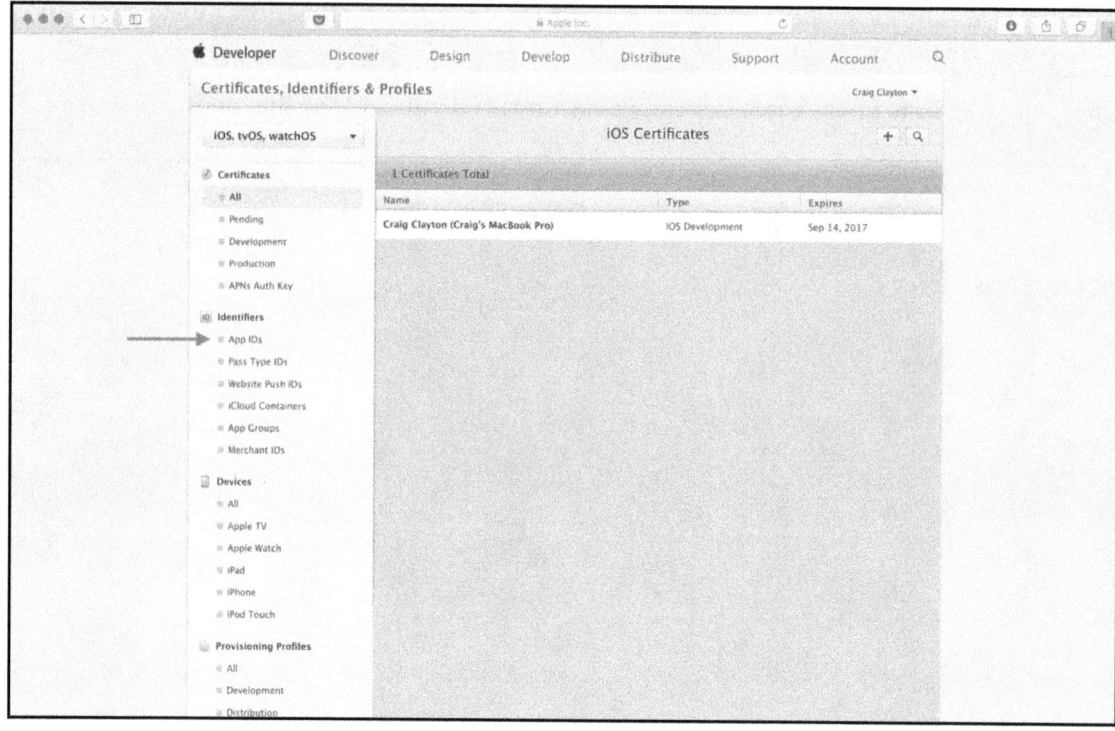

Chapter 29

4. Click on the + button at the top-right of the screen:

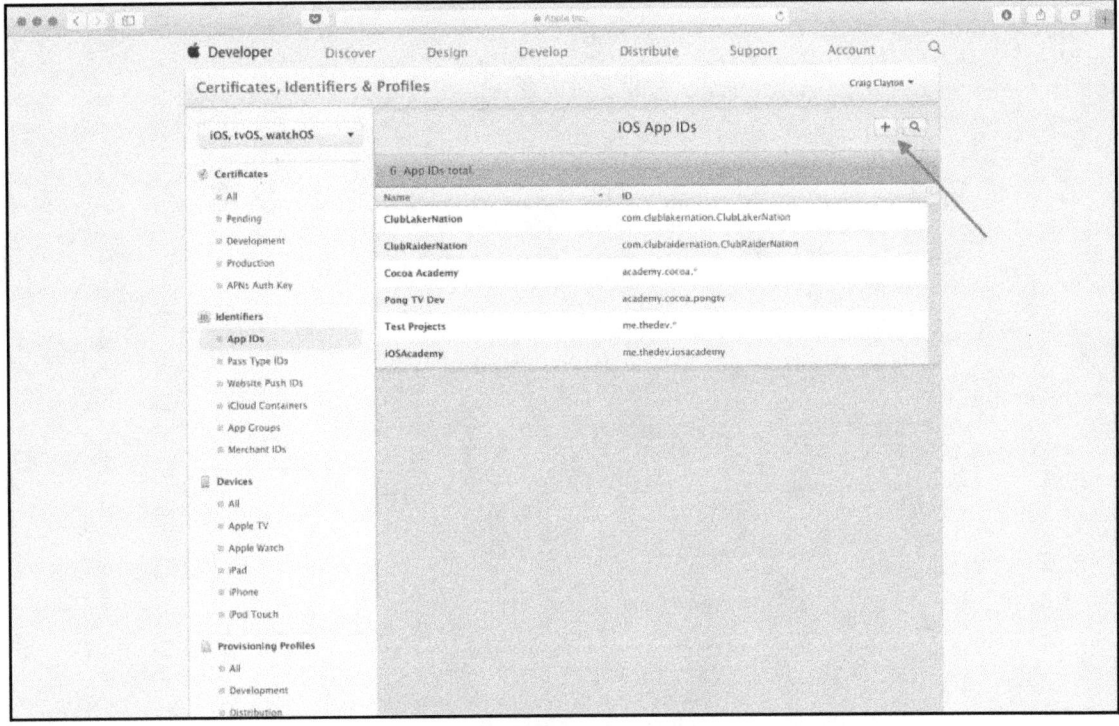

[741]

5. The **Registering an App ID** screen will appear, as follows:

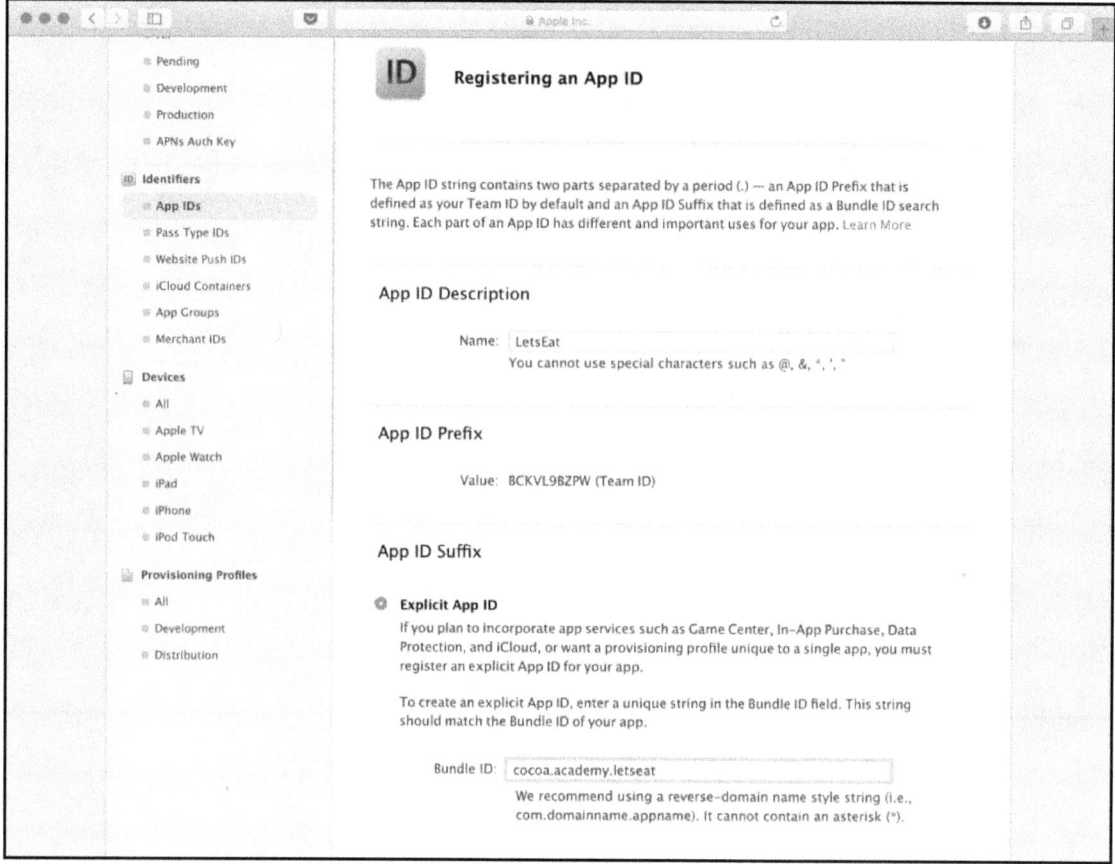

6. In the top part of the **Registering an App ID** screen, as seen in the preceding screenshot, add the following:

   - **Name**: Update this field under **App ID Description** as `LetsEat`.
   - **Explicit App ID**: This field under **App ID Suffix** should be selected.
   - **Bundle ID**: This field under **App ID Suffix** should be filled with your details entered in it.

Make sure that the **Bundle ID** follows the standard naming convention: `com.yourcompanyname.letseat`. Your **Bundle ID** should be the same ID that you set up when we created the project. For example, mine is `cocoa.academy.letseat`.

7. Next, in the bottom part of the **Registering an App ID** screen shown as follows, select the **App Services** that the app requires and then click **Continue**.

Our project does not have any **App Services**, but this is where you would set them if a future app required them:

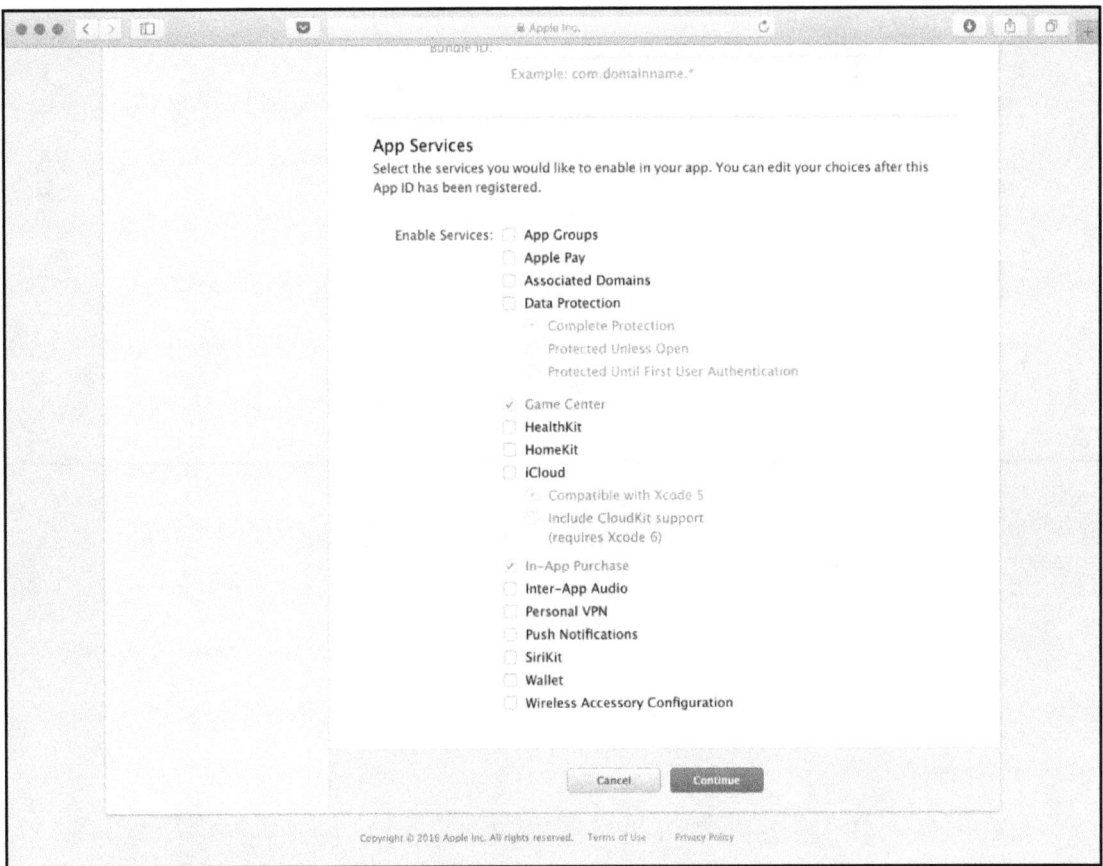

Beta and Store Submission

If you later decide to add **App Services**, you can do so inside of Xcode. You would select the project under **Targets** and then select the **Capabilities** tab and modify as necessary:

After verifying your App ID information, click **Register**:

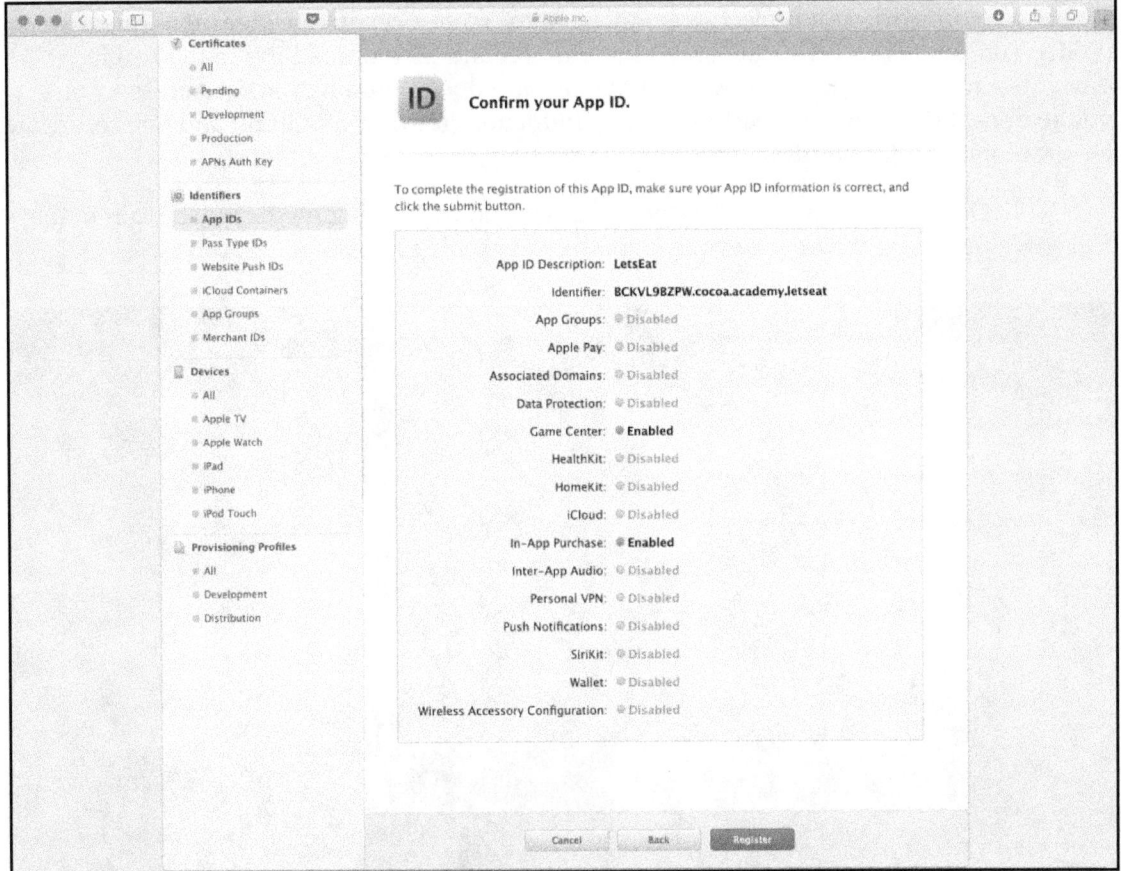

Your App ID is now created. Now let's look at what certificates are and how to use them.

Creating a certificate signing request

Whenever you work on a project, you will need to create a **certificate signing request** (**CSR**). You create this certificate on your computer and then upload it into the Apple developer account. You then download this file and open it into **Keychain Access** when you're done. Let's create one certificate for production (for the App Store) and one certificate for development (for building locally):

1. Open Keychain Access (which you can find by clicking on the search icon in the upper-right corner of your menu bar and typing `Keychain Access`):

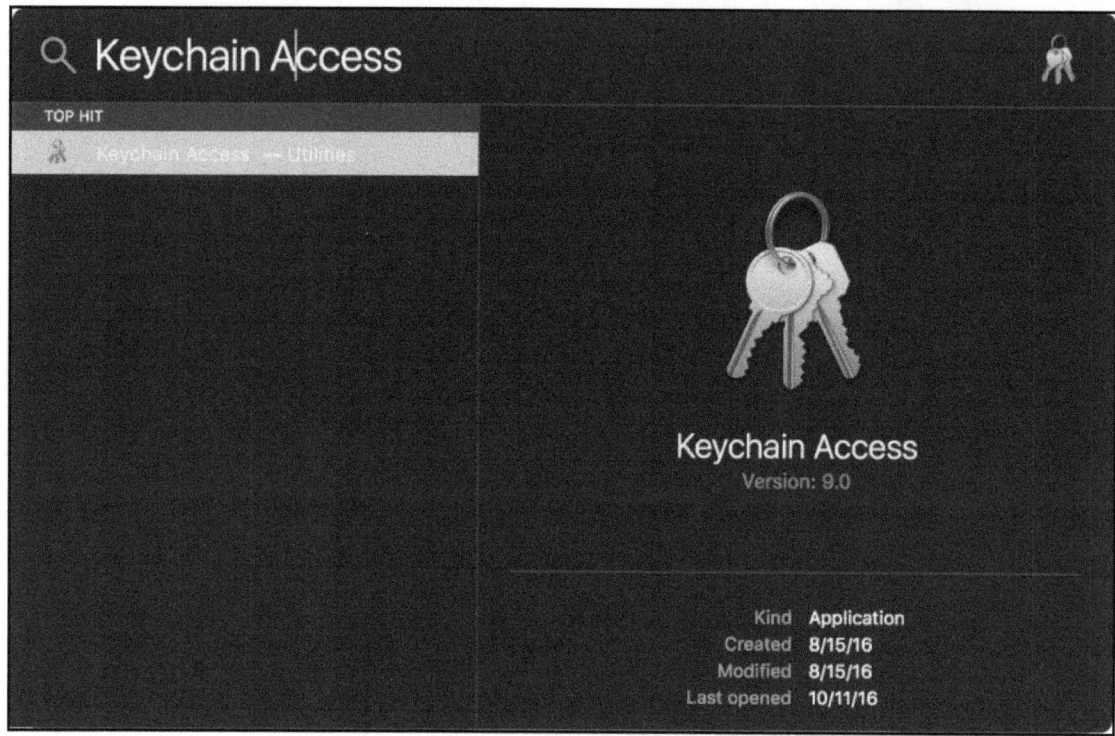

2. In the menu bar, while in Keychain Access, select **Keychain Access | Certificate Assistant | Request a Certificate From a Certificate Authority...**:

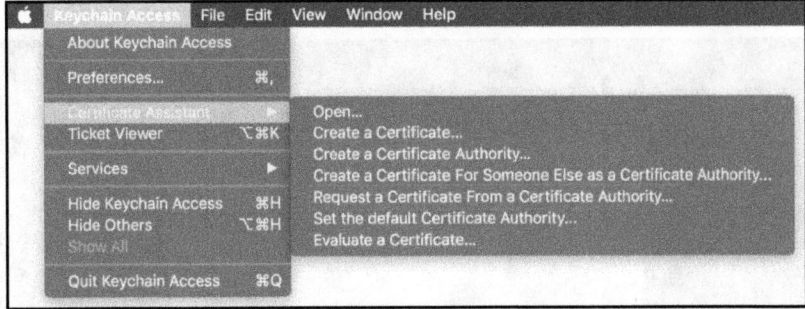

3. Enter your email address for **User Email Address** and the app name for **Common Name**, and then select **Saved to disk** under **Request is**:

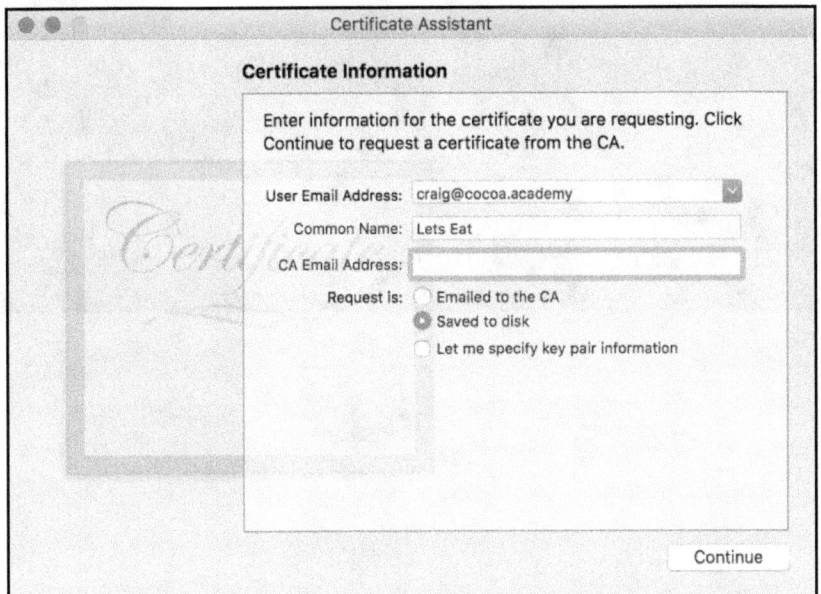

4. Then, click **Continue**.
5. In the screen that appears, enter the certificate name, select a save location and click **Save**, as follows:

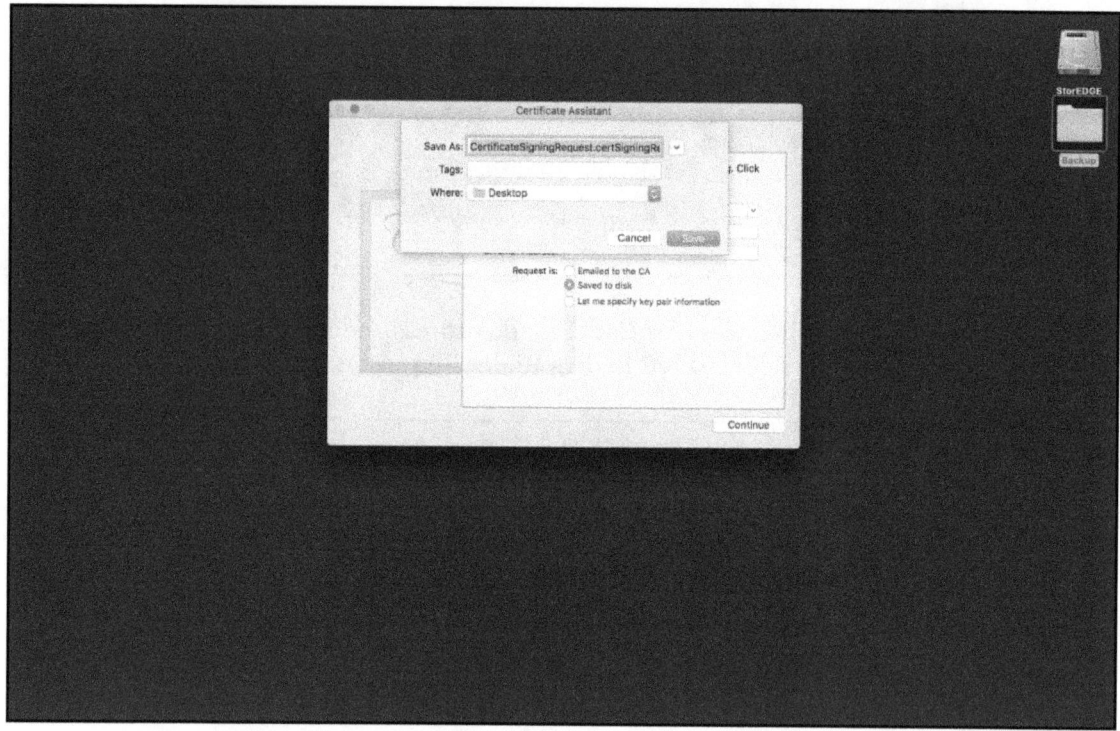

6. Click **Done**, export the certificate and save it to your computer:

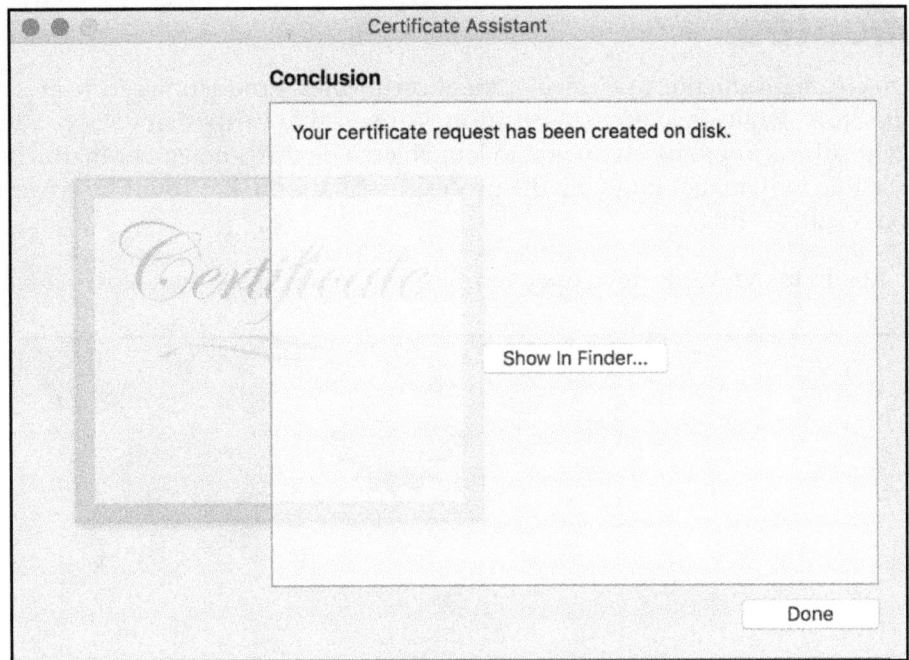

Creating production and development certificates

We need to create production and development certificates. Production certificates are used for the App Store, while development certificates are used to verify that you are a team member who allows apps signed by you to launch on a device. Remember that Xcode 9 can now handle this for you, but knowing the process is still useful. Let's start by creating a production certificate first:

1. Log in to the Apple developer account, and you will see the following screen:

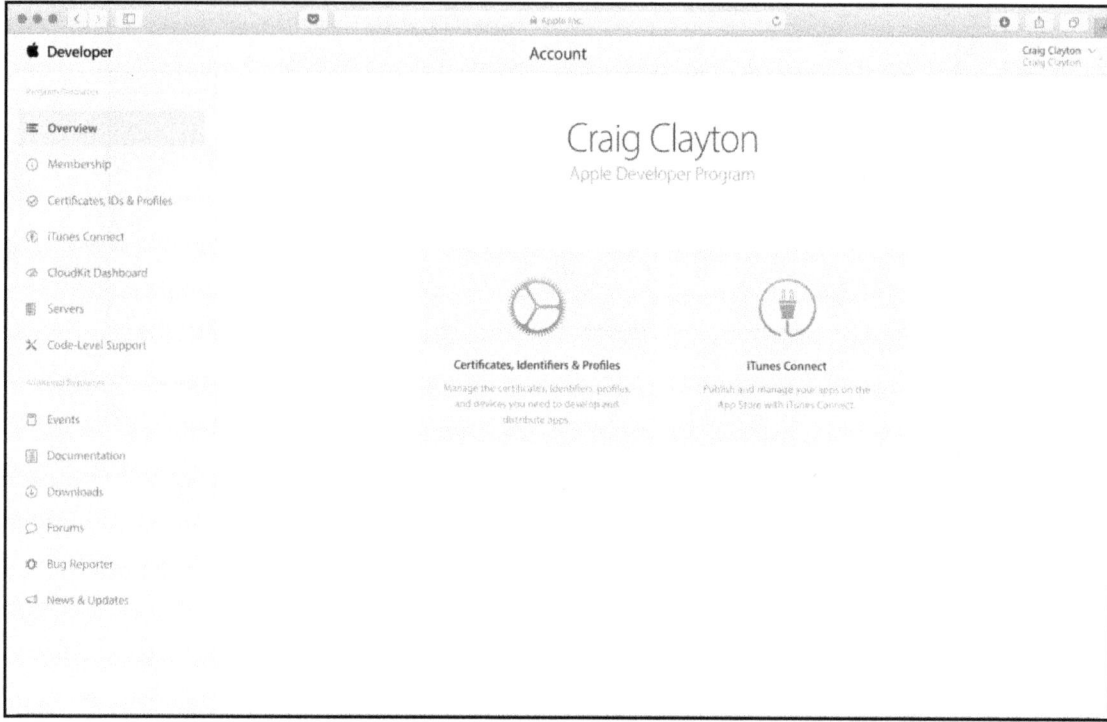

2. Click **Certificates, Identifiers & Profiles**, and then under **Certificates**, select **All**.
3. Click on the + button at the top-right of the screen:

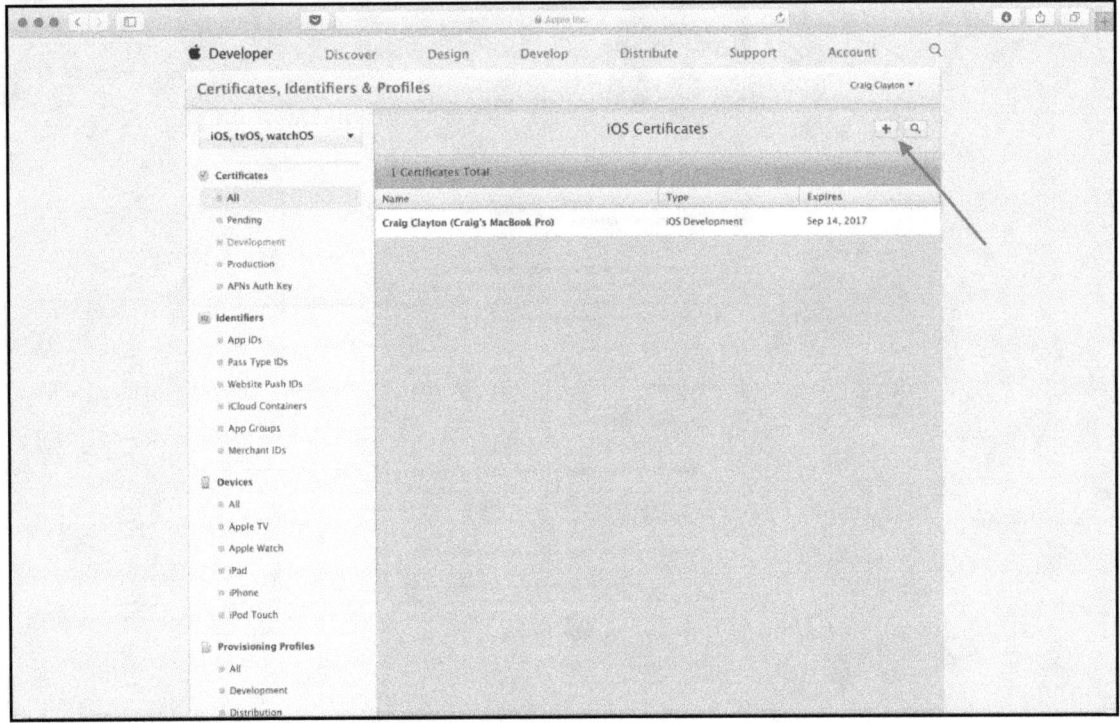

Beta and Store Submission

4. In the screen that appears, select **App Store and Ad Hoc** under **Production** and then click **Continue**:

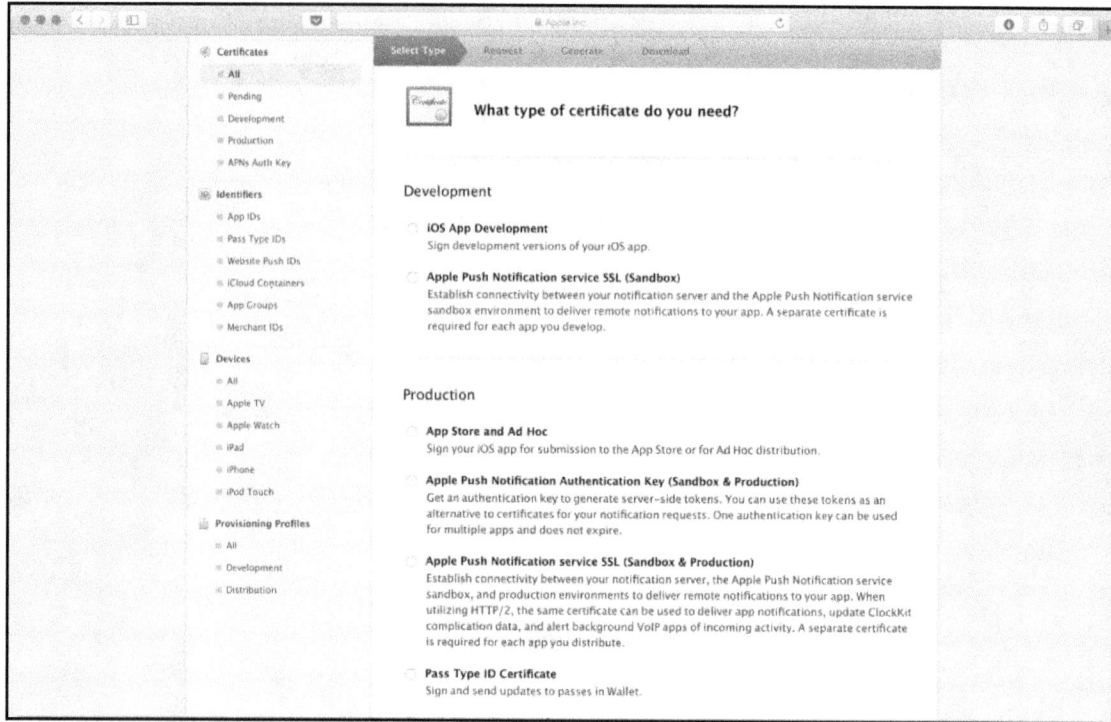

Chapter 29

5. The following screen then lists the steps required for creating a CSR file (which we have already created). Click **Continue**:

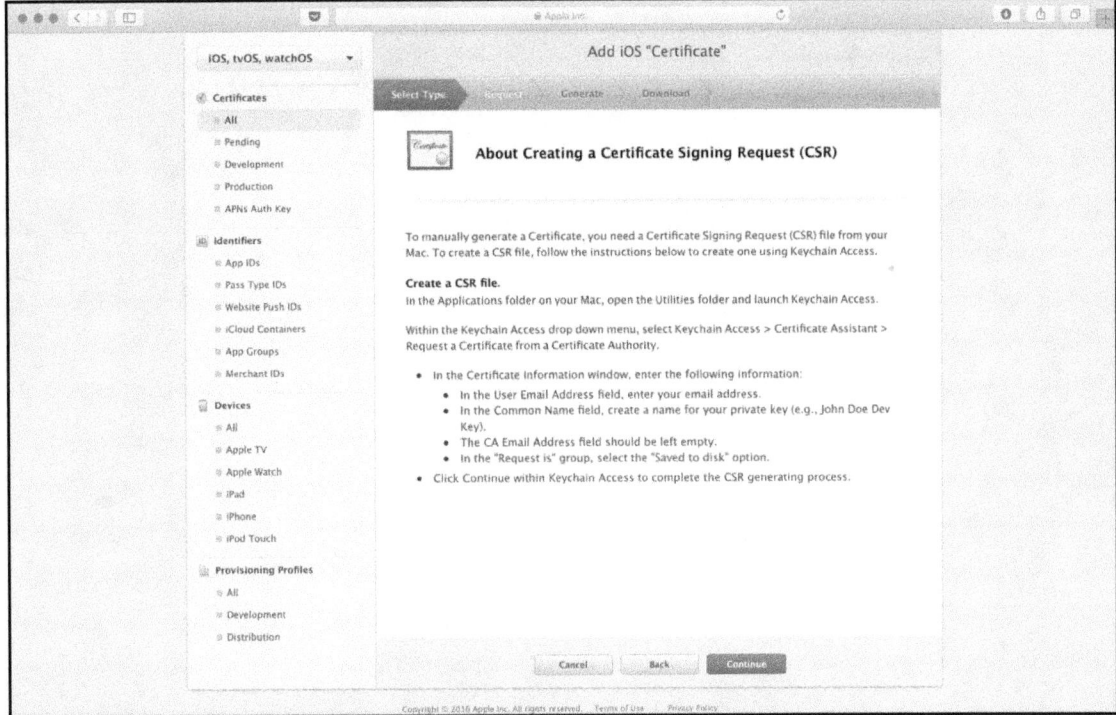

6. Upload the CSR created earlier by selecting **Choose File** under **Upload CSR file**, selecting the certificate file you saved, and clicking **Open**. Then, click **Continue**:

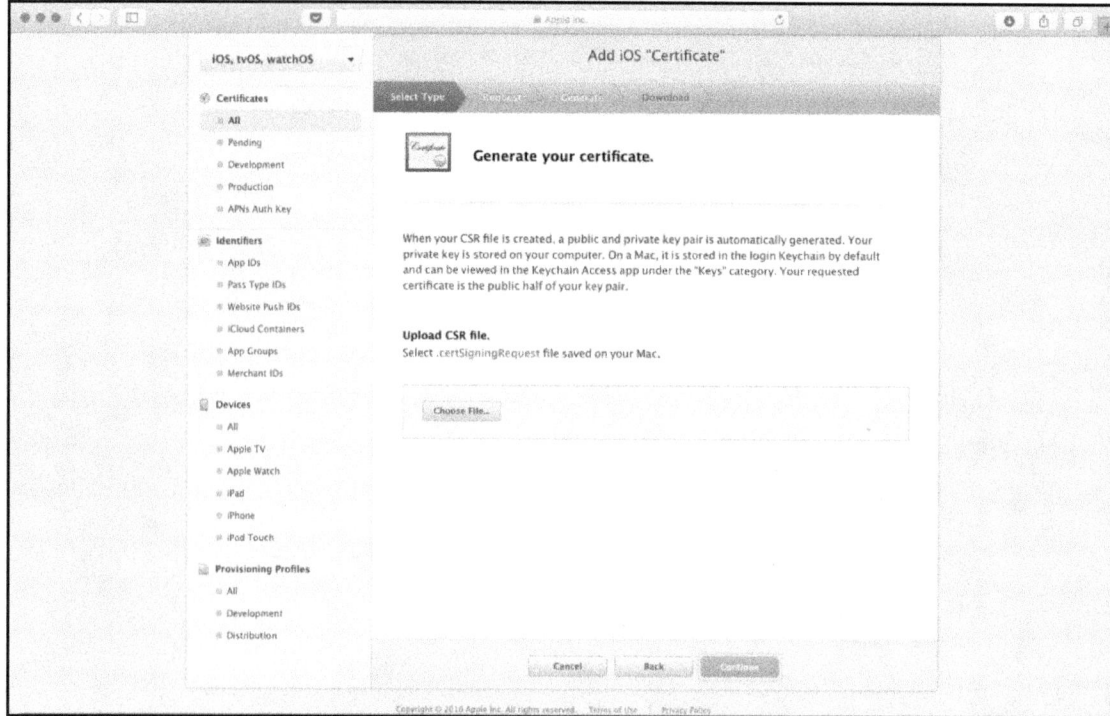

7. Next, download the certificate:

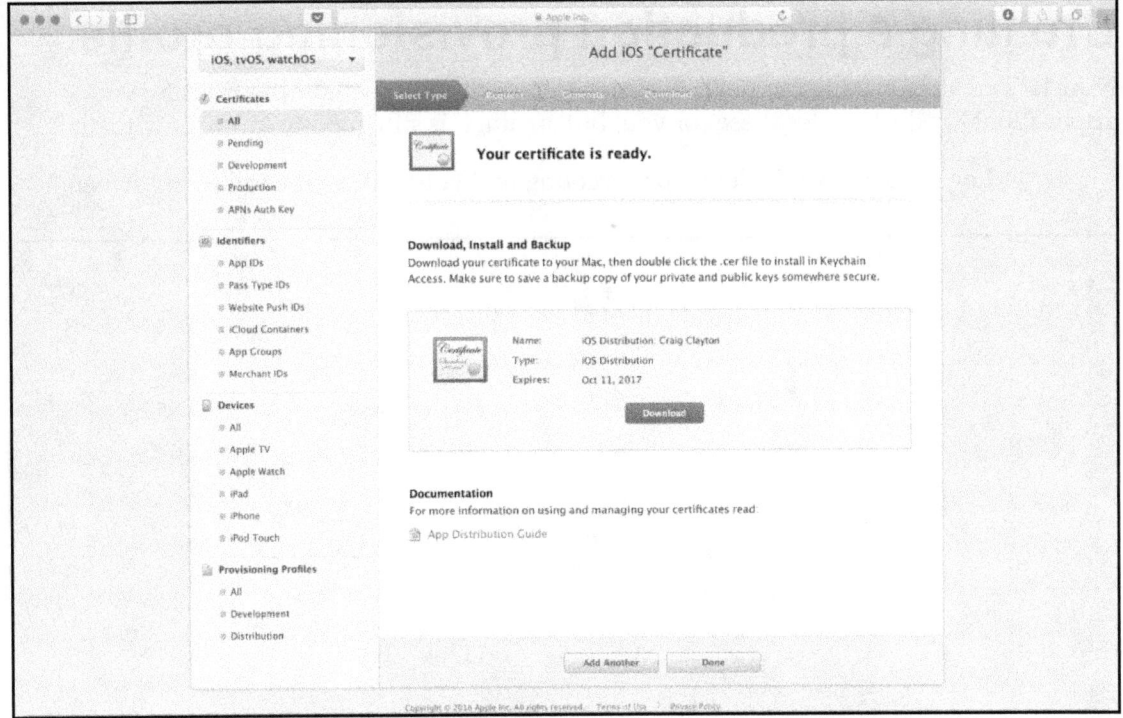

8. Then, install the downloaded certificate by double-clicking it.

For the development certificate, you will need to repeat these steps again, except in the step where you choose the type of certificate you need, instead of selecting **App Store and Ad Hoc** under **Production**, you will select **iOS App Development** under **Development**. All the other steps will be the same.

Creating a production provisioning profile

Now let's create a production provisioning profile, which is used for distributing your application. Xcode 9 creates these for you, but, again, it is still good to know how to do it:

1. Log in to the Apple developer account, and you will see the following screen:

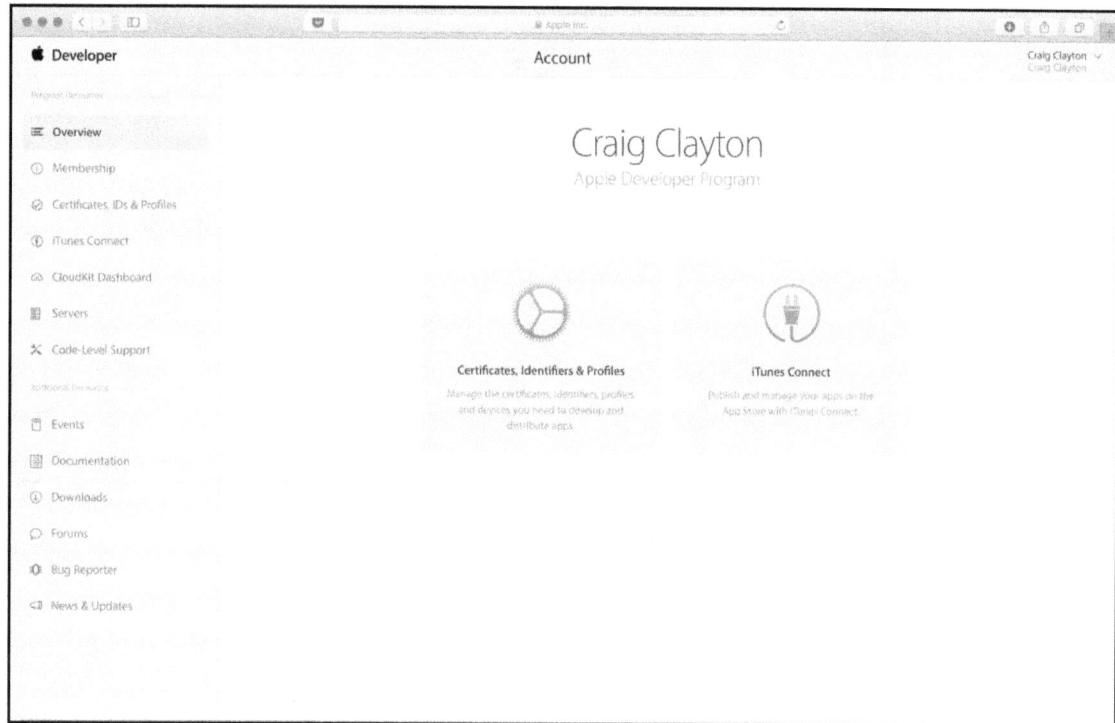

2. Click **Certificates, Identifiers & Profiles**, and under **Provisioning Profiles**, select **All**.
3. Click on the + button at the top-right of the screen:

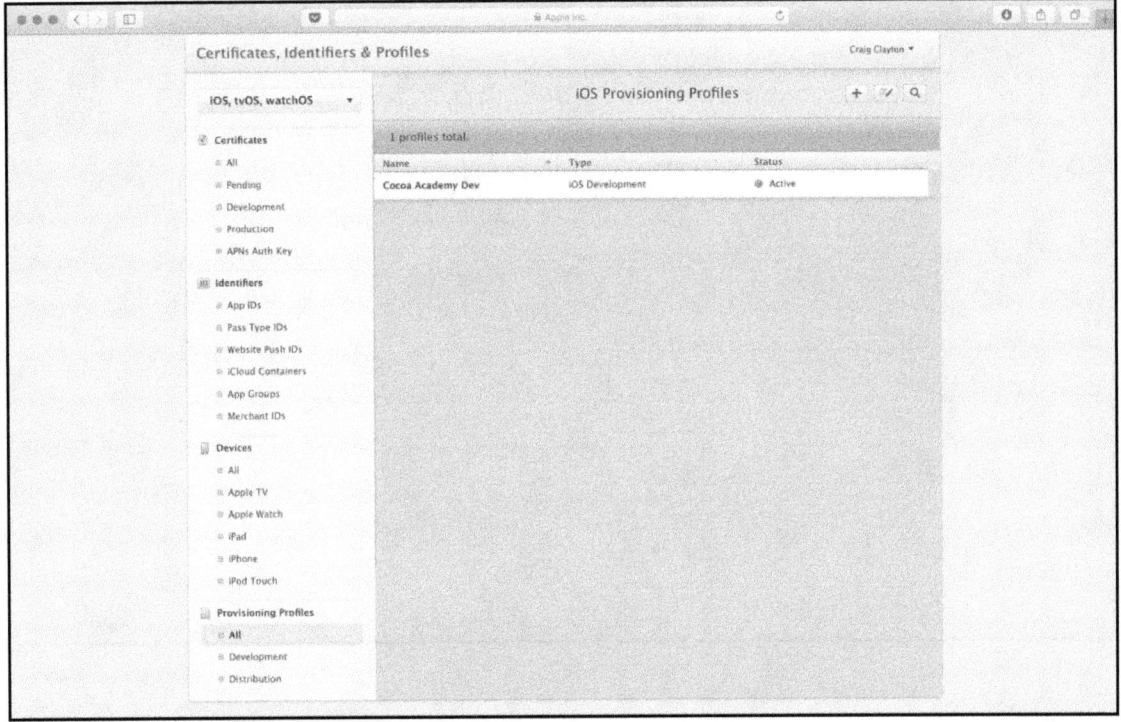

4. Select **App Store** under **Distribution** and then click **Continue**:

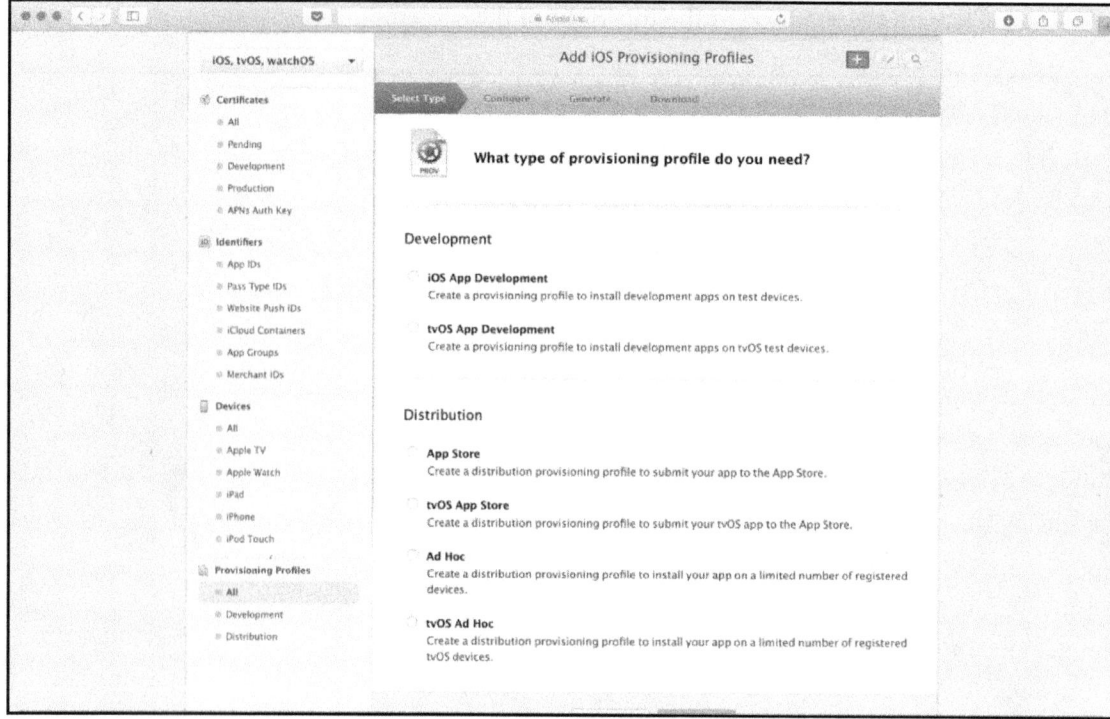

Chapter 29

5. Select the **Bundle ID** created earlier and then click **Continue**:

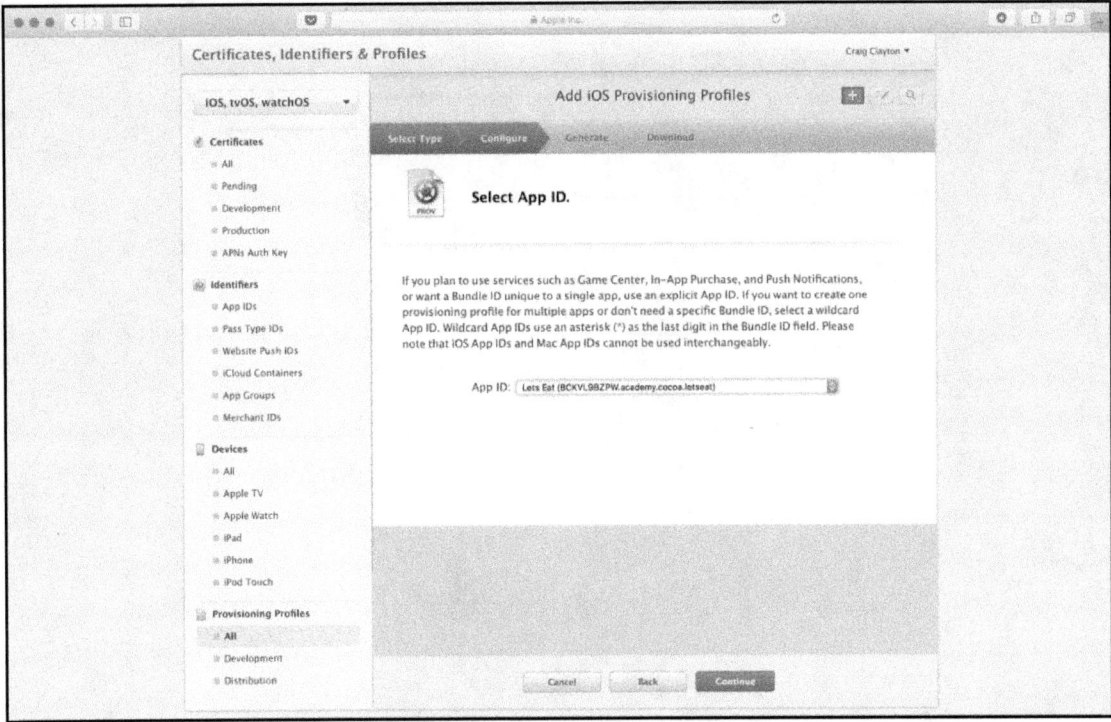

Beta and Store Submission

6. Next, select the certificate created earlier and then click **Continue**:

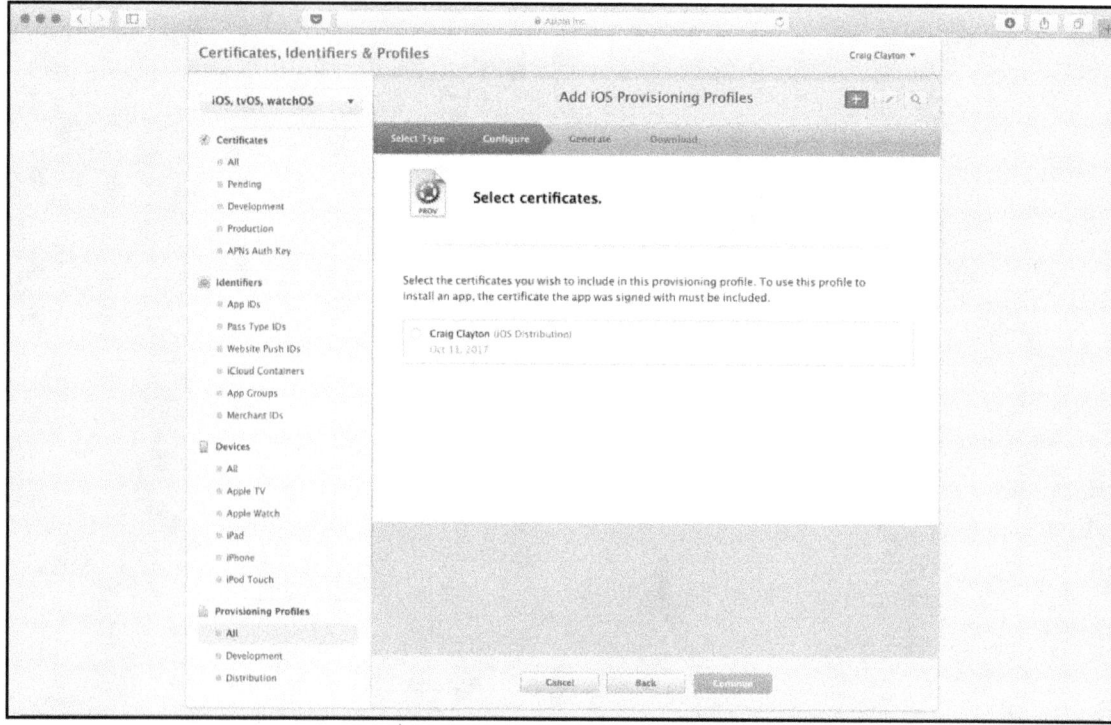

7. Next, enter the **Profile Name**, **Lets Eat Prod**, and click **Continue**:

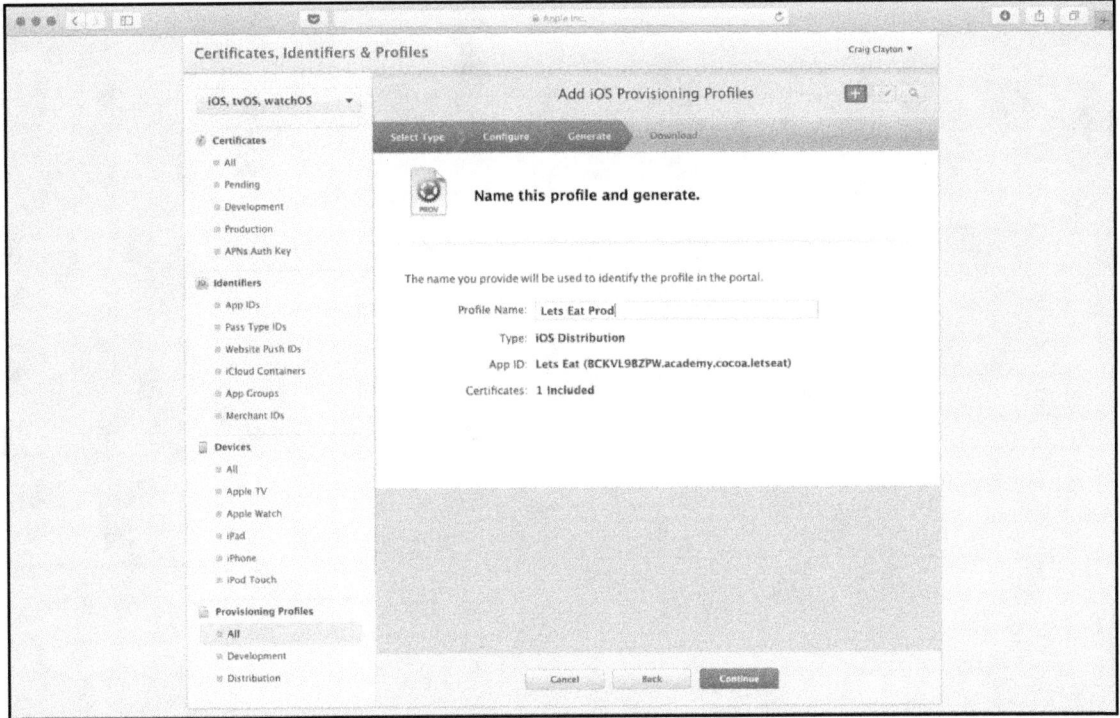

Beta and Store Submission

8. Download the certificate:

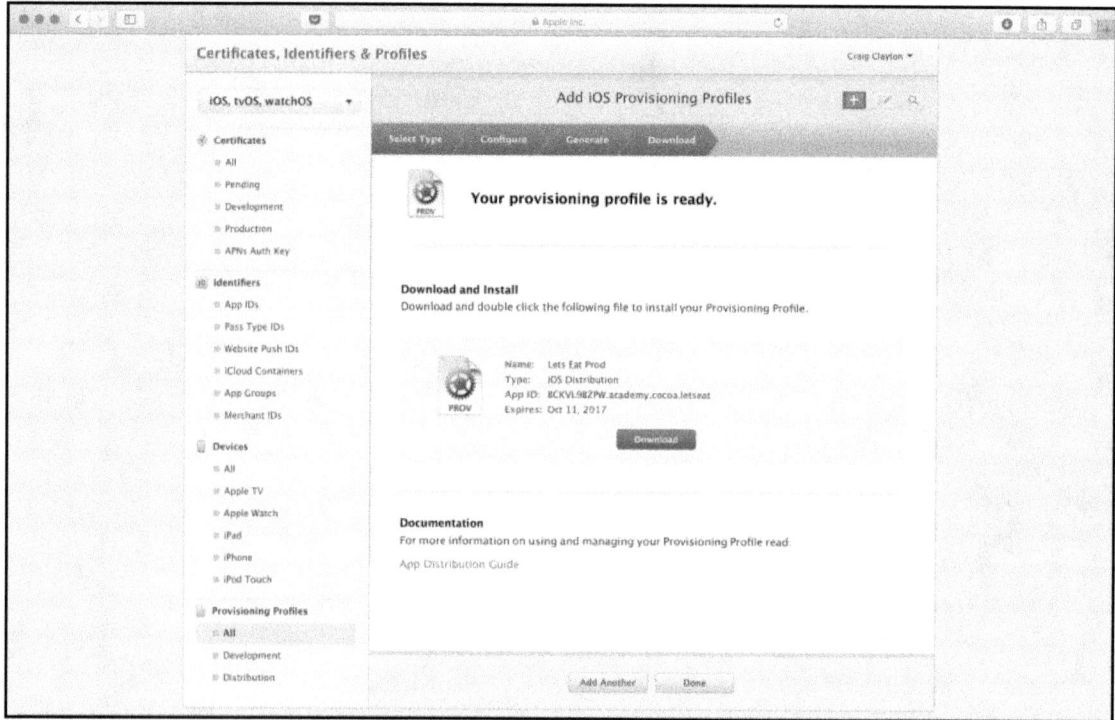

9. Install the downloaded certificate by double-clicking it.

Creating a Development Provisioning Profile

Now let's create a development provisioning profile, which is used for building apps on your device using Xcode:

1. Log in to the Apple developer account.
2. Click **Certificates, Identifiers & Profiles**.
3. Next, under **Provisioning Profiles**, click **All**.
4. Then, click on the **+** button at the top-right of the screen.
5. Next, select **App Store** under **Distribution** and then click **Continue**.
6. Select the **Bundle ID** created earlier and click **Continue**.
7. Next, select the certificate created earlier and then click **Continue**.
8. Enter the **Profile Name**, `Lets Eat Dev`, and click **Continue**:

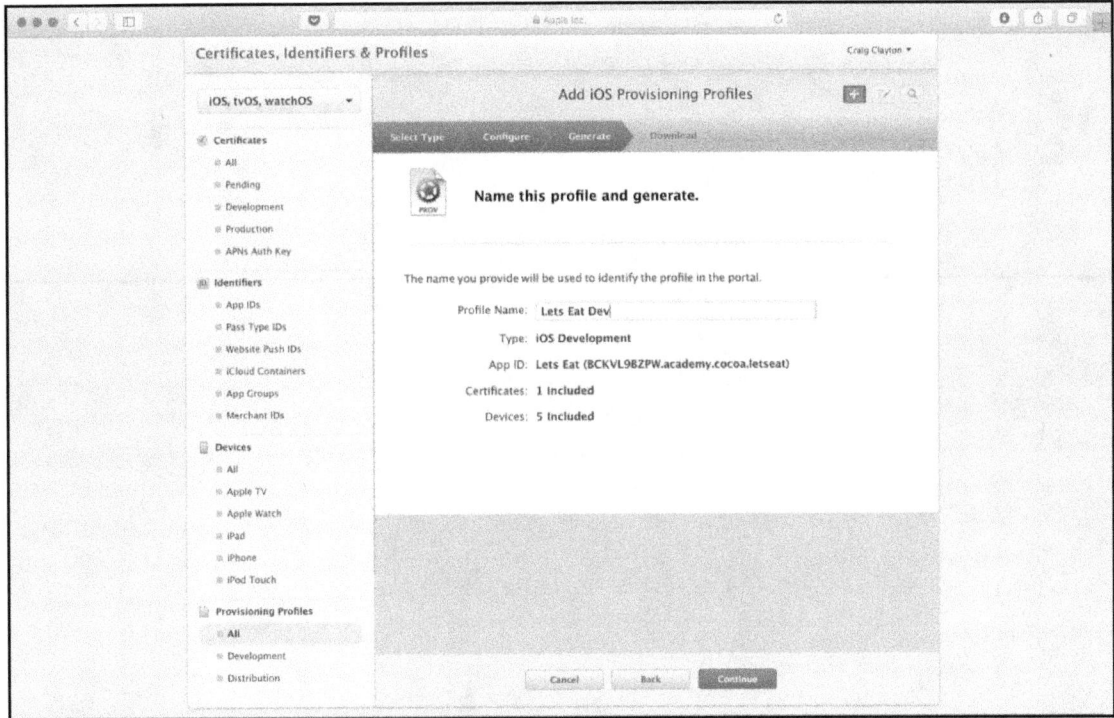

Beta and Store Submission

9. Select the devices you wish to use or choose **Select All**:

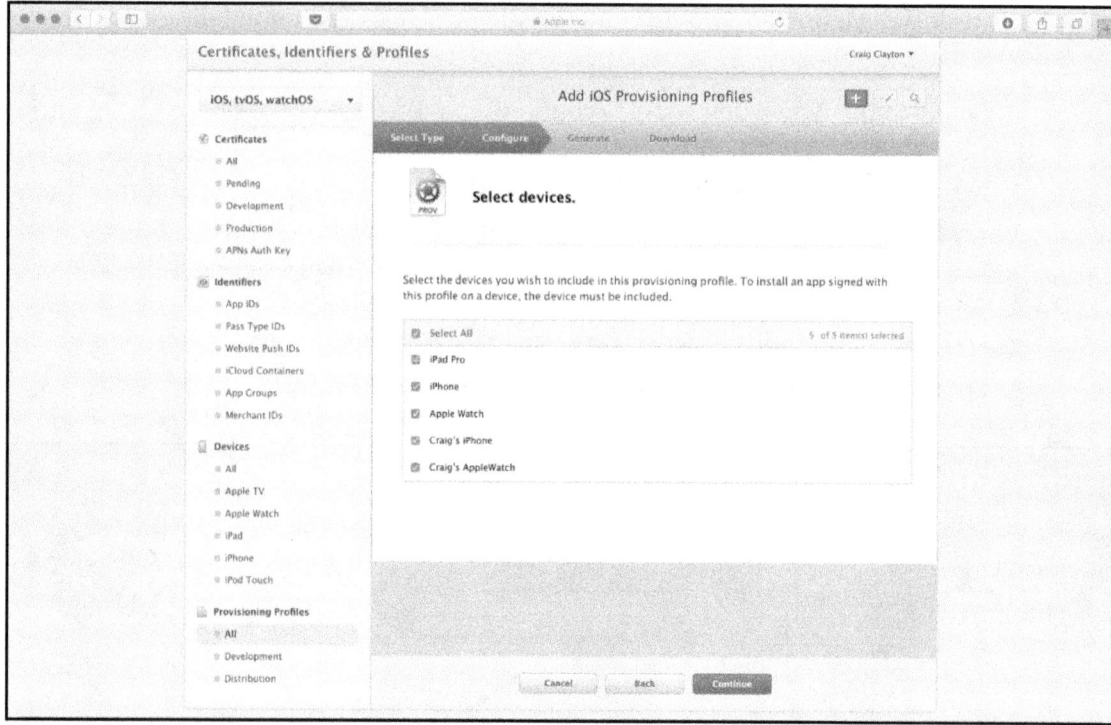

10. Download the certificate:

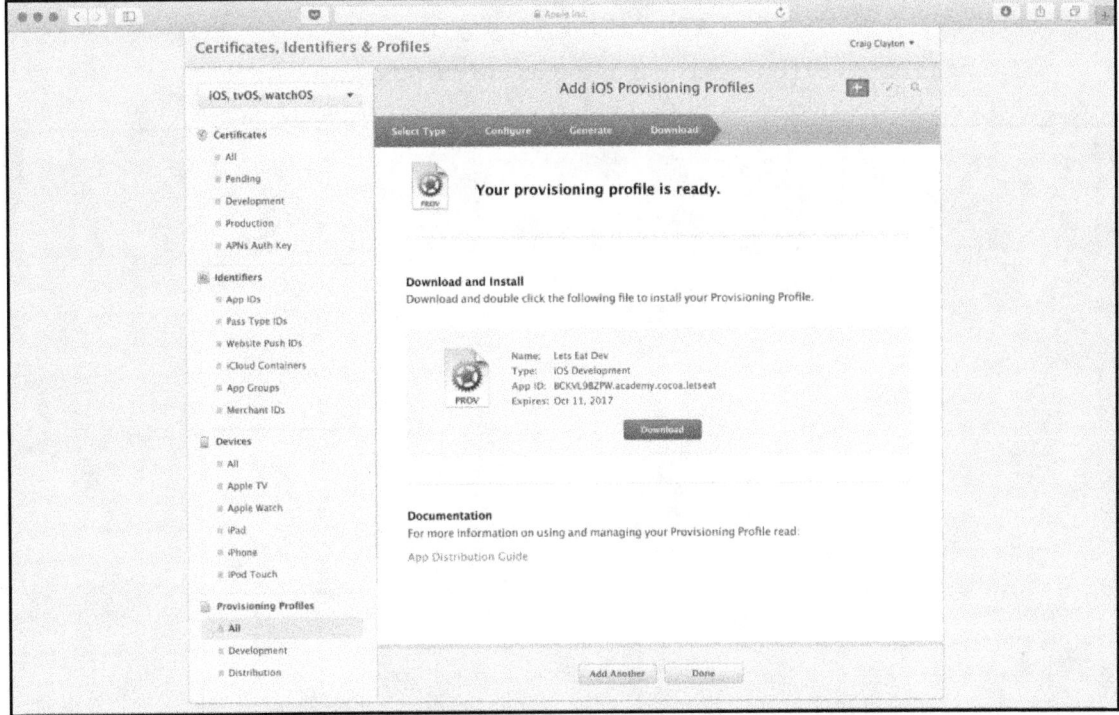

11. Install the downloaded certificate by double-clicking it.

Creating an App Store listing

Next, we are going to create the App Store listing:

1. Log in to your iTunes account and select **My Apps**:

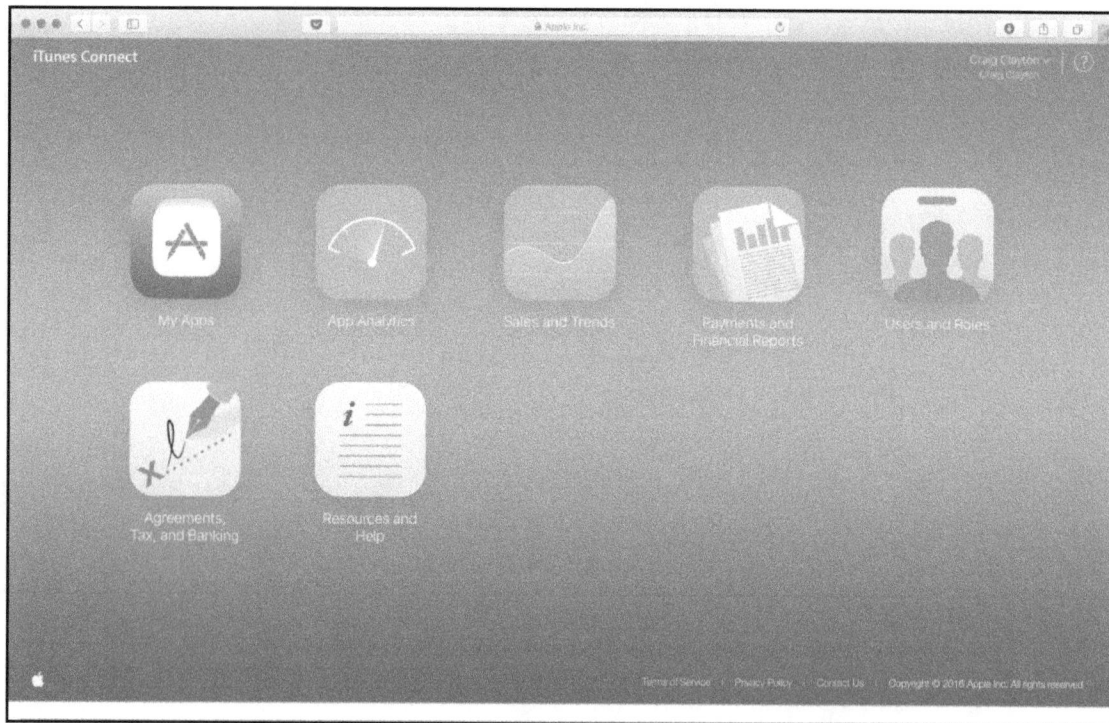

Chapter 29

2. Click on the + button at the top-left of the screen:

3. Select **New App**:

4. Enter your app details and then hit **Create**:

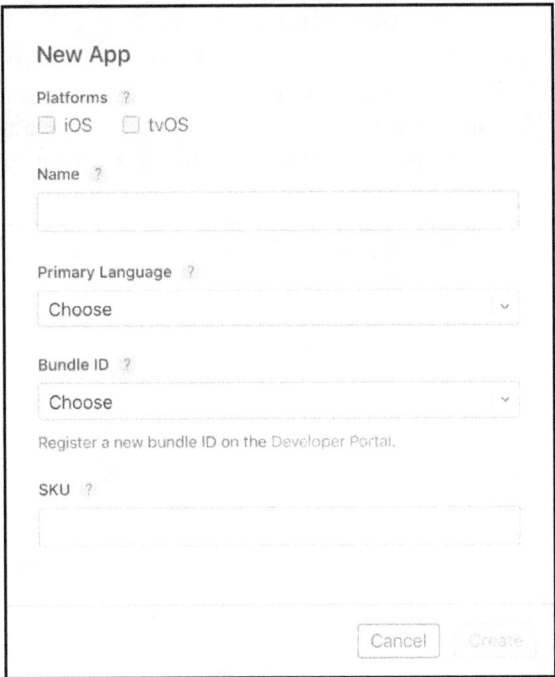

The app will now be listed in your iTunes account.

Creating an archive build

When you submit your app to the App Store, you need to create an archive. This archive will also be used for internal and external testing, which we will address shortly. When your archive is complete, you will upload it to the App Store. Let's create an archive now:

1. Open Xcode, select the project, and enter the following information:
    - Under **Identity**, update the **Version** and **Build numbers** to 1.1 and 2, respectively.
    - Under **Signing**, ensure **Automatically manage signing** is checked.

Beta and Store Submission

- Under **Signing**, select **Team**.
- For minor builds, you want to increment your **Version number** by `0.1` and your **Build number** by `1`. In some instances, developers make their **Version numbers** three digits (for example, `1.1.2`). This is all based on your business and how you want to handle **Version numbers**. If you are performing a major update, then you typically increment your **Version number** by `1`.

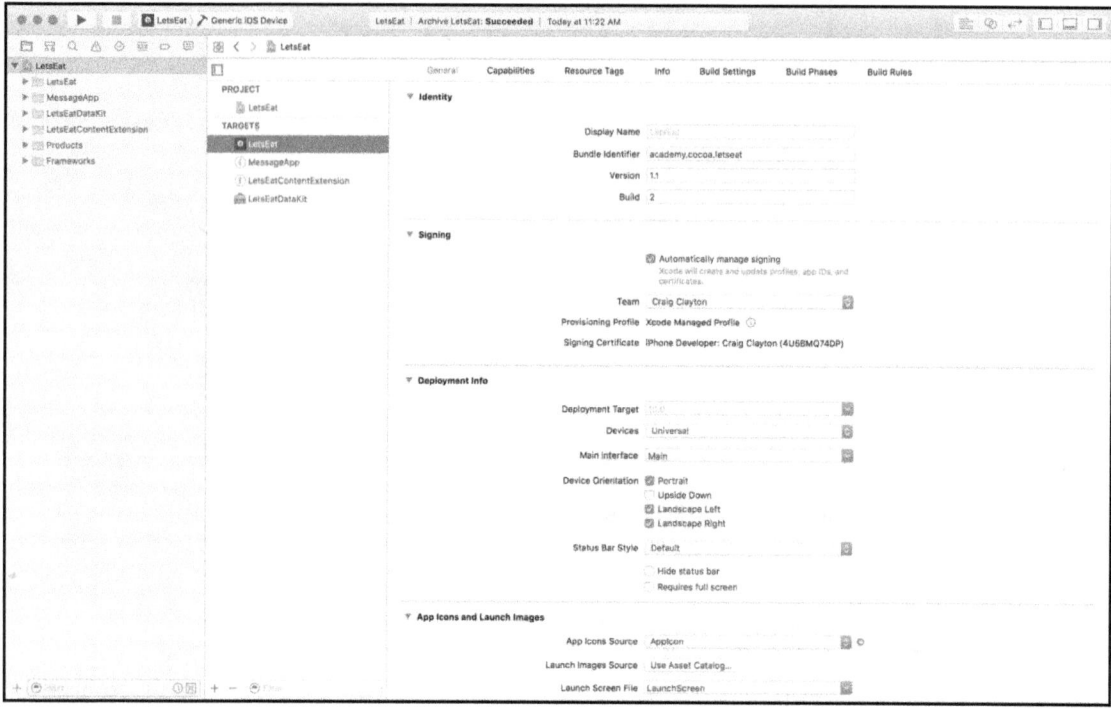

Chapter 29

2. Select **Generic iOS Device** as the build destination:

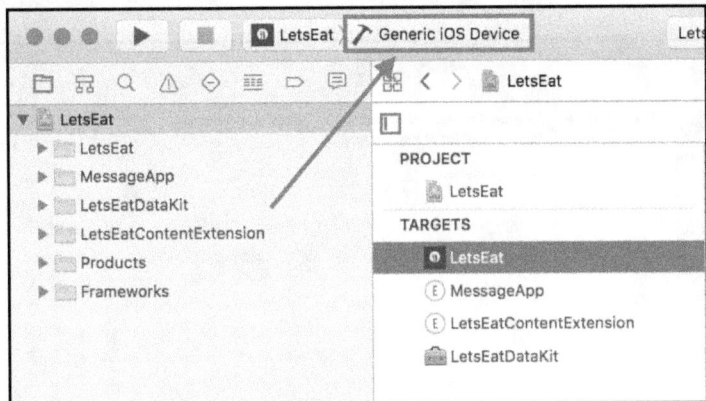

3. Update your `Info.plist` by adding `ITSAppUsesNonExemptEncryption`, making its type `Boolean`, and setting its value to `NO`. The value should be `NO` unless you are using some special encryption. Since our app does not have special encryption, we will set our value to `NO`.

4. Select **Product** | **Archive**:

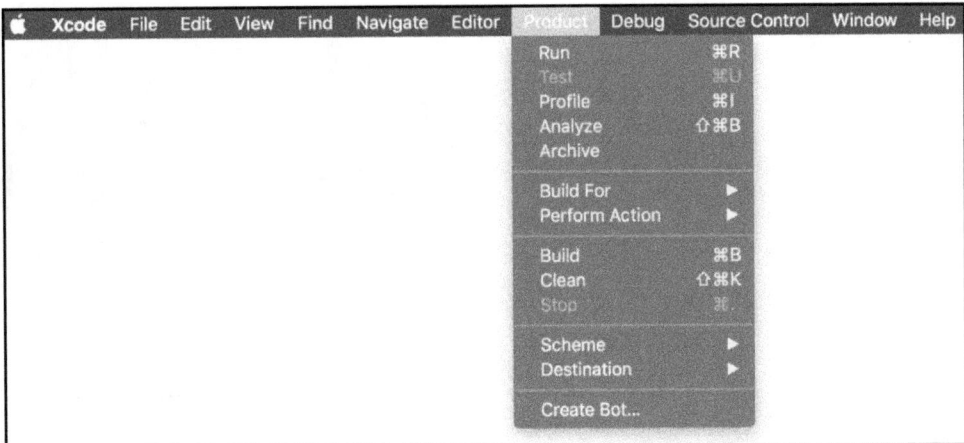

Beta and Store Submission

5. Under the **Archives** tab in the screen that appears, select your **Development Team** and then hit **Choose**:

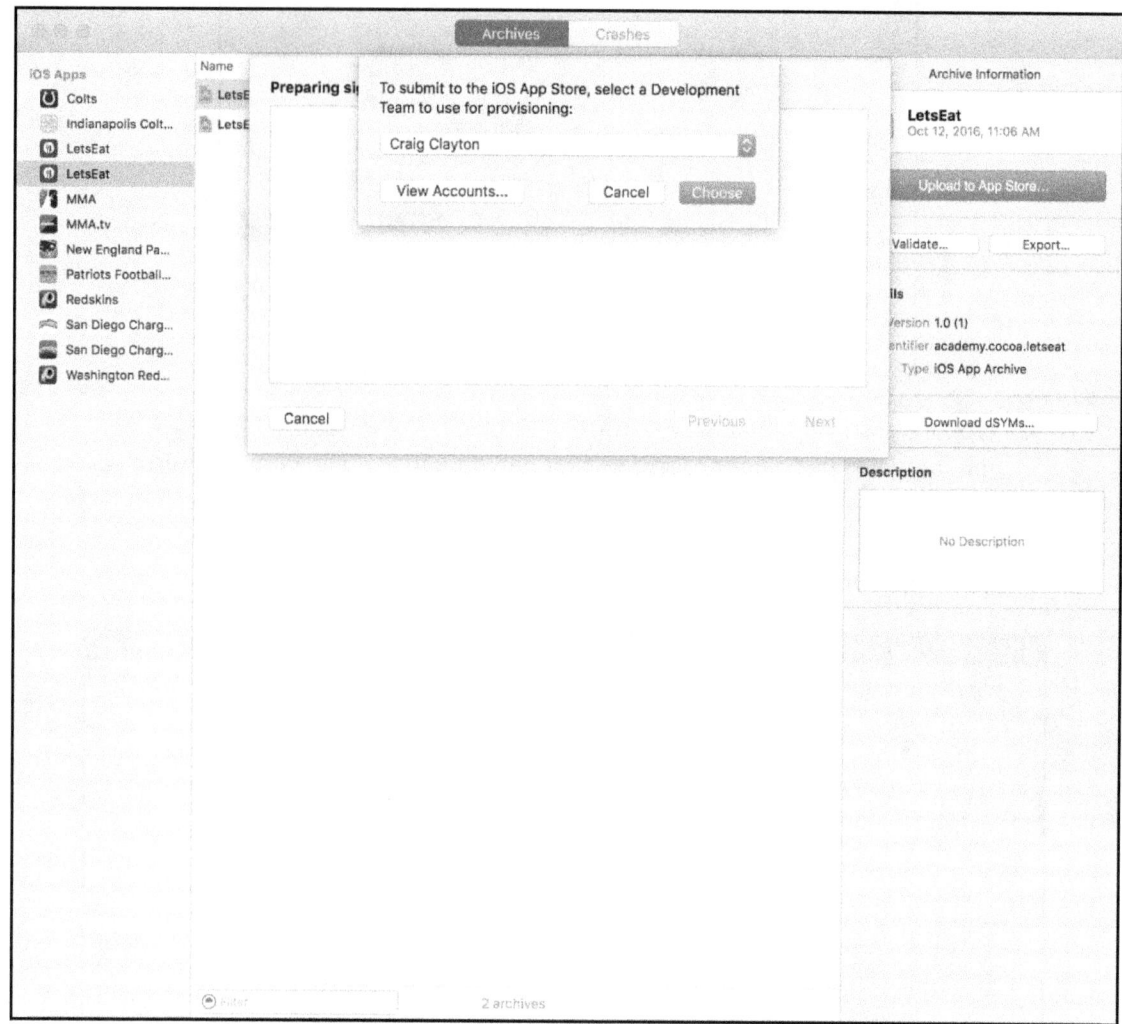

6. Your IPA file will now be created, so now click **Upload**:

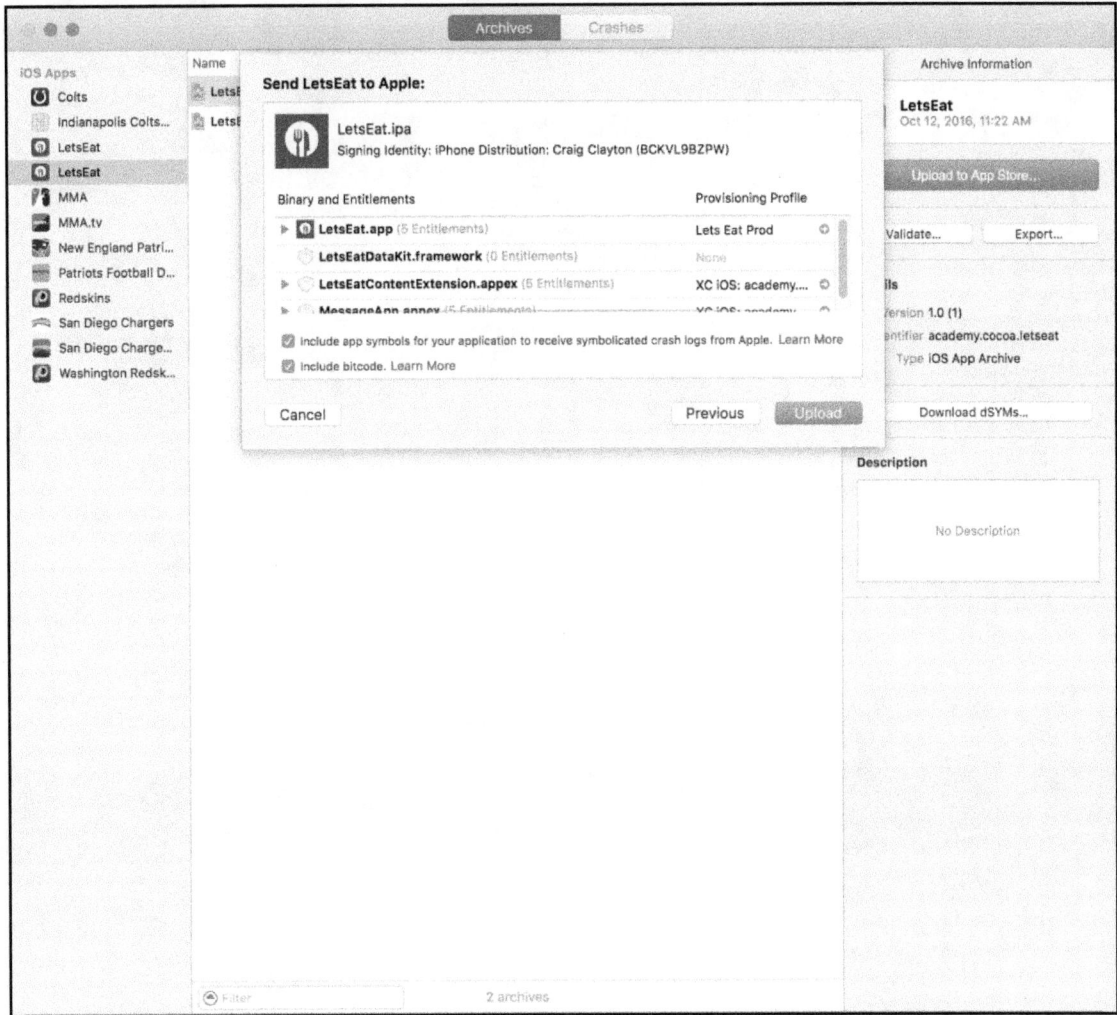

Beta and Store Submission

7. You will see uploading begin, as shown in the following screenshot:

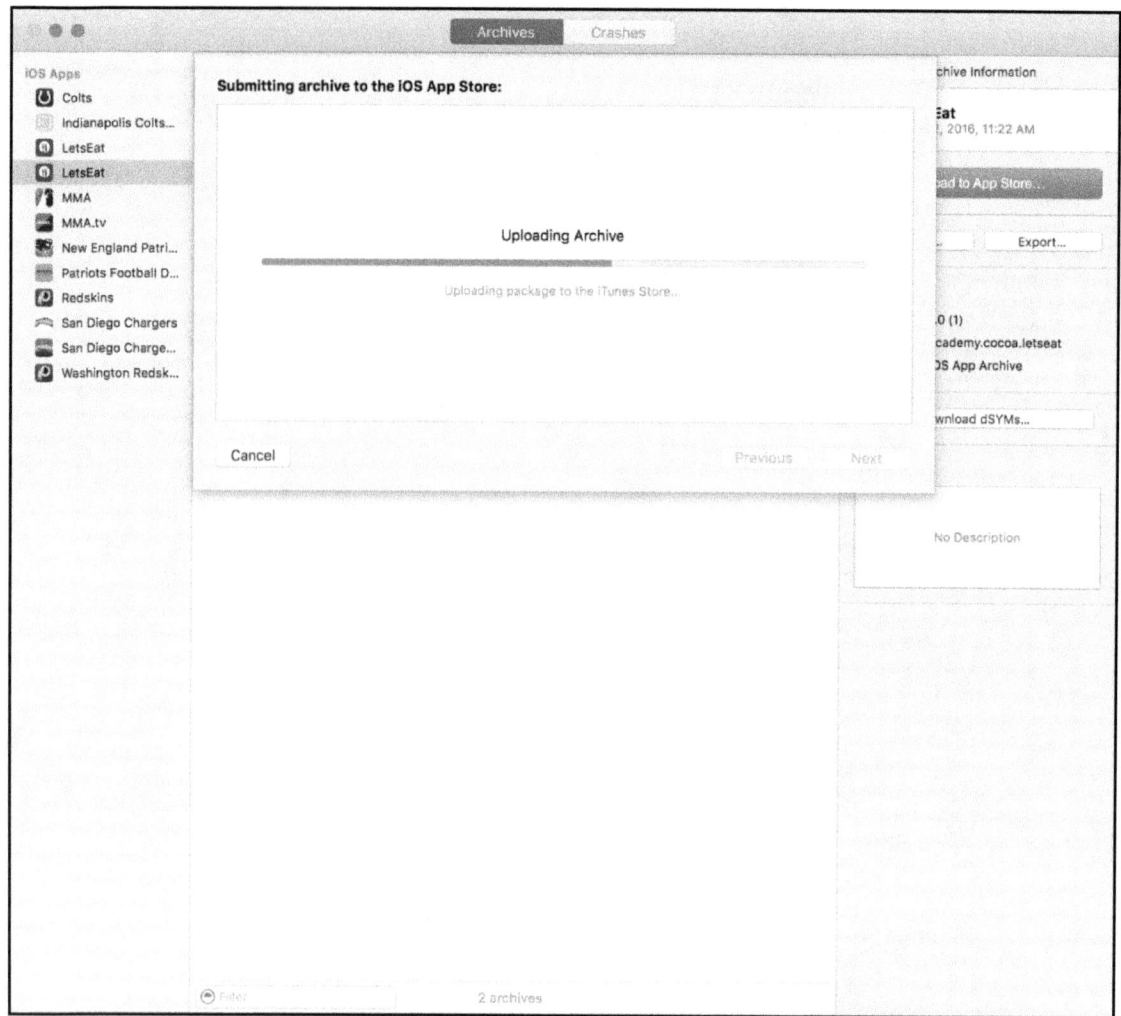

8. Then, when your upload is successful, you will see the following:

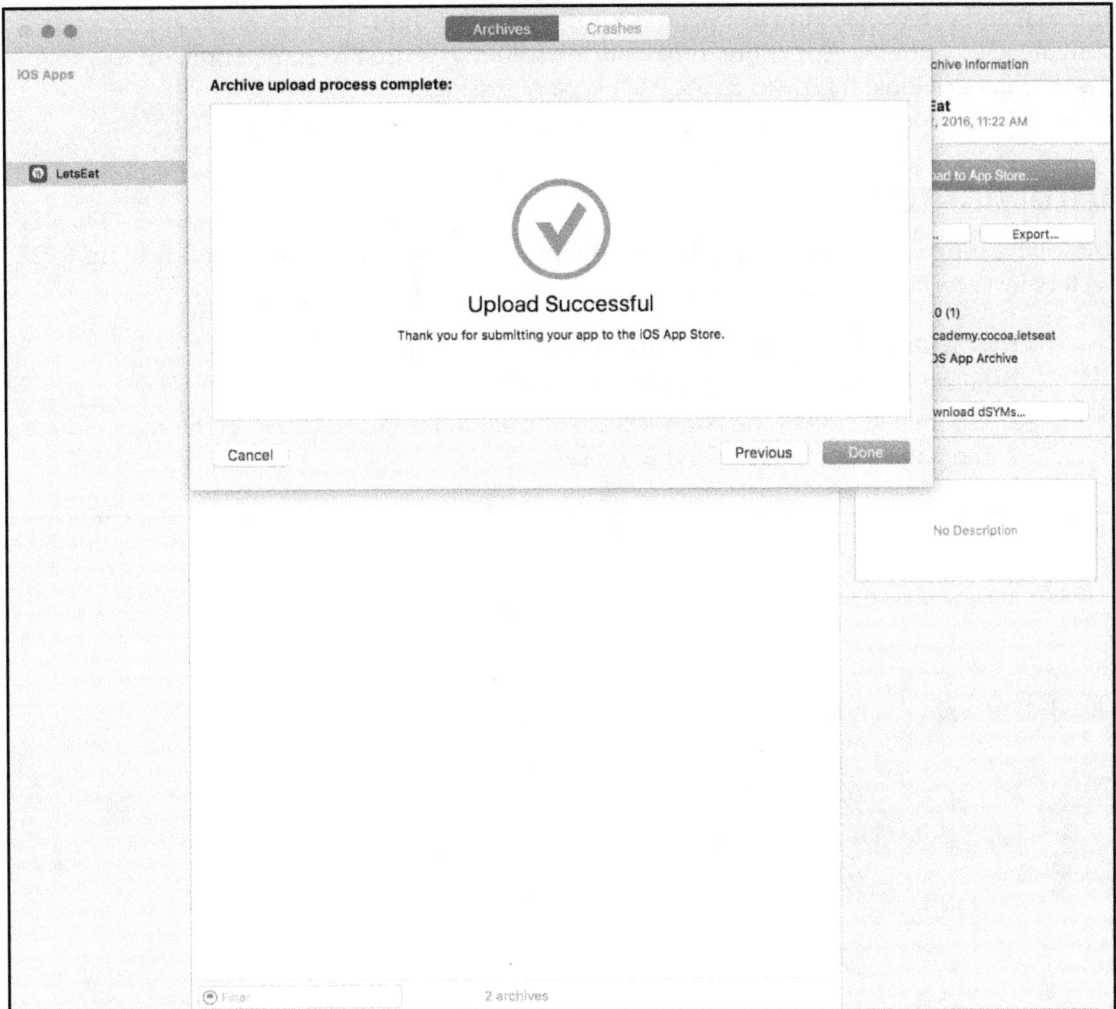

9. You will receive an email when your app is either approved or rejected. If rejected, once you fix the issues, you can resubmit it in the same manner by updating the archive and following the steps laid out previously.

Beta and Store Submission

Internal and external testing

Internal and external testing use what is known as **TestFlight**. The *TestFlight* app can be downloaded from the App Store. Email addresses are required to sign people up to *TestFlight*. Let's look at how to create each type of testing.

Internal testing

Internal testing does not go through a review process. You can only send builds to up to 25 testers for internal testing. Let's begin:

1. Log in to your iTunes Account and select **My Apps**.
2. Select your *Let's Eat* app and then *TestFlight*.
3. On the left side of the page, select **Internal Testing**, and then on the right side of the page, click **Select Version to Test**:

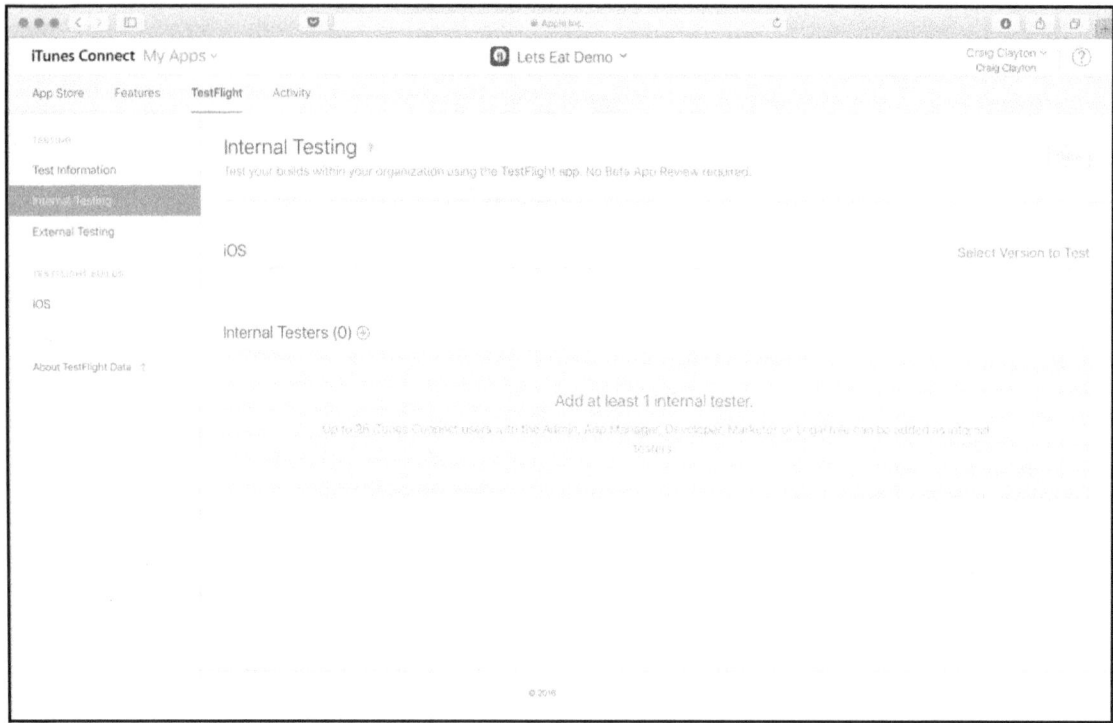

4. Then, select the version you want to test and click **OK**:

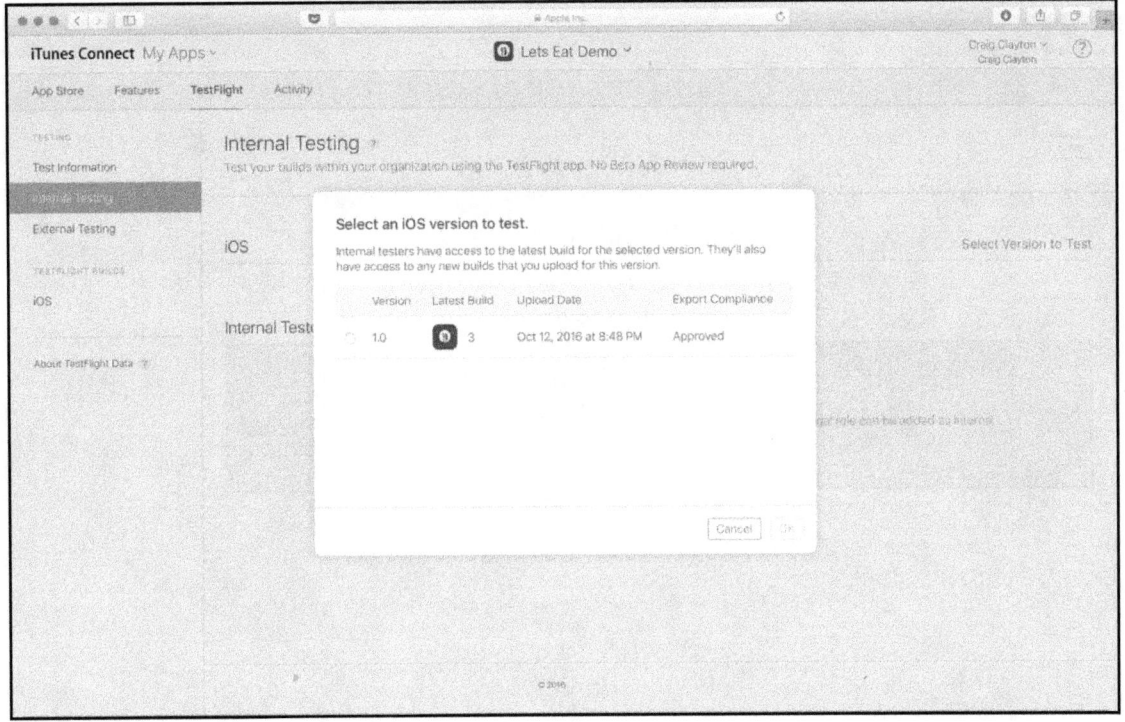

Beta and Store Submission

5. You will now see the following screen:

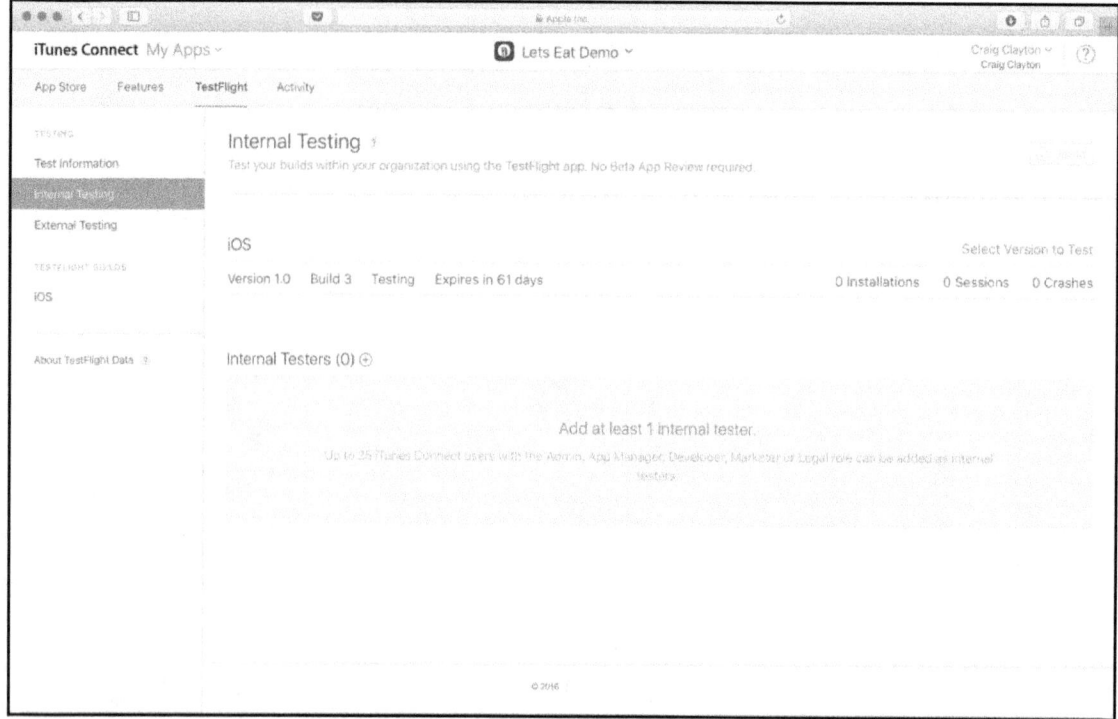

6. Finally, click the **+** button next to **Internal Testers** and add your **Internal Testers**:

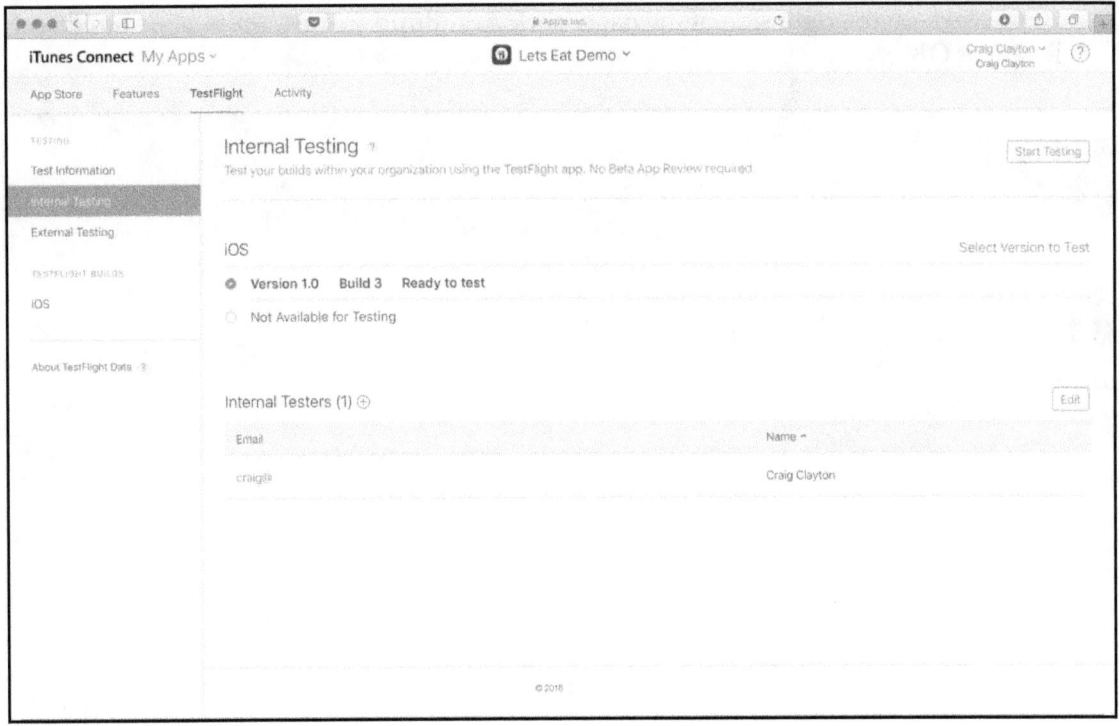

External testing

External testing may or may not go through a review process, but with external testing you can have up to 2,000 testers. For external testing, follow these steps:

1. Log in to your iTunes account and select **My Apps**.
2. Select your *Let's Eat* app and then *TestFlight*.
3. On the left side of the page select **External Testing**.

Beta and Store Submission

4. Next, on the right side of the page, click **Add Build to Test**, select your build and hit **OK**:

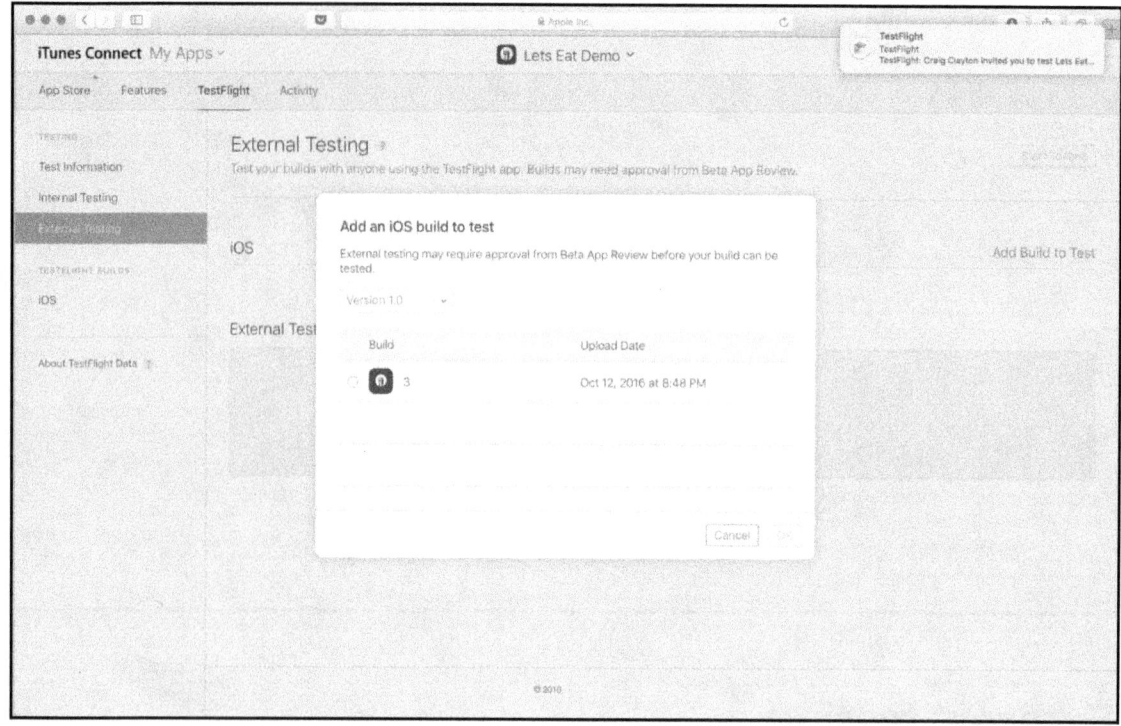

5. Finally, click the + button next to **External Testers** and add your external testers:

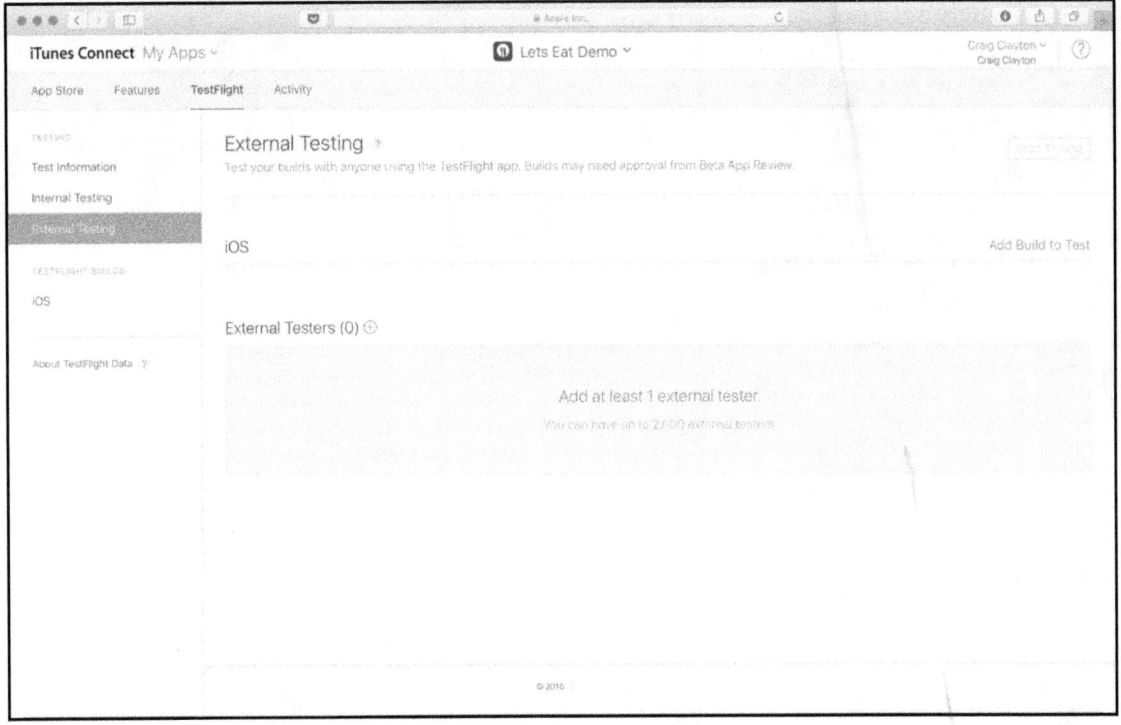

6. When you are done adding testers, click the **Start Testing** button, and you will see the following screen. You will need to complete the information requested as follows:

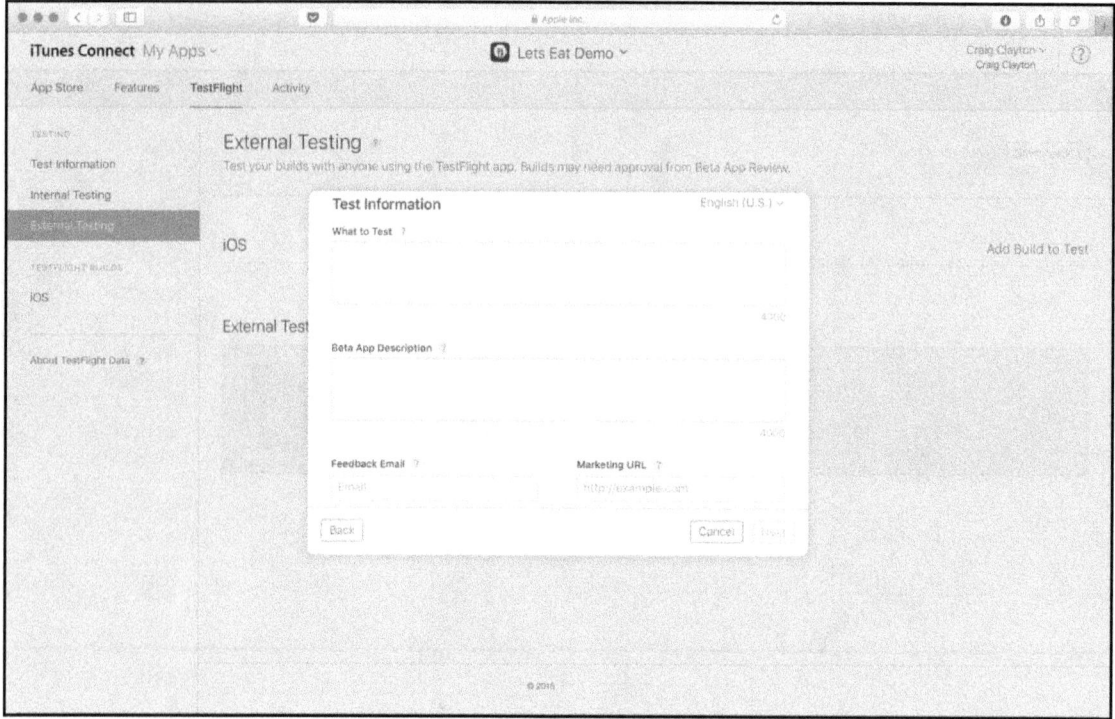

7. Next, submit your app to Apple for review; you will receive an email when it is either approved or rejected. If rejected, once you have fixed the issues, you can resubmit it in the same manner by updating the archive and following the steps laid out previously.

Summary

You have now completed the entire process of building an app and submitting it to the App Store. If you have gone from beginning to end, congratulate yourself, because it is truly a big feat.

At this point, all you can do is wait for Apple to review your project. The next week or so will be the most nerve-wracking (at least it was for me). Don't worry if your app gets rejected, because it happens to the most experienced of developers and is often fixable. Apps can be rejected for minor reasons that are easy to fix; however, you do not want to work for months on a project and miss something big that Apple will never approve. So, do your research as to what is and is not acceptable to Apple. When you submit your apps to the App Store, please reach out to me on Twitter (`@thedevme`) to let me know—I would love to see what you have built.

Other Books You May Enjoy

If you enjoyed this book, you may be interested in these other books by Packt:

Mastering Swift 4 – Fourth Edition
Jon Hoffman

ISBN:978-1-78847-780-2

- Delve into the core components of Swift 4.0, including operators, collections, control flows, and functions
- Create and use classes, structures, and enumerations
- Understand protocol-oriented design and see how it can help you write better code
- Develop a practical understanding of subscripts and extensions
- Add concurrency to your applications using Grand Central Dispatch and Operation Queues
- Implement generics and closures to write very flexible and reusable code
- Make use of Swift's error handling and availability features to write safer code

Swift 4 Programming Cookbook
Keith Moon

ISBN: 978-1-78646-089-9

- Explore basic to advanced concepts in Swift 4 Programming
- Unleash advanced features of Apple's Xcode 9 IDE and Swift Playgrounds
- Learn about the conditional statements, loops, and how to handle errors in Swift
- Define flexible classes and structs using Generics, and learn about the advanced operators, and create custom operators
- Explore functionalities outside of the standard libraries of Swift
- Import your own custom functionality into Swift Playgrounds
- Run Swift on Linux and investigate server-side programming with the server side framework Vapor

Leave a review - let other readers know what you think

Please share your thoughts on this book with others by leaving a review on the site that you bought it from. If you purchased the book from Amazon, please leave us an honest review on this book's Amazon page. This is vital so that other potential readers can see and use your unbiased opinion to make purchasing decisions, we can understand what our customers think about our products, and our authors can see your feedback on the title that they have worked with Packt to create. It will only take a few minutes of your time, but is valuable to other potential customers, our authors, and Packt. Thank you!

Index

3
3D Touch quick actions
  adding 673, 674, 675, 676, 677, 678, 679, 680, 681, 682, 684, 685
  dynamic 674
  static 674

A
address section
  creating 277, 278
annotations
  adding 419
  creating 419
API 454
API Manager file
  exploring 456, 457
API Manager
  creating 454
App Store listing
  creating 766, 767, 769
Apple
  supported intents 715
apply filter view controller
  creating 542, 543, 544, 546, 549
apps
  drag, accepting from 701, 702, 703, 705, 706
archive build
  creating 769, 771, 772, 773, 774, 775
array
  about 93, 94
  creating, with initial values 95
  element count, checking 101
  empty array, checking 102, 103
  empty array, creating 94
  items, adding 96, 97, 99
  items, removing 108, 110
  iterating 107
  mutable array, creating 95
  value, retrieving 103, 106
auto layout 147
Auto Layout
  adding, for Photo Filter View 313
  adding, to cell 585, 586
  adding, to Explore cell 260, 261
  adding, to Explore header 256, 258
  adding, to headers 279
  adding, to Photo Filter cell 315
  adding, to photos section 283, 284
  adding, to Restaurant cell 265, 266, 267
  adding, to Review cells 294, 295, 296, 297, 298

B
basic notifications 646
Boolean
  about 35
  creating 40
bugs
  detecting 37
bundle identifier
  creating 739, 740, 741, 742, 743, 744, 745
buttons
  adding, to notifications 662, 663, 664

C
cell UI
  setting up 584
cell
  connecting to 371
  setting up 211, 272
certificate signing request (CSR)
  creating 746, 747, 748, 749
classes 343

closed Range 77, 78, 79
code
  organizing 438, 439
Collection View cells
  about 352, 353, 354
  data, obtaining 355
Collection View Controller
  about 143, 352, 353, 354
  adding 196, 197, 198, 199
  cell, setting up 209, 210
  outlets, hooking up 199, 200, 201, 202, 204, 205
comments 42
comparison operators 48
constants
  about 36
  versus variables 42
control flow
  about 80
  for...in loop 81, 82, 83, 84
  repeat...while loop 89, 90
  while loop 86, 87, 88
controllers
  about 343
  Collection View cells 352, 353, 354
  Collection View controllers 352, 353, 354
  creating 344, 345, 346, 347, 348, 349, 350, 351
  data source 356, 358
  data, obtaining into Collection View 355
Core Data 555, 556
Core Data manager
  updating 692, 693, 694, 696, 697, 698, 699
custom annotations
  creating 424, 427
custom color
  creating 205, 206, 207, 208
custom initializer 363
custom UI
  adding, to notifications 665, 666, 667, 668, 669, 670

D

data manager
  working with 400, 401

data model
  creating 557, 558, 559, 560, 562
data source
  adding, to Table View 387, 389, 390, 391
data types
  about 33
  Booleans 35
  floating-point numbers 35
  integers 34
  strings 33
data
  adding, to property list 395, 396, 397, 398
  displaying, in static Table View 505, 506, 508
  obtaining 368, 369, 370
  passing, to restaurant detail 433, 434
Debug panel 37
decrement operation 47
delegate
  adding, to Table View 387, 389, 390, 391
development certificate
  about 750
  creating 755
development provisioning profile
  creating 763, 764, 765
dictionary
  about 112
  creating 112, 114
  elements, adding 114, 117
  elements, updating 115, 116
  item, accessing 118
  items count, checking 122
  items, removing 124, 125
  keys, iterating over 120, 121
  values, iterating over 119, 121
drag
  accepting, from apps 701, 702, 703, 706
  accepting, from user 705
DRY (don't repeat yourself) 415

E

empty array
  checking 102, 103
  creating 94
Explore 591, 592, 593, 595, 596, 597, 599
Explore cell

Auto Layout, adding to 260, 261
Explore Collection View cell
  setting up 258, 259, 260
Explore header
  Auto Layout, adding to 256, 258
  setting up 251, 252, 253, 254, 255, 256
Explore tab
  storyboard, creating for 327, 328, 329, 330, 331, 332, 333
ExploreData.plist 361
ExploreDataManager.swift 364, 365, 366, 367, 368
ExploreDataManager
  refactoring 418
ExploreItem.swift 362, 363, 364
ExploreViewController
  refactoring 439, 440, 441
extension 363
external testing 779, 782

F

favorites
  adding 686
  model object, creating 687, 688, 689, 690, 691
files
  creating 159, 160
filter cell
  creating 539, 541
filter items
  dragging 706, 707, 710, 711
  dropping 707, 710, 712
filter scroller
  creating 535, 536, 537, 539
filters 531, 533, 535
floating-point numbers
  about 35
  adding 38
folders
  creating 401, 402, 403, 404, 405
food reviews
  about 511
  rating control setup 523
  ratings, displaying in custom UIControl 513, 514, 515, 518
  review form controller creation 524, 526, 529

touch events, adding 519
unwind segues setup 522
for...in loop 81, 82, 83, 84
functions
  about 64
  example 64, 65, 66, 67, 69, 70, 71, 72

G

grid
  updating 215, 216

H

half-closed Range 79, 80
headers
  Auto Layout, adding to 279
Hungarian notation 41

I

IBOutlets
  UI elements, hooking up 372, 373, 374, 375
  UI, hooking with 372
if statements 51, 52, 53, 54, 55, 56, 57
iMessages
  about 612
  assets, updating 617
  crashing 637, 639
  extension, creating 613, 614, 615, 616
  framework, creating 623, 624, 625, 626, 627, 628, 629
  message cell, connecting 631, 632
  reservations, sending 640, 642
  restaurants, displaying 633, 634, 636
increment operation 47
inheritance 340
integers
  about 34
  variables, creating with 37
Integrated Development Environment (IDE) 7
internal testing 776, 777
items
  accessing, in dictionary 118
  adding, to array 96
  array, adding 97, 100
  count, checking 122

removing, from array 108, 110
removing, from dictionary 124, 125
removing, from set 137

J
JSON file 454, 455

L
let constant 39
Let's Eat app
  about 148
  creating 154, 157
  Explore tab 148
  Locations view 150
  Map tab 153
  Restaurant detail 152
  Restaurant listings 150
  setup 154
local sessions 702
location cell 268
location data manager
  creating 399
location list
  about 458
  Done button, unwinding 463, 464, 465
  Header view, adding 460
  last selected location, obtaining 466, 467, 468
  selected location, passing to Explore View 461, 462
location listing 600
Location View Controller class
  creating 383, 384
Location View Controller
  Table View, connecting with 384, 385, 386
location
  adding, to Table View 392, 393
  setting 458, 459

M
managed object context (moc) 570
managed object model
  about 556
  Core Data manager 568
  creating 557, 558, 559, 560, 562

entity auto-generation 564
  item review 566
  Restaurant Photo Entity 565
map annotations
  base class, creating 415, 416
  code, refactoring 417
  Map Data Manager, creating 413
  MKAnnotation 407, 408
  restaurant annotation 408, 409, 410, 411, 412
  setting up 407
Map Data Manager
  creating 413
Map Kit View 244, 245, 246, 247, 248
Map tab
  storyboard, creating for 325
map to restaurant detail
  about 428, 432, 433
  storyboard reference, creating 429, 430, 431
Map View Controller
  creating 419, 421, 423
MapViewController
  refactoring 447, 448, 449, 450, 451
MARK comment
  using 442, 443
Messages UI
  Auto Layout, adding to cell 622
  implementing 618, 619, 620, 621
MKAnnotation 407, 408
modal
  adding 217, 218, 220, 221, 222, 223
  Bar Button Items, updating 225
  Cancel button, unwinding 226
  first Table View, adding 227
Model View Controller (MVC)
  about 142, 147
  architecture 335
  classes 337, 338, 340, 341, 342
  Controller camp 336
  Model camp 336
  setting up 337
  structures 337, 338, 340, 341, 342
  View camp 336
model
  about 360, 361
  ExploreData.plist 361

ExploreDataManager.swift 364, 365, 366, 367, 368
ExploreItem.swift 362, 363, 364
mutable array
  creating 95

N

navigation button
  adding 499, 500, 501, 502, 503, 504
Navigation Controller 144
no data
  handling 482
non-local sessions 702
notifications
  buttons, adding 662, 663, 664
  custom UI, adding to 665, 666, 667, 668, 669, 670
  customizing 656
  displaying 653, 654, 655, 656
  images, embedding 656, 657, 658, 659, 660, 661
  permission, obtaining 646
  setting up 648, 650, 651, 652

O

one-sided Range operator 85
operations, integers
  about 45
  comparison operators 48
  decrement 47
  increment 47
optional binding 62
optionals
  about 58
  adding, to Playgrounds 59, 60, 61, 62
  need for 63
overall rating
  adding 587, 588

P

permission
  obtaining 550, 551
persistent store coordinator 556
Photo Filter cell
  Auto Layout, adding to 315
Photo Filter View cell
  creating 314, 315
Photo Filter View
  adding 309, 310, 311, 312
  Auto Layout, adding for 313
photos section
  about 280, 282
  Auto Layout, adding to 283, 284
photos
  saving 578, 579, 580, 583
Playground project
  creating 50, 76, 77
Playgrounds 30, 31, 32, 33
print() 37
production certificate
  about 750
  creating 750, 751, 752, 753, 754
production provisioning profile
  creating 756, 757, 758, 759, 760, 762
property list (plist)
  creating 394, 395
  data, adding to 395, 396, 397, 398

R

Ranges
  about 77
  closed Range 77, 78, 79
  half-closed Range 79, 80
repeat...while loop 89, 90
restaurant annotation
  creating 408, 409, 410, 411, 412
restaurant cell class
  creating 474, 475
Restaurant cell
  Auto Layout, adding to 265, 266, 267
  setting up 261, 262, 263, 264, 265
restaurant data manager
  creating 478, 479
restaurant detail
  data, passing to 433, 434
  updating 608, 609
restaurant list cell outlets
  setting up 475, 476, 477
Restaurant List View

adding 230
cell, setting up 231, 232, 233, 234, 235, 236, 237
outlets, hooking up 230, 231
restaurant list
  location, passing to 470, 471
restaurant listing 377, 378, 379, 380, 601, 602, 603, 604, 605, 606
RestaurantDetailViewController
  setting up 491, 492, 494, 495, 496, 497, 498
RestaurantViewController
  refactoring 443
Review cells
  Auto Layout, adding to 294, 295, 296, 297, 298
Review storyboard
  setting up 316
reviews section 288, 289, 290, 291
Reviews section
  about 285, 286, 287
  reservation header 302, 303
  reservation information 299, 300
  reservation times cells, updating 298, 299
Reviews View
  adding 240
  reviews, viewing 241, 242
reviews
  creating 316
  saving 575, 576, 577

S

section headers
  about 211, 212, 213, 214
  creating 273, 274, 275, 276
segue 147
sets
  about 126
  checking, for item content 130
  creating, with array literal 127
  empty set, creating 127
  intersecting 134
  items, adding 128
  items, removing 137
  iterating over 131
  joining 136
  mutable set, creating 128

Siri
  about 714
  capabilities, enabling 716, 718, 720, 721, 723
  intent handler, updating 726
  testing 728, 730, 732, 734
  users, creating 725, 726
static Table View
  Auto Layout, adding for reviews creation 322
  cell, updating 319
  data, displaying in 505, 506, 508
  Review form, creating 318
  Reviews cell, updating 319
  UI elements, positioning 319, 320
storyboard reference 326
storyboard
  about 146
  app assets, adding 166, 167, 168, 169, 170, 172, 173, 174, 175, 176, 177, 178
  app logo, adding onto screen 184, 185, 186, 187
  creating, for Explore tab 327, 328, 329, 330, 331, 332, 333
  creating, for Map tab 325
  launch screen, creating 179, 180, 181, 182, 183
  Navigation Controller, adding 188, 189, 190, 191
  refactoring 324
  setting up 161, 162, 163, 164, 165
  updating 178
string interpolation 44
strings
  about 33
  concatenating 43
  variables, creating with 36
Swift 43
Swift types 338

T

Tab Bar Controller 145
Table View Controller 142
Table View
  code 387
  connecting, with Location View Controller 384, 385, 386
  data source, adding 387, 389, 390, 391

delegate, adding 387, 389, 390, 391
locations, adding to 392, 393
TestFlight app 776
testing
external testing 779, 782
internal testing 776, 777
type inference 43
type safety 43

U

UI elements
hooking up, with IBOutlets 372, 373, 374, 375
UI setup
auto layout 147
Collection View Controller 143
Model View Controller (MVC) 147
Navigation Controller 144
segue 147
storyboard 146
Tab Bar Controller 145
Table View Controller 142
terms 142
View Controller 142

V

value type 340
value
retrieving, from array 103, 106

variables
about 36
creating, with integers 37
creating, with strings 36
versus constants 42
View Controllers
about 142
setting up 307, 308

W

while loop 86, 87, 88

X

Xcode interface
about 13
debug panel 15
Generic iOS Device 18
iOS Device 18, 20, 22
navigator panel 14
standard editor 14
toolbar 15, 16, 17
utilities panel 15
window pane controls 25, 27
wireless connection 23, 24
Xcode
about 7
downloading 8
launching 10, 11

CPSIA information can be obtained
at www.ICGtesting.com
Printed in the USA
LVHW06s1216170718
584024LV00040B/149/P